MOON

FIJI

MINAL HAJRATWALA

Contents

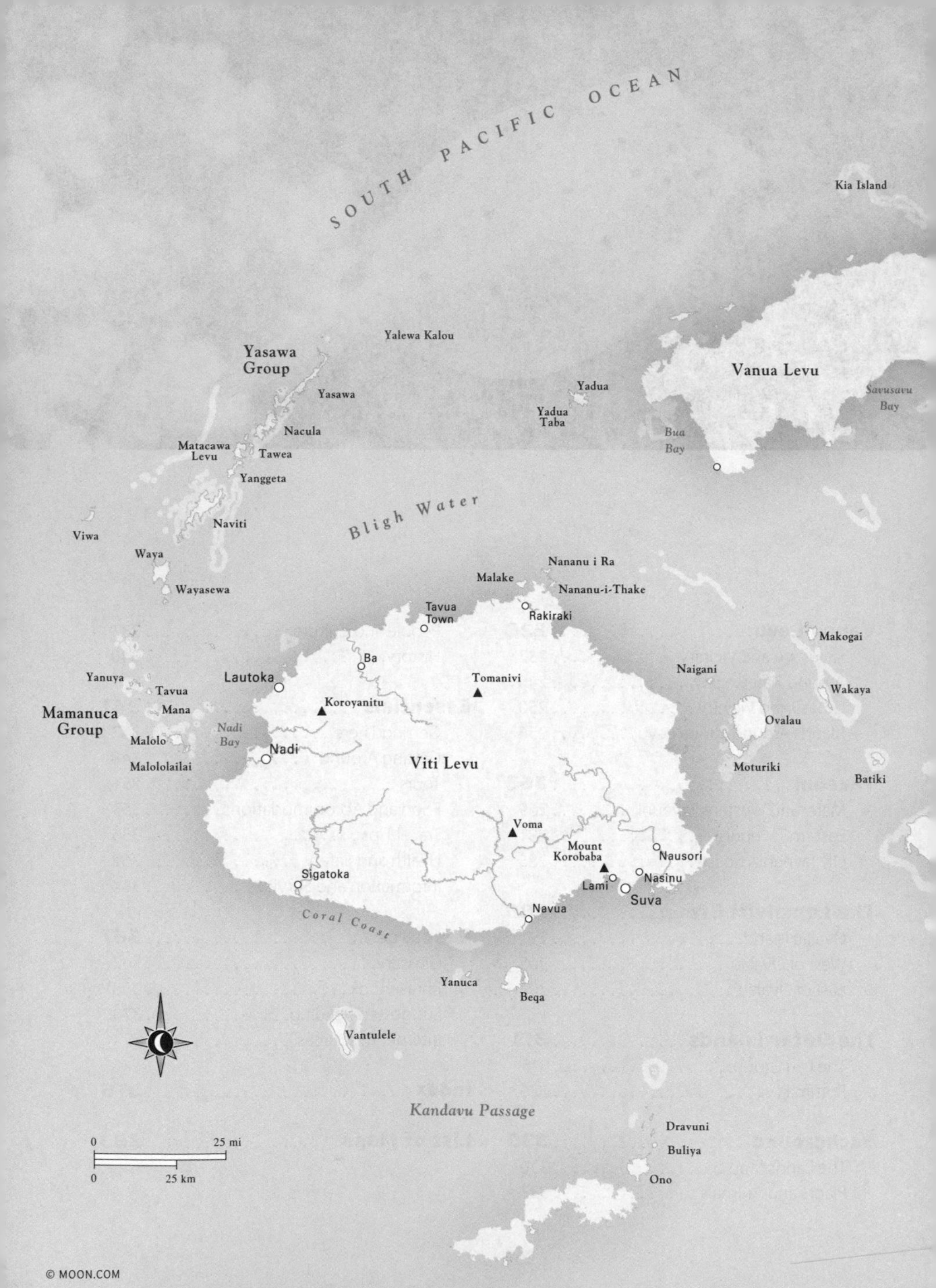
SOUTH PACIFIC OCEAN
Kia Island
Yalewa Kalou
Yasawa Group
Yasawa
Nacula
Matacawa Levu
Tawea
Yanggeta
Naviti
Viwa
Waya
Wayasewa
Yadua
Yadua Taba
Vanua Levu
Savusavu Bay
Bua Bay
Bligh Water
Nananu i Ra
Malake
Nananu-i-Thake
Tavua Town
Rakiraki
Makogai
Ba
Tomanivi
Naigani
Wakaya
Lautoka
Koroyanitu
Yanuya
Tavua
Mana
Mamanuca Group
Malolo
Nadi Bay
Nadi
Malololailai
Viti Levu
Ovalau
Moturiki
Batiki
Voma
Mount Korobaba
Nausori
Nasinu
Lami
Suva
Sigatoka
Navua
Coral Coast
Yanuca
Beqa
Vantulele
Kandavu Passage
Dravuni
Buliya
Ono
0
25 mi
0
25 km

THE FIJI ISLANDS

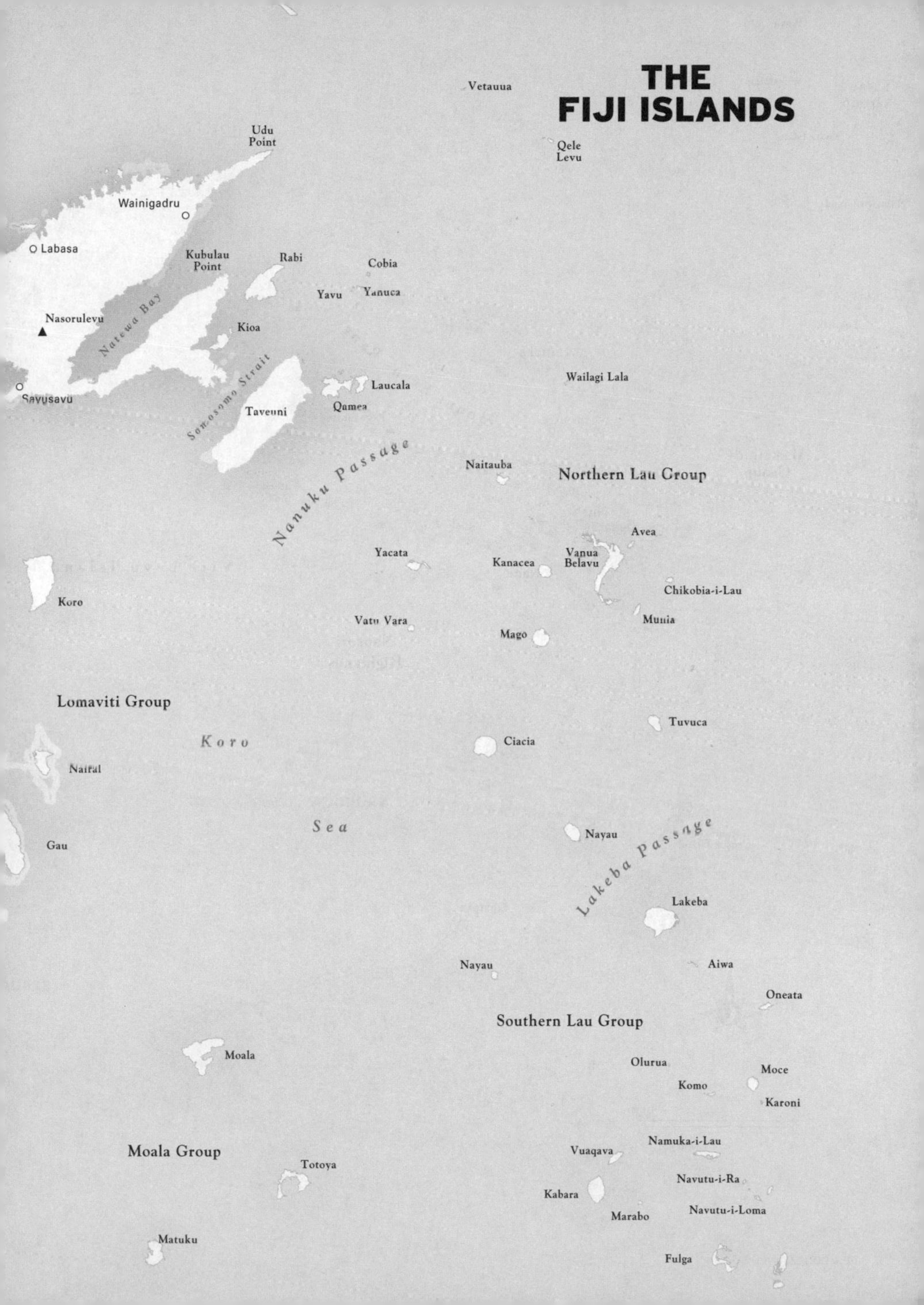

Vetauua
Udu Point
Qele Levu
Wainigadru
Labasa
Kubulau Point
Rabi
Cobia
Yavu
Yanuca
Natewa Bay
Nasorulevu
Kioa
Somosomo Strait
Savusavu
Laucala
Qamea
Taveuni
Wailagi Lala
Nanuku Passage
Naitauba
Northern Lau Group
Avea
Yacata
Kanacea
Vanua Belavu
Koro
Chikobia-i-Lau
Vatu Vara
Munia
Mago
Lomaviti Group
Koro
Tuvuca
Ciacia
Nairai
Sea
Nayau
Lakeba Passage
Gau
Lakeba
Nayau
Aiwa
Oneata
Southern Lau Group
Moala
Olurua
Moce
Komo
Karoni
Namuka-i-Lau
Moala Group
Vuaqava
Totoya
Navutu-i-Ra
Kabara
Navutu-i-Loma
Marabo
Matuku
Fulga

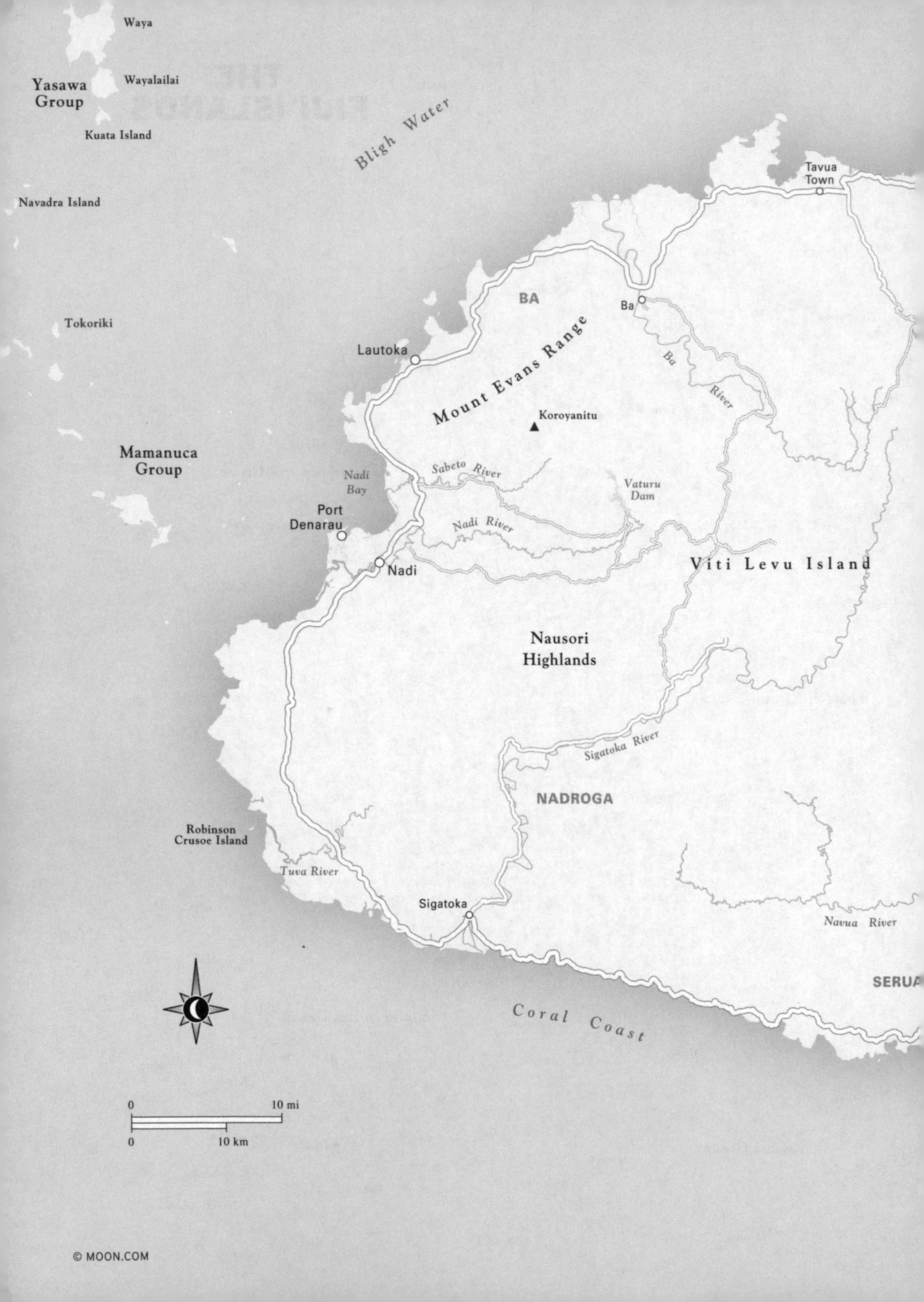
Waya
Yasawa Group
Wayalailai
Kuata Island
Bligh Water
Navadra Island
Tavua Town
BA
Ba
Tokoriki
Mount Evans Range
Lautoka
Ba River
Koroyanitu
Mamanuca Group
Nadi Bay
Sabeto River
Vaturu Dam
Port Denarau
Nadi River
Nadi
Viti Levu Island
Nausori Highlands
Sigatoka River
NADROGA
Robinson Crusoe Island
Tuva River
Sigatoka
Navua River
SERUA
Coral Coast
0
10 mi
0
10 km
© MOON.COM

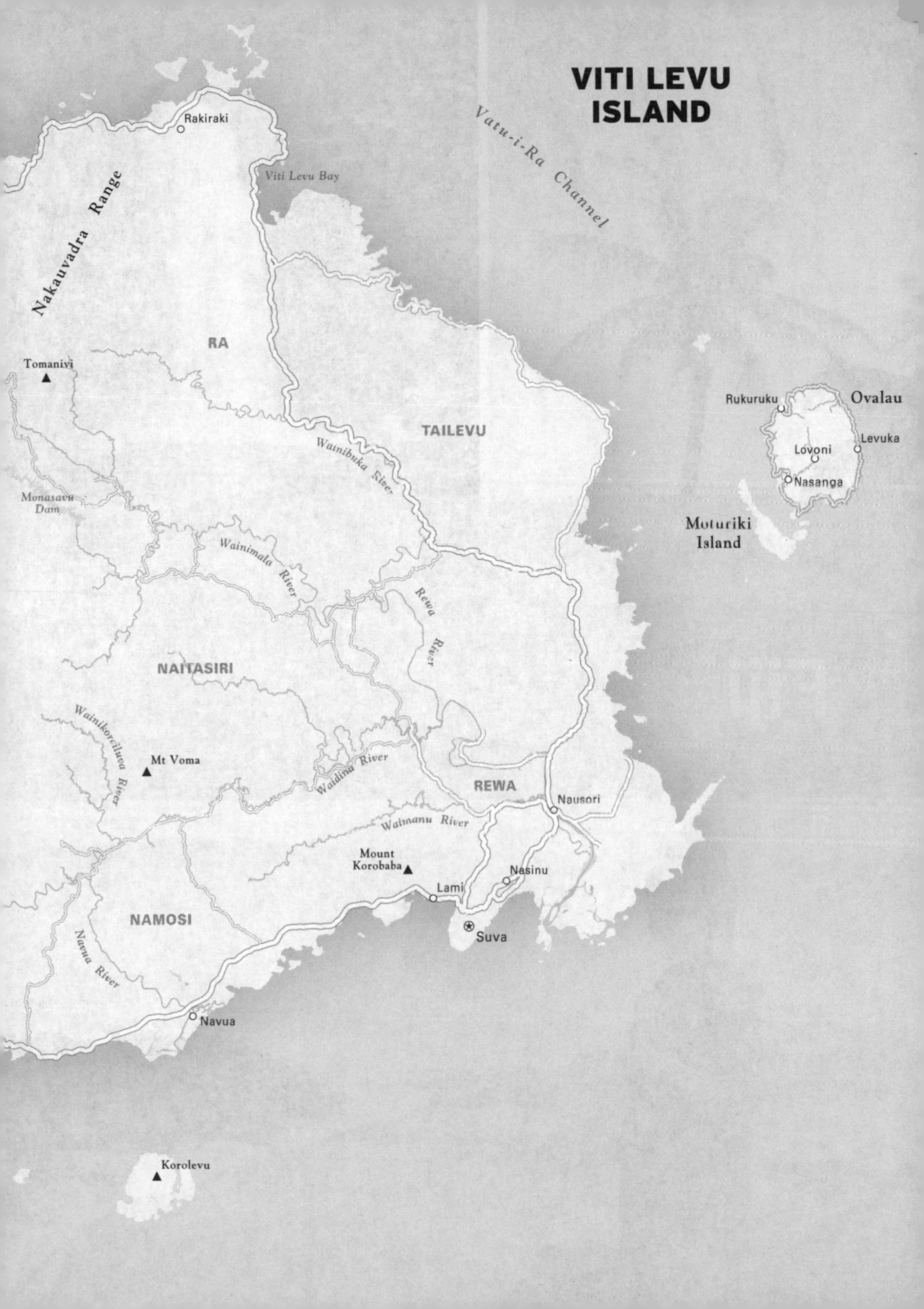

VITI LEVU
ISLAND
Vatu-i-Ra Channel
Rakiraki
Viti Levu Bay
Nakauvadra Range
RA
Tomanivi
TAILEVU
Wainibuka River
Monasavu Dam
Wainimala River
Rewa River
NAITASIRI
Wainikoroiluva River
Mt Voma
Waidina River
REWA
Nausori
Wainanu River
Mount Korobaba
Nasinu
Lami
Suva
NAMOSI
Navua River
Navua
Korolevu
Rukuruku
Ovalau
Levuka
Lovoni
Nasanga
Moturiki Island

DISCOVER

Fiji

One of the most remote archipelagoes in the world, Fiji is where you go when you want—need—to get away from it all. Famous for its flawless beaches, deep-sea wonders, and cocktails in coconuts, this collection of 300-plus jewel-like islands hosts treasures that would take a lifetime to explore.

More than 70 percent of the earth is water, and there's nowhere better to experience this gorgeous truth than Fiji. No less than 33 barrier reefs form decorative halos around the hundreds of islands, home to thousands of colorful marine species, many unique to these waters.

Away from the sea, more adventures await. Try dramatic waterfall trekking, spelunking large limestone caves, zip-lining through old-growth vesi rainforests, and white-water rafting through river gorges lined with black volcanic walls.

Fiji's rich and diverse landscape is matched by its mix of cultures. This is where Polynesia and Melanesia meet, from iTaukei warrior dances to Indian temples. It's one of the few nations in the world where indigenous people

Clockwise from top left: a beach sunset; one of the Bouma waterfalls on Taveuni; a bilibili raft on Sonaisali Island; the honeybee goby; banners streaming from the Sri Siva Subrahmaniya Swami Temple in Nadi, a path to the beach in Pacific Harbour.

have retained most of their land and time-honored traditions. Everyone speaks English as well as their own mother tongue, and Fijians are famously friendly and social. You just might find yourself sharing an intoxicating bowl of kava with new friends on the deck of a boat.

It's time to learn your first Fijian word: *Bula!* Hello, welcome, come on in.

Clockwise from top left: having fun on Natadola Beach; a bull shark in the Beqa Lagoon; Navala village on Viti Levu; coconut warning at the Lawaki Beach House on Beqa Island.

FALLING
OBJECTS

10 TOP EXPERIENCES

1 **Find Your Beach Paradise:** Get ready to enjoy some of the best beaches in the world (page 29).

^
^
^

2 Discover Underwater Treasures: Dubbed the "soft coral capital of the world" by oceanographer Jacques Cousteau, Fiji offers teeming reefs around every island (page 33).

3 Take a Hike: From coastal treks to incredible volcanic vistas, spectacular scenery awaits those who are willing to walk for it (page 34).

4 Catch Epic Waves: Surf some of the world's best breaks, including the famous **Cloudbreak** (page 36).

5 **Ride the Rapids:** Rush down the thrilling **Navua River** as it cuts through dramatic volcanic gorges (page 157).

>>>

6 **Visit Picture Perfect Islands:** Live out your fantasies of movie glamour on *The Blue Lagoon*'s **Nanuya Lailai** (page 111) in the Mamanucas and on *Cast Away*'s **Modriki Island** (page 100) in the Yasawas.

>>>

7 **Explore Contemporary Art and Culture:** Experience Fiji's local art scene by watching a performance from the high-octane dance artistes of **VOU** (page 47) or seeing vibrant paintings in the **art galleries of Suva** (page 174).

8 Village Homestay: Get way, way off the grid and be welcomed like a family member at **Namosi Eco Retreat,** north of Pacific Harbour on Viti Levu (page 159).

<<<

9 Adventure at Bouma National Heritage Park: Snorkel pristine waters, hike to lush jungle waterfalls, or take a beautiful coastal walk at one of Fiji's best nature reserves (page 281).

>>>

10 Polish Your Binoculars: You're going to see (and hear) some unique feathered species (page 274).

<<<

Planning Your Trip

Where to Go

Nadi and Vicinity

As the site of Fiji's international airport, Nadi is the country's **gateway,** with lots of glassy storefronts and cultural sights. It's a great place to acclimate while exposing your taste buds to everything from cheap street snacks to Fiji's emerging nouveau **cuisine.** Just a tiny hop over a small bridge is resort-rich **Denarau Island,** a fun and safe place to party, relax, try a new water sport, or embark on a half-day excursion to the western islets. South is the historic **Momi Bay** gun battery, and inland is the mountainous **Sleeping Giant** jungle, with zip-lining and a 35-acre eco-park.

The Mamanuca and Yasawa Islands

For the romantic beaches of the travel brochures, spend a day or a week at these enticing archipelagoes an easy hop from Nadi. Most of Fiji's **island resorts** are here, with clear waters, golden or white sands, and dazzling reefs. These mini-paradises have seduced generations of global audiences through productions such as *The Blue Lagoon, Cast Away,* and season 33 onward of *Survivor.* You don't have to earn a superstar salary, though, to visit their natural beauty by cruise, catamaran, or seaplane.

The Coral Coast

The southern flank of Fiji's main island, Viti Levu, is the **Coral Coast,** where Fijian tourism began. Dozens of resorts, hotels, and hostels stretch along 50 miles of beach, with plenty of places to tempt travelers to pause—whether for a scenic round of golf at world-famous **Natadola,** a challenging sand hike over the **Sigatoka Sand**

hibiscus flowers

Dunes, a snorkel and barbecue on the beach, or an array of other tours and activities available in this developed region. At the eastern end, **Pacific Harbour** is a hub for sea-based action sports, while the stunning **Navua River** beckons to white-water rafters.

Suva and the Kadavu Group

The largest and most cosmopolitan city in Oceania, **Suva** offers tons of culture, shopping, and eating. Fiji's largest museum, hippest nightclubs, and numerous historic buildings are here. To the north, a tiny well-kept rainforest at Colo-i-Suva and a reef frequented by spinner dolphins offer outdoor adventure. Offshore, lush **Kadavu Island** offers access to the virtually untouched Great Astrolabe Reef.

Northern Coast and Interior Viti Levu

On Viti Levu's northern half, seascapes give way to vast sugar plantations and lush volcanic forests intercut by networks of rivers and streams. The paved two-lane Kings Highway makes for comfortable travel to sugar city **Lautoka** and sleepy **Rakiraki.** Avid hikers can choose from several glorious, virtually tourist-free treks up into the lush mountains and sweeping valleys of the interior **Nausori Highlands** and Fiji's highest peak, **Mount Tomaniivi. Nananu-i-Ra Island** is a favorite of scuba divers, windsurfers, and backpackers.

Vanua Levu

The heart of the "friendly north," Fiji's second-largest island feels worlds away from Viti Levu. **Savusavu** is a picturesque town with an active, friendly marina scene, and two spectacular highways sweep north through mountains and east along a verdant coast. There's plenty to do here, whether it's visiting a pearl farm, enjoying a thermal mud bath, or going on a scenic search along the **Hibiscus Highway** for the elusive Natewa silktail bird.

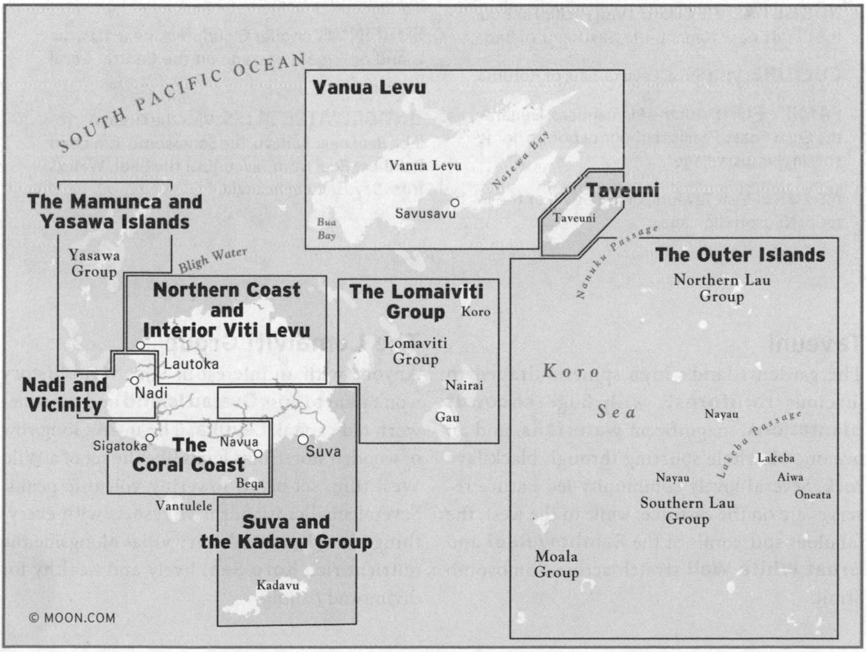

If You're Looking for...

the beach on Denarau Island

- **ADRENALINE:** Visit the Navua River near Pacific Harbour or the Sleeping Giant near Nadi.
- **BUDGET ADVENTURE:** Visit Pacific Harbour, the Coral Coast, Nananu-i-ra, Savusavu, or Beqa.
- **CULTURE:** Visit Suva, Levuka, Lau, or Rotuma.
- **FAMILY FUN:** Visit the Mamanucas, Denarau, the Coral Coast, Pacific Harbour, or book a homestay in Namosi village.
- **NATURE:** Visit Taveuni, Colo-i-Suva, or the interior Nausori Highlands.
- **ROMANCE:** Visit the Blue Lagoon in the Yasawas or an adults-only resort in the Outer Islands or Lomaiviti Group.
- **SURFING:** Conquer Cloudbreak near Tavarua Island or Frigate Passage off the Central Coral Coast.
- **UNDERWATER BLISS:** Visit the Great Astrolabe Reef near Kadavu, the Somosomo Strait and Rainbow Reef from Taveuni, or the Bligh Waters from Savusavu or Rakiraki.

Taveuni

The garden island's high spine is draped in luscious **rainforest,** with huge **coconut plantations,** magnificent **waterfalls,** and an oceanic blowhole spurting through black lava rock. Several lovely community-led nature reserves are on the east side, while to the west, the fabulous soft corals of the **Rainbow Reef** and **Great White Wall** stretch across Somosomo Strait.

The Lomaiviti Group

Anyone with an interest in Fiji's vivid history won't want to miss **Ovalau Island** and the time-worn old capital, **Levuka.** The town's long row of wooden storefronts looks like the set of a Wild West film, set below towering volcanic peaks. Several smaller islands have resorts with everything from dorms to luxury villas alongside the nutrient-rich **Koro Sea,** lively and healthy for diving and fishing.

The Outer Islands

Words like *pristine, untouched,* and *idyllic* were invented for these little-known islands in the **Lau Group** and **Moala Group** to the east and **Rotuma Island** far to the north. It's worth the extra effort to travel where few tourists go in order to experience some of the most fantastic beaches, therapeutic mineral springs, and stunning limestone formations in the world.

Know Before You Go

High and Low Seasons

Fiji has great weather year-round, so there is no special travel season. There's a **hotter, more humid season** November-April, and a **cooler, drier time** May-October. March is the hottest and rainiest month, and July is the coolest and driest. The risk of **cyclones** is highest during the wetter season, sometimes shutting down sea and air travel for a few days per year.

Family-oriented resorts may be more crowded during Australian and New Zealand school holidays (one week each in January, April, and July). Check availability, especially if you have your heart set on a particular spot.

If you're a scuba diver, it's useful to know that the best **diving** conditions occur April-October, with the calmest seas in April and May. Visibility is tops June-October, then slightly worse November-March due to river runoff and plankton growth. The marine life is most bountiful July-November.

Surfing is possible throughout the year, with the biggest swells out of the south March-October.

May-October is the **yachting** season, with the trade winds blowing reliably out of the southeast.

Visas and Officialdom

Citizens of most countries do not need a visa to enter Fiji; see the list of exempt nations at www.fijihighcom.com. Travelers should be prepared to show:

- a passport valid for at least six months after arrival;
- a ticket for departure from Fiji and the appropriate visa or document for entering their next destination; and
- up-to-date vaccinations for tetanus, hepatitis A, and hepatitis B.

For stays of more than four months, see the additional visa requirements in the Essentials chapter.

Transportation

Fourteen international airlines either fly to Fiji or have codeshare agreements, with frequent service from Auckland, New Zealand; Brisbane, Melbourne, and Sydney, Australia; Honolulu, Hawaii; Los Angeles and San Francisco, California; Guam; Samoa; and Tonga.

Within Fiji, a combination of **flights, boats, taxis, buses,** and possibly **car rentals** will serve you well. Depending on whether you value time or money more, you can fly across the main island in less than an hour or drive across it in four. The round-the-island local bus is scenic and a great bargain as long as you can handle occasional bumpiness and proximity to fellow travelers. Private taxis are not prohibitive; day rates for a driver and car are often about the same as a day's car rental alone.

Ferries and motorboats are the way most people travel to the outlying islands, and most are equipped comfortably enough for tourists. Commercial flights also go to some islands. Seaplanes, engaged by exclusive resorts to bring passengers onto their own landing strips, are an option if price is no object.

The Best of Fiji

With 300-plus islands to choose from, planning a trip to Fiji can seem daunting. The following itineraries can be used independently or combined to create the best *bula* vacation for you.

The route I recommend to friends and family visiting Fiji for the first time is to arrive in Nadi on Viti Levu, fly straight to the garden island of Taveuni, then fly back to Viti Levu via Suva, spending a couple of days in the capital before heading west along the Coral Coast back to Nadi.

Viti Levu: Greatest Hits

You can have a fantastic, diverse trip to Fiji while exploring all that Fiji's largest island has to offer. To maximize your time on Viti Levu, fly straight to Suva after you arrive in Nadi, and enjoy meandering along the coastal route back to Nadi.

Suva

DAY 1

Arrive in Nadi in the early morning and walk across a driveway to the domestic terminal for the first flight to Suva. (Be sure to book your international ticket all the way through to Suva so that you won't be charged extra for luggage on the domestic leg.) After the hour-long flight, take a 15-minute taxi ride from the airport to the elegant, restful **Grand Pacific Hotel,** where you can enjoy a royal brunch buffet before crashing to recuperate from your jet lag.

When you surface again, you might take a relaxed, self-guided walking tour of the various colonial monuments in the area, including the **Fiji Museum.** Pay special attention to the huge *drua*, the double-hulled canoe in the museum's main hall. For dinner, venture into the bustle

the pool at the Grand Pacific Hotel

of downtown—either a 3-minute taxi ride or a 20-minute walk—and have a casual meal in the food court at **Tappoo City,** where everyone in your group can choose their own dining adventure amid an array of vegetarian, fish, and meat purveyors in Fijian, Indian, East Asian, or continental style. If you still have energy, stop by the **Piano Bar** at the **Holiday Inn** for a nightcap and dessert, and be serenaded by local singers, before turning in at the Grand Pacific just next door.

DAY 2

Walk or take a taxi to the bus station and enjoy a quick breakfast at one of the roadside stalls (the mince pies at **Hot Bread Kitchen** are tasty). Catch the bus to **Colo-i-Suva,** a small rainforest just outside of Suva, spotting some of the rare birds that nest in this sanctuary. You can go for a scenic, not-too-strenuous 90-minute hike here, adding a little time for waterfall swims if you like. Then grab lunch at **Colo-i-Suva Rainforest Eco Resort,** located at the rainforest entrance.

In the afternoon, let history come to life by booking a sail on the **Drua Experience,** an authentic, handcrafted double-hulled canoe modeled on the 1913 canoe in the museum. It was this sort of vessel that's believed to have carried the early Melanesians to Fiji in 500 BC. On the tour, you'll enjoy a swim at historic and scenic **Nukulau Island** before sailing back. Dine and socialize at **Eden Bistro & Bar,** where the daily specials might feature anything from sashimi to curries to burgers; you're likely to make some new friends in this cheerful, relaxed joint.

The Coral Coast

DAY 3

After a couple of days in Suva, it's time to get completely off the grid. Rent a car in town that you can return in Nadi, and then drive up into the foothills to spend a night at the **Namosi Eco Retreat.** You'll stay in your own hut next to an indigenous village, and cook, converse, and splash in the river with new friends. Children especially love this place.

Alternatively, take a bus or taxi for the half-hour trip from either Pacific Harbour or Suva to the wharf town of Navua, arriving around noon. Across from the bus station, board a motorboat to go down the **Navua River** and across the open

The Drua Experience offers tours in a traditional double-hulled canoe in Suva Harbour.

sea to peaceful little **Lawaki Beach House.** Enjoy the golden sands as well as fresh meals of fish caught by the owners and vegetables from their organic hillside farms, and take an occasional snorkel out to the reefs that encircle the island and the entire **Beqa Lagoon.**

DAY 4

After breakfast, continue west to the Coral Coast. The paved road, fine scenery, and numerous interesting stops make this one of Fiji's best road trips. After about two hours of driving, pause at the **He-Ni-Uwa Restaurant.** You might wish to work up an appetite by taking a horseback ride with the family-owned **Fiji Coral Coast Horse Riding Adventures,** which also owns the restaurant. Choose from a 40-minute beach ride, a 90-minute beach/mountain ride, or a 2-hour rainforest ride that includes a waterfall dip; they all include a fine lunch at the restaurant.

After lunch, continue about half an hour to the **Sigatoka Sand Dunes National Park,** a unique coastal ecosystem formed over millennia. Enjoy a beautiful, moderately strenuous 45-minute hike from the visitors center through the dunes and back. Back on the road, after about 30 minutes of driving, you'll arrive at the big island's most gorgeous beach, **Natadola.** This is the perfect spot to relax for the rest of the afternoon—you've earned it! Take photos, drink from a freshly cracked coconut, lounge on the beach, and perhaps have a massage at one of the open-air tables. When your stomach starts rumbling again, pop into the open-air bar and restaurant of the **Natadola Bay Golf Course** and enjoy stunning views of the southern coast; try the Sigatoka River prawns and the lime-passion fruit cheesecake.

From here, drive about 45 minutes north and check into the posh **Marriott Resort Momi Bay,** which, although a chain, is worthwhile for its location and gorgeous over-water *bures.*

Nadi and Vicinity

DAY 5

Enjoy a big breakfast at the hotel, relax with a morning swim in the infinity pool or on the beach, then check out and head 20 minutes north to the historic **Momi Battery Historic Park.** Here you can marvel at the two huge antique cannons used to defend Fiji during World War II and the even more stunning view of the southern islands.

Drive about half an hour north to one of the resorts on **Denarau Island** (upscale) or **Wailoaloa Beach** (budget) for an afternoon of sun, swimming, lazing, and perhaps a massage with only-in-Fiji organic coconut and floral lotions. If a jolt of adrenaline fits your mood better, book an excursion north to **Sleeping Giant Zip Line Fiji.** You'll be picked up from your hotel and whisked to a 35-acre adventure park with five zip lines, where you can fly through the jungle canopy at a maximum speed of 40 kph.

For a social evening with locals, try the old-fashioned **Nadi Club** in town. It's a drinking society, distinguished by the fact that **Felix Fastfood,** attached to the club, serves tasty Indian and fusion meals (chicken, lamb, duck, goat, and fish) for around F$5.

DAY 6: DAY TRIP TO THE MAMANUCAS

For a glimpse of some of Fiji's most spectacular outer islands, take a day cruise that includes lunch on one of the **Mamanuca Islands.** You could lounge on the beach and paddleboard off the coast of **Modriki Island,** made famous by the movie *Cast Away,* or Jet Ski out to **Cloud 9,** a floating pizzeria in clear deep waters perfect for parasailing and kayaking. There are a dozen possibilities depending on whether your mood is booze cruise, romantic private cove, or family fun.

All embark from the **Marina at Port Denarau,** which is conveniently also full of restaurants, so you can have your choice of dinner and an indulgent dessert when you return. One good choice is **Bonefish Seafood Restaurant,** a pioneer of Fijian nouveau cuisine, where signature dishes include a seafood chowder spiked with brandy and a Yasawa lobster grilled in a sweet chili sauce. To keep the party going, you could board the open-air **Bula Bus** and use your unlimited rides to go bar-hopping among all the fancy resort bars on Denarau till the wee hours.

DAY 7

Spend your last day taking in the sights and sounds of Nadi. To take a taste of Fiji home with you, sign up for a class with the **Flavours of Fiji Cooking School,** which starts at the **Nadi Market,** where locals from all over the islands come to sell their fruits and vegetables. Then the chef-teachers take you to the pro kitchen on Denarau, where you learn to prepare an 11-item lunch—and eat it.

Afterward, browse for souvenirs at the **Handicraft Market** and the glassy storefronts of downtown. Stop by the prominent **Sri Siva Subrahmaniya Swami Temple,** the largest and most colorful Hindu temple in the South Pacific. Eat your last Fijian meal at **Tu's Place,** savoring local classics such as *kokoda* (ceviche made with coconut milk) and *rourou* (taro leaf balls), before heading to the airport to drop off your rental car and fly out.

With More Time

THE GREAT ASTROLABE REEF

If you have two more nights, pause between Suva and the Coral Coast for an excursion to **Kadavu Island.** (You could do this in one night, if absolutely necessary, but you'd regret it!)

Fly directly from Suva into Vunisea Airport and be whisked to **Matava,** one of Fiji's original eco-resorts, right on the stunning Great Astrolabe Reef. The resort's on-site diving and fishing operators are award-winning, so you could spend the afternoon doing your activity of choice (divers, be sure to allow 24 hours before your next flight). Kayaking is also excellent here. Delicious meals are included, and you can easily spend a couple of days in and around your beautiful *bure.* The comfortable decks are perfect for spotting Kadavu's four endemic bird species, while the snorkeling in the marine reserve just opposite is superb.

parasailing in the Mamanucas

The Yasawas: Relaxation and Romance

If you're looking for glorious time away from the crowds, you'll find it just off the coast of Nadi, above the Mamanucas. The Yasawas offer gorgeous beaches, romantic views, and—best of all—privacy.

Day 1

Arrive at Nadi Airport in the wee hours, catch a taxi to have a hearty breakfast at **Taste Fiji** in town when it opens at 0630 sharp, then go by taxi to **Port Denarau** in time for the 0830 sailing of the high-speed ***Yasawa Flyer*** catamaran. Admire the stunning island and sea views or catch a nap on the 4.5-hour journey to the end of the line: lovely little **Nacula Island.** It's a long travel day, but once you check in at the **Blue Lagoon Beach Resort,** the hardest part is over, and you can fall asleep to the sound of waves in one of the most gorgeous parts of the world.

Day 2

Check with the resort's boat crew to find out when the tide will be right to visit the two must-see sights in this area: the fabulous **Blue Lagoon** cove and the freshwater cave plunge on **Sawa-i-Lau Island.** Enjoy these excursions for part of the day, then relax, hike, or try some watersports on Nacula Island or one of the nearby neighbors, **Tavewa** and **Nanuya Lailai.**

Day 3

After breakfast and a lazy morning, catch the afternoon catamaran to **Naviti Island** and enjoy one of the beaches (the best one is on the southwest coast). Check into the **Botaira Beach Resort,** have dinner, and hang out with the staff and other guests, perhaps over a bowl of kava.

Day 4

After breakfast, hike about 40 minutes to the

dramatic scenery around the Blue Lagoon in the Yasawas

Nanuya Lailai in the Yasawas

Find Your Beach Paradise

the exclusive Vomo Island

BEST ALL-AROUND BEACH

- **Natadola, Coral Coast** (page 121): Viti Levu's most scenic beach also offers massages, coconuts, and tranquility.

BEST BEACH STARRING IN A MOTION PICTURE

- **Blue Lagoon, Nanuya Lailai Island, Yasawas** (page 111): Turquoise waters and dramatic rock formations have seduced many Hollywood producers.
- **Modriki Island, Mamanucas** (page 100): You may find a volleyball named Wilson on this uninhabited, paradisiacal island.

BEST FOR A COASTAL WALK

- **Lavena, Taveuni** (page 282): The farther you stroll, the more waterfalls you'll see.

BEST FOR ROMANCE

- **Yasawa Island, Yasawas** (page 116): Enjoy a creamy white beach, a private gourmet picnic, fluffy towels, and no one else in sight.

BEST FOR SNORKELING

- **Nanuya Balavu and Drawaqa Islands, Yasawas** (page 107): These gorgeous beaches face a channel with fast-moving schools of colorful fish and (Apr.-Nov.) huge migrating manta rays.

BEST FOR SWIMMING

- **Devodara Beach, Vanua Levu** (page 247): Fine white sand leads out to a protected natural swimming lagoon.

BEST FOR WATER SPORTS

- **Nananu-i-Ra Island, Viti Levu** (page 223): With strong winds from both directions, this tiny island is great for windsurfing.
- **Pacific Harbour, Viti Levu** (page 146): This is the best beach for jet-skiing and other motorized action sports.

BEST FOR WHEN YOU WIN THE LOTTERY

- **Vomo Island, Mamanucas** (page 101): White-sand beaches—and butlers—tend to your every need.

BEST OFF THE BEATEN TRACK

- **Kadavu Group** (page 195): All of the islands in the Kadavu Group, in the southernmost reaches of Fiji, are gorgeous and worth the trek.

BEST TO DO NOTHING ON

- **Lawaki, Beqa Island** (page 154): The calm and scenic Beqa Lagoon is lovely for relaxing in a hammock.

island's highest point, then head over to the scenic **Honeymoon Point** for postcard-perfect views. Scuba diving and snorkeling are beautiful in this region, and easy currents make the diving suitable for beginners. You have a good chance of swimming alongside angel-like manta rays April-July.

Day 5

Catch the afternoon catamaran to one of the middle Yasawa islands—**Waya, Wayasewa, Viwa,** or **Kuata.** White-sand beaches, lovely reefs, and small scenic peaks mean that the swimming, snorkeling, scuba diving, and hiking are all terrific on these isles. The **Octopus Resort** is a solid midrange place on a lovely beach, but there are plenty of other great choices at various price points on these islands.

Day 6

Spend the day on your island or take a little boat trip to one of the others in this area. You might visit a **Fijian village** (with permission or on an organized trip), experiencing the *sevusevu* ceremony and getting a glimpse of traditional iTaukei (indigenous) culture. A 90-minute round-trip hike up the volcanic plug that is Vatuvula Peak, on Wayasewa Island, rewards you with sweeping 360-degree views of Viti Levu in the distance and the numerous small isles that make up the Mamanucas and Yasawas. Or hop in a kayak—usually available free from your resort—and circle Wayasewa in a fabulous all-day trip, with a picnic lunch at the secluded beach cove of your choice.

Day 7

The afternoon Awesome Adventures catamaran will take you back to Denarau Island. Have an authentic but luxurious dinner at the marina, just a few meters from where you disembark, at **Nadina Fijian Restaurant;** the lobster and chargrilled octopus are favorites. You can pick up a few souvenirs in the marina shops before boarding the Yellow Bus connection or a taxi to take you to Nadi International Airport in time for your night flight.

Taveuni and Vanua Levu: Back to Nature

Taveuni, otherwise known as the Garden Island, lives up to its name, with lush forests, waterfalls, and spectacular diving. It's best paired with neighboring Vanua Levu, Fiji's second largest island and home to the scenic and cultural Savusavu.

Day 1

You'll probably arrive at Nadi International Airport in the middle of the night. Change a good chunk of money at the exchange office in the arrivals hall, then walk over to the departures hall to await the morning flight to **Taveuni.** Keep your camera out; the landing at tiny Matei airstrip is spectacular. Get picked up by the van (complimentary) from **Nakia Resort & Dive,** then check into your *bure* and have lunch and perhaps a quick hammock nap at the resort. Make bookings (paid) to use the hotel's van and driver for the next couple of days. In the afternoon, take in the sights of the western side of the island: the natural waterslide at **Waitavala Sliding Rocks,** the **international date line,** and the surprising **Matamaiqi Blowhole** (at high tide only). Enjoy an open-air sunset dinner (reservations essential) at **Paradise Taveuni Resort** on the way back before turning in for a well-earned rest.

Day 2

Fish rise early, so in the morning, head out by boat on the resort's catamaran on a dive or snorkel trip to the **Rainbow Reef,** consistently rated as one of the world's top dive sites. Return to your *bure* for a shower and lunch. In the afternoon, book the hotel's car and driver to take a 30-minute drive up the slope of **Des Voeux**

dramatic coastline around the Matamaiqi Blowhole on Taveuni

Peak, the only place where the bright red tagimoucia flower—subject of many a tragic, romantic legend—grows. If you prefer to hike it, allow four hours round-trip, take plenty of water, and plan to be down well before dark. Enjoy dinner in town at everyone's favorite spot, the **Tramonto** (reservations essential), with a superb view of the **Somosomo Strait.**

Day 3

Have breakfast at the resort and ask for a picnic lunch to be packed for you. Head east to **Bouma National Heritage Park** for a wonderful hike to one, two, or three waterfalls, depending on your energy level; even sloths like me can enjoy the 10-minute stroll to the first set of falls, and the cool pool below feels fantastic in the tropical heat. Then go east to the **Lavena Coastal Walk** along Taveuni's best beach, where you can enjoy your picnic in one of the gazebos, lounge around, or enjoy a gorgeous 5-kilometer beach hike or kayaking trip. This may be the evening to try **kava** after dinner at your accommodation; most likely, the staff at your hotel will gladly help you partake.

Day 4

Get an early start by catching an 0730 ferry (either the Miller or Grace shipping company, depending on day of the week) across the Somosomo Strait to the eastern tip of Vanua Levu, then a bus from the dock to picturesque little **Savusavu.** The whole trip takes about six hours, with gorgeous scenery along the way. From Savusavu's main bus station, it's a quick F$10 or less taxi ride to your bungalow at **Daku Resort.** Soak off your travel aches with a thermal mud plunge in the emerald jungle with **Savusavu Tours;** you could add a horseback ride through the rainforest to reach the mud pools if you like. Afterward, meet yachties at the bar at the **Copra Shed Marina,** and enjoy a drink over the water as the sun sets. Walk five minutes to the other end of town to sample Indo-Fijian specialties at an unassuming gem, the **Taste of Hidden Paradise Restaurant.** After dinner, stroll along the safe waterfront back to your accommodation, pausing occasionally to gaze up at the stars and watch the moon rise over the water.

Day 5

After breakfast at Daku, take the 0930 tour of the

Best Value Resorts

These resorts—neither dirt cheap nor luxury—strike the perfect balance between your wallet and your dream. Most are owner-operated, and those that aren't have attentive management on-site to take care of your needs. With discounts available through their own websites or third-party sites, you can typically stay at these places for US$50-150 for two people per night.

Note that Suva doesn't really have "resorts"; it has hotels/motels. The Outer Islands don't have resorts that qualify for value.

NADI AND VICINITY

- **The Palms, Denarau** (page 70): Spacious, modern apartments with fully equipped kitchens, suitable for groups, making a great base from which to explore the Nadi area while saving money on meals.
- **Sapphire Bay, Vuda Point** (page 77): Huge four-bedroom, three-bathroom villas that sleep up to 12 people, a short drive from the Nadi Airport, with kitchens, a private pool, and stunning views of the western isles—so you can bring everyone you love with you.

THE MAMANUCA AND YASAWA ISLANDS

- **Coral View Island Resort, Tavewa Island** (page 112): One of the nicest budget places to stay in Fiji, with *bures* as well as dorms, on a secluded beach with a mostly under-35 crowd.
- **Blue Lagoon Beach Resort, Nacula Island** (page 115): Villas as well as dorms near fabulous white-sand beaches and clear lagoons.
- **Octopus Resort, Waya Island** (page 107): Family friendly with a great beach.

CORAL COAST

- **Bedarra Beach Inn, central Coral Coast** (page 141): Clean and bright, with a good restaurant, it's across the road from a small private beach good for swimming and snorkeling at high tide.
- **The Uprising, Pacific Harbour** (page 150): Popular with young, active travelers, it has plenty of water sports, a party vibe, and a range of hearty food.

Lawaki Beach House on Beqa Island

- **Lawaki Beach House, Beqa Island** (page 154): Located on an idyllic beach, it's small and quiet, locally run, and far more affordable than other options on the same incredible Beqa Lagoon.

VANUA LEVU

- **Daku Resort, Savusavu** (page 242): Friendly and active, an ideal base for tours and activities.
- **Siga Siga Sands, Hibiscus Highway** (page 247): Your own bungalow, spaced well away from others, on the island's best lagoon beach.

TAVEUNI

- **Paradise Taveuni Resort** (page 281): Attentive service, pleasant grounds, and easy boat access for divers, fishers, and snorkelers; no beach.
- **Garden Island Resort** (page 280): On the beach, with air-conditioning and four-star comfort.

LOMAIVITI GROUP

- **Leleuvia Island Resort** (page 305): An ecotourism leader set among miles of pristine sanctuary waters, with an art gallery and traditionally constructed buildings and canoes.
- **The Baystay, Ovalau** (page 303): Cozy, on a small beach cove, and with good meals prepared fresh by attentive on-site owners.

J. Hunter Pearls Farm by boat, including a snorkel amid giant clams in the refreshing bay around **Nawi Island.** Rinse off at the hotel, check out, and catch a cab along with your luggage to have lunch at **Surf and Turf,** on the back side of the Copra Shed Marina, whose chef learned the trade at the uber-luxurious resorts in this area before opening this popular spot. Then head by taxi for the 15-minute ride to the airport and the quick 45-minute flight back to Nadi or Suva.

Underwater Treasures: Diving and Snorkeling

TOP EXPERIENCE

Fiji's seemingly endless seas are a diver's paradise. The coral reefs that surround most of the islands are home to hundreds of hard and soft coral species as well as thousands of fish species, with new ones being discovered all the time. Larger marine animals include sharks, manta rays, barracuda, sea turtles, and even migrating humpback whales. With visibility of 35 meters or more, and dramatic underwater topography that ranges from tranquil coral gardens set in protected lagoons to challenging tunnels, walls, and pinnacles, Fiji offers a plethora of options for divers and snorkelers of all skill levels.

Easy Diving

If you're a beginning or occasional diver, you're looking for gentle currents and spectacular sea life at relatively shallow levels, as well as experienced dive instructors and divemasters who can give you extra attention when you need it. You'll find all of that at resorts in the **Mamanucas, Yasawas,** and on the **Coral Coast.** The best diving here is in less than 15 meters of sea, with healthy reefs and an awe-inspiring array of

colorful marinelife

soft corals in the Mamanucas

Take a Hike

With an extinct volcanic peak at the center of every island, the hiking on Fiji is accessible and rewarding. Even on the smallest islands, be sure to walk around the coast as far as you can before the cliffs or mangroves stop you, and up to the highest point for views of sparkling seas and isles.

- The high peaks of Viti Levu are **Mount Tomaniivi** (page 220) and **Mount Batilamu** (page 215), each possible to scale in a day; **Talanoa Treks** (page 216) based in Suva, leads well-organized group hikes guided by men and, increasingly, women from the highland villages.
- An unusual hike is up and down (and up, and down, and...) the rolling **Sigatoka Sand Dunes** (page 128), some of which are 50 meters high; for every two steps up a dune you'll slide a step down, but on the downward slopes you can pretend you're sledding.
- An easier hike/stroll is at **Colo-i-Suva Forest Park** (page 191), near Suva Airport, where native birds nest.
- On Vanua Levu, the **Waisali Rainforest Reserve** (page 236) has many native arboreal species, including the giant kauri trees.
- On Taveuni, there's beautiful hiking at **Bouma National Heritage Park** (page 281). Explore the **Vidawa Rainforest,** the **Bouma waterfalls,** and along the **Lavena coast**—trips are all organized by local village guides in a model sustainable ecotourism project.
- Also on Taveuni, don't miss the iconic trek up the volcanic slopes of **Des Voeux Peak** (page 271), with views of **Lake Tagimoucia.**

lush Mount Tomaniivi

colorful fish and corals. These resorts are good places to learn, as they see a lot of divers, the sites are well mapped, and their instructors are experienced in teaching.

The following sites are great for beginners:

- Around **Navini Island** (page 91) in the Mamanucas, the calm waters have been a no-fish area for many years, leaving abundant marinelife for divers to see.
- Around the movie-famous Blue Lagoon, off **Nanuya Lailai Island** (page 111) in the Yasawas, even beginners can snap photos of the spectacular underwater topography. Encounters with sea turtles, reef sharks, and eagle rays are common.
- The **Stingray site** (page 135) off the Coral Coast is barely a minute's boat ride offshore, and you're likely to spot the resident school of barracuda right away, just a few meters below the surface. There are also abundant lionfish, trevally, and colorful angelfish and butterflyfish.

Advanced Diving

For divers comfortable in deeper, stronger waters, Fiji has an array of stunning possibilities. Almost anywhere you go, you'll find treasure. Most of these regions also have some easy dives, but you'll need to be a powerful swimmer and confident in the water to dive the most exciting sites.

- The **Namena Marine Reserve** (page 256), south of Savusavu on Vanua Levu, has it all: big fish such as tuna, barracuda, mantas, and sharks, as well as soft corals and pristine reefs.
- **Vatu-i-Ra Conservation Park** (page 223) encompasses a small island and more than 100 square kilometers of reefs north of Rakiraki on the northeastern coast of Viti Levu. This is a protected corridor for humpback whales migrating August-October, and has spectacular walls, soft corals, and thousands of schooling fish.
- West of Taveuni, in the **Rainbow Reef** (page 272), you swim through a tunnel to the immense, showy **Great White Wall,** a bottomless vertical seascape teeming with multicolored coral and swarming fish, including some rare species.
- The enormous **Great Astrolabe Reef** (page 197) off Kadavu, south of Suva on Viti Levu, features spectacular walls of hard corals, with caves, canyons, and abundant marinelife that includes manta rays and sharks.
- The following two sites are somewhat less accessible, except by liveaboard boat: **Cakaulevu Reef** (page 252), off northern Vanua Levu, is the third-longest barrier reef in the world, with dramatic outer walls and passages in strong currents. In the Outer Islands you'll find the largely unexplored reefs around the **Lau Islands** (page 315), where your dive group might map a new and unknown site—or even a new species.

Snorkeling

While scuba diving is a pricey hobby, snorkeling is free once you have a mask, and you can do it as often as you like. Most dive shops will take snorkelers along for a nominal fee if the boat's not full. There are countless places around Fiji where you can snorkel straight out to the reef: the Mamanuca Group, Coral Coast, Beqa Island, Kadavu Island, and many other shores.

Three fantastic snorkel spots are:

- Off Taveuni's east coast, the **Waitabu Marine Park** (page 281) is a biodiverse sanctuary with a stunning 1,198 species of reef fish, including silvertip reef sharks, with knowledgeable local snorkel guides.

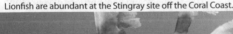

Lionfish are abundant at the Stingray site off the Coral Coast.

Catch Epic Waves

Fiji's surfing is ideal for experienced riders who love the big waves. Bring your own board; there's only one place that rents good boards, the Fiji Surf Shop in Nadi.

- The world-famous **Cloudbreak** (page 95), host to championship events, is the place to be, whether on a surf package stay at Tavarua Island or on a day trip from the Coral Coast.
- **Frigate Passage** (page 135), off Beqa Island, is accessible from the Coral Coast, Beqa, Kadavu, and nearby Yanuca Island.
- **Qamea Island** (page 287) off Taveuni is home to a budget-oriented surf camp and, unlike the two huge swells above, is suitable for beginners as well.
- Beach break surfing (as opposed to more challenging reef break surfing) is possible at the mouth of the Sigatoka River near **Kulukulu** (page 130).

a surfer at world-famous Cloudbreak

- The mouth of the **Sigatoka River** (page 130) is Fiji's finest **windsurfing** spot, followed by **Nananu-i-Ra Island** (page 223) off the Sunshine Coast; conditions are best June-August.

- Near Savusavu on Vanua Levu, in the sheltered bay tucked behind Nawi Island, you can snorkel virtually on top of giant clams 1.5 meters wide and learn about pearl-growing on a tour with **J. Hunter Pearls** (page 236).
- **Beqa Lagoon** (page 154), which consists of the little island of Beqa encircled by 190 kilometers of coral reefs, showcases an incredible diversity of hard and soft coral gardens filled with every color and size of fish imaginable, as well as sea turtles and reef sharks. If you stay at any of the Beqa resorts, the reefs are just a 10-minute swim straight out from your hotel. Otherwise, a number of tour operators in Pacific Harbour and along the Coral Coast bring you here by boat.

Underwater Logistics

CERTIFICATION

Worldwide, two organizations train scuba divers, but in Fiji, only **PADI** (www.padi.com) offers dive instruction. If you just want to try it out, you can take a half-day **Discover Scuba session,** where you learn a few basics and then dive while being held by an instructor. To get certified, it's ideal to do the textbook and pool portions of your **Open Water Certification course** at home and save the open-water dives for your trip, so that you don't have to spend your vacation in a classroom. If you're a certified diver but you haven't dived in a while, you can take a half-day refresher course on your first day (all PADI dive centers around the world are required to offer this).

HEALTH AND SAFETY

Fiji's weather allows for safe year-round diving, though if a storm makes the water choppy, captains may decide to cancel boat trips on certain days. PADI certification requires that you be **fit enough** to tread water for 10 minutes and to swim 200 meters (eight laps of an Olympic-size swimming pool) without stopping. People with ear, heart, lung, and respiratory conditions (including asthma) should consult a doctor to see if it's safe for you to dive. **Do not dive** while under the influence of alcohol, kava, or medications that impair your cognitive functioning, or if you have a stuffy nose due to a cold, flu, sinus infection, or allergy flare-up.

Fiji has no stinging jellyfish, but **coral cuts** can sting badly, and **shark injuries** have been reported during dives where sharks are lured into dive areas.

ECOLOGICAL CONCERNS

The **global coral crisis** hasn't spared Fiji. Travelers can help by never touching coral (a bit of oil from your skin can kill a whole colony), respecting the boundaries of designated reef regeneration areas, and speaking up to educate other tourists and tour operators when you see someone hurting the reefs. **Ask dive operators** whether they anchor at moorings, which are preferred rather than dragging an anchor over the reefs. If you have strong snorkeling or diving skills (including enough control to avoid brushing reefs with your hands and fins), you might enjoy joining a resort's **coral-planting project** for an afternoon; the Cousteau Resort near Savusavu, Hideaway Resort on the Coral Coast, and Makaira Resort on Taveuni have model projects.

COSTS

A **one-tank boat dive** in Fiji ranges F$99-199, depending largely on the luxury level of your boat and crew. Add F$25-75 if you're **renting gear,** for a full kit that includes wet suit, tanks, BCD vest, mask, and fins. If you're staying in one place and planning to dive for several days, look into **package discounts;** the more you dive, the less you'll pay per tank.

DIVING WITH CHILDREN

Many experienced dive instructors don't teach children, feeling that preteens lack the maturity to handle the unnatural state of being away from real air without panicking, thus endangering themselves, other divers, and aquatic life. However, the international dive education program PADI offers a pool-only **Bubblemaker program** for children as young as 8, and allows children 10-14 to be certified as **Junior Open Water divers.** In practice, Fiji operators have been known to allow 8- and 9-year-olds to get "certified" and go on accompanied dives.

As a parent, only you can determine what risks you're willing to take. But it's a good idea to (a) ask the dive instructor whether he or she is experienced with teaching children, and (b) make sure your children can handle the experience. Are they comfortable in water? Do they listen to instructions? Is there a language barrier that might inhibit communication?

dive shop at the end of the rainbow

Experience Fijian Culture

A lot of experiences are marketed as "the real Fiji," but the savvy traveler can tell the difference between a staged song-and-dance routine and a truly meaningful performance or work of art. To weight your experience toward the latter, look where contemporary Fijians of all walks of life are living, advocating, creating art, and leading the way for the world to live sustainably.

Above all, enjoy your time in Fiji with respect and curiosity. Most Fijians are happy to answer earnest questions about their families, communities, and concerns.

VISUAL ART

- Traditional arts are well represented and explained at the **Fiji Museum** in Suva, and at the various handicrafts markets where you can bargain hard. For a view of culture-makers today, check out the **art galleries** of Suva as well as the unique **Waisiliva Artists Collective** gallery on Leleuvia Island.

DANCE

- Almost every resort offers a *meke* performance, with singing and dancing that's presented as authentically Fijian. Traditionally a *meke* was a participatory celebration or pre-battle preparation to propitiate a tribe's protective deity, but tourists don't have time for that kind of rite. So these days, *meke* performers blend their resort shows with more dramatic hula and Tongan dance forms to keep the attention of crowds. One dance company creating contemporary choreography, incorporating stories of Fijian life and challenges today, is Nadi-based **VOU Dance Company,** whose professional and student dancers perform original works all across Fiji as well as internationally.

LOCAL STAYS

- Several small accommodation owners are passionate about sharing traditional Fijian ways and Fiji's nature with travelers, through personal interaction and loving explanation: **Kauwai Guesthouse** and **Bobo's Farm** on Ovalau, **Namosi Eco Retreat** near Pacific Harbour, and **Bobby's Nabogiono Farm** on Taveuni.

TOUR OPERATORS

- **Talanoa Treks** on Viti Levu offers hiking and village stay experiences you won't find anywhere else in the world. **Savusavu Tours** on Vanua Levu arranges mud-pool excursions and other adventures along the Hibiscus Highway.

HISTORY

- The Fiji Museum is also a good place to delve into Fiji's dramatic history. Walking tours around colonial **Suva** and the old capital, **Levuka,** a World Heritage Site, bring to life the often-violent clashes of civilizations that created the rich cultural mix that is today's republic.

RELIGION

- Faith is deeply meaningful to most Fijians, and a fine way to connect is to visit a service. Whether at a **church, temple,** or **mosque,** if you respect the etiquette and follow the lead of local worshippers, you'll be warmly welcomed. Sunday morning church choirs give moving performances throughout Fiji. On the northern Viti Levu coast, **Lautoka** is a great place to tour Fiji's diverse range of religions.

MARKETPLACES

- Every large town has a **daily produce market** where growers come to sell their fruits and vegetables, and there's usually a kava corner and fish area as well. The markets are busiest on Saturdays, when vendors from more distant areas join the hubbub. Bargaining is welcome here, but the prices are cheap anyway. **Handicrafts markets** in Suva and Nadi sell a range of goods, some handmade, others imported from China.

EVENTS

- The country's largest fair is the August **Hibiscus Festival** in Suva, where other large events such as **Fashion Week** are also held. In the old capital, **Levuka,** an annual commemoration re-creates the historic events of October 10, 1874, when Fiji's chiefs signed their country over to Queen Victoria. Sports fans will be interested in the **Fiji International Golf Tournament**, held at scenic Natadola Golf Course every August, and **rugby** and **soccer** tournament showdowns at the stadium in Lautoka.

Nadi and Vicinity

Visitors flying into or out of Fiji will land in Nadi, the gateway to the western island archipelagoes, the rest of the country, and even most of the South Pacific. But Nadi is worth more than a pass-through.

Nadi (pronounced NAN di, rhymes with candy) is Fiji's third-largest city, with a population just over 50,000, but it is second only to Suva in cultural importance and diversity. Here, Fiji's diverse indigenous, Indian, Asian, and white populations all find a niche, making Nadi a great place to acclimate to the country.

The surrounding cane fields have been largely replaced by hotels and shops; you'll find pretty much anything you need in these shiny glass storefronts, from duty-free electronics imported directly from Asia to

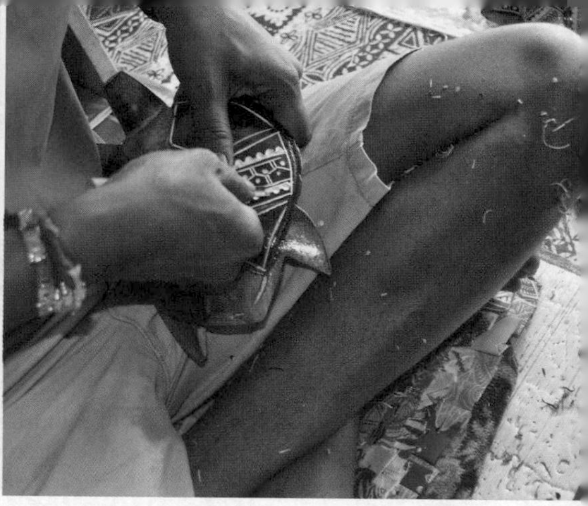

Look for ★ to find recommended sights, activities, dining, and lodging.

Highlights

★ **Sri Siva Subrahmaniya Swami Temple:** The largest and most colorful Hindu temple in the South Pacific is open to visitors (page 43).

★ **See a Dance Show:** See a contemporary performance by **VOU** (page 47) in Nadi or one of the **cultural shows** (page 65) on Denarau Island.

★ **Foodie Fiji:** Modern chefs are creating imaginative twists on old standbys, using traditional techniques and fresh ingredients from soil and sea (page 54).

★ **Cloud 9:** You can eat delicious pizza, dance to a DJ, and kayak at this artificial floating island off of Port Denarau (page 62).

★ **Foothills of the Sleeping Giant:** With garden walks, zip-lining, and natural mud pools, this natural wonderland is easily accessible from Nadi (page 71).

★ **Momi Battery Historic Park:** The British six-inch guns installed here in 1941 are of historical interest—but the views of the offshore islands are even more appealing (page 78).

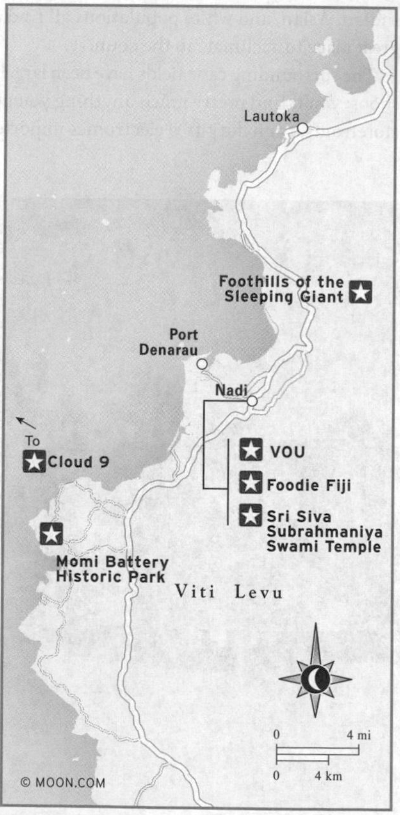

Find Your Beach

The beaches in this area aren't the best in Fiji, but they're lovely for your first and last glimpses of beach life.

- **Wailoaloa Beach** (page 46): Separated from Nadi's main street by the airport runway, this is a fine stopover on your way into or out of the country. There's cheap, tasty food all along the shore, plenty of backpacker-friendly bars in the hotels, and a lovely view out to the Mamanuca Islands.
- **Denarau Island:** The best (artificial) white-sand beaches are at the Sofitel (page 69) and the Hilton (page 69). These are more pleasant for swimming than the murky waters of Wailoaloa, though there can be clumps of seaweed on the seabed.
- **Vuda Bay** (page 74): From the Vuda Point Marina you can stroll onto a long **coral beach** with excellent views of the Mamanuca Islands.

locally manufactured souvenirs, clothes, and groceries. The city's thriving culinary scene encompasses everything from cheap street snacks to nouveau cuisine, making it one of the best places in Fiji for foodies. Both the Nadi Handicraft Market and the Nadi Market, the latter a bustling open-air warehouse where vegetables and fruits are sold, are excellent places to while away a couple of hours taking in the sensory stimuli.

From Nadi, it's a tiny hop over a small bridge to resort-rich Denarau Island. Denarau has boomed in recent years and now houses a range of orderly eateries and shops. It's a popular option for those less interested in authenticity than convenience and upscale amenities. The Marina at Port Denarau has a fun mall and is the embarkation point for most water sports, cruises, and trips to the Mamanuca and Yasawa Islands.

Inland and north of Nadi, the mountainous Sleeping Giant jungle is home to a 35-acre eco-park, zip lines, an orchid garden, and mud baths for soaking away your travel stress.

Half an hour south of Nadi, Momi Bay feels like another world. It's well worth visiting for the peerless view from a historic gun battery that housed thousands of soldiers during World War II.

PLANNING YOUR TIME

The Nadi area has four distinct regions to explore, each worth about a half day, so you can see all of the highlights in two full days. You could stay in any of these places and easily commute to the others. The outlying areas, north and south, have excellent scenery but few food options, so a good strategy would be to enjoy those areas in the mornings. Return to Nadi or Denarau Island for lunch, afternoon activities, and dinner.

If you're staying just one or two nights in Nadi, you could stay either in town or near the airport. If you'll be in the area for a few more days, go west or south to a resort with a view.

If you have more time in Nadi, a huge selection of day cruises, sightseeing tours, and adventure activities are available, and the city makes a convenient base for exploring the western part of Viti Levu as well as the western islands. There are bus tours to gardens, valleys, mountains, and beaches. You can go snorkeling, golfing, and fishing as often as you like.

Be warned that many international flights arrive at the crack of dawn, while most hotels guarantee check-in only at 1500. Pack a swimsuit in an accessible location if you want to wait at your hotel's pool while your luggage sits at the bell desk, or a day pack if

Previous: a pool overlooking Sonaisali Beach; an orchid in the Garden of the Sleeping Giant; woodcarver Ashish Chand at the Nadi Handicrafts Market.

Nadi and Vicinity

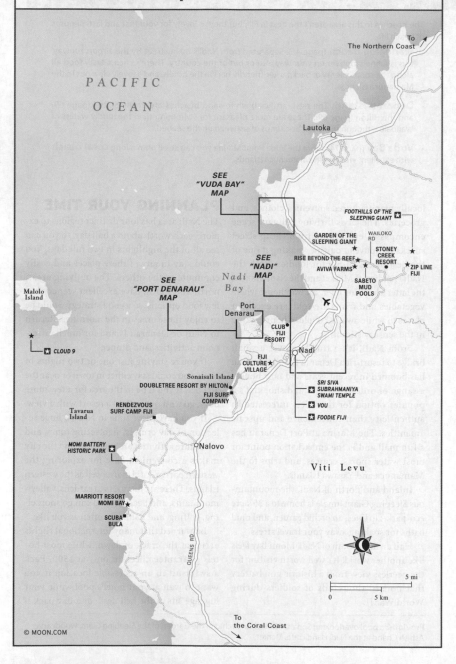

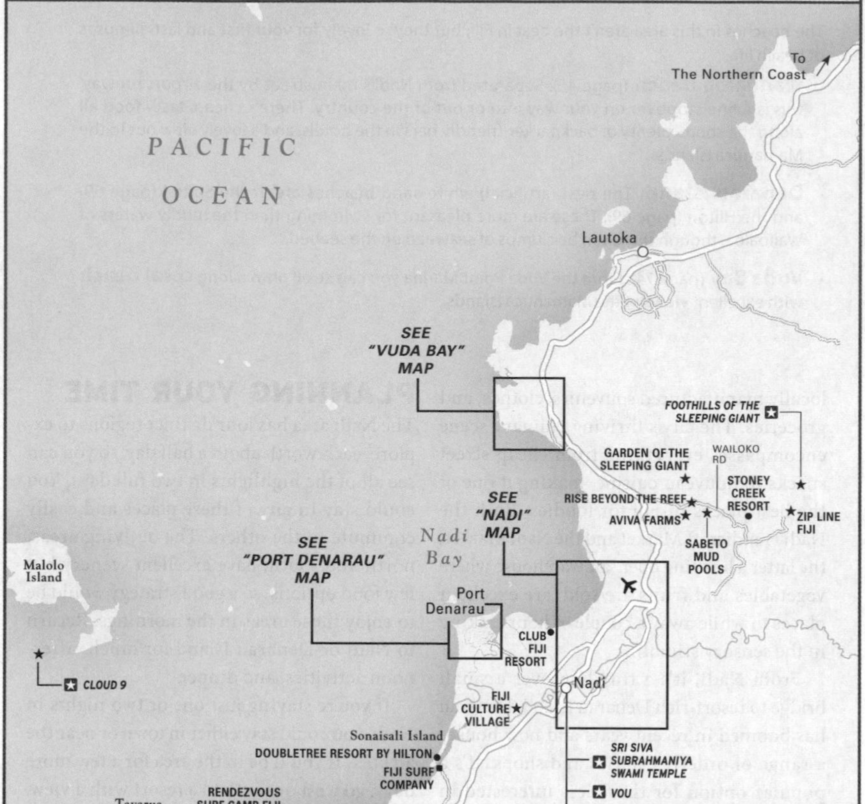

Two Days Around Nadi

DAY 1

Have breakfast at **Wing Hing Restaurant,** then spend the morning in town, taking in the nearby **Nadi Market** and **Sri Siva Subrahmaniya Swami Temple.** Pack a few snacks for the afternoon and head south to spend a couple of hours visiting **Momi Battery Historic Park.** Head back to Nadi for dinner at one of the city's many restaurants. If you still have energy, check out **Smugglers Cove** on Wailoaloa Beach.

DAY 2

Head north for some adventure with **Sleeping Giant Zip Line Fiji** and some relaxation at the **Sabeto Mud Pools.** Spend the later afternoon shopping at the **Marina at Port Denarau.** End the day with the Lomani Wai show at the **Radisson** (reservations essential), which includes an inauthentic but thrilling fire dance performance, kava, and a fancy dinner with your toes in the water, creating the sensation that you're afloat in a few inches of water.

you plan to power through your jet lag and enjoy a morning in town or sightseeing. Some larger resorts work hard to ease the wait with meal coupons or even massage vouchers; it doesn't hurt to inquire about freebies if you're inconvenienced.

Nadi

If you want to be where the action is, you won't be bored in Nadi. The main downtown strip, Queens Road, merges seamlessly into the northern neighborhoods of Martintar and Namaka and then the airport, with shiny and not-so-shiny stores, restaurants, and accommodations from budget to midrange along the way. Due west from Martintar is Wailoaloa Beach, which hugs Nadi Bay and is a longtime favorite of backpackers and flashpackers. A cluster of hostels and hotels is tucked between the beach and the airport runway.

SIGHTS

Nadi Market

For a glimpse of the "real Fiji," visit **Nadi Market,** off Hospital Road between downtown Nadi and the bus station. It's open daily, except Sunday, but it's busiest on Saturday, when city folk and villagers mix to buy and sell the week's produce. Various tour companies include a market visit as a stop on a half-day or full-day tour, though you don't really need a guide to point out the pretty vegetables and fruits. One corner of the market is assigned to *yaqona* (kava) vendors, and it's possible to order a whole bowl of the root beverage for about a dollar (locals will gladly help you finish the bowl). Some market stalls sell a few homemade souvenirs, and cheap eateries fill the surrounding streets; observe what others are having and order the same.

A fun way to see the market is with the chef-teachers of the **Flavours of Fiji Cooking School** (5 Denarau Industrial Estate, tel. 675-0840, reservations@flavoursoffiji.com, http://flavoursoffiji.com, F$180 adults/F$130 children), who can add a market tour prior to your cooking course. They'll point out unique ingredients that you'll be cooking later, as well as answer any questions about how to select the perfect pineapple and the ripest guava.

★ Sri Siva Subrahmaniya Swami Temple

The **Sri Siva Subrahmaniya Swami**

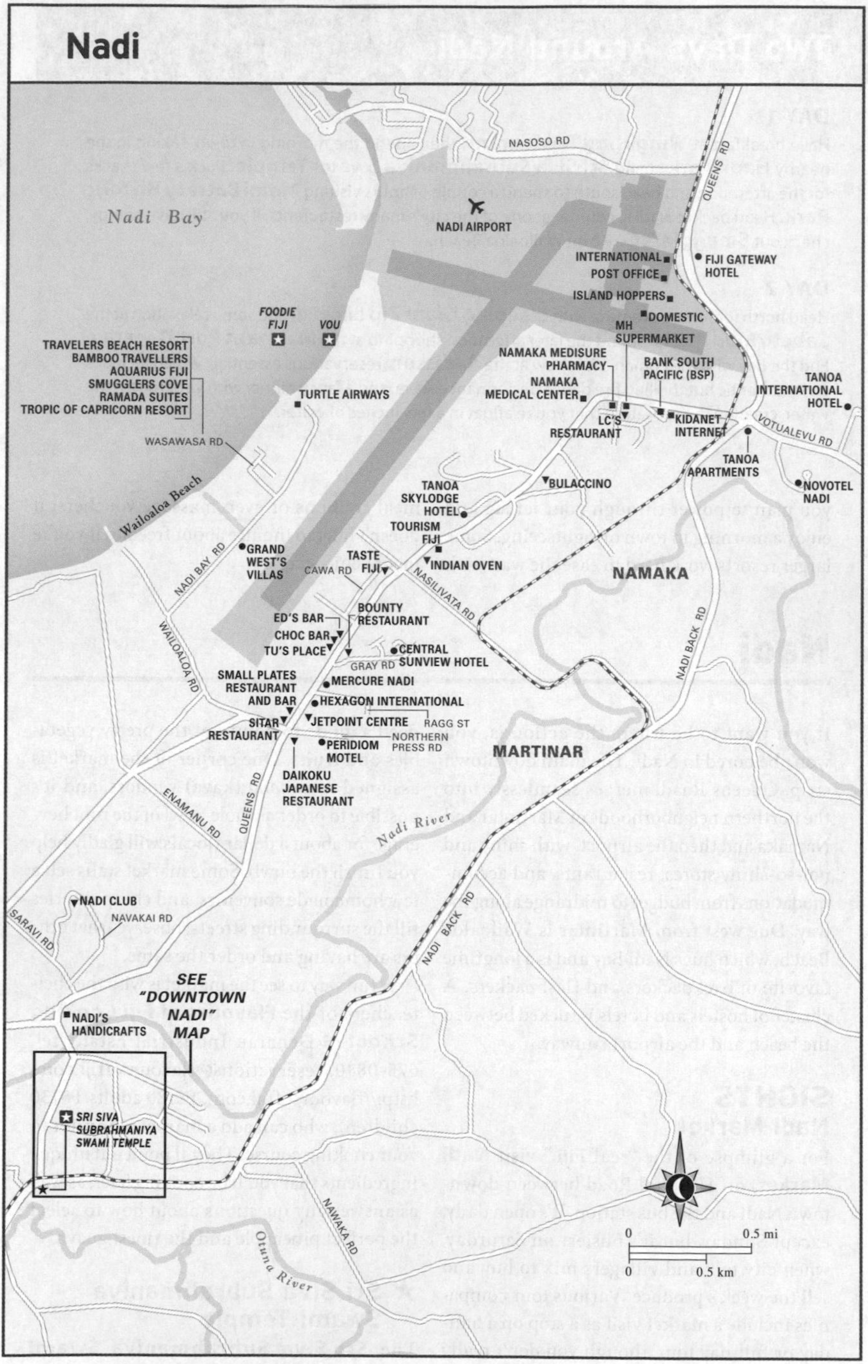
Nadi
Nadi Bay
NASOSO RD
QUEENS RD
NADI AIRPORT
INTERNATIONAL
POST OFFICE
FIJI GATEWAY HOTEL
ISLAND HOPPERS
DOMESTIC
MH SUPERMARKET
FOODIE FIJI
VOU
TRAVELERS BEACH RESORT
BAMBOO TRAVELLERS
AQUARIUS FIJI
SMUGGLERS COVE
RAMADA SUITES
TROPIC OF CAPRICORN RESORT
TURTLE AIRWAYS
NAMAKA MEDISURE PHARMACY
NAMAKA MEDICAL CENTER
BANK SOUTH PACIFIC (BSP)
TANOA INTERNATIONAL HOTEL
LC'S RESTAURANT
KIDANET INTERNET
VOTUALEVU RD
WASAWASA RD
TANOA APARTMENTS
NOVOTEL NADI
BULACCINO
Wailoaloa Beach
TANOA SKYLODGE HOTEL
TOURISM FIJI
INDIAN OVEN
NADI BAY RD
GRAND WEST'S VILLAS
CAWA RD
TASTE FIJI
NASILIVATA RD
NAMAKA
NADI BACK RD
WAILOALOA RD
ED'S BAR
BOUNTY RESTAURANT
CHOC BAR
TU'S PLACE
CENTRAL SUNVIEW HOTEL
GRAY RD
SMALL PLATES RESTAURANT AND BAR
MERCURE NADI
HEXAGON INTERNATIONAL
SITAR RESTAURANT
JETPOINT CENTRE
RAGG ST
NORTHERN PRESS RD
PERIDIOM MOTEL
MARTINAR
DAIKOKU JAPANESE RESTAURANT
ENAMANU RD
Nadi River
NADI CLUB
NAVAKAI RD
SARAVI RD
SEE "DOWNTOWN NADI" MAP
NADI'S HANDICRAFTS
SRI SIVA SUBRAHMANIYA SWAMI TEMPLE
NAWAKA RD
Otunu River
0
0.5 mi
0
0.5 km

Downtown Nadi

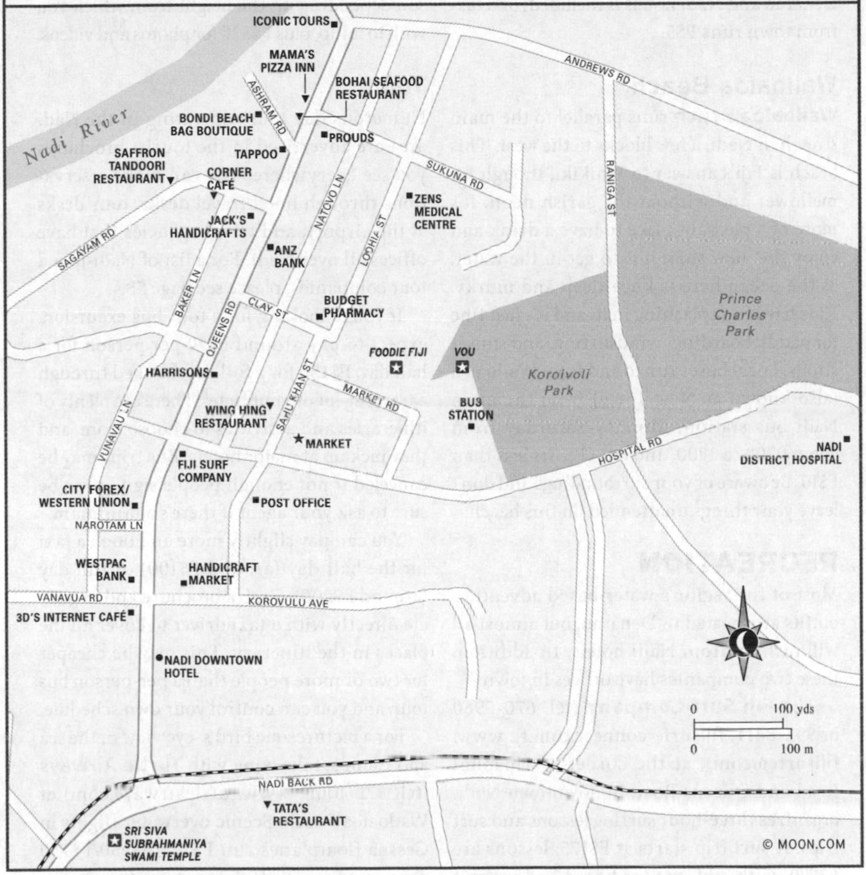

Temple (open during daylight hours, F$5), off Queens Road at the south entrance to town, is the largest Hindu place of worship in the South Pacific. Erected in 1994 by skilled workers from South India, the entire brick and concrete building is covered in intricate, colorfully painted sculptures. This temple is dedicated to Muruga (also known as Subrahmaniya), the mythical general who led the gods to victory over the demons; on the ceiling outside the three-story main sanctum is a fresco of a six-faced Lord Muruga riding a peacock. Visitors must remove their shoes, and there's a strict dress code. If your shoulders and legs aren't covered, you'll have to pay to rent a sulu to cover yourself.

Fiji Culture Village

Fiji Culture Village (Lot 1, Nacaqara, tel. 620-0116 or 804-4800, res@fijiculturevillage.com, www.fijiculturevillage.com, Mon.-Sat. 0830-1700) opened in late 2017 to cater to visitors who want a quick, entertaining glimpse of culture. Just past the southern edge of Nadi on the main road, Chinese businessman Peter Pan has created this faux village with several *bures* and amphitheater seating on a scenic spot overlooking the Nadi River. Admission is F$90 adults, F$45 children ages 5-12. With a *lovo* lunch, it's F$140/F$85. Pickup from Denarau and Nadi hotels is included, or a taxi from town runs F$5.

Wailoaloa Beach

Wailoaloa Beach runs parallel to the main stretch in Nadi, a few blocks to the west. This beach is Fiji's answer to Waikiki, though far mellower and without the garish neon. It's more of a pleasant place to have a drink and enjoy the view than it is to get in the water, as the ocean here is knee-deep and murky. Kids have fun splashing in it, and it's just fine for paddleboarding, windsurfing, and sunset strolls. Local buses run to and from Wailoaloa (also known as New Town) from the main Nadi bus station, Monday-Saturday from about 0700 to 1700, and a taxi costs less than F$10. Be aware of your surroundings and don't leave your things unattended on this beach.

RECREATION

Most of the region's water-based adventure outfits are located in Denarau, but almost all will pick up from Nadi hotels. In addition, these two companies have offices in town:

The **Fiji Surf Company** (tel. 670-5960 or 992-8411, fijisurf@connect.com.fj, www.fijisurfco.com), at the corner of Hospital Road and Queens Road in downtown Nadi, organizes three-hour surfing lessons and surf trips. A surf trip starts at F$175; lessons are F$270, with add-ons for board and wetsuit rental. Its surf school teaches all ages, and also has a local program that makes the sport accessible to Fijian children. You can purchase the ultimate souvenir here: a Fiji-made surfboard designed just for local wave conditions, with colorful tapa patterns. Owner Ian Ravouvou Muller is a passionate advocate for the local surfing scene and a peerless guide, having arranged his business and life around surfing a single wave—Cloudbreak, in the Mamanucas.

Skydive Fiji (tel. 672-8166, www.skydivefiji.com.fj), opposite the Hexagon International in Martintar, offers tandem skydiving jumps from a small plane every two hours daily 0800-1600. It's F$525-780 per person depending on the height from which you wish to jump, plus F$220 for photos and videos.

Tours

Numerous day tours operating in the Nadi area are advertised in the tourist brochures you see everywhere. You can make reservations through hotel travel desks, tour desks at the airport, and travel agencies that have offices all over Nadi. For a list of Nadi-based tour companies, please see page 58.

If you're looking for a tour bus excursion, expect to pay around F$70 per person for a half day, F$150 for a full day, booked through a travel agent or your hotel. There are plenty of itineraries and activities to choose from, and they pick up at major hotels. Bus trips may be canceled if not enough people sign up, so be sure to ask your agent if there's a minimum.

You can pay slightly more and book a taxi for the half day (around F$100) or full day (around F$200). Grab a brochure and negotiate directly with a taxi driver to cover all the places in the itinerary. This may be cheaper for two or more people than a per-person bus tour, and you can control your own schedule.

For a picturesque bird's-eye view of the sea and islands, take wing with **Turtle Airways** (tel. 672-1888, www.turtleairways.com) at Wailoaloa Beach. Scenic overwater flights in Cessna floatplanes run F$275/F$550/F$750 per person for 20/40/55 minutes (minimum of two and a maximum of six passengers with a combined weight of 460kg).

You can also fly with **Island Hoppers** (tel. 672-0410, www.islandhoppersfiji.com), which has a separate terminal behind the airport post office and another office at Port Denarau. Helicopter tours around Nadi and the Mamanucas run for 10, 15, 20, or 30 minutes, starting at F$275 per adult and F$165 per child.

SHOPPING

Nadi is a good place to pick up both souvenirs and necessities, as shops there cater to locals,

TOP EXPERIENCE

★ VOU: Think Locally, Dance Globally

VOU draws on tradition to create exuberant, modern choreography.

On a side street in Nadi across from Prince Charles Park is a glass storefront filled with an unruly jumble of costumes, bits of stage sets, and, at any given time, dancers in various stages of stretching, rehearsing, laughing, and planning. This is the home of Fiji's vibrant, internationally renowned dance company and school, **VOU** (32 Naicker St., tel. 670-0693, info@voufiji.com, www.voufiji.com).

The company's name means "new" in the iTaukei language, but many of the works are actually a hypnotic, explosive blend of old and new. Since ancient times, dance has played a vital role in Fijian cultures, used to beseech deities to safeguard crops, bless sea voyages, and protect warriors in battle. Traditionally, dances were created anew for each occasion by the tribe's choreographer, a shaman who based his creations on dreams he received from the supernatural world. Today this sacred occupation is dying out, as children educated in Western ways seek more lucrative careers. This means the loss of not only new dances, but also generations of choreography.

Through its unique research-based dance programs, VOU rigorously trains young dancers in modern technique, then sends them back to their village communities to collect what they can of traditional chants and gestures, as well as the lore that inspires them. By blending traditional and contemporary forms of dance, music, and theater, the company's dancers are not only creating innovative work, but keeping Fijian dance alive in a cosmopolitan context.

In 2016, after Cyclone Winston tore through Fiji, many of the dancers returned to their villages to help rebuild—and to document the people's stories. The resulting hour-long show, *Are We Stronger Than Winston?*, is a poignant meditation on climate change that won the Edinburgh Fringe Festival's Sustainable Practice Award in 2016.

The company's ambitions are only growing. A children's program providing affordable tuition to talented young dancers now serves 250 students. International programs offer foreign choreographers a chance to study Fijian dance and work with the VOU dancers. Student and company dancers perform hundreds of shows a year across Fiji and as far afield as Australia, New Zealand, Indonesia, India, Malaysia, the United States, Guam, New Caledonia, Canada, China, Latvia, Lithuania, Slovenia, France, England, Austria, and Scotland.

To catch a show, check the **event listings** on the group's website and Facebook page.

not just tourists. Shops are open 0900-1700 Monday-Saturday unless otherwise noted. Supermarkets are open on Sundays. The main shopping area is the three-block section of Queens Road between the Nadi Handicraft Market at the south end and the Nadi River crossing at the north end.

The **Nadi Handicraft Market** (Mon.-Sat. 0800-1800), opposite the Nadi Hotel just off Queens Road, provides the opportunity to buy directly from handicraft producers. Choose wisely among the cheap mass-produced goods, and bargain down to half the stickered "tourist price." Artisans include Ashish Chand, an Indo-Fijian who learned the craft of woodcarving as a child from his indigenous neighbors, and Salote (she uses only one name) from the Lau Islands, whose labor-intensive weavings have been featured in a BBC documentary. The ice cream stall at the far end of the market sells $1 cones and an assortment of snacks, as well as useful behind-the-counter items such as cigarette papers and chewing gum.

Before bargaining at the market, you might stop in at one of the several large curio emporiums along Queens Road to get an idea of what's available and how much your preferred items should cost. The shiniest is **Jack's Handicrafts** (tel. 670-0744, www.jacksfiji.com, Sun. 0800-1300). Close to the bridge over the river is **Nadi's Handicrafts** (tel. 670-3588), with a wide and relatively inexpensive selection. Alongside curios, **Prouds** (tel. 670-0531, 670-1077, or 777-7836, www.prouds.com.fj) and **Tappoo** (tel. 670-1022, www.tappoo.com.fj) also sell imported luxury goods, including perfumes and handbags, of the type usually seen in airport duty-free shops. All of the curio places sell touristy beachwear and other Fiji-branded clothing.

For more clothing options, try the locally owned two-story **Harrisons** (tel. 670-0097) and, just off the strip on Ashram Road, an outlet of the upscale Australian resort wear company **Bondi Beach Bag Boutique** (tel. 777-5442, www.bondibeachbagco.com).

To avoid pricey hotel minibars, buy your own bottles and snacks at the **MH** (tel. 670-0033) or **RB Patel** (tel. 339-1899) supermarkets. For kava, you can stop by the 24-hour **Praveen's Kava Shop** (tel. 346-0016).

If your lodging has cooking facilities, pick up the day's catch by following the "fresh fish" sign from the main road at the junction to Namaka village.

NIGHTLIFE

Smugglers Cove (tel. 672-6578, daily 1600-2300), a resort on Wailoaloa Beach, has a popular beachside bar for tourists, backpackers, and trendy locals. It's a good place to strike up a friendly conversation, and you can grab a bite from the in-house restaurant.

The nightclub at the **Novotel** (tel. 672-2000), near the airport, is safe with a relatively upscale clientele. A live band plays Friday and Saturday starting at 2030.

Ed's Bar (tel. 672-4650, cover F$5), a little north of the Mercure Hotel in Martintar, has a long daily happy hour 1200-2100. You'll enjoy chatting with the friendly staff and meeting the trendy locals and surfers who hang out here. There are three pool tables in a section that opens at 1700.

After Dark Night Club (daily 2000-0300), in Namaka just northeast of MH, hosts a mostly indigenous Fijian crowd. It plays newly released music.

White House Nightclub (tel. 831-8106, daily 1800-0300, admission F$5) is located in Jetpoint Centre in Martintar, walking distance from many of the Martintar hotels. This popular spot fills up around 2300. It's generally safe, though carrying excessive cash is not advised. A separate lounge area offers a more relaxed environment for a drink, laid-back music, and chatting with locals.

Also in the Jetpoint Centre is **Ice Bar** (tel. 672-7123, Mon.-Sat. 1800-0300, Sun. 1900-0200, cover F$5), popular with younger partygoers and the Indo-Fijian crowd. It has a

1: Sri Siva Subrahmaniya Swami Temple in Nadi **2:** Flavours of Fiji Cooking School **3:** the Nadi Handicraft Market.

1

PENSONIC
2

3

Retail Therapy

Most chain stores offer coconut-based beauty products.

You can hardly be a tourist in Fiji without encountering a **Jack's, Tappoo,** or **Prouds** store, as they have outlets in many hotels, on every main thoroughfare, and even aboard the larger ships. Prices are fixed, and there's little variation in price across locations. The branches in downtown Nadi and downtown Suva occupy the largest square footage and thus offer the most selection.

All offer similar ranges of replica handicrafts, souvenirs, jewelry, coconut-based beauty products, and *bula* wear for children and adults. **Jack's** and **Tappoo** have branched out into the food business, standardizing menus and cuisines with impressively consistent quality. **Prouds** sells designer goods such as you'd find in an airport duty-free store (perfumes, brand-name purses, etc.) and is also the sole licensed outlet for **J. Hunter Pearls,** the only pearls grown in Fiji. (Pearls you see in other stores come from Tahiti or farther afield.)

Three smaller chains—**Nagindas, Harrisons,** and **Cloudbreak**—are also found in many towns and offer Fiji-inspired clothing lines, with Cloudbreak geared a little more toward swimwear and water sports.

Much of the clothing that looks local is indeed made in Fiji, but an increasing amount of made-in-China wear is being imported. Specialized sportswear from Australia and elsewhere is often expensive. Clothing is generally true to American sizing and goes up to at least 2XL in both men's and women's, but you may need to ask a clerk to bring out the larger sizes from the stockroom.

Every major town has an **MH** supermarket (formerly Morris Hedstrom, and often still referred to by locals as "Morris"), with groceries, toiletries, and household goods. Its bakery is handy for quick breakfasts and lunches on the go. Less ubiquitous but equally clean and well stocked is the **RB Patel** supermarket chain.

balcony where you can drink alfresco. Ice Bar isn't overly busy or crowded unless an event is being held at the club, making it a nice spot for a hassle-free and relaxing evening.

You're welcome to drink alongside local members at the **Nadi Club** (Lodhia St., tel. 670-0239, www.nadisportsclub.com, Mon.-Thurs. 1000-2200, Fri.-Sat. 1000-2300, Sun. 0900-2100). **Felix Fastfood** (Mon.-Thurs. 0700-2200, Fri.-Sat. 0700-2300, Sun. 1000-2100, F$5), attached to the club, serves tasty Indian meals (chicken, lamb, duck, goat, and fish). The Indian-style chop suey is substantial.

FOOD

Breakfast

Several places along Sahu Khan Street, near the market, serve a good cheap breakfast of egg sandwich with coffee. The **Wing Hing Restaurant** (tel. 670-1766, Mon.-Sat. 0630-1830) is the best of these.

Bulaccino (Queens Rd., tel. 672-8638, www.bulaccino.com, Mon.-Fri. 0800-1630, Sat.-Sun. 0800-1500), next to the bridge, is a European-style coffee-and-cake place with a nice terrace overlooking the Nadi River. It's good for breakfast. Other meals run F$12-20. There's a computer with Internet access that costs F$3 per 30 minutes.

Corner Café (Sagayam Rd., tel. 670-3131, Mon.-Sat. 0800-1700), behind (and owned by) the two-story Jack's Handicrafts store on Queens Road, has air-conditioning, free (if slow) Wi-Fi, espresso drinks, pastries, and a good café menu for breakfast and lunch. Try the lamb kebab roll (F$14) and mango smoothie (F$7).

Fijian

★ **Taste Fiji** (Cawa Rd., Martintar, tel. 890-1197 or 867-0470, Mon.-Sat. 0630-1800, Sun. 0700-1400, taste@tastefiji.com, www.tastefiji.com) serves up hearty breakfasts and lunches (F$8-23) with local touches: Fijian honey on a stack of pancakes, local *ota* fern salad, or caramelized Vuda pork belly over sesame rice.

★ **Tu's Place** (Queens Rd., Martintar, tel. 672-2110, ratuf@connect.com.fj, daily 0700-2230, F$15-F$50) is more upscale. If you like pancakes, come for breakfast. Later in the day, try the *kokoda* or the *rourou* (taro leaf) balls with grilled fish in coconut sauce.

Indo-Fijian

Hearty fare is found at ★ **Saffron Tandoori Restaurant** (Sagayam Rd., tel. 670-3131, Mon.-Sat. 1100-1430 and 1730-1930, Sun. 1730-1930), also owned by Jack's Handicrafts. At dinner, the seafood and meat entrées average F$39, or you can order something from the grill. The service is efficient, the selection of dishes is large, and fish-and-chips are available for the kids.

Another real find is **Tata's Restaurant** (Nadi Back Rd., tel. 670-0502, Mon.-Fri. 0730-1700, Sat. 0730-1600), on Nadi Back Road around the corner east of the Siva temple. Most dishes are listed on a blackboard; the curries (F$5-7) are a great value. Though this place is surrounded by automotive workshops, the outdoor seating is pleasant.

The brightly lit **Indian Oven** (Colonial

sweets on display at an Indo-Fijian bakery

Plaza, Namaka, tel. 834-7205, indianovenfiji@gmail.com, daily 1100-2300) is popular with flight crews who come for the late-night curries and tandoori dishes.

East Asian

★ **Small Plates Restaurant and Bar** (Queens Rd., tel. 672-3888, daily 1600-2300, F$8-25), located opposite the Jetpoint Centre in Martintar, can easily be missed because of the high hedges surrounding the front garden. It's open daily for lunch and dinner, and specializes in Asian-influenced small plates. Favorites include the salt-and-pepper squid and the eggplant with chili bean paste.

★ **Bohai Seafood Restaurant** (Queens Rd., tel. 670-0178, daily 1000-2200, F$6-18), upstairs at the junction of Queens and Ashram Road, offers a large selection of Chinese dishes, curries, and seafood at good prices. Plenty of local Asians eat here, which is a good sign. Portions are generous, and the deep-fried okra are heavenly. Allow extra time for prawns and crab cooked to order.

The atmospheric **Daikoku Japanese Restaurant** (tel. 670-3623, www.daikokufiji.com, Mon.-Sat. 1200-1400 and 1800-2130), at the corner of Queens Road and Northern Press Road in Martintar, is the place to splurge on teppanyaki dishes (F$26-33) cooked right at your table. The sashimi and sushi are also good. Ask for the special seafood sauce.

Sitar Restaurant (tel. 672-7722, daily 1100-1500 and 1800-2200), at the corner of Queens Road and Wailoaloa Road, serves Thai dishes (F$17-20) and Indian *thalis* (F$9-13).

The **Bounty Restaurant** (79 Queens Rd., tel. 672-0840, www.bountyfiji.com, daily 0900-2300), located a little north of the Mercure Hotel in Martintar, has local and Asian dishes and hamburgers for lunch, and steaks and seafood for dinner. Lunch specials here start at F$12, while dinner plates are F$16-33. Lobster is F$45. The dining room has lots of local color and the terrace is very popular during happy hour (daily 1600-1900).

LC's Restaurant (2 Hillside Rd., tel. 672-8181, daily 1100-1430 and 1800-2130) is located behind the MH supermarket in Namaka. This friendly restaurant is popular for family-style Cantonese fare. The décor is simple and meals are reasonably priced.

Western

Mama's Pizza Inn (Queens Rd., tel. 670-0221, daily 1000-2300, F$8-28), at the north end of downtown opposite the Mobil service station, serves good pizza. Mama's has two other outlets, in Colonial Plaza in Namaka (tel. 672-0922) and in the Marina at Port Denarau (tel. 675-0533), but the downtown branch is tastiest. It's a good choice if you're with a group and want to keep your costs down.

The **Ed's Bar** complex (Queens Rd., tel. 672-4650) in Martintar is a fun place. You can dine on appetizers at the bar, such as a plate of six big, spicy barbecued chicken wings for F$6.50. Otherwise, go through the connecting door into the adjacent **Choc Bar** (Mon.-Sat. 1200-2300, Sun. 1630-2300) or "Chocolate Bar," which serves lunch for F$6.50 (try the sui beef bone soup). At dinnertime there are blackboard specials, such as a pot of garlic prawns (F$29) or a T-bone steak (F$32). Burgers start at F$8, curries at F$12, and fish-and-chips at F$15.

ACCOMMODATIONS

Many Nadi hotels offer free airport transfers, although sometimes it's only the trip *from* the airport that is free. Check when making your reservation or ask one of the uniformed tour guides (stationed at the exit of the customs area of the airport) whether a driver from your hotel is present.

The Queens Road hotels in Nadi, Martintar, and Namaka may experience street noise, especially if they abut a bar or disco; ask for a room on the quiet side of the hotel. Plenty of budget and midrange accommodations line the shore at Wailoaloa, making it a popular scene for flashpackers. If you're looking at dorms in this area, be sure to check how many people (and their snores) will be sharing your room and bathroom, and whether the dorms are mixed or gender-segregated.

Many mid-priced hotels regularly discount their official rack rates for walk-in bookings, and you could pay considerably less than the published rates listed here. Even when booking in advance, you may be able to bargain them down if you're staying several nights; look online for "stay a night free" deals and talk to the front desk if you're interested in three-night and five-night packages.

Downtown Nadi, Martintar, and Namaka

UNDER US$50

The nicest backpacker place in Martintar is the two-story, 18-room **Central Sunview Hotel** (14 Gray Rd., Martintar, tel. 672-4933, hsunviewmotel@connect.com.fj). An air conditioned room for a single or couple is F$75; with two double beds, F$100. Breakfast is included, cooking facilities are available, and it's clean, quiet, and friendly. The Wi-Fi often doesn't work.

Nadi Downtown Hotel (Queens Rd., Nadi, tel. 670-0600, www.nadidowntownhotel.com) is in the center of Nadi, between the Handicrafts Market and the temple. Its main attraction is the price: It starts at F$70 for a single or double with fan/air-conditioning, including private bath. The eight-bed dormitory is F$20 per person. These rates include a toast-and-coffee breakfast and are easily reduced with bargaining. This place looks seedy from the outside, but with recent renovations the rooms are fine. A cozy little 24-hour bar is in back.

Peridiom Motel Accommodation (Northern Press Rd., Martintar, tel. 672-2574, www.peridiommotelfiji.com) is worth considering if you want cooking facilities. The standard units with double bed start at F$50, while the two rooms with one double and one single are F$80. The family room runs F$90-120 depending on the size of your group (up to five adults). All units are in a long, single-story block and have air-conditioning.

Hexagon International (Queens Rd., Martintar, tel. 672-0044, www.hexagonfiji.com) is a sprawling complex of two- and three-story blocks with three semi-rectangular swimming pools and a bar and restaurant. The 27 standard air-conditioned rooms with private bath and fridge are F$85 double, the 54 larger deluxe rooms F$160, the four family rooms and four studio apartments F$190, and the 24 two-bedroom apartments with kitchen F$290. Internet access is F$4.50 per half hour.

★ **Tanoa Skylodge Hotel** (Queens Rd., Namaka, tel. 672-2200, www.tanoaskylodge.com) is just two kilometers south from the airport, constructed on spacious grounds in the early 1960s and renovated in 2014. The 14 standard rooms are F$100 single or double; the 37 superior rooms with towels and TV are F$130/F$160 for single/double; and the two family rooms with cooking facilities are F$180. It's clean and the scheduled airport transfers are free. The on-site Gordy's Country Diner has main dishes from F$25, and happy hour at the bar is 1730-1830. There's a small swimming pool. Wi-Fi is free if you book online; otherwise it is F$8 an hour.

US$50-100

Mercure Nadi (Queens Rd., Martintar, tel. 672-2255, www.mercure.com), an Accor Hotels property halfway between the airport and town, is one of Nadi's nicest large hotels. This appealing three-story building has 85 air-conditioned rooms, each with a terrace; rates are F$166 single or double and F$195 for deluxe/family rooms. A third person can be added for F$50, and a F$95 late checkout rate allows you to keep your room until 1800, if it's available. Lots of well-shaded tables and chairs surround the swimming pool. There's a Rosie Holidays desk, a spa, and a taxi stand. Airport transfers and use of the tennis court are free for guests. Wi-Fi is a steep F$11.50 per hour.

Directly opposite the airport and within easy walking distance of the domestic terminal is the two-story, colonial-style **Fiji Gateway Hotel** (Queens Rd., Namaka, tel. 672-2444, www.fijigateway.com). The Gateway (formerly a Raffles) has 22 standard

★ Foodie Fiji

Fijian restaurants once served up unimaginative copies of continental cuisine. But these days, a new generation of innovative chefs is creating a modern Fijian palate, offering fresh twists on classics.

Star ingredients are ocean and river **fish, coconut** in all its forms, ***duruka*** (a cane shoot with a texture and mild taste similar to water chestnuts), **nama** ("sea grapes," a type of seaweed), and **root vegetables** such as sweet potato, taro, and cassava. ***Ota,*** a fiddlehead fern grown in the mountains, creates an interesting texture in salads and vegetarian side dishes.

Look for fancy iterations of ***kokoda,*** Fiji's version of ceviche, in which the "cooking" agent is vinegar instead of lime and is mellowed out with fresh coconut milk. Desserts are also a must, utilizing the **tropical fruits** that are abundant year-round, from pineapple mousse to dragonfruit sorbet. Don't miss the pineapple, papaya, and watermelon that populate every market and buffet spread, as well as passion fruit and mango in season.

Fiji's bartenders and bar designers have poured on the creativity, too, so you can wash it all down with an only-in-Fiji **cocktail** or mocktail, typically featuring **local rum** distilled in Lautoka plus coconut, ginger, tropical fruit, raw sugar, and/or chili pepper.

The best places to experience modern Fijian cuisine in Nadi are:

- **Tu's Place** (Cawa Rd., Martintar, tel. 890-1197 or 867-0470, Mon.-Sat. 0630-1800, Sun. 0700-1400, taste@tastefiji.com, www.tastefiji.com) serves up hearty breakfasts and lunches with local touches.
- **Taste Fiji** (Queens Rd., Martintar, tel. 672-2110, ratuf@connect.com.fj, daily 0700-2230) serves local dishes in an upscale environment.

The marina in Port Denarau has two nouveau restaurants next to each other in a pleasant waterfront setting:

- **Bonefish Seafood Restaurant** (Marina at Port Denarau, tel. 675-0197, www.bonefishfiji.com, daily 1100-2200) is known for its excellent seafood and use of local ingredients.
- **Nadina Fijian Restaurant** (Marina at Port Denarau, tel.675-0290, Mon.-Sat. 0800-2300) features fresh takes on traditional iTaukei (native Fijian) dishes.

If you'd like to give Fijian cooking a try yourself, the professional and well-organized **Flavours of Fiji Cooking School** (5 Denarau Industrial Estate, tel. 675-0840, reservations@flavoursoffiji.

rooms without TVs at F$125 single or double, 46 larger deluxe rooms at F$215, poolside rooms at F$240, and 7 suites at F$295. Only the deluxe rooms can be reserved through the hotel's website; they can accommodate a third person for F$25. There are two swimming pools. The Gateway's bar is worth checking out if you're stuck at the airport waiting for a flight, but the restaurant is pricey. Wi-Fi is free in the lobby, F$15 per day in your room. A Rosie Holidays desk is here.

Novotel Nadi (Votualevu Rd., tel. 672-2000, www.novotel.com) is a sprawling two-story Accor property with mountain views from the spacious grounds on Namaka Hill. The 127 air-conditioned rooms with patio or balcony and fridge begin at F$175 single or double, but can be considerably cheaper when booked through the Novotel website. Walk-in discounts are also possible. Two children under 13 are accommodated free when sharing their parents' room. A swimming pool is available, and there's a nine-hole executive golf course on the adjacent slope. A Rosie Holidays desk is here.

People on brief prepaid stopovers in Nadi are often accommodated at the two-story **Tanoa International Hotel** (Votualevu Rd., tel. 672-0277, www.tanoainternational.com), a few hundred meters inland. It's a cut

You'll see plenty of fish served up with flare.

com, http://flavoursoffiji.com, F$180 adults/F$130 children) on Denarau offers market tours plus half-day cooking classes. You'll create and eat up to 11 Fijian and Indo-Fijian dishes in an immaculate kitchen with personal stations—all in just three hours thanks to the fine chef-teachers, who come in at dawn to chop and prep your ingredients in individual portions. Groups of 8 or more receive a discount.

To re-create a taste of Fiji at home, pick up a copy of *Kana Vinaka: Contemporary Island Cuisine*, a colorful **cookbook** by chef Colin Chung. The Hawaii native has trained numerous Fijian chefs and hoteliers in creating dishes that make the best of local sea and land produce. Impress your friends by preparing neo-Fijian dishes such as spicy steamed fish on eggplant pillows, or papaya-coconut pie.

If you love cooking shows, let Fiji's top chef, the affable Lance Seeto, take you on a foodie tour of a different island and dish in each episode of ***Taste of Paradise*** (www.tasteofparadise.tv).

above the Novotel, but no off-site shops or restaurants are within walking distance of either property. The 148 air-conditioned rooms with fridge are F$116/132/152 (standard/superior/executive single or double). Children under 12 stay free. A swimming pool and fitness center, floodlit tennis courts, and an ATS Pacific tour desk are on the premises.

OVER US$100

★ **Tanoa Apartments** (tel. 672-3685, www.tanoahotels.com) is off Votualevu Road, on a hilltop overlooking the surrounding countryside. Opened in 1965, this property was the forerunner of the Tanoa hotel chain owned by local businessman Yanktesh Permal Reddy. The 20 self-catering apartments begin at F$320; weekly, monthly, and walk-in rates discounted up to 50 percent are often available. Facilities include a swimming pool and tennis courts. For those who get the discount, Tanoa Apartments is a top pick for its comfort and location—close to the action but secluded from the commercial strip.

Wailoaloa Beach

Wailoaloa Beach (sometimes known as New Town Beach) is to flashpackers what Denarau Island is to wealthy tourists on upscale package tours. The properties listed below are right on the beach on Wasawasa Road unless otherwise noted.

UNDER US$50

★ **Bamboo Travellers** (tel. 672-2225, bamboobackpackers@gmail.com, http://bambootravellers.com/) is a friendly hostel with its own dive shop, fast Wi-Fi, and live acoustic music every night. Young solo travelers will have no trouble meeting new friends, perhaps over kava, and the travel desk here is knowledgeable about budget accommodations on other islands. Beds start at F$16 for a fan-only coed dorm, and go up to F$26 for an air-conditioned female dorm. An array of other room types start at F$60 (fan only, shared bathroom, no view). A separate mansion, 100 meters down the beach, has air-conditioned rooms and a quieter vibe; the priciest room here is the Tropic Oceanfront Superior, at F$155 (sleeps up to five, easier if some of them are children). Everything is clean, though aged.

Tropic of Capricorn Resort (tel. 672-6607) is a pleasant, welcoming place. The manager, Mama Selena, has traveled the world and is a lot of fun to meet. The old building facing the figure-eight swimming pool contains six-bed and eight-bed dorms with fan at F$26 per person, as well as an air-conditioned double (F$85). The newer three-story building erected between the pool and beach is all air-conditioned; it includes an 8-bed dorm on the ground floor and a 10-bed dorm in the middle floor, both F$6 per person, as well as two doubles at (F$90/F$135). Higher-priced rooms have fridges, TVs, and balconies. Breakfast is included.

The **Aquarius Fiji** (tel. 672-6000, www.aquariusfiji.com) is a large mansion with four standard rooms at F$145 double and four ocean-view rooms at F$195. A third person pays an extra F$25. The pair of two-bed dorms are F$30 per person, and the 6- and 12-bed dorms are F$47 per person. All rooms are air-conditioned. Breakfast is included with the dorms but not with the rooms. Aquarius has a swimming pool right on the beach and a party atmosphere.

Travelers Beach Resort (tel. 672-3322, beachvilla@connect.com.fj) has five air-conditioned "ocean wing" rooms with views in an older building that are F$90/110 single/double; two other rooms in this building are designated as "beachfront" rooms and overlook both the pool and the beach, at F$115/135. Other rooms, at various rates/sizes, are spread among several two-story buildings across the road and are a block back from the beach. The two 16-bed dorms cost F$25 per person. All rates include a light breakfast and tax. There's a restaurant-bar and swimming pool near the beach with a Polynesian show on Fridays.

Smugglers Cove Horizon Beach Resort (tel. 672-2832, www.horizonbeachresortfiji.com) is a large, wooden two-story building across a field from the beach. Dorm beds start at $42 for a fan-only 34-person dorm, and go up to $52 in the 16-bed air-conditioned "girls sanctuary." The 14 rooms with bath begin at F$95 single or double with air-conditioning, and go up to $295 for an ocean-view room with a balcony. No cooking facilities are provided, but there's a mid-priced restaurant/bar and a miniature swimming pool. Probably the biggest draw is that guests here are allowed to use all the amenities at the much pricier Smugglers Cove resort next door.

US$50-150

The focal point for young backpackers is ★ **Smugglers Cove Beach Resort** (tel. 672-6578, www.smugglersbeachfiji.com). The four garden-view rooms are F$180 single or double and the 16 ocean-view suites are F$295, including continental breakfast. There's an evening activity every night except Monday at the trendy beachfront restaurant, including fire dancing three times a week. The bustling tour desk offers all the standard Nadi activities, and there's a snazzy swimming pool.

A kilometer southwest of the other hotels on Wailoaloa Beach is **Club Fiji Resort** (Wailoaloa Rd., tel. 670-2189, www.

clubfiji-resort.com). The 24 thatched duplex bungalows, all with verandas, private baths, solar hot water, and fridges, are priced according to location: F$130 single or double for a garden unit, F$160 ocean view, or F$190 on the beach. The eight "beachfront villas" are actually rooms in a two-story building (F$270 double with air-conditioning). Food and drink costs here quickly add up, with main plates at the club's restaurant costing F$18-33. Special events include a Sunday-night beach barbecue (F$22-34). The only other dining options within an easy walk are **JB's On the Beach,** which has a nice view from its deck, and the **Beachside Resort.** There's a small, clean swimming pool.

Grand West's Villas (Nadi Bay Rd., tel. 672-4833) comprises 10 studios at F$210, 10 one-bedroom apartments at F$230 single or double, and 20 two-bedroom apartments at F$320 double in several two-story blocks. These spacious, self-catering apartments are a reasonable value, but the location is poor—the beach is too far away and the airport runway too close. Some units are rented to locals on a long-term basis. Two tennis courts, a swimming pool with a waterslide, and an ATS Pacific desk are on the grounds. The adjacent **New Town Shopping Center** (daily 0630-2100) sells alcohol and groceries at normal prices.

OVER US$150

In 2018, the four-star **Ramada Suites** (http://ramadabeachfiji.com, F$487-874), a joint project with Smugglers Cove next door, opened on the beach. The F$15 million development includes a mix of studio and one- and two-bedroom apartments. Free Wi-Fi and airport transfers are included with all rates, and there are deals for guests who stay more than four nights. The beach and restaurants are at Smugglers Cove, but the Ramada has its own bar with fine views of the western islands.

An even more upscale hotel is set to gentrify the waterfront in late 2019. The five-star **Pullman Nadi Bay Resort and Spa** is Wailoaloa's bigger project, an $80 million investment by the Gokal Group (which also owns the Peninsula Hotel in Suva), operated by the international Accor chain under its high-end brand for business travelers. The only five-star property in Nadi proper, the Pullman will try to give the Denarau hotels some competition with a promised 234 rooms, 16 suites, six restaurants and bars, two swimming pools, a day spa, shops, and a 400-seat conference center.

INFORMATION AND SERVICES

Tourism

There are no visitors centers with objective information for tourists in Fiji. **Tourism Fiji** (tel. 672-2433, www.fiji.travel.com) has a marketing office in Colonial Plaza, Namaka; you can pick up brochures in the lobby, but it's not set up to deal with the general public. The website has extensive but often outdated accommodations listings.

Instead, a host of private travel agencies provide information, generally skewed toward earning themselves commissions. Even the information desk at the international airport is staffed by tour agents who will steer you toward their own cubicles for even the simplest requests. If you're booking with a foreign tour company, chances are they've outsourced your trip to one of these inbound travel agencies; you might be able to cut out the middleman and save money if you don't mind some long-distance emails.

The agents are friendly and helpful, but always keep in mind that they only promote properties and sights that pay them commissions. If budget is a consideration it's a good idea to compare rates and call operators directly. If an agent warns you not to go somewhere, it may be because he or she doesn't get an adequate commission from the place.

Be sure that you leave their offices understanding which vouchers you need for which trips, and make sure any important details are in writing (two twin beds, not one king bed, for example; breakfast, Wi-Fi, etc.). It can be difficult to get a refund from an agent if something goes wrong. The best arbiter of disputes is probably your international credit card.

That said, when you do want someone to plan a trip or an excursion for you, the following Nadi-based agencies are reputable:

Iconic Tours (Queens Rd. at Andrews Rd. intersection next to Kia Motors, tel. 920-4246 or 902-7163, www.iconictoursfiji.com, Mon.-Fri. 0700-1700, Sat. 0900-1400) caters to budget travelers for day trips in and around Nadi and backpacker stays in the western islands. Owners Sunny and Preti worked for larger tour companies before setting up shop on their own.

Treks & Tours By Locals Fiji (tel. 931-3134 or 731-3134, toursbylocalsfiji@gmail.com) arranges custom guided itineraries for six hours for up to four people at F$400; tours include an air-conditioned vehicle, bottled water, and a guide. Admission fees and meals are extra.

Argo Travel & Foreign Exchange (269 Queens Rd., tel. 670-2308) has an office in town; it exchanges money and books local, regional, and international flights.

Rosie Holidays (at Nadi Airport and many resorts, tel. 672-2755, www.rosiefiji.com) works with most of the upscale resorts and many foreign travel agencies, catering to international visitors with special touches such as garlands and welcome drinks. Rates, especially for longer multiday packages, can be more expensive than those at other agencies. The airport office (tel. 672-2935, airport@rosie.com.fj) is staffed 24 hours. **ATS Pacific** (at Nadi Airport and many resorts, tel. 672-2811, www.atspacific.com), **Coral Sun Fiji** (at Nadi Airport, tel. 934-4411, www.coralsunfiji.com), and **Fiji's Finest Tours** (Port Denarau, tel. 675-0646, www.fijisfinesttours.com) all offer similar tours and services; compare rates or go with the one that's most convenient to you.

Better known as PVV Tours, **Pacific Valley View Tours** (tel. 670-0600, www.pvvtours.com), based at the Nadi Downtown Backpackers Inn, is similar. It specializes in obtaining discounted prices at upscale resorts near Nadi (including Sonaisali and Shangri-La's Fijian Resort). Prices vary here and bargaining might work.

Tourist Transport Fiji (TTF, at Nadi Airport, tel. 672-3311, www.touristtransportfiji.com) handles the "Feejee Experience" backpacker bus tours around Viti Levu.

Immigration

Visa extensions can be arranged at the **immigration office** (tel. 672-2263, Mon.-Fri. 0830-1230), upstairs near the Pacific Sun check-in counter in the departures hall at Nadi Airport.

Health

Zens Medical Centre (40 Lodhia St., behind Prouds in downtown Nadi, tel. 670-3533, 670-7525, 708-0209, or 999-6003, nadi@zensmedicalcentre.com, www.zensmedicalcentre.com, 24 hours daily) has X-ray, dental, and minor surgical equipment. Call for ambulance service. It is affiliated with the **Namaka Medical Center** (Queens Rd., tel. 672-2288, Mon.-Sun. 0730-2400), located near the Grand Melanesian Hotel.

For nonemergencies, **Dr. Ram Raju** (DSM Center, 2 Lodhia St., tel. 670-1375, Mon.-Fri. 0800-1700, Sat. 0800-1300) is a family doctor specializing in travel health.

The outpatient department at **Nadi District Hospital** (tel. 670-1128), inland from the Nadi bus station, is open Monday-Thursday 0800-1630, Friday 0800-1600, and Saturday 0800-1200.

Namaka Medisure Pharmacy (12 Namaka Lane, tel. 672-8851) is open 24/7.

Budget Pharmacy has locations in downtown Nadi (Queens Rd., tel. 670-0064) and in Namaka (Queens Rd. near Westpac Bank, tel. 672-2533). Both are open Monday-Friday 0800-1900, Saturday 0800-1530, and Sunday 0900-1230.

Money

ATMs can be found all over Nadi. **City Forex/Western Union** (tel. 672-6396) has a 24-hour exchange counter in the arrivals concourse at Nadi International Airport.

If you have a choice among banks, look for the many outlets of the **Bank South Pacific (BSP),** which does not charge a foreign exchange commission and has the lowest ATM fees. Other options are the **Westpac Bank** (there's one opposite the Nadi Handicraft Market) and the **ANZ Bank** (near MH), both of which charge F$5 commission to exchange currency. Banks in Fiji are open Monday-Thursday 0930-1530, Friday 0930-1600.

To avoid fees and lines, or if you need weekend service, go to **Exchange and Finance Fiji Limited** (tel. 670-3366, Mon.-Fri. 0800-1700, Sat. 0800-1600, Sun. 1000-1400), located between the ANZ Bank and MH. It changes cash without commission at a rate comparable to the banks.

Internet

Many hotels offer Wi-Fi, either for free (at least in the lobby or public areas) or for an hourly or daily fee. Some also have terminals you can use, often in the business center. If you're at a big resort, check in advance whether signing up for the chain's loyalty program will give you free Wi-Fi. It's almost never fast enough for streaming, and at cheaper places, it may not be fast enough for much of anything.

3D's Internet Café (Queens Rd., tel. 670-8700, Mon.-Sat. 0700-1900, Sun. 0900-1830) offers Internet access as well as a range of printing and copying services and game stations.

Kidanet Internet (New Shop & Save Plaza, Namaka, tel. 670-6496, www.kidanet.com.fj, Mon.-Thurs. 0830-1615, Fri. 0830-1600) charges F$1.90 for 60 minutes.

Phone

The best place to get a temporary SIM card for your mobile phone is right inside the international arrivals terminal at Nadi Airport. Fiji's two main providers, Airtel and Vodafone, both have counters there and are efficient in getting you set up within 15 minutes or so. Plans sold at the airport include international calling and texting, unlike what's available in town. Both carriers are similar on Viti Levu, but if you're traveling to other islands, note that Vodafone is better on Taveuni and Airtel is better on Ovalau. If you're staying longer than 30 days, you can buy the SIM card here and top it off later online or at a retail outlet in one of the towns.

Post

Nadi has two large post offices, one next to the market in central Nadi (tel. 670-0001), and another between the cargo warehouses directly across the park in front of the arrivals hall at Nadi Airport (tel. 672-2045). Both are open Monday-Friday 0800-1600, Saturday 0800-1300.

Laundry

Dhoby's Laundry (tel. 672-3061, Mon.-Sun. 0800-1700), at the end of Northern Press Road beside Sunny Travelers Inn, charges F$8 a kilogram to wash, dry, and fold your laundry. Ironing is separate.

The Laundromat (tel. 672-6208, Mon.-Sun. 0700-2000) in Martintar, next to Bounty Restaurant, will wash (F$5) and dry (F$7) up to six kilograms of laundry.

GETTING THERE AND AROUND

Air

Nadi International Airport (www.airportsfiji.com/nadi_aiport.php) is Fiji's largest air hub. Compact and modern, it underwent extensive renovations in 2017. The international terminal is divided into an arrivals hall—with numerous tour agency offices and a separate area for car rental companies—and a departures hall, with check-in counters. Food on the arrivals side is limited to a mediocre cafeteria; stick with the more hygienic hot items. It's better to walk over to the nice café in the departures area. If you're outbound, the options are better after security, with a small food court that includes Indian food and a Burger King. A Jack's Handicrafts is at the gate for last-last-minute shopping.

The domestic terminal is located outside across a wide driveway from the international terminal, and also has a serviceable cafeteria. City buses, long-haul buses, taxis, and parked cars all have their own designated areas outside.

Sea

Although Denarau Island is the main port, the hyperbolically named Fantasy Jetty in Wailoaloa serves a few budget operators. The **Ratu Kini Cruiser** (tel. 999-1246 or 672-1959, diveratukini@gmail.com) and the **Mana Flyer** (tel. 930-5933) are speedboats that shuttle backpackers to Mamanuca accommodations. Both can arrange special trips for groups as well.

Bus

Local buses start their routes at the central **Nadi Bus Station,** on Hospital Road between the Nadi Market and Koroivoli Park. For Wailoaloa Beach, look for hourly buses marked Wailoaloa or Newtown. Most routes go frequently on weekdays (dawn to dusk), less frequently on Saturdays, and not at all on Sundays. Fares start at 70 cents and can be paid on board. You don't have to have exact change, but it's appreciated. Drivers and passengers are generally helpful in guiding you to the right bus and alerting you to your stop.

The airport also has a bus hub with frequent routes into town, to Wailoaloa/Newtown, and to points north.

Taxi

Taxis around Nadi are quite cheap provided the driver uses the meter. Make sure it's working before you get in.

For day trips, you can negotiate a taxi for your own private tour for about F$30 an hour, or F$180 for the whole day, making this a better option than a package tour if you have two or more people. Going through your hotel's bell desk will get you a higher price—the fancier your hotel, the higher the quoted taxi rate. For the best deal, find a talkative, friendly driver with a good car at a taxi stand in town, at the airport, or outside a budget hotel.

If you prefer to preplan your airport transport but don't want to book a whole package, you might try **Fiji Transfers** (http://fijitransfers.com/). For an online booking fee (Australian $15), they will connect you with a local driver who will be given your flight number and will wait for you at the airport, even if your flight is delayed. You pay the driver directly, and your group is taken directly to your hotel anywhere in Nadi, Denarau, or all the way to the Coral Coast. Prices are in line with what high-end hotels charge for airport transfers; you'd likely find it cheaper to hop into a local taxi, but this takes out the guesswork and ensures you a comfortable air-conditioned ride. You can even request a salusalu flower garland greeting for each member of your party (F$5 pp).

Car

The roads in Fiji are generally good, and if you can adjust to driving on the left side of the road, you should have no trouble. Half a dozen agencies have booths in the airport's 24-hour car rental center, but many of them will tell you that they have no cars available; make reservations in advance. The local companies tend to have lower rates but older cars. If you're not already at the airport, most companies will deliver the car to your hotel or give you a free transfer to the airport to pick up your car. If you're planning to drive into the interior mountains and villages, ask for a four-wheel drive, as some of the roads are steep and unpaved.

There's a lot of fine print when it comes to renting a car in Fiji:

- Drivers must be over 21 and have a valid driver's license from their home country, but some companies charge more for drivers under 26.

- You'll pay extra if you want to return a car to a different place from where you picked it up.
- Some companies forbid taking a rental car on the inter-island car ferries; be sure to ask if you plan to do this.
- The prices quoted below are for a single day; rates go down by as much as 50 percent for multiday rentals.
- A stamp duty of F$10 per rental is levied on top of all taxes and fees.

Here's a complete list of rental car companies operating from the Nadi airport:

- **Avis** (tel. 672-2233 or 999-1451, info@avis.com.fj, www.avis.com.fj) has vehicles from a compact (F$123) to an eight-seater luxury SUV (F$331).
- **Budget** (tel. 672-2735, reservations@budget.com.fj, www.budget.com.fj) has options from subcompacts (F$82) to a five-seater SUV (F$165). Note that Budget has a higher age threshold; you must be 25 or over and have held your license for two years.
- **Bula Car Rentals** (tel. 670-1209, 990-8990, or 999-9718, reservations@bulacarrentals.com.fj, www.bulacarrentals.com.fj) can be booked directly or through Tappoo shops. A scooter is F$89 and a subcompact is F$99, with rates increasing up to a nine-seater van for F$219. You can also book a chauffeur for F$70 a day, from 0800 to 1700, with 48 hours advance notice.
- **Europcar** (tel. 672-5957 or 999-3407, reservations@europcarfiji.com.fj, europcarfiji@connect.com.fj, www.europcar.com.fj) has subcompacts (F$67) up to small SUVs (F$106).
- **Satellite Rent-A-Car** (tel. 670-2109 or 999-2109, satelliterentals@connect.com.fj, www.satelliterentacar.com.fj) has compacts (F$159) up to 11-seater vans (F$350).
- **Thrifty Car Rental** (tel. 672-2755, www.thriftyfiji.com) has three categories: compact sedan (US$92), midsize hatchback (US$154), and five-seater SUV (US$201). Rosie Holidays operates joint desks with Thrifty in many hotels.
- **True Blue Rent-A-Car** (tel. 670-7470, 999-7368, or 929-7368, renttrueblue@connect.com.fj, www.truebluerentacar.com) has vehicles ranging from a hybrid Toyota Prius (F$90) to a 4WD SUV (F$180). The minimum rental is two days.

Denarau Island

Denarau is perfect for those times when you don't want to have some sort of authentic, rugged experience—you just want to be and act like a tourist. The upscale resorts, golf course, water park, and marina on this constructed island, six kilometers west of downtown Nadi, are so posh you wouldn't guess that it all used to be mangrove swampland.

Filled in and developed at great expense over the past few decades, the resulting beaches are an ecological travesty but are pleasant for cocktails, kayaking, and stand-up paddleboarding. Most hotels offer free equipment to their guests. You won't see anything if you snorkel here, and the waves aren't strong enough for surfing. Only the Sofitel and Hilton have lovely (man-made) white-sand beaches, pleasant for swimming, though there can be clumps of seaweed on the seafloor. There are volleyball nets at the Hilton. Depending on the tides, the other beaches can range from light brown to a dark, nearly black sand, so most guests spend their swim time in the pool. You're welcome to use the beach anywhere along the shoreline, and if you act like you belong, no one will you stop you from taking a dip in the sprawling hotel pools.

There are no local villages on the island,

Port Denarau

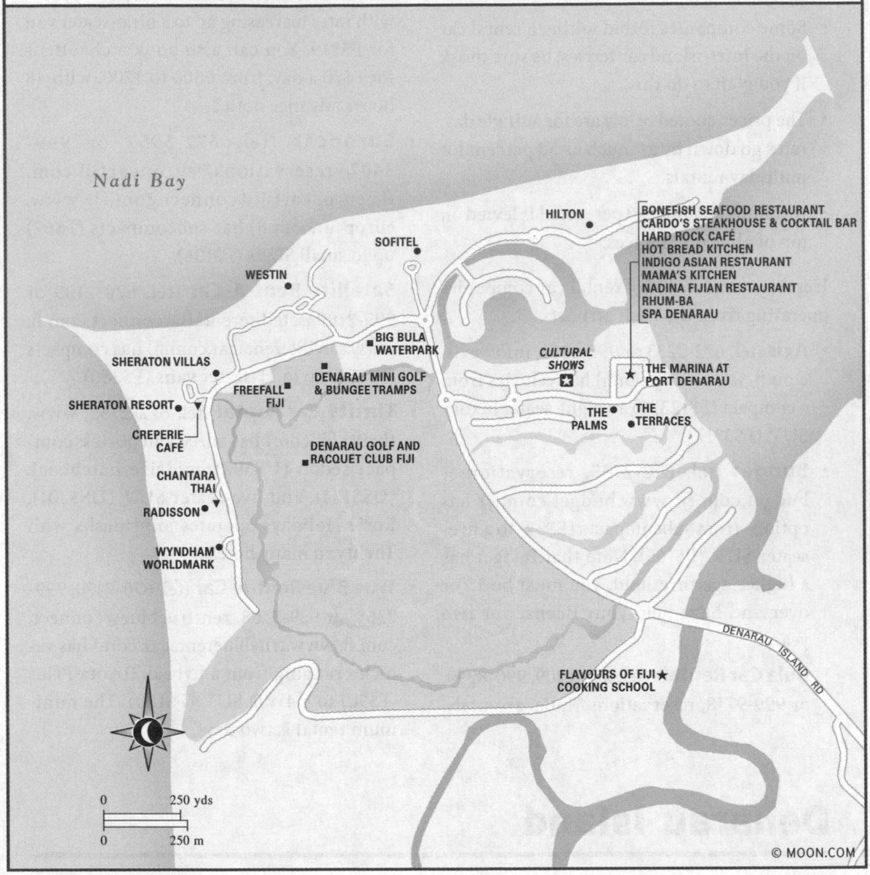

only some gated communities where well-heeled Fijians and expats own vacation homes.

SIGHTS

The Marina at Port Denarau

There's nothing quite like **The Marina at Port Denarau** (www.portdenarau.com.fj) anywhere else in Fiji. This outdoor mall has everything you need for an afternoon of noshing and shopping, as well as planning the rest of your stay in Fiji. It's amusing to have a beer on a terrace here and watch the tour groups embarking or disembarking from their catamarans and cruise vessels. A booth in the center, next to the Hard Rock Café, offers freebies and heavily discounted activities (such as a $99 Jet Ski package for $5) if you'll sit through a 90-minute sales pitch for a timeshare at the Wyndham resort. They'll be most interested in you if you say you're staying at an expensive hotel and are from Australia or New Zealand.

★ Cloud 9

If Tom Hanks and his rotund pal Wilson had had a surfboard in the movie *Cast Away,* they could have caught just a few waves from their island out to Fiji's floating pizzeria,

One Day in Denarau

infinity pool at the Hilton Fiji Beach Resort & Spa

Start your day with an energy-boosting smoothie, cappuccino, and bacon-and-egg crepe at the **Creperie Café** outside the Sheraton. Then buy your F$8 Bula Bus pass in the market just a few steps away, and you're ready to slay the day. Cross the street to play a round of golf at **Denarau Golf and Racquet Club Fiji** or, if you have kids, miniature golf at **Denarau Mini Golf & Bungee Tramps.**

When your stomach starts to growl, ride the Bula Bus 10 minutes to the **Marina at Port Denarau** for a leisurely waterfront lunch and day-drinking at **Bonefish Seafood Restaurant.** Here you can sample a nouveau cuisine dish such as sweet-chili Yasawa lobster or an exemplary fish-and-chips, and wash it down with a Fiji rum cocktail.

In the marina, browse for souvenirs and beachwear at **Cloudbreak** or **Harrisons,** and stop by the carousel of tour desks to plan any future excursions. Then enjoy a unique seashell massage (F$151 for 60 minutes) at **Spa Denarau,** with aromatherapy oils distilled from Fiji's special flora

Later in the afternoon, change into a swimsuit and board the Bula Bus to the **Hilton Fiji Beach Resort & Spa,** where you can lounge in the infinity pool and enjoy a gorgeous view of the Mamanuca Islands. You might enjoy local ice cream (try the pineapple flavor!) poolside. The beach here is perfect for a long stroll and a dip, with lounge chairs and volleyball nets on the way to the adults-only bar at the far end, perfect for sunset cocktails.

Rinse off with a quick shower poolside, and then hop on the bus again to catch the Lomani Wai show at the **Radisson** (reservations essential). Enjoy an inauthentic but thrilling fire dance performance, kava, and a fancy dinner with your toes in the water, creating the sensation that you're afloat in a few inches of water. Hop back on the Bula Bus and feel free to ride it all the way around the island for your last adventure of the night.

★ **Cloud 9** (Roro Reef, tel. 869-7947, book@cloud9.com.fj, www.cloud9.com.fj, daily 1000-1700). But this double-decker artificial "island" is more than just a pizzeria; it bears all the hallmarks of civilization, including a DJ, sunbeds, and fully stocked bar, in addition to the wood-fired oven serving up a range of handmade carnivorous, vegetarian, and even gluten-free pies (F$20-35). You can swim or kayak in the clear, deep waters around the island. A six-hour package deal costs F$229, including bus transport from Nadi and Denarau hotels, a F$60 food and drink credit, and the boat trips (leave the marina at 0915 and leave Cloud 9 at 1400). Children receive a 10 percent discount. It's also possible to add parasailing (F$455) or Jet Skiing (F$536); prebooking is essential so that an instructor can be on hand.

RECREATION

The **Big Bula Waterpark** (tel. 776-5049, www.bigbulawaterpark.com.fj, daily 1000-1700), on Resort Drive opposite the Sofitel and Westin, is a water play arena with inflatables and waterslides. Aside from the pools at the bottom of the slides, there's no swimming pool. Admission is F$110 adults, F$95 children 6-12, F$60 children under 5, and F$70 seniors over 70. A family package for any configuration of four people is F$370, and renting a towel for the day is F$8. A free Bula Bus pass (worth F$8) comes with every entry ticket. You must wear swimsuits in the pools, but oddly, you must wear socks on rides, and you'll be given some if you don't have any. There are a few kid-friendly activities such as hair braiding and henna tattoos, and grown-ups can buy beer, but it's really best for travelers who will be happy zooming down the same slides multiple times. Bring your own picnic, as the on-site café is slow and mediocre.

Denarau Golf and Racquet Club Fiji (opposite the Westin Resort, tel. 675-9710, www.westindenarauisland.com/denarau-golf-racquet-club, daily 0700-2200) is a par-72 golf course designed by Eiichi Motobashi, incorporating a unique Pacific theme with bunkers in the shape of marine creatures. Fees are F$130/F$160 for 9/18 holes, including cart rental, with discounts for multiday packages. Reservations are highly recommended. There are also 10 tennis courts here (F$25/hour), and you can rent racquets and balls.

At **Denarau Mini Golf & Bungee Tramps** (tel. 903-9920, daily 0830-1600), you can play 18 holes on a cute course dotted with carved turtles and traditional iTaukei (indigenous Fijian) canoes. Rates are F$25 adults, F$22 children, or F$65 for a group of two adults and two children. Use of the "bungee tramp," a large bungee cord with a trampoline underneath, is F$17 per person.

Freefall Fiji (Denarau Golf & Racquet Club, tel. 776-7073, www.freefallfiji.com) offers tandem skydiving jumps with a jumpmaster from a small plane. You're picked up from your Nadi or Denarau hotel and taken to the Skydive Centre, located next to the Denarau golf course. There you're treated to complimentary refreshments (if your stomach's not

yachts at Port Denarau

already full of butterflies) and given a safety briefing before driving to the Nadi launchpad. You can jump from 10,000 feet for 30 seconds of freefall (F$765), or from 14,000 feet for 70 seconds of freefall (F$845), landing in a drop zone in front of the golf course clubhouse. Photo/video packages are extra.

All of the hotels have day spas for your grooming and relaxation needs. But a better value is the **Spa Denarau** (tel. 675-0312 or 675-0314, spadenarau@connect.com, www.spadenarau.com), tucked into a corner of the Marina at Port Denarau, on the parking lot side between the liquor store and the boat terminal. Products from the high-quality Pure Fiji brand are used in all treatments, which include massage, mani-pedi, waxing, facials, and after-sun hair therapy. Try the "Beqa Hot Stone Therapy," an 80-minute massage (F$192) whose name refers to the island where stones are heated for fire walkers, or the 90-minute Guava Nourishing Wrap (F$203), where you're scrubbed down with raw sugar, coated with a guava mask high in vitamin C, and treated to a scalp massage, leaving you polished and glowing.

ENTERTAINMENT AND NIGHTLIFE

Bars

Because the island's accommodations are built facing west and north, sunset cocktails abound. The Bula Bus and the abundance of resort bars make Denarau a fine site for those inclined to bar-hopping. The **Wyndham, Sheraton,** and **Sofitel** have swim-up bars in their pools. The **Radisson's lobby bar** has imaginative Asian-inspired cocktails. The beach side of the **Hilton** has a lovely panoramic view of the Mamanuca Islands.

At the marina, the **Rhum-Ba** (tel. 770-7486, www.rhum-ba.com, Sun.-Fri. 1000-2300, Sat. 0800-2300, closed Mon.) on the far south end specializes in rum drinks but also has beers on tap. You won't get a sunset view from this end of the island, but you can sit out on the balcony to watch fish swimming toward the lights below at night. If you must, the **Hard Rock Café** (tel. 675-0032, www.hardrock.com/cafes/fiji, daily 1100-2200) does its thing and has happy hour drink specials 1500-1800 daily, with a pleasant outdoor courtyard and a view of the yachts. Local bands play covers every evening.

Inland, the **Denarau Golf & Racquet Club** (tel. 675-0777, Restaurant.Fiji@starwoodhotels.com) is the island's go-to sports bar, a vast complex with multiple screens and seating areas, and plenty of beers on tap. Be warned that the food is substandard, and it's overcrowded and slow whenever big Australia or New Zealand sports events are being broadcast.

★ Cultural Shows

Any day of the week, you can catch a show in Denarau. A free performance in the center court of the marina mall, daily at 1730, incorporates Fijian, Samoan, and Tongan styles and culminates in acrobatic fire dancing.

Hotel shows include meals and require reservations:

The **Sofitel** (tel. 675-1111) offers Polynesian entertainment on Fridays and a Fijian *meke* on Saturdays ($95 buffet dinner).

At the **Wyndham Worldmark,** the Seafront Restaurant (tel. 675-0722) has a *meke*-plus-*lovo* buffet dinner (F$55) on Tuesday and a Polynesian show with fire dancing on Friday, both at 1830 (F$55).

A Beqa Island fire walking show is presented at the **Westin** (tel. 675-0000) on Wednesdays and Saturdays at 1830 as part of the buffet dinner (F$111.25).

The **Hilton** (tel. 675-6800) has fire dancing and kava on Tuesdays and Saturdays at 1830, and you can opt for either the F$110 buffet or order dinner a la carte.

Perhaps the most elaborate option is the **Lomani Wai** experience at the **Radisson** (tel. 675-6677, restaurants@radissonfiji.com), on Monday nights only. If you just can't get enough of being in the pool, this is the dinner for you. Tables are set in a few inches of water, and fire dancers perform while you eat. Kava is included in the fixed-price menu at

Meke, Fire Walking, and Fire Dancing

An array of activities in Fiji fall under the heading of "cultural show," but few bear much relation to traditional practices. As long as you're not an anthropologist, it's worth taking in at least one during your time in Fiji. Here's a primer:

- An authentic *meke* is a village's song-and-dance ceremony to honor the gods as part of a momentous event, such as a harvest or a battle.
- *Fire walking* on hot coals originated as a religious ceremony, practiced (in two separate traditions) by both Fijian and Indian devotees on a spiritual journey.
- *Fire dancing* is not a Fijian tradition, but has been incorporated to add thrills to some shows.

dancers at the nightly show at the Marina at Port Denarau

At tourist venues, you'll see elements of all of these blended with showier Polynesian performance forms such as Samoan dance and Hawaiian hula. Most large hotels have at least one night a week where they offer a show, often alongside a *lovo* (traditional pit-roasted feast) and a shared kava bowl. Some exuberantly invite participation, while others seek only applause; unless you're invited onstage by a dancer, don't get up and boogie.

F$135 per adult, F$55 per child age 4-12. It's all a little hokey, but it's good fun. The Radisson also has a *meke* in the Blu Restaurant on Wednesday and a fire show on Friday at 1830 (F$39 for salad bar buffet, or you can order from the a la carte menu).

FOOD

The Radisson boasts Denarau's only Thai restaurant, ★ **Chantara Thai** (tel. 675-6677), with an imaginative street food-style menu created by Bangkok chef Jasmine Chawengchote. Dishes range from F$24 for tom kha soup to F$46 for sizzling softshell crab. The four-course progressive dinner menu is worth the F$75 splurge.

Outside the Sheraton, the **Creperie Café** (tel. 776-1012, daily 0800-2130) serves up fresh savory and sweet crepes (F$12-14) in a breezy open-air environment. Oddly, there's also packaged sushi.

For low-cost meals the Marina at Port Denarau is your best bet. **Hot Bread Kitchen** has tasty chicken and lamb pies (F$4), as well as Fijian specialties such as cream buns and coconut twist pastries. Other options are fried chicken meals (F$6-12) at **Chicken Express** or pizza (F$10-30) at **Mama's Kitchen.**

Among the pioneers of imaginative Fijian cuisine is ★ **Bonefish Seafood Restaurant** (Marina at Port Denarau, tel. 675-0197, www.bonefishfiji.com, daily 1100-2200, F$18-52). This restaurant has a sleek bar and boasts 95 percent local ingredients, most from its own farm. Signature dishes include a seafood chowder spiked with brandy and cream, Yasawa lobsters grilled in a sweet chili sauce, and the Happy Monkey dessert: four scoops of Fijian vanilla ice cream, hot fudge, salted almonds, and jungle bananas.

A similar look, feel, and price range can be found at Bonefish's two sister restaurants next door. All have spacious outdoor eating areas with lovely sunset views, and all of them are operated by Jack's, so you get good quality and service at premium prices. **Indigo**

Asian Restaurant (tel. 675-0026, www.indigofiji.com, daily 1100-2200) has a range of vegetarian and meat dishes, including a signature chili crab and an upscale version of *khichdi,* a Gujarati comfort food that's like a spicy risotto. **Nadina Fijian Restaurant** (tel. 675-0290, Mon.-Sat. 0800-2300) offers tasty, seasonal local specialties like chargrilled octopus salad and plenty of coconut milk concoctions.

If you're craving an expensive continental meal, go to **Cardo's Steakhouse & Cocktail Bar** (tel. 675-0900, daily 0700-2300, F$28-49). From the outdoor tables, you can enjoy a charbroiled steak while eavesdropping on the talented local bands who play pop-rock covers at the overpriced Hard Rock Café.

ACCOMMODATIONS

Two types of accommodations line the northern and western shores of Denarau Island: regular hotel rooms, and apartments stocked with fully equipped kitchens. Most are operated by international chains, giving the island a groomed feel, and have travel desks to book excursions for you. You can save significantly if you join their free loyalty programs. Many hotels are "cashless," meaning that you charge everything to your room or, if you're a day visitor, to a tab that you pay off before you leave. The apartments are ideal for families or groups of adults, especially if you have a longer stay or don't want to pay high resort prices for food and drink.

Don't be deterred by the US$200-and-up rack rates quoted here. The Denarau hotels mark up their regular prices so that they can hold near-constant sales. You'll find deep discounts on their websites and third-party sites, and even bigger price slashes if you sign up for a package tour or a three-nights-for-the-price-of-two deal.

When choosing accommodations, consider how long you'll be staying and what amenities you'll truly use. Are you a family or group of adults on a budget using Denarau your launching point for excursions throughout the area? You might like the relatively economical Terraces and the Palms, located next to the marina, where every unit comes with a modern kitchen and in-room laundry, but no beach. Looking for a secluded, romantic interlude? Try the adults-only area at the far end of the Hilton, which has its own kid-free rooms, restaurant, pool, and stretch of beach. Planning to while away your days on the golf course? The Sheratons and the Westin, as well as the golf club, are all owned by the Starwood Group, so guests have cashless access to facilities and restaurants across all of the resorts, and package golf deals are sometimes available.

Clockwise, from southwest:

It's a bit complicated to book one of the 136 spacious self-catering apartments at the ★ **Wyndham Worldmark** (tel. 675-0442, denarau.reception@wyn.com, www.wyndhamvrap.com), but it's worth the effort. This spot has the best of all worlds: a huge apartment with kitchen, an ocean view, and a resort-like atmosphere that is relaxed about rules. Most of the accommodations are privately owned or timeshare units, so check third-party websites for owners renting out their units. Booking directly, you could get a one-bedroom apartment that sleeps four for F$722 or a two-bedroom that sleeps six for F$955, or score a cheap deal if you meet certain financial criteria and are willing to sit through a 90-minute sales pitch during your stay (www.holidaysbywyndham.com.au/). The new or refurbished apartments are lovely; avoid the older, non-refurbished units. The large beachside pool compensates for the poor beach, and includes an adults-only pool area with a swim-up bar. There's a Mexican restaurant near the pool. Because most guests are owners, there's a more relaxed feel than in a hotel; no one will object if, for example, you want to take your own drinks and snacks to the pool.

Radisson Blu Resort (tel. 675-6677, reservations@radissonfiji.com, www.radisson.com/fiji) is a big hotel that sometimes seems too busy for its management and staff. It has 270 sizable rooms and suites in a maze

1

2

3

of three-story blocks around a huge swimming pool that opens to the beach. Rooms start at F$410 single or double and increase to F$914 for a two-bedroom suite. Be warned that rooms listed as having an ocean or pool "view" may in fact have just a sliver of a view, probably not worth the premium. An impressive faux waterfall faces the reception, with the day spa on an island in the pool below. Six food outlets and extensive children's facilities are scattered around the hotel. A perk: If your flight lands at dawn but your room isn't available till afternoon, the Radisson works hard to ease the wait, with coupons for free or discounted meals and activities on arrival day. Suites have a washer and dryer in the unit.

Next along the Denarau resort row is the **Sheraton Fiji Resort** (tel. 675-0777, www.sheraton.com/fiji). The 292 rooms begin at F$420 single or double; for the presidential suite it's F$1,800. Built as a state-of-the art resort in 1987, it's aging, but still worthwhile if you find a great value deal and don't plan to have all of your meals at the slow, pricey restaurant. The two-story hotel includes a shiny shopping arcade and is conveniently located halfway along resort row, near a small strip of cafés and a grocery store. The kids' club for both the Westin and Sheraton is located here.

Between the Sheraton and the golf club is the affiliated **Sheraton Denarau Villas** (tel. 675-0777, www.sheraton.com/denarauvillas). The 82 condos have kitchenettes, washers/dryers, TVs, and lounges, starting at F$925 for a two-bedroom suite and going up to F$1,500 for a three-bedroom villa. There are plenty of children's activities. The swimming pool and bar face the beach.

Westin Denarau Island (tel. 675-0000, www.westinfiji.com) has 271 spacious rooms from F$420 single or double, up to $1,800 for the Royal Suite. Facilities include a swimming pool and spa. There's no kids club here. The ground-floor oceanfront rooms open directly onto the beach; those wanting privacy should ask for an upstairs room. Built in 1975 before being taken over by the Westin chain in 2006, the layout is more old-school Fijian, as opposed to the modern architecture of the rest of Denarau. The breakfast buffet is better here than at the Sheraton.

Sofitel Fiji Resort (tel. 675-1111, reservations@sofitelfiji.com.fj, www.sofitelfiji.com) is a series of three-story blocks with a long swimming pool winding along the artificial beach. Rooms range from a single or double at F$408 to the luxurious Imperial Suite for F$1,348. Family rooms, starting at F$568 for one queen bed and two bunk beds, might be a good option for young families wanting a hotel rather than an apartment vacation. The Mandara Spa (tel. 675-7870, www.mandaraspa.com) runs a nine-*bure* spa village on the property.

Hilton Fiji Beach Resort & Spa (tel. 675-6800, fijibeachresort.reservations@hilton.com, www.fijibeachresortbyhilton.com) has more of an outer-island feel than the other mega-resorts. Every room has an ocean view, and the long, calm beach has picturesque views of the Mamanuca Islands. Many rooms also have a barbecue grill on the terrace, so you can buy and grill local fish and meats if you like. A standard single or double starts at F$500, up to F$2,685 for a penthouse suite with kitchenette and laundry. The complex of pools includes a beautiful, large infinity pool whose serenity is periodically interrupted by activities such as "Fijian" aqua aerobics (shout "Bula!" after every move). You can take out hotel paddleboards and kayaks for free. A series of 23 two-story white cubes start at F$600 for a studio and rise to F$2,150 for a three-bedroom. An extensive kids' club is balanced out by an exclusive adults-only area.

The Terraces (tel. 675-0557, www.theterraces.com.fj), near the Marina at Port Denarau, overlooks the third hole of the golf course on Denarau Island. It's intimate, with only 30 self-catering town houses in a series of three-story blocks; there's no jostling for buffet lines here. Rates are F$485/625/725 for one/

1: fresh ginger sorbet cocktail **2:** soaring with Sleeping Giant Zip Line Fiji **3:** vessels of all sorts docked at Port Denarau.

two/three bedrooms. All have in-unit washers and dryers; some of the kitchens don't have ovens. There's free Wi-Fi and a swimming pool but no beach.

The Palms (tel. 675-0104, reservations@thepalmsdenarau.com, http://thepalmsdenarau.com/) is the only Fijian-owned accommodation on Denarau. It's the closest to the Marina at Port Denarau—just across the parking lot—which is ideal if you're planning on early-morning scuba or surf trips. Newer than the Terraces, the apartments at the Palms have high ceilings and snazzy modern appliances in their kitchens. Rates are F$560/$680/$850 for one/two/three bedrooms. There are also a few studios, without kitchens, at F$420 for one or two people. All have in-unit washers and dryers. There's free Wi-Fi and a swimming pool but no beach.

INFORMATION AND SERVICES

At the Marina at Port Denarau, if you go right instead of going into the main entrance, you'll find a food-court-like array of **tour desks** offering various expeditions to the Mamanuca and Yasawa Islands. For the best tour options. This is a good spot to pick up brochures and ask questions in person.

Fiji's Finest Tours (tel. 675-0046, www.fijisfinesttours.net) will allow you to **store luggage** here in a secure room behind their tour desk for F$10 per day, even if you're not traveling with them. It's a good option if you're taking a boat out to the islands for a couple of days but don't want to lug everything.

An **ATM** is just inside this entrance, and there are machines in the lobbies of most of the hotels.

GETTING THERE AND AROUND

The $1 **Westbus,** known as "the yellow bus," is an easy way to reach Denarau Island, with buses leaving Nadi's main bus station every 10 minutes from 0500 to 2300 daily, stopping at designated bus stops all over the island including the marina.

Within Denarau, the open-air, hop-on-hop-off **Bula Bus** allows you to travel all day for F$8, or for four days for F$24; children under 12 travel free with an adult. Buses operate on a loop every 15 minutes from 0730 to 2330 daily. The only catch is that the drivers don't handle money; you have to buy your pass inside one of the hotels, the marina, the supermarket in front of the Sheraton, or the golf club.

Taxi trips originating on Denarau are on a strict and expensive fee schedule. Metered taxis and outside car services are not allowed to pick up on the island at all, thanks to a monopoly contract with the local Fijian landowners. You'll have to either pay the listed fee—there's a complex schedule of rates based on each hotel's location and your destination—or take the yellow bus to a point outside Denarau where you can get in a regular taxi.

North of Nadi

Almost as soon as you pass the Nadi Airport, you're in a whole different Fiji. Cane fields blanket the landscape, and historical sites—including the shore where the first humans landed in Fiji—await.

To your right, the city gives way to the lush, forested foothills of the Sabeto Mountains, better known as the Sleeping Giant for the shape the hills make when viewed from the coastal route. Here you can take in nature with a lowlands horseback ride through Fiji's first agritourism organic farm, an orchid tour or mud pool bath in the mid-level jungle, or a zip line adventure starting at the heights.

To your left is the sloping curve of Nadi Bay, with glimpses of stunning views out to the Mamanuca Islands. Hug the coastline to reach Vuda Bay, a peaceful beach area with sweeping views that has emerged as one of the best hidden values in Fiji.

★ FOOTHILLS OF THE SLEEPING GIANT

Whether you're longing to slow down or feeling a need for speed, the gorgeous green region where the Sabeto River flows down from the Sabeto Mountains has something for you From lolling about in warm mud like a satisfied wild piglet to zip-lining through the rainforest at 40 kph like a screechy parrot, several different nature adventures are possible in these hills.

It isn't possible to reach the Sleeping Giant itself (Mount Batilamu) from its steep western face; you have to access it from the north via Lautoka, through the gateway village of Abaca in the Koroyanitu National Heritage Park (see page 214).

Sleeping Giant Zip Line Fiji

Sleeping Giant Zip Line Fiji (Holika Rd., tel. 992-7018, sleepinggiantzipline@gmail.com, www.ziplinefiji.com) is a 35-acre adventure park with five zip lines. You'll fly through the jungle canopy at a maximum speed of 40 kph (25 mph) along lines that are 80-160 meters long. If you book directly through the website, it's F$199 per adult, F$149 per child age 4-12. The rate includes pickup from a Denarau hotel, a sandwich lunch and nonalcoholic beverages, a guided hike through a rain tree jungle to two waterfalls (wear a swimsuit), and unlimited rides. The zip lines operate rain or shine, but some of the walking trails may close in heavy rain. Note that you can't arrive independently; you'll have to be picked up or be part of a tour.

Garden of the Sleeping Giant

Five kilometers north of Nadi Airport is the turnoff to Wailoka Road, which leads to the **Garden of the Sleeping Giant** (Mon.-Sat. 0900-1700, Sun. 0900-1200, F$12 adults, F$6 children). It's also known as Perry Mason's Orchid Garden because Canadian American actor Raymond Burr established the garden in 1977. The brochure claims that 2,000 kinds of orchids are kept in these gardens at the foot of the hills. That figure may be a slight overstatement, but the orchids are indeed gorgeous and abundant.

Aviva Farms

Less than a kilometer west from the garden, along Wailoko Road, is **Aviva Farms** (Wailoko Rd., Sabeto, tel. 922-4179 or 620-6222, livaitora@gmail.com, http://agrotour.wixsite.com/avivafarms). This may be the best place to go horseback riding in Fiji, with well-cared-for horses and 54 acres of farmland to explore. It's also a lovely introduction to Fiji's native flora and its medicinal and edible uses.

Founder Livai Tora was the originator of agritourism on Fiji, starting in 1997 when he inherited what was then a sugarcane plantation from his father. Livai planted 20 indigenous species and 4,000 organic papaya trees, and added horseback riding to provide an additional sustainable income stream. Hundreds of young rural Fijians have come over the years to learn organic farming practices. A guided indigenous species tour is F$10 per person (daily 0900-1630), while 90-minute horseback rides (0900, 1200, or 1500) are F$50 for adults, F$25 for children 12 and under. Prebooking is required for all visits. Horse races are held at the on-site racetrack once a quarter, in a fair-like environment with food and drink; inquire about attending or even competing. The farm is two kilometers east of the Queens Road.

Rise Beyond the Reef

Just across the street from Aviva Farms is the headquarters and pleasant shop of **Rise Beyond the Reef** (Wailoko Rd., Sabeto, tel. 777-5742, http://risebeyondthereef.org, Mon.-Fri. 1000-1600), a nonprofit that works with women from remote areas to handcraft home textiles and goods. Proceeds fund development and sustainability efforts in communities that are far away from tourist money. Shopping here is a fine way to support these efforts and take home well-crafted souvenirs; the group's Instagram account (@rise_beyond_the_reef_fiji) shows the process behind some of the crafts, such as solar botanical printing and curing *kuta* grass for weaving. In the adjoining office, you can custom-order linens and prints for weddings and special events.

Sabeto Mud Pools

A kilometer east of Rise Above the Reef are the **Sabeto Mud Pools** (Wailoko Rd., Sabeto, tel. 834-0088, Mon.-Sat. 0900-1700, F$20). There are four pools: one filled with mud, the other three with hot water for various phases of rinsing and soaking. After you're all softened up, you can opt for a massage in the six-table open-air massage *bure* (F$30 for one hour). Bring your own towel or rent one for F$5.

Tours

Tour operators from Nadi offer trips here and to Vuda Bay at various rates and with different itineraries; for example, **Rosie Holidays** (tel. 672-2755, www.rosiefiji.com) offers a four-hour Vuda Lookout/Viseisei village/Garden of the Sleeping Giant tour for F$67 per person. **ATS Pacific** (tel. 672-2811, www.atspacific.com), **Coral Sun Fiji** (tel. 672-3105, www.coralsunfiji.com), and **Great Sights/Tourist Transport Fiji** (tel. 672-3311, www.touristtransportfiji.com) offer the same kind of day tours as Rosie with slight variations. Mud pool excursions can run F$75 if booked through a Nadi agency. It's likely cheaper to arrange your own trip and enjoy being on your own schedule.

A fun option is the quad-bike tour offered by **Go Dirty Tours** (tel. 992-8162, http://godirtytoursfiji.com). They entail off-roading on dirt tracks, and you really do get dirty. Those with valid driver's licenses can drive, while others can ride in the back. One trip takes you to the mud pools (F$329) and another to the zip line (F$399). Children 6-12 pay half price. Rates include pickup at Nadi, Denarau Island, and Coral Coast hotels. If you'd like to talk to someone in person, the main office is near the airport at Lot 31, Waqavuka Road, Namaka Industrial, Nadi; sales desks are also at the Wyndham Worldmark on Denarau; the Horizon Beach Resort on Wailoaloa Beach; and the Hideaway Resort on the Coral Coast.

Food and Accommodations

The only eating and staying option here is the **Stoney Creek Resort** (Sabeto Rd., tel. 672-2206, www.stoneycreekfiji.net), six kilometers east of Queens Road along the same road as (and before) the zip line park. It's seen better days and guests have complained about maintenance issues. Two *bures* with indoor hot tubs are rented at F$145 double, two rooms behind the restaurant are F$110 double, and a hilltop dormitory is F$33 per person. Continental breakfast in the restaurant-bar is included and there's a swimming pool, sometimes sticky with algae. Many dogs share the grounds. The large garden restaurant bakes pizza (F$16-26), seafood

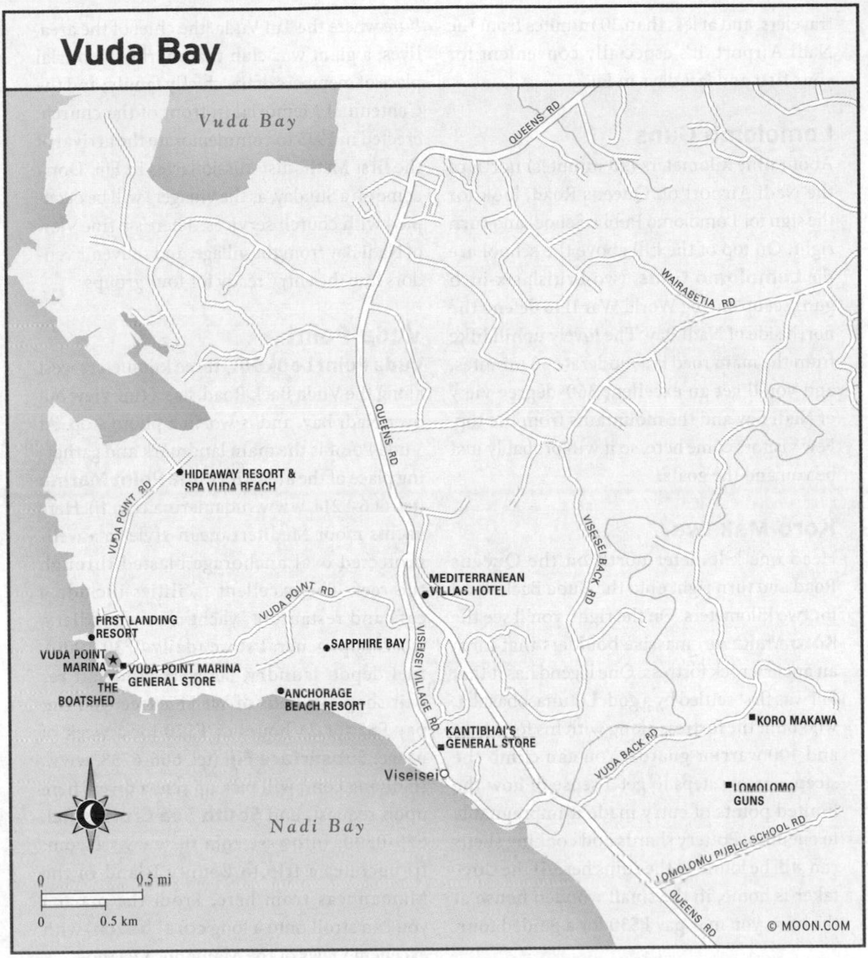

(including lobster at F$65), and bread in a wood-fired stone oven.

Getting There

If you're not going with a tour operator, you can take a taxi from Nadi to this area (F$10-20 one-way, or F$30 an hour if you want the driver to stay with you as you tour around). Renting a car is also an option. Either way, you'll want a 4WD vehicle because some of the roads can become slick with a bit of rain.

By bus, take any of the frequent Lautoka-Nadi locals and ask to be dropped off at the Wailoko Road junction (F$2.40), then walk or accept a ride to your destination. It's three kilometers to the farthest point, the Sabeto Mud Pools.

VUDA BAY

As Nadi and Denarau boomed over the past few years, developers set their sights north. The area overlooking pretty Vuda Bay is now home to a range of budget and luxury destinations. Some of the latter are real values, with much better rates than comparable resorts on small islands; a few also have kitchens and are suitable for large groups. The area is now worth consideration for budget and midrange travelers, and at less than 30 minutes from the Nadi Airport, it's especially convenient for your first and last days in Fiji.

Lomolomo Guns

About nine kilometers (20 minutes) north of the Nadi Airport on Queens Road, look for the sign for Lomolomo Public School and turn right. On top of the hill above the school are the **Lomolomo Guns,** two British six-inch guns set up during World War II to defend the north side of Nadi Bay. The lovely uphill hike from the main road is a moderate 30 minutes, and you'll get an excellent 360-degree view of Nadi Bay and the mountains from the top. Few visitors come here, so it will probably just be you and the goats.

Koro Makawa

Head one kilometer north on the Queens Road and turn right onto the Vuda Back Road for two kilometers. On the right, you'll see the **Koro Makawa,** massive boulders that form an ancient rock fortress. One legend has it that Fiji was first settled by a god, Lutunasobasoba, who built the fortress along with his four sons and 100 warrior guards. You can climb the steep, narrow steps to get a sense of how the limited points of entry made it impregnable to enemies. Pottery shards and cooking shells can still be found in the ruins here. If the caretaker is home, in the small wooden house at the base, you may pay F$30 for a guided tour.

Viseisei Village

Back on the Queens Road, cross the Vuda River and take the first left to head west onto the Vuda Back Road. Here, **Viseisei village** is said to be the first settlement in Fiji. According to one legend, the gods Lutunasobasoba and Degei landed their great canoe, the *Kaunitoni,* at Vuda Point, where the oil tanks are now. Most visitors arrive on sightseeing tours, and if you come on your own, you should ask permission to visit of anyone you meet. A guide will accompany you, and you should pay F$10 for your group. The tour will include the traditional *bure* where the Tui Vuda, the chief of the area, lives; a giant war club that marks the burial place of members of the chiefly family; and the Centennial Memorial in front of the church, erected in 1935 to commemorate the arrival of the first Methodist missionaries in Fiji. Don't come on a Sunday, as the villagers will be occupied with church services. There's a fine view of Nadi Bay from the village, and souvenir vendors line the entry ready for tour groups.

Vuda Point

Vuda Point Lookout, three kilometers west along the Vuda Back Road, has a fine view out over Nadi Bay, and is worth a photo stop. At Vuda Point is the main landmark and gathering place of the area, the **Vuda Point Marina** (tel. 666-8214, www.vudamarina.com.fj). Here yachts moor Mediterranean-style in a well-protected oval anchorage blasted through the reef. The excellent facilities include a café and restaurant, yacht club, chandlery, workshop, general store (daily 0730-1900), fuel depot, laundry, showers, and sail repair shop. An hour of Wi-Fi is free; you can pay F$5 for 24 hours or F$20 for a week of usage. **Subsurface Fiji** (tel. 666-6738, www.fijidiving.com) will pick up scuba divers here upon request, and **South Sea Cruises** (tel. 675-0500, info@ssc.com.fj, www.ssc.com.fj) operates a trip to Bounty Island in the Mamanucas from here. From the marina you can stroll onto a long **coral beach,** with excellent views of the Mamanuca Islands.

Food

★ **The Boatshed** (Vuda Point Marina, tel. 666-8214, www.vudamarina.com.fj, daily 0700-2200) is the area's prime gathering spot, with open-air tables looking out on the water and an extensive bar menu. Alongside standards such as burgers and fish-and-chips are delicious adventures such as the lobster pizza (F$29) and coconut-crusted walu fish

---

1: Hideaway Resort & Spa Vuda Beach **2:** a WWII gun barrel at Momi Battery Historic Park **3:** a horse on Sonaisali Island **4:** the lagoon at Momi Bay.

1

2

3

4

served on wild fern leaves (F$22). Don't miss the homemade ginger ice cream. There's live music occasionally.

If you're staying in a self-catering accommodation and haven't stocked up on groceries in Lautoka or Nadi, you'll end up either at the **Vuda Point Marina General Store,** which is lovely but designed for tourist wallets, or at **Kantibhai's General Store** (next to Viseisei village), which is cheaper and has a more local feel, with offerings such as live chickens.

Accommodations

UNDER US$150

Mediterranean Villas Hotel (tel. 666-4011, www.villas.com.fj, from F$99/140 s/d), on Vuda Hill overlooking Viseisei village near Vuda Point Junction on Queen's Road, has six uniquely decorated self-catering villas with fridges. There's a pool, but the beach is far from here. The view of Nadi Bay is good. Local buses between Lautoka and Nadi stop nearby.

Two kilometers down Vuda Road from Mediterranean Villas is the **Anchorage Beach Resort** (tel. 666-2099 or 999-2099, anchorage@connect.com.fj, www.anchoragefiji.com, F$251-493). It's on a hilltop just before the descent to First Landing Resort, a 15-minute walk along the cane railway line or beach from Viseisei. Anchorage has an array of rooms and villas ranging in price depending on size and location. All units are air-conditioned, and each has a fridge and balcony. Only the apartments have cooking facilities (other guests must use the restaurant). The views across Nadi Bay are nice and there's a swimming pool. The Anchorage can be noisy when local guests are present. It's built on a slope, so rooms listed as "beachside" or "oceanfront" are right on a coral beach that's fine for swimming at high tide (bring reef shoes) but is too murky for snorkeling. Rooms listed as "ocean view" and "mountain view" are about 100 meters uphill; rides to and from the beach by cart can be arranged. Meal plans are F$62/F$89 for two/three meals, but you may want to try it out for a day first, as guests have complained about the quality and service.

First Landing Resort (tel. 666-6171, www.firstlandingfiji.com) is next to the Vuda Point Marina. The 14 aging duplex units facing the swimming pool are F$185 single or double, while the 18 duplex beachfront units go for F$270 (extra persons F$48). All units have fully screened porches and are equipped with a fridge and coffeepot (but no cooking facilities). Connecting doors make the units ideal for large families or small groups. Three units are wheelchair-accessible. One beach villa opposite the reception has its own kitchen and pool at F$520 double. Prices are negotiable. A cooked breakfast is included in all rates. The beach here is much better than those in and around Nadi, but you'd only call it good at high tide. The snorkeling is poor. **Subsurface Fiji** (tel. 666-6738, www.fijidiving.com) offers scuba diving. Airport transfers are F$30/45 single/double one-way. First Landing is okay for a night or two, but you'd be making a mistake to plan your whole vacation around it.

OVER US$150

★ **Hideaway Resort & Spa Vuda Beach** (tel. 776-6777, reservations@hideaway.com.fj, http://hideawayfiji.com/vuda-resort) opened in late 2017 for adults only (16 and older). Unlike its always-a-party sister property on the Coral Coast, the vibe here is serene and relaxed. The pool opens onto lovely Vuda Bay beach, where the kayaking is mellow and the views are excellent. It's 20 minutes north of Nadi Airport and just a few minutes from the Vuda Bay Marina. Listed rates for suites start at F$775 and *bures* with private pools at F$975, but third-party websites often offer deals at less than a third of the price. The full meal plan is a good deal for drinkers, as it includes alcohol. Transfers to the Yasawa Islands are easily arranged using the house boat. Children are permitted if you book all 21 rooms at the resort—perhaps for a wedding in the 30-seat open-air chapel.

★ **Sapphire Bay** (U.S. tel. 888/640-7927, http://sapphirebayfiji.com, US$499) has three spacious villas available as the first stage of a planned real estate development overlooking Nadi Bay. Each 3,500-square-foot villa has four air-conditioned bedrooms and three bathrooms; they sleep up to 12 people in an array of bedroom configurations and common-area daybeds, making it an economical choice for large families or groups. Each villa also has a fully equipped kitchen and a private infinity pool with stunning views surrounded by a deck for al fresco dining. There's no daily cleaning service, but a washer and dryer are in each villa. If you're cooking, stock up on the way, as there are no supplies within walking distance. You can also opt to have a chef come and prepare meals. The airport transfer is included, but meals and additional rides are extra. A five-minute track leads down to the beach. The Wi-Fi is poor, but you're given a mobile phone to use during your stay.

Getting There

A taxi from Nadi to the Vuda Point Marina runs about F$20.

Local buses between Lautoka and Nadi take the Vuda Back Road and stop at Viseivisei village. Southbound buses from Lautoka stop at the Vuda Point Marina. Northbound buses from Nadi, however, turn off onto the Viseivisei village bypass road; from there, it's a scenic 25-minute walk up the road to the marina.

South of Nadi

SONAISALI ISLAND

This flat, low island tucked in close to the mainland lacks any compelling geographic features, but offers quiet respite and a fine view of the Mamanuca Islands. The **Fiji Surf Company** (tel. 670-5960 or 992-8411, www.fijisurfco.com) owns a jetty just across from the island, making this a convenient place to stay if you plan to join their surf trips. At just 15 minutes south of Nadi, it's also a reasonable stayover if you want—or need!—to squeeze in a bit more beach time before your international flight.

DoubleTree Resort by Hilton

Opened as a local resort in 1992, and completely revamped by Hilton in 2016, the **DoubleTree Resort** (tel. 670-6011, http://doubletree3.hilton.com) is somewhat sterile but also a good bargain, at about half the price as places offering similar amenities in Denarau. Access is via a three-minute speedboat ride across a calm river; travelers with limited mobility are asked to call ahead to arrange assistance. All rooms have an ocean view and are air-conditioned, with fridges. A prepaid breakfast buffet package runs F$60 per room. The main building houses rooms (F$239) with two queen beds each and balconies. Duplex *bures* (F$314-434) are spacious and come with private balconies, one or two king beds, and either a partial or "premium" (unobstructed) ocean view. The black-sand beach is clean and pleasant, with a designated swimming area and one of the longer walkable coastlines on Viti Levu. There's not much to see while snorkeling. Activities include a kids' club, volleyball, a large swimming pool, and free kayaking and paddleboards. For a fee you can book a sunset horseback ride, Jet Ski, or day trip to another island. Dinner reservations are required; the fare is serviceable, if predictable—pizzas, burgers, and so on, with very little local flair.

Getting There

Any taxi can drop you here, but Nasautorotoro Taxi operated by Korovuto village, which owns the island, has a monopoly on outbound taxis; it's F$30 to Nadi town or F$45 to the airport. The company also operates a F$8 shuttle to town Monday through Saturday, departing from Sonaisali Island at 1030 and from Jack's Handicrafts in Nadi at 1400.

MOMI BAY

Momi Bay, 29 kilometers southwest of Nadi, features spectacular views and a historic battlement. Surfers flock here for easy access to some of the greatest breaks in the world. Nonsurfers can enjoy a couple of days at a resort here, or a pleasant half-day trip from Nadi. There are no restaurants outside of the handful of hotels, but there are a few roadside barbecue and fruit stands. Water access is rocky, without any real beaches, keeping the area off the beaten path for tourism.

★ Momi Battery Historic Park

On a hilltop overlooking the bay are two British guns named after Queen Victoria (1900) and King Edward VII (1901). The huge guns, 15 centimeters in diameter and more than 7 meters long, were recycled from the Boer War. They were set up here in 1941 by the New Zealand Army as the Allies and Japan battled island by island through the South Pacific. According to records revealed after the war, Japan's invasion of Fiji was planned and scheduled for June 1942—but then the Imperial Army decided to try to secure the island of Midway first. When the Battle of Midway turned disastrous for Japan, the invasion of Fiji was first deferred, then abandoned. Locals now use the concrete bunkers to shelter during cyclones and tsunamis.

A shiny new visitors center (tel. 628-4356, daily 0900-1700, F$5) offers excellent context (and clean bathrooms). The entry fee includes explanations by a friendly guide, who will also show you the now-empty rooms where the new technology of radar was used to aim the guns.

From atop the battlements, you get a panoramic view of the famous surf island, Tavarua, as well as other islands in the Mamanuca Group, the gorgeous turquoise over the shallow reefs, and the surrounding countryside. On a clear day you can see northwest as far as the Yasawas.

Recreation

The coastline here is just a 15-minute boat ride from world-renowned surf sites: Cloudbreak (Saturdays only), Restaurants, Swimming Pools, and more.

Surfers can book a four-hour boat trip via **Rendezvous Surf Camp Fiji** (Lot 1, Uciwai Rd., tel. Henry at 948-9258 or Inia at 973-3502, surfcloudbreakfiji@gmail.com, www.fijirendezvous.com, F$90). If you're not staying at Rendezvous, a car will pick you up from Nadi hotels for an additional fee (depending on hotel), or you can make your own way there by taxi or bus. With five surf boats, they can accommodate most schedules.

Scuba Bula (tel. 628-0190, www.scubabula.com), with an office across from the Marriott, can handle to up to 24 divers at a time, from beginner to advanced. The cost is F$205/285 for one/two tanks, or F$825 for a PADI certification course (minimum of two people). Divers experience lots of fish/shark action at Navula Lighthouse, and there's great drift diving at Canyons (the guides really know their spots). When there's space, snorkelers are welcome to go along at F$50 per person.

Food

There are no restaurants in the Momi Bay region, and the hotels don't take day visitors, so plan to eat elsewhere or bring a picnic.

Accommodations

Rendezvous Surf Camp Fiji (Uciwai Rd., tel. 948-9258, 777-6038, or 973-3502, surfcloudbreakfiji@gmail.com, www.fijirendezvous.com) is a clean budget property that requires a two-night minimum, which is what you'd need to enjoy a full day of surfing. Accommodation choices include a bed (F$35) in a four-bed single-sex dorm; a private room with double bed and shared bathroom (F$60 for 1-2 people); and two larger rooms with double and single beds and en suite bathrooms, suitable for up to three people ($120 for fan only, $150 for the only air-conditioning on the property). There's free Wi-Fi, kayaking, a small pool, and a mandatory meal plan with breakfast and dinner at $40/day. Food is hearty and the beer is cheap. A four-hour surf trip costs F$90; gear rental and lessons are extra, and discounts are available for multiday packages. Freediving and spearfishing are possible at some of the surf sites. Rendezvous will book you a F$50 airport transfer, but for more than one person, you're better off taking a taxi for the same amount for your entire party. Or take the $2 Uciwai bus from Nadi and get off at the Rendezvous signpost on Queens Road, then call the lodge for a complimentary pickup for the five-kilometer ride down a winding gravel road to the coast.

Marriott Resort Momi Bay (tel. 670-7000, www.marriott.com) opened in 2017 after many years of construction and negotiation snafus, and it became instantly famous for its gorgeous over-water *bures*. They're built onto a long wharf and rent for US$1,100 a night; a regular room is but US$441. Swimming is best in the family pool or adults-only infinity pool, although there is also a beach and lagoon. Three on-site restaurants offer an assortment of fine Asian, Indian, Fijian, and continental food. A F$10 shuttle to Nadi runs Tuesdays and Thursdays.

Getting There

Half-day trips to the Momi Battery Historic Park, some including lunch, are sold by numerous tour companies and hotel travel desks, but it's easy enough to visit on your own or make it your first stop on your way toward the Coral Coast. A taxi from Nadi will cost F$40-55 one-way and takes about 40 minutes. A local bus costs F$2 and departs from the Nadi bus station on weekdays at 0800, 1330, or 1730, and Saturdays at 0745, 1300, and 1700 (no bus on Sundays and holidays). It's a pleasant drive in a rental car; some inner roads are gravel, but are well maintained.

The Mamanuca and Yasawa Islands

Some of the South Pacific's finest beach-bumming, snorkeling, diving, surfing, and sailing await you in the western islands of Fiji. From Nadi, it's just half an hour by boat to the southern tip of the gorgeous Mamanuca Islands, a string of 20 mini-paradises arcing north and east. Beyond that are the soaring volcanic peaks of the Yasawas, Fiji's watery western border, once out of reach to all but the most intrepid backpackers.

Now both archipelagoes offer a range of accessible options, from cruises to backpacker hostels to multiday resort packages. Family-friendly resorts abound, with special activities including scuba for children as young as eight. For those seeking a more grown-up vibe, several adults-only resorts have opened in the last few years, with some

Highlights

Look for ★ to find recommended sights, activities, dining, and lodging.

★ **Surfing Cloudbreak:** Next to Tavarua and Namotu Islands, Fiji's most famous surfing wave awaits those willing to attempt it (page 95).

★ **Modriki Island:** You'll find white sand, an emerald lagoon, and maybe even a volleyball named Wilson on this uninhabited, *Castaway* island (page 100).

★ **Kayaking the Yasawas:** The gentle, sparkling waters of Fiji's western edge are a sea kayaker's delight (page 104).

★ **Hiking Vatuvula Peak:** The invigorating hike up this towering volcanic plug provides a superb view of Wayasewa and Kuata Islands, with Viti Levu on the horizon (page 103).

★ **Swimming with Manta Rays:** April is the best month to see huge manta rays migrating through the channel between Nanuya Balavu and Drawaqa Islands (page 108).

★ **Blue Lagoon:** The world-famous lagoon on **Nanuya Lailai Island** has stunning, shallow turquoise waters cupped in picturesque rock formations—it's even more beautiful than in the movies (page 111).

★ **Cave Swimming at Sawa-i-Lau Island:** Enjoy a dip in a dramatic limestone sea cave that's been featured both in legend and film (page 115).

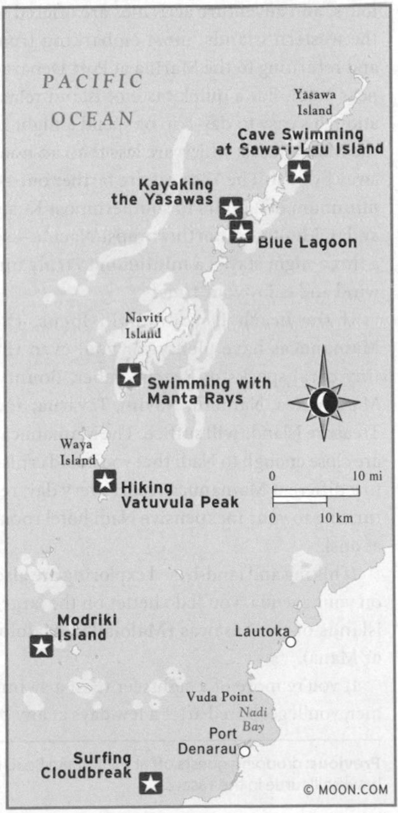

of the most romantic beaches in the world as backdrop.

Active travelers will find plenty to fill their days and stretch their muscles. There's diving and snorkeling, of course, with these areas comprising some of the planet's most pristine undersea environments. Also famous is the surfing on world-renowned breaks such as Cloudbreak. Hiking is possible on several of the dormant volcanic peaks, and usually rewards you with fantastic views of turquoise waters. Sportfishing is available in many areas. Many resorts include the use of nonmotorized equipment such as snorkeling gear, kayaks, and paddleboards in your room rate.

PLANNING YOUR TIME

A huge selection of day cruises, sightseeing tours, and adventure activities are offered to the western islands, most embarking from and returning to the Marina at Port Denarau near Nadi. For a quick taste of island relaxation, it's easy to day-trip or spend a night in the Mamanucas, which are less than an hour away by boat. The Yasawas are farther out—a minimum of 2 hours to southernmost Kuata and 4.5 hours to northernmost Nacula—so a three-night stay is a minimum to truly unwind and enjoy your time.

If the beach is your main focus, the Mamanucas have plenty for you; even the tiny coral specks of Beachcomber, Bounty, Matamanoa, Namotu, Navini, Tavarua, and Treasure Islands will suffice. The Mamanucas are close enough to Nadi that you could cruise to a different Mamanuca resort every day, returning to your inexpensive Nadi hotel room at dusk.

If hiking and land-based exploring are also on your agenda, you'll do better on the larger islands of the Yasawas (Malolailai, Malolo, or Mana).

If you're more of a sightseer than a swimmer, you'll get bored after a few days at any of these islands; you might prefer an organized cruise. There's little in the way of shopping or entertainment out on the islands, although the larger resorts make valiant attempts at entertaining you with bars, performances, excursions, and *lovo* feasts. Bring small bills if you intend to shop at the local handicraft markets, most of which offer a selection of cheap jewelry, potholders, and the like.

Don't schedule a return to Nadi on the same day you must catch an international flight, as bad weather can lead to the cancellation of all boat trips, especially if a cyclone warning has been issued. December-April is the official cyclone season, but the fast-moving storms can also occur in November, May, and June.

GETTING THERE

Most travelers take the fast catamarans that leave daily from the Marina at Port Denarau in Nadi. The priciest resorts will arrange for you to take their private seaplanes when you book your reservation. You can also book your own seaplane or helicopter transfer and take in stunning aerial views of turquoise shoals and shores. Alternatively, choose to save some money on one of the budget ferry/"seabus" options.

Air

Turtle Airways (tel. 672-1888, evanson.jr@gmail.com, www.turtleairways.com), next to the golf course at Wailoaloa Beach in Nadi, runs a seaplane shuttle to both archipelagoes. Traveling to the main Mamanuca resorts costs F$330 per person one-way (minimum of two passengers); to the Yasawas, F$380 per person one-way. Baggage is limited to one 15-kilogram suitcase plus one carry-on, or 185 kilograms maximum body weight and luggage per couple, as the Cessna seaplane has a strict weight maximum. There is no set schedule; whatever Mamanuca or Yasawa resort you book with will coordinate your flights

Previous: dropping guests off at the Botaira Beach Resort; Blue Lagoon beach at Nanuya Lailai Island; a hawksbill turtle in the Yasawas.

according to your arrival in Nadi to minimize your layover time.

Feel like a star by flying with **Heli-Tours** (Marina at Port Denarau, mobile tel. 992-4940/home tel. 675-0255, www.helitoursfiji.com), which has provided aerial views for media such as *The Chronicles of Narnia*, several BBC specials, and a Bollywood beverage commercial. They offer door-to-door transfers to your island resort in either an R44 Robinson helicopter (seats three) or an AS355 Twin Squirrel (seats six). Flights range from F$395 per adult for the closest Mamanuca islands to F$1,780 for the farthest Yasawa spot. There are discounts for children and groups. The heliport is located just outside the bridge to Denarau, and all flights include pickup in an air-conditioned van from the airport or your hotel. Scenic day flights and adventure trips are also available via their website or at the sales office, located at Port Denarau where the boat tour desks are.

Sea

MAMANUCAS

If you're booking travel to the Mamanucas through a hotel tour desk in Nadi, chances are you'll end up on a vessel belonging to **South Sea Cruises** (tel. 675-0500, info@ssc.com.fj, www.ssc.com.fj, staffed by phone daily 0700-2000). The high-speed shuttles leave Denarau several times a day. Book through your island hotel to increase the chances that your room will be ready when you arrive, or DIY at www.ssc.com.fj; just enter your dates and desired port(s). Rates range from F$90 (Bounty) to F$160 (Vomo) one-way, and include free bus pickup from the Nadi airport, many Nadi hotels, or (on Denarau) the Westin and Wyndham. Children ages 5-15 are half price on all trips; under 5 travel free. See the "Day Cruises" section below for organized cruises offered by the same company. Be prepared to wade on and off the boat in ankle-deep water.

Golden Charters (tel. 992-1999 or 999-5999, bookings@goldenchartersfiji.com, www.goldenchartersfiji.com) offers charter transfers for up to five people on the *Lady Rose* speedboat. Rates range from F$550 (Bounty) to F$990 (Vomo), and include transfers from Denarau hotels; pickups from elsewhere cost extra. The boat is also available for day cruising through the Mamanucas, including snorkeling, fishing, dolphin-watching, and other activities, at F$800 for four hours or F$1,400 for a full day.

Budget travelers, especially those staying in Wailoaloa or coming directly from Nadi Airport, have two options for getting to the Mamanucas with no frills. The **Ratu Kini Cruiser** (tel. 999-1246 or 672-1959, diveratukini@gmail.com), a small, basic ferry owned by the backpacker-oriented Ratu Kini Dive Resort, departs Fantasy Jetty daily at 0930 for F$85 one-way. The **Mana Flyer** (tel. 930-5933) is a water taxi speedboat that departs Fantasy Jetty daily at 1130 (F$80 one-way); staff respond most quickly to messages via the Facebook page. Both operators serve Beachcomber, Bounty, Treasure, Malolo, and Mana Islands. Service includes bus transfers to Nadi hotels. Reservations are recommended.

YASAWAS

To reach the Yasawa Islands, most travelers take the "yellow boat," the *Yasawa Flyer II*. It's operated by **Awesome Adventures** (tel. 675-0499, www.awesomefiji.com), which is owned by South Sea Cruises. It zips up and down the Yasawa chain daily, with a couple of Mamanuca stops as well. If you'd like to travel direct to the Yasawas with no fuss, you can book the Welcome and Departure packages and be whisked off from Nadi Airport. The free bus transfer from Nadi Airport leaves at 0650 from the bus lot outside the Arrivals terminal, and you can also arrange transfers from most Nadi and Denarau hotels. One-way fares from Denarau range US$49-94 (children are half price).

To visit multiple islands with Awesome Adventures, save money with the multi-day **Bula Pass,** starting at US$218 for five days and unlimited hops. The boat leaves Denarau at 0830, arriving at the farthest

Yasawa

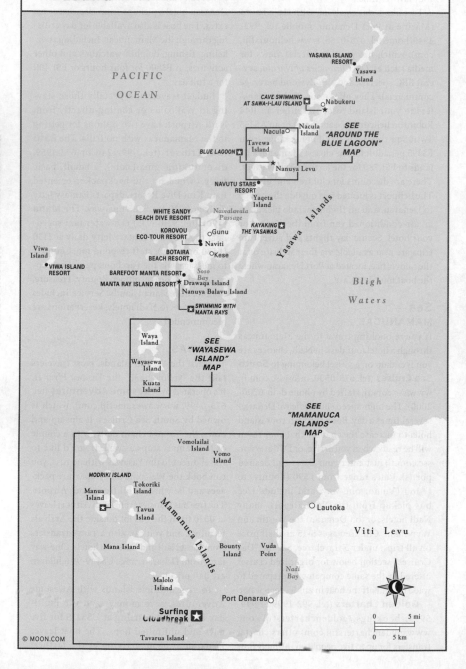

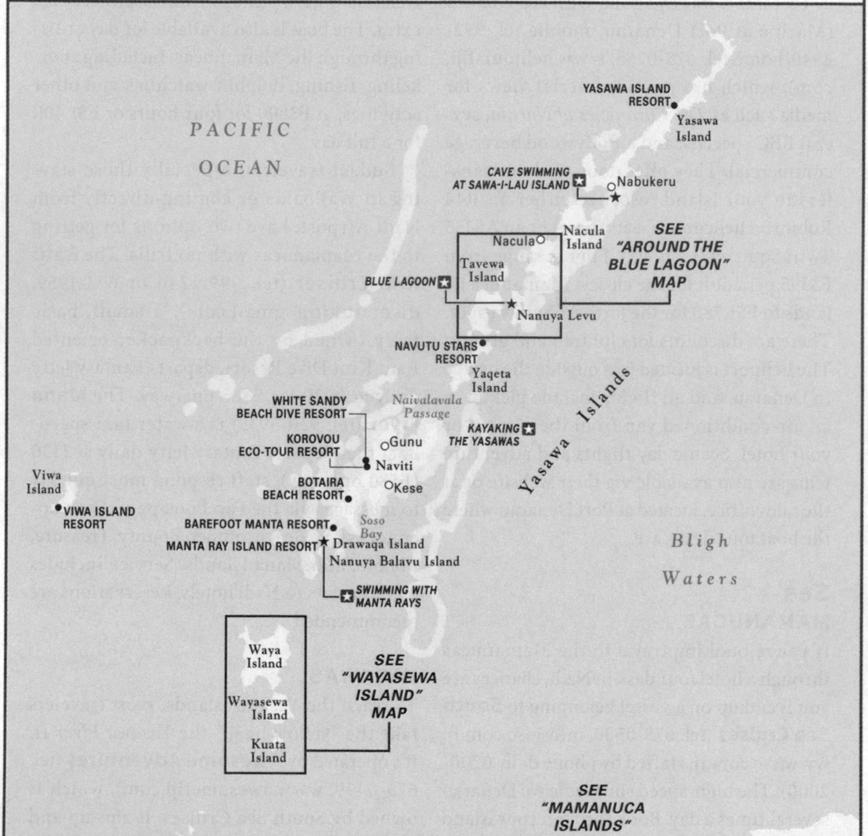
PACIFIC
OCEAN
YASAWA ISLAND
RESORT
Yasawa
Island
CAVE SWIMMING
AT SAWA-I-LAU ISLAND
Nabukeru
Nacula
Nacula
Island
SEE
"AROUND THE
BLUE LAGOON"
MAP
Tavewa
Island
BLUE LAGOON
Nanuya Levu
NAVUTU STARS
RESORT
Yaqeta
Island
Yasawa Islands
WHITE SANDY
BEACH DIVE RESORT
Naivalavala
Passage
KAYAKING
THE YASAWAS
KOROVOU
ECO-TOUR RESORT
Gunu
Naviti
Viwa
Island
BOTAIRA
BEACH RESORT
Kese
VIWA ISLAND
RESORT
BAREFOOT MANTA RESORT
Soso
Bay
MANTA RAY ISLAND RESORT
Drawaqa Island
Nanuya Balavu Island
Bligh
Waters
SWIMMING WITH
MANTA RAYS
Waya
Island
SEE
"WAYASEWA
ISLAND"
MAP
Wayasewa
Island
Kuata
Island
SEE
"MAMANUCA
ISLANDS"
MAP
Vomolailai
Island
Vomo
Island
MODRIKI ISLAND
Tokoriki
Island
Manua
Island
Mamanuca Islands
Tavua
Island
Lautoka
Viti Levu
Mana Island
Bounty
Island
Vuda
Point
Nadi
Bay
Malolo
Island
Port Denarau
Surfing
Cloudbreak
0
5 mi
0
5 km
Tavarua Island
© MOON.COM

Find Your Beach

Local vessels moor on Nacula Island in the Yasawas.

MAMANUCAS

- **Modriki Island** (page 100): The **best overall beach** in the Mamanucas is on this tiny paradisiacal island (where Tom Hanks was famously cast away).
- **Small resort islands:** Beachcomber, Bounty, Castaway, Matamanoa, Navini, South Sea, and Tokoriki all have **excellent snorkeling** in their lagoons, especially at high tide.
- **Mana Island** (page 97): Mana has fine beaches on the northern, southern, and western sides.
- **Malololailai Island** (page 91): The best beach is in front of the Plantation and Lomani resorts.
- **Vomo Island** (page 101): If you're looking for luxury, the western beach on Vomo Island is superb. The island is only accessible to guests of the island's resort.

YASAWAS

- **Nanuya Lailai Island** (page 111): The **Blue Lagoon Beach** on this island is the **best overall** in the Yasawas (and where Brooke Shields made a Hollywood splash).
- **Nacula Island** (page 113): On a **budget,** you can't beat the glorious beach (and the price) on this island, where you can stay in a dorm at either Oarsman's Bay Lodge or Blue Lagoon Beach Resort.
- **Waya Island** (page 105): The high white beach in front of Octopus Resort on the northwest coast is the best on this larger island.
- **Nanuya Balavu** and **Drawaqa Islands** (page 107): The channel between these two small islands is **great for snorkeling,** especially when manta rays visit April-November.
- **Yasawa Island** (page 116): If you're able to shell out for the **luxurious** Yasawa Island Resort that offers exclusive access to this island, you'll be rewarded with creamy white sands.

point, Nanayu Island, at 1330. Then it turns right back around and docks in Denarau at 1745. Note that some resorts charge a F$10 water taxi fare to collect you from the *Yasawa Flyer.* Also, many resorts in the Yasawas have a two-night minimum, and none take walk-ups; you'll be asked if you have a reservation before you disembark.

For an all-inclusive, multi-island experience, budget travelers can check out the **Bula Combo Pass** offered by Awesome Adventures. Passes are valid for 5-15 days and can be used for travel on certain South Sea Cruises trips (only Bounty, Treasure, Beachcomber, and South Sea Islands) as well as all Awesome Adventures vessels to the Mamanucas and Yasawas. Your pass is activated on the first day of travel, and you can island-hop as much as you like, as long as you make boat and accommodation reservations 24 hours ahead. Be sure to book well ahead during peak periods, though. The travel desk on board the boat can help you make reservations and amend your plans along the way, as well as extend your pass *before* it expires by upgrading to a longer pass. Your pass expires as soon as you return to Denarau, even if that's before the last day. Passes can be used at the following resorts: South Sea Island (dorm), Naqalia (12-bed dorm and *bure*), White Sandy (dorm and *bure*), Long Beach (dorm and garden *bure*), Wayalailai (20-bed dorm and private lodge), Safe Landing (dorm and *bure*), Nabua Lodge (dorm and *bure*), and Gold Coast (dorm and *bure*). Meals, of varying quality and quantity, are included in the hotel rates. Drinks and bottled water tend to be cheaper on the boat than on the islands. Choose your accommodation level by a rating system of one or two "coconuts": one is very basic (must bring your own towel and soap), while two offers minimal amenities; none of the accommodations are fancy. The pass ranges in price depending on what you choose, starting at US$487 for 4 nights in dorms, up to US$2,230 for 14 nights in single rooms.

An alternative to the *Yasawa Flyer* is the 46-seat **Fiji Seabus** (tel. 666-2648, 924-9770, or 904-3723, www.seabusfiji.com, tavewaseabus@coral.com.fj), also known as the Tavewa Seabus or simply the "red seabus." The comfortable, fast catamaran was built in Navua and offers the quickest ride from Viti Levu to the famed Blue Lagoon area of the Yasawas. It departs from Lautoka, which cuts a couple of hours of sea time from your journey. Fares are F$100 for the closer islands (Nanuya, Yaqeta, Vuaki, Matacawalevu, Naisisili, Tavewa, Malakati, and Nacula), F$120 for the middle islands (Navotua, Tamusua, and Nabukeru), and F$160 for the farthest (Dalomo, Teci, Bukama, YIR). Locals get a discount of about 30 percent. It departs at 0800 daily from Lautoka Kings Jetty and is operated by Coralview Resort on Tavewa Island.

The Mamanuca Islands

The Mamanuca Islands are a paradise of eye-popping reefs and sand-fringed isles shared by traditional Fijian villages and jet-age resorts. The white-coral beaches offer superb snorkeling, though some reefs were washed out by Cyclone Winston and are still recovering; ask about local conditions when you arrive on your island, and guides will point you toward the best spots. These islands are in the lee of big Viti Levu, which means you'll get about as much sun here as anywhere in Fiji. Some of the South Pacific's finest scuba diving, surfing, sportfishing, and yachting await you.

DAY CRUISES

General Information

To enjoy the islands for a day, you have options—many options, as an island day trip is one of the most popular activities in Fiji for tourists and well-heeled islanders alike.

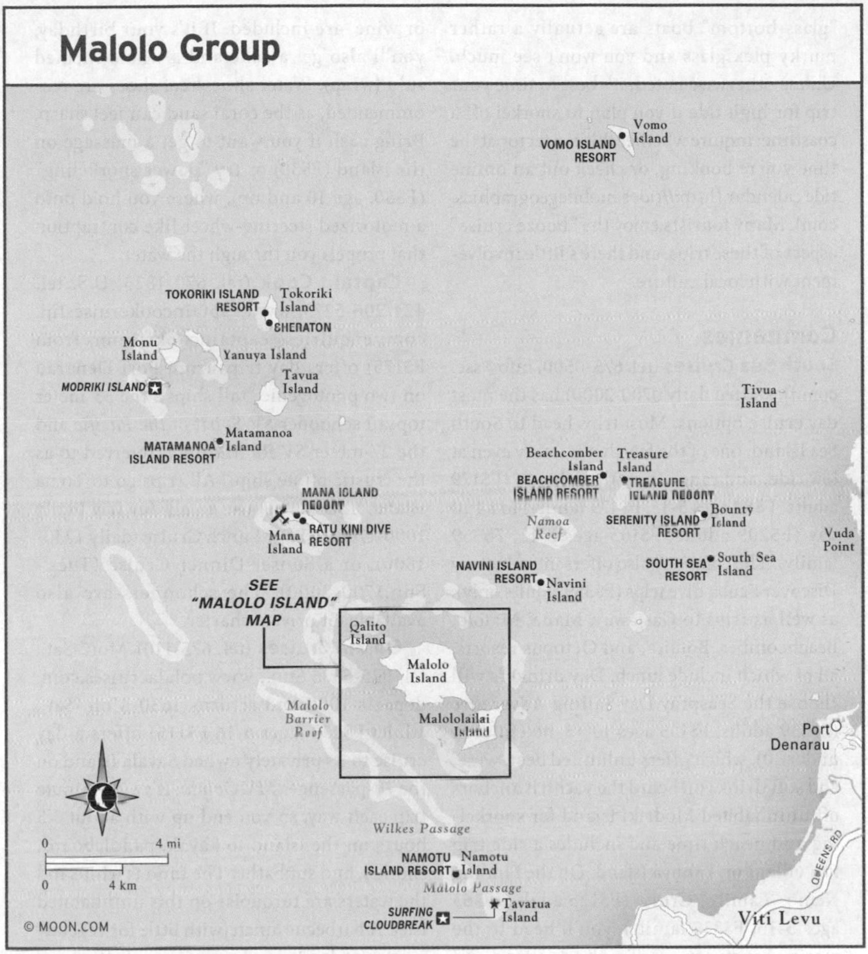

Choose and prepay your trip by contacting one of the tour operators below in advance, book through a hotel travel desk, or go directly to the tour operators' area at the Marina at Port Denarau, where sales staff for the various companies will be glad to explain all your options.

Virtually all of the day cruises include free bus transfers from most Nadi hotels, as well as from Coral Coast hotels at additional cost. If you're taking one of these buses, be sure to board the correct one by showing your printed confirmation email or voucher; several companies have similar names and logos.

Once you're at the port, check in at your tour desk and you'll be given the actual cruise ticket. You'll then exit the tour desk area to the docks, perhaps be offered a complimentary beverage while you wait, and eventually give the ticket to a crew member as you board the boat. Some parts of this process may seem chaotic, but the employees are usually efficient and will point you in the right direction.

The cruises include free snorkeling gear, but they do run out occasionally, so don't be slow to select yours. Kayaks and stand-up paddleboards are also usually free. Scuba and other activities may be extra. The "glass-bottom" boats are actually a rather murky plexiglass and you won't see much. Unless otherwise noted, it's best to time your trip for high tide if you plan to snorkel off a coastline; inquire whether this is a factor at the time you're booking, or check out an online tide calendar (http://tides.mobilegeographics.com). Many tourists enjoy the "booze cruise" aspect of these trips, and there's little involvement with local culture.

Companies

South Sea Cruises (tel. 675-0500, info@ssc.com.fj, staffed daily 0700-2000) has the most day cruise options. Most trips head to South Sea Island, one of the few that is lovely even at low tide, and range from three hours (F$179 adults, F$89 ages 5-15, F$479 family) to a full day (F$209 adults, F$105 ages 5-15, F$559 family). The company also offers introductory Discover Scuba dive trips (F$359, adults only), as well as trips to Castaway, Mana, Malolo, Beachcomber, Botaira, and Octopus resorts, all of which include lunch. Day drinkers will choose the Seaspray Day Sailing Adventure (F$239 adults, F$155 ages 10-15, no children under 10), which offers unlimited beer, wine, and soft drinks on board the yacht; it anchors off uninhabited Modriki Island for snorkeling and beach time and includes a side trip to a village on Yanuya Island. On the Finding Nemo "Family" Cruise (F$125 adults, F$63 ages 5-15, F$335 family), you'll head to the marine sanctuary near South Sea Island and hop on a semisubmersible vessel; it's sort of like a floating aquarium, except you're the one behind glass while the fish roam free. Family rates, where offered, include two adults plus up to three children.

Oceanic Schooner Co. (tel. 670-2443, www.whalestale.com.fj, departs 1000 and returns 1700 daily, adults F$229, ages 11-16 F$169, ages 5-10 F$119, ages 4 and under free) sails to privately owned Schooner Island on the 30-meter *Whale's Tale,* built at Suva's Whippy Shipyard in 1985. A champagne breakfast and gourmet lunch served buffet-style aboard ship, including Fijian beer or wine, are included. If it's your birthday, you'll also get a cake and a whale-themed sulu (wrap). Water shoes/reef shoes are recommended, as the coral sand can feel sharp. Bring cash if you want to get a massage on the island (F$30) or try "power snorkeling" (F$80, age 10 and up), where you hold onto a motorized steering-wheel-like contraption that propels you through the water.

Captain Cook (tel. 670-1823, U.S. tel. 424/206-5275, www.captaincookcruisesfiji.com, enquiries@captaincookfj.com, from F$175) offers day trips from Port Denarau on two photogenic "tall ships": the 33-meter topsail schooner *SV Spirit of the Pacific* and the 27-meter *SV Ra Marama,* referred to as the "rustic pirate ship." All trips go to Tivua Island. You can choose an all-day trip (daily 1000-1700), a Lazy Lunch Cruise (daily 1230-1800), or a Sunset Dinner Cruise (Tues.-Sun.1700-2000). The schooners are also available for private charter.

Oolala Cruises (tel. 675-1101 Mon.-Sat., tel. 925-5336 Sun., www.oolalacruises.com, departs 1000 and returns 1630 Mon.-Sat., adults F$230, ages 6-16 F$115) offers a day cruise to its privately owned Savala Island on the 70-passenger *MV Oolala.* It's a 75-minute trip each way, so you end up with about 3.5 hours on the island to kayak, paddleboard, snorkel, and sunbathe. The sand is white and the waters are turquoise on this uninhabited islet. A barbecue lunch (with little for vegetarians), soft drinks, and morning and afternoon tea are included. You can pay extra for a massage on the island. Beware that the company has questionable ecological practices: Staff pick up starfish and sea cucumbers to show to tourists, drop breadcrumbs to draw fish to the glass-bottom boat, and hand-feed baby sharks with sausage and chicken to attract them close to shore.

THE TINY ISLANDS

Most of the tiny islands only take about 30-45 minutes to reach from Nadi. South Sea Island, Beachcomber Island, and Bounty Island are the most popular with day-trippers. Wadigi and Castaway Islands off of Malolo are a bit farther, and will take about 1.5 hours to reach.

Tivua Island

The tiny **Tivua Island** is a pleasant place to spend a day. It's affordable and very safe, and is the first stop on many multiday cruises.

The island is owned by **Captain Cook Cruises** (tel. 670-1823, reservations@captaincook.com.fj, www.captaincookcruisesfiji.com), which has exclusive rights to run trips here. On a day trip, you'll arrive on one of two tall sailing vessels, the *Ra Marama* or the *Spirit of the Pacific*. Aside from lolling on the beach beds and hammocks with your drinks, you can take a trip in the company's somewhat murky glass-bottom boat or snorkel with one of their Fijian marine biologists. Certified divers can go on a nearby wreck dive, but Cyclone Winston washed out the reefs here.

The full-day trip leaves Denarau at 1000 and returns at 1700 for F$229 per adult. One child 3-9 years old can pay just F$59 with an adult fare; otherwise, children 3-15 years old pay F$129. A Captain's Club for children is included, along with a buffet lunch and non-motorized water sports. For the "lazy lunch" cruise, it's a 1230 departure and 1830 return, and the price is about F$30 less.

Overnight stays in a beach *bure* run F$100 per person for just two guests, less if there are additional guests (up to six people max). There's limited (and often no) electricity, and all water must be shipped in to the island, so your showers are likely to be cold and short. But you're guaranteed silence, privacy, meals cooked to Captain Cook's Australian standards, and gently lapping waves all to yourself until the next day's batch of cruisers arrive.

South Sea Island

South Sea Island is one of the smallest Mamanucas—a sandbank reminiscent of shipwreck cartoons from newspapers. It's a *very* popular day destination thanks to South Sea Cruises, as well as a party island for young backpackers. It's often overcrowded and not as clean as it could be, but if you enjoy swimming and socializing, you'll have a good time. The beach here is nice, even at low tide.

South Sea Island Resort (tel. 651-0506, www.ssc.com.fj, F$150 pp) packs 30 people into a thatched dormitory upstairs in a two-story building. Good buffet meals and lots of water sports are included in the rate. The developers have constructed an unnecessary and tacky little swimming pool in the center of the island. Boat transfers from Nadi on the *Tiger IV* are F$135 each way, but many guests use the free stopover allowed here on *Yasawa Flyer* tickets to the Yasawa Islands.

Beachcomber Island

Since the 1960s, **Beachcomber Island** has been "Club Med on a budget" for thousands of young travelers. The island is so small that you can stroll around it in 10 minutes, but there's a white-sand beach and buildings nestled among coconut trees and tropical vegetation. A beautiful coral reef with well-fed fish extends far out on all sides, and scuba diving is available through Subsurface Fiji.

Beachcomber Island Resort (tel. 666-1500, www.beachcomberfiji.com) still has its trademark sand-floor bar, dancing, and floor shows four nights a week, but the average guest has become a little older in recent years—and the prices have crept up too. These days, the bar closes and the music goes off at 0100. Parasailing, waterskiing, Jet Skis, and other sporting activities are available for an additional charge. Accommodations include all meals served buffet-style. Most young backpackers opt for the big, open mixed dormitory where the 42 double-decker bunks (84 beds) cost F$119 a night. Secure lockers are provided. The 16 simple lodge rooms at F$275/365 single/double (fridge and fan provided) are a good compromise for slightly older, budget-conscious couples. You can also get one of 16 thatched ocean-view *bures* with ceiling fan, fridge, and private facilities for F$399/479/598 single/double/triple (add F$50 for the six beachfront units). The *bures* are okay for young families, as children under 12 enjoy slightly reduced rates. Drinks at the bar are pricey, so a duty-free bottle purchased upon arrival at the airport will come in handy here.

Bounty Island

Bounty is bigger than Beachcomber (it takes about 30 minutes to walk around), with a bit more nature to explore and a bit less partying. The snorkeling here is amazing, with lots of marine life. Reef Safari offers scuba diving excursions here.

In late 2018, **Serenity Island Resort** (tel. 999-9382 or 910-3500, reservations@serenityisland.com.fj, www.serenityisland.com.fj, F$350-475 d) took over the rundown Bounty Island Resort and gave it a complete makeover to rave reviews. Three categories of air-conditioned bures, with and without ocean views, are clustered along a fine beach with good snorkeling. Wi-Fi and flatscreen satellite TVs are included. Jet-Skis, paddleboards, and kayaks are for rent, and day trips to go fishing or to Cloud 9 (off Port Denarau south of Nadi) can be arranged for a fee. A meal plan is F$155 per person, but a la carte meals at F$20-50 may be a better deal. Meals are tasty and generous. Transfers via the Vuda Point Marina cost F$150 per adult each way from the Nadi Airport, or F$100 for just the boat ride if you make your own way to Vuda. Children age 3-11 receive a 50% discount on meals and transfers.

Treasure Island

Beachcomber's little neighbor, **Treasure Island,** offers *bures* set on white sands in a lush setting. Despite its tropical greenery, the island's insect population is controlled by a large and benevolent community of geckos.

Treasure Island Resort (tel. 666-1599, www.treasureisland-fiji.com) is popular among packaged vacationers from New Zealand and Australia. The resort is owned in part by the Tokatoka Nakelo landowning clan, which also supplies most of the workers, although the management is European. The 68 *bures* are all air-conditioned and have three categories: Oceanview *bures* at F$880 (max three adults), the Ocean Front *bures* at F$1,007 (max three adults), and the Premium Beachfront *bures* at F$1,227 (max four adults). Add F$217 per adult per day for the meal plan (accompanying children under 12 eat for free); without it, the resort's restaurants are overpriced. A kids' club attends to guests under 15. Some nautical activities such as windsurfing, sailing, and canoeing are included, and

snorkelers near Vomo Island

there's a swimming pool. Scuba diving with Subsurface Fiji is extra.

Navini Island

Navini Island is a 2.5-hectare coral isle that makes a perfect first stop in Fiji if you're looking to be spoiled. Unlike the party spots, it's ideal for those looking for a quiet holiday. Only overnight guests are accepted (no day-trippers). There's abundant marinelife for snorkelers and divers to see, as fishing has been banned here for many years.

★ **Navini Island Resort** (tel. 666-2188, www.navinifiji.com.fj) is a secluded eco-resort with just 10 beachfront *bures* nicely ensconced in the low island's shrubbery. Rates start at F$698 double for a fan-cooled unit with a motel-like bathroom; the Deluxe Premiere *bure* is F$794 and includes an outdoor shower; the two-bedroom *bure* is F$831; and the family *bure* is F$1,045. Deals are available for stays of more than a week and for children. The compulsory and excellent two-/three-meal package is F$147/162 per person per day. Everyone gets to know one another during predinner cocktails and by eating together at long tables at fixed times. In the evening, you can also request private candlelit dining on the beach in front of your *bure*. Free morning boat trips are offered, as are snorkeling gear, paddleboats, sailboats, and kayaks. Scuba diving with Subsurface Fiji can be arranged, and the snorkeling right off the beach is good at high tide. Car/boat transfers from Nadi via the Vuda Point Marina are arranged anytime upon request (F$171 pp one-way).

Wadigi Island

The tiny **Wadigi Island** off the western coast of Malolo belongs entirely to you throughout the duration of your stay. It's a magical way to fulfill a fantasy of having a totally exclusive, all-inclusive island of your very own—but you'll pay top dollar to do so.

Wadigi Island Villa (tel. 672-0901, www.wadigi.com) costs F$4,300 per couple, with up to six persons maximum per villa (minimum stay three nights). Included in the rate are all meals, drinks, and sporting equipment, such as kayaks, windsurfing rigs, surfboards, fishing rods, and snorkeling gear. Deep-sea fishing, guided surfing trips, and scuba diving (with Subsurface Fiji) cost extra.

Castaway Island (Qalito Island)

Don't confuse this **Castaway Island** for the place where the Tom Hanks hit was filmed—that's Modriki Island. But no one will know what you're talking about if you refer to this 174-hectare island by its official name, **Qalito.** Just west of Malolo, it's known by its only resort, which was Fiji's first in the outer islands and remains one of the most popular. This resort sells out well in advance thanks to Australian vacationers who return year after year. Even the South Sea Cruises day trips sell out because only 20 guests per day are allowed to land on the island.

Castaway Island Resort (tel. 666-1233, www.castawayfiji.com) sits on a sandy point at the western end of the island. The 66 closely packed thatched *bures* sleep four at F$1,236 and up. The generous all-meal plan is F$169 per adult (F$86 for children under 13). The *lovo* and *meke* are on Wednesday night, the beach barbecue on Saturday. Among the free nonmotorized water sports are sailing, windsurfing, paddleboats, tennis, and snorkeling; scuba diving and fishing are extra. There's a swimming pool. Castaway is marketed to families with small children, but only four persons are allowed per *bure*—and infants count. A 10-person family *bure* will cost F$3,524. A free kids' club operates daily 0900-2100 with lots of fun activities for those aged 3-12.

MALOLOLAILAI ISLAND

Malololailai, or "Little Malolo," is the second-largest island in the Mamanuca group at eight kilometers around. Inland are rounded, grassy hills. In 1880, an American sailor named Louis Armstrong purchased Malololailai from the Fijians for one musket; in 1964, Dick Smith bought it for many muskets. You can still be alone at the beaches on the far side of the island, but with three growing resorts, a marina, a nine-hole golf course, and lots more timeshare condominium projects in the pipeline, it's becoming overdeveloped. An airstrip across the island's waist serves as a hub for charter flights to the region's resorts. Plantation Island Resort has a better beach and is more all-inclusive than neighboring Musket Cove Resort, which is more of a do-it-yourself kind of place and popular with yacht travelers. Lomani Island Resort is for adults only.

For **yachters:** Musket Cove's marina provides yachters with water, clean showers, and fuel. There's a bar on Ratu Nemani Island, a tiny coral islet connected to the marina by a floating bridge. Yachts can use the Musket Cove marina moorings or moor stern-to, Mediterranean-style, at a daily rate. There is a restriction of 1.8 meters draft at low tide at the entrance to the marina. The marked anchorage is protected and 15 meters deep, with good holding. Most of the boats in June's Auckland-to-Fiji yacht race end up here just in time for Fiji's prestige yachting event, the President's Cup. In mid-September, there's a yachting regatta week at the resort.

Accommodations

Plantation Island Resort (tel. 666-9333, www.plantationisland.com), on the west side of Malololailai, is one of the largest resorts off Nadi. It belongs to the Raffles Group, which also owns the Lomani Island Resort here and the Fiji Gateway Hotel in Nadi. The 142 rooms are divided between 41 air-conditioned hotel rooms in a two-story building and 101 individual or duplex *bures*. Rates start at F$725 single or double for one of the 26 garden hotel rooms and increase to F$1,085 for a deluxe beachfront *bure*. The rooms have fridges but no cooking facilities, so add F$92 per person for buffet breakfast and dinner. A supermarket is at the airport end of the resort. Plantation Island Resort works hard to cater to families, with two children under 12 accommodated free when sharing with their parents, and a children's meal plan at F$32 for guests under 12. Babysitting services are available, and there's a 20-meter waterslide and two pools. Free activities here include snorkeling gear, windsurfing, paddleboats, leaky kayaks, and Hobie Cat sailing. Daily snorkeling and fishing trips are offered at no charge; scuba diving is extra. Greens fees at Plantation Island's golf course toward the airport are reasonable, and clubs and cart are for hire. In 2019 a $10 million upgrade and construction of a new restaurant, pool, and 40 additional rooms was underway.

Musket Cove Island Resort (tel. 666-2215, VHF channel 68, www.musketcovefiji.com) opened in 1977 and has been built hodgepodge, so accommodations here vary widely. This is one of the few Mamanuca resorts that provide cooking facilities for its guests, and it's popular with yachties. Full kitchen facilities are provided in the 16 two-bedroom villas, costing F$1,150 (maximum four guests). The 21 garden and lagoon *bures* (F$665 s/d) and the 12 beachfront *bures* (from F$935 s/d) have breakfast bars. The six air-conditioned rooms (F$318 s/d) upstairs in the resort's administration building do not have cooking facilities. Musket Cove's well-stocked grocery store sells fresh fruit and vegetables (but no alcohol), and a coin laundry is near the store. A F$125 per adult (F$55 per child under 12) meal plan is available at any of the food and beverage outlets, including Dick's Place Restaurant by the pool. Entertainment is provided every night except Sunday. The resort has a wellness spa, Makare, that you can book upon arrival. Activities such as snorkeling, windsurfing, canoeing, kayaking, and line fishing are free for guests. Paid activities include the Hobie Cats and waterskiing, scuba diving, yacht cruises, deep-sea sportfishing, and dolphin-watching trips.

On the southwestern coast of Malololailai, **Lomani Island Resort** (tel. 666-8212, www.lomaniisland.com) is intimate and upscale, with eight deluxe suites in a two-story building at F$795 double and four Hibiscus suites at F$925. Beachfront *bures* are F$1,095 and beachfront pool *bures* are F$1,250. Tax and a full American breakfast are included; lunch and dinner are F$175 per person. Children under 16 are not accepted here.

Getting There

A separate catamaran service operates to Malololailai Island on the **Malolo Cat** (tel. 675-0207, reservations@malolocat.com, https://malolocatfiji.com). One-way is F$80 for adults, F$40 for children age 2-15, including bus pickup from the Nadi airport and from most Nadi and Denarau hotels. The boat leaves Denarau at 0730, 1030, 1400, and 1730. You're only allowed to carry two bottles of liquor per person. Of the company's three boats, the two newest fiberglass ferries were built by indigenous boatbuilders on Malololailai Island itself.

MALOLO ISLAND

At low tide, you can wade from Malololailai to nearby **Malolo Island,** largest of the Mamanuca Group. Yaro, one of two Fijian villages on Malolo, is known to tourists as the "shell village" for what the locals offer for sale.

Accommodations

The **Funky Fish Beach Resort** (tel. 628-2333, www.funkyfishresort.com) on the south coast is a flashpacker place. The 16-bed dorm is F$55 per person, or it's F$119 for a double room with shared bath in the dorm. A small thatched beach *bure* with private bath starts at F$317 double; it's F$583 for the one-bedroom family *bure* or F$634 for a two-bedroom, self-catering beach *bure* for up to four people. The three-meal plan runs F$110 per person. The boat transfer from Denarau is F$282 round-trip or F$141 one-way for adults and half price for children ages 3-12. Even with the extras, this is still a good value compared to the other places on Malolo Island. Funky Fish has a pool as well as a fine beach, and it makes a good base for surfing and scuba diving. The three-hour round-trip hike to an old Fijian fort provides a 360-degree view.

Malolo Island Resort (tel. 666-9192, www.maloloisland.com) is at Malolo's western tip, a 20-minute walk from Walu Beach at low tide. The resort is owned by the Whitton family of Nadi, which also runs Rosie Holidays. It offers four family *bures* at F$2,100 per night double, and three other categories of *bures* start at F$750 per person. All but the family bungalow are duplexes, so don't expect much privacy, despite the price. Up to two children under 12 can stay with their parents for free and there's a kids' club on-site. The full meal plan costs F$170 per person (half price for children under 12). Malolo Island Resort has a two-tier freshwater swimming pool, and most nonmotorized water sports are included in the rate. Scuba diving with Subsurface Fiji costs extra.

Even more upscale is the adults-only **Likuliku Lagoon Resort** (tel. 666-3344, www.likulikulagoon.com), just over the point from Malolo Island Resort. It's also owned by Rosie Holidays, which promotes it heavily to honeymooners. The packages here depend on the location of your *bure*. There are four categories: Garden Beachfront (F$1,990 d), Beachfront (F$2,400 d), Deluxe Beachfront (F$2,800 d), and Over the Water, a Tahitian-style over-water *bure* with glass floors (F$3,200 d). Included are taxes, meals (drinks extra), and nonmotorized water sports. Children under 17 are not permitted. The lagoon has been partly dredged to provide deeper swimming areas, but at low tide the over-water bungalows are over mud. Likuliku Lagoon Resort is off limits to nonguests.

★ **Six Senses Fiji** (tel. 666-5028, reservations-fiji@sixsenses.com, www.sixsenses.com, from F$2,000) is the newest luxury resort on the island, opened in 2018 on a white-sand beach on the island's western side. The resort emphasizes sustainability, local art, and surfing. It is 100 percent solar powered by Tesla batteries and has its own rainwater collection and reverse osmosis water facility, meaning your drinking water doesn't arrive in the plastic bottles that are the bane of the Pacific Ocean. Throughout, you'll find contemporary art curated by Suva's 21K Art Gallery and crafts produced by Rise

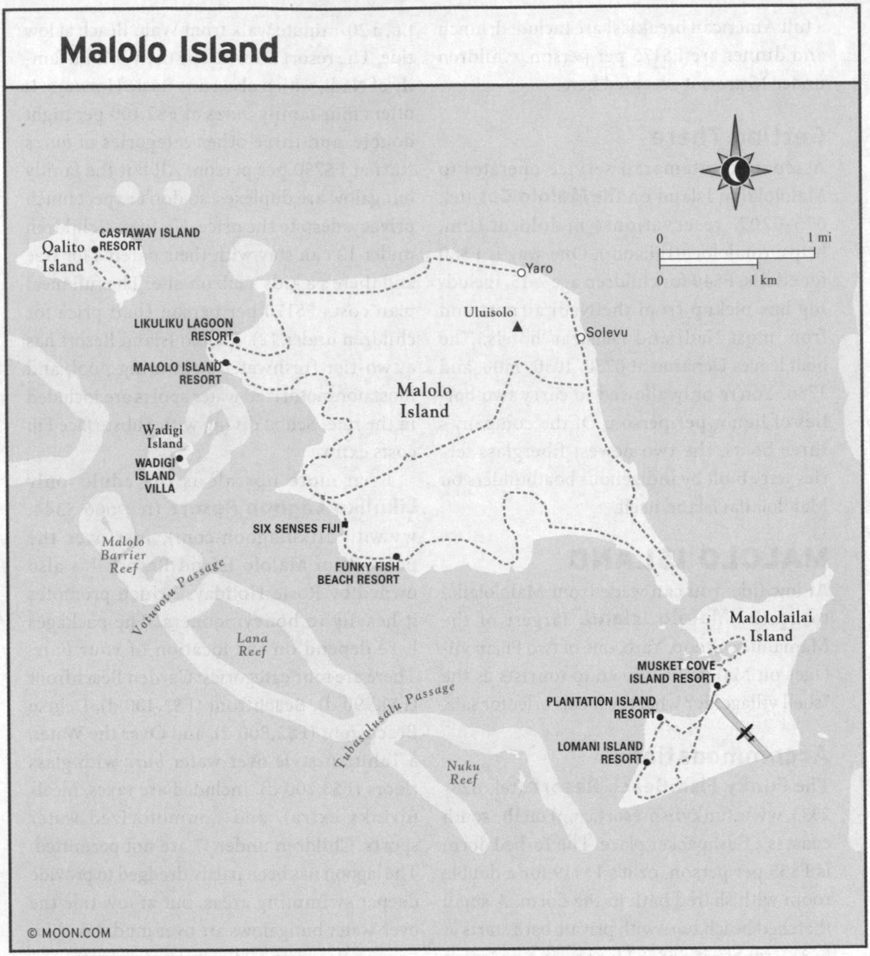

Beyond the Reef, a nonprofit that employs Fijian women in remote communities.

At Six Senses, surf lessons and trips, including to Cloudbreak, are with the high-end international company **Tropicsurf** (http://tropicsurf.com). Tropicsurf offers learn-to-surf programs as well as eco-friendly Firewire boards for resort guests, making this one of the few places in Fiji where you don't need to BYO surfboard. Additional amenities include an outdoor movie theater, Asian- and Pacific-themed restaurants, a pizzeria, a kids' club, and a "Wellness Village" complete with spa, yoga pavilion, and an outdoor hill circuit course. Rates start at F$2,000 for a one-bedroom villa with private pool, and go up to F$7,900 for a five-bedroom residence that sleeps 10. Meal plans are F$160/230 for two/three meals, half price for children 6-11. An "inclusive" plan with three meals plus daily yoga, massage, and drinks is F$600.

THE SURFING CAMPS: TAVARUA AND NAMOTU ISLANDS

The small islands of **Tavarua** and **Namotu** offer luxury and constant access to high-end surfing at the famous Cloudbreak and

Restaurants waves. There's also exhilarating scuba diving here on the Malolo Barrier Reef and the passages around tiny Namotu, which is known as "Magic Island" for the rich stream of nutrients swept in by strong currents.

Surfing

Less experienced surfers will find Fiji more welcoming in summer (November-March), when the swells are shorter in duration and the winds are lighter. But it's not for absolute beginners, as most of the breaks are atop prickly coral reefs, requiring control and confidence in the water. For safety reasons, surfers in this part of Fiji are expected to have at least three years of experience in a variety of conditions; there are no lessons at these resorts. Expert surfers come in winter (April-October), when huge swells originating in New Zealand can range as high as three meters.

★ CLOUDBREAK

Fiji's most famous surfing spot is **Cloudbreak,** a hollow left-breaking wave on the Navula Reef at the south end of the Mamanuca Group. An exposed reef break, it's regularly voted one of the 10 most challenging waves in the world. At five meters, Cloudbreak is the thrill of a lifetime; at two meters, it's a longboarder's paradise. Cloudbreak barrels best in a southwest offshore wind, with tube rides of up to 200 meters possible. In summer, it has flat days, but otherwise Cloudbreak is consistently perfect.

Tavarua Island Resort formerly had exclusive access to the wave, but since 2010 it's been required to open Cloudbreak on Saturdays to surfers from the mainland; Rendezvous Surf Camp Fiji, at Momi Bay (see Nadi chapter), leads trips.

OTHER SPOTS

Namotu Left is a world-class reef break that's more forgiving than its fearsome, famous neighbor. The powerful right barrel of **Wilkes Passage** is good anywhere from one to three meters. Rounding out the scene is **Swimming Pools,** a playful full-wraparound right break on the leeward side of Namotu Island that, with its crystal-blue water and sheltered position, has to be one of the world's most remarkable breaks.

Scuba Diving

Both pelagic and reef fish abound in the canyons, caves, and coral heads around Namotu, but in some places the action has been distorted by scuba operators who regularly feed the fish. The outer slopes of Namotu, where the reef plunges 1,000 meters into the Pacific abyss, feature turtles, reef sharks, and vast schools of barracuda, with visibility up to 50 meters. Dolphins also frequent this area. Bigger fish, manta rays, and oceangoing sharks are often seen at **The Big W** on the outer edge of the Malolo Barrier Reef, where vertical walls drop a spectacular 70 meters. Also along the outer barrier reef are the pinnacles of **Gotham City,** so called for the batfish seen here, along with brilliantly colored soft corals and vast schools of tropical fish.

Accommodations

South of Malololailai, **Tavarua Island Resort** (tel. 670-6513, www.tavarua.com) is the South Pacific's most famous surfing resort and *the* place to go for top U.S. surfers. It caters to affluent, older surfers rather than a young party crowd. Guests are accommodated in 14 beach *bures* with hot showers and private baths, plus two larger family *bures.* Facilities include a lagoon-style swimming pool and a large hot tub. On off days you can get in some deep-sea fishing, windsurfing, snorkeling, or scuba diving (extra charge). Bookings must be made six months in advance through **Tavarua Island Tours** (U.S. tel. 805/686-4551, Fiji tel. 776-6513, www.tavarua.com) in Santa Barbara, California. The minimum stay is one week.

Just across Malolo Passage on tiny Namotu Island is **Namotu Island Resort** (intl. tel. 310/584-9900, U.S. tel. 888/669-7873, www.namotuislandfiji.com), which runs a "Blue Water Sports Camp" for surfers. All

1

2

3

4

guests arrive on a Saturday via seven-night package tours from Los Angeles, costing US$2,727-US$3,339 per person depending on accommodation. The rate includes meals (drinks extra), airport transfers, snorkel and fishing gear, and unlimited access to the local surf breaks. Surfers must bring their own boards. All U.S. reservations must go through Waterways Travel in Santa Monica, California (www.waterwaystravel.com). Local bookings from within Fiji are possible only in the off-season, January and February, if space happens to be available—unlikely, as the island only takes 25 guests at a time. Children under 12 are not accepted. Scuba diving with Subsurface Fiji and massages cost extra.

MANA ISLAND

Grassy rounded hilltops, white-sand beaches, and crystal-clear waters make **Mana** one of the most beautiful islands in the Mamanuca group. It's also the only other resort island in the Mamanucas (other than Malolo) inhabited by Fijian villagers.

Set 32 kilometers northwest of Nadi, Mana is divided by a high fence erected down the middle of the island, with the large Mana Island Resort on the western side and a slew of low-budget backpacker hostels in the Fijian village on the eastern side. There's some tension between the Japanese investors who run the resort and the Fijian villagers who accommodate the backpackers. Shoestring travelers are most unwelcome anywhere in the resort, including the restaurants, shops, bars, and dive shop. In contrast, tourists from the resort are quite welcome to order cheap drinks or meals at the backpacker camps.

Recreation

There are lots of lovely **beaches** all around the island, most of them empty because the packaged tourists seldom stray far from their resort. The long white beach on the northeast side of the island is deserted. At the resort, the snorkeling is better off South Beach at low tide and off North Beach at high tide, but the nicest is Sunset Beach at the western end of Mana. There's a great view of the Mamanucas and southern Yasawas from the highest point on the island, a 10-minute hike from the backpacker camps, and splendid snorkeling on the reef. The Mana Main Reef is famous for its drop-offs, with visibility never less than 25 meters. You'll see turtles, fish of all descriptions, and the occasional crayfish.

One of the world's most famous reef shark-encounter venues is **Supermarket,** a 30-meter wall just west of Mana Island. Grays, whitetips, and blacktips are always present, and you might even see a tiger shark. Divemasters from either Ratu Kini or Mana Island resort hand-feed sharks more than two meters long.

Accommodations

Mana Island Resort (tel. 665-0423, www.manafiji.com, F$320-800) is by far the biggest of the tourist resorts off Nadi, with a spa and daily kids' club program. The numerous tin-roofed bungalows and suites range in price depending on amenities and views. Children under 13 sleep free if sharing with one or two adults. About half the guests here are Japanese. Some nonmotorized water sports are included, along with paid scuba, waterskiing, wakeboarding, banana riding, and other exotic activities. Resort restaurants are pricey (entrées from F$28). Live entertainment is presented nightly, and there's a Fijian *meke* on Tuesday and a Polynesian show on Friday. **Aqua Trek Mana** (tel. 670-2413, www.aquatrekdiving.com) serves guests at Mana Island Resort.

Right up against the big resort's security fence are the reception and dining areas of **Ratu Kini Dive Resort** (tel. 672-1959 or 999-1246, diveratukini@gmail.com, www.ratukinidiveresort.com.fj). The large accommodations buildings are 100 meters back in the village. You can camp for F$18 per person, and two mixed dormitories, with 14 and 12 beds each, cost F$35 per bed. A group

1: Tivua Island at the southern end of the Yasawas **2:** kayaking around Vomo Island **3:** marinelife in the Yasawas **4:** Modriki Island.

Diving Outfitters

Divers explore a wreck in the Malolo Barrier Reef.

A few dive operators serve the Mamanuca and Yasawa islands. Some operate from western Viti Levu and others are based out of the island resorts. They can be rather arbitrary about their rates, depending on how busy they are and where you're staying. Some hotels have prearranged discounts with certain dive shops.

Generally, the more days you dive, the less you'll pay per day. A two-tank boat dive can range F$99-199 per person, plus F$25-50 if you need to rent gear. Safety and expertise isn't much of a concern, as Fiji is a primo location where divemasters from all over the world want to work. But you'll get what you pay for in terms of amenities: the more expensive operators typically have faster and more comfortable boats, better surface-interval snacks, and more staff to help you haul your gear on and off.

If you're traveling during a busy time, such as the Australia and New Zealand school holidays—or if you have your heart set on a particular experience—be sure to make your dive reservations in advance. Otherwise, you can go with the flow and inquire about local conditions and timing when you arrive.

Subsurface Fiji (tel. 664-5911, mobile tel. 999-6371, www.fijidiving.com) will pick up divers at Port Denarau daily at 0830 and 1400, at the Vuda Bay Marina by arrangement, or from the following Mamanuca resorts: Musket Cove, Plantation Island, Lomani Island, Funky Fish, Tropica Island, Malolo Island, Likuliku Island, Wadigi Island, Navini Island, Namotu Island, and Tavarua Island. Rates vary depending on your pickup location. The two-day PADI certification course is F$990 (minimum two persons). Children eight years and up are accepted at their scuba school.

Reef Safari (tel. 675-0566, www.reefsafari.com) books scuba diving day trips from Nadi to islands in the Mamanuca Group. For beginners, it's F$150 per person for the tour, lunch, drinks, and an introductory Discover Scuba dive. Certified divers pay the same for two dives. Dive trips in the Yasawas are from a base at Manta Island Resort.

Aqua Trek Mana (tel. 670-2413, www.aquatrekdiving.com) serves guests at Mana Island Resort; **Viti Watersports** (tel. 670-2412, www.vitiwatersports.com) is based at Matamanoa Island Resort; and **Tokoriki Diving** (mobile tel. 972-4068, www.tokorikidiving.com) is at Tokoriki Island Resort. Nonguests can dive with them if the boat is not already filled with guests of the host hotel.

might like to book the entire five-bed dorm, which is air-conditioned and has its own bathroom, at F$55 per person. Private rooms in the main house are F$190 (some have en suite bathrooms), cottages are F$220 per couple, and a thatched family *bure* in the backyard is F$250 for two adults plus F$32 for up to two more people (children under 12 are half price). Have a look around at check-in before committing yourself, as all of the rooms are different. Breakfast is included but other meals cost extra (on Wednesdays or Thursdays they prepare a *lovo*). Full-day boat trips and two-hour snorkeling trips can be arranged if four people want to go.

Getting There

Charter flights service the island and land at a terminal that's a seven-minute walk west of Mana Island Resort. To get to the backpacker lodge, head for the wharf, from which the security fence will be visible.

Mana is the only Mamanuca island with a wharf, so you don't need to take off your shoes when you disembark from a boat. By catamaran, **South Sea Cruises** runs a day trip from Nadi, including lunch at Mana Island Resort (adults F$235, children under 16 F$129).

Accommodations with their own shuttle boats depart from Fantasy Jetty at Wailoaloa Beach. Ratu Kini requires guests to book on either the Ratu Kini Cruiser, which leaves Fantasy Jetty daily at 0930 and leaves Mana island daily at 1130 (F$160 round-trip including bus transfer from Nadi hotels), or on the South Sea Cruises ferry, which leaves Port Denarau daily at 900, 1200, and 1500 (F$128 one-way). The Ratu Kini Cruiser is less comfortable but takes only 30 minutes, while the South Sea ferry takes 90 minutes because it stops at several other islands. A private charter can also be arranged. Alternatively, Ratu Kini will arrange a transfer from the *Yasawa Flyer* at Beachcomber Island for F$110 for a solo traveler or F$90 per person for more than one. It's best to book your boat transport with the hotel at the time you make your reservation.

The **Mana Flyer** (tel. 930-5933), a low-cost speedboat, departs Fantasy Jetty daily at 1130 (F$80 one-way including pickup from Nadi hotels), and returns sometime in the afternoon; schedules vary according to tides and passenger bookings. They respond most quickly to messages via their Facebook page.

THE OUTER ISLANDS

Matamanoa Island

To the northwest of Mana Island is charming, tiny **Matamanoa Island,** which is just big enough to hold a resort—and it's for adults only. It only takes about 90 minutes to reach here on the high-speed catamaran *Cougar* (F$155 one-way, departing Port Denarau at 0915 and 1515), but it feels a world away from the big island. A volcanic cone on the northwest coast offers a hike with a view, while the white-sand beach stretches around the rest of the island.

Matamanoa Island Resort (tel. 672-3620, www.matamanoa.com) has 13 air-conditioned motel-style rooms at F$649 single or double, 14 split-level villas at F$1,039, and 19 *bures* at F$1,149. A third adult can be added to the villas and *bures* for F$165. Children under 16 are not accepted. All *bures* feature tapa-lined ceilings and private gazebos with plunge pools, and because the resort occupies both sides of the island, you can request either a sunrise or sunset view. The beach is complemented by an infinity swimming pool and spa, and there are tennis courts, a library with board games, and various sorts of boating excursions available. A full breakfast is included, and you can buy meals a la carte (lunch entrees average F$25 and dinner entrees average F$55), or purchase a dinner-only or all-meals plan. Complimentary afternoon tea and happy hour snacks are served at the bar. Rooms were renovated in 2015, while the common areas were upgraded in early 2018. Loud cruise-ship-style entertainment is put on at mealtimes and during the evening. Scuba diving is with **Viti Watersports** (tel. 670-2413, www.vitiwatersports.com), although the snorkeling is better than the diving.

Behind the Scenes: *Cast Away*

In early 2001, moviegoers worldwide got a taste of the beauty of Fiji's westernmost islands from Robert Zemeckis's film ***Cast Away,*** starring Tom Hanks as a FedEx employee traveling on a company jet that crashes in the Pacific. He spends four years alone on the island with just his volleyball for company. *Cast Away* was filmed in two stages—eight months apart, to allow Hanks to lose weight and grow a raggedy beard to play the character after years of rough living—with the second portion shot on location on tiny **Modriki Island.**

To avoid environmental damage and potential controversy, Zemeckis was careful to have veteran naturalist and author Dick Watling do an environmental impact assessment before the filming, and the film crew followed Watling's recommendations carefully. Later, when naturalists from the World Wide Fund for Nature in Suva investigated the affair, they gave Zemeckis and his team high marks.

To see the island in person, day cruises to Modriki can be booked at Port Denarau or through hotel tour desks in Nadi, or for guests at resorts on nearby Matamanoa and Tokoriki Islands.

TOP EXPERIENCE

★ Modriki Island

Matamanoa is the closest resort island to **Modriki,** the uninhabited island seen in the Tom Hanks film *Cast Away.* On this paradise island, green volcanic slopes fall to a high white beach facing a broad lagoon perfect for snorkeling. You'd probably need a guide to find the rare crested iguanas that dwell high up in the island's trees. The endangered hawksbill turtle is often seen in the lagoon off Modriki. Sheer cliffs on the back side of the island make it impossible to walk right around Modriki.

The schooner ***Seaspray*** (tel. 675-0500, www.ssc.com.fj) operates all-inclusive day cruises to Modriki, and passengers have a chance to go ashore for snorkeling or exploration. You can board the *Seaspray* at Matamanoa (F$209) or Mana (F$209), or do it as a day trip from Nadi (F$239), departing the Denarau Marina at 0900. Lunch and drinks are included, and any Nadi tour desk can book the trip (Nadi hotel transfers are included).

Tokoriki Island

Tokoriki is the farthest Mamanuca island from Nadi, and the most private and secluded. Its two resorts are more or less opposites in style and feel; both are upscale. At the center of the island is a 94-meter-high hill offering good views of the Yasawa and Mamanuca groups. The fast catamaran *Cougar* leaves Port Denarau for Tokoriki daily at 1515 (F$110 pp each way).

Scuba diving is available with **Tokoriki Diving** (www.tokorikidiving.com) at several sites, including the reef just off the western coast.

ACCOMMODATIONS

★ **Tokoriki Island Resort** (tel. 666-1999, www.tokoriki.com) occupies the western shore of the island and has 36 spacious *bures,* ranging F$1,350-1,795 depending on whether you choose fan-cooled or air-conditioned. The ten Sunset Pool villas with private pools are F$1,850, and include complimentary laundry and daily canapés in your *bure.* All have outdoor showers and hammocks. The three-meal plan is F$250 per person and includes champagne. There's also a wedding chapel and two pools. The beach has good swimming but a lot of seaweed. Nonmotorized water sports such as reef fishing, windsurfing, and Hobie Cats are free; sportfishing is available at additional charge. The resort swept up number one ratings in 2017 from various travel magazines and websites, and requires full payment with no cancellation 45 days before arrival. Children under 12 are not accepted.

The **Sheraton** (tel. 666-7707, www.sheratontokorikiisland.com/) occupies the southwestern corner of the island with 101 guest rooms, ranging F$475-995 depending on view and amenities. Some rooms have plunge pools. The beach is down a flight of stairs, but the pool has a swim-up bar. There are several (expensive) restaurants, mini golf, and, at opposite ends of the resort, a playground for children and an adults-only area (no pool, though). There's a fee for all water sports, including snorkel gear and nonmotorized equipment.

Vomo Island

This pretty island is only accessible to guests of the luxurious Vomo Island Resort. Standing alone midway between Lautoka and Wayasewa Islands, 87-hectare Vomo is a triangular high volcanic island with a white beach around its western side. The view from the top of the hill is spectacular.

Since 1993, the coral terrace and slopes behind this beach have been the site of the **Vomo Island Resort** (tel. 672-7297, res@vomo.com.fj, www.vomofiji.com), managed by Sofitel. The 29 air-conditioned duplex and freestanding villas with individual hot tubs start at F$2,375 for two people, including all meals, nonalcoholic beverages, nonmotorized activities, Wi-Fi, and daily laundry service. Deals are occasionally available, such as a free fifth night if you book four nights. The swimming and snorkeling is excellent, and the nine-hole pitch-and-putt golf course is free to guests. If you *still* need to get away from it all, you can book a special excursion to neighboring Vomo Lailai ("Little Vomo") for F$300 per couple. You'll be left completely alone with a picnic, sun loungers, and a two-way radio that you can use to call the boat back to be "rescued." Wedding packages start at F$3,900 per couple.

The Yasawa Islands

Twenty jewel-like volcanic islands scattered across 135 square kilometers make up the Yasawas—the first land that Captain William Bligh sighted in 1789 following the mutiny on the HMS *Bounty*. In the lee of Viti Levu, the Yasawas are dry and sunny, with beautiful, isolated beaches, cliffs, bays, and reefs. The waters are crystal clear and almost totally shark-free. The group was romanticized in the *Blue Lagoon* movies about a pair of child castaways who grow up and fall in love on a deserted isle.

More than two centuries after Bligh's arrival, increasing numbers of ferries and mini cruise ships ply the islands, but there are still few motorized land vehicles or roads. The Yasawas were once a haven for backpackers seeking cheap beach stays, and there are still a few budget options, but the islands have upscaled over the past decade.

PLANNING YOUR TIME

The most structured way to visit the Yasawas is to take a three-, four-, or seven-day mini cruise. You'll sample at least one island in the morning and another in the afternoon each day, hitting the highlights and having access to all manner of included activities.

You can achieve similar results yourself, with more flexibility and less money, via a Bula Pass on the *Yasawa Flyer*. With two or three nights at several different resorts, supplemented by half-day trips to smaller islands, you can easily visit several islands in a week. A good plan is to go straight from Port Denarau to the farthest point, Nacula, on your first day, and then slowly work your way back down to Nadi. This has two advantages: First, you'll get an idea of where you want to stop on the southbound trip from what you see on the way north. Second, because the return boat passes in the afternoon, you'll get an extra morning on the beach at all stops. There will be no need to get up early to catch the northbound boat, and everyone who is leaving will have left by the time you get to your resort (you won't have to hang around waiting for someone to vacate their room).

If both of those sound like too much bopping around, you can choose a single resort as your home base. In case you get bored, you can always make a day trip to other islands in the vicinity.

MONEY

Don't expect to be able to use your credit card everywhere in the Yasawas, although certain upscale resorts are now "cashless" and accept *only* credit cards. Changing foreign currency may not be possible, either. It's best to bring sufficient Fijian currency to cover drinks, excursions, equipment rentals, and snacks. Also, take care where you leave your money while out of the room or on the beach, as theft is not unheard of. Always lock your bags when leaving your room.

CRUISES

Blue Lagoon Cruises (tel. 670-5006 Mon.-Sat. 0730-1700, cruisecentre@bluelagooncruises.com, www.bluelagooncruises.com) offers a reasonably luxurious way to see the greatest hits of the Yasawas via the 68-passenger *Fiji Princess.* You can choose a four-night trip starting on a Monday, taking in the Blue Lagoon and Sawa-I-Lau as well as manta rays (when in season); a three-night trip starting on a Friday, taking in Modriki Island and village visits on Soso Bay and Naukacuvu Island; or combine them to spend seven nights on board. Diving is possible for an extra fee at two of the seven ports.

Captain Cook (tel. 670-1823, U.S. tel. 424/206-5275, enquiries@captaincookfj.com, www.captaincookcruisesfiji.com) offers similar itineraries on the 140-person *Reef Endeavour,* which was built in Suva in 1996 and is showing its age. The boat is shabbier than Blue Lagoon's, and the square pool is uninviting, but the friendly crew makes the voyage a pleasant experience. There's a three-night cruise to the Mamanuca and southern Yasawa Islands, including Modriki; a four-night cruise to the northern Yasawas, including the Blue Lagoon and Sawa-i-Lau; or the option to combine them into a seven-night trip. Diving is possible almost every day in the Yasawas for an extra fee.

Most of the Yasawas are a bit too far for day cruises from Nadi, but if you don't mind being on a boat for a few hours—or if you're already at Beachcomber or Treasure Island—you could enjoy a day trip to the Yasawas courtesy of **South Sea Cruises** (tel. 675-0500, info@ssc.com.fj, staffed 0700-2000 daily). A full-day cruise will take you to the idyllic Botaira Beach Resort (F$250; add $25 if you want lobster in your lunch). Or enjoy the white-sand beach and honeycomb rock formations of Barefoot Kuata (F$235).

KUATA ISLAND

Kuata is the *Yasawa Flyer II*'s first stop in the Yasawa Islands. Like neighboring Wayasewa and Waya, it's a scenically spectacular island with a nice beach, though without any Fijian villages. You can climb to the island's summit (171 m) in about 30 minutes for a great sunrise or sunset view.

Barefoot Kuata (tel. 776-3040, www.barefootkuatafiji.com) is part of the international scuba-oriented chain of Barefoot lodges. It's a backpacker place with dormitories of four or six beds at F$60-82 per person, 15 basic thatched *bure* with private bath at F$182 double, and a family *bure* at F$399. A mandatory F$99 per person fee includes three meals per day. An optimal snorkeling area is located at the southwest tip of Kuata. Look for the cave near the seabird rocks at the point itself. You'll pay F$20-25 per person for the transfer from the *Yasawa Flyer II.*

WAYASEWA ISLAND

Also known as Wayalailai ("little Waya"), the roundish **Wayasewa Island** is just five kilometers in diameter. It's the middle isle of a group of three and has two excellent peaks,

Wayasea Island

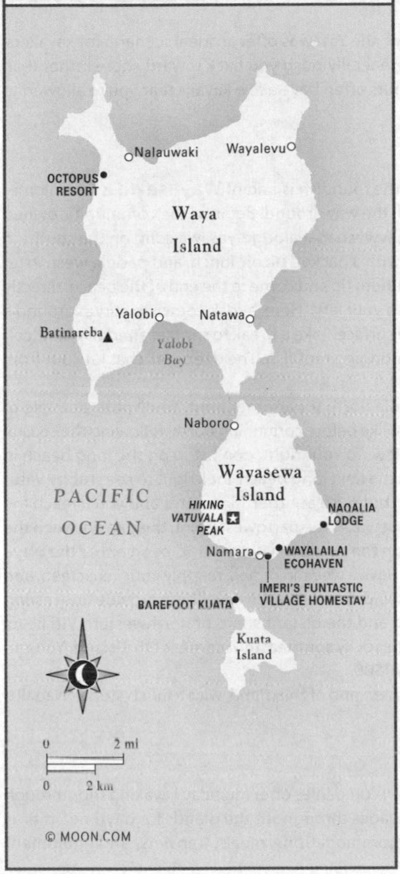

one of which is a great climb. The old village on the southern end was damaged in a landslide in 1985, leading the government to relocate many families to the northern end. The villages are still linked, though, and belong to the Tagova clan, which is connected with the Vuda Point residents on Viti Levu. The Friday-afternoon rugby at the Naboro village school on the northern end is fun to watch. The community owns and operates both lodges on the island.

★ Vatuvula Peak

The most popular hike on Wayasewa is to the top of **Vatuvula Peak** (349 m), the fantastic volcanic plug hanging directly over Wayalailai Ecohaven. The steep, well-trodden path circles the mountain and comes up the back, taking about 1.5 hours total excluding stops from the resort (a guide really isn't necessary). From the top of Vatuvula, you get a sweeping view of the west side of Viti Levu, the Mamanucas, and the southern half of the Yasawa chain—one of the scenic highlights of the South Pacific. From Vatuvula, you can trek northwest across the grassy uplands to another rock with a good view of Yalobi Bay (also known as Alacrity Bay). Guides from the Naqalia Lodge lead a sunset summit trip at 1600 daily.

Accommodations

Wayalailai Ecohaven (tel. 603-0215, 932-3446, or 936-3744, wayalailai@connect.com.fj, www.wayalailairesort.com) is spectacularly situated on the south side of Wayasewa opposite Kuata Island. This large backpacker camp is built on two terraces, one 10 meters above the beach and the other 10 meters above that. The lower terrace has the double, duplex, and dormitory *bures,* while the upper terrace accommodates the restaurant-bar and the former schoolhouse of Namara village, now partitioned into 14 tiny double rooms. Simple rooms with shared bath and open ceiling in the school building are F$70 per person (a good option for singles), while the five *bures* with private bath and a small porch are F$200 double (add F$70 for additional persons over six years old). The camping space nearby is F$55 per person. The minimum stay is three nights. Upon arrival, ask the staff to change the sheets if they haven't already done so. Three meals are included in all rates (but drinks cost extra). Wednesday evening, a *lovo* is prepared. An electric generator is used in the evening, and water is always available. Informal musical entertainment occurs nightly, and because this resort is collectively owned by the village, the staff is like one big family. The pleasant atmosphere makes up for the rather basic accommodations. There's lots to see and do at Wayalailai,

★ Kayaking the Yasawas

Nestled between barrier reefs and land masses, the Yasawas offer an ideal scenario for kayakers: the waters are relatively calm, and the tides generally push you back toward shore rather than out to rougher seas. Resorts and organized tours often have a few kayaks that you're allowed to take out for as long as you can paddle.

SELF-GUIDED ITINERARY

If you'd like to go out on your own for a day, the roundish island of **Wayasewa** is five kilometers in diameter, just the right size to kayak all the way around. Begin at the community-owned **Naqalia Lodge** (tel. 624-0532 or 672-4274, www.naqalialodge-yasawa.com) on the southern end after breakfast. Be on the water by 0900 with a packed picnic lunch, and paddle west. After about 45 minutes, you'll round the island's southern tip and come to the end of the beach, directly across from the northern tip of Kuata Island (to your left). Here, a rocky outcrop curves around a plush reef that rises to within a few feet of the surface. Take a break to snorkel amid the multicolored hard and soft corals and a rainbow of thronging reef fish. The deep wall that juts out from the coastline is home to reef sharks and turtles.

Back in your kayak, continue east and paddle north for another hour. You'll pass a couple of small beaches where you can take a break if you like before continuing north, following the coastal curve as **Waya's Yalobi Bay** comes into view. To your right, don't stop on the long beach in front of Yamata village without permission. At the next long beach, look right to see stubby Vatuvula Peak rising behind it. You could rest here, but push another 15 minutes and you'll reach the perfect lunch stop, at the northern tip of Wayasewa. At the narrowest point, the gap between the islands becomes a sandbar at low tide. Picnic on the sandbar if it's low tide, or on either the Waya or Wayasewa side of the beach if it's high tide. Have a wee dip or nap, reapply your sunscreen, and continue south along the eastern side of the island. Several beach coves here provide fine resting places, as well as scenic views of Naviti Island and the distant shore of northwestern Viti Levu. Paddle hard with your left arm as you round the rocky southeastern corner of the island. You can comfortably make it back to Naqalia Lodge by 1500.

This trip is also possible starting on the northern end of the island, with a lunch stop at Naqalia; call ahead to make arrangements.

GUIDED OUTFITTERS

For a more immersive experience, two Australian companies offer multiday kayaking trips through the Yasawas. Both have arrangements with villages throughout the islands for daytime visits as well as overnight camping. All sevusevus, accommodations, meals, transfers, and equipment

with hiking and scuba diving being the main activities. The resort's dive shop, Dive Trek Wayasewa, offers a PADI open-water certification course. For groups of six or more, there are snorkeling trips to a reef halfway to Vomo. **Rabua's Travel Agency** (tel. 672-6306, dreammakertravel@yahoo.com), based at Nadi Airport, takes Wayalailai bookings.

★ **Naqalia Lodge** (tel. 624-0532 or 672-4274, www.naqalialodge-yasawa.com) is a friendly, community-owned lodge near the southeast tip of Wayasewa Island. The five beachfront *bures* with private bath are F$330 double, and there's a 10-bed dorm at F$130 per person over the age of six. Camping is F$70 per person with your own tent. Meals and afternoon tea are included in all rates. The beach is good, and there's an even better one with great snorkeling over the ridge from the lodge.

In the village next to the lodge, an enterprising young woman and her family began taking homestay visitors in 2017. **Imeri's Funtastic Village Homestay** (tel. 766-7571, imerigalo72@gmail.com, F$114 pp) offers a room without a door, fresh local meals

kayaking around Tivua Island

(including two-person tents, life jackets, and dry bags) are included. Itineraries are approximate, as you'll go with the flow as dictated by winds and tides. Both operators offer one trip for women only each year.

Southern Sea Ventures (Aus. tel. 02/8901-3287, ssvtrips@southernseaventures.com, www.southernseaventures.com, 8 days AU$2,495 or 11 days AU$2,795, May-October) offers adventurous kayaking trips with at least two open-ocean crossings. Trips begin with a briefing and overnight at the Mercure Hotel in Nadi, after which you board the 0830 *Yasawa Flyer* to go directly to Tavewa Island, near the azure Blue Lagoon. After camping overnight at a village, the kayaking begins. Single kayaks are standard, with a double kayak along for emergencies. An average of 5-6 hours a day of paddling takes in several islands, including the Sawa-i-Lau swimming cave.

World Expeditions (U.S. tel. 800/567-2216, www.worldexpeditions.com/Fiji) offers a seven-night kayak tour with 3-4 hours of kayaking daily for US$2,290 per person. A typical trip starts in Nadi and goes to Tavewa, Nacula, Sawa-i-Lau, and Vawa Islands, camping on beaches everywhere before turning back for the return journey. Double kayaks are provided, with some single kayaks available. An 11-day trip, with 5-6 hours of paddling a day, is US$2,490.

at F$35/day, a friendly welcome, and a location just 30 seconds from the beach. There's no hot water, but there is a little bit of Wi-Fi and solar power for charging devices. You're an honorary family member for the time you stay there, and village attire is required.

Getting There

Wayasewa is close enough to kayak from Kuata in about half an hour. From Waya, it's only about 15 minutes by kayak, and in low tide you can even walk across a sandbar. Most visitors take the *Yasawa Flyer II* to Kuata, then arrange pickup by boat to Wayasewa (F$25 each way).

WAYA ISLAND

The high island clearly visible to the northwest of Lautoka is **Waya,** closest of the larger Yasawas to Viti Levu (just 60 kilometers away). At 579 meters, it's also the highest island in the chain. The beaches are very nice, and four Fijian villages are sprinkled around Waya: Nalauwaki, Natawa, Wayalevu, and Yalobi. The rocky mass of Batinareba (510 m) towers over the western side of Yalobi Bay.

1

2

Cyclone Winston's eye passed directly over Waya and most of the island suffered heavy damage, including its major **coastal trail** from Yalobi to Nalauwaki village. The trail is still there, with spectacular views and a range of terrain, but it's tough going; it's mainly used by locals out of necessity now. Check with locals before heading out. It takes 2 hours from Yalobi to Nalauwaki village, and another 2-3 hours to make it round-trip. To make the return journey, head to Octopus Resort, a 10-minute walk west of Nalauwaki over a low ridge, from where it's possible to hike down Waya's west coast and across Loto Point. Due to rocky headlands lapped by the sea, you can only go down the west coast at low tide, thus one must set out from Yalobi at high tide and from Octopus at low tide.

Accommodations

On a high white-sand beach in Likuliku Bay on northwestern Waya is ★ **Octopus Resort** (U.S. tel. 800/518-0949, Aus. tel. 02/8319-9189, www.octopusresort.com). This popular and long-standing flashpacker resort tries hard to cater to both ends of the market. The 14 comfortable but not luxurious *bures* come in several categories: five bungalows with shared bath (US$113 d), four beachfront "point" *bures* (US$344), "premium garden" *bures* (US$216), a deluxe beachfront suite (US$475), and, for families or groups, two- or three-bedroom villas (US$599/US$1,003). The minimum stay is two nights and a generator provides electricity. All rates include tax and the compulsory meal plan. Drinks are extra.

Octopus has its own dive shop, which offers PADI certification courses. The snorkeling here is best at high tide. Watch out if you're swimming, as the bottom drops off fast.

VIWA ISLAND

Viwa Island sits alone, 30 kilometers west of the main Yasawa chain. Most of the inhabitants live in Naibalebale village at the southwest end of the island. The beach here is fabulous, and the only resort is high-end.

The upscale ★ **Viwa Island Resort** (tel. 603-0066, www.viwaislandresort.com) has deluxe beachfront *bures* (F$1,038 s/d) and three executive beachfront *bures* (F$1,115 s/d). In 2015, a group of six divers who were former customers loved it so much that they bought it outright—only to be hit with Cyclone Winston in 2016. The resort underwent $4.5 million in repairs and refurbishing, with guests praising the personal attention and referring to it simply as "paradise." In 2018 the diver-owners turned over day-to-day management to an outside company. All units are air-conditioned and come with coffeemakers and fridges. There are two (all-inclusive) meal plans available at F$190, or you can order a la carte. The resort is an hour by boat from Octopus Island Resort, via a F$160 each-way transfer from the *Yasawa Flyer*. Children under 12 are not accepted.

NANUYA BALAVU AND DRAWAQA ISLANDS

The main draw of these two islands is the manta-rich channel between them, though the beaches are lovely any time of year, and there's good diving and snorkeling in the region. Long skinny boomerang-shaped **Nanuya Balavu** has one affordable resort at its northern tip, and across the channel, molar-shaped **Drawaqa** has a simple resort at its northern tip as well. Both have their own dive operators. The *Yasawa Flyer II* comes directly to both resorts.

Accommodations

★ **Manta Ray Island Resort** (tel. 664-0520, www.mantarayisland.com) on Nanuya Balavu Island sits on a point between two nice white beaches. The "jungle" *bures* with private baths are F$195 single or double. The small "tree house" *bures* with shared baths jut out from a hillside amid trees, and at F$128 are perhaps the most charming budget rooms in the country. The 32-bed dorm is F$49 per person; camping is F$36 per person. The compulsory

1: Vatuvula Peak on Wayasewa Island **2:** Yalobi Bay on Waya Island.

Swimming with Manta Rays

Manta rays abound in the Bligh Waters around the Yasawas.

April-November, huge manta rays migrate via the channel between **Nanuya Balavu** and **Drawaqa Islands,** just south of Naviti Island. The rays, called *vai* in Fijian, come for the nutrient-rich plankton that are concentrated in the swift currents here. Gliding alongside these serene creatures, whose wingspans can reach seven meters, is a true encounter with the majesty of the undersea world.

The best way to see the mantas is to stay at a resort on Nanuya Balavu or Drawaqa. During manta season, the resorts send out staff in a boat to look for rays. When they're spotted, the boat zooms back to shore, a drum is sounded and everyone rushes onboard to be whisked to the channel. You hop into the water with your snorkel and let the strong current carry you, the plankton, and the manta rays in the same direction. A guide comes into the water to point out reef sharks and other interesting sealife, and the boat picks you up wherever you've drifted after half an hour or so.

The strong current here calls for caution and strong swimming skills on the part of snorkelers. Let the guide know to keep track of you if you're nervous. Never touch the rays; they're not poisonous, but their fins are powerfully muscled and can smack you.

It's also possible to take your chances via a day trip by seaplane from Nadi, or a boat trip from one of the Naviti Island resorts. This may involve more waiting than swimming time, but it's well worth it if you get even just a few minutes with the mantas.

buffet meal package is F$59 per person extra. All the usual parties and activities are put on for the youthful backpacking guests. The focus here is on water sports rather than land-based activities like hiking. You can snorkel with manta rays in season at high tide.

Pacific Island Air (tel. 672-5644, reservations@pacificislandair.com, www.pacificislandair.com) offers a seaplane day trip to Manta Ray Island Resort for F$799 per person. It includes lunch, resort access, and swimming with manta rays in season, or a guided snorkel trip if the manta rays are not around. The flight leaves Nadi Airport's domestic terminal at 0830 and returns at 1530.

Barefoot Manta Resort (tel. 670-1823, www.barefootmantafiji.com), on a fine beach on Drawaqa, is not part of the international

Barefoot chain, and guests are a little older and the atmosphere quieter than at Manta Ray. Accommodations range from F$60 for a bed in a four-person dorm to F$399 for a "family safari room," a canvas tent on a platform large enough for a queen bed and two twin bunk beds. Meals are included in all rates, but an additional F$105/F$55 per adult/child (age 4-11) is added for each day. Most rooms have shared bathrooms and outdoor showers. There's a two-night minimum stay. Snorkeling gear and kayaks are free, but you should bring your own towel.

NAVITI ISLAND

Naviti is one of the few Yasawa islands large enough to offer a range of accommodations and activities. Shuttles from Nadi cruise right up the western side of the island, where most of the resorts are found.

Recreation

The **beach** on Natuvalo Bay, where the backpacker resorts are located, is rather poor. You can swim only at high tide, and there isn't much for snorkelers to see.

There's a shady, well-trodden **path** that takes about 40 minutes to climb from the beach southeast up to a huge mango tree atop a ridge; a few hundred meters past the tree is a grassy hill with great views as far as Wayasewa. The trail continues to Kese village, and is best enjoyed right after breakfast while it's still relatively cool.

A much easier walk is to **Honeymoon Point,** the peninsula overlooking the north end of Natuvalo Bay. The trail begins next to White Sandy Beach Dive Resort and takes only 15 minutes. You'll have a view of the entire west side of Naviti, plus the long, low island of Viwa at the 11 o'clock position on the horizon, far to the west. For better swimming and snorkeling than what's available right in front of the resorts, head to Honeymoon Beach.

Reef Safari (tel. 675-0566, www.reefsafari.com.fj), based at the Manta Ray Island Resort on Nanuya Balavu Island, provides scuba diving services to all of the resorts on Naviti; prices vary depending on where you're staying.

Accommodations

The **Botaira Beach Resort** (tel. 603-0200 or 670-7002, www.botaira.com, F$654 d), on the southwest side of Naviti, faces one of the island's best beaches. Botaira has 11 upscale *bures* with bath; meals and some sporting activities are included in the rate. The snorkeling is great, with manta rays in June and July. **South Sea Cruises** (tel. 675-0500, info@ssc.com.fj) sells hurried day trips to Botaira from Nadi at F$275, including a lobster lunch (drinks are extra).

The island's largest resort is **Korovou Eco-Tour Resort** (tel. 665-1001, korovoultk@connect.com.fj). It caters to the backpacking masses, and there's nothing particularly ecological about it. The 14 *bures* with private bath are F$200 double while the 32-bed dorm is F$80 per person. The *bures* come in a variety of thatched and duplex styles, so you might ask to see a couple of them before deciding. All prices include three basic meals. A spacious restaurant with a large deck is right above the beach and a swimming pool. Activities include snorkeling with manta rays (F$25) and an evening fire-dancing show. A generator provides electricity in the evening.

The **White Sandy Beach Dive Resort** (tel. 666-4066), on the beach next to Korovou, has only a handful of neat little bungalows with tin roofs at F$150 double, including very good meals. The dorm is F$65 per person. One-/two-tank dives start at F$90/170, with the price varying slightly depending on the site. They can also take you snorkeling at a plane wreck in three meters of water or with manta rays. A boat trip around the island with stops at both of these sites is also possible. Snorkeling gear is for rent.

All three resorts include afternoon tea in their prices and provide free transfers from the ferry to shore. Drinking water is scarce, and you'll be expected to buy bottled water.

Behind the Scenes: *The Blue Lagoon*

Two children are stranded by shipwreck, forced to grow up on a gorgeous deserted island. Once they figure out how to survive, they end up exploring their sexuality with each other as teenagers. Oh, and they're cousins.

It's not much of a premise, but this storyline has been made into four different movies over a century, bringing fame and tourists to an incredibly gorgeous inlet of a remote Fijian island. The films are all based on a 1908 novel by Henry de Vere Stacpoole, a doctor with extreme literary ambitions. Having served as a ship's medic for a few years in the tropics (probably not Fiji, though), he set many of his 30 novels on tropical islands, in addition to his native Ireland.

Nostalgia for an idyllic "primitive" state of humankind led him to write his 13th and most successful novel, *The Blue Lagoon*. He set it in the Marquesa Islands and wrote two sequels. Its purple prose inspired a 1923 silent film starring Molly Adair and Dick Cruickshanks, shot in Honolulu. A 1949 British remake starring Jean Simmons and Donald Houston was shot in the Yasawas, on Matacawa Levu Island, and became the seventh-highest-grossing release in Britain that year.

It was the American remake in 1980 that made Fiji's Blue Lagoon cove famous, along with its young stars Brooke Shields and Christopher Atkins. Director Randal Kleiser was given license to shoot the high-budget film with unknown stars on the heels of his incredibly successful debut *Grease*. He based the production on Nanuya Levu Island (Turtle Island), whose millionaire owner was a cable-television entrepreneur, giving him a cameo as a sailor in the film. The sexy love-making scenes that caused a scandal—Shields was only 14 at the time of shooting, not even old enough to see the R-rated film—were shot in the sheltered Blue Lagoon off neighboring Nanuya Lailai Island. In a pique of teen emotion, Shields's character, Emmeline, runs away to the beautiful limestone cave on Sawa-i-Lau Island.

As with the other Blue Lagoon iterations, no local culture ever intrudes upon the Victorian-era storyline; the only reference to actual Fijians is a hint of threatening natives on the other side of the island, but this plotline is never developed. The movie was released to critical jeers but became North America's ninth-biggest box office grosser of the year, and cinematographer Néstor Almendros was nominated for an Oscar.

Return to the Blue Lagoon, a 1991 sequel starring 15-year-old Milla Jovovich, followed the plot of one of the novel's sequels, picking up a generation later. The son of the original two lovers is stranded with his foster-sister, and similar themes ensue. It was filmed on Taveuni Island.

Lifetime television revisited the story for a 2012 movie, *Blue Lagoon: The Awakening,* which was shot in Trinidad. It's set in contemporary times; "Emmeline" becomes "Emma," and the two teens are high school classmates rather than relatives. Atkins makes a reappearance as a teacher-chaperone on the class trip that strands the pair.

YAQETA ISLAND

Yaqeta Island is a pleasant **adults-only option** for spending time in the Yasawas if you're neither the 1 percent nor a backpacker. Unfortunately, the muddy tidal beach is poor—but the only resort's pool is nice and the architecture is pretty.

The upscale **Navutu Stars Resort** (tel. 664-0553, www.navutustarsfiji.com, F$500-850) on the west side of Yaqeta has nine thatched *bures* in a mix of Mediterranean and Fijian styles. The target clientele is romance-seeking couples, and children under 16 are not usually accepted. Rates include continental breakfast; a la carte lunch and dinner are F$90/115/170 vegetarian/light/gourmet per person extra. You'll save about 10 percent by paying in U.S. cash rather than Fiji dollars for meals, drinks, and incidentals. Nonmotorized sporting activities are included in the basic rates. Massage is offered, with the first massage free.

The *Yasawa Flyer II* comes directly to the resort for F$221 each way. By plane, there are two charter options (fares are per person, one-way, and there's a two-person minimum): Pacific Seaplane, F$465, luggage limit 20kg per person, which lands on the resort beach; or Turtle Airways, F$380, luggage limit 15kg per person, which lands on nearby Turtle Island, where you catch a free boat transfer to Navutu.

AROUND THE BLUE LAGOON

TOP EXPERIENCE

★ Nanuya Lailai Island

Nanuya Lailai, between Tavewa and Nanuya Levu Islands, is best known for **Blue Lagoon Beach** on the island's west side. Dramatic rock formations adorn the curving coastline, which wraps around warm shallow waters and soft white sands, making this beach a standout even in lovely Fiji. Hollywood has aided the reputation of this picturesque beach, so it is often visited by cruise-ship passengers, and many yachts anchor just offshore.

Unfortunately, the snorkeling here is now substandard, as daily hordes of tourists have damaged the reefs, though islanders have been trying to restore the coral life with the assistance of the Ministry of Fisheries.

Westside Watersports (tel. 666-1462), also known as Yasawa Dive, serves all the resorts on the island from its dive center on the beach at Nanuya Island Resort. Its two dive boats, *Absolute II* and *Aftershock*, go out at 0900 and 1330; where you'll dive depends on the wind. Aside from the spectacular underwater topography, encounters with sea turtles, reef sharks, and eagle rays are fairly common.

ACCOMMODATIONS

Since 2000, the island's seven families, related to the Naisisili people on Nacula, have established a half-dozen small **backpacker resorts** along Enandala Beach on Nanuya Lailai's east side. Expect water shortages (bring bottled water), a lack of electricity (this could change), and no credit cards accepted. Transfers from the *Yasawa Flyer II* to Nanuya Lailai are F$25 per person each way. It's only a 10-minute walk across the island from the backpacker camps to Blue Lagoon Beach. To avoid conflicts with the powerful tour operators, your hosts may ask you to stay away from the groups of cruise-ship passengers swimming in the Blue Lagoon—the beach is long enough for everyone. All accommodation prices include meals.

Sunrise Lagoon Resort (tel. 995-1341, sunriselagoon@gmail.com), at the north end of Enandala Beach, charges F$155 double in 10 thatched *bures* with shared bath and F$185 in one garden *bure* with private bath. Both the seven-bed family beach *bure* and a 14-bed dorm are F$75 per person. At last report, Sunrise Lagoon was the only backpacker resort on Nanuya Lailai with electricity, but opinions about the place vary considerably. This resort is well promoted by the Nadi travel agents, so it's usually overflowing with young guests.

On a long stretch of beach next to Sunset Lagoon is **Seaspray Resort** (tel. 666-8962) with two simple *bures* with shared bath at F$120 double, plus a 10-bed dorm at F$70 per person. Lighting is by kerosene lamp, but the outdoor eating area is nice and the food okay. We've heard reports of petty theft from the dorm at Seaspray.

The **Gold Coast Inn** (tel. 776-0212, goldcoastinn@connect.com.fj, F$150), on the beach right next to Seaspray, has seven *bures* with private bath. It's less crowded than the other places and the rooms and food are also better.

The ★ **Nanuya Island Resort** (tel. 666-7633, www.nanuyafiji.com), right on the famous Blue Lagoon Beach, is the pearl of Nanuya Lailai. It's one of the nicest beach resorts in Fiji and far more upscale than the places just mentioned. The eight small hillside *bures* are F$260 double, while the four deluxe beach *bures* run F$410. All units have private baths and 24-hour electricity. The rates include a light breakfast, but all other meals are a la carte (mains F$20-34) and no meal plan is available. The food is excellent. There are numerous activities. Westside Watersports has a dive shop here, which is great if you're a diver. If you're not, the comings and goings of speedboats can be a nuisance. There's a lovely reef just 30 meters offshore, but few large fish, probably due to overfishing. Another drawback is the shortage of beach chairs (you almost have to be there at 0700 to reserve one). The staff here are great, and excellent musicians to boot.

Nanuya Levu Island

In 1972, American cable-TV millionaire Richard Evanson bought 200-hectare **Nanuya Levu Island** for US$300,000. Evanson played a sailor in the 1980 *Blue Lagoon,* much of which was filmed here.

Evanson's **Turtle Island Resort** (tel. Fiji 672-2921 or 666-3889, U.S. tel. 800/255-4347, Aus. tel. 04/1790-3209, www.turtlefiji.com, US$2,499 d) was one of the first luxury destinations in the Yasawas. Many of the staff are his descendants; Evanson had a string of five Fijian wives and a collective nine children. Richard Evanson Jr., known as "Junior," now runs the resort. Only 14 fan-cooled, two-room *bures* grace Turtle, and with a staff of 70 to serve a maximum of 28 guests, you're guaranteed attentive service. There's a cliffside pool and the beach is only a few steps away.

The room rate includes meals, drinks, and laundry service, and a private seaplane brings you to the island from Nadi. You can often find airfare-and-hotel packages for less than the rack rates quoted here. Meals are served at remote and romantic locations or taken at the community table. Children can come during family weeks in April, June-July, and December-January, and those under five get their own nanny. Sports such as sailing, snorkeling, canoeing, windsurfing, deep-sea fishing, horseback riding, guided hiking, moonlight cruising, and one tank per day of scuba diving are all included in the rate. To spend the day on any of 14 secluded beaches, just ask, and you'll be dropped off. Later, someone will be back with lunch and a cooler of wine or champagne (or anything else you'd care to order over the walkie-talkie).

Matacawa Levu Island

Matacawa Levu, west of Nanuya Levu, has less tourist infrastructure than its neighbor, but is a beautiful site for travelers with low expectations and simple needs.

Long Beach Resort (993-4177, www.longbeachfiji.com) stands on a point at the end of the long white beach on Matacawa Levu's south side. It has four simple *bures* at F$250 double, including meals; it's an extra F$95 for a third person. A much better unit with private bath is F$280. The eight-bed dorm, arranged in four double bunks, costs F$120 per person with meals. At low tide, you can walk to nearby Deviulau Island, and good snorkeling is available.

The **Isa Lei Glampsite** (tel. 939-6862) opened on the northern beach in 2017. Situated just meters from a reef, it's good for snorkeling and, at US$70 for a two-adult tent, it's an economical option. The canvas tents sleep two and there are shared cold shower facilities. However, guests have experienced problems with insufficient food quantities and being charged higher-than-expected excursion fees. If the owners can iron out these issues, it's an idyllic site.

TAVEWA ISLAND

Tavewa's main selling point is its proximity to two must-see Yasawa sites, the Blue Lagoon and the Sawa-i-Lau cave. The beach here isn't great, but boat trips to the world-famous Blue Lagoon Beach are free for resort guests. The boat trip to the Sawa-i-Lau caves requires a minimum of five people willing to pay F$70 per person.

Tall grass covers the hilly interior of this two-kilometer-long island. Tavewa is in the middle of the Yasawas, and from the summit, you can behold the long chain of islands stretching out on each side, with Viti Levu in the distance. The summit offers the best view of the adjacent Blue Lagoon, and the sunsets can be splendid.

Nestled in a cozy valley on a secluded beach with high hills on each side, ★ **Coral View Island Resort** (tel. 666-2648 or 925-8341,

Nanuya Levu Island

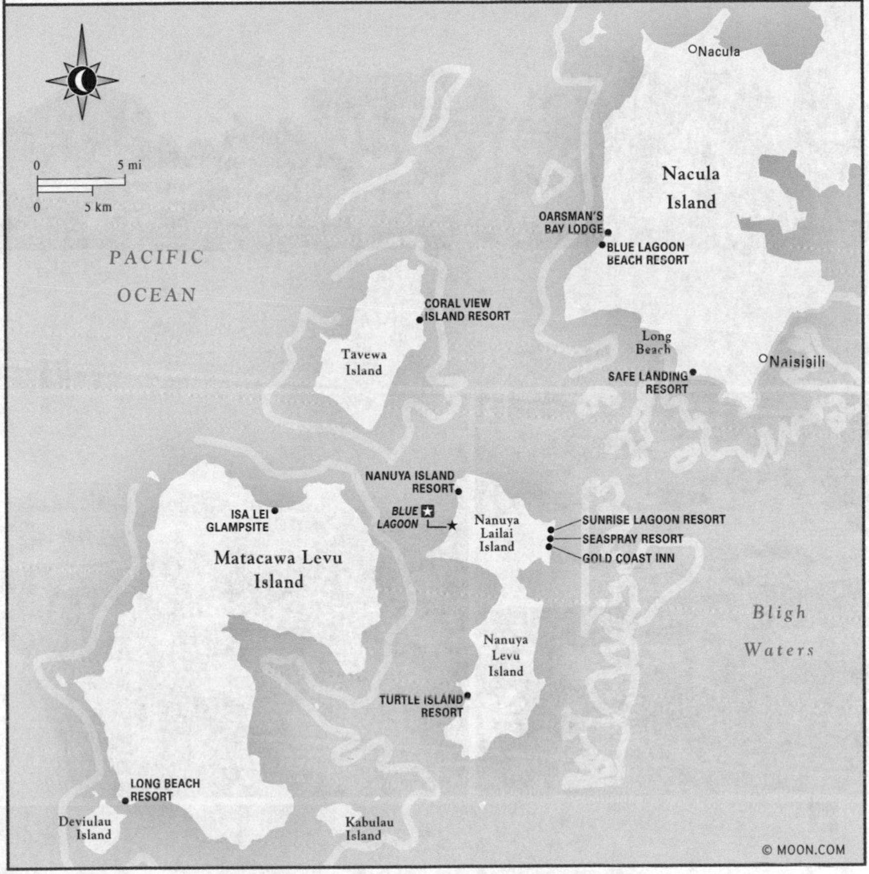

www.coralview.com.fj) is one of the nicest low-budget places to stay in Fiji. It has 14 deluxe *bures* with private bath and fridge from F$220-270 double and three 10-bunk dorms at F$77 per person. Discounts are offered for children under 14. Mosquito nets are supplied and there's 24-hour electricity. Included in the price are three decent meals and transfers to/from the *Yasawa Flyer II*. Coral View is a place where people come to relax and socialize. The staff is genuinely friendly, and most guests tend to be under 35.

Dive Yasawa Lagoon (www.diveyasawalagoon.com), based at Coral View, charges F$175/210 for one/two tanks and holds PADI certification courses for F$850.

NACULA ISLAND

The third largest of the Yasawas, **Nacula** is home to four villages and four resorts. Fabulous white-sand beaches and clear lagoons make it a fine place to anchor your Yasawas stay. **Long Beach,** at the southwest end of Nacula, is one of the loveliest in Fiji. Nacula Bay has a beautiful lagoon perfect for swimming and snorkeling. Water-taxi transfers to/from the *Yasawa Flyer II* cost F$20-25 per person one-way.

1

2

3

4

Accommodations

★ **Blue Lagoon Beach Resort** (tel. 776-6223, www.bluelagoonbeachresort.com.fj) is a project of the owners of Octopus Resort on Waya Island, replicating their popular formula of plenty of family-friendly activities and abundant food in a gorgeous location. It's on safe, swimmable Long Beach, adjacent to Oarsman's Bay Lodge on Nalova Bay. The seven well-constructed beachfront villas range NZ$159-519 double; those away from the bar are quietest at night. To sleep in one of the two six-bed dorms costs NZ$29. The compulsory three-meal plan at the restaurant-bar is NZ$80 per person (or NZ$60 for children under 13).

Oarsman's Bay Lodge (tel. 672-2921, www.oarsmansbayfiji.com) is on the same glorious beach. There's a 13-bed dormitory above the restaurant-bar at F$41 per person, six self-contained bungalows with solar panels ranging F$315-390 double, and two large family bungalows sleeping six at F$510. Camping with your own tent costs F$41 per person. The compulsory meal plan is F$98 per person extra. Paddleboats, kayaks, and snorkeling gear are loaned free. Most of the workers hail from Nacula village on the north side of the island, and resort profits go to village projects. If you're staying at Safe Landing or one of its neighbors and wish to visit Oarsman's for the day, it takes a bit more than an hour to walk along a shortcut trail across the island to/from Suntan Beach. It's easy to walk there along the beach only at low tide; at high tide, you'll need to wade part of the way.

Safe Landing Resort (tel. 744-9248) is on a white-sand beach tucked between two headlands. Fan-cooled bungalows are F$150 for two people, with private bathrooms and direct access to the beachfront lagoon. It's a fine spot with good swimming at high tide, though the beach at Oarsman's Bay Lodge is much better. The snorkeling isn't that great in this area because there's little coral. Safe Landing is owned by the Vola Vola family of nearby Naisisili village. Guests are welcome to attend the Sunday service in Naisisili.

Oarsman's and Safe Landing have many things in common. Both were built in 2000 with interest-free loans provided by the owner of Turtle Island Resort. To ensure that the loans are repaid, both resorts are now managed by Turtle Island, and bookings are controlled by the **Turtle Island office** (tel. 672-2921, nacula@hotmail.com) at Nadi Airport. To further control finances, all accounts at Oarsman's must be paid by credit card (cash is not accepted anywhere, not even at the bar). Both resorts operate on "Bula Time" (one hour ahead of Fiji time) to give guests an extra hour of daylight.

1: the Blue Lagoon's dramatic seascape **2:** wares for sale on Naviti Island **3:** the view of Nanuya Lailai Island from Nanuya Island **4:** a sunset view of Nacula Island.

★ SAWA-I-LAU ISLAND

The large limestone cave of **Sawa-i-Lau,** illuminated by a crevice at the top, is filled with a clear, deep pool where you can swim. An underwater opening leads back into a smaller, darker cave (bring a light). In the 1980 film *The Blue Lagoon,* Brooke Shields runs away to this very cave.

Tourists are told various tales about the cave's significance. One has it that the cave was once the home of the serpent god, but it lost its spiritual strength after being "blessed" by missionaries. Another tells how a young chief once hid his love in this cave when her family wished to marry her off to another. Each day, he brought her food until they could both escape to safety on another island.

All of the resorts and tour operators in the area run trips to Sawa-i-Lau, where the landowning tribe allows access via permit. Depending on where you're staying, the expedition may be included or cost up F$150. Yachties should present a *sevusevu* to the chief of Nabukeru village, just west of the cave, to visit. It's 20 slippery stone steps up on the outside, then 20 even wetter stone steps down to the metal ladder into the pool.

YASAWA ISLAND

If you reach **Yasawa Island,** the northernmost island in this group, you'll be rewarded with 11 lovely beaches, the highlight being a creamy white beach on the upper west side of the island. This 22-kilometer-long island features the oldest resort in the Yasawas—and can only be visited by booking with said resort, the only one on the island. It's also home to the Tui Yasawa, high chief of all of the Yasawa Islands villages, who resides at Yasawairara village on the north end of the island. There are six villages altogether.

Accommodations

For many years, the Fiji government had a policy that the Yasawas were closed to land-based tourism development, and it was only after the 1987 coups that approval was granted for the construction of **Yasawa Island Resort** (tel. 666-3364 or 672-2266, www.yasawa.com, enquires@yasawa.com.fj). Most of the employees come from Bukama village, which owns the land where this Australian-owned resort opened in 1991. It was rebuilt after a devastating fire in 2009. The spacious accommodations consist of six air-conditioned *bure* suites costing F$2,163 for up to three adults; 10 one-bedroom deluxe suites are F$2,563; a two-bedroom unit is F$3,625; and a honeymoon unit is F$4,625. Meals and Wi-Fi of variable quality are included. Alcoholic drinks can be added to your package at the time of booking for F$180 per adult per night.

Included activities include kayaks, stand-up paddleboards, tennis, guided walks, village visits, half-day trips to the Blue Lagoon and Sawa-i-Lau, private beach picnics, guided snorkeling, and use of a catamaran. Scuba diving, sportfishing, and massage cost extra.

Guests arrive on a chartered flight (25 minutes from Nadi, F$475 each way) to the resort's private airstrip. Children under 12 are welcome at the resort only during designated family weeks throughout the year.

the entry to the Sawa-I-Lau sacred cave

The Coral Coast

Southern Viti Levu, known as the Coral Coast, is where Fijian tourism began—specifically, on the sands of Korolevu. The original 1950s resort, with affordable private thatch huts nestled amid lush greenery at ocean's edge, has given way to dozens of resorts, hotels, and hostels for every budget along 50 miles of beaches that line the main island's southern shore. The road from Nadi to Suva travels along the coast, with plenty of places to tempt travelers to pause—whether for a quick roadside coconut, a couple of hours of spelunking, or a few days of oceanside relaxation.

While the region has a developed tourist infrastructure, with plenty of sea- and land-based activities and easy transportation, it also retains a bit of the wild. At various roadside stands you can haggle over the

Highlights

Look for ★ to find recommended sights, activities, dining, and lodging.

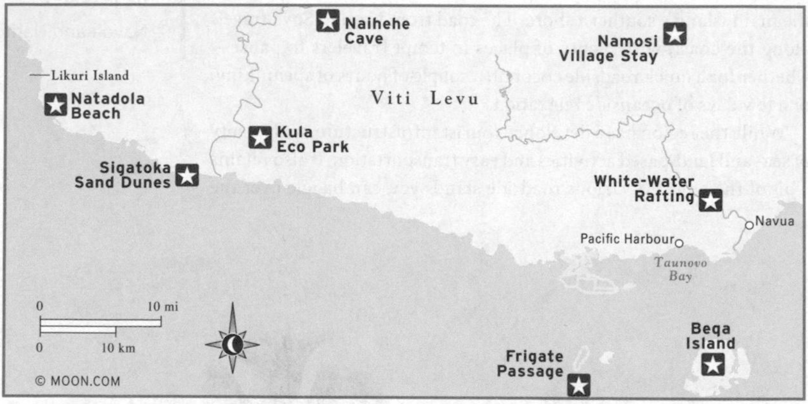

★ **Natadola Beach:** One of the world's most beautiful beaches, this long stretch is ideal for sunbathing, water sports, and beachside massages (page 121).

★ **Sigatoka Sand Dunes:** Hiking trails climb and cross these dunes, offering excellent views of the coast and local vegetation (page 128).

★ **Naihehe Cave:** A pleasant trip upriver takes you to a cave where you can see sparkling stalactites, underground springs—and an actual platform and oven used for ancient cannibal practices (page 130).

★ **Kula Eco Park:** See the country's birds, bats, and iguanas in a lovely tropical setting (page 134).

★ **Frigate Passage:** Killer waves and stunning cerulean horizon make this a favorite spot for experienced surfers—and divers love the undersea life, too (page 135).

★ **Beqa Island:** With its peaceful beaches, lush landscape, and small resorts, Beqa is the perfect place to relax away from the crowds (page 154).

★ **White-Water Rafting:** Emerald waterfalls and stunning black volcanic gorges line the upper **Navua River,** which alternates between tranquil currents and heart-racing rapids (page 157).

★ **Namosi Village Stay:** The best village stay in Fiji is in a guest *bure* at **Namosi Eco Retreat,** high in the rocky green mountains above Pacific Harbour (page 159).

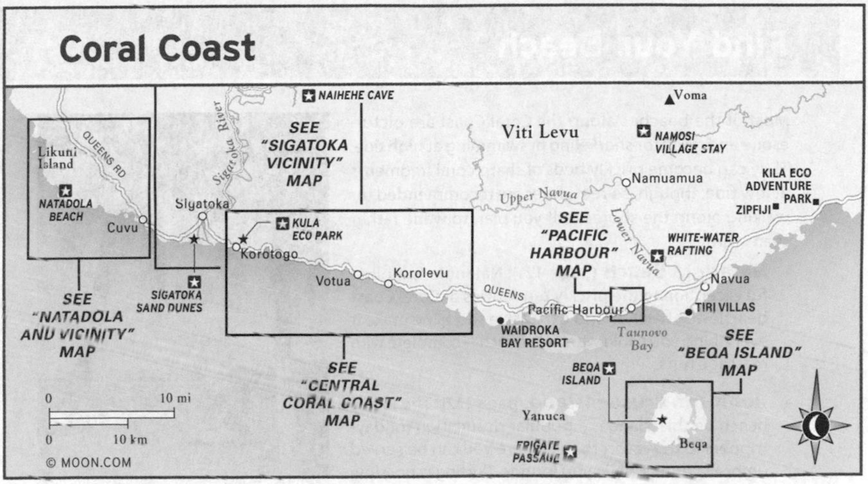

catch of the day with local fishers and other enterprising folk. Depending on where you choose to stay and go, you can have the sensation of discovering a hidden gem.

The easternmost point of the Coral Coast is Pacific Harbour, once a backwater whose main attraction was a hokey fire-walking show, now reinvented as a watersports hub with a healthy nightlife. Farther east, on the way to Suva, lie the Namosi Highlands and the gorgeous Navua River, home to Fiji's finest river trips. Navua is also the gateway to lush, peaceful Beqa Island. This region is close enough to Suva, just an hour away, that it's a popular weekend getaway for city dwellers and can even serve as a base from which to make day trips into the capital.

PLANNING YOUR TIME

Many tourists spend their entire Fiji vacation on the Coral Coast. All the large resorts offer a wide range of nautical activities and entertainment, and they're better positioned for land-based sightseeing than resorts on smaller islands. There are also budget properties for backpackers and independent travelers. For variety, chose one resort at the western end (closer to Nadi) and another toward the east (closer to Suva). The possibility of rainfall and the lushness of the vegetation increase as you move east.

If you're staying in Nadi, it's also easy to organize your own self-guided day tour of the Coral Coast by rental car, taxi, bus, or a combination. One possible itinerary is to take an express or local bus to the Sigatoka Sand Dunes National Park visitors center on Queens Road. After a hike over the dunes, catch another bus on to Sigatoka town for lunch along with some shopping and sightseeing, and then hail a taxi to visit the Tavuni Hill Fort. Plenty of buses cover the 61 kilometers from Sigatoka back to Nadi until late in the evening. All of this will cost you far less than the cheapest half-day tour, and you'll be able to mix freely with people going about their daily commutes.

GETTING THERE AND AROUND

All the Nadi tour companies (see page 58) as well as those in Pacific Harbour offer day tours of Coral Coast highlights, but these are often hurried affairs that involve more time in

Previous: Taunovo Bay near Pacific Harbour; firewalkers on the beach at Pacific Harbour; wild hibiscus on Beqa Island.

Find Your Beach

Most of the beaches along the Coral Coast are picturesque and good for snorkeling or swimming at high tide. They can become prickly beds of sharp coral fragments at low tide, though, so reef shoes are recommended for walking along the shores or if you plan to wade rather than swim.

- **Natadola Beach** (page 121): Natadola is a blissful exception to the prickly tendencies of Coral Coast beaches. Soft sands and expansive shoreline make it everything you could want in a beach—complete with massage huts.
- **Robinson Crusoe Island** (page 122): The lovely beach on this island is a popular destination for day-trippers to the resort there, where you can be served umbrella drinks while you lounge. Surfing is possible on Likuri and at the mouth of the Sigatoka River, near **Kulukulu** village.
- **Sigatoka Sand Dunes** (page 128): Those who make the hike can enjoy the gorgeous coast and beach on the other side.
- **Beqa Island** (page 154): This quiet island off Pacific Harbour boasts lovely, sandy coastlines protected by the tranquil Beqa Lagoon. Expert surfers can go out from this beach or from Yanuca Island to reach the fast, hollow tube of Frigate Passage.

a beach along the central Coral Coast

the car than anything else. For more than one person, it's cheaper to hire a taxi, and you can choose your own pace. It's also easy to drive yourself, as the Queens Road is smoothly paved all the way to Suva. Buses are frequent along this route, and the express buses stop everywhere you'd want to stop.

Bus

Coral Sun Express (7 Yasawa St., Lautoka, tel. 672-3105 or 999-2708) is a quick and economical way to travel along the southern route, as it stops only at major hotels. The air-conditioned, once-daily bus departs from the Suva at the Holiday Inn at 0715 and arrives at Nadi Airport four hours later. The return trip leaves from the Nadi Airport international arrivals terminal at 1300. If it's very busy, they may add a second bus departing half an hour later. The cost one-way is F$25 per person if you call Coral Sun to book directly or just show up. You'll pay F$5 more if you book through an agency or your hotel's travel desk.

Other buses from Nadi labeled "Suva Express" are equally comfortable and make about twice as many stops. These are about F$18 direct from Nadi Airport to Suva's main bus station, less if you're only going part of the way. They stop at the Sigatoka Sand Dunes, Sigatoka town, Kulukulu village, Baravi Handicrafts, and other major sites along the Queens Road. **Pacific Transport** (tel. 670-0044) has express buses daily at 0720, 0750, 0900, 1300, 1640, 1750, 1820 and 1850. Only the 0900 bus begins its run at Nadi, so you have the best chance of getting your choice of seats (the others originate in Lautoka). **Sunbeam Transport** (www.sunbeamfiji.com, tel. 666-2822) buses leave at 0930, 1010, 1100, 1200, 1335, 1505, and 1610 daily.

There are also plenty of slow local buses that travel the Queens Road. Catch them at the main bus station in either Suva or Nadi airport; it's best to inquire there for routes and times, as options are numerous. Beware of taxi drivers hustling for fares at the bus station who may claim untruthfully that there's no bus going where you want to go.

Taxi

A taxi from Nadi all the way to Suva along the Queens Road costs about F$200 one-way. A partial journey, round-trip, should be less; to Natadola, expect to pay about F$100 for up to four passengers. If you'd like to meander, negotiate a flat rate and let the driver know you'll be stopping for lunch, sightseeing, and/or beach time along the way. Write out a list of the places you might like to stop, and show it to the driver beforehand so he can't demand more money later.

If you're starting in Suva, you can go to the **East-West Shuttle Service** on the waterfront behind the Civic Centre and the Olympic Pool to nab a seat in a shared taxi for F$25 direct to Nadi, or book the whole four-seat car for F$100. You can make a full day of it by hiring the car to Nadi for around F$200 with lots of stops along the way; again, write down your list.

Once you're on the Coral Coast, local taxis based in Sigatoka and elsewhere make it easy to get around. A taxi service that operates near the Outrigger is **Classic Sounds Taxi & Tours** (tel. 934-1773, classicsoundequip@gmail.com).

Car

If you're not renting a car in Nadi, you can rent one in a few places on the coast:

Thrifty Car Rental (tel. 652-0242) has desks at the Outrigger, Warwick, Naviti, and Hideaway resorts. Cars are US$92-US$201 per day.

Coastal Rental Cars (tel. 652-0228, www.coastalrentalcars.com.fj), on Korotogo Back Road near the traffic circle at Korotogo, rents cars from F$89 a day plus a one-time F$10 government surcharge, a 5 percent credit card surcharge, and a F$60 surcharge if you want to drop the car off in Suva

Several other places, including the Beach Side Restaurant and the Bedarra Inn, rent cars for a negotiable F$65-90 a day plus insurance.

Natadola and Vicinity

Viti Levu's southwest corner is blessed with the island's finest beach, which has only recently been developed for first-world tourism. Queens Road crosses rolling, pine-clad hills near here, but to see the sands one must leave the highway. This area is popular among day-trippers as well as golfers who come for the gorgeous course, which offers ocean views from every hole. Offshore, Robinson Crusoe Island is a small resort island catering to young travelers. It is home to Fiji's largest hotel, one of the original island resorts.

SIGHTS

★ Natadola Beach

The long, white sandy beach here is easily the best on Viti Levu. Natadola has long been a popular picnic spot for day-trippers from the nearby Shangri-La resort and for those breaking the long journey from Nadi to Suva. Care should be taken while swimming in the ocean here, as the waves can be unexpectedly strong. For beginning surfers, the small left point break at Natadola is good, but always be aware of the currents and undertow. The left-hand breaks outside the reef are only for the experienced.

There are several massage shacks, of which the most permanent is **Beach Blue,** which offers massage at F$40 per half-hour, as well as snorkel rental and other amenities. The Beach Blue team will also gladly prepare a *lovo* feast for you and your travel companions; stop by in the morning to make arrangements for

Natadola and Vicinity

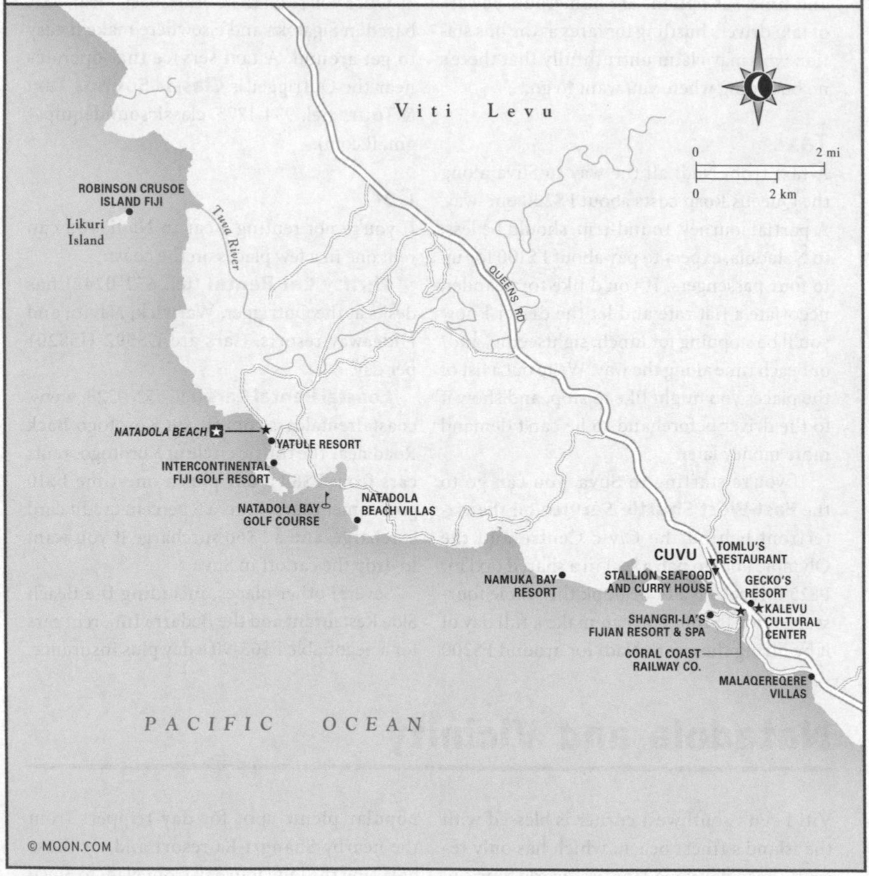

the evening or the next day. To Jet Ski off the beach, contact **Sunny Watersports** (tel. 940-9487, info@sunnyfiji.com); be sure to specify that you want a Natadola-based rental, as they also run Jet Ski trips from Denarau.

Robinson Crusoe Island

There was no real Robinson Crusoe, of course, and the fictional protagonist of Daniel Defoe's 1719 novel was marooned on an equally fictional desert island off Trinidad. This island's moniker is said to honor a wrecked yacht named the *Robinson Crusoe* whose captain named his cat "Friday" after the native assistant in the story, but even this is likely a myth. Whatever the case, the beach here is fantastic, and there's plenty to feed, water, and entertain you should you be washed ashore here for a few hours or days.

Officially known as Likuri Island, this is a good alternative to the better-known Mamanuca resorts. Half-day trips to the island are offered by **Robinson Crusoe Island Fiji** (tel. 679-6535, 628-1999, or 776-0999, reserve@rcifiji.com, www.robinsoncrusoeislandfiji.com, daily 0830-1245, F$119 adults, F$55 ages 5-14). Trips include snacks, a 30-minute river cruise, and some guided activities on the island. Beverages, massages, and certain activities are extra, and hotel pickup depends on your location. For a more thematic adventure, you can choose the Culture Day Tour (1000-1600 Tues., Thurs., and Sun., F$199 adults, F$85 ages 5-14), which includes a *lovo* lunch, or the Village & Mud-Crab Catching Tour (1000-1600 Mon., Wed., and Sat., F$219 adults, F$85 ages 5-14). Family rates and an add-on sunset dinner cruise are also available for all tour options.

Other Sights

Train buffs will be interested in the *Fijian Princess,* a restored narrow-gauge railway originally built to haul sugarcane. It's permanently parked at the station on the highway opposite the Shangri-La resort. Trips for tourists were discontinued in 2017; to check the train's status, ask any hotel tour desk or call the **Coral Coast Railway Co.** (tel. 652-0434).

Across the road from the train station is the **Kalevu Cultural Center** (tel. 652-0200, daily 0900-1700), an interesting and well-curated set of *bures* that display elements of Fijian and Pacific Island culture. The one-hour guided tour is F$30 per person, but you can walk in and show yourself around without any problem. For groups of 25 or more, a full day at the center can be arranged for F$80 per person, with a *lovo* lunch, dance show, and tours of the Fiji, Samoa, Tonga, Rotuma, New Zealand, and Kiribati "villages"; contact e-sales@geckoresort.com.

RECREATION

Reef Safari (tel. 675-0566, www.reefsafari.com.fj, F$170/260 for one/two tanks including gear rental) offers resort-based dive trips for guests at only two resorts in the area, Robinson Crusoe Island Fiji and Shangri-La's Fijian Resort & Spa. See these listings under Accommodations for more information.

At the par-72 **Natadola Bay Golf Course** (tel. 673-3500, www.natadolabay.com), 15 of the 18 holes hug the coast. Redesigned in 2016 by champion Vijay Singh, who hails from Lautoka, the course now hosts the **Fiji International** tournament every August. The views are stunning, even from the open-air bar and restaurant (open to the public) that overlooks the course; try the Sigatoka River prawns (F$33) or the lime-passion fruit cheesecake (F$12). Greens fees start at F$45 for 9 holes, up to F$210 for an all-inclusive package including club rental. Guests staying at the InterContinental receive a discount. Tee times start at 0720. Be prepared for strong winds, especially in the afternoon.

Coral Coast Fishing Charters (tel. 780-6303 or 742-3732, contact@coralcoastfishingcharters.com, www.coralcoastfishingcharters.com) leads trips on the 15-passenger, 28-foot Faizan. Captain Fai is a third-generation fisherman in the area, and he and crew member Bento have been fishing together in Cuvu Bay for 25 years. For two people, it's F$290/435/570 for 4/6/8 hours. Large groups and children receive discounts. Trips include snacks, drinks, and free transfers from any hotel between Denarau Island and the Warwick Hotel. A four-night package at Gecko's Resort with two full days of fishing is F$2,120 per person including airport and boat transfers.

FOOD

★ **Stallion Seafood & Curry House** (tel. 958-3905 or 921-3590, Old Queens Hwy., Cuvu, reservations@stallionsseafoodandcurryhouse.com, www.stallionsseafoodandcurryhouse.com, Mon.-Sat. 1100-1630 and 1700-2230, Sun. 1700-2130, F$5-78) was launched in 2017 by Sippu, a longtime chef at the Shangri-La. Located in Cuvu just five minutes from the resort (F$5), it's serious competition to that property, serving up five-star tastiness in a more relaxed and personal environment. Drink and food prices are a fraction of what you'd pay at the resort, and the menu includes fresh locally caught seafood, local produce, and a wide selection of local traditional Fijian and Indian dishes. There's a play area for kids.

TomLu's Restaurant (tel. 652-0729,

Lovo Feasts

Chefs remove steamed leaves of a *lovo*, revealing the foil packets inside.

More than a millennium ago, Pacific Islanders invented a way of deliciously slow-roasting meats and root vegetables without pots, pans, or any special equipment other than what nature provides. The method gives remarkably consistent results, so your choice of *lovo* experience depends largely on atmosphere and accompaniments rather than taste. Whether you're on the beach at Natadola, in a village up in the mountains, or at a fancy hotel, the *lovo* is a culinary tradition that unites the country.

To make a *lovo*, first dig a shallow pit. Stack some dry coconut husks in it and set them on fire. Once it's going well, heap coral stones on top. Meanwhile, wrap up your food in freshly cut banana leaves. When most of the husks have burnt away, place the food bundles on the hot stones (careful, don't touch them!): fish and meat below, vegetables above. The size of your feast will determine the size of your fire; you can roast anything from a chicken to a whole pig (stuff the pig with leaf-wrapped hot stones, so that it cooks from the inside out as well). Cover the whole thing with more leaves, which will create steam inside, and stones to hold them in place. Then kick back with your beverages of choice for about 2.5 hours.

Queens Rd., Voua, daily 1230-2200) serves up fresh Chinese-ish seafood that gets rave reviews—whole snapper in cognac butter, curried mud crab, garlic lobster—all at a fraction of resort prices. It's about a 10-minute, F$10 taxi ride from the Shangri-La. Service can be slow, so be prepared to relax and wait.

ACCOMMODATIONS

Under US$50

Namuka Bay Resort (tel. 707-0243, info@namukabaylagoonresort.com, www.namukabaylagoonresort.com) is on a nice coral beach at Naidiri, about halfway between Natadola Bay and the Shangri-La, six kilometers off Queens Road via a gravel road. A bed in the dorm *bure* goes for F$33 per person, while standard rooms are F$119. There's also a freestanding villa (F$280) for four people, and a large villa with two master bedrooms renovated in 2017 (F$550). It's a family-run place, and goats, cows and chickens share the grounds. Meals—including fresh-from-the-source milk and eggs—are included, and there's electricity 0600-1800. A free tour of a local cave is included.

Robinson Crusoe Island Fiji (tel. 628-1999/776-0999, www.robinsoncrusoeislandfiji.com) on Likuri Island caters to a young and active crowd. Not to be confused with Crusoe's Retreat (close to Pacific Harbour), Robinson Crusoe has a dorm *bure* with 14 beds upstairs for F$59 per person. The simple thatched *bures* with shared bath start at F$89 for the *Bure* Lailai and go up to F$448 for the Family Lodge, which sleeps up to five adults. Daily meal plans are an additional F$70 per adult and F$40 per child. Included in the rates are kayaks, snorkel gear, handline fishing, and evening entertainment in the Pirates Nightclub. Transfers from Nadi, including bus and boat, are F$150 per person, round-trip, crossing the small channel from the Tuva River Jetty at 1000 and 1630 daily. Scuba diving with **Reef Safari** (tel. 675-0566, www.reefsafari.com.fj) is F$170/260 for one/two tanks including gear rental.

US$50-100

★ **Gecko's Resort** (tel. 652-0200, geckosales@connect.com.fj, www.fijiculturalcentre.com), at the Kalevu Cultural Center on Viti Levu across the highway from the entrance to Shangri-La's Fijian Resort, is a clean, friendly motel with 23 rooms, each with a single and queen bed (F$180); breakfast is included. There's Wi-Fi at F$10/hour, but you're better off with F$12 for 8 hours or F$19 for 24 hours. Rooms can be connected (at the same rate) if you have a group of 4-6. A kidney-shaped pool compensates for the lack of a beach. Some weekends see a Samoan fire-dancing performance. Meals and drinks here are reasonably priced, especially during happy hour (daily 1700-1900), and many guests from the Shangri-La stroll over for a change of pace. Likewise, massages and other treatments at the hotel's Relaxation Hut are a bargain compared to its massive neighbor: F$120 for a 90-minute hot-stone massage, or F$20 for a child's mani-pedi (age 10 or younger). Bicycles are available for rent.

Yatule Resort (tel. 672-8004, sales_marketing@yatulefiji.com.fj, http://yatulefiji.com) offers 50 villas at F$288 for a pool-view room (you can book two and connect them), a beachfront *bure* (F$317), and a larger deluxe beachfront *bure* (F$397). Call ahead if you'd like to have dinner at the **Na Ua** restaurant, which has all the usual items as well as specials from the tandoor (Indian oven). It's the closest hotel to the lovely Natadola Beach; the property is tucked behind the InterContinental's back gate, where a guard is stationed to make sure no one sneaks into the posh resort.

Natadola Beach Villas (tel. 905-2585, peter@healthpak.co.nz, www.natadolabeachvillas.com.fj) is a good choice if you're staying awhile and would like a full kitchen. The four freestanding cottages lack charm but are clean, air conditioned, and include a full-size fridge, stove, and four-person dining table; they start at US$300 per night for a couple, with a four-night minimum. Configurations range from a double bed to a six-person villa with two master bedrooms. It's within walking distance of Natadola Beach, and there's a supermarket at the turn-off from the main road.

Over US$150

Eight miles southwest of Natadola along the Queens Highway, **Shangri-La's Fijian Resort & Spa** (tel. 652-0155, www.shangri-la.com/yanucaisland/fijianresort) occupies all 40 hectares of beautiful Yanuca Island (not to be confused with another island of the same name west of Beqa). It is connected to Viti Levu by a short causeway that you can walk across, but guests are usually transported via golf cart. Opened in 1967, this Malaysian-owned complex of three-story concrete buildings is still Fiji's biggest hotel.

The 442 air-conditioned rooms start at F$570 single or double in the "lagoon view wings," F$600 in the "ocean view wings," and F$1,025 for the "Lagoon Bure." Included is a buffet breakfast for two people per room. A third adult is F$75, but two children 18 or under who share their parents' room stay free (kids 12 and under also eat for free). This makes Shangri-La's Fijian an ideal

1

2

3

4

choice for families—and there are hordes of kids, as well as an active kids' club. There's even a 25-meter-by-25-meter water park. Shangri-La's Fijian often has cheap room specials, but meals are overpriced, and service can be indifferent. There's a mini-golf course, tennis courts, numerous restaurants and shops, and three swimming pools (including one for adults only). You can't help feeling a bit herded as you join the mass migrations from buffet breakfast to soft sandy beach to noisy pool. **Reef Safari** (tel. 675-0566, www.reefsafari.com.fj) leads dives to Nabaibai Passage, Barracuda Drift, the Wall, Golden Reef, the Pinnacles, and other fine sites that are just a few minutes from the resort jetty.

The flashy **InterContinental Fiji Golf Resort** (tel. 673-3300, www.intercontinental.com) at Natadola has 216 spacious rooms and suites with cable TV, mini-fridges, bathtubs, and terraces. Rates vary depending on whether you have a garden, pool, lagoon, or beachfront view, the last of those being the most coveted: Rooms are F$609-1,112, executive suites with private plunge pools are F$988-1,129, and two-bedroom suites are F$1,597-1,950. Discounts are available through the hotel website. There are also 55 more expensive villas in a separate Club InterContinental area, high on the hill with sweeping views of Natadola Bay, with plunge pools or spa baths. The sprawling property has four pools, three restaurants, two bars, a kids' club, gym, spa, dive shop, and business center. Five hundred people can sit down to dinner in the resort's conference center. The resort abuts the famed golf course, so you can wake up and stroll over to your tee time. Guests here receive a discount on golf fees.

Malaqereqere Villas (tel. 652-0704, www.malaqerevillas.com) stands on a hill overlooking Cuvu Bay, 500 meters off Queens Road and 2.5 kilometers east of Shangri-La's Fijian Resort. The four deluxe villas, each with three bedrooms, two bathrooms, kitchen, fridge, and lounge, are F$365 single or double, F$735 for 3-6 persons. There's a minimum stay of three nights. The local walk-in rate is about 40 percent lower than this and there are usually online specials. There's a swimming pool.

Sigatoka and Vicinity

The main town along the Coral Coast is Sigatoka (sing-a-TOE-ka, population 11,000), a busy little spot with plenty of eateries and bars as well as places to stock up on supplies. Sigatoka is the main business center for the Coral Coast and headquarters of Nadroga/Navosa Province, and you can catch buses going both east and west here. The palatial Hare Krishna temple on the hillside above Sigatoka offers a fine view of the sea and river confluence.

The town has a picturesque riverside setting and is pleasant to stroll around. Sigatoka has a 24-hour gas station with mini-mart, and plenty of shops, ATMs, and Internet cafes. Its market is not massive, but it's the country's best—full of fresh fruit and vegetables of astounding variety, and a good place to stock up if you plan to cook. Most travelers will probably just pass through on their way to a beach resort.

For sightseers, the unique Sigatoka Sand Dunes are absolutely worth a stop. If you're lingering in the area, take a drive, taxi ride, or organized tour upriver from town into the wide valley known as Fiji's "salad bowl," where rich market gardens line the Sigatoka River, the country's second largest. Vegetables are grown in farms on the western side of the valley, while the eastern bank is planted with sugarcane. Small trucks use the good dirt road up

1: the Natadola Bay Golf Course **2:** Cuvu Bay
3: the water lily pond at Gecko's Resort
4: Natadola Beach.

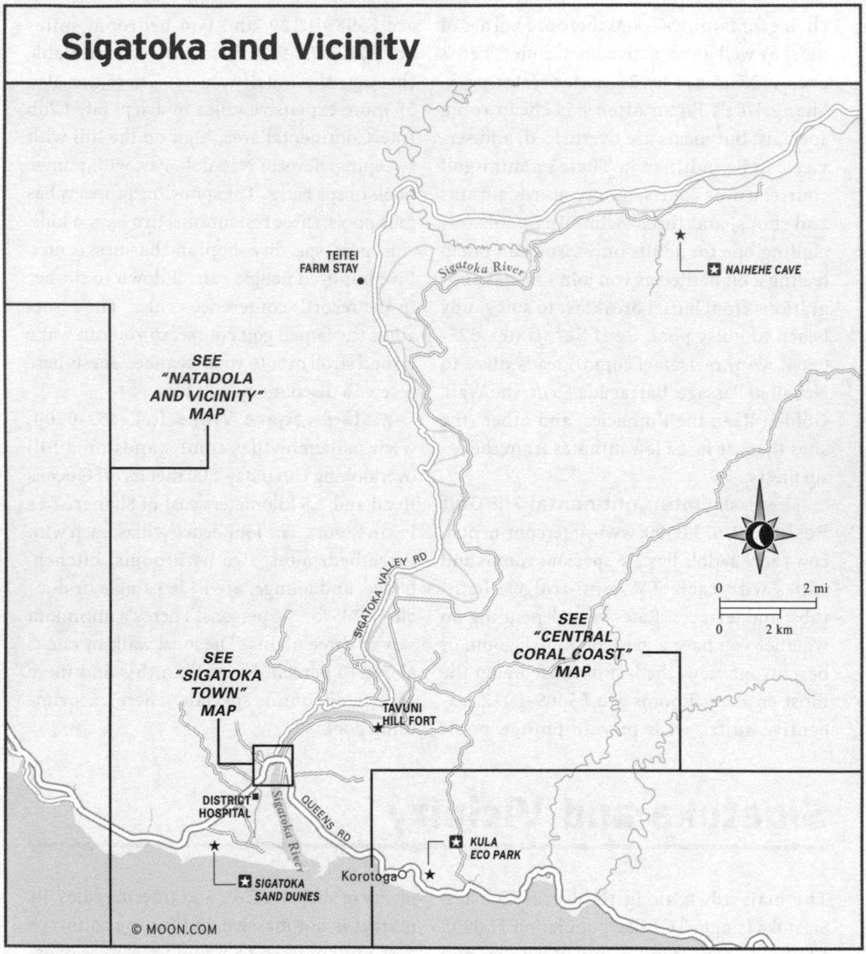

the west side of the river to take the produce to market, so you can drive right up the valley in a normal car or taxi. The shark god Dakuwaqa is said to dwell in the river.

SIGHTS

★ Sigatoka Sand Dunes

Spreading five kilometers west from the mouth of the Sigatoka River, the incredible 20-meter-high **Sigatoka Sand Dunes** separate the cane fields from the beach. This unique ecosystem was formed over millennia as sediment delivered by the river was blown back up onto the shore by the southeast trade winds. It's a fascinating, evocative place, protected as a national park since 1989 through the efforts of the National Trust for Fiji.

If you're lucky, you might find that the winds have uncovered a 3,000-year-old potsherd or even human bones from ancient burials. Giant sea turtles come ashore here to lay their eggs. A mahogany forest was planted here in the 1960s to prevent sand from blowing onto Queens Road, and there are also dry beech and casuarina forests.

There are two official trails you can take: a two-kilometer, 45-minute hike, or a more

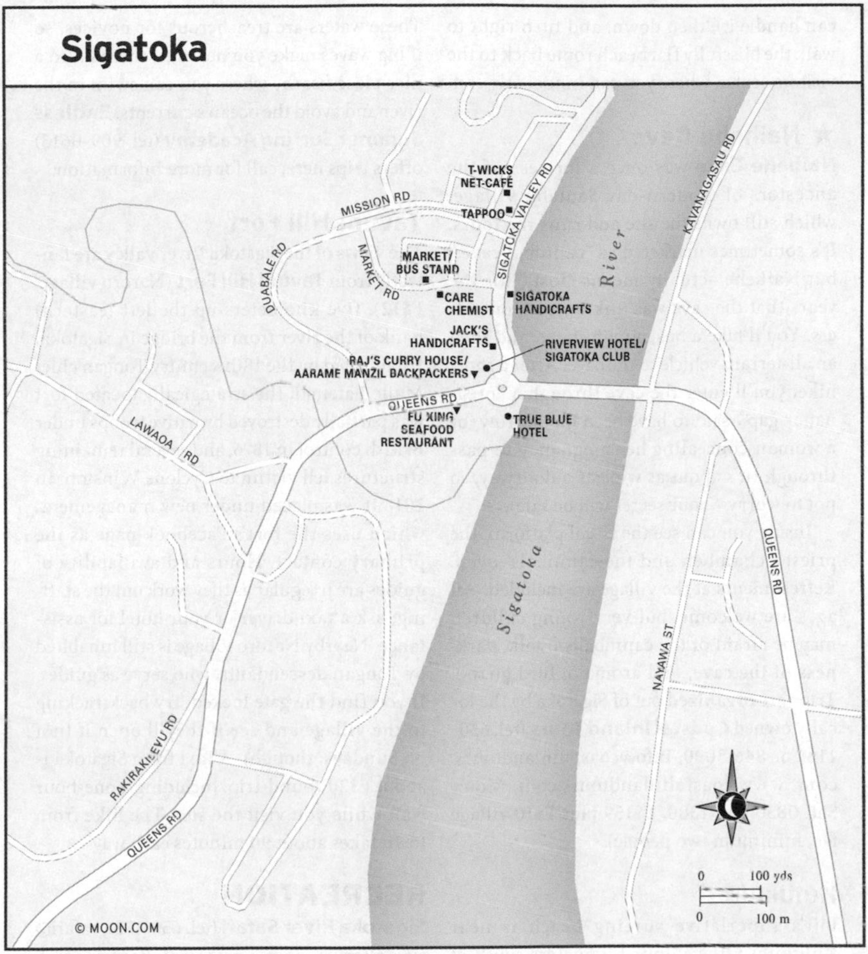

challenging five-kilometer, two-hour hike. Don't underestimate the challenge. Fiji's Olympic gold-winning rugby team trained by running up and down the dunes daily—a real workout!

The official way in is to pay F$10 and enter through the **visitors center** (Queens Road, tel. 652-0243, www.nationaltrust.org.fj, daily 0800-1800, entry ends at 1400). The visitors center is rather dingy, and the real archaeological treasures were long ago moved to the Fiji Museum in Suva. The center is located about seven kilometers east of Shangri-La's Fijian Resort and four kilometers west of Sigatoka, and most buses (except for certain express buses) will make a stop here.

Unofficially, there's a back route through Kulukulu village. To find it, if you're traveling from Nadi toward Sigatoka, go past the visitors center and then look for a small white sign indicating the village road. Turn right and proceed past the Salvation Army building on your right and a mini-mart on your left. Then look to your right for a small red-and-yellow Hanuman temple. Turn right immediately and drive a couple hundred meters on a gravel driveway. This sand dune is the back way into the park. Climb up (if your quads can handle it), then down, and turn right to walk the blissfully flat beach route back to the visitors center, where you can innocently exit.

★ Naihehe Cave

Naihehe Cave was once a fortress of the ancestors of modern-day Sautabu village, which still owns the site and runs the tours. It's sometimes marketed as "cannibal cave," but Naihehe actually means "lost," for the years that the cave was unknown to outsiders. You'll take a bus, a motorboat, and then an all-terrain vehicle to the cave. After a short hike, you'll enter the cave through a "pregnancy gap," said to have been too narrow for a woman concealing her pregnancy to pass through (it's about as wide as a doorway, so not to worry—your secret will be safe).

Inside you can see the ritual platform, the priest's chamber, and the cannibals' oven. Refreshments at the village are included. All ages are welcome, but very young children may be afraid of the cannibalism talk, darkness of the cave, and aroma of bird guano. Trips are organized out of Sigatoka by the locally owned **Coastal Inland Tours** (tel. 650-1161 or 846-3090, info@coastalinlandtours.com, www.coastalinlandtours.com, Mon.-Sat. 0830 and 1300, F$159 plus F$10 village fee, minimum two people).

Kulukulu

Fiji's superlative surfing beach is near Kulukulu village, four kilometers south of Sigatoka, where the Sigatoka River breaks through Viti Levu's fringing reef to form the Sigatoka Sand Dunes. The surf is primarily a river-mouth point break with numerous breaks down the beach (which is accessible by land only if you climb over the high dunes). It's one of the only places for beach-break surfing on Viti Levu, with no boat required. When the wind comes up in the afternoon, the windsurfing in this area is fantastic, as you can either sail "flat water" across the river mouth or do "wave jumping" in the sea (which has an all-sand bottom and big rollers during high winds). You can also bodysurf here. These waters are treacherous for novices, so if big waves make you nervous, there's also a nice place nearby where you can swim in the river and avoid the ocean's currents. **Endless Summer Surfing Academy** (tel. 909-0613) offers trips here; call for more information.

Tavuni Hill Fort

The views of the Sigatoka River valley are fantastic from **Tavuni Hill Fort** (Naroro village, F$12), five kilometers up the left (eastern) bank of the river from the bridge in Sigatoka. Established by the 18th-century Tongan chief Maile Latemai, the strategically located fort was partially destroyed by native troops under British control in 1876, and several remaining structures fell victim to Cyclone Winston. In 2018 it was placed under new management, which uses the fort's Facebook page as the primary contact. Hours and availability of guides are irregular as they work out the staffing; ask a taxi driver or your hotel for assistance. Nearby Naroro village is still inhabited by Tongan descendants, who serve as guides. If you find the gate locked, try backtracking to the village and see if they'll open it (not on Sundays, though). A taxi from Sigatoka is about F$20 round-trip, including a one-hour wait while you visit the site. The hike from town takes about 90 minutes each way.

RECREATION

Sigatoka River Safari (tel. 650-1721, safari@sigatokariver.com, www.sigatokariver.com), with a desk in the Tappoo shop in Sigatoka, runs a boat 60 kilometers up the river. Four-hour tours operate daily, except Sunday, at 0845 and 1300 (F$249 pp, including lunch and transfers from most Coral Coast and Nadi resorts). The company has a sweet backstory: It was cofounded by an Australian who fell in love with Fiji while on holiday as a child and the Fijian man who befriended him while working as a security guard at a resort. Fifteen villages participate in the business, which brings tourism revenue deep into the interior. Trips visit a different village every day to spread the impact. This tour offers an easy

Seasonal Fruits and Vegetables

pineapple at a roadside market

Fijian food is characterized by a handful of year-round staples—coconut, taro, fresh fish—and an abundance of rotating seasonal fruits and vegetables. To eat like a local, look for these items in season on menus and in markets:

- **Ivi** (Tahitian chestnut): March-April, October-November
- **Kangkong** (local watercress): January-April
- **Kavika** (rose apple): October-February
- **Mango:** August-March
- **Moca** (amaranth): September-March
- **Moringa pods** ("drumsticks"): June-October
- **Ota** (fiddlehead fern shoots): January-May
- **Passion fruit:** April-August
- **Soursop:** October-April
- **Uto** (breadfruit): November-April

way of seeing a bit of the river and meeting those who own the land while enjoying an exciting speedboat ride.

Coastal Inland Tours (tel. 650-1161 or 846-3090, info@coastalinlandtours.com, www.coastalinlandtours.com) offers four tours, including the unique Naihehe "cannibal cave" tour (see above). Other tours include a cruise up the river, a farm-and-village tour to the "salad bowl," and a trip to the Biausevu Waterfall east of Sigatoka along the Queens Highway.

Gold Coast Tours (tel. 993-9720 or 625-1568, goldcoasttoursfiji@yahoo.com, www.goldcoasttoursfiji.webs.com, F$190 adults, half price children 3-12), based at Bedarra Inn, runs a half-day trip from Nadi to Sigatoka and its surroundings. It's a fine way to see the area if your time is limited or you don't wish to organize your own transport. Stops include the sand dunes and a local market, school, beach, temple, pottery workshop, and coconut home decor workshop (with opportunities to buy, of course). Bargain hard, as prices can be inflated depending on where you say you're staying.

SHOPPING

Sigatoka has ubiquitous souvenir shops and a colorful local market in the center of town (Market Rd., Mon.-Sat. 0700-1700) with a large handicraft section (especially on Wednesday and Saturday).

Jack's Handicrafts (tel. 650-0810, www.jacksfiji.com) facing the river sells the traditional handmade Fijian pottery made in Nakabuta and Lawai villages near Sigatoka.

The **Sigatoka Handicraft Center**, in a shack beside the river opposite Jack's, is a good place to buy *masi* cloth, carvings, and other souvenirs. It's managed by local women.

For quality snorkeling gear and Internet access, try **Nats** (tel. 650-0064), upstairs between the Bank of the South Pacific and Big Bear on the street facing the river.

FOOD

A number of snack bars around the bus station and market dispense greasy fast food and sandwiches to bus passengers during their 15-minute stops here. If you have more time, try one of the town's many restaurants.

Jacks Coffee Shop (Mon.-Fri. 0830-1700), outside of Jack's Handicrafts, offers lunch specials for F$4-9. It's also a good breakfast place.

Fu Xing Seafood Restaurant (tel. 650-2151, daily 1000-2200), above Jack's Handicrafts, serves family-style Chinese food at large round banquet tables. The emphasis is on seafood, but the giant menu covers everything. Locals love the Mongolian sizzling chicken/beef/shrimp platters (F$20).

For Indian dishes, there's **Raj's Curry House** (tel. 650-1470, Mon.-Sat. 0800-2200), on Queens Road next to the Riverview Hotel. There are two sections here: a cheap fast-food side and an overpriced regular restaurant. The curries listed on the restaurant menu cost F$10-25. A couple of vegetarian dishes are available.

The restaurant downstairs at **Sigatoka Club** (tel. 650-0026, Mon.-Sat. 1000-2300, Sun. 1000-2200, F$7-8), across the street from the Riverview Hotel, serves good meals daily from 0900 to 2200. The club's bar is always fine for a beer or a game of pool on one of the three tables. The picnic tables outside next to the river are especially good for people-watching. A more expensive tourist restaurant is upstairs.

ACCOMMODATIONS

★ **Teitei Farm Stay** (863-8944, akka1980@gmail.com, https://ffwrfromfiji.wordpress.com, F$105 adults, F$50 children 5-12) is a 30-acre working farm in Fiji's "salad bowl," the Sigatoka River valley. Guests stay in a three-bedroom cottage. There's no Wi-Fi, and the shower has cold water, but hot water is available for a bucket bath. All meals (five per day, mostly from the farm) and farm activities are included. Alcohol is frowned upon. It's surrounded by Indo-Fijian farms and beautiful mountains, but the real attraction is the fertile farm itself: There are chickens, ducks, geese, honeybees, fish, coconuts, sandalwood, cassava, papayas, pineapples, ginger, lemons, corn, peanuts, bananas, sweet potato, sorghum, guava, breadfruit, jackfruit, cashews, duruka...and more. Teitei aims to preserve traditional Fijian permaculture practices, such as terrace planting and intercropping (pairing crops that grow well together). Guests who stay three nights or longer receive free pickup in Sigatoka town; otherwise, a taxi from town to Teitei is F$25 for the 19.2-kilometer ride. Farmwork volunteers who can cover their own costs may apply for long-term stays.

1: overlooking Sigatoka **2:** shopping in Sigatoka **3:** climbing up the Sigatoka Sand Dunes **4:** the beach at the Sigatoka Sand Dunes.

1

2

3

4

In town, **Aarame Manzil Backpackers Accommodations** (tel. 864-1682) above Raj's Curry House is a good low-cost option but is only sometimes open.

Riverview Hotel (tel. 650-0318, F$80 s/d), facing the highway bridge in town, has six rooms with bath and balcony and air-conditioning. A large public bar is downstairs, so be prepared for noise.

True Blue Hotel (Queens Rd., tel. 650-1530, www.truebluehotel.com, F$91), above the Sigatoka Club across the traffic circle from the Riverview, has nine air-conditioned rooms with private bath that can accommodate up to three people; breakfast is included. It can get loud here due to the bar-nightclub below.

Information and Services

The **District Hospital** (tel. 650-0455) is 1.5 kilometers southwest of Sigatoka along the road to Nadi.

Dr. Aida Gerona and Dr. Rudy Gerona (tel. 652-0128) work out of an office on Sigatoka Valley Road, facing the river near the old bridge. They're open weekdays 0830-1600, Saturdays 0830-1300. A dentist is next door.

Care Chemist (tel. 652-0393), at the market square, is open 0800-1730 Monday-Saturday.

ATMs are at the ANZ Bank opposite the bus station, the Westpac Bank, and Bank South Pacific. **Western Union Currency Exchange** (Mon.-Fri. 0800-1800, Sat. 0800-1600), between Jack's Handicrafts and the Riverview Hotel, changes money at rates similar to the banks, without commission.

T-Wicks Net-Cafe (tel. 652-0505), on Sigatoka Valley Road, offers Internet access for F$1 per hour. It's open Monday-Friday 0830-1800 and Saturday 0830-1600.

Public toilets are available at the bus station, at Tappoos, and at Chicken Express (next to BSP).

Central Coral Coast

The 80-kilometer stretch between Sigatoka and Pacific Harbour is the heart of the Coral Coast, with long reef-lined beaches and accommodations of all types all along the Queens Highway, as well as some fun sights and a handful of lovely beach-side restaurants. Distances between the resorts are great, but frequent buses ply the highway, and there are plenty of sightseeing options via your hotel's tour desk, private taxis, or your rented car.

A cluster of inexpensive places to stay and one large American-run resort are located about eight kilometers east of Sigatoka; of these, only the Outrigger on the Lagoon, Sandy Point Beach Cottages, and Tubakula Beach Resort are right on the beach itself.

Farther east, the sugar fields of western Viti Levu are replaced by coconut plantations with rainforests creeping up the green slopes behind. Once you reach **Taunovo Bay,** the accommodations tend to cater to a more upscale crowd, and cooking facilities are usually not provided for guests. These places draw heaps of Australians and New Zealanders on packaged beach holidays who intend to spend most of their time unwinding. The Beachouse, the Mango Bay Resort, and Waidroka Bay Resort cater to the flashpacker market.

SIGHTS

★ Kula Eco Park

Opposite the Outrigger hotel, a small road leads to **Kula Eco Park** (tel. 650-0505, www.fijiwild.com, daily 1000-1600, F$40 adults, F$20 ages 11 and under), known to locals as Kula Bird Park. It's a beautiful place to stroll around for a couple of hours, and a must for bird-watchers. It's the only place you can see the *kula* lorikeet, the Kadavu musk parrot, the goshawk, flying fox fruit bats, and other fauna in near-natural settings. From the reception pavilion, a shaded walkway passes a half-dozen aviaries and displays in the valley, and then loops back through the hillside forest and several additional aviaries. Numerous small bridges cross the seasonal stream that winds through the park. If you pause, the call of the barking pigeon, the shrill cry of the honeyeater, and songs from a host of other unseen creatures may reach your ears. Aside from the birds, 140 floral species have been identified in this verdant park. Kula Eco Park has a captive breeding program for the endangered crested iguana and peregrine falcon.

Savu Na Mate Laya Waterfall

The 65-foot-high Savu Na Mate Laya Waterfall, located deep in the forest just off the Queens Highway, is a lovely half-day diversion. Access is through Biausevu village, which owns the falls and welcomes visitors Monday-Saturday. The closest major landmark is the Warwick Hotel on the Queens Highway; to reach the falls from there, go one kilometer east and pass the Korolevu police post and post office on your right, then take the first road inland (right turn). Go three kilometers to Biausevu village. You must pay F$30 per person for admission and a guide, who will expect an additional tip. It's a pleasant half-hour hike on a paved trail lined with giant ferns and red ginger, and your guide can point out medicinal herbs along the way. The trail crisscrosses several streams, so wearing footwear that can get wet is a must, or you can hire a horse from the village for an additional fee. At the falls, there's a toilet and changing hut, and a shallow area of the large, crystal-clear pool has been segregated with rocks so that young children can splash around in it safely. Bring drinking water.

Organized trips to the falls are available through operators such as **Coastal Inland Tours** (Sigatoka, tel. 650-1161 or 846-3090, info@coastalinlandtours.com, www.coastalinlandtours.com, F$139) and **Lino Cappuccino Tours** (200 meters along the beach from the Warwick, tel. 802-9142 or 938-7101). These tours typically include transport from Sigatoka or Coral Coast hotels, a kava ceremony, horseback riding, and sometimes lunch at a village home; check to make sure they include the village/waterfall fee as well.

★ Frigate Passage

Fiji's most underrated surfing wave could be the left-hander in **Frigate Passage.** This consistently fast and hollow tube is like Cloudbreak near Nadi but without the crowds. It breaks on the western edge of the Beqa Barrier Reef and isn't for beginners. Conditions are ideal May-November, when waves reach 1-5 meters.

Matanivusi Surf Resort (tel. 360-9479, www.surfingfiji.com) and **Waidroka Bay Resort** (tel. 992-4944, www.waidroka.com) take guests on the 40-minute boat ride to the wave; if you're staying elsewhere, you can call them to book day trips if space is available. The actual location is southwest of Yanuca Island. Confusingly, there are two islands named Yanuca off the Coral Coast: One, off the western side near Natadola, is home to the Shangri-La Fijian Hotel, and is usually called simply the Shangri-La. This is the other one, and it's known only as Yanuca Island. It's off the eastern end of the Coral Coast, somewhat close to Pacific Harbour and Beqa Island.

Beneath the waves, Frigate Passage is also one of the top scuba-diving sites on the Coral Coast. All of the Coral Coast resorts and scuba shops lead trips here, where big schools of fish are drawn by a vigorous tidal flow that washes in and out of the passage. The fish are the main attraction, but there are also large, attractive coral heads. The strong currents make the area unsuitable for beginning divers.

SPORTS AND RECREATION

Diving

Dive sites along the coast offer a range of experiences. Beginners can see a resident school of barracuda and a huge lionfish population at the shallow, easy **Stingray site,** as well as a hard-coral carpet and frequent eagle rays

Central Coral Coast

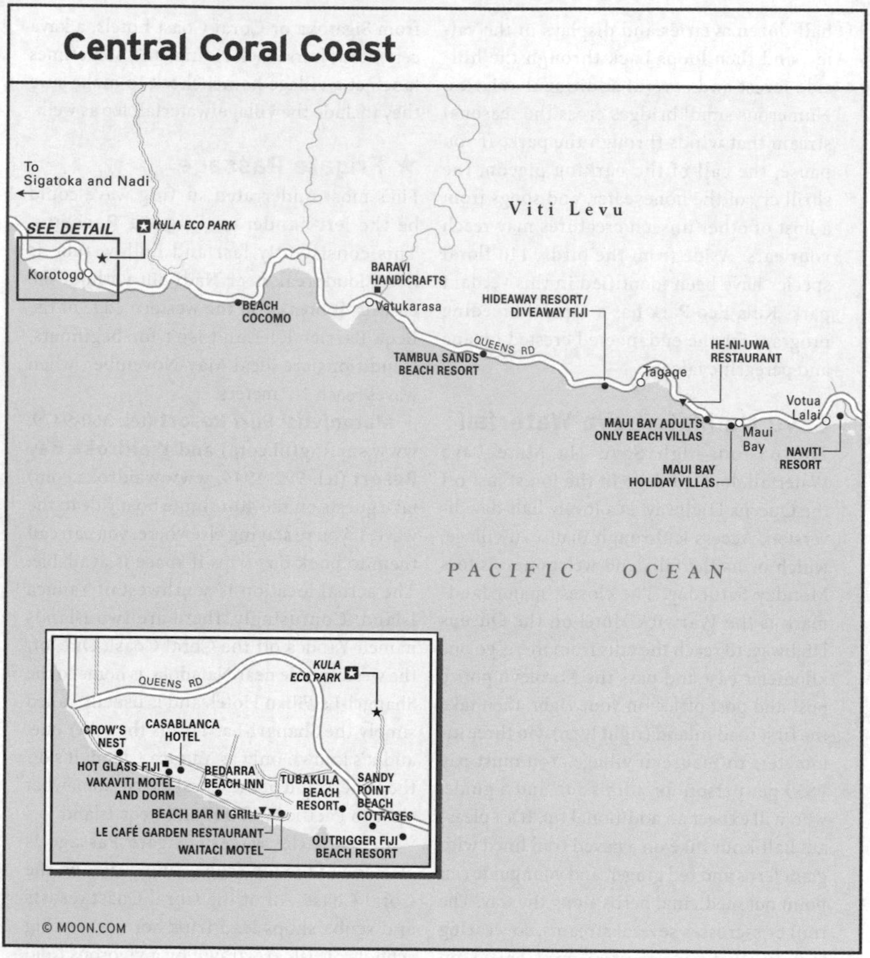

at Ras Bula. Advanced divers can plunge through a narrow gorge to an underwater canyon at Gunbarrel, filled with reef sharks herding snapper and surgeonfish, and the Maze, with swim-throughs and tunnels that twist round and about, culminating in an 11-meter vertical chimney.

Diveaway Fiji (tel. 931-6883/926-3112, info@diveaway-fiji.com, www.diveaway-fiji.com, 0730-1600 Mon.-Sat.), with a jetty at the Hideaway Resort, is the main dive operator on the Coral Coast. It's F$180/260 for one/two tanks inclusive of gear, with discounts for more diving. It's also one of the few dive operations in Fiji to offer PADI advanced and rescue courses. An outer reef snorkeling trip is F$50 per person. Pickup can be arranged from all nearby hotels.

Off-Roading

Coral Coast Adventures (tel. 650-1751 or 834-7250, info@coralcoastadventures.com, www.coralcoastadventures.com) rents two-seater dune buggies for a three-hour guided tour (F$259 adults) inland on the hill trails north of the Queens Highway. Helmets, seatbelts, drinks, and snacks are provided, and it's a fun way to get beyond the resorts. The

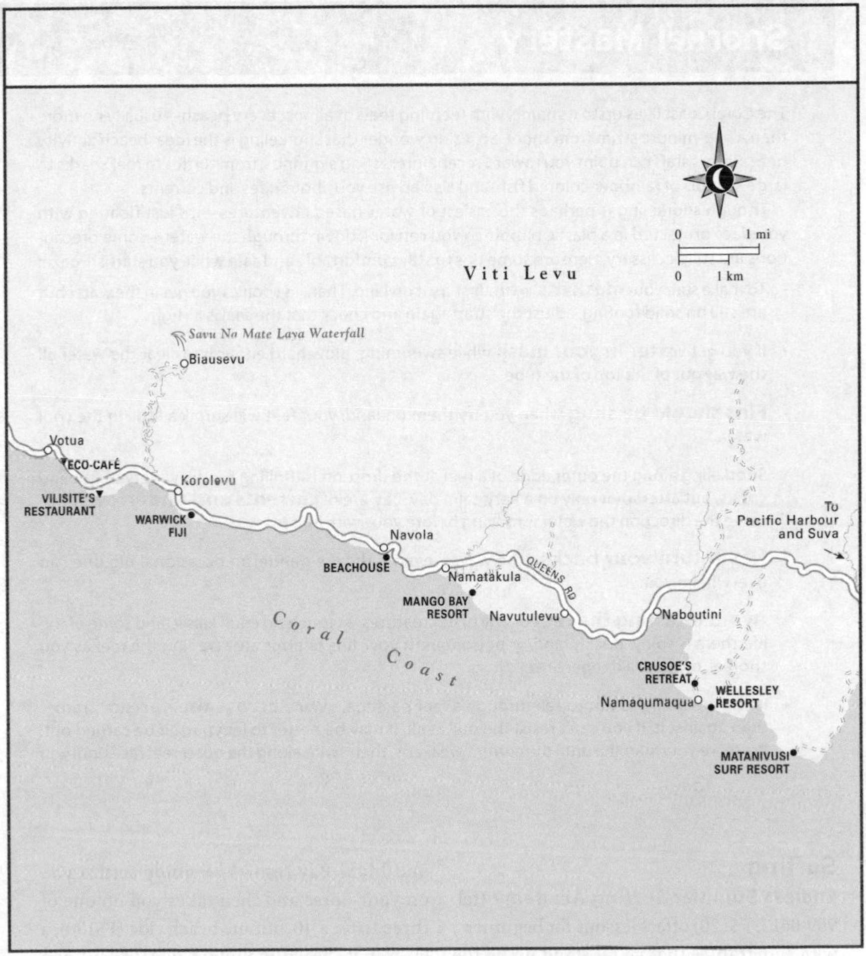

four-wheel, all-terrain vehicles are a cross between a lawnmower and a bumper car; videos on the Facebook page give an accurate sense of what this experience is like. The ride can be dusty or muddy, but that just makes the waterfall dip all the more refreshing. Only adults can drive the dune buggies, and they must have a valid driver's license from their home country. Children taller than 120 centimeters are allowed as passengers; those under age 15 pay F$149. Groups with two adults plus two children pay a family rate of F$729. Trips must be prebooked and can be arranged any day except Sunday.

Fishing

Mango Bay Fishing Charters (tel. 653-0069 or 992-8903, info@mangobayresortfiji.com, www.mangobayresortfiji.com) takes fishers on the *Mango Princess,* a 28-foot fiberglass motorboat built in Fiji. It's F$310 per person per day for a four-person charter. Or you can rent the whole boat, with up to seven passengers, for F$1,100/1,800 per half/full day. Transfers are not included but can be arranged for a fee. Whatever you catch becomes the property of the Mango Bay Resort, which will cook it for you upon request, but you can also ask to take fresh fillets with you.

Snorkel Mastery

The Coral Coast lives up to its name, with teeming reefs at almost every beach—usually no more than a five-minute swim from shore. So it's no wonder that snorkeling is the ideal beach activity here. Resort staff can point you toward recent interesting sightings, from turtles to reef sharks to large schools of rainbow-colored fish, and also advise you about tides and currents.

Though snorkeling is perhaps the easiest of water-based adventures—it's just floating with your face protected in a plastic bubble so you can look down through the water—some precautions are still necessary. Here are some tips to stay comfortable and safe while you starfish-gaze:

- To make sure your **mask fits well,** first try it on land. Then, as soon as you get in the water but are still on solid footing, adjust the strap again and check that the seal is airtight.
- If you get **water in your mask** while swimming, blow hard enough to clear the water all the way out of the top of the tube.
- **Fins should be snug** when you try them on land; your feet will shrink a little in the cool water.
- Snorkeling along the outer edge of a reef at the drop-off is thrilling for the variety of fish and corals, but attempt it only on a very calm day. Beware of **currents and undertows.** Observe the direction the water is moving before you swim into it.
- **Never turn your back** to the waves, even if they're gentle; an occasional big one can overwhelm you.
- **Avoid touching the reef** or any of its creatures, as touching coral kills it, and some of the life there is spiny, prickly, and/or poisonous. If your fins or arms are scraping the reef as you snorkel, move to a deeper area.
- If you are dragged out to sea through a reef passage, **swim across the current,** rather than against it. If you can't resist the pull at all, it may be better to let yourself be carried out. Preserve your stamina until the current weakens, then swim along the outer reef face until you

Surfing

Endless Summer Surfing Academy (tel. 909-0613, F$120) offers lessons for beginners, with a guarantee that you'll stand up by the end of your 90 minutes. Instructors are certified by the Fiji Surf Association and will meet you at the beach of your choice, depending on where you're staying. You can also rent boards or take longer surf trips with them to popular places in the area, including the Frigate Passage and Kulukulu.

Horseback Riding

The family-owned **Fiji Coral Coast Horse Riding Adventures** (tel. 950-2961, fjcoralcoasthorseridin@gmail.com) is located at the **He-Ni-Uwa Restaurant,** off the Queens Highway between the Hideaway and Maui Bay resorts. A guide settles you on your horse and then takes you on one of three trips: a 40-minute beach ride (F$180), a 90-minute beach/mountain ride (F$240), or a 2-hour rainforest ride that includes a waterfall dip (F$280). Prices include resort pickup/drop-off and a fine lunch at the restaurant.

Glassblowing

A fun new addition to the Coral Coast scene is **Hot Glass Fiji** (tel. 909-3200, alice@hotglassfiji.com, www.hotglassfiji.com, Tues.-Fri. 1000-1500), near the Kula Eco Park and the Outrigger hotel. Owners Alice and Alex Hill patiently guide you through learning a new skill, and you'll take home a unique souvenir you make yourself. Choose from the "quick slick" class (F$195, 30 minutes), where

Snorkeling is great along the Coral Coast.

find somewhere to come back in. Or use your energy to attract the attention of someone on a boat or on shore.

- Consider **buying snorkel gear at home.** Free masks given to resort guests are typically the old-fashioned type with plastic (rather than silicone) skirt seals and simple j-style tubes (rather than one-way valves). The newer, full-face snorkel masks aren't available in Fiji.
- **Snapping your own photos** underwater has never been easier. Few tourists bother with expensive underwater cameras these days, as waterproof casings are an affordable way to convert your camera phone, GoPro or similar camera, or even a larger SLR for blue-green beauty shots. Be sure to get a waterproof wrist strap so that your device doesn't float away from you.

you make a pre-shaped paperweight, drinking glass, vase, or dish; a sandcasting class (F195, 1 hour), where you design and create your own mementos (gecko? cannibal club?) from red-gold liquid glass; and glassblowing technique (F$390, 1-4 hours depending on your group's size), where you make three separate items. It's best not to go on your last day, as it takes a day for your glass creation to cool from its 1,000°C working temperature. You can pick it up the next day or have it delivered to a Coral Coast hotel, or have it posted to you at home for a fee.

SHOPPING

Vatukarasa village, between Korotogo and Korolevu, is notable for both its quaint appearance and for **Baravi Handicrafts** (Queens Road, tel. 652-0364, daily 0700-1800). Baravi carries a wide selection of Fijian handicrafts at fixed prices that are lower than the Fijian chain stores. There's also coffee on hand. Two other Vatukarasa handicraft shops are just west of Baravi.

FOOD

All of the larger hotels along the coast have restaurants that are open to nonguests. Barbecue stalls and fruit stands are also frequent, and are a delicious way to sample local fare.

Arranged west to east, here are a few notable eateries:

Facing the beach just east of the Outrigger is the **Beach Bar n Grill** (tel. 902-5979, F$20), serving Western dishes as well as specialties such as chili prawns and coconut seafood curry. To dine on lobster, order in the morning and one will be caught just for you.

Le Café Garden Restaurant (tel. 652-0877, daily 1000-2200) is between the Beach Bar n Grill and the Waitaci Motel. Pizzas are F$9-19, mains F$16, specials F$7. Happy hour is 1700-1900. Under Swiss management, this place has class.

★ **He-Ni-Uwa Restaurant** (tel. 932-9179, daily 0800-2000), off the Queens Highway in Valase between the Hideaway and Maui Bay resorts, serves up Fijian favorites such as fish-and-chips, curry crab, *kokoda,* and *babakau.* If you've been fishing, owners Apenisa and Kinisalote Vunitasiri will cook up your catch of the day. Try the fresh lemonade. The beach view is stunning, especially at sunset. Calling ahead is recommended.

The lovely little ★ **Eco-Café** (tel. 785-3953 or 807-8928, eco.cafe@yahoo.com, http://ecocafe-fiji.info, Wed.-Sat. 1700-2200, Sun. 1200-2200, F$9-F$38) is a two-story bamboo lodge located right on the beach in Votua, just west of the Coral Lagoon Resort. Fijian dishes include river mussels in coconut cream (F$26), and there are also sandwiches, burgers, pasta, and wood-fired pizzas. Almost everything is organic and local.

Vilisite's Restaurant (Queens Rd., tel. 653-0054, daily 0800-2200), by the lagoon between the Warwick and Naviti resorts at Korolevu, is better known as "Felicity's place." The favorite lunch dish is fish-and-chips; there's also chop suey or curries. Dinner consists of a choice of six set seafood menus (F$20-45). The champagne sunsets here 1800-1900 are unforgettable. Vilisite's gift shop has good prices on handicrafts and there are rooms for rent.

ACCOMMODATIONS

Under US$50

Vakaviti Motel and Dorm (Sunset Strip, tel. 650-0526, www.vakaviti.com), next to the Crow's Nest, has four self-catering units facing the pool at F$80 single or double. The five-bed family *bure* with one double and three single beds is F$90 double. Children under 12 are free. The six-bed backpacker dorm is F$20 per person. Stay a week and the eighth night is free. Facilities include a swimming pool and a large lending library/book exchange at the reception. Day trips to Natadola Beach are arranged.

Casablanca Hotel (Sunset Strip, tel. 652-0600), next door to Vakaviti, is a two-story hillside building on the inland side of Sunset Strip. Its eight rooms with cooking facilities and arched balconies begin at F$85/95 single/double and F$150 for the family room that sleeps up to four adults. Have a look at a few rooms, as they do vary.

Just west of the Outrigger at Korotogo is the **Waitaci Motel** (tel. 650-0278, F$80 s/d), with three large A-frame bungalows and two rooms below the reception in the main building. Cooking facilities are provided. The swimming pool and charming management add to the allure. A third person can be accommodated for F$20.

US$50-100

Tiny ★ **Beach Cocomo** (tel. 936-7063 or 650-7333, beachcocomofiji@gmail.com, www.beachcocomofiji.com, F$150 queen, F$175 king) has just two fan-cooled cottages, a Korean owner-chef, and the feeling of having stumbled upon a secret hideaway. It's three kilometers east of Malevu village, tucked into a secluded strip of beach just off the main Queens Highway, on spacious grounds that are shaded with palm trees. It's an extra F$92 if you want to take all your meals there. Food is cooked to order and you can request sushi, Korean, or Fijian specialties; no alcohol is served, but you can bring your own. There's no Wi-Fi or TV.

A bit east of the Outrigger and right on the beach, ★ **Tubakula Beach Resort** (Queens Rd., tel. 650-0097, www.fiji4less.com) offers a holiday atmosphere at reasonable rates. The 22 pleasant A-frame bungalows with fan, cooking facilities, and private bath—each capable of sleeping three or four—start at F$126 double for those near the highway. Renovated bungalows are F$139 double poolside, F$153 garden, or F$180 beachfront (extra persons are F$24 each, with a maximum of five). One self-catering house has three rooms with shared bath (F$63/69 s/d). The "Beach Club" dormitory consists of eight rooms, each with five or six beds at F$28 a bed (there's a small discount for students and HI card holders); these units are not new or fancy, but they are a good value.

Tubakula caters to independent travelers, with a communal kitchen plus a swimming pool, restaurant, game room, nightly videos, and a mini mart. To allow the lagoon coral to regenerate undisturbed, motorized water sports are not offered. Ask about the Tuesday night *lovo* (underground-oven feast) at Malevu village, 500 meters east. The snorkeling here is good, there's surfing and scuba diving nearby, and bus or taxi excursions are available.

Crow's Nest (Sunset Strip, tel. 650-0230, www.crowsnestfiji.com), a few hundred meters southeast of the traffic circle, has 18 split-level duplex bungalows with cooking facilities, verandas, and thin walls. The eight "executive" units are F$135 single or double, while the 10 self-catering units are F$145, plus F$25 per extra adult to four maximum. The restaurant up the hill faces the swimming pool. The nicely landscaped grounds are just across the road from the beach, with good views over the lagoon from an elevated perch.

Sandy Point Beach Cottages (Queens Rd., tel. 650-0125, www.sandypointfiji.com) shares a beach with the adjacent Outrigger. Three fan-cooled beachfront units and one garden bungalow with full cooking facilities are F$90/110 single/double and a five-bed cottage is F$160. Set in spacious grounds right by the sea, Sandy Point has its own freshwater swimming pool.

US$100-150

The clean and classy ★ **Bedarra Beach Inn** (77 Sunset Strip, tel. 650-0476, frontdesk@bedarrafiji.com, www.bedarrafiji.com, $210 d), a bit west of the Outrigger on the Lagoon, has 21 spacious air-conditioned motel-style rooms with fridges in a two-story block. All rooms have a sea view. It's just a few steps across the road and down to a pleasant beach with good snorkeling at high tide, and kayaks and snorkel gear are available for guests. A swimming pool, video room, and lounge round out the facilities. At 1700 daily, a band performs in the comfortable restaurant, which is open 0700-2100. Happy hour with half-price drinks is 1700-1900 daily, and you can order chef's specials such as tandoori beef kebabs (F$29). You can also be served dinner right on the beach. There's a spa with offerings such as a coconut aromatherapy massage (60 minutes, F$89) and a marine-extract detox body wrap (90 minutes, F$150).

The popular ★ **Beachouse** (Queens Rd., tel. 992-9500, www.fijibeachouse.com)—with only one "h" in its name—is on a palm-fringed white beach just off Queens Road, between Navola and Namatakula villages. Fan-cooled cottages (F$175-195) are scattered around a wide lawn. Each has its own en suite bathroom, and the showers are private but open-air, meaning you may share space with lizards and critters. There are also a few air-conditioned suites with king beds (F$195), and a fan-cooled dormitory with six bunk beds (F$48). The cottages and dorm are wheelchair-accessible, but the suites are up a flight of stairs. Breakfast, afternoon tea, and daily yoga are included. Meals in the restaurant (open until midnight) consist of fish-and-chips, burgers, and vegetarian fare.

The British reality-TV series *Celebrity Love Island* once filmed here, its crew constructing a pool and Fijian-style movie set by the beach. Swimming in the ocean is good at high tide, and staff will take you out to the nearby reef in their launch for snorkeling (but watch for strong currents). There's a lending library, free SkyTV and Internet in the lobby, a travel center, and a bush track up into the hills behind the resort. Despite the party vibe, Beachouse tries to be a good neighbor, and the hammocks are made by local villagers; you can buy one to take home (F$250-300). Staff member Elenor will wash, dry, and fold your laundry

1

2

3

4

for F$15 per load. A three-hour horseback tour to a waterfall is F$80 including lunch.

Tambua Sands Beach Resort (Queens Rd., tel. 650-0399, res.tambuasands@warwickhotels.com, www.warwickhotels.com/tambua-sands, F$218-252), operated by Warwick in an attractive location facing the sea, conveys a feeling of calm and peace. The 31 bungalows are all the same, clean and roomy with either a double bed or two single beds, fridge, and mini-patio, with either a garden view or beachfront. There's a bar and restaurant, swimming pool, and live music many evenings.

★ **Crusoe's Retreat** (tel. 650-0185, www.crusoesretreat.com), by the beach four kilometers off Queens Road from Naboutini, is the most isolated place to stay on the Coral Coast (and is not to be confused with Robinson Crusoe Island). The 29 large *bures* each have two double beds, an antique fridge, and a porch. The 17 "seaview" bungalows up on the hillside are from F$234 double, while the 11 "seaside" *bures* start at F$321. Only units 1-6 have thatched roofs (no. 1 is the closest to the beach). Prices include a buffet breakfast, afternoon tea, and nonmotorized sports such as kayaks, sailboards, and paddleboards. It's cheaper to order from the menu at the restaurant than to buy a meal plan. The on-site dive shop charges F$250 for one/two tanks including gear, but this isn't a dive resort.

Wellesley Resort (tel. 603-0664, www.wellesleyresort.com.fj, F$279 d) is near Namaqumaqua village, 4.5 kilometers off Queens Road down the same bumpy access road as Crusoe's Retreat. The Wellesley is set in a narrow valley that opens onto a lovely white beach (one of the Coral Coast's best) facing a protected lagoon. There's also a large swimming pool. The 15 spacious rooms are aligned in a long block well back from the beach. Rates include a light breakfast and tax. Airport transfer is free if you stay three or more nights. Meals are available a la carte or you can opt for the all-inclusive packages. It's easy to get to either the Wellesley or Crusoe's Retreat by taking a public bus to the Warwick Fiji at Korolevu and a taxi from there (about F$15-20).

Built in 2017, ★ **Maui Bay Holiday Villas** (Queens Rd., tel. 650-7110 or 797-0945, roselyn@mauibayholidayvillasfiji.com, www.mauibayholidayvillasfiji.com, F$250), next to the Total gas station, has 20 two-bedroom motel-style apartments with full kitchens arranged around a large freeform swimming pool. Each apartment is spacious, clean, air-conditioned, and has a king bed, two twin beds, and three daybeds; they can sleep a total of seven, making Maui Bay an excellent value for a large family or group. Conveniently, a restaurant, bar, and supermarket are attached. The beach is 100 meters down the road.

US$150-200

Just down the road from Maui Bay Holiday Villas is a sister property with a completely different feel, the upscale **Maui Bay Adults Only Beach Villas** (Queens Rd., tel. 650-7110 or 797-0945, roselyn@mauibayholidayvillasfiji.com, www.mauibayholidayvillasfiji.com). Here, four gleaming private villas right on the beach cater to couples only. It's F$575 for garden view, F$650 for ocean view, and F$750 for the "honeymoon" villa with private plunge pool (you also get complimentary fruit and sparkling wine). The villas have simple modern furnishings, and a chef prepares custom meals.

Waidroka Bay Resort (tel. 992-4944, www.waidroka.com) is up the steep, rough gravel road leading to the Dogowale radio tower between Korovisilou and Talenaua, four kilometers off Queens Road. Operating since 1995, Waidroka has earned a reputation as one of Fiji's top surfing resorts, as several breaks are just a five-minute boat ride from the resort, and they'll ferry you out there at F$50 per person for two hours of surfing. Accommodations include five oceanfront

1: Maui Bay Adults Only Beach Villas **2:** a *bure* at Tambua Sands Beach Resort **3:** glassworker Laisa at Hot Glass Fiji **4:** the beach in front of Bedarra Beach Inn.

bungalows with private baths, fans, bamboo walls, and covered decks at F$276 single/double with continental breakfast. The two superior bungalows are F$356 for single/double, F$432 for triple. The optional meal plan is F$100 per person a day (cooking facilities are not provided). There's also a swimming pool, outdoor bar, yoga cabana, and spa. Movies are shown in the jungle bar at night. Waidroka's beach is mediocre but snorkeling trips can be arranged. Waidroka's dive boats have powerful engines that enable them to reach Frigate Passage in just 20 minutes. Surfers pay F$132 pp including lunch, while cuba diving is F$140/220 for one/two tanks, plus F$40 for equipment rental. There's a F$340 minimum for the boat to go, either with a combination of surfers and divers, or by an individual paying a flat fee. Sportfishing is also offered. Surfers or divers staying elsewhere can be picked up at Korovisilou village on Queens Road for F$20. Reservations are necessary, as the Waidroka Bay Resort is often full.

★ **Mango Bay Resort** (tel. 653-0069, info@mangobayresortfiji.com, www.mangobayresortfiji.com) occupies lovely grounds behind a sparkling white beach near Namatakula village, almost exactly halfway between Nadi and Suva. There are 10 colorfully painted thatch-roof beachfront *bures* with private bath; the ones in the back row are "standard" (F$329) and the ones in front are "superior" (F$349). In 2016, 10 garden lodges were added across a grassy field (F$230). There's no air-conditioning, though breakfast is included. Children under 12 are usually not accepted. When the hotel is full, there are plenty of parties and activities for the young traveler, including snorkeling (high tide only), kayaking, water sports, sportfishing, tours, hiking, rafting, horseback riding, diving, bonfires, DJ dancing, and an outdoor cinema. The lagoon-shaped pool has a swim-up bar. The on-site Mango Bay Fishing Charters has a fiberglass boat for fishing trips.

The 116-room **Hideaway Resort** (Queens Rd., tel. 650-0177 or 992-5181, reservations@hideawayfiji.com, www.hideawayfiji.com) at Korolevu is set on a palm-fringed beach. Some cottages have king beds, others a queen plus a single bed; prices vary by proximity to the beach (F$385-599). The two-bedroom villa (F$623) is a good deal for a larger group, with one king bed in a bedroom, two singles in another bedroom, and the option of adding two more single beds to the living area. A full buffet breakfast is included in all rates, and children under 12 stay and eat free. Be prepared

the beach at Hideaway Resort

for a lively holiday camp atmosphere, especially around the resort's huge oceanside pool. Some rooms get a lot of disco noise from the bar or traffic roar from the adjacent highway. This big resort provides zany cruise ship-style entertainment nightly. Sundays at 2000, the charming Tagaqe Village Choir sings hymns. The Rosie Holidays desk arranges other trips and Thrifty Car Rental bookings. The main restaurant overlooks the pool and beach, and has a giant menu including very good *kokoda* (F$17.50) and pizzas (F$21). From January to May, surfing is possible on a very hollow right in the pass here (not for beginners), and you can rent a board for F$75. Guests can use coin-operated washers and dryers.

The 254-room **Outrigger Fiji Beach Resort** (Queens Rd., tel. 650-0044, www.outrigger.com/fiji, F$345-1,450) is a large hotel built to look like a Fijian village, sprawling down the hillside from Queens Road to a sandy beach. The four-story main building closest to the road has air-conditioned rooms with ocean views and balconies, and scattered around the grounds are 52 thatch-roofed modern cottages, priced according to proximity to the beach. The large family *bures* have a king bed and two single beds. Most guests book ahead through the Outrigger website and pay a lot less than the rack rates listed, so look for specials. Wheelchair-accessible rooms are available. Romantic couples and throngs of children share the huge million-liter swimming pool beside the ho-hum beach. There are tons of resort-style activities and excursions, with everything from coconut bowling to yoga to nightly themed dinners. Even if you're not staying here, you can come for the Fijian buffet and *meke* Tuesdays and Saturdays (F$69) or the seafood buffet with Polynesian show Sundays (F$76). There's a convenience store, restaurant, bar, café with takeaway baked goods, and Thrifty Car Rental and Rosie Holidays desks, and wireless Internet is available at fair prices. A tunnel under the highway near the tennis courts leads to Kula Eco Park.

Over US$200

★ **Matanivusi Surf Resort** (tel. 360-9479, www.surfingfiji.com F$560 pp, three-night minimum), on a fine white-sand beach five kilometers off Queens Road from Vananiu village, is a top pick for surfers who want comfort and convenience but don't need ultra luxury. It has eight attractive duplex units. Included are three meals and boat rides to select surfing and snorkeling spots. A swimming pool is near the restaurant. Most of the 16 guests come to surf at Frigate Passage (F$80 pp) or on three smaller waves closer to the resort. Transfers from Nadi Airport are F$350 for two persons round-trip.

Naviti Resort (Queens Rd., Korolevu, tel. 653-0444, info.naviti@warwickhotels.com, https://warwickhotels.com/naviti-resort) has 220 spacious air-conditioned rooms and suites in a series of two- and three-story blocks, as well as some villas. Its facilities include two swimming pools, a small fitness center, a nine-hole golf course, five floodlit tennis courts, a beauty center, lobby ATM, and a boutique. Scuba diving is available through South Pacific Adventure Divers. Rates start at F$450 for two adults plus two children under 12, though the website often has discounts of 40 percent. The price includes all meals with unlimited wine or beer, plus many activities; rooms without meal plans often work out to be more expensive. The Naviti is one of the more wheelchair-accessible resorts on this coast.

Warwick Fiji (Queens Rd., 653-0555, info.fiji@warwickhotels.com, www.warwickhotels.com/fiji-resort), on a lovely beach on Queens Road six kilometers east of the Naviti, is one of the largest hotels on the Coral Coast. Erected in 1979, it's now owned by the same Hong Kong-controlled company as Naviti and Tambua Sands, and there's a shuttle bus running among them. Rooms start at F$625 for two adults and three under-12 children, but discounts of 40 percent are often available on the website. Units 1-9 are family beachfront *bures*; 10-20 are "normal" beachfront, with one queen and one single bed; and the remainder are garden view *bures* with one double and two single beds. Families can book two interconnected *bures*. All-inclusive meal plans are available, and children under 12 eat breakfast free when accompanied by adults. There's a kids' club (0900-2100, ages 3-12) with plenty of activities, an adults-only pool, daily entertainment, and free Wi-Fi in the public areas. There are several restaurants and bars, including a Japanese restaurant and swim-up bars in the pools.

Pacific Harbour

Marking the eastern end of the Coral Coast, and about an hour's drive (49 kilometers) southwest of Suva, Pacific Harbour is a condo development that now has a number of hotels along a nice sandy beach. In the early 1970s, Canadian developers built and sold most of the original villas to Australian and Hong Kong investors. Good paved roads meander between the landscaped lots and the golf course. Curving canals in the residential neighborhoods, set up to drain what was once a swamp, have residents' boats tied up to mini-docks.

There are no sights per se, but Pacific Harbour offers lots to do, varied accommodations and food, and convenient transportation. It has become a mini-hub for adventure activities such as Jet-Skiing and river rafting, without the overly corporate manicuring of Denarau.

RECREATION

Scuba Diving

The 65 kilometers of barrier reef around the 390-square-kilometer Beqa Lagoon south of Pacific Harbour feature multicolored soft corals and fabulous sea fans at Sidestreets, and an exciting wall and big fish at Cutter Passage. Sulfur Passage on the east side of Beqa is equally good. The top dive sites just north of Yanuca Island, such as Soft Coral Grotto, Caesar's Rocks, and Coral Gardens, are easily accessible from Pacific Harbour.

Beqa Adventure Divers (tel. 345-0911, www.fijisharkdive.com), based at the marina behind the Pearl, pioneered shark dives in the Beqa Lagoon. They regularly hand-feed eight species of sharks, including bull sharks, and participate in research tagging projects in the Shark Reef Marine Reserve area. Shark dives are Monday, Tuesday, Thursday, Friday, and Saturday morning and cost F$450, including two tanks and a marine park fee. Coral dives are Wednesday and Sunday mornings, as well as Monday, Tuesday, Thursday, and Friday afternoons (F$400). Gear rental is F$50/day. Multiday dive discounts and accommodation packages at the Pearl or the Uprising are available.

Aqua-Trek Beqa (tel. 345-0324 or 994-2475, www.aquatrek.com) at the Club Oceanus marina is an efficient operation with good rental equipment. Shark dives are Monday, Wednesday, Friday, and Saturday and cost F$270 including two tanks and a marine park fee. Coral dives are Tuesday, Thursday, and Sunday, and cost F$210 for two tanks. Gear rental is an additional F$40/day. Committed divers can book package deals, including accommodations at Club Oceanus, the Pearl, or the Uprising. U.S. customers can book dive packages directly and discuss options by calling 800/541-4334.

Fishing

Freedive Fiji (tel. 777-2815, U.S. tel. 310/927-7698, charters@freedivefiji.com, www.freedivefiji.com) offers day charters as well as overnight and multiday trips for game fishing (from the boat) or spearfishing while freediving. The 30-foot vessel is equipped with ice lockers and speargun racks and accommodates up to six people. A half-day trip (four hours) to Beqa Lagoon and Frigates Passage is F$1,400, and a full day (eight hours) is F$2,400. Lunch, fruit, and cold drinks are

Pacific Harbour

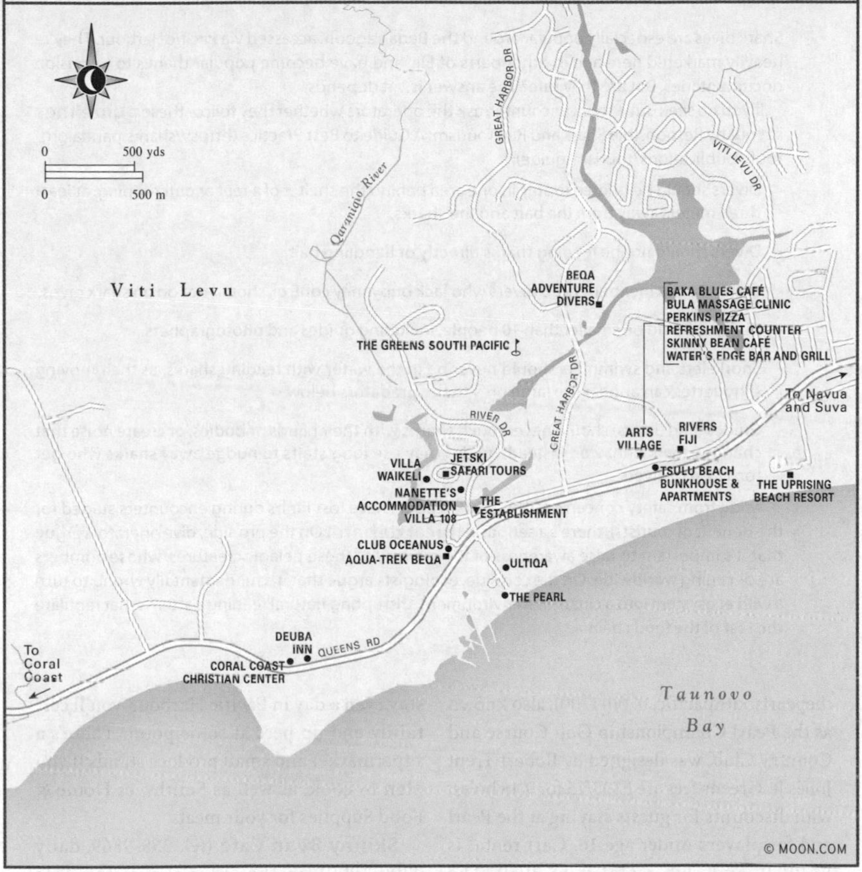

provided. Longer trips can be arranged to Kadavu with overnight beachfront stays, and fishers are asked to share a portion of their catch with the villages that own the fishing rights to the reefs, along with an additional levy per passenger (fees vary depending on the exact itinerary).

Jet Ski Tours

Jetski Safari Tours (15 Belo Circle, Pacific Harbour, tel. 345-0933 or 992-0994, sales@jetski-safari.com, www.jetski-safari.com) operates from the Bayly Beach Estate in Pacific Harbour. Call ahead to check availability and timing. It's F$110 for 15 minutes, F$190 for half an hour, and F$350 for an hour rental, per person, with two people per Jet Ski. If you're comfortable on a Jet Ski already, the four-hour excursion to Beqa Island (F$320/580 per person for double/solo use) is a better value. Children 6-16 must be accompanied by an adult. Jet-Skiing is dependent on weather and ocean conditions, so always call to check expected conditions a day before.

Golf

The 18-hole, par-72 championship **The Greens South Pacific** (tel. 773-0475, golf@

Shark Diving: Do or Don't?

Shark dives are especially popular around the Beqa Lagoon, accessed via Pacific Harbour. They're heavily marketed here and in other parts of Fiji, and have become popular thanks to television documentaries. But are they safe? The answer is...it depends.

If you do seek out a shark encounter, ask the operators whether they follow these **guidelines** set out by Responsible Shark and Ray Tourism: A Guide to Best Practice (https://sharks.panda.org/tools-publications/tourism-guide):

- Divers should be briefed to stay in one area behind the shelter of a reef or outcropping, at least three meters away from the bait and the sharks.
- Divers should not be feeding sharks directly or handling bait.
- Children, and inexperienced divers who lack buoyancy control, should not go on shark dives.
- Groups should be smaller than 10 people, including guides and photographers.
- Snorkelers and swimmers should never be in the water with feeding sharks, as their moving silhouettes can appear like large prey to the predators below.
- Guides (and divers) should never touch sharks with their hands or bodies, or create noise that changes shark behavior. Instead, guides may use long staffs to nudge away sharks who get too close to divers.

Aside from safety concerns (Fijian shark feeders have lost limbs during encounters staged for the benefit of tourists), there's a serious **ethical debate.** On the pro side, dive operators argue that it's important to raise awareness of the majesty of these pelagic creatures, whose numbers are declining worldwide. On the con side, ecologists argue that it's fundamentally wrong to turn a wild ecosystem into a circus-like environment, disrupting natural feeding patterns that regulate the rest of the food chain.

thepearlsouthpacific, 0700-1700), also known as the Pearl Championship Golf Course and Country Club, was designed by Robert Trent Jones Jr. Greens fees are F$35/75 for 9/18 holes, with discounts for guests staying at the Pearl and for players under age 16. Cart rental is F$30/50, and club rental is F$30/50. The clubhouse is a couple of kilometers inland off Queens Road. Persons dressed in jeans, bathing suits, or shoes with metal spikes are not allowed on the course. Collared shirts and golf shoes are required. The bar is open 0900-1730.

FOOD

Pacific Harbour's once-grand **Arts Village** (tel. 345-0065), conceptualized as a cultural showcase and replica "village," is now a rather sad outdoor mall, but its restaurants are the redeeming factor. It's also where you'll go for ATMs, a cybercafé, a massage place, and a laundry service. It's a landmark, and if you stay even a day in Pacific Harbour, you'll certainly end up here at some point. There's a supermarket and small produce stands if you plan to cook, as well as Smithyees Home & Food Supplies for your meats.

Skinny Bean Café (tel. 358-9869, daily 0700-1900) on the outer rim of the Arts Village, between the two banks, has espresso drinks, guava smoothies, toasted sandwiches, and free Wi-Fi for customers.

The long-standing ★ **Oasis Restaurant** (tel. 345-0617, daily 0930-2130, lunch F$6-14, dinner F$16-40), in the Arts Village marketplace, serves sandwiches, salads, and burgers at lunchtime, and more substantial main courses for dinner. The daily catch—perhaps fresh mud crab in chili, or whole fried nuqa fish—is a good bet, and people from as far as Suva come for the beef curry. A large selection of paperbacks is for sale at F$2 a book. It's pleasant sitting at the tables next to the

Guides use rods to nudge sharks away from divers.

If you choose to do a shark dive, remember that you're a visitor in their world, and seeing even one shark in the wild is a wondrous experience. Instead of staged drama, you might seek out **non-interfering dive trips**—available in almost every reef area of Fiji, though rarely advertised—in which knowledgeable local guides can take you to areas where sharks naturally converge for cleaning, mating, or feeding. See "Joining the Great Fiji Shark Count" on page 225.

pond outside. On the weekends they host local bands and have an open mic.

The **Baka Blues Café** (tel. 345-0041, stella@bakabluescafe.com, Tues.-Sun. 1100-2200, F$35-55) is the only place in Fiji you can get a taste of the American South, with a funky New Orleans-style jazz club environment, and a barbecue lover's menu that spans everything from Kansas City spare ribs to Texas rib-eye to Carolina pulled pork. The cocktails are creative and most weekends have live music.

The Refreshment Counter (Mon.-Fri. 0600-1900, Sat.-Sun. 0600-1700) at the Pic'n Pac Supermarket in the Arts Village marketplace serves sandwiches at F$2, and chicken or fish-and-chips for F$4.80. There's also ice cream.

The **Water's Edge Bar and Grill** (tel. 345-0145, Mon.-Thurs. 0930-1600, Fri.-Sat. 0930-2030), between Tsulu and the marketplace, has a large terrace overlooking the front pool. They serve Indian dishes (F$14-24) including curries (F$16), as well as pizza (F$19), and pasta (F$18-28).

Perkins Pizza (tel. 345-2244, daily 0930-2100, F$19-27), on the side of the Arts Village marketplace facing the highway, has 20 varieties of pizza.

Outside the Arts Village, near the police post, is a welcome addition: **The Establishment** (corner of Hibiscus and River Drives, tel. 773-0028, http://establishmentfiji.com, daily 1100-2200, dinner entrees F$20-26). It serves all-day breakfast, burgers, salads, and other standards as well as alliterative nightly specials: Taco Tuesday, Thai Thursday, and Seafood Saturday.

The restaurant at **The Uprising** (Beach Rd., tel. 345-2200, www.uprisingbeachresort.com, daily 0700-2300) has a beach party environment, with generous portions and something for everyone: fish-and-chips, bangers and mash, *ota and kuita* (octopus), and so on. There are always burgers, pizzas, and a curry of the day. Thursdays are island night from 1930 onward, with a "Polynesian" fire-knife show and buffet. Happy hour (1600-1800 daily) gets lively with cheap drinks and the bonus of free Wi-Fi. The house band plays live music 1800-2100 on Tuesdays, Thursdays, Saturdays, and Sundays. On the last Friday of the month, there's a DJ and dance party.

Pacific Harbour's most exclusive restaurant is **Seduce** (tel. 345-0022, Tues.-Sat., F$45-75) at the Pearl, specializing in fish and beef dishes. There are special prix fixe dinners on holidays, and sometimes a *lovo*. Reservations, and formal or smart-casual dress, are required.

ACCOMMODATIONS

Under US$50

One kilometer west of the bridge at Pacific Harbour is the friendly **Coral Coast Christian Center** (Queens Rd., tel. 345-0178, www.christiancampfiji.org). It offers four five-bed rooms called "Kozy Korner" rooms, with a good communal kitchen and cold showers at F$15/28/41 single/double/triple. The four adjoining motel units go for F$40/55 single/double, complete with private bath, kitchen, fridge, and fan. The two family units are F$45/62/77 single/double/triple (plus F$10 for air-conditioning). Camping costs F$9 per person. A small selection of snack foods is sold at the office. The camp is just across the highway from long, golden Loloma Beach, which has good snorkeling. Watch your valuables if you swim there. On weekends the property is often fully booked by church groups. No alcohol is permitted on the premises.

Next door, **Deuba Inn** (Queens Rd., tel. 345-0544, theislander@connect.com.fj) has eight small rooms with shared bath at F$45/50 single/double, and five self-catering units at F$80/90 for four/five people. Camping space costs F$15 per person. The restaurant serves good meals, and the Sand Bar (closed Mon.) is handy if you're staying at the "dry" Christian Center next door.

Tsulu Beach Bunkhouse & Apartments (tel. 345-0065) occupies the top floor of a mock-colonial two-story building at the Arts Village. You can choose between apartments, rooms, and air-conditioned dorms, but they're all rather run-down. Bunk beds in dorms are F$25-30, rooms with shared bath are F$63 single or double, and rooms with private bath are F$85. Children are not allowed in the rooms, so the self-catering apartments (F$96/126/285 one/two/four bedrooms) are for families. Guests have access to a communal kitchen and lounge. The Ritz Kona Café opposite the reception serves breakfast. To reach the beach, cross the highway and walk west a hundred meters till you're opposite the post office, then turn left down the lane to the beach.

★ **The Uprising Beach Resort** (Beach Rd., tel. 345-2200, www.uprisingbeachresort.com), a little east of the Arts Village, is set right on a long beach that stretches west to the mouth of the Qaraniqio River. The 24-bed dormitory at the back of the property is F$35 per person. The six attractive thatched beachfront *bures* are F$180 single or double, while the six garden-view *bures* are F$160 double. The *bures* are spacious and accommodate up to four (the third and fourth person are F$20 each). You can pitch your own tent near the dorm or on the sandy beach at F$20 per person. A light breakfast is included. Facilities include a swimming pool, open-air restaurant-bar, laundry service, and free Internet-enabled computers at the reception. It's an upbeat party spot for locals as well as tourists, with frequent live music.

US$50-150

Clean, comfortable, and ideally situated for divers, ★ **Club Oceanus** (Atoll Place, tel. 345-0498, http://club-oceanus-resort-fj.book.direct, F$150-250 s/d) is home to Aqua-Trek Beqa dive shop. The 10 rooms in a long block have baths, fans, TVs, and full cooking facilities (use of the air-conditioning is F$10 extra). The room closest to the water has an extra loft space and is priced the same as the doubles, so it's the best value. The manager can organize scuba diving discounts for you. The property is quite pleasant, with spacious riverside grounds and a tiny pool. Breakfast is included at the on-site Brizo's Bar and Grill, which also serves drinks, lunch (F$12-22), and dinner (F$19-F52).

Nanette's Accommodation Villa 108 (108 River Dr., tel. 331-6316 or 345-2041, www.nanettes.com.fj or www.nanettespacificharbour.com, $150 d), beside Dive Connections, has four rooms with private bath. Continental breakfast is included. Communal cooking facilities and a fridge are provided, and there's a sheltered swimming pool out back. It's one of Pacific Harbour's best values.

Villa Waikeli (Belo Circle, tel. 345-0328, www.airbnb.com/rooms/5039736, US$62) is a large, modern home designed by an architect. The Cockburn family manages it, and there are two fan-cooled rooms for rent with a bathroom shared between them. A cooked breakfast, laundry, and Wi-Fi are included. It's rather upscale with a modern lounge and garden, and the hosts are as engaged or nonintrusive as you prefer. The villa overlooks the Qaraniqio River, a five-minute walk to the Pearl and to the beach.

Harbor Property Services Ltd. (tel. 345-0959, www.fijirealty.com), with an office at the Arts Village, rents out 22 of the privately owned Pacific Harbour villas at F$180-300 for up to six persons. All villas have kitchens, lounges, and washing machines, and some also have a pool. The minimum stay is three nights, and there's a reduction after a week. A one-time cleaning fee of F$50 is charged, plus F$9 a day for gas and electricity. **Resort Homes** (tel. 345-0034, www.resorthomesfiji.com), also at the Arts Village, offers similar properties at F$1,000 a week and up.

Over US$150

Pacific Harbour's largest hotel is **The Pearl** (Queens Rd., tel. 773-0022, www.thepearlsouthpacific.com), a three-story building launched as a Travelodge in 1972. After several changes of ownership and expansions, it's now a 4.5-star resort, conference center, and spa. The location couldn't be better, at the mouth of the Qaraniqio River between Queens Road and a long, sandy beach, on attractive grounds and with a sloped swimming pool. The marina has moorings for yachts. Marina- and ocean-view rooms have

The Pearl is next to a marina in Pacific Harbour.

full glass windows and tiny patios, but none of the rooms are very far from the beach. Rates range from F$400 for a garden room to F$950 for the penthouse suite. There are several eateries to choose from, all with fine views of the marina, pool, or sea. The sesame tuna with pawpaw (papaya) salsa over wok-fried noodles (F$43) is an unlikely but delicious blend of flavors, and the cassava fries (F$10) are addictive. There's a kids' club 1100-1800, for ages 4-12, with plenty of activities such as fish feeding, Fijian language games, and coconut bowling. The hotel is also a popular place for Suva's fancier class to hold weddings and celebrations, and it has a convenience store, a Jack's souvenir shop, and a Senikai Spa.

Most of the units at the **ULTIQA Fiji Palms Beach Resort** (Queens Rd., tel. 345-0050) have been sold as part of a timeshare scheme, but two-bedroom, two-bathroom apartments are sometimes available on a casual basis at F$200/1,200 a day/week (Sat.-Sat.). There's a massage *bure*, pool, and restaurant, and the resort is right next door to the Pearl, sharing the same beach on the other side of the river. The rooms are modern and clean, with air-conditioning, fully equipped kitchens, patios, and washers/dryers—making this a high-value option for travelers who don't need a lot of organized activities. Each apartment sleeps up to six with one queen bed, two twin beds, and a double sofa bed in the living area. The entire property is no-smoking.

Tiri Villas (50 Rovodrau Rd., tel. 345-0552, www.tirivillas.com) is among the mangroves near the mouth of the Deuba River, four kilometers east of Pacific Harbour. The adjacent mangrove forest may interest bird-watchers. The six well-constructed beach villas are F$340 double, the five garden villas are F$245, and the three group villas (which have five twin beds) are F$204. Rates include breakfast, and there's a happy hour at the Pacific Breeze restaurant/bar overlooking Rovodrau Bay 1700-1900 daily. There's a private beach and pool. Tiri Villas is three kilometers down a gravel road off Queens Road from Moti Lal and Sons. A taxi from the highway will charge F$6. The entire property is no-smoking.

INFORMATION AND SERVICES

Rosie Holidays (tel. 345-0655) in the Arts Village can make any required hotel or tour bookings, and they also represent Thrifty Car Rental. Call ahead if you want to pick up a car here.

Both ANZ Bank and Bank South Pacific have **ATM machines** in the Arts Village marketplace. The Bank South Pacific also has a branch open weekdays 0930-1600.

The main Pacific Harbour **post office** is next to the Arts Village.

R.L. Laundromat (tel. 918-7823, daily 0900-1700), at the Arts Village, charges F$5 to wash, F$1.50 to dry and fold your clothes for you.

TRANSPORTATION

All of the Queens Road express buses between Nadi and Suva stop opposite the entrance to the Pearl, a kilometer from the Arts Village. The slower Galoa buses and some other local buses will stop right in front of the Arts Village itself (advise the driver beforehand), which is closer to the Uprising hotel.

The air-conditioned Fiji Express leaves from the front door of the Pearl for Suva at 1050 and 1615 (F$10) and for Nadi at 0810 and 1625 (F$20). Cheaper and almost as fast are the regular Pacific Transport express buses, which stop on the highway outside the Pearl: to Nadi Airport at 0750, 0930, 1035, 1315, 1605, and 1835 (148 km, three hours, F$12), and to Suva at 1015, 1100, 1155, 1555, 1930, and 2115 (49 km, one hour, F$4.85). Sunbeam Transport buses to Lautoka stop here at 0830, 1100, 1210, 1415, and 1515.

Your Holiday Massage

a massage *bure* on Sonaisali Island

Masseuses in Fiji are trained in a number of ways: in villages, on the job, via a three-month course at Fiji National University in Suva, or through an in-house beauty school run by the Senikai Spa chain, which operates in many hotels. In villages next to major resorts, generations of women pass on the skill to each other. Masseurs in Fiji are rare, as it's considered a female occupation.

The basic style is Swedish, although you may find other offerings. Most use heated coconut oil scented with Fijian flowers such as jasmine or frangipani. Unscented oils and lotions are unheard of; if you're scent-averse or allergic, bring your own preferred massage oil and the staff will bemusedly accommodate you.

You'll typically be asked to undress except for your underwear and lie under a sheet or a couple of towels. Higher-end places will give you a pretty sulu to wrap around yourself. Open-air beachside massages don't require undressing.

The price can vary wildly, from F$40 or whatever you can negotiate with someone on the beach, to F$200 at a five-star hotel. Quality, of course, also varies, but you'll find the masseuses accommodating if you know what you want.

- The tiny **Bula Massage Clinic** (Shop 10B, Arts Village, tel. 345-0024 or 805-8603) in Pacific Harbour offers a unique 75-minute "octopus" massage (F$180), with four women rubbing you down at the same time.
- In Suva, the luxurious **Pure Fiji Day Spa** (52 Karsanji St., Vatuwaqa, tel. 338-3611, spa@purefiji.com, www.purefiji.com/spa-info/) takes bookings Monday-Saturday for a range of facials and massages (F$50-385) using its signature plant-extract products. The spa is between two solariums where the company grows its organic produce for creating lotions and soaps.
- **High-end hotels** may offer a complimentary 10-minute foot massage to get you into the spa, or a massage discount if your room isn't ready when you arrive. It's worthwhile to ask if there are any such offers when you check in.

★ Beqa Island

Beqa (MBENG-ga) is a quiet, laid-back island only 10 kilometers south of Viti Levu but feels worlds away. The beaches are soft and uncrowded, and there's little to do but enjoy the natural beauty of sand and sea. The island is home to the famous Fijian fire walkers; Rukua, Naceva, and Dakuibeqa are fire-walking villages. Nowadays, the fire walkers perform mostly at hotels on the Coral Coast, although the local resorts occasionally stage a show.

At low tide, you can hike part of the 27 kilometers around the island: the Rukua to Nawaisomo and Dakuni to Naceva portions are not hard, but the section through Lalati can be difficult. Malumu Bay, between the two branches of the island, is thought to be a drowned crater. Climb Korolevu (439 m), the island's highest peak, from Nawaisomo or Lalati. Kadavu Island is visible to the south of Beqa.

DAY TRIPS

Rivers Fiji (tel. 345-0147, info@riversfiji.com, www.riversfiji.com) offers day trips (US$217 pp) to Beqa Island in two-person, sit-on-top sea kayaks. You can opt for a round-trip transfer from your hotel (F$45-65 per person, from anywhere between Nadi and Suva) or meet at the Rivers Fiji office, next to the Arts Village in Pacific Harbour. You cross to Beqa by catamaran, then explore a tiny uninhabited island and paddle into Malumu Bay. Hundreds of fruit bats cling to the trees deep inside this cliff-lined bay. A secret mangrove tunnel provides an escape south to the great blue beyond. Lunch is on a calm, white-sand beach, and there's a break to sunbathe or snorkel before heading back. If you're lucky, on the return trip you might see pilot whales and dolphins alongside your boat. In the U.S., you can book this trip through the river tours company OARS (U.S. tel. 209/736-0597, http://oars.com). Children under eight are not allowed.

Jetski Safari Tours (15 Belo Circle, Pacific Harbour, tel. 345-0933 or 992-0994, sales@jetski-safari.com, www.jetski-safari.com) operates half-day excursions to Beqa Island at F$320 per person, with two people per Jet Ski; if you want one to yourself, it's F$580. Tours leave the Bayly Beach Estate in Pacific Harbour at 0820, after a safety briefing, and then cross the open ocean of the Beqa Passage. There's a stop on Beqa Island for snorkeling and a beach picnic lunch before returning four hours later.

ACCOMMODATIONS

You won't see marketing materials anywhere for the fine little ★ **Lawaki Beach House** (tel. 992-1621 or 368-4088, info@lawakibeachhousefiji.com, www.lawakibeachhousefiji.com), on the western shore, which relies on word of mouth and repeat visitors rather than agency bookings. It's the kind of place you wish would get more business and wish you could keep secret so that you'll always be able to get a room. Facing the golden sands of **Lawaki Beach**, it's one of the few hotels in Fiji owned by an indigenous Fijian, lovingly tended by Sam Tawake, from nearby Naceva village, and his Swiss wife, Christine. There are a handful of *bures* for one or two people (F$100-180) and one six-bed family *bure* or dormitory at F$60 per person. If you're alone and there's an empty *bure*, they'll often upgrade you from the dorm. To camp (with your own tent) is F$40 per person. A mandatory meal plan is F$72 per adult and F$55 per child, and meals are fresh and lovely.

Visits and tours of the organic hillside farms can be arranged, and fishing, surfing, scuba diving, table tennis, and a demonstration of Beqa's famous fire walking are available for a fee. But mainly the thing to do is come here and sit in a hammock, pet a dog or two, and take an occasional snorkel out to the reef. Boat transfers from Navua are F$40

Beqa Island

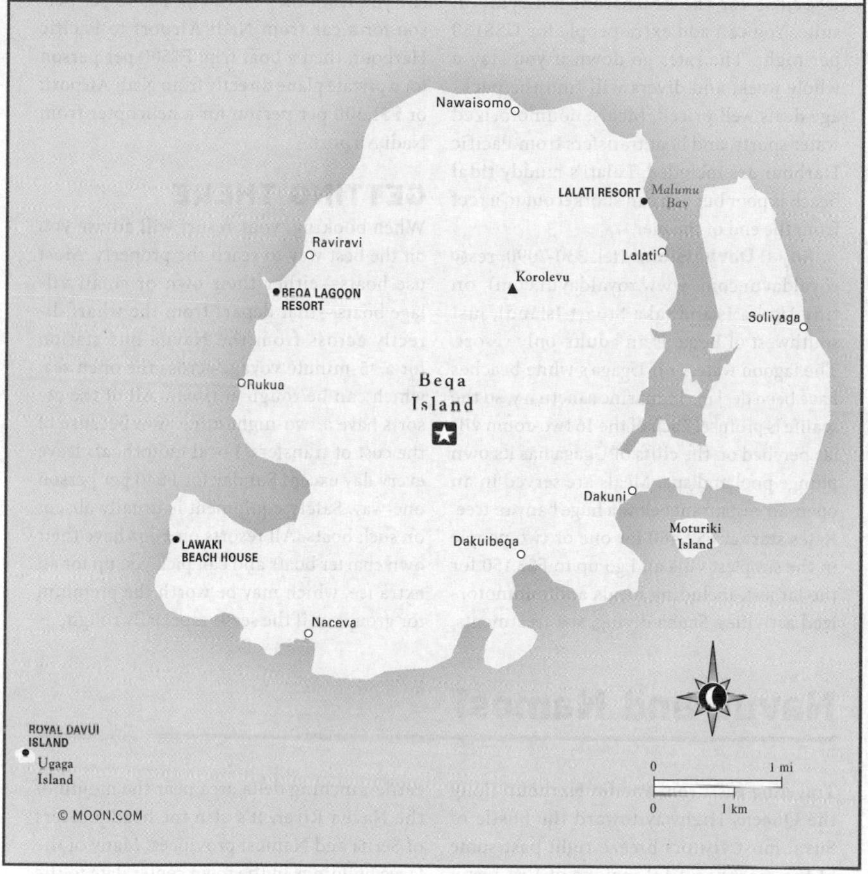

if you take a local boat departing Monday-Saturday around noon, or you can charter the *Lawaki Delight* for up to eight people for F$315.

Beqa Lagoon Resort (tel. 330-4042, www.beqalagoonresort.com) on the west side of Beqa between Raviravi and Rukua villages dates back to 1991. The gardens and central pond are lovely, and there's an infinity swimming pool near the restaurant. There's also an open-air spa. Scuba diving in the Beqa Lagoon and surfing runs to Frigate Passage are the main reasons people come here. Each of the 12 beachfront *bures* has a private courtyard and plunge pool, starting at US$499 per person, double occupancy (singles pay more). A two-bedroom unit is good for two couples or a family at F$439 per person. All rates include three meals (not drinks) and round-trip transfers from either Nadi or Suva airport.

Lalati Resort (tel. 368-0453, www.lalatifiji.com), at the north opening of Malamu Bay, was one of Fiji's first eco-resorts, with rainwater collection, a gray-water irrigation system for the landscaped gardens, and composting toilets. As it ages, it's more like a decent 3.5-star dive resort than a luxury retreat. A three-night package (the minimum stay) starts at US$1,122 for one person or US$1,320 for two people in a cottage, up to US$2,835 for the beachfront honeymoon suite. You can add extra people for US$160 per night. The rates go down if you stay a whole week, and divers will find the package deals well priced. Meals, nonmotorized water sports, and boat transfers from Pacific Harbour are included. Lalati's muddy tidal beach is poor but you can snorkel out to a reef from the end of the pier.

Royal Davui Island (tel. 330-7090, res@royaldavui.com, www.royaldavui.com), on tiny Ugaga Island (aka Stuart Island), just southwest of Beqa, is an adults-only resort. The lagoon waters off Ugaga's white beaches have been declared a marine sanctuary, so the sealife is profuse. Each of the 16 two-room villas perched on the cliffs of Ugaga has its own plunge pool and spa. Meals are served in an open-air restaurant below a huge banyan tree. Rates start at F$2,460 for one or two people in the simplest villa and go up to F$3,150 for the largest, including meals and nonmotorized activities. Scuba diving, spa treatments, sportfishing, and semisubmersible rides all cost extra. Transfers are expensive and insulate you from the rest of Fiji: F$300 per person for a car from Nadi Airport to Pacific Harbour, then a boat trip; F$500 per person for a private plane directly from Nadi Airport; or F$1,300 per person for a helicopter from Nadi Airport.

GETTING THERE

When booking, your resort will advise you on the best way to reach the property. Most use boats—either their own or small village boats—that depart from the wharf directly across from the Navua bus station for a 45-minute voyage across the open sea, which can be rough at times. All of the resorts have a two-night minimum because of the cost of transfers. Local motorboats leave every day except Sunday for F$40 per person one-way. Safety equipment is usually absent on such boats. All resorts on Beqa have their own charter boats and can pick you up for an extra fee, which may be worth the premium for groups or if the sea is especially rough.

Navua and Namosi

Traveling east from Pacific Harbour along the Queens Highway toward the bustle of Suva, most visitors breeze right past some of the most beautiful regions of Viti Levu. If you take your time on this drive, you'll be rewarded with several interesting stops. The Navua River offers a plethora of water-based activities for the adventurous, while the jungles and mountainous highlands of Namosi are some of the most welcoming interiors of Fiji.

NAVUA

The bustling riverside town of **Navua,** 39 kilometers west of Suva, is the market center of the mostly Indo-Fijian rice-growing and dairy cattle-ranching delta area near the mouth of the Navua River. It's also the headquarters of Serua and Namosi provinces. Many of the large buildings in the town center date to the early 20th century, when this was an important sugar milling town.

For visitors, Navua town is only important as the gateway to the fabulous Navua River. The lower Navua below Namuamua is navigable in large outboard motorboats, while rubber rafts are used on the much faster upper Navua through the narrow **Navua River Gorge.** Either way, a river trip will give you a memorable glimpse of emerald-lush southeastern Viti Levu. All buses between Suva and Nadi stop at Navua.

TOP EXPERIENCE

★ White-Water Rafting

Rivers Fiji (tel. 345-0147, info@riversfiji.com, www.riversfiji.com) leads exciting white-water trips on inflatable kayaks or rafts through the stunning Navua River gorge. Trips start at the office behind the Arts Village in Pacific Harbour, but pickups can be arranged from elsewhere on the Coral Coast or from Suva. An all-day trip is required to see the lush, remote Upper Navua River (US$239, Mon., Wed., and Fri. 0645-1800), which is fed by as many as 70 waterfalls. The river slices a deep chasm through rainforest and formidable black volcanic canyons, some as narrow as five feet wide—just enough for your inflatable raft. Other trips include inflatable kayaking on the gentler Middle Navua River (US$185, Tues., Thurs., and Sat.) and a combination of kayaking through the Wainikoroiluva ('Luva) River in the Namosi Valley, followed by an exhilarating ride in a motorized punt down the lower Navua Canyon (US$179, Tues., Thurs., and Sat.). There's also an eight-day trip that combines these and adds in some sea kayaking and zip-lining, with overnight village stays (US$2,899 pp, based on double occupancy; $550 single supplement).

Rivers Fiji adheres to ecotourism best practices such as "Leave No Trace" (packing out all garbage generated by the trips) and working with local village residents as river guides and staff. All trips include helmets, life jackets, snacks, lunch, and transfers. Because the waters can be rough, children under age eight are not allowed. Booking online via the website nets you an immediate 10 percent discount.

Discover Fiji Tours (tel. 346-0380, 346-0480, 924-8133, or 710-3330, discoverfiji@connect.com.fj, www.discoverfijitours.com) offers a dizzying array of river trips, the most heavily marketed of which is the rather staged Jewel of Fiji tour, which features a "warrior" escort, kava ceremony, waterfall swim, 30-minute ride on a woven *bilibili* raft, and a trip down the river on a motorized canoe. It's often filled with cruise ship passengers. More adventurous travelers should opt for the "Namosi 2" or "Serua 3" trips, which take you upriver in a motorboat and let you come downriver part of the way in a rubber white-water raft. Discover Fiji's prices vary widely depending on time of year, size of your group, and who you book through; for the best rate, send an email ahead of time and then compare with the price quoted to you by your hotel or travel agency.

Zip-Lining

ZipFiji (tel. 930-0545, www.zip-fiji.com) has set up 16 connecting zip lines through a private section of the canopy over the Wainadoi River valley and rainforest. It's a two-kilometer, hour-long thrill ride that lets you travel at speeds up to 60 kph. There's some hiking through the rainforest on the way to the platforms, and guided tree climbs, rappelling, and a cave tour are also offered. The rate for bookings directly through the website is F$235/person (children pay the same as adults), plus pickup/drop-off. Travelers report getting better deals and packages through hotels, sometimes as low as F$90, so shop around.

KILA ECO ADVENTURE PARK

About 22 kilometers west of Suva is **Kila Eco Adventure Park** (tel. 331-7454, kilatours@kilaworld.com, www.kilaworld.com, daily 1000-1630). Its marketing materials are aggressive (Killer Giant Swing! Leap of Faith Zipline!), but it's actually a scenic jungle park with 10 kilometers of paths, waterfalls, picnic *bures,* a botanical garden, and a freshwater pool. The basic entry fee is F$12.50. You can add activities such as a guided hike, rappelling, zip-lining, a ropes course, and a 12-meter-high giant swing for F$60 per activity, or opt for an inclusive half-day or full-day package. There are discounts for groups of 5 or 10, and for a family of two adults and two children under age 15 (F$480 all day, all activities). Hotel guests report that it's best to take a taxi, as booking a transportation-included

1

2

package from a hotel will cost you double or triple the price of admission.

NAMOSI

Inland from Kila is **Namosi village,** spectacularly situated below massive **Mount Voma**, with sheer stone cliffs on all sides. You can climb Mount Voma in a day for a sweeping view of much of Viti Levu. It's steep, but not too difficult. Allow at least four hours for the roundtrip hike to the 927-meter high peak. Inquire at the village to hire a guide. While you're there, the old Catholic church in the village is worth a visit.

TOP EXPERIENCE

★ Namosi Village Stay

A truly special experience, and the best village stay anywhere in Fiji, is ★ **Namosi Eco Retreat** (tel. 928-9378, 942-9141, 721-3201, bookings@trusupfiji.com, www.trusupfiji.com/namosieco), high in the rocky mountains of the Namosi Highlands. It's the brainchild of resident Danny Jason, who enlisted his home village in hosting tourists for homestays. As demand increased, they decided to build a separate set of dedicated *bures*, giving guests more privacy and comforts such as cushy mattresses. The ten *bures* are made in the traditional way, with thatch roofs and bamboo walls, and have a nearby dining hall, kitchen, and bathroom.

Guests live alongside villagers and learn how to cook on an open fire, catch prawns and river fish at night, and pick crops. The village is especially welcoming to families with children. Amenities such as massages and *mekes* can be arranged. There's just enough electricity that you can have a hot shower, but not enough to keep your devices running 24/7, which gives you a chance to enjoy village-style leisure activities: yoga and meditation on the mountain, waterfall hikes, rafting on a handmade *bilibili* (river raft), horseback riding, and river volleyball.

Getting There

From the Queens Highway at Kila Park Navua, turn up the road and drive for about an hour. It's better to go on transport arranged by the retreat, though, so that you don't miss a turn and are sure to be in a vehicle capable of traversing the rougher parts of the road.

1: Lawaki Beach House on Beqa Island **2:** Namosi Eco Retreat.

Suva and the Kadavu Group

The pulsing heart of the South Pacific, Suva is the largest and most cosmopolitan city in Oceania. Occupying a peninsula at the southeastern corner of Viti Levu, it is wetter and greener than the coast to the west, and here the emphasis is less on beach life and more on cultural and natural attractions. The city's port is always jammed with ships bringing goods and passengers from afar. Busloads of commuters and outer-islanders stream through the busy market bus station near the docks, while locals, tourists, and expat Aussies and Kiwis wander the shops and sights. Red soil, meandering creeks, and lush taro greens swirl through it all; in the early years, the streets were paved with coral.

A multiracial city of 173,000—a fifth of Fiji's total population and

Look for ★ to find recommended sights, activities, dining, and lodging.

Highlights

★ **Fiji Museum:** The outstanding exhibits in this museum, located on the site of the original village of Suva, bring Fiji's history and culture to life (page 167).

★ **Grand Pacific Hotel:** Historic and elegant, this lovingly restored Edwardian-style edifice—once a centerpiece of colonial Suva—welcomes visitors for a dip in the pool, a scenic sunset cocktail or high tea, and a glimpse back in time (page 169).

★ **Drua Experience:** Sail the waters around Suva on a real Fijian double-hulled canoe, handmade of vesi hardwood and bamboo (page 170).

★ **Colo-i-Suva Forest Park:** Enjoy some of the most accessible rainforest hiking—complete with waterfalls and swimming holes—in the South Pacific (page 191).

★ **Diving the Great Astrolabe Reef:** Virtually untouched, the fourth-largest barrier reef in the world is rich with manta rays, soft and hard corals, and pelagic and reef fish (page 197).

★ **Kayaking the Great Astrolabe Reef:** See both the reef and the Kadavu Group's wild, unspoiled coasts by paddling these calm, clear, turquoise waters (page 198).

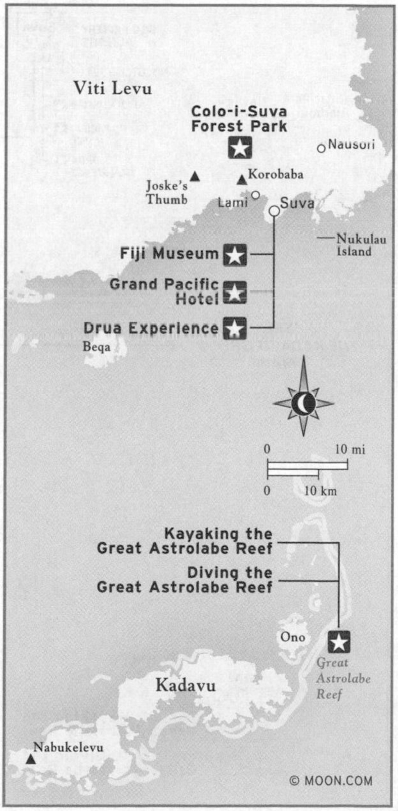

Suva and the Kadavu Group

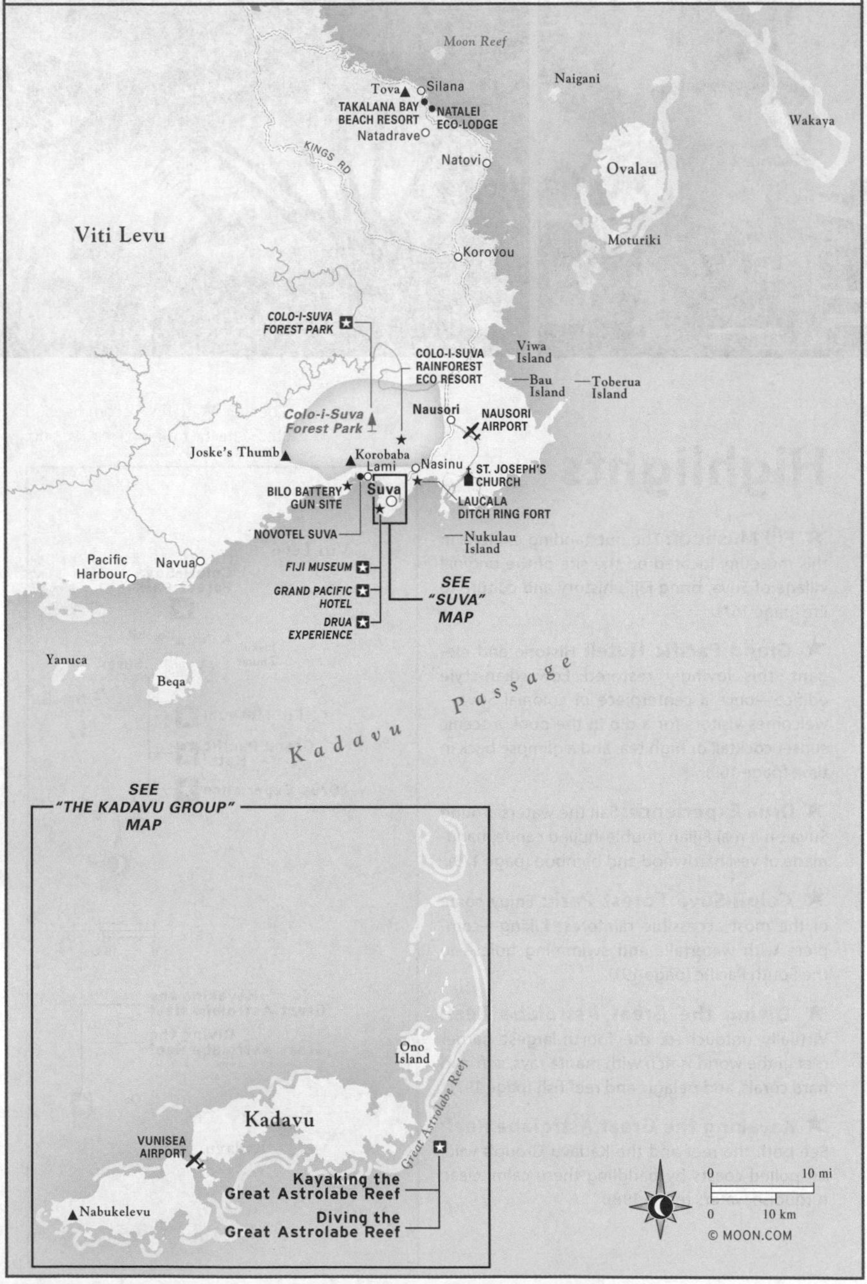
Moon Reef
Naigani
Wakaya
Tova
Silana
TAKALANA BAY BEACH RESORT
NATALEI ECO-LODGE
Natadrave
KINGS RD
Natovi
Ovalau
Viti Levu
Moturiki
Korovou
COLO-I-SUVA FOREST PARK
Viwa Island
COLO-I-SUVA RAINFOREST ECO RESORT
Bau Island
Toberua Island
Colo-i-Suva Forest Park
Nausori
NAUSORI AIRPORT
Joske's Thumb
Korobaba
Lami
Nasinu
ST. JOSEPH'S CHURCH
BILO BATTERY GUN SITE
Suva
LAUCALA DITCH RING FORT
NOVOTEL SUVA
Nukulau Island
Pacific Harbour
Navua
FIJI MUSEUM
GRAND PACIFIC HOTEL
DRUA EXPERIENCE
SEE "SUVA" MAP
Yanuca
Beqa
Kadavu Passage
SEE "THE KADAVU GROUP" MAP
Ono Island
Great Astrolabe Reef
Kadavu
VUNISEA AIRPORT
Kayaking the Great Astrolabe Reef
Diving the Great Astrolabe Reef
Nabukelevu
0 10 mi
0 10 km
© MOON.COM

Find Your Beach

- **My Suva Picnic Park** (page 169): Suva itself has no beaches, though this park along the seawall offers fine views of the sea and modern playground equipment.
- **Nukulau Island** (page 169): Out in Laucala Bay to the west of Suva, this tiny island is a great picnic spot with fine beaches for swimming.
- **Kadavu Group** (page 195): For truly special beaches, travel far south of Suva to the gorgeous white sands of the Kadavu Group, adjacent to spectacular snorkeling and diving at the Great Astrolabe Reef.

nearly half the urban population—Suva has been Fiji's commercial and political capital since the British moved the government here from Levuka in 1882. It's now a brash, up-to-date city with American-style food courts and some of the best restaurants and bars in the country. Yet despite the banks, boutiques, and Internet cafés, Suva still has a small-town feel, and you can easily walk around it in a day. About the only thing Suva lacks is a beach—though it does boast a lovely harbor, bay, and sea views all around.

To the north and east are verdant mountains that catch the trade winds, so a bit of warm tropical rain falls almost every day in Suva and the neighboring towns of Lami, Nasinu, and Nausori. The last of those is the site of the Suva airport, as well as lovely small rainforest with a startling array of birdlife, just minutes from the urban center.

Here too you'll find the gateway ports to the eastern islands, which are mellow and restful compared to the massive resorts of the west. Suva is also a jumping-off point for the southern island group of Kadavu, where small resorts nestled amid volcanic isles fringe the virtually untouched Great Astrolabe Reef.

PLANNING YOUR TIME

Although you can see all of Suva's main sights in a single busy day, it's preferable to spend two or three days in the city to soak up the lively atmosphere. Suva Market and the downtown area, the Fiji Museum, and a boat trip into Suva Harbour could each fill half a day. The main town is very walkable, and you can easily get to all of the other attractions by city bus or taxi. Sundays are quiet, with most shops and restaurants closed except for inside the malls and hotels. It's worth dressing up to attend church and hear the marvelous choral singing.

If you're in Suva for a long stay, pack an umbrella for both the rainy mornings and hot sunny afternoons. December-April you can expect at least some rain every day.

North of the city are the eastern gateways out of Viti Levu: the airport, and ferry landings for ships headed to Ovalau, Vanua Levu, and Taveuni. From a pleasant rainforest just a hop from the airport to the playgrounds of spinner dolphins, there are treasures here worth exploring. Traffic can get congested; allow extra time for airport trips during rush hour, approximately 0800-1000 and 1500-1800.

Previous: a *drua* (double-hulled canoe) in Suva Harbour; the clock tower at Thurston Gardens; kayaks at Colo-i-Suva Rainforest Eco Resort.

Suva

The southern stretch of downtown retains the atmosphere of the long-gone British Raj, with its lawn bowling grounds, presidential palace, botanical garden, and other historical sites. The downtown core is about the only place in Fiji where you'll see a building taller than a palm tree, as growing numbers of high-rise offices and business hotels overlook the historic retail district and market.

From sea level, the city rises to hilly residential areas. The outlying areas offer a plethora of academic institutions where Pacific Islanders from all over come to study: the Fiji School of Medicine, the University of the South Pacific (USP), and the Fiji Institute of Technology are all here. Additionally, the headquarters of many regional organizations and diplomatic missions have been established here.

The North Suva sites are about a 15-minute taxi or bus ride from downtown. The remainder of the city sights can be seen in a pleasant half-day walking tour, including a couple of hours in the museum. For a deeper dive, you can take a boat trip to historic Nukulau Island.

SIGHTS

North Suva

The story of Suva starts once upon a time, before recorded history, with the **Laucala Ditch Ring Fort** (on Sekoula Rd. at Tagimoucia Place, tel. 331-9637, lbssfiji@gmail.com). This twin ring fortification covers 1.16 hectares in the Laucala Beach area on the outskirts of Suva. Not much is known about the people who built it, and to be honest, there's not much to look at here—you can see a well-defined ditch and four causeways—so visiting may be of interest only to the most avid history buffs. But there's a proposal to reconstruct a historically accurate version and add a cultural center here.

Cross the peninsula to the Queens Road to see the picturesque **Suva Cemetery,** where the graves decorated with colorful sulus are a favorite for visiting photographers. Suva's four World War I and five World War II casualties are buried here. These days, graves are dug by prisoners at the neighboring **Suva Prison,** a concrete block built in 1913. The prison also runs art workshops, and the **Tagimoucia Art Gallery** (www.corrections.gov.fj/tagimoucia-art-gallery, tel. 330-3512, Mon.-Fri. 1000-1500) exhibits and sells artworks created by prisoners. Nearby is the prominent **Fosters Brewery.**

Opposite the prison is the **Royal Suva Yacht Club** (http://thegalleyfiji.com, tel. 720-0810, Tues.-Sun. 0700-1500 and 1700-2100, closed Mon.), founded in 1940. The security guard may be able to suggest someone willing to sign you in. Remove your hat as you enter the building. The club's restaurant is a treat and the bar has some of the most affordable drink prices in Suva; you'll meet some yachties, and maybe you'll find a boat to crew on.

Take Waimanu Road on the way back downtown so that you can pass by **Borron House,** built in 1927 by one of the early plantation owners. It was converted to a guesthouse for distinguished official visitors from abroad; former U.S. First Lady Eleanor Roosevelt and Great Britain's Princess Anne are among those who've rested at the stately manor.

South Suva

THURSTON GARDENS

Most visitors start their dig into the past at **Thurston Gardens** (admission free), the site of the original village of Suva. When the British co-opted Suva as their capital in 1882, they evicted the village and moved it to Suva Vou, or "new Suva," across the harbor. The

Suva

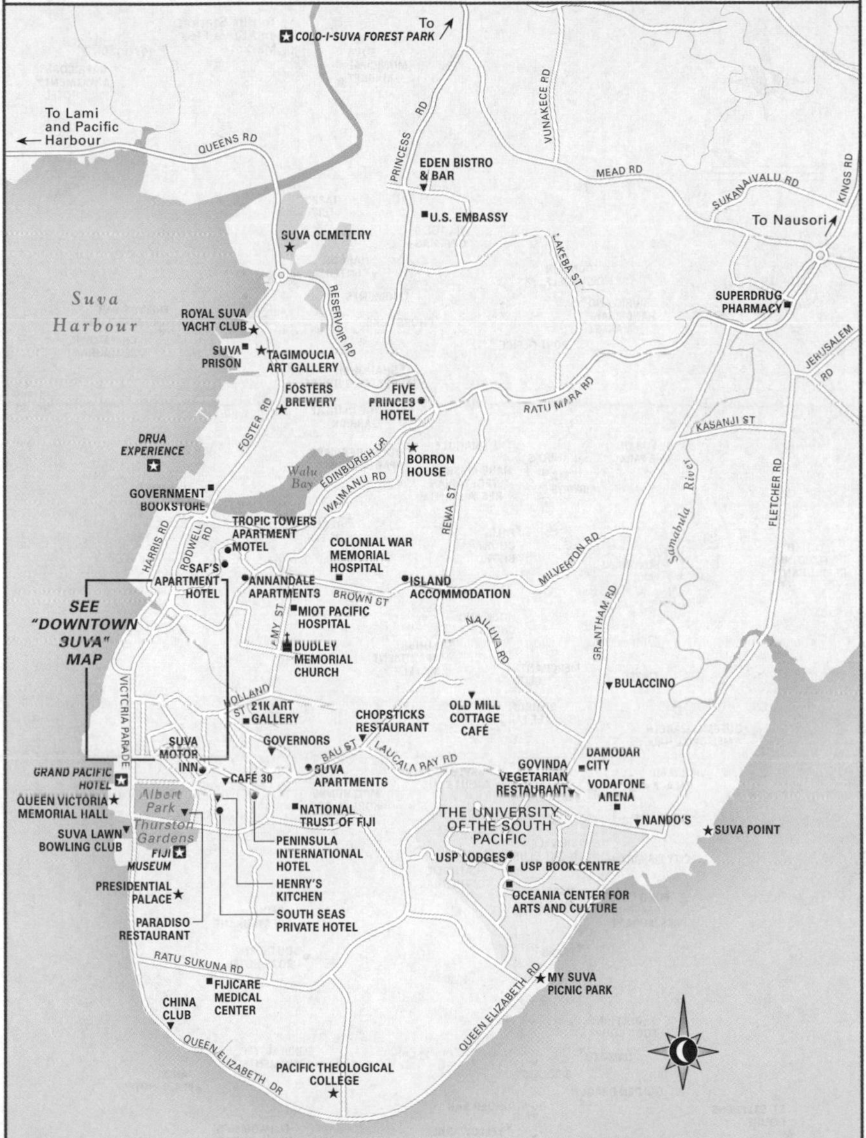
COLO-I-SUVA FOREST PARK
To
To Lami and Pacific Harbour
QUEENS RD
PRINCESS RD
VUNAKECE RD
EDEN BISTRO & BAR
MEAD RD
SUKANAIVALU RD
KINGS RD
U.S. EMBASSY
To Nausori
SUVA CEMETERY
LAKEBA ST
Suva Harbour
RESERVOIR RD
SUPERDRUG PHARMACY
ROYAL SUVA YACHT CLUB
SUVA PRISON
TAGIMOUCIA ART GALLERY
JERUSALEM RD
FOSTERS BREWERY
FIVE PRINCES HOTEL
RATU MARA RD
FOSTER RD
KASANJI ST
DRUA EXPERIENCE
EDINBURGH DR
BORRON HOUSE
Walu Bay
WAIMANU RD
FLETCHER RD
GOVERNMENT BOOKSTORE
REWA ST
Samabula River
HARRIS RD
RODWELL RD
TROPIC TOWERS APARTMENT MOTEL
COLONIAL WAR MEMORIAL HOSPITAL
MILVERTON RD
SAF'S APARTMENT HOTEL
ANNANDALE APARTMENTS
BROWN ST
ISLAND ACCOMMODATION
SEE "DOWNTOWN SUVA" MAP
MIOT PACIFIC HOSPITAL
GRANTHAM RD
AMY ST
NAILUVA RD
DUDLEY MEMORIAL CHURCH
VICTORIA PARADE
BULACCINO
HOLLAND ST
21K ART GALLERY
OLD MILL COTTAGE CAFÉ
CHOPSTICKS RESTAURANT
GOVERNORS
BAU ST
LAUCALA BAY RD
SUVA MOTOR INN
DAMODAR CITY
GOVINDA VEGETARIAN RESTAURANT
GRAND PACIFIC HOTEL
CAFÉ 30
SUVA APARTMENTS
VODAFONE ARENA
QUEEN VICTORIA MEMORIAL HALL
Albert Park
NATIONAL TRUST OF FIJI
THE UNIVERSITY OF THE SOUTH PACIFIC
NANDO'S
SUVA POINT
Thurston Gardens
SUVA LAWN BOWLING CLUB
PENINSULA INTERNATIONAL HOTEL
FIJI MUSEUM
USP LODGES
USP BOOK CENTRE
PRESIDENTIAL PALACE
HENRY'S KITCHEN
OCEANIA CENTER FOR ARTS AND CULTURE
PARADISO RESTAURANT
SOUTH SEAS PRIVATE HOTEL
RATU SUKUNA RD
MY SUVA PICNIC PARK
FIJICARE MEDICAL CENTER
CHINA CLUB
QUEEN ELIZABETH DR
PACIFIC THEOLOGICAL COLLEGE
0
0.5 mi
0
0.5 km
© MOON.COM

Downtown Suva

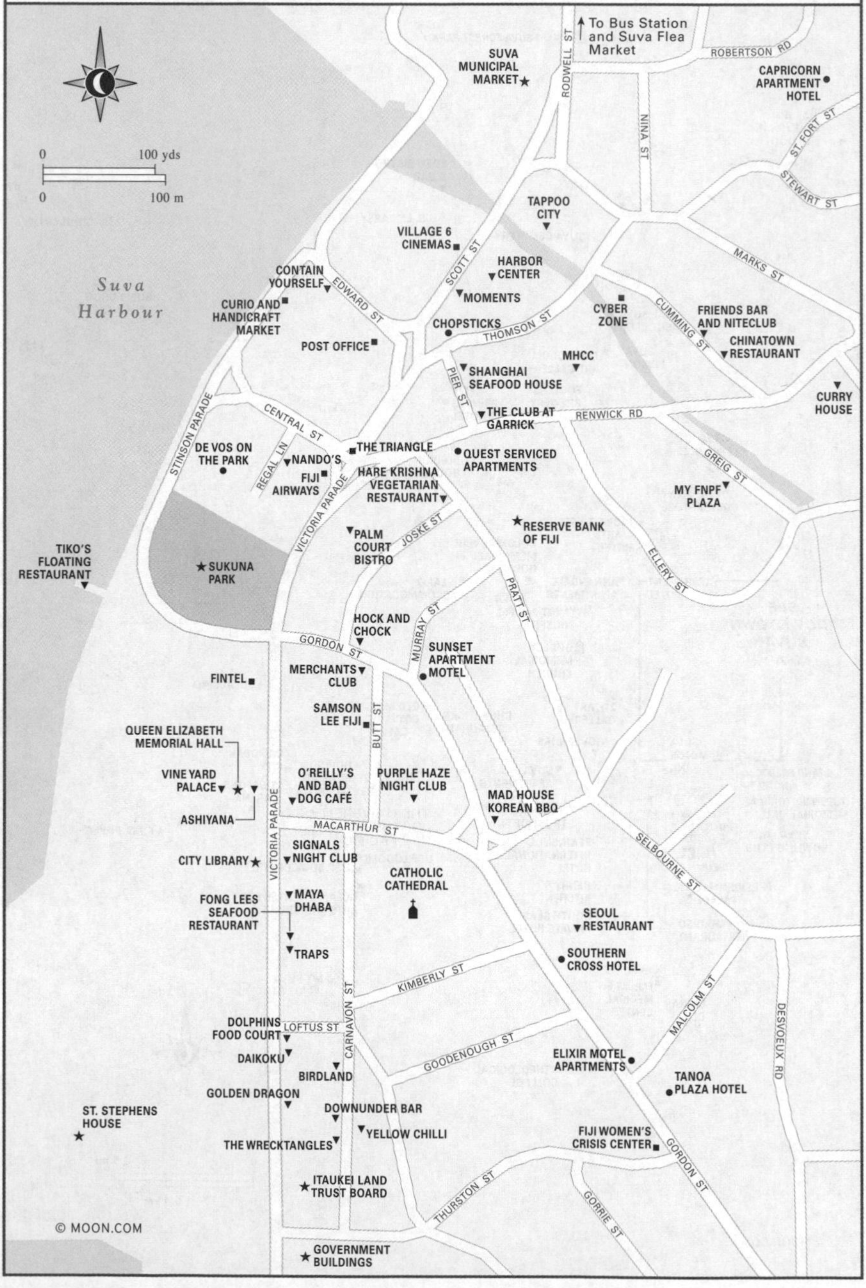

To Bus Station and Suva Flea Market
SUVA MUNICIPAL MARKET
ROBERTSON RD
CAPRICORN APARTMENT HOTEL
RODWELL ST
NINA ST
ST. FORT ST
STEWART ST
0
100 yds
0
100 m
TAPPOO CITY
VILLAGE 6 CINEMAS
SCOTT ST
HARBOR CENTER
MARKS ST
CONTAIN YOURSELF
EDWARD ST
MOMENTS
Suva Harbour
CURIO AND HANDICRAFT MARKET
CHOPSTICKS
THOMSON ST
CYBER ZONE
CUMMING ST
FRIENDS BAR AND NITECLUB
CHINATOWN RESTAURANT
POST OFFICE
MHCC
SHANGHAI SEAFOOD HOUSE
PIER ST
CURRY HOUSE
STINSON PARADE
CENTRAL ST
THE CLUB AT GARRICK
RENWICK RD
THE TRIANGLE
QUEST SERVICED APARTMENTS
GREIG ST
DE VOS ON THE PARK
REGAL LN
NANDO'S
FIJI AIRWAYS
HARE KRISHNA VEGETARIAN RESTAURANT
MY FNPF PLAZA
VICTORIA PARADE
RESERVE BANK OF FIJI
JOSKE ST
PALM COURT BISTRO
TIKO'S FLOATING RESTAURANT
SUKUNA PARK
ELLERY ST
PRATT ST
MURRAY ST
HOCK AND CHOCK
GORDON ST
SUNSET APARTMENT MOTEL
MERCHANTS CLUB
FINTEL
SAMSON LEE FIJI
BUTT ST
QUEEN ELIZABETH MEMORIAL HALL
VINE YARD PALACE
ASHIYANA
O'REILLY'S AND BAD DOG CAFÉ
PURPLE HAZE NIGHT CLUB
MAD HOUSE KOREAN BBQ
VICTORIA PARADE
MACARTHUR ST
SELBOURNE ST
CITY LIBRARY
SIGNALS NIGHT CLUB
CATHOLIC CATHEDRAL
FONG LEES SEAFOOD RESTAURANT
MAYA DHABA
SEOUL RESTAURANT
TRAPS
SOUTHERN CROSS HOTEL
KIMBERLY ST
CARNAVON ST
MALCOLM ST
DESVOEUX RD
DOLPHINS FOOD COURT
LOFTUS ST
DAIKOKU
GOODENOUGH ST
ELIXIR MOTEL APARTMENTS
BIRDLAND
TANOA PLAZA HOTEL
GOLDEN DRAGON
DOWNUNDER BAR
ST. STEPHENS HOUSE
YELLOW CHILLI
THE WRECKTANGLES
FIJI WOMEN'S CRISIS CENTER
GORDON ST
ITAUKEI LAND TRUST BOARD
THURSTON ST
GORRIE ST
© MOON.COM
GOVERNMENT BUILDINGS

SUVA AND THE KADAVU GROUP
SUVA

grounds became botanical gardens in 1913, but as they are below sea level, drainage is poor and the trees, though labeled, are suffering. The clock tower was erected in 1918.

★ FIJI MUSEUM

Inside Thurston Gardens is the well-curated **Fiji Museum** (tel. 331-5944 or 331-5043, fijimuseum@kidanet.net.fj, www.fijimuseum.org.fj, Mon.-Sat. 0930-1600, adults F$10, children under 13 and students F$5), founded in 1904. The museum's centerpiece is a double-hulled canoe, or *drua,* made in 1913. Each oar is massive, meant to be plied by four men. There's also a bamboo house raft *(bilibili),* whale-tooth necklaces, and a collection of original war clubs, spears, and cannibal forks. The history galleries beyond the museum shop and upstairs have a rich collection of exhibits about the many peoples who have come to Fiji, including Tongans, Europeans, Solomon Islanders, and Indians. The rudder from the HMS *Bounty* is on display. An air-conditioned room upstairs contains an exhibition of tapa cloth. At the museum entrance is the open-air **Ginger Kitchen** juice bar, which serves smoothies (F$8.50), breakfast items, and sandwiches.

ALBERT PARK

Just across Ratu Cakobau Road from the main gates of Thurston Gardens is **Albert Park,** where the first trans-Pacific flight—from California to Australia—made a pit stop in 1928. A plaque mounted on a white pedestal marks the spot. Today it's used for rugby and cricket matches; for welcoming dignitaries such as the queen or the pope; and for large public ceremonies such as Fiji Day (every October 10, which marks the date that in 1874 Fiji was ceded to the British, and the date in 1970 when it regained its independence). On Sundays and Christian holidays the bleachers fill with impressive choirs.

GOVERNMENT BUILDINGS

Continue north along Victoria Parade to Suva's largest edifice, the imposing **Government Buildings** (1939), once the headquarters of the British colonial establishment in the South Pacific. They now serve as Fiji's parliament, High Court, and executive branch offices. A statue of Chief Cakobau stares thoughtfully at the building. Next door is the headquarters of the **iTaukei Land Trust Board,** which administers much of Fiji's land on behalf of indigenous landowners.

the Fiji Museum in Thurston Gardens

A City of Festivals

Children race model *drua* canoes in Suva Harbour during the annual Hibiscus Festival.

Suva loves a party, and large festivals have proliferated in the decade since the government opened the stadium in Nasese to non-sporting events. Rechristened the Vodafone Arena, it hosts the following celebrations, which draw tens of thousands of revelers:

Hibiscus Festival (tel. 331-1168 or 999-4423, www.hibiscusfiji.com, August): Fiji's grandest event fills the expansive grounds of the Vodafone Arena with stalls, games, concerts, and carnival revelers for a full week. It coincides with Fijian school holidays, so almost everyone in Suva as well as plenty of outsiders stop by. Each day has a different theme, and each night features a pageant. Many of the pageant contestants are sponsored by local businesses, leading to titles that don't exactly roll off the tongue, like the Vodafone Hibiscus Second Runner-Up Miss Solar Energy Solutions. On Thursday a sellout crowd comes to see the fabulous Miss Adi Senikau pageant, a contest for trans women and drag performers; the talent segment is worth the F$25 admission for the sheer range of performances, from melodramatic lip-sync numbers to truly poignant original songs and traditional dance parables. Stop by the ticket booth early in the week if you want to attend. The other pageants are also fun to observe, at least for a little while, and don't require advance booking. Another highlight of the festival is the annual Veitau Waqa traditional boat race, held in Suva Harbour by the Pacific Blue Foundation to celebrate ancient boat-making skills. It's irritatingly difficult to look up a schedule, but locals seem to just know; ask your concierge, taxi driver, or really anyone.

Fiji Fashion Week (tel. 708-8898, info@fijifashionweek.com.fj, www.fijifashionweek.com.fj, end of May or beginning of June): This festival is a must-see extravaganza for the trendy and stylish. The main events take place at the Vodafone Arena in Suva, but there are also events in other cities. If you'd like to volunteer or even model, you can inquire at models@fijifashionweek.com. Amateur and commercial designers come from all over the South Pacific for runway shows as well as workshops and mentorship by pros from New Zealand and Australia. The designs incorporate local fabrics and techniques in far more creative ways than what you'll see in any tourist shop.

Fiji Showcase (tel. 331-4766, July): Local manufacturers show off their wares to retail buyers and the public at this fun event. Overseas and Fijian entertainers, food stalls, and carnival rides draw crowds of families to the biggest trade show in the South Pacific. No tickets are necessary.

★ GRAND PACIFIC HOTEL

Across the main road is the statuesque **Grand Pacific Hotel** (584 Victoria Parade, tel. 322-2000, info@gph.com.fj, www.grandpacifichotel.com). There's nothing like it anywhere else in the South Pacific isles. Built in 1914 to accommodate the privileged passengers of the Union Steamship Company of New Zealand, it was the destination of choice for noble guests to Fiji all the way up to Queen Elizabeth II, for whom grand balls were held here during her visits in 1953 and 1973. Ownership squabbles led to a period of decline until it shuttered in 1992, and soldiers had to move in to keep it free of squatters. In a joint nonprofit venture, it was lovingly restored and reopened in 2014, and now it offers a glimpse of the old Suva with all the modern-day conveniences.

It's worth a wander inside just to see the old-time photographs and wall of fame of illustrious visitors. Unlike many of the other fancy hotels in Fiji, GPH doesn't screen out nonguests; you can even take a dip in the pool if you want. Continue through the lobby and out past the pool, and you'll see a view of the entire harbor. Peer across the bay for a view of **Joske's Thumb,** a volcanic plug. The restaurant and lounge here are excellent, and will accommodate off-menu requests if needed; I watched a couple order vegetarian stir fry noodles in mid-afternoon, even though there was nothing Chinese on the menu. Happy hour is 1630-1830.

PRESIDENTIAL PALACE

Exiting the hotel, turn right (south) on Victoria Parade and continue past Thurston Gardens to the **Presidential Palace,** a Georgian mansion with immaculate flowering gardens. Formerly called Government House, it was the residence of a century of British governors who reigned over Fiji, and now houses the president and his family. The first building on this site went up in 1882, but lightning burned it down in 1921. It was rebuilt in 1928 and is a replica of the old British governor's residence in Sri Lanka. You can't go in, but the sole guard changes shifts every two hours in a somber ceremony. If you happen to be in Suva at the end of the month, you can watch the larger changing-of-the-guard ceremony, as the old guard bows to and welcomes the new guard.

ALONG THE SEAWALL

For a much longer stroll, you can walk south along the seawall past several schools, including the stately **Pacific Theological College.** After half an hour, you'll arrive at **My Suva Picnic Park,** a F$1 million project that added children's play equipment and manicured floral gardens to the seafront area. It stretches about 1.6 kilometers to **Suva Point,** at the end of Laucala Bay Road where it intersects with Beach Road. This is the best area in Suva to spot shorebirds, who roost on the jetty at high tide and shift to the exposed southern shore at low tide. There's also a good view of Nukulau Island. There's no shade on this walk, so it's best to do this early in the day.

NUKULAU ISLAND

Nukulau Island (www.lands.gov.fj), a tiny reef island southeast of Suva, has a history as colorful as Alcatraz or Ellis Island. It was the residence of the very first U.S. consul to Fiji; when his house caught fire on July 4, 1849, he demanded compensation from the reigning head of Fiji. Unable to afford the astronomical sum of US$40,000, Ratu Cakobau refused to cede land to the Americans—as the consul had hoped—and instead opened negotiations with the British. This set in motion a chain of events that led to Fiji becoming a British colony in 1874. The British then began importing indentured laborers from India in earnest, and converted Nukulau to a quarantine and immigration station; between 1879 and 1916 some 60,537 Indians arrived in Suva, most pausing for two weeks' quarantine on Nukulau. Eventually the island was converted to a park, though from 2000 to 2006 it was closed to the public while it served as a high-security prison for leaders of a military coup.

Today Nukulau is a pleasant picnic spot

and an easy day trip from Suva. You can inquire about boats at Walu Bay; the typical rate is F$15 per passenger, plus a required fee of F$2 per person for 24 hours on the island. Upon arrival you'll turn your permit over to the caretaker, who will give you a brief orientation to the rustic campsites, barbecue stands, public toilets, and best swimming areas. Bring everything, including drinking water, and firewood if you intend to cook.

★ DRUA EXPERIENCE

The finest way to visit Nukulau is with the **Drua Experience** (www.druaexperience.com, tel. 991-7248 or 920-3862), aboard a real Fijian double-hulled sailing canoe. It took two years to handcraft the 51-foot *i Vola Siga Vou* out of vesi hardwood and bamboo using traditional methods, modeled on the ancient canoe housed in the Fiji Museum. It launched in 2016 on the Navua River. A full-day excursion, including a fish fry on the beach at Nukulau, is F$250/person, with a minimum of 6 passengers and a maximum of 10. If you're solo, give them a call and they'll add you to an existing trip. Half-day sunset cocktail trips (F$175) or quick one-hour jaunts (F$75) are also possible. Most trips leave from Walu Bay and can, by arrangement, drop you at any of the waterfront hotels or restaurants in Suva.

Central Suva

Just north of the Holiday Inn, turn left and follow the waterfront path. You'll pass **St. Stephens House** on the waterfront, a historic building that is destined to become the new National Centre for Contemporary Arts. Funds for the multi-year project were allocated in late 2017, and the UK is helping to renovate the space so that it can house visual exhibitions of contemporary art, as well as dance and performance space. As the path curves back to Victoria Parade, on your left you'll see **City Library,** which opened in 1909 as one of the 2,509 public library buildings that American industrialist Andrew Carnegie gave to communities in the English-speaking world. Next are the picturesque **Queen Victoria Memorial Hall** (1904), later Suva Town Hall and now a restaurant complex with takeaway and dine-in options, and the colonial-style **Fintel Building** (1926), which is the nerve center of Fiji's international telecommunications network.

Farther north along the waterfront is **Sukuna Park,** a favorite site for political demonstrations, church rallies, and afternoon workout groups. At the junction of Renwick Road, Thomson Street, and Victoria Parade is a small park known as **The Triangle,** home to a white obelisk bearing four inscriptions: "Cross and Cargill first missionaries arrived 14th October 1835; Fiji British Crown Colony 10th October 1874; Public Land Sales on this spot 1880; Suva proclaimed capital 1882."

Inland a block on Pratt Street is the **Sacred Heart Cathedral** (1902), built of sandstone imported from Sydney, Australia. Between the Triangle and the cathedral is the towering **Reserve Bank of Fiji** (1984), which is worth entering to see the currency exhibition (www.rbf.gov.fj, Mon.-Fri. 0900-1600). On the corner of Thomson and Pier Streets opposite the post office is the onetime **Garrick Hotel** (1914), with wrought-iron balconies upstairs. This is the older part of downtown, and the original arches and arcades now house a busy array of clothing, electronics, and housewares stores.

The largest retail produce market in the Pacific, the colorful **Suva Municipal Market** off Rodwell Road next to the bus station, is a good place to browse fresh produce of every kind. Bundles of kava roots are sold upstairs. On the street outside, Fijian women sell fresh pineapple and guava juice. From Thursday to Saturday the marketplace is even more lively, as farmers from Tailevu and as far as Nadroga come to sell their fresh produce.

West Suva

Just west of Lami on the Queens Highway, a sign marks the World War II-era **Bilo**

Hannah Dudley's Legacy

a portrait of Hannah Dudley surrounded by artifacts that belonged to her

One of the few Methodist missionaries to successfully proselytize among Fiji's Indian community was an Englishwoman named Hannah Dudley, who had previously worked in India. An individualist unwilling to follow the usual rules for white evangelists laid down by the male-managed mission of her day, "our Miss Dudley" (as her fellow missionaries called her) worked in Suva among the indentured Indian laborers from 1897 to 1913. Dudley adopted their vegetarianism as a step toward godliness, and she visited the area's Hindu and Muslim women in their own homes, as only a woman could. Through her Bible classes, she soon created a circle of Indian converts in Suva.

Although conditions for the Indians of her day were harsh, Dudley didn't protest to the colonial authorities, as some other Methodist missionaries had. She instead turned her own home into an orphanage, and her Indian converts called her *mataji*, "respected mother." When Dudley returned to Calcutta in 1905 to work with the Bengali Mission, she took her Indo-Fijian orphans along. In 1934, members of the Indian Methodist congregation in Suva erected the **Dudley Memorial Church** on the spot where she first preached. The cream-colored building, strongly influenced by Indian architecture with its domes and central Moorish arch, stands at the corner of Toorak Road and Amy Street, just up the hill from downtown Suva.

Battery Gun Site (tel. 331-5944 or 331-5043, www.rfmf.mil.fj/bilo-battery-historical-site, Mon.-Sat. 0930-1600, F$5 adults, F$3 children). Travel 1.7 kilometers along gravel Bilo Road, past Namuka village, to reach the historical site. The concrete structures that held the four long cannons, installed in 1941 to defend Suva Harbour, are set in a pleasant parklike environment that once housed Fijian, New Zealand, and U.S. troops. The site is maintained by the Fiji Museum.

ENTERTAINMENT AND EVENTS

Nightlife

Suva's numerous nightclubs all require neat dress (no shorts or flip-flops). Nothing much happens at the clubs until after 2200. The bars are more casual, depending on location. By law, public nightclubs and bars in Fiji are required to close by 0100, but in practice many stay open until nearly dawn. Almost all have an active Facebook presence, so you can browse the photo albums to get a sense of the vibe of the various clubs.

Alas, Suva's nightlife is uncomfortable for women traveling alone. You could try going unescorted at opening time for a quiet predinner drink, but after dark, go in a group or stick to the hotel bars; otherwise you're likely to get too much attention of the wrong kind. Good options for solo women are the cozy **Piano Bar** at the **Holiday Inn,** which often presents rather good jazz singers, and the bayside **Na Toba Bar** beyond the pool at the **Grand Pacific Hotel,** which has only canned music but incredible views and a safe path for a night stroll.

CLUBS

Traps (305 Victoria Parade, tel. 331-2922, Mon.-Fri. 1700-0100, Sat. 1700-0300) is Fiji's largest nightclub, with four themed bars and a *bure,* with a capacity of 800 people. It opened in 1984 and has undergone several makeovers. It draws a young Fijian crowd, as the drinks (try the "Kavikazi," a blend of kava and Captain Morgan rum) are reasonably priced and the music is trendy. One of the bars has karaoke. There's happy hour until 2000. Fridays and Saturdays are *the* nights to be there, with a live DJ, but Mondays, Wednesdays, and Thursdays have live music starting at 2200.

Signals Night Club (255 Victoria Parade, tel. 331-3590), opposite the Suva City Library, is a popular dance spot for Asian seamen. Gay male travelers will feel comfortable here.

Birdland Sports Bar and R&B Club (6 Carnarvon St., tel. 330-3833) has outstanding live jazz from 2000 on Sundays. On other nights, there's recorded music. It's a late-night place where people come after they've been to the other clubs. The bar is relatively safe and the crowd here is friendly.

Purple Haze Night Club (Butt and MacArthur Sts., closed Sun.-Tues.), above the Merchants Club, is a predominantly Indo-Fijian disco with a mostly male crowd. There is a cover charge of F$5.

The upscale **Downunder Bar** (54 Carnarvon St. tel. 330-2538, daily 1800-0500) has Australian-themed decor and two pool tables. Happy hour is 1700-2100. There's live music some nights.

The Wrecktangles (54 Carnarvon St., tel. 999-1386, Wed.-Sat. 1800-0500) is a popular country-and-western club with live entertainment. The crowd here is a bit older than in some of the other clubs and it's something of a hangout for Rotumans and iTaukei civil servants.

The **Golden Dragon** (379 Victoria Parade, tel. 331-1018) is frequented by university students and islanders from other parts of the Pacific (such as Samoa, Tonga, Vanuatu, the Solomon Islands, and Papua New Guinea).

Bar 66 (tel. 870-6071, closed Sun. and Mon.), above Dolphins Food Court (entrance off Loftus Street), has some of the city's cheapest drinks, making it very popular with university students—as well as minors.

Liquids Night Club (tel. 330-0679), upstairs in the Harbor Center (access from beside Wishbone restaurant outside on the Nubukalou Creek side of the building), is crowded with local sports teams on weekends. During the week, local businessmen unwind and network in the separate lounge area.

Be aware that the places north of Nubukalou Creek are considerably rougher than those mentioned above. Among these, **Friends Bar and Niteclub** (38 Cumming St., tel. 330-0704) has a happy hour 1700-2000. Security is tight, as this is a popular bar for local rugby club players, off-duty military officers, and youthful Fijian crowds.

BARS

O'Reilly's Bar (5 MacArthur St., tel. 331-2322), just off Victoria Parade, has a happy hour daily 1700-2000. It's a nice relaxed way to kick off a night on the town, with a big-screen TV, pool table, and canned music. This bar is popular with the trendier locals and has special events on Fridays and Saturdays.

A block up MacArthur from O'Reilly's is **The Merchants Club** (15 Butt St., tel. 330-4256). Founded by Indian business owners in

LGBTQ Pride in Fiji

Transgender peer educators work with the Fiji Ministry of Health to raise awareness about HIV.

In May 2018, Fiji made history as the first country in the Pacific to host an LGBTQ Pride parade. Fifty participants marched in Lautoka, the nation's second-largest city, after Suva police had denied annual requests to hold a parade in the capital since 2012. The Lautoka parade, an associated sports day, and a policy conference coincided with the International Day Against Homophobia, Biphobia, and Transphobia.

Former president Ratu Epeli Nailatikau gave a supportive talk at one of the events, but current Prime Minister Frank Bainimarama has stated that gay couples should move to Iceland (!), as gay marriage would not be legalized in Fiji in his lifetime. That dichotomy shows the transitional stage that Fiji is in with regard to attitudes toward its lesbian, gay, bisexual, transgender, and queer community.

Although traditional communities had room for everyone, and the Fijian constitution guarantees equality for sexual and gender minorities, the intense Christianization of the iTaukei (indigenous) population over centuries of missionary presence has led to some extremely conservative attitudes toward sexuality and gender roles. There's no overt culture war going on—same-gender sexuality was decriminalized in 2010, and LGBTQ identity hasn't been a flashpoint for violence—but families and mainstream religious authorities in Fiji are often intolerant toward their queer kin.

Nevertheless, LGBTQ Fijians and their allies have been working toward change. There are three aspects of the movement: an advocacy and visibility movement, largely based in Suva, that has ties to feminist and anti-gender-violence organizations; a health emphasis, originally funded by international anti-HIV programs, including some medical providers from the LGBTQ community itself; and a transgender community that has tendrils everywhere, as trans folks live even in tiny towns and villages. A major corporation sponsors an annual transgender beauty pageant in Suva at the nation's largest celebration, the Hibiscus Festival.

Many queer Fijians have found employment in the hospitality, retail, and service sectors. As a tourist, it's not hard to strike up a conversation, especially if you're open about your own status without making assumptions. Public displays of sexuality, though, are rare among people of all sexual persuasions in Fiji; it's respectful to keep it strictly G-rated in front of mixed groups.

The Facebook pages of the **Rainbow Pride Foundation** (tel. 918-7474), **DIVA for Equality** (www.divafiji.com), and **Haus of Khameleon** (www.hausofkhameleon.org) are good sources of information about upcoming public events.

1952, before they were allowed into the white bars, it retains an old-school, mostly male club environment, with snooker and poker rooms in the back and a large dining room presided over by framed black-and-white portraits of the founders. (Mention the author of this guide, and they'll point you to my grandfather's picture.) Properly dressed overseas visitors are welcome, and the curries are excellent. The hours are needlessly complicated, but basically you can go at dinnertime any weekday, and all day on weekends: Monday and Tuesday 1700-2130, Wednesday and Thursday 1630-2230, Friday 1630-2300, Saturday 1100-2230, Sunday 1100-1900.

The Club at Garrick (tel. 330-8746, Mon.-Sat. 1100-2100), upstairs in a colonial building at the corner of Pier Street and Renwick Road, gathers a rather rowdy Fijian clientele around a long Wild West-style bar. There's a pool table and great people-watching over downtown Suva from the balcony.

The bar at the **Suva Lawn Bowling Club** (tel. 330-2394, Mon.-Sat. 0900-2100, Sun. 0900-1700), facing the lagoon opposite Thurston Gardens and just off Albert Park, is a very convenient place to down a large bottle of Fiji Bitter after visiting the museum. You can sit and watch the bowling, or see the sun set over Viti Levu.

Cinema

With its large Indo-Fijian community, Suva is a good place to catch a Bollywood movie with English subtitles. Two multi-screen cinemas showing both English and Indian films now serve the city. Downtown, there's **Village 6 Cinemas** (12 Scott St., tel. 330-6006), and near the USP campus is **Damodar Cinemas** (Grantham Rd., tel. 327-5100). Matinees start around 1030 and the last show is usually around 2100. Regular tickets are F$7 adults, F$5.50 children under 12; you can upgrade to premium seats. All shows are discounted F$1 on Tuesdays. Both theaters are owned by the same company; see http://damodarcinemas.com.fj for current listings. Aside from Hollywood and Bollywood blockbusters, you can sometimes catch independent films from Australia, New Zealand, and Samoa.

TOP EXPERIENCE

ARTS AND CULTURE

The **Oceania Center for Arts and Culture** (tel. 323-2832, www.usp.ac.fj, Mon.-Fri. 1000-1600) at the University of the South Pacific has gallery exhibitions and hosts frequent events, from locally written and produced plays to poetry readings to dance classes for children. Any of the frequent buses that stop in front of the Vanua Arcade, opposite Sukuna Park on Victoria Parade, will bring you directly to campus (get off when you see a McDonald's on the left). From Laucala Bay Road, follow the main walkway to the library. Across a wooden bridge behind the library, past the university bookstore, is a traditional Fijian *bure* called the Vale ni Bose, which is used for workshops and seminars. To the left of the *bure* is the gallery. As you walk, look around and enjoy the beautiful 72.8-hectare campus, founded in 1968 and jointly owned by 12 Pacific countries. More than 70 percent of the 22,000 students here are from Fiji; the rest are on scholarships from every corner of the Pacific.

21K Art Gallery (21 Knollys St., tel. 902-7408, info@21kgallery.com, www.21kgallery.com, 1100-1500 Wed.-Thurs., or by appointment) opened in May 2017 to showcase the work of five contemporary Fijian artists whose careers have spanned 25 years or more, and who have international reputations. Temporary exhibits of other artists also take place. It's a lovely, small space, and well worth a visit.

The vintage **Suva Prison**, built in 1913, is home to the **Tagimoucia Art Gallery** (www.corrections.gov.fj/tagimoucia-art-gallery, tel. 330-3512, Mon.-Fri. 1000-1500). It exhibits

1: produce at the daily Suva Flea Market **2:** award-winning artist and inmate Aisake Amoe at the Tagimoucia Art Gallery **3:** the historic Grand Pacific Hotel.

1

2

3

and sells artworks created by prisoners during rehabilitative art workshops.

A beautifully designed source of information and profiles of Fijian artists is the online magazine **ArtTalk** (tel. 777-6820, https://artalkfiji.com), founded by local curator Peter Sipeli. The magazine's Facebook page (@artalkfiji) is a good source of information about upcoming events involving Suva's culturati. Sipeli also runs the spoken-word poetry scene in Suva; inquire about performing at or attending an open mic night at **The Poetry Shop** (thepoetryshopfiji@gmail.com), which holds occasional events at various venues.

SHOPPING

In downtown, **Cumming Street** is Suva's busiest shopping street. Expect to obtain a 10-40 percent discount at the "duty-free" shops here by bargaining. Be wary when purchasing gold jewelry, "pearls," and "gemstones"; if the deal seems too good to be true, it is.

Markets

The large **Curio and Handicraft Market** (Mon.-Sat. 0800-1700) on the waterfront behind the post office is a good place to haggle over crafts. Amid the ubiquitous masks and faux cannibalism tools are treasures like the palm-fiber weavings of Lau islander Neomai Vakarau (stall 54). The grandly named Stamp World (stall 37, tel. 995-5062 or 332-0917, stephenj@connect.com.fj, 0900-1200 only) is packed full of wares for collectors of stamps, coins, and postcards from Fiji and throughout the Commonwealth. Throughout the market, do bargain hard and scrutinize the goods for quality—a hand-painted map of Fiji on tapa cloth may be quoted at anywhere from F$50 to F$300. Prices shoot up if a cruise ship is in port. Don't display your dollars or follow touts into blind alleys outside the market.

The **Suva Flea Market** on Rodwell Road opposite the bus station may be the cheapest place in Fiji to buy a sulu. Grass mats woven from *pandanus* (screw pine) leaves and tapa bark cloth are other items to consider, and there are several good little places to eat. Unlike the handicraft market, the vendors here won't try a hard sell on you. Haggling is welcome.

Malls

Two retail giants serve as landmarks, occupying entire blocks of downtown Suva:

Morris Hedstrom City Center is known by all as **MHCC—The Meeting Point** (Renwick Rd, tel. 919-6969, www.mh.com.fj, daily 0900-2100). Fiji's largest mall, it is anchored by the MH supermarket on the ground floor, and has useful Digicel and Vodafone outlets in case your mobile phone needs topping off.

Tappoo City (Thomson St., tel. 331-5422, www.tappoo.com.fj, Mon.-Sat. 0900-2000, Sun. 1000-1800) is a silvery spaceship-like six-story structure that houses a full-service department store. There are clothing sections, household goods, a M.A.C. makeup counter, a spa, and a good bookstore.

North of the city center, near the Vodafone Arena, is the **Damodar City** mall (Grantham Rd., daily 0800-2100). Shops, restaurants, cinemas, and a 24-hour McDonald's here serve the university population.

Clothing and Accessories

Pacific Islands Art (PIA) Fashion (tel. 330-0783 or 664-0085, sales@pacificislandsart.com, http://pacificislandsart.com), with locations in Palm Court and the QBE Insurance Arcade, specializes in Tahitian designs hand-printed on a range of apparel, from men's sleeveless T-shirts to women's spandex dresses.

Samson Lee Fiji (Shop 1, LICI Building, tel. 941-5137, samsonleefiji@gmail.com, Mon.-Fri. 0930-1730, Sat. 1000-1500), opposite the *Fiji Times* parking lot, features creative clothing and accessories made by an established local designer. Lee has dressed several Hibiscus pageant winners and is one of the few Fijian designers to post creations regularly on Instagram (@samsonleefiji).

Aladdin's Cave (tel. 330-1005), facing the Palm Court Bistro in the mall behind Air New Zealand, has one-of-a-kind jewelry, purses, scarves, pillow covers and wind chimes. Prices are reasonable considering that everything is handmade.

Books and Music

Suva's number one bookstore is the **USP Book Centre** (tel. 323-2500, www.uspbookcentre.com, Mon.-Fri. 0800-1800, Sat. 0830-1300) at the main Laucala Bay university campus. Not only does it have one of the finest Pacific sections in the region, but it stocks the publications of several dozen publishers affiliated with the university, and you can turn up some truly intriguing items.

Books R Us (Level 4, Tappoo City, tel. 999-6648) is one of the few bookstores in Suva that only specializes in books and not stationery. It has all manner of fiction and nonfiction, from fantasy to diet books to lifestyle and self-help books. There's also a small counter on the ground floor of Tappoo City that sells a line of children's books about Fiji starring an appealing character named Tui.

The **Fiji Museum** shop sells several excellent books about Fiji and Pacific history at reasonable prices, as well as scholarly journals.

The **Coconut Frond,** at the back of the Suva Flea Market on Rodwell Road, has a large stock of used paperbacks.

The **Government Bookstore** (Foster Rd., Walu Bay, tel. 331-5504, Mon.-Fri. 0800-1600,) sells Fijian dictionaries, history books, and grammar texts at low prices.

Procera Music Shop (68 Suva St., tel. 330-3365), just above downtown, sells cassettes (yes, really) and CDs of local Indian and Fijian music.

Gear

Bob's Hook Line & Sinker (14 Thomson St., tel. 330-1013), on a street-side corner of the Harbor Center, sells quality snorkeling and fishing gear.

RECREATION

Hiking

For a bird's-eye view of Suva and the surrounding area, spend a morning climbing to the volcanic plug atop **Mount Korobaba** (429 m), the region's highest peak. Take a Shore bus to the cement factory beyond the Novotel at Lami, and then follow the dirt road past the factory up into the foothills. After about 45 minutes on the main track, you'll come to a fork just after a sharp descent. Keep left and cross a small stream. Soon after, the track divides again. Look for a trail straight up to the right where the tracks rejoin. It's a 10-minute scramble to the summit from here. The route can be confusing, so it's better to hire a local guide than try to find the way on your own.

A far more challenging climb is to the top of **Joske's Thumb,** a volcanic plug 440 meters high that lies 15 kilometers west of Suva. Take a bus to Naikorokoro Road, and then walk inland 30 minutes to where the road turns sharply right and crosses a bridge. Follow the track straight ahead and continue up the river till you reach a small village. It's necessary to request permission of the villagers to proceed, and to hire a guide. From the village to Joske's Thumb will take just less than three hours. The trail can be wet and muddy, and includes a couple of stream crossings. The last bit is extremely steep, and ropes may be necessary. Even Sir Edmund Hillary failed twice to climb the Thumb, succeeding only 30 years later, after he scaled Everest.

Talanoa Treks (tel. 998-0560, info@talanoa-treks-fiji.com, https://talanoa-treks-fiji.com) offers excellent guided hikes into interior Viti Levu, departing from and returning to Suva. There are day trips as well as overnight village stays up to four nights, and you get the chance to explore areas of Fiji that see less than a hundred tourists a year. Owners Marita and Matt Manley are passionate hikers who have hiked all over the island since coming to Suva in 2006 and, upon invitation by chiefs they met while hiking little-used trails in the highland villages, worked to set up cooperative ventures in which local guides and chiefs help run the trekking company. Custom itineraries are possible if your dates don't match scheduled trips.

Running

The **Suva Marathon Club** (tel. 998-0560, bula@suvamarathon.org, www.suvamarathon.org) holds 5K training runs year-round and a full marathon in July. Regular fun runs begin at 1715 Thursdays weekly, and 0700 on the first Saturday of the month, starting at the seawall outside the Suva Lawn Bowling Club on Queen Elizabeth Drive. There are 3K, 5K, 7K, and 10K loops, and it's a fun way to see the city and meet people. For your warm-up or cooldown, modern stretching and strength-training equipment has been installed at the southwest corner of Albert Park. On Saturdays there's a friendly post-run meetup at Ginger Kitchen, the café outside the Fiji Museum. Facebook and Twitter (@suvamarathon) are the best sources of upcoming event information, while the website has registration information for the marathon itself. Running for health is a relatively new pastime for Fijians, and the club's founding in 2014 has introduced the activity to an enthusiastic crowd—so you're likely to see first-timers, kids, and even pets at the runs.

Scuba Diving

Suva has no regular dive shops, although **Dive Center Ltd.** (tel. 330-0599), facing the Royal Suva Yacht Club, fills scuba tanks. It doesn't rent equipment or offer diving.

FOOD

Suva is the best place in Fiji to sample an array of foods, from quick bites to upscale cuisine. Most restaurants are closed on Sundays except in the major malls and hotels, but the Chinese and Korean eateries stay open. Vegetarians will find that Indian and Chinese places offer the most options, though others will try to accommodate.

Fast Food

A dizzying array of eateries—Fijian, Indian, Chinese, Middle Eastern, pizza, and more—fill the food courts of downtown Suva. You can satisfy your appetite by popping into any of the many arcades: the **Harbor Center** (daily 0700-1800) along Nubukalou Creek between Scott and Thomson Streets; **Dolphins Food Court** (tel. 330-7440) at FNPF Place, Victoria Parade, and Loftus Street; or the top floor of **My FNPF Plaza** (Mon.-Fri. 0900-1930, Sat. 1000-1800) on Grieg Street, where you can find Suva's only Sri Lankan food stall. The most diverse food courts are atop **Tappoo City** (Thomson St., Mon.-Sat. 0900-2000, Sun. 1000-1800) and **MHCC** (Renwick Rd., daily 0900-2100), which also has a good bakery on the ground floor serving meat pies.

If you're arriving in Suva by bus or boat, prices in the food court at the **Suva Flea Market,** just opposite the station, can't be beat. You can sit at wooden picnic tables in a covered courtyard.

Daily 1700-0500, **barbecue vendors** on Edward Street opposite the post office sell takeaway chicken, chops, sausages, and eggs hot from their grills (F$7). You'll see a steady stream of cars and taxis stopping here to pick up dinner.

An inexpensive **snack bar** (tel. 330-1443, Mon.-Fri. 0800-1730, Sat. 0800-1530) with outdoor concrete picnic tables is at the harbor side of the Handicraft Market. A chow mein or a rump steak will run F$6-10 and the portions are gargantuan. It is packed with locals around lunchtime.

Fijian

★ **Old Mill Cottage Café** (49 Carnarvon St., tel. 331-2134, Mon.-Sat. 0700-1700, F$5-12), behind the Dolphins Food Court, draws employees from nearby offices at lunchtime for the inexpensive curried freshwater mussels, curried chicken livers, fresh seaweed in coconut milk, taro leaves creamed in coconut milk, and fish cooked in coconut milk. It's also very good for breakfast.

Henry's Kitchen (24 Williamson Rd., tel. 360-6908, Mon.-Sat. 0700-1700, F$8.50-14.50)

1: a view across Suva Harbour **2:** *kokoda* (ceviche in coconut milk) at the Grand Pacific Hotel **3:** woven wares at the Curio and Handicraft Market.

1

2

3

was an institution at the Suva Lawn Bowling Club. It relocated in 2017 to one of the oldest colonial-era institutions in Fiji, the Union Club. Specialties include the seafood platter, *dalo* (taro root), and *rourou* (taro leaves).

Green Leaf (in the My FNPF Plaza food court, no phone) specializes in healthy Fijian food and fruit smoothies. Try the *kokoda* (ceviche) with *nama* (sea grapes) or the baked *kai* (freshwater mussels).

Indian

★ **Yellow Chilli** (53 Carnarvon St., tel. 331-0063, http://yellowchilli.restaurantwebexpert.com, dinner daily 1800-2200, lunch Mon.-Sat. 1100-1500) is in a charming old house with limited seating; dine early or call for reservations. The ambience is a cut above other Indian restaurants in Fiji, and unlike most, this one serves wine and beer.

Trendy **Maya Dhaba** (281 Victoria Parade, tel. 331-0045, daily 1100-1500 and 1730-2200) serves a good variety of spicy South Indian dishes priced F$10-18. *Thalis* are F$10-12.

Takeaway chicken (F$10) is popular at **Ashiyana** (tel. 331-3000, Tues.-Sat. 1130-1430 and 1800-2200, Sun. 1800-2130), in the old town hall on Victoria Parade. North Indian meats and breads are prepared in a tandoor.

Hare Krishna Vegetarian Restaurant (16 Pratt St., tel. 331-4154, Mon.-Sat. 0800-1730), at the corner of Pratt and Joske Streets downtown, is an acceptable option for strict vegetarians. It serves snacks, sweets, and 14 flavors of ice cream (F$2 cone) downstairs, and lunch (F$9.50 for the all-you-can-eat vegetarian *thali*) upstairs.

A tastier spot for vegetarians is ★ **Govinda Vegetarian Restaurant** (Laucala Bay Rd., tel. 327-0186, Mon.-Sat. 1100-1500), near the Vodafone Arena. Here the outstanding combination lunch *thali* is F$10.50, or you can have a la carte dishes, sweets, ice cream, milk shakes, and masala tea.

A cheap and popular place is the **Curry House** (44 Waimanu Rd., tel. 331-3756, www.curryhousefiji.com, Mon.-Fri. 0730-1800, Sat. 0730-1600). The special vegetarian *thali* (F$5) makes for a good lunch, and the chicken curry and meat samosas are favorites. Try the takeaway *rotis*.

Saffron Tandoori Restaurant (tel. 327-0017, www.saffronfiji.com, daily 1100-2300), owned by Jack's, serves up an array of tasty dishes—including specialties of regional Indian cuisine—in an upscale mall environment at Damodar City. It's up one flight of stairs (no elevator). The deep-fried okra, duck curry, and soft minced lamb kebabs offer flavors you won't find elsewhere.

Chinese

★ **Fong Lees Seafood Restaurant** (293 Victoria Parade, tel. 330-4233, daily 1200-1400 and 1800-2200) is next to Traps Bar. The spicy eggplant in fish sauce is excellent (and truly spicy), and the squid, prawn, and crab dishes are delicately prepared. Prices start around F$18 but can go up to F$80 for lobster and other catch-of-the-day specials.

Chopsticks Restaurant (68 Thomson St., tel. 330-0968, daily 1030-1430 and 1800-2200, under $F15), upstairs in the Honson Building, is a bit hard to find. It's above J. Maneklal and Sons Ltd., but the entrance is farther along the street, next to the MHCC driveway. Meals are individually prepared and reasonably priced, though the décor is basic.

Next door is the pricier **Shanghai Seafood House** (Pier Street, tel. 331-4968, daily 1130-1430 and 1800-2230, F$22-80), above Lotus Money Exchange. The balcony overlooks Pier Street, and the menu is massive. A second outlet at Damodar City is buffet-style (F$17-F$25).

Suva's most imposing Chinese restaurant is the 300-seat **Vine Yard Palace** (tel. 331-5546, Mon.-Sat. 1130-1430 and 1800-2200, Sun. 1730-2200, F$8-48), in the old town hall next to the public library on Victoria Parade. A lunch buffet (F$14) is served weekdays 1130-1430.

China Club (Queen Elizabeth Dr. and Charlton Ave., Nasese, tel. 331-1257, Mon.-Fri. 1800-2230, Sat.-Sun. 0900-1500 and 1800-2230) serves a popular *yum cha*, or brunch, on weekends. It features a small-plate format (F$3.50-F$7) in which you can choose among items such as steamed dumplings, spicy fried squid, and flavorful rice porridges and soups. Large plates are F$18-60; try the yellow chicken or the giant crabs (seasonal).

ChinaTown Restaurant (83 Cumming St., tel. 330-8868, Mon.-Sat. 1100-1430 and 1800-2230, Sun. 0900-1500 and 1800-2230) also serves *yum cha* Sunday brunch, and is popular for takeaway dinner. The crackling pork is a must-try. It's located in the Parshotam Building; look for the large sign.

Korean

Seoul Restaurant (63 Gordon St., tel. 330-3605, Mon.-Fri. 1200-1500 and Mon.-Sun. 1800-2200), tucked above the Southern Cross hotel, offers a quiet setting for traditional Korean dishes as well as DIY barbecue at your table. The Sunday barbecue buffet is popular, and the staff here are sweet and helpful in guiding locals through the adventure of this relatively new cuisine to Fiji.

Mad House Korean BBQ (43 Gordon St., tel. 800-3444, Mon.-Fri. 1300-2200, Sat.-Sun. 1800-2200) is a pleasant, modern place with a picture menu. Bibimbap, soups, and hot pots are F$13-F$25; barbecue meats are F$25 and come with side vegetables and pickles.

Japanese

For upscale Japanese food, it's **Daikoku** (359 Victoria Parade, tel. 330-8968, www.daikokufiji.com, Mon.-Sat. 1200-1400 and 1800-2200, F$10-58), upstairs in FNPF Place. The teppanyaki dishes are artistically prepared right at your table. Reservations are suggested.

Sakura Sushi Train (Damodar City, Grantham Rd., tel. 802-5537, Mon.-Sun. 1100-1500 and 1700-2200), on the top floor of the Damodar City mall, is a typical Japanese sushi bar, tamed for local palates. It also does hot pots and soups.

Continental

Tiko's Floating Restaurant (tel. 331-3626, Mon.-Fri. 1130-1400 and 1730-2200, Sat. 1800-2200) is housed in the MV *Lycianda*, an ex-Blue Lagoon cruise ship launched at Suva in 1970 and now anchored off Stinson Parade behind Sukuna Park. Steaks (F$30) and seafood mains (F$18-45) are good. Lobster or a mountain of crabs will run F$55-60. An all-you-can-eat salad bar is included. It's a romantic spot, and you can feel the boat rock gently in the waves.

Nando's (tel. 330-1040, daily 1100-2200), on Regal Lane opposite the Sea Salt Restaurant, is a South Africa-based franchise famous for its spicy Portuguese flame-grilled chicken (F$12/18 for a quarter-/half-chicken meal). Pour on as much peri-peri sauce as you like. There's a second Nando's location at 237 Laucala Bay Road, opposite the Fiji Post National Stadium.

The whimsically named ★ **Bad Dog Café** (219 Victoria Parade, tel. 331-2800, Mon.-Sun. 0900-2200) has two locations in Suva City, one downtown next door to O'Reilly's and the other at Damodar City. This trendy bar-and-grill serves wine, margaritas, sangria (F$18 for a jug), and 26 different beers. The menu features seven varieties of pizza (F$15-22), burgers (F$17), pasta (F$15-22), steaks (F$25-35), and other mains (F$12-21), or group platters to share (F$30-55).

At Gordon and Joske Streets, **Hock and Chock Fish and Chips** (tel. 368-1071, Mon.-Sat. 0830-2000, Sun. 0830-1400) serves upscale fish-and-chips (F$8/12 small/large). Chicken-and-chips is F$10/F$13, and steaks are F$22-30. This place is also good for breakfast.

★ **Eden Bistro & Bar** (11 Bureta St., tel. 338-6246) serves breakfast (0830-1000), lunch (1130-1500), and dinner (1700-2230) daily amid a friendly and relaxed setting. The eclectic menu can range from sashimi to curries to burgers, and there are daily specials (F$8-75). Reasonable drink prices keep people hanging out well before and after dinner.

Paradiso Restaurant (Albert Park, tel. 777 2303, suvalawnbistro@gmail.com, Tues.-Sat. 1000-2100, Sun. 900-1500) serves up

Italian specialties, such as pasta and wood-fired pizza (F$12-37), in an airy environment surrounded by greenery. Adjacent is the Suva Lawn Tennis Club. There's a full bar and happy hour specials (1700-1900), sometimes accompanied by live music.

Governors (Knolly St., tel. 337-5050, Mon.-Sun. 0730-1430, Wed.-Sat. 1800-2130) is a museum-themed restaurant. Breakfast and lunch (F$10-28) are better than dinner (F$18-35), and reservations are encouraged. The menu includes pancakes, sliders, wraps, and fish steaks.

Café 30 (30 McGregor, tel. 310-0148, Mon.-Fri. 0900-1600, Sat. 0800-1500, F$12-29) is a quaint family dining room that's popular for brunch and lunch. Try the pulled pork and the fresh seasonal desserts.

Cafés

Bulaccino (Garden City, Grantham Rd., tel. 327-5010, www.bulaccino.com/suva, Mon.-Fri. 0730-1700, Sat.-Sun. 0800-1600) offers espresso drinks, all-day breakfast, pastries, and a lunchtime sandwich menu. Organic avocados, honey, and other produce come from the family's farm outside Nadi. Try one of the substantial Viti bowl smoothies (F$12), an only-in-Fiji superfood mix of coconut, honey, and fruits of your choice.

For a big American-style cooked breakfast (F$10.80), try the **Palm Court Bistro** (tel. 330-4662, Mon.-Fri. 0700-1630, Sat. 0700-1330), in the Queensland Insurance Arcade behind Air New Zealand on Victoria Parade. Their burgers and sandwiches are good.

The **Focaccia Café** (Mon.-Fri. 0700-1700, Sat. 0800-1500), in the Vanua Arcade on Victoria Parade opposite Sukuna Park, serves lunch and cooked breakfast (including coffee) for F$5-7. Smoothies are F$4.50-6, coffee drinks F$3-4.50.

Moments (3 Scott St., Dominion House, tel. 997-7796, Mon.-Sat. 0700-2000, Sun. 0900-1800) is a relaxed yet modern café in the heart of downtown and perfect for a cappuccino, smoothie, or fresh juice (F$5-9). The pastries, meat pies, and focaccia sandwiches (F$5-13) are good for lunch or snack time.

★ **Contain Yourself** (Edward St. next to the post office, tel. 948-1681, Mon.-Fri. 0700-1000) is a fun little open-air café made out of a repurposed shipping container. You can feel pampered here while you watch the harbor and market action. Fresh fruit smoothies, coffee drinks, lasagna, and frittatas are on offer. Try the moli-ginger juice (F$5.70), made from the citrusy Tongan pomelo fruit.

ACCOMMODATIONS

Suva offers a wide variety of places to stay, from low-budget to grand luxury. Prices drop as you leave the city center, but watch out for too-good-to-be-true rates; some hotels (not listed here) northeast of downtown cater to hourly "guests."

Under US$50

The historic 42-room ★ **South Seas Private Hotel** (6 Williamson Rd., tel. 331-2296, www.fiji4less.com), one block east of Albert Park, is a quiet place with a pleasant veranda and a large communal kitchen. It originally housed workers involved in laying the first telecommunications cable across the Pacific; it later served as a girls hostel. In 1983 it was converted for backpackers. A bed in a five-bed dorm is F$26, a fan-cooled room with shared bath is F$49/63/75 single/double/triple, and a better room with private bath is F$81 double (there's only one). You'll receive a F$1 discount if you have a youth hostel, VIP, or Nomads card. For a refundable F$10 deposit, you may borrow a plate, mug, knife, fork, and spoon, but there's a constant shortage of pots and pans. It's possible to leave excess luggage at the South Seas for free while you're off visiting other islands, but you should lock your bag securely. The staff changes money at bank rates. It's worth it to catch a taxi here from the bus station the first time (F$4-5).

Saf's Apartment Hotel (100 Robertson Rd., tel. 330-1849) has a mixed local and foreign clientele. The 40 rooms with bath in this three-story concrete building are F$30 single or double downstairs, F$40 upstairs, or F$50 with TV and cooking facilities (F$10 extra for air-conditioning).

Tropic Towers Apartment Motel (86 Robertson Rd., tel. 330-4470, www.tropictowers.com) has 34 air-conditioned apartments with cooking facilities, fridges, and TVs in a four-story building, starting at F$64/78 single/double downstairs and F$76/92 upstairs. The airy upstairs rooms are a much better value than those downstairs, as some are quite large. The 13 "budget" units in the annex are F$43 single or double with shared bath. A bar and coffee lounge are on the premises and a swimming pool is available for guests.

An alley at the end of Anand Street leads straight up to **Annandale Apartments** (265 Waimanu Rd., tel. 330-9766). The 11 smaller rooms downstairs with fridges and private baths are F$55 single or double, while the 12 spacious one-/two-bedroom apartments upstairs with balconies, TVs, air-conditioning, and cooking facilities are F$80-90 for up to three or four people.

Anyone with business at the University of the South Pacific should see if there's room at **USP Lodges** (Laucala Bay Rd., tel. 321-2614, usplodges@usp.ac.fj), though the units are often taken up by students on a long-term basis. The accommodations here are in two clusters: Reception/check-in for all units is at the Upper Campus Lodge, overlooking the Botanical Garden on the main campus, where there are six small flats with TVs and cooking facilities at F$66/75 single/double. Down beside Laucala Bay near the School of Marine Studies is Marine Lodge, with five self-catering units with TVs at F$72/85 single/double.

US$50-100

The simple ★ **Island Accommodation Suva** (56 Extension St., tel. 331-6316, islanda40@yahoo.com) is tucked behind the Colonial War Memorial Hospital and is the residence of choice for visiting medical students and doctors. It's an excellent value. The four airy upstairs rooms (F$180 s/d, but you can easily add a third person) have their own bathrooms and share a kitchen and spacious living room. Some have verandas. Breakfast is cooked for you, and you can prepare lunches and dinners yourself. Downstairs are three self-catering apartments (F$220). All rooms have private baths and air-conditioning.

Just up the hill from downtown, the **Capricorn Apartment Hotel** (7 St. Fort St., tel. 330-3732, www.capricornfiji.com) has 34 spacious air-conditioned units with cooking facilities, fridges, and local TV beginning at F$140 single or double. A room upstairs is F$15 more, a one-bedroom flat is F$160, and the two-bedroom apartment is F$260. The three- and four-story apartment blocks edge the swimming pool, and there are good views of the harbor from the individual balconies. It's a good choice for families.

Twenty self-catering units owned by the National Olympic Committee are available at **Suva Apartments** (17 Bau St., tel. 330-4280, fasanoc@fasanoc.org.fj, $115), where a minimum two-week stay is required. All rooms are air-conditioned. The apartments are popular with visiting athletes and business travelers, so the residence is fairly quiet. By staying here, you help support organized sports in Fiji.

The four-story **Sunset Apartment Motel** (tel. 330-1799), at the corner of Gordon and Murray Streets, has standard rooms for F$110 single or double and deluxe rooms at F$145. Add a third person for $F35.

The four-story **Elixir Motel Apartments** (77 Gordon St., tel. 330-3288, plantworld@connect.com.fj), at the corner of Gordon and Malcolm Streets, were extensively renovated in 2017, and have their own restaurant and bar. A standard suite is F$151 single or double, and two-bedroom apartments with kitchen range F$183-214. A family suite, for two adults and two children under age 12, is F$330.

US$100-150

The **Southern Cross Hotel** (63 Gordon St., tel. 331-4233, southerncross@kidanet.net.fj) is a high-rise concrete building. The 32 air-conditioned rooms accommodating up to three people start at F$336 for a standard room on the 4th floor, or a bit more (F$370) for the deluxe rooms on the 2nd, 3rd, and 5th floors; ask for a walk-in discount. There is also a one-bedroom apartment for F$447. The restaurant on the 6th floor serves Korean dishes.

The 10-story **Tanoa Plaza Hotel** (Gordon St., tel. 331-2300, www.tanoahotels.com), formerly known as the Berjaya Hotel, at the corner of Malcolm and Gordon Streets, is the tallest hotel in Fiji. The 48 superior rooms are F$225 single or double, eight deluxe rooms run F$355, and four penthouse suites are F$685. All rooms have fridges, TVs, and fairly comfortable beds, and all face the harbor. The air-conditioning helps muffle the noise from inside and out. The Tanoa Plaza has a business center and conference facilities for groups of up to 200 people, plus a swimming pool behind the building.

The ★ **Suva Motor Inn** (Gorrie St., tel. 331-3973, www.hexagonfiji.com), a three-story complex near Albert Park at the corner of Mitchell and Gorrie Streets, has 36 air-conditioned studio apartments with kitchenettes at F$225 for a single or double; add a third person for F$35. The nine two-bedroom apartments capable of accommodating five persons are F$400. A courtyard swimming pool with waterslide and waterfall faces the restaurant-bar (happy hour 1700-1900). The house band is good. This property is well worth considering by families who want a bit of comfort.

The **Peninsula International Hotel** (MacGregor Rd., tel. 331-3711, www.peninsula.com.fj), at the corner of MacGregor Road and Pender Street, is a four-story building with a swimming pool. The 100 air-conditioned rooms underwent a much-needed facelift in 2018. Rates are F$200-260 single or double, and deluxe rooms that sleep three are F$310. A family suite is F$310 for the first two people, F$30 each for up to two more people.

De Vos on the Park (Sukuna Park, tel. 330-5005, http://devosonthepark.com) is a former YWCA that's been converted to a 24-room hotel. Some of the suites are quite large, accommodating up to six people, and include lounges, balconies, and sea or park views. Rates range F$218-399 for up to two adults, plus F$80/F$35 per additional adult/child. De Vos is finding its niche and is aiming for upscale business travelers, but you have to pay for Internet. The **Sportsman's Bar**, with a huge flat-screen TV, gets lively during rugby matches.

Quest Serviced Apartments (Renwick Rd., tel. 331-9118 or 331-9119, stay@questsuva.com, www.questsuva.com) has 54 apartments on the 6th and 7th floors of the Suva Central building. It's the most upscale option in the heart of downtown. It's quiet and well constructed, and all units were modernized in 2017. Rates are F$256 for a studio or F$342 for a one-bedroom; join the units to form a two-bedroom, two-bath apartment for F$524. All units have a fridge, but the TVs may only pick up local stations. There is free parking, cable, and Internet, as well as paid breakfast, pantry-stocking, and dry-cleaning options.

The **Five Princes Hotel** (5 Princes Rd., tel. 338-1575, www.fiveprinceshotel.com) is housed in an elegant 1920 mansion in Samabula South. Aviator Harold Gatty bought the property in 1949 and later it became a bed-and-breakfast known as Tanoa House. The three air-conditioned rooms in the main building are F$280 double, while the four self-catering cottages in the garden go for F$310.

The **Novotel Suva** (Queens Rd., tel. 336-2450, www.novotelsuva.com.fj) at Lami, on the Bay of Islands seven kilometers west of Suva, includes a 600-seat convention center, a bayside swimming pool, and floating seafood restaurant (try the marinated raw fish). The 108 rooms with private bath, fridge, and air-conditioning in this tasteful two-story building start at F$235 double for standard garden/ocean view or F$260 superior ocean view. Two children under 16 can share a parent's room for free. Many cruising yachts anchor here, and the location is the most picturesque of any Suva hotel. Though this property is far from the center, bus service into Suva is good and a taxi into the heart of town is less than F$15.

Over US$150

For glorious old-fashioned luxury, there's nothing like the ★ **Grand Pacific Hotel** (584 Victoria Parade, tel. 322-2000, info@gph.com.fj, www.grandpacifichotel.com). Rack rates start at F$549 for a double room, with a range of options all the way up to F$2,088 for the Royal Suite, but you can almost always find deals that drop the price to a third of that. The hotel's main restaurant, which has indoor and poolside seating areas, is a popular place for local bigwigs to meet and make deals. Visiting rugby players, actors, and business types mix it up with tourists. You can order a bowl of kava to share or enjoy a filet mignon. For a real taste of the colonial lifestyle, dress up and savor the pastries at the Sunday High Tea (1400-1600, F$55 pp). The little Swiss Bakery out front (daily 1000-2100) is a bit too fussy to satisfy any real appetite, but it makes decent cappuccinos on the veranda, and also serves lamingtons, a bright pink coconut-covered Australian cake. Rosie Holidays has a travel desk inside, and **Global Pacific Tours** (tel. 866-4060, sammyali29@yahoo.com) handles airport transfers and day rentals of cars and drivers from an office just outside.

Next door to the Grand Pacific is the 130-room **Holiday Inn Suva** (501 Victoria Parade, tel. 323-6006, www.holidayinn.com). Formerly a Travelodge, it's a big American-style place with 76 air-conditioned standard rooms with fridges and TVs beginning at F$449 single or double; 34 renovated superior garden rooms at F$467; and 20 superior sea-view rooms at F$521. The swimming pool behind the two-story buildings compensates for the lack of a beach, and the view of Viti Levu from here is splendid. A Rosie Holidays tour desk is at the hotel, and there's a Mediterranean restaurant, a cozy piano bar, a fitness center, and three conference rooms.

INFORMATION AND SERVICES

Tourism

Brochures, but not much else, are available from the **Ministry of Tourism** (tel. 330-2060, www.tourism.gov.fj), on Level 3 of the Civic Tower behind the City Library.

Discount Flight Centre (tel. 331-7207) is efficient and has various offices around Suva: at MHCC in the ground floor supermarket area, across the road at Dominion House, at Mid-City Mall, and at Damodar City mall.

Rosie Holidays (46 Gordon St., tel. 331-4436, www.rosiefiji.com), near Sarita Flats and in a few hotels, books tours, transfers, and accommodations all around Fiji. The **ATS Pacific** tour desk (tel. 331-2287, www.atspacific.com) in the lobby of the Holiday Inn does the same.

To book or change flights, you can drop by the offices of **Air New Zealand** (tel. 331-3100) in the Queensland Insurance Center, 9 Victoria Parade; or **Fiji Airways** (tel. 330-4388) in the Colonial Building on Victoria Parade.

The **South Pacific Tourism Organization** (FNPF Plaza, Victoria Parade, 3rd Fl., tel. 330-4177, www.south-pacific.travel) provides information on other countries in the region.

History

Beneath the bustling modern town is a grand history, much of which is being painstakingly preserved by the **National Trust of Fiji** (tel. 330-1807, info@nationaltrust.org.fj), a good source of information on historical sites in Fiji. From prehistoric ruins, through the colonial encounter, to the arrival of indentured Indian workers, several centuries of stories are embedded in the geography of Suva—if you just know where to scratch the surface.

The library of the **Bureau of Statistics** (tel. 331-5822, www.statsfiji.gov.fj, Mon.-Fri. 0800-1300 and 1400-1600), on the 5th floor of the Ratu Sukuna House at Victoria Parade and MacArthur Street, has many interesting technical publications on the country. Ask for a free copy of "Fiji Facts and Figures."

Maps

The **Map Shop** (tel. 331-8631, CK Patel Building, 94 Raojibhai Patel St., Mon.-Fri. 0800-1600) of the Lands and Survey Department sells detailed island-by-island maps of Fiji. It's tucked behind the back entrance to the building, up a flight of stairs. It's cash only and they generally don't have change. If you want your map laminated, order three days in advance. A complete list of maps for sale and current prices is at www.lands.gov.fj (click on the "Map Shop fees" link). Simpler maps are available for purchase at post offices.

The **Fiji Hydrographic Office** (top floor, Amra St., Walu Bay, tel. 331-5457, Mon.-Fri. 0800-1630) sells navigational charts of the Yasawas, Kadavu, eastern Vanua Levu, and the Lau Group at F$23 per sheet. All other areas are covered by British navigational charts of Fiji, which are sold by **Carpenters Shipping** (22 Edinburgh Rd., tel. 331-2244, www.carpship.com.fj), across from the BP service station, for a whopping F$104 each; it's better to buy these overseas.

Money

There are plenty of ATMs throughout Suva: at the massive bank headquarters that you can't miss while strolling around Victoria Parade, outside the Village 6 Cinemas, and inside the shopping malls and food courts. The main banks have dedicated foreign exchange counters. You might also check the rates at private exchange offices such as **MH Money Express** (50 Thomson St., tel. 322-8811, Mon.-Fri. 0830-1730, Sat. 0830-1500), **Lotus Foreign Exchange** (30 Thomson St., tel. 331-9755, Mon.-Fri. 0830-1700, Sat. 0830-1300) opposite the Westpac Bank, and **UAE Exchange** (53 Waimanu Rd., tel. 331-8133). All are similar.

If you need a quick infusion of funds, **GlobalEX** (Victoria Parade at Gordon St., tel. 331-4812, Mon.-Fri. 0800-1730, Sat. 0800-1400) is a Western Union agent. Money can be sent to you here from almost anywhere in the world through the Western Union network.

For those still using travelers checks, the **Bank South Pacific** (BSP, tel. 331-4400, www.colonial.com.fj, Mon.-Fri. 0900-1600, Sat. 0900-1400) has a commission-free Bureau de Change on Renwick Road at Pier Street.

Internet

If you're content to stick to bankers' hours, **Fintel** (158 Victoria Parade, tel. 331-2933, www.fintelfiji.com, Mon.-Fri. 0830-1700, Sat. 0900-1700) is also your best bet for Internet. As Fiji's main telecommunications provider, it provides very fast access in a comfortable air-conditioned room at F$2 for 30 minutes, or F$3 an hour.

For those middle-of-the-night webchats with another time zone, go to the 24-hour **SkyNet Café,** on Gordon Street near Victoria Parade. The 40 computers are available at F$5 an hour.

Other options, at F$4 an hour, are the comfortable, air-conditioned **Connect Internet** (10 Thomson St., tel. 330-0777, www.connect.com.fj, Mon.-Fri. 0800-2200, Sat. 0900-2000, Sun. 0900-1800), opposite the General Post Office, and the bustling **Cyber Zone** (3rd Floor, 107 Cumming St. at the corner of Thomson St., 992-3373, Mon.-Sat. 0800-2000), a favorite of gamers.

Free Wi-Fi hot spots are at My FNPF Plaza in the food court near the inexplicable gigantic plaster *tyrannosaurus rex*, as well as at Tappoo City.

Phone

Fintel, the **Fiji International Telecommunications** office (158 Victoria Parade, tel. 331-2933, www.fintelfiji.com, Mon.-Fri. 0830-1700, Sat. 0900-1700) is the best place in Suva to make long-distance calls. Its Kidatalk (www.kidatalk.com.fj) system allows you to phone many countries at F$1 for 10-20 minutes, after which it's F$0.11 for each additional minute. No phone card is required. You can also send faxes here.

Telecom Fiji (tel. 330-4019, www.tfl.com.fj)

Eco-Volunteering

Volunteers of the It's Time Foundation installed solar panels at Rabi High School.

If you'd like to spend some time in Fiji volunteering, you could inquire in these offices, which operate out of Suva. Volunteers with scuba certification and marine biology backgrounds are particularly welcome.

- **NatureFiji-MareqetiiFiji** (Flat 1, 249 Rewa St., tel. 310-0598, support@naturefiji.org, http://naturefiji.org) works on biodiversity projects and holds occasional public activities, such as planting endangered palm species, or a scavenger hunt for kids to find six animals that live amid mangrove roots; the website has upcoming events. Overseas members can join to support for F$50 annually, and the website's store is a great source for books on Fijian bird and plant life (they ship internationally).
- Several nongovernmental organizations (NGOs) sit side by side in a Suva suburb. The **National Trust for Fiji** (3 Ma'afu St., tel. 330-1807, www.nationaltrust.org.fj) manages several nature reserves and historical sites around Fiji. Its neighbor, the regional office of the **World Wide Fund for Nature** (4 Ma'afu St., tel. 331-5533, www.wwfpacific.org.fj), funds various projects in support of wildlife and wild habitats throughout the South Pacific. Next door is the South Pacific Country Program of the **Wildlife Conservation Society** (11 Ma'afu St., tel. 331-5174, www.wcs.org).
- The **Pacific Blue Foundation** (tel. 839-0473, http://pacificbluefoundation.org) operates conservation and cultural projects on Beqa, Lau, and elsewhere. It also has an office in La Jolla, California (U.S. tel. 858/534-8947).
- The **It's Time Foundation** (Aus. tel. 02/8003-4143, www.iitime.org) installs solar panels at rural schools, replacing expensive and polluting diesel generators. Volunteers with electrician skills are particularly needed.

operates a telephone center on Scott Street next to Village 6 Cinemas.

Health

Suva's **Colonial War Memorial Hospital** (Extension Rd., tel. 331-3444), about a kilometer northeast of the center, is available 24 hours a day for emergencies and has Fiji's only **Hyperbaric Unit** (tel. 321-5525), with an entrance off Waimanu Road.

Miot Pacific Hospital (120 Amy St., tel. 330-3404, www.miotpacifichospitals.com.fj) provides vastly superior service and state-of-the-art facilities and is open 24 hours a day. Local drivers may know it by its old name, Suva Private Hospital. It's F$35/F$110 to see a general practitioner/specialist, and the pharmacy is excellent.

Mitchells Clinic (tel. 337-1133, mitchellsclinic@connect.com.fj), on level 4A of Tappoo City, is run by two Australian-trained general practitioners, Dr. Rosemary Mitchell and Dr. Krupali Rathod Tappoo. They can deal with travelers' ailments as well as women's health and pediatric care.

FijiCare Medical Center (123 Amy St., tel. 331-3355, Mon.-Fri. 0830-1300 and 1400-1800, Sat. 0830-1130) has several foreign doctors (one female) on its roster. Consultations are F$35.

A dentist is **Dr. Abdul S. Haroon** (Epworth House, Ste. 12, tel. 331-3870), off Nina Street and just down the hall from Patterson Brothers.

SuperDrug Pharmacy has three locations: one in Nabua (opposite Westpac Bank at the traffic crossing, tel. 338-7766), others at MHCC and MY FNPF Plaza. All are open daily 0900-2000.

Fiji Women's Crisis Center (88 Gordon St., tel. 331-3300 answered 24 hours, www.fijiwomen.com, center hours Mon.-Fri. 0830-1630, Sat. 0900-1200), opposite the Tanoa Plaza Hotel, offers free and confidential counseling and other services for women and children who require immediate help.

Public Toilets

Public toilets are just outside the Handicraft Market on the side of the building facing the harbor; in Thurston Gardens; on the ground floor of the FNPF Dolphin Plaza at the corner of Loftus and Vicoria Parade; in My FNPF Plaza on Stuart Street (there is a set of toilets on every level close to the lifts); in the food court area at Tappoo City; on the food court level at the Harbor Center (F$0.30); at MHCC Food Court (F$0.20); beside Nubukalou Creek off Renwick Road; and between the vegetable market and the bus station.

The public toilets in Sukuna Park (Mon.-Sat. 0800-1535) cost F$0.80; you can shower here for F$1.30.

Laundry

Since 1930, **Suva Electric Laundry** (31 Knollys St., tel. 330-1442, Mon.-Fri. 0730-1745, Sat. 0800-1400) has been providing brisk wash-dry-fold service, with no chitchat. Drop off your bag (no need to count items; it's F$3 per kilogram) in the morning and pick it up by 1730.

A similar facility on the other side of town is **Flagstaff Laundry & Drycleaners** (62 Bau St., tel. 330-1214).

TRANSPORTATION

Getting There

AIR

From Nadi, both **Fiji Link** (www.fijiairways.com) and **Northern Airways** (www.northernair.com.fj) fly daily to Nausori Airport, north of Suva. Regular flights to Suva are scheduled from Labasa, Taveuni, Cicia, Vanuabalavu, Savusavu, Kadavu, and Lakeba.

Nausori Airport (tel. 672-5777, www.airportsfiji.com/nausori_airport.php) is Fiji's second-largest airport, and a hub for flights to the eastern islands. There's a café that serves pastries, sandwiches, samosas, and coffee. The ANZ Bank at the airport has an ATM. **Avis** (tel. 337-8361) and **Budget** (tel. 330-2450) have car rental desks in the terminal. There is no luggage storage facility or lockers.

A taxi between Suva and the airport will run about F$25. You can save money by taking a taxi from the airport only as far as Nausori (4 km, F$3.50), then hopping a local bus to Suva from there (19 km, with service every 10 minutes until 2200 for F$2.10). It's also possible to catch a local bus to Nausori (F$0.70) on the highway opposite the airport about every 15 minutes. When going to the airport, catch a local bus from Suva to Nausori, then take a taxi to the airport.

You can catch Sunbeam Transport express

buses from Nausori to Lautoka at 0635, 0715, 0855, 1240, 1405, and 1745 (246 km, 5.5 hours, F$19.40).

CAR

By road, the quickest route from Nadi is the southern way, along the Queens Road through Sigatoka town and the Coral Coast. It's a mostly smooth two-lane road with beautiful coastal views at some spots, and takes about four hours. You could also opt for the northern Kings Road, taking in a different set of sights on your way back; count on six hours of drive time. Don't get talked into a daylong road trip all the way from Nadi to Suva and back—that's eight full hours in a vehicle.

BUS

The **Coral Sun Express** (7 Yasawa St., Lautoka, tel. 672-3105 or 999-2708) is a comfortable, economical way to travel the southern route, as it stops only at major hotels. The air-conditioned, once-daily bus departs Suva from the Holiday Inn at 0715 and arrives at Nadi Airport four hours later. The return trip leaves from the Nadi Airport international *arrivals* terminal at 1300. If it's very busy, they may add a second bus departing half an hour later. The cost one-way is F$25 per person if you call Coral Sun to book directly. You'll pay F$5 more if you book through an agency or your hotel's travel desk.

Express Sunbeam and Pacific Transport buses are equally comfortable but make about twice as many stops as the Coral Sun Express. These are F$18 direct from Nadi Airport to Suva's main bus station. There are also plenty of slow local buses that travel the Queens Road. Catch them at the main bus station in either Suva or Nadi airport; it's best to inquire there for routes and times, as options are numerous.

TAXI

A taxi from Nadi to Suva along the Queens Road costs about F$200 one-way. If you'd like to meander, negotiate a flat rate and let the driver know you'll be stopping for lunch, sightseeing, and/or beach time along the way. Write out a list of the places you might like to stop, and show it to the driver beforehand, so he can't demand more money later on.

In Suva, you can go to the **East-West Shuttle Service** on the waterfront behind the Civic Centre and the Olympic Pool to nab a seat in a shared taxi for F$25 direct to Nadi, or F$100 for the whole four-seat car. You can make a full day of it by hiring the car to Nadi for around F$200, with lots of stops along the way; again, write down your list.

YACHTING FACILITIES

Many yachts anchor off the **Novotel Suva** in Lami, a recognized cyclone anchorage.

The **Royal Suva Yacht Club** (tel. 331-2921, VHF channel 16, www.rsyc.org.fj), on Foster Road between Suva and Lami, offers visiting yachts such amenities as mooring privileges, warm showers, laundry facilities, a restaurant and bar, email, and the use of club services. There have been reports of thefts from boats anchored here, so lock up anything of value.

Getting Around

CAR

Car rentals are available in Suva from **Avis** (at Nabua, tel. 337-8361, www.avis.com.fj), **Budget** (123 Foster Rd., Walu Bay, tel. 331-5899, www.budget.com.fj), **Carpenters Rentals** (Foster Rd. across from the Mobil station, tel. 331-3644, www.carpenters.com.fj), **Central** (295 Victoria Parade, tel. 331-1866), **Dove** (64 Votua Road, off Ono St., tel. 331-1755, doverentals@connect.com.fj), **Hertz** (Nausori Airport,, tel. 992-3923, www.hertzfiji.net), and **Thrifty** (46 Gordon St., tel. 331-4436, www.rosiefiji.com). If you're driving, note that parking meters in downtown Suva streets must be fed F$0.20 every 15 minutes weekdays 0800-1630, Saturdays 0800-1230.

BUS

For travel within and around the Suva area, Suva's main bus station, near the harbor and the market, offers transport in every direction. It can be a little confusing, as there are numerous companies, and timetables are not posted. Most drivers know where a certain bus will park, so just ask. There's continuous local service until about 2100. From anywhere in Suva and the vicinity, you can jump on any bus headed toward downtown Suva and wind up back at the market.

TAXI

Taxis are easy to find and relatively cheap. All taxis in Suva are required to have working meters and have a day rate and a night rate. From 0600 to 2200, flag fall is F$1.50 and then it's F$0.50 a kilometer. From 2200 to 0600, flag fall is F$2 plus F$0.50 a kilometer. Waiting time costs F$0.10 a minute. Fares average less than F$5 in the city center and less than F$15 out to the suburbs. Drivers are not obliged to use their meters for trips over 16 kilometers, so you'll need to negotiate a fare. To hire a taxi for a city tour might cost about F$25 an hour.

Nausori Taxi (tel. 330-4178), based at the taxi kiosk in the parking lot at the Holiday Inn, offers a shuttle service from Suva to Nausori Airport at F$10 per person. Trips are scheduled daily at 0445, 0845, 1300, 1530, and 1645; you must make a reservation the day prior.

Other taxi services are **Angel Taxi** (tel. 356-0087), **Regent** (tel. 331-2100) and **CWM** (tel. 331-1137).

North of Suva

The outposts north of Suva are home to numerous Fijian villages, but for tourists, they're mainly of interest as departure points for elsewhere. The town of Nausori is home to Fiji's second-largest airport and isn't much of a destination itself, but close by is the lovely Colo-i-Suva Forest Park, which most people visit as a day trip from Suva. The park is also home to the only accommodation option near the airport, the Colo-i-Suva Rainforest Eco Resort.

The docks of Bau Landing and Natovi provide ship passage to the eastern islands. The islands of Bau and Viwa are rich with history. Toberua Island is the only resort-style destination, with a fine reef.

NAUSORI

Most visitors know **Nausori** only for its airport, which serves Suva and eastern Fiji. The town is situated on the Rewa River, 19 kilometers northeast of Suva. It's Fiji's third-largest town, with a predominantly Indo-Fijian population of 47,500.

Sights

To go between the airport and Suva, you cross Fiji's largest river, the Rewa. In 1937 the nine-span **Rewa River Bridge** was erected here. In 2006, it was replaced by Fiji's longest and widest bridge, 425 meters long and four lanes wide, built with F$30 million in European Union aid.

At the end of the old Rewa bridge, the **Syria Monument** (1983) commemorates the wreck of an iron sailing ship, the *Syria*, on Nasilai Point in May 1884. Fifty-seven of the 439 indentured Indian laborers aboard ship at the time drowned. The monument tells the story of the rescue.

Several ATMs and food stalls are clustered around the bustling **Nausori Market,** on Verrier Street across from the bus station. A block over is an MHCC supermarket, a Westpac bank with an ATM, and a Pizza King restaurant.

The river delta is busy with motorboat traffic to villages upstream, where the only site of interest is Naililili village. There, French Catholic missionaries built **St. Joseph's Church** in 1905 of solid limestone, with stained glass windows. Inquire at nearby Nakelo Landing or Wainibokasi Landing to find a boat headed upriver.

Getting There

Nausori is home to the second-largest airport in Fiji, the **Nausori Airport** (tel. 672-5777, www.airportsfiji.com/nausori_airport.php). It's the gateway airport to Suva as well as a hub to the eastern islands.

A taxi between Suva and the airport will run about F$25. You can save money by taking a taxi from the airport only as far as Nausori town (4 km, F$3.50), then hopping a local bus to Suva from there (19 km, with service every 10 minutes until 2200 for F$2.10). It's also possible to catch a local bus to Nausori (F$0.70) on the highway opposite the airport about every 15 minutes. When going to the airport, catch a local bus from Suva to Nausori, then take a taxi to the airport.

You can catch Sunbeam Transport express buses from Nausori to Lautoka at 0635, 0715, 0855, 1240, 1405, and 1745 (246 km, 5.5 hours, F$19.40).

★ COLO-I-SUVA FOREST PARK

The lovely **Colo-i-Suva Forest Park** (tel. 332-0211, daily 0900-1600, F$5), at an altitude of 122-183 meters, offers 6.5 kilometers of trails through the lush forest flanking the upper drainage area of Waisila Creek. It's close to the airport and well worth a half-day excursion before your flight: You can hike, take a dip in one of the waterfalls or natural swimming pools, and have a picnic. The mahogany trees you see here are natives of Central America and were planted after the area was logged in the 1950s, with the park opening in 1973. With the lovely green forests behind Suva in full view, this is one of the most breathtaking places in all of Fiji, and you may spot a few native butterflies, birds, reptiles, and frogs. The park is so unspoiled that it's hard to believe that you're only 11 kilometers from the city.

For families, the **Lower Pools** are ideal, with a children's swimming area for tots; the more adventurous can launch from a rope swing and drop into the water below. For a less populated spot, head to the **Upper Pools;** a pleasant half-kilometer nature trail begins here. Both falls have their own parking areas.

For a **longer hike,** start at the trailhead just east of the forestry station, then follow the left (northern) fork along the Big Dakua Trail. Take the detours to the Lower Pools and Upper Pools if you wish. Returning to the main trail, head back west along the left (southern) fork, which is the Falls Trail. After about 400 meters, you'll reach Waisila Falls, a pretty 15-meter waterfall with several tiers and a fine pool for swimming, as well as a picnic shelter. The whole loop (minus the detours) is about two kilometers of hilly terrain—you could race through it in an hour, but it's more pleasant to linger.

Security has improved here since a police post was set up, but you must still keep an eye on your gear if you go swimming in the pools. Muggings are also not unknown in this park. Although the park doesn't have any tourist information, you can see a map and birders' guide online (http://coloisuva.com/index.php/activities/birdwatching) or buy an informative, full-color bird guide for F$5 at **Colo-i-Suva Rainforest Eco Resort** (tel. 332-0562, 891-3111, 927-3472, or 783-9163, info@coloisuva.com.fj, www.coloisuva.com), 50 meters from the entrance to the park, across from the police post. Consider picking up food or spending the night at this well-managed lodge, which has an attractive restaurant-bar (tel. 332-0562) overlooking a small lake. Keep your muffin crumbs to yourself and instead ask for free pellets to feed the tiny tilapia. Happy hour specials are 1700-1900. They may be willing to store your luggage behind the desk while you hike.

Colo-i-Suva is easily accessible on the Sawani or Serea buses (F$1.75), which leave from the westernmost lane at Suva Bus Station every hour (Sunday every two hours). The last bus back to Suva leaves at about 1800. A taxi will be F$15-F$20. Try to come on a dry day, as it's even rainier here than in Suva and the creeks are prone to flooding.

Accommodations

★ **Colo-i-Suva Rainforest Eco Resort** (tel. 332-0562, 891-3111, 927-3472, or 783-9163, info@coloisuva.com.fj, www.coloisuva.com), near the entrance to Colo-i-Suva Forest Park, 11 kilometers north of Suva, is the closest accommodation to Nausori Airport and caters well to the traveler who values cleanliness and enjoys escaping the city. The rack rates are high to account for agency commissions: They range from F$109 for a fan-cooled budget double, through a variety of room configurations all the way up to F$335 for a luxurious two-bedroom air-conditioned *bure* with a lake-view deck. Booking direct yields you an immediate discount of at least 25 percent, and prices drop to about half of rack rates for longer stays. There's free Wi-Fi, and every window opens onto a lush forest scene. If you're staying a while, you can get your own mailbox here with a key. Owners Val Salama and Brian Riches are on-site and attentive to everyone's needs. The large thatched restaurant-bar overlooks a former rock quarry that has been converted into a lovely lake teeming with tiny tilapia. At breakfast, try the coconut-flour pancakes (F$13.50). Happy hour is 1700-1900. Colo-i-Suva can be reached on the Sawani or Serea buses (F$1.15), which leave Suva bus station and stop at the police post directly across the road from the lodge. A taxi will cost F$12.

BAU ISLAND

Bau, a tiny eight-hectare island just east of Viti Levu, has a special place in Fiji's history, as this was the seat of high chief Ratu Cakobau, the first head of united Fiji. At its pinnacle, Bau had a population of 3,000, and more than 20 temples stood on the island's central plain.

You can see everything on the island in an hour or so. Note the great stone slabs that form docks and seawalls around much of the island, which once accommodated Bau's fleet of hundreds of war canoes. The graves of the Cakobau family and many of the old chiefs lie on the hilltop behind the school. The large, sturdy stone church near the provincial offices was the first church in Fiji. Inside its nearly one-meter-thick walls, just in front of the altar, is the old stone once used for human sacrifices, today the baptismal font. Now painted white, this font was once known as Ratu Cakobau's "skull crusher," and it's said that a thousand brains were splattered against it. Across from the church are huge ancient trees and the thatched Council House on the site of the onetime temple of the war god Cagawalu. The family of the late Sir George Cakobau, governor-general of Fiji from 1973 to 1983, has a large traditional-style home on the island.

Getting There

To get to Bau, take the bus (five daily) 11 kilometers west from Nausori to Bau Landing, where outboards provide transport the island. Be aware that Bau is not considered a tourist attraction, and from time to time visitors are prevented from going to the island. It's important to get someone to invite you across, which they'll do willingly if you show a genuine interest in Fijian history. Bring a big bundle of *waka* for the *turaga-ni-koro* and ask very politely to be shown around. There could be some confusion about who's to receive the *sevusevu*, however, as everyone on Bau is a chief! The more respectful your dress and demeanor, the better your chances of success. If you're told to contact the Ministry of Fijian Affairs in Suva, just depart gracefully, as that's their way of saying no. After all, it's up to them.

VIWA ISLAND

A good alternative if you aren't invited to visit Bau itself is **Viwa,** where a single Fijian village stands. To reach the island, hire an outboard at Bau Landing; if you're lucky, you'll be able to join some locals who are going.

Before Ratu Cakobau adopted Christianity in 1854, Methodist missionaries working to

1: hiking through the rainforest at Colo-i-Suva
2: a pond at Colo-i-Suva **3:** the Tailevu Coast, seen at sunset from aboard the ferry to Ovalau Island.

1

2

3

convert him and his people resided on Viwa, just across the water from Bau. Here the first Fijian New Testament was printed in 1847; Reverend John Hunt, who did the translation, lies buried in the graveyard beside the church that bears his name.

TOBERUA ISLAND

The tiny reef island of **Toberua** off the eastern tip of Viti Levu measures barely 250 meters long at its widest point. Toberua doesn't get much rain so there are no mosquitoes. There's golfing on the reef at low tide, and it's a unique experience to snorkel among the sea snakes just offshore. It's open only to guests of the resort here.

Created in 1968, **Toberua Island Resort** (tel. 992-9190 or 992-9590, reservations@toberua.com, www.toberua.com) was one of Fiji's first luxury outer-island resorts. The thatched *bures* all have ocean views and are designed in the purest Fijian style, and the resort's small size means peace and quiet. The rate is NZ$385-567 for a family-friendly *bure* designed for two adults and two children. A daily meal plan with very good food is NZ$110 per adult and NZ$60 per child age 2-12 ordering from the children's menu. A la carte is also possible but there are no other dining options on the island. Large families or groups may want to consider the three-bedroom, three-bathroom villa, with three king beds and four single beds, at NZ$1,505 per night. You can also book the whole island, for 36 adults, for NZ$13,000 per night. The par-32 course has nine holes from 90 to 180 meters, and clubs and balls are provided. Scuba diving is F$200/350 for one/two tanks. Most other activities are free, including snorkeling, sailing, windsurfing, and kayak trips to a bird sanctuary or mangrove forest, and there's a swimming pool.

The resort arranges transfers from Suva airport by car and boat at NZ$155 per person.

THE TAILEVU COAST

The **Tailevu Coast** on the eastern coast of Viti Levu is remote and harder to access, but pretty in its own right. The main attraction here is dolphin-watching at Moon Reef.

About an hour's drive (52 km) north of Nausori is **Natovi,** terminus of ferry services from Vanua Levu and Ovalau. If you're headed to the islands, or if you're driving from Suva toward the Sunshine Coast, you might break your journey here and enjoy a day or two completely off the grid.

Note that Cyclone Winston severely damaged this area in 2016, and the facilities have been slow in recovering.

Mount Tova

You can climb **Mount Tova** (647 m) for a sweeping view of the entire Tailevu area. Starting from Silana village, or Nataleira a couple of kilometers southeast, it will take about three hours to go up and another two to come back down. An experienced hiker might be able to find the way, but it's better to hire a guide in one of the villages.

Waidina Waterfall

In 2016 the region saw thousands of visitors due to a rumor that the **Waidina waterfall** had miracle healing powers. At the peak of the craze, all 27 of the village's households were hosting guests who would stay and bathe for several days until the waters healed them of their various maladies; the chief had to restrict bathing hours. Today a sign from the main road at the village of Natadradave still points out the falls, and someone will be happy to direct you toward the five-minute walk. On a hot day, a dip in the icy green pool below the two-tier waterfall is certainly restorative.

Dolphin-Watching

The main attraction in the region is **Moon Reef,** the only reef in Fiji that's home to spinner dolphins. Day trips from Suva, including ground transportation and lunch, are arranged by **Dolphin Watch Fiji** (tel. 991-6338, takalana@gmail.com) for F$215 per person. A boat takes you out in the morning, when the dolphins enter the reef; they surface to greet and race with the boat. Snorkeling is done at another site along the reef, so as not to disturb the dolphins. You also see them frolicking on your return trip before they depart to hunt at sea in the afternoon. Trips are discounted to F$60 per person if you don't need transportation from Suva.

Accommodations

Takalana Bay Beach Resort (tel. 991-6338 or 356-0295, takalana@gmail.com, takalana.blogspot.com) is a large country estate standing on a lush garden hilltop that overlooks Vatu-i-Ra Passage, with good views of the Lomaiviti Group of islands and Vanua Levu. It's an off-the-grid, family-run destination with home-cooked food (meals are included in the room rate); there is often no hot water or electricity. Dorm rooms with shared bathroom are F$115 single or F$220 double; a private room or *bure* with bathroom is F$250, and a family *bure* for two adults and two children is F$285. Mosquito nets are provided.

Nearby **Natalei Eco-Lodge** (tel. 354-8905, 943-1787, or 991-6338, nataleieco@gmail.com, F$185 s/d) has eight traditional thatched Fijian *bures* along a black-sand beach. It's run by the residents of the surrounding village, who take personal pleasure in guiding you as you enjoy their region. The food here is abundant, and if the six-person *bure* is empty, you can ask for an upgrade even if you're just two people.

Getting There

It's easier to approach from the southern (Suva) side than from the northern route, which has a rougher road. Catch the local air-conditioned express buses (Flying Prince Transport, Inter-Cities Bus Ltd., Sunbeam Transport, or Vatukoula Express, F$12-14) from Suva's main western bus station to Korovou town, in Tailevu, and then take a taxi/van to your lodge. Even if you're coming from Rakiraki, it's better to drive south into the interior on Kings Road to Korovou, and then head up the coast. If you're renting a car, you'll want a 4WD vehicle, as the final stretch of the trip, from Lawaki village to the lodges, is unpaved.

The Kadavu Group

At 450 square kilometers, **Kadavu Island** is Fiji's fourth largest, and one of its least developed. A mountainous, varied island with waterfalls plummeting from the rounded, forested hilltops, Kadavu is outstanding for its vistas, beaches, and reefs. The three hilly sections of Kadavu are connected by two low isthmuses, with the sea biting so deeply into the island that on a map its shape resembles that of a wasp.

Just northeast of the main island is the fabulous **Great Astrolabe Reef,** which stretches nearly 100 kilometers. Right on the reef is **Ono Island,** just 30 square kilometers. Nearby **Galoa** and **Yaukuve Levu** round out the group, along with some uninhabited islets.

The Kadavu group is all about quiet island life. Some 12,000 indigenous Fijians live in 70 villages across the group, working mostly as farmers, fishers, and loggers who harvest nonnative pine for export. Most of the island's dozen or so small resorts are located on the watery channel between Kadavu and Ono.

KADAVU ISLAND

The only town in the group is tiny **Vunisea** on Kadavu Island. Located at the junction between the eastern and central sections, Vunisea is the provincial headquarters of Kadavu Province. The airstrip and wharf on Kadavu are each a 10-minute walk in different directions from the center of town. There's a police station, hospital, and post office/telephone office (Mon.-Fri. 0800-1500) that sells some groceries and stationery. It also houses a small branch of the Bank South Pacific—but there's no ATM and it doesn't

The Kadavu Group

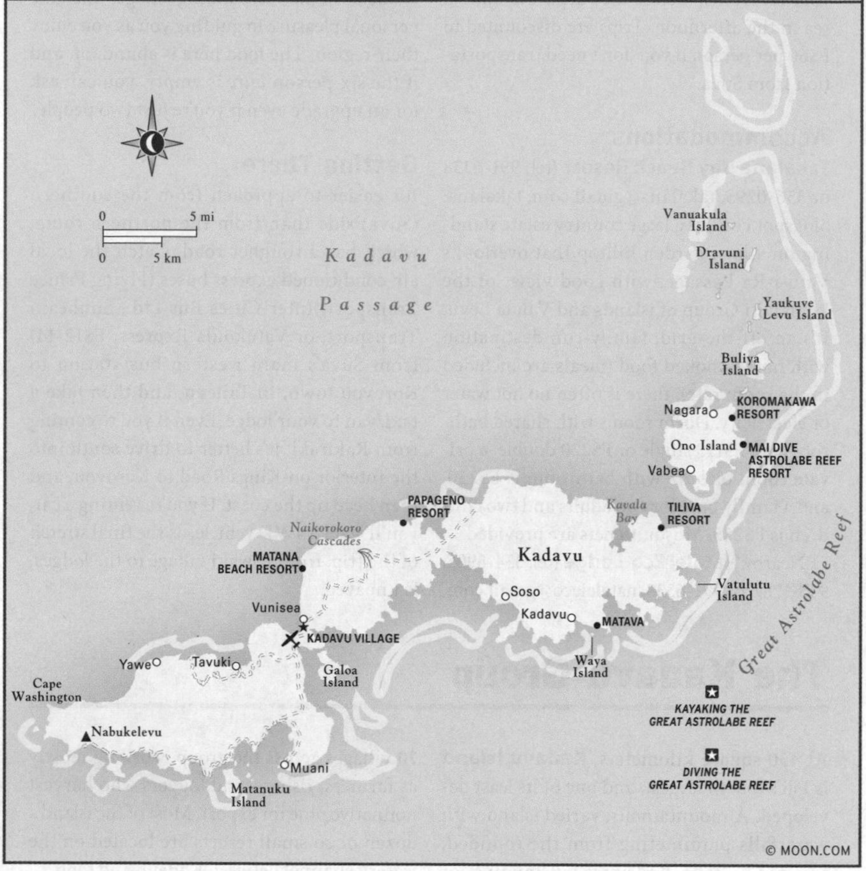

deal in foreign currency, so change enough money before coming.

It's common to get around Kadavu by foot or by boat, as the roads are few and don't always connect. The main road runs along the south coast from Vunisea to the southwestern tip, home to **Nabukelevu**—a 838-meter-high volcanic cone, also known as Mount Washington, that is the most prominent feature on the landscape. Petrels nest in holes on the north side of the mountain. There are no trails going up, as the volcano is believed to have been active as recently as the 1600s. Quakes and landslides are not infrequent, and local oral history recalls the volcano's terrors. It towers above the fine surf of scenic **Cape Washington.**

Along the northern coast of Kadavu are the villages of Nalotu, Yakita, and Naqalotu at Yawe, where traditional Fijian **pottery** is still made. Women shape the pots with a paddle, glaze them using sap from mangroves, and then fire them without a kiln over an open fire.

GREAT ASTROLABE REEF

The **Great Astrolabe Reef** stretches unbroken for 100 kilometers along the east side of Kadavu. One kilometer wide, this reef is rich in coral and marinelife, and because it's so far from shore, it still hasn't been fished out. The reef surrounds a lagoon containing 10 islands, the largest of which is 30-square-kilometer Ono. The reef was named by French explorer Dumont d'Urville, who almost lost his ship, the *Astrolabe*, here in 1827.

RECREATION

★ Diving and Snorkeling

Numerous openings on the west side of the reef, and a teeming lagoon never more than 20 meters deep, makes this a favorite of scuba divers. Toward the southern end, divers and snorkelers can go by boat to glide among manta rays year-round (unlike the Yasawas, where mantas are seasonal) at a natural manta cleaning station. The Astrolabe is exposed to unbroken waves generated by the southeast trade winds, and diving conditions are often dependent on the weather and tides. Currents are to be expected in places like Naiqoro Passage, but they're not as strong as those at Taveuni. A vertical drop-off of 10 meters inside the reef and 1,800 meters outside, with visibility up to 75 meters, make the Astrolabe a diver's dream. The hard and soft corals on the outer side of the reef are truly spectacular, but most of the corals inside the reef are dead. This barrier reef is also famous for its caves, crevices, and tunnels, which advanced divers will enjoy.

Your dive operator will depend on where you stay:

Dive Kadavu (www.divekadavu.com) operates out of Matana Beach Resort. The morning two-tank boat dive is F$180 without gear. Lodging packages start at US$585 for a nondiver or US$935 for a diver (six tank dives included) for five nights. This was the first dive operation in Fiji to create and use moorings rather than dropping reef-damaging anchors at dive sites, and they have exclusive access to the pristine corals of the Motu Marine Protected Area.

Mad Fish Dive Centre (http://scuba-diving-fiji.com) operates out of Matava and is the only dive operator located directly on the Great Astrolabe Reef. Diving starts at F$150 per tank, plus F$50 for gear. All-inclusive dive-and-stay packages start at F$2,640 per person, double occupancy, for five nights (eight tanks included).

the Great Astrolabe Reef

Return of the Humpbacks

For most of recorded history, Fiji was the breeding grounds of a tribe of humpback whales that made an annual migration north from New Zealand. However, a massive whaling operation in the 1970s knocked the tribe back to just 35 survivors. The vastly diminished tribe stopped coming to Fiji, instead going to Tonga, which has capitalized on their presence with whale-watching (rather than harpooning) expeditions.

Fiji declared itself a whale and dolphin sanctuary on March 11, 2003. A decade later, the whales—having recovered a portion of their earlier numbers—seemed to have forgiven the bloody past and began returning to Fijian waters to calve. Today, adult humpback whales and their babies can be spotted at various times of the year throughout the Somosomo Straits, the Lomaiviti Passage, the Yasawas, and around the islands of Nananu-i-Ra, Taveuni, Beqa, and Kadavu.

A humpback breaches the waves of western Fiji.

On Ono Island, the **Koromakawa Resort** (tel. 603-0782, info@koromakawa.com.fj, www.koromakawa.com.fj) offers its guests a manta ray snorkeling expedition and boat diving with a PADI instructor (US$45 per dive, minimum two divers).

Also on Ono Island, **Mai Dive Astrolabe Reef Resort** (Aus. tel. 02/8005-3845 or 04/1623-5084, info@maidive.com, www.maidive.com) is one of the few sites in the Kadavu Group where snorkelers have as many great options as divers; trips are guided by resort staff and are for guests only.

★ Kayaking and Canoeing

Kadavu offers an idyllic scenario for paddling: The barrier reef breaks the swells, leaving the shorelines calm. Most resorts include free kayaks for you to take out. Two operators run kayak and canoe trips for serious paddlers:

Sea-Kayak Fiji (New Zealand office hours 0900-1800 at tel. 21/752-855, info@tamarilloactivetravel.com, http://seakayakfiji.com) guides tours around Kadavu's wild, unspoiled coasts. In between kayaking, you'll snorkel in lagoons, stroll through rainforests, and swim in waterfall pools. The no-camping tours start at the Kadavu airport and include overnight stays in small resorts, with en suite bathrooms and hot showers guaranteed. Guides are indigenous Kadavu islanders, and you can opt for a village homestay if you wish. Trips are arranged for private groups of 2-14 people so you can customize your itinerary and meal preferences. A motorized support boat carries your luggage and provisions, and gives you a ride if you get tired of paddling. Sample itineraries are four nights for NZ$2,280 per person and six nights for NZ$2,595 per person; groups of six or more receive a discount. If you're already staying on Kadavu, you can opt for a day kayaking trip (or use it to transfer yourself and your luggage from one resort to another). The company is skillfully run by New Zealander Anthony Norris and Kadavu village chief Ratu Bose, who is a descendant of the very first Fijians to land on Kadavu two millennia ago.

Astrolabe Reef Outrigger Adventures (tel. 744-1144, fijitom@icloud.com, www.paddlefiji.com) offers multiday trips on OC1 and OC2 canoes for groups of 2-6 people, up to nine nights (US$3,695/person). Children get a discount of about 10 percent.

Accommodations are at the middle to upper range of Kadavu, and a support boat carries your luggage from place to place. Aside from paddling, your trip can include hiking, snorkeling, swimming with mantas, a *lovo* feast, and even diving or surfing by prearrangement. Day trips from Kadavu or Ono resorts can also be arranged.

Fishing

Bite Me Gamefishing Charters (tel. 603-0685, info@matava.com, http://gamefishingfiji.com/) operates out of Matava resort and holds over 50 national and world records for sportfishing. They fish the Great Astrolabe Reef and nearby areas for giant trevally, wahoo, yellowfin, sailfish, mahi mahi, marlin, and dogtooth tuna aboard the twin-engine *Bite Me Too*. Serious anglers can choose package expeditions starting at F$4,485 per person, double occupancy, for four days of fishing plus seven nights in a traditional oceanfront *bure* at Matava. For dabblers, rates start at F$1,000, inclusive of taxes, for a half-day charter of up to six people.

Surfing

Surfing is possible at **Vesi Passage** near Matava Resort (boat required), but there are no organized outfitters. Only experienced should consider it.

Bird-Watching

Few islands of this size anywhere in the Pacific have as much endemic biodiversity as Kadavu, which lacks predators such as mongoose. The **birdlife** is rich; you'll easily spot the famous red-and-green Kadavu musk parrots. Four other endemic species on the island are the Kadavu velvet fruit dove, the crimson shining-parrot, the Kadavu honeyeater, and the Kadavu fantail. You won't find certain species found elsewhere in Fiji such as mynahs, bulbuls, and cane toads. There's no need to hike for hours into the jungle, as the avifauna frequent areas near the resorts and villages all over the island, with little road traffic to disturb them. Birders report exceptional results in the rainforests behind Matana Beach Resort and the Matava resort. From the airport at Vunisea, it's a quick stroll to a fine birding area; turn inland onto Namara Road and walk about 300 meters past a five-way roundabout, continuing along the unpaved Namara Road to see clusters of the endemic species, as well as many others.

Hiking

Kadavu's **waterfalls** offer spectacular rewards for jungle hikers. Two kilometers south of the Vunisea airstrip by road, then a 10-minute uphill hike inland, **Waikana Falls** is a perfect spot for a refreshing dip on a hot day, as cool spring water flows over a 10-meter high rocky cliff between two deep pools. Other favorites are near **Kadavu Village** (a two-minute walk from the village), near **Kavala Bay** where the big ferries land (a 30-minute walk), and the stunning series of falls with large pools at the **Naikorokoro Cascades** on the north coast (a rigorous 45-minute walk or 15-minute boat ride plus a 1-kilometer hike from either Papageno or Matana resort, as it's in between them). If you're not with a group, you may be asked to pay an admission fee of F$5 and seek permission from the village chief.

A newly completed project is the **Vatulutu Trails**, a network of paths across little Vatulutu Island at the eastern tip of Kadavu. You'll need to have a boat from your hotel drop you at one end; from there it's a strenuous but gorgeous three-hour hike to the other. On the way are some of the finest viewpoints in the entire archipelago, unusual rock formations, and interesting subtropical forests, with good snorkeling on the eastern beach nearest the Great Astrolabe Reef. Take water. You can hike back to return, or arrange to be picked up at the beach.

FOOD

The only restaurants in the Kadavu Group are inside hotels or resorts. Most are open to nonguests. In Vunisea, a coffee shop at the airstrip opens for flights. In town, a

Turtle Callers

the turtle calling ceremony on Kadavu Island

If you happen to be on Kadavu at the right time, you may be invited to a ceremony conducted by the famous **turtle callers** of Kadavu Island. There's a strict protocol: no pointing, no talking, and no taking photos (though the islanders may snap shots of you with their phones). The several variations of the turtle-calling legend hold that once upon a time, there was a war between villages on the island. Hostages were taken in battle, but they turned into turtles and escaped via the sea. When their great-great-great descendants call to them, they come to protect and assist them. If, after the ceremonial singing and clapping, you happen not to see the turtle beaks rising amid the waves, the chief is likely to tell you that your eyesight simply isn't sharp enough. The ceremony occurs irregularly and is by invitation only, but tourist groups frequently attend; ask at your accommodation or tour agency to find out whether an invitation can be arranged.

half-dozen small general stores sell canned goods. **Vunisea Market** is open Monday-Saturday 0800-1600 and offers cooked meals, hot coffee, and stacks of fruit. A stall at the market sells roti, pies, and juice.

ACCOMMODATIONS

Kadavu

Matana Beach Resort (tel. 368-3502, www.matanabeachresort.com), not to be confused with the more expensive Matava eco-resort, is located at Drue, six kilometers north of Vunisea. *Bure* accommodations start at US$100 per person for a quad share in a two-bedroom beachfront *bure*, and run to US$160 in a single hillside "ocean-view" *bure*. Rates include three meals, all taxes, and airport transfers. Windsurfing rigs, kayaks, and paddleboards are free. The snorkeling off Matana's golden beach is good, and the Namalata Reef is straight out from the resort (the east end of the Great Astrolabe Reef is an hour away). Last-minute specials are often available. Many of the guests are scuba divers on all-inclusive packages with **Dive Kadavu** (www.divekadavu.com). Packages start at US$585 for a non-diver or US$935 for a diver (including six tank dives) for five nights. If you're not on a package, the morning two-tank boat dive is F$180 without gear.

The 16-room **Papageno Resort** (tel.

603-0466, connect@papagenoresortfiji.com, www.papagenoresortfiji.com) is on the north side of Kadavu, 15 kilometers east of Vunisea and accessible only by boat. A thin strip of beach opens onto a rocky shore. Rooms start at F$429 for a two-person garden room in a long block; it's F$529 for the deluxe oceanfront *bure*. The palatial royal *bure* has four bedrooms for a large family or group of up to 10 people. Airport transfers (F$100 per person) are free with three or more nights' stay. The resort uses solar and hydroelectrical power, with a backup diesel generator ensuring 24-hour electricity. The friendly and accommodating staff, tasty meals made of local seafood and organic vegetables, and the efficient German management make this a fine off-the-grid small resort.

Tiliva Resort (tel. 333-7127 or 724-8776, www.tiliva-resort.com), near Tiliva village east of Kavala Bay on the northern coast of Kadavu, faces a white-sand beach with good swimming and snorkeling and has a nice view of Ono. Tiliva has five spacious fan-cooled twin bungalows at F$280, and one honeymoon beachfront bungalow at F$350 double (ask for an upgrade if it's empty). All meals in the restaurant-bar overlooking the resort are included, as well as airport transfers if you stay three nights or more. Tiliva had a dip in service, but energetic new management installed in 2017 has things looking up. It has an active volunteer program and works with medical volunteers to inoculate and treat local residents.

★ **Matava** (tel. 603-0685, info@matava.com, www.matava.com), not to be confused with Matana Beach Resort, is located on the southeast side of Kadavu. It was one of Fiji's first eco-resorts, with solar power, a spring-water system, catch-and-release fishing trips, and an organic garden with beehives. There's no beach in front, but the snorkeling in the marine reserve off tiny Waya Island, just opposite, is fine. The beautiful fan-cooled *bures*, with full decks for bird-watching, are scattered among verdant hillsides. Many are up strenuous paths, but there are three *bures* below on the beach. Bed-and-breakfast rates are F$540 for the six thatched oceanview *bures* or F$660 for the four honeymoon *bures*. Most guests come on all-meals-included packages, which range from three nights at F$1,065 per person to seven nights at F$2,485 per person (double occupancy). All rates include airport pickup. There is no kids' club, and children under seven are served an early dinner and not permitted in the restaurant-bar area after 1900, but "informal" babysitting can be arranged. The onsite **Mad Fish Dive Centre** (http://scuba-diving-fiji.com/) is the only dive operator located directly on the Great Astrolabe Reef. Diving starts at F$150 per tank, plus F$50 for gear. All-inclusive dive-and-stay packages start at F$2,640 per person, double occupancy, for five nights (eight tanks).

Ono

Koromakawa Resort (tel. 603-0782, info@koromakawa.com.fj, www.koromakawa.com.fj) is on a long white beach on the northeast side of Ono Island. Its modern two-bedroom cottage is 275 square meters, surrounded by a large deck and overlooking an artesian well pool, and includes meals with wine served in the dining room of the main house of this 20-acre estate. Only one couple or family (up to four people) at a time is accepted here, and there are kayaks, hammocks, snorkeling gear, and a volleyball net. The rate is US$250 per adult for the first two adults; additional adults are US$120 per night and children are US$80 per night. Included are airport transfers, picnics on a nearby uninhabited island, visits to the village and bird sanctuary, babysitting, daily laundry service, and one manta ray snorkeling expedition. One of the on-site owners is a PADI instructor, and boat diving is offered at US$45 per dive (minimum two divers). A private wedding can be arranged, with the village minister presiding and local dancers as celebrants, for US$795-1,495.

Mai Dive Astrolabe Reef Resort (Australia tel. 02/8005-3845 or 04/1623-5084, info@maidive.com, www.maidive.com), on the east side of Ono Island, is one of the few sites in the Kadavu Group where snorkelers have as many great options as divers. There are three stand-alone beachfront cabins and, in the main lodge, two adjoining rooms that can be connected to accommodate a family or two couples. All of the rooms are just meters from a beach with a reef that's good for snorkeling. Meals in the restaurant are served at a common table. There's a five-day minimum stay. Rates start at F$800 and the entire resort can be booked for F$2,950 per night for as few as 8 people—up to a max of 18 people, though that would be a squeeze. Three meals and all taxes are included, but you pay F$70 per person round-trip for the 90-minute speedboat ride from the airport.

GETTING THERE AND AROUND

Air

Fiji Link (tel. 672-0888, www.fijiairways.com) flies to Kadavu's tiny Vunisea Airport, also known as Namalata Airport, on the central eastern side. Flights go to and from Suva (F$106 one-way) on Mondays, and to and from Nadi (F$232 one-way) most other days. During busy periods, the airline may separate you from your luggage or fellow travelers with a follow-up flight within 30 minutes or so; everyone on Kadavu is used to this flexibility and will know how to handle the change of plans, so don't fret. You may find it economical to book your international flight to/from Kadavu directly, so that the local leg will be included.

Island Hoppers (tel. 672-0410, reservations@islandsalesfiji.com, www.islandhoppersfiji.com) offers charter flights to the Kadavu airport for small groups on your own schedule.

Most resorts are a boat ride away from the airport at Vunisea, on the central-eastern side. Prearrange your boat transfer to be picked up from the airport by resort staff. Depending on the tide, you may have to walk out to the boat in ankle-deep water to board. It's a scenic ride between 45 minutes and 2 hours, depending on your final destination, so keep your sunscreen, sunglasses, hat, camera, and waterproof jacket handy. Boats vary in terms of comfort level and safety equipment; in rough weather everything could get wet.

Pacific Island Air (tel. 672-5644, reservations@pacificislandair.com, www.pacificislandair.com) flies charter 6-seat or 10-seat amphibious seaplanes from Nadi Airport to land directly at the beach in front of certain resorts in Kadavu.

Sea

If you're not flying in, you have one tourist option and one local option.

Twice a year, **Captain Cook** (tel. 670-1823, U.S. tel. 424/206-5275, enquiries@captaincookfj.com, www.captaincookcruisesfiji.com) runs an 11-day cruise aboard the 140-passenger *Reef Endeavour* that includes stunning views of the islands and a day stop at Vunisea. A turtle-calling ceremony is conducted for the tour group's benefit. There's an optional local fishing trip for an additional fee. Diving is also possible.

Goundar Shipping (tel. 330-1035, 330-1020, or 773-1035, goundarshipping@kidanet.com.fj, www.goundarshipping.com) is only of interest to low-budget travelers headed for Waisalima who can disembark at Kavala Bay. It links Suva with Kadavu Island once a week. The *Lomaiviti Princess II* departs from Muaiwalu Port (commonly known by its old name, Narain Jetty) at Suva's Walu Bay on Wednesday at 2200. After arriving in Vunisea by 0600 on Thursday, it pauses for four hours, then travels onward to Kavala Bay, on the western end of Kadavu, arriving by 1300. It departs Kavala at 1500 and returns to Suva at 2100. This essential island service transports passengers, fuel, fresh produce, animals, building supplies, and more. The timetable is only a rough guideline. Take seasickness precautions before boarding, especially during the windy season April-August.

Car

There are a few roads in Kadavu, but there is no road from Vunisea to the eastern side. Occasional carriers ply the rugged, muddy roads of west Kadavu. There are no buses or car rental agencies. It's best to have your accommodation arrange your transport.

Northern Coast and Interior Viti Levu

To escape the tourist hordes, head to Viti Levu's winding northern coast and mountainous interior. Here, seascapes give way to vast sugar plantations and lush, volcanic forests intercut by networks of rivers and streams. Here, too, are chances to encounter a Fijian way of life that isn't all about tourism.

Just 35 minutes northeast of Nadi, the bustling sugar city of Lautoka is a lesser-used departure point for the Yasawas. The jagged mountains behind it are part of Koroyanitu National Heritage Park and include the Sleeping Giant himself, Mount Batilamu. The paved two-lane Kings Road, which heads west from Lautoka all the way around the coast to Suva in the southwest, is as pretty and comfortable as the southern Queens Road, and far less traveled.

Highlights

Look for ★ to find recommended sights, activities, dining, and lodging.

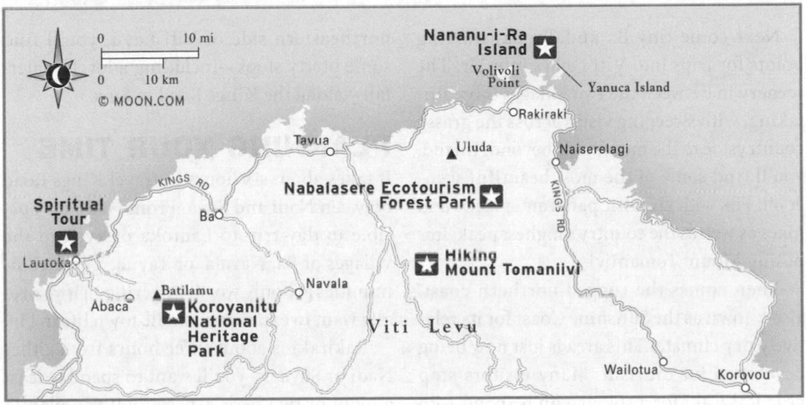

★ **Spiritual Tour of Lautoka:** This traditional Indo-Fijian town is the perfect place to take a tour of Muslim, Sikh, and Hindu places of worship, all just a few minutes' stroll from one another (page 207).

★ **Koroyanitu National Heritage Park:** The mountainous region behind Lautoka offers spectacular views, hiking, and waterfalls for intrepid overnighters and day-trippers alike (page 214).

★ **Hiking Mount Tomaniivi:** A rigorous six-hour round-trip hike takes you through meadows and streams to the peak of Fiji's highest mountain, where you'll be rewarded with a 360-degree summit view of all of Viti Levu (page 220).

★ **Nananu-i-Ra Island:** For the best beaches and underwater activities along the northern coast, look no further than this small island (page 223).

★ **Nabalasere Ecotourism Forest Park:** Head to one of Fiji's newest natural sanctuaries for an invigorating day hike, waterfall swim, and village visit (page 227).

Northern Coast and Interior Viti Levu

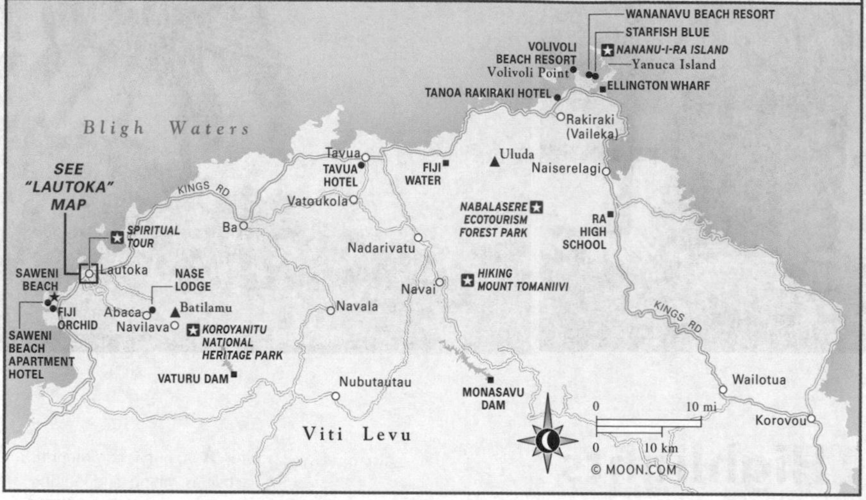

Next come tiny Ba and Tavua, starting points for trips into Viti Levu's interior. The scenery in between the two villages is breathtaking, with sweeping vistas across the grassy countryside to the mountains beyond. Inland, you'll find some of the most beautiful scenery in Fiji, with fantastic panoramic views and hikes as well as the country's highest peak, imposing Mount Tomaniivi.

Then comes the rugged northern coast, also known as the Sunshine Coast for its relatively dry climate. This area is just now being developed for tourism. Many visitors stop near Rakiraki for a sojourn on Nananu-i-Ra Island, where the beaches, snorkeling, windsurfing, and hiking are all excellent. Some of Fiji's best scuba diving is along this portion of the coast.

If you continue south along the northeastern side of Viti Levu, you'll find some pretty stops—including a lovely waterfall—along the Kings Road to Suva.

PLANNING YOUR TIME

It takes about six hours to travel Kings Road between Nadi and Suva. From Nadi, it's possible to day-trip to Lautoka or even to the villages of Ba, Navala, or Tavua. These communities are only worth lingering in if you really want to experience small-town life in Fiji.

Rakiraki is about three hours from either Nadi or Suva, so you'll want to spend at least a night or two here, especially if you plan to visit Nananu-i-Ra Island.

Avid hikers will want to allocate at least a couple of days to visit some glorious, virtually tourist-free trails in the lush mountains of the interior.

Previous: waterfalls at Nabalasere Ecotourism Forest Park; detail of a house in Navala village; the beach at Volivoli Bay.

Find Your Beach

- **Lautoka:** The best beach near Lautoka is **Saweni Beach** (page 209), behind the Saweni Beach Apartment Hotel.
- **Sunshine Coast:** The best coastal beaches are along the northernmost peninsula, about halfway between Nadi and Suva. The beach at **Volivoli Point** (page 221) is attached to a resort, where you can have a posh lunch and cocktails. If you have your own transportation, the **adjacent bay** is free and just as picturesque for a picnic and a dip.
- **Nananu-i-Ra Island:** A quick boat ride from the mainland, this island has long, white beaches that are open to all. The island is a favorite of **windsurfers,** who enjoy the breeze from the open ocean on both sides (page 223).

Lautoka

Fiji's third-largest city, **Lautoka,** is the focus of the country's sugar and timber industries, a major port, and the Western Division and Ba Province headquarters. A row of towering royal palms line the main street, and Marine Drive offers a lovely seaside walk.

Lautoka grew up around the iTaukei (indigenous) Fijian village of Namoli, and today the temples and mosques standing prominently in town reflect the city's significant Indo-Fijian population.

Because Lautoka doesn't depend on tourism, you'll get a truer picture of ordinary life here than you would in Nadi. There's plenty of shopping and eating, and the town is a pleasant place to wander around.

The jagged mountains behind Lautoka form Koroyanitu National Heritage Park. Tour operators from Nadi and Lautoka will take you to Abaca, the park's gateway village, and into the park itself, which is full of hiking and climbing opportunities.

SIGHTS

★ Spiritual Tour of Lautoka

Lautoka's status as Fiji's largest settlement for Indo-Fijians, combined with its small, flat, pedestrian-friendly town center, makes it a perfect place to take a miniature tour of Indian religions. Cover your shoulders and knees when you enter these sites, and if a service is in progress, non-believers should remain outside. Hours vary depending upon observances, but they are generally open during daytime hours.

JAME MOSQUE

From the market, walk south on Yasawa Street to the photogenic **Jame Mosque** (Vitogo Parade, next to Churchill Park), a prominent symbol of Lautoka's large Indo-Fijian population. Non-Muslims who are conservatively dressed can visit the mosque outside of the five daily prayer times; remove your shoes. During the crushing season (June-Nov.), narrow-gauge trains rattle past the mosque, bringing cane to Lautoka's large sugar mill.

SIKH GURDWARA

Follow the railway line east along the main road, Vitogo Parade, for about 300 meters. After the cinemas, you'll come to the **Sikh Gurdwara** (24 Vitogo Parade), rebuilt after a smaller temple fell to arson in 1989. To enter, you must wash your hands and cover your head (kerchiefs are provided at the door). Don't bring cigarettes or liquor into the compound. The teachings of the 10 Sikh gurus are contained in the Guru Granth Sahib, the holy book prominently displayed in the temple.

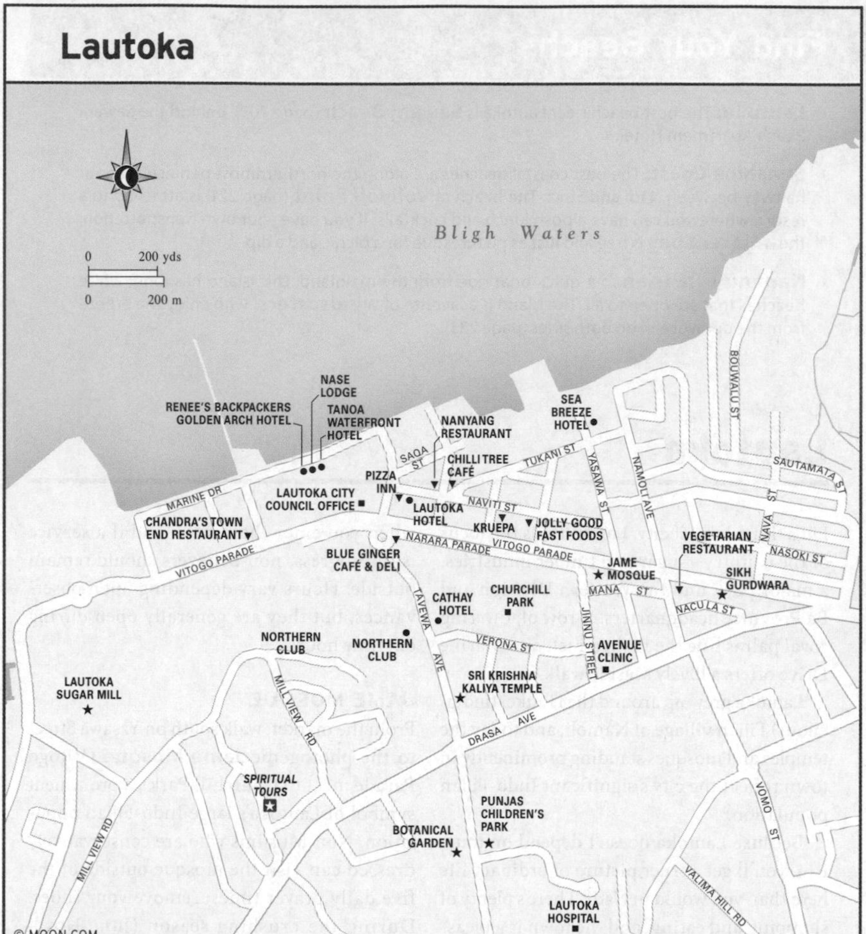

SRI KRISHNA KALIYA TEMPLE

Go back the way you came along Vitogo, but turn left to go south onto Namoli Avenue, then right (west) on Drasa Avenue. After about 600 meters, you'll arrive at the **Sri Krishna Kaliya Temple** (5 Tavewa Ave., tel. 666-4112, daily until 1800), the most prominent Krishna temple in the South Pacific. The International Society for Krishna Consciousness (ISKCON) runs this temple, which is unique in that it's the only temple named for a serpent deity—Kaliya, who was subdued by the god Krishna. Remove your shoes before entering. A mural inside shows Krishna dancing on the snake. Legend has it that Krishna exiled him to an island known as "ramnik deep," which devotees here believe was Fiji. If it's Sunday, you can enjoy a brief chanting service at noon and a vegetarian feast at 1300 (free, donations appreciated).

Botanical Garden

Lautoka's **botanical garden** (Thomson Crescent, weekdays 0800-1700, free) sits half a kilometer south of the Krishna temple opposite the hospital. It's a pleasant, shady spot with an array of plants. There are numerous

From Cane to Crystals

Sugar cane grows abundantly around Lautoka, the "sugar town" of Fiji.

The **Lautoka Sugar Mill,** once the largest in the Southern Hemisphere, was founded in 1903 as part of the Colonial Sugar Refinery company. It's busiest June-December, with trains and trucks constantly depositing loads of cane to be fed into the crushers. Molasses from the mill is the main raw material for South Pacific Distillery, just south on Nadovu Road, which makes Bounty rum, Regal gin, Royal whiskey, and Tribe vodka. The fertilizer factory across the highway uses mill mud from the sugar-making process. To the north, beyond the conveyor belts used to load raw sugar onto the ships, is a veritable mountain of pine chips ready for export to Japan, where they are used to make paper.

The mill no longer offers tours, but **here's how it works:** Cane arrives by train and is fed through a shredder, then into a row of huge rollers that squeeze out the juice. The crushed fiber (bagasse) is set aside and burned to fuel the mill or processed into paper. The juice, now fiber-free, gets an infusion of lime to preserve it and prevent discoloration, and is then heated. Impurities settle to the bottom and are filtered out to be used as fertilizer, while the clear juice carries on through a series of evaporators. It is boiled and the steam sucked away by a vacuum, reducing it to a thick syrup. The syrup is boiled again under greater pressure in a vacuum pan, forming raw sugar crystals. The mix then enters a centrifuge, which spins off the remaining goop as molasses—used by distilleries or in animal feed. Finally, the still-moist crystals are tumble-dried using hot air in a rotating drum. What emerges is the raw Fiji sugar you can find in packets all over the Pacific.

birds in the gardens, and picnic tables are provided. **Punjas Children's Park** (daily 1000-1800, free), across the street from the gardens, is perfect if you're with children under 12, and it has a snack bar.

Saweni Beach

The best beach in the area is **Saweni Beach,** aside a north-facing bay about 10 kilometers south of Lautoka. The beautiful white sand and the view are sometimes marred by uncollected litter and drunken revelers, and picnickers arrive by the carload from Lautoka on weekends. Bird-watchers can observe waders on the flats. A concrete platform here is all that remains of a World War II-era American flying boat base. A bus from bay No. 14 at the Lautoka bus station runs to the apartment hotel on the bay six times a day. Otherwise, any of the local Nadi buses will drop you off a 10-minute walk away. A taxi from Lautoka is F$10-12.

ENTERTAINMENT AND NIGHTLIFE

Lautoka's nightclubs cater almost exclusively to locals, and can be rough and unsafe, especially for women. One good bet for foreign visitors is the **Ashiqi Nite Club** (2 Naviti St., Fri.-Sat. 2000-0100, F$5 cover), off the inner courtyard at the Lautoka Hotel. The more exclusive **Northern Club** (11 Tavewa Ave., tel. 666-2469, Mon.-Sat. 1000-2300, Sun. 1200-2200) has an atmospheric colonial-style bar, and its restaurant (daily 1000-1500 and 1700-2130, F$9-20) serves excellent meals.

Village 4 Cinemas (Namoli Ave., tel. 666-3555, www.damodarcinemas.com.fj) play the latest English and Bollywood hits. Tickets are F$7 (F$6 on Tuesdays). The last show starts around 2100.

SPORTS AND RECREATION

Lautoka is a sports city, and every Saturday you can catch exciting rugby or football (soccer) games at the stadium in **Churchill Park** (Rockingham Beach Rd.). Local matches are F$10 general admission, F$20 wooden grandstand, F$30 main grandstand, and are available for purchase at the stadium or the **Lautoka City Council office** (169 Vitogo Parade, tel. 666-0433 or 1000-1500); they don't sell out. For more information or to purchase advance tickets to upcoming international tournaments and special events, see the websites and Facebook pages of **Fiji Rugby** (www.fijirugby.com, Apr.-Sept.) and the **Fiji Football League** (www.fijifootball.com.fj, Feb.-Oct.).

At the **Northern Club** (11 Tavewa Ave., tel. 666-2469, Mon.-Sat. 1000-2300, Sun. 1200-2200), you can use the large swimming pool and play tennis with purchase of a one-week pass (F$15).

SHOPPING

Lautoka's big, colorful **market** (next to the bus station, Mon.-Fri. 0700-1730, Sat. 0530-1600) is busiest on Saturdays. Handicrafts are sold at stalls along the Naviti Street side of the market.

FOOD

Indian

Unpretentious ★ **Minaxi Hot Snax** (56 Naviti St., tel. 666-1306, Mon.-Fri. 0830-1730, Sat. 0830-1600, F$9) may be the number one place in Fiji to sample South Indian dishes; the *dosa* (rice pancake) and *idli* (steamed rice cake), served with coconut chutney, make a great brunch. You can also get ice cream and sweets.

★ **Kruepa Vegetarian Restaurant** (42 Vidilo St., tel. 666-0591, kruepa@gmail.com, Mon.-Sat. 0800-1800, F$2-F$11), in spacious premises kitty-corner to MH, is the place to go for North Indian-style street food. If you're eating in, try the savory *pani puri* (puffed bread stuffed with chutney and potato), the samosas, or the *thalis* (combination plate meals). For road-trip snacks, ask for a half pound of *muruku* or *chevdo* at the counter—spicy, fried, trail-mix-like treats. The sweets and ice cream are also good. Service is brisk and brusque, but people come from as far as Nadi and Tavua to get their fix here.

Cafés

The best cappuccino in town is at the centrally located **Blue Ginger Café & Deli** (Elizabeth Square near the post office, tel. 907-6553, Mon.-Fri. 0800-1800, Sat. 0800-1700, F$7-12), where you can also get grilled wraps, burgers, sandwiches, and cheesecake. There's Wi-Fi, but you must spend a minimum F$25 to use it.

More upscale is the air-conditioned **Chilli Tree Café** (tel. 665-1824, Mon.-Sat. 0730-1600), at the corner of Nede and Tukani Streets. A good, filling breakfast is F$11, plus there are cakes and specially brewed coffee. You can "build your own" salad and sandwich.

Casual

Jolly Good Fast Foods (60 Naviti St., tel. 666-9980, daily 0800-2200, F$8-15), opposite the market, is a great place to sit outside in the covered garden and read a newspaper over a coffee. The best dishes are listed on the "made to order" menu on the wall beside the cashier: fish, chicken, mutton, or prawns. Portions are large.

Chandra's Town End Restaurant (15 Tukani St., tel. 666-5877, Mon.-Sat. 0630-1900, Sun. 0800-1700), on the ocean side of the bus station, serves cheap meals like fish-and-chips (F$5) or meat and rice (F$6).

MH Supermarket (Vidilio and Tukani Sts., tel. 666-2999, Mon.-Sat. 0800-1800, Sun. 0800-1300) is Lautoka's largest grocery. At the back, a food court offers the usual fish or chicken and chips, hot pies, ice cream, and breakfast specials.

Chinese

Nanyang Restaurant (4 Nede St., tel. 665-2668, Mon.-Sat. 1100-1500 and 1800-2200, Sun. 1800-2200, F$16-30) dishes out Lautoka's top Chinese meals in flashy surroundings.

Pizza

Seaview Restaurant (2 Naviti St., tel. 666-4592, daily 0800-2100, F$9-37) is the only place in Lautoka to get pizza, as well as a range of other items. It's a pleasing spot with air-conditioning located in the Lautoka Hotel. It has a good bar.

ACCOMMODATIONS

Under US$50

Renee's Backpackers Golden Arch Hotel (17 Naviti St., tel. 666-0033, homenaway@connect.com.fj) has 11 rooms that run F$50/60 single/double, or F$70 for the self-contained family room that accommodates five. Most (but not all) of the rooms are air-conditioned but none have private bath.

To be close to the action, stay at the 38-room **Lautoka Hotel** (2 Naviti St., tel. 666-0388 or 666-0126, www.cjsgroup.com.fj/lautoka), which has a nice swimming pool. It's F$25 per person to stay in the 10-bed dorm; rooms start at F$45 double for a spacious fan-cooled older room with shared bath and go to F$100 with private bathroom, fridge, and tea-making facilities in the newer wing. The rooms with private bath are good, but the shared-bath rooms above the reception in the old building are subjected to a nocturnal rock beat from nearby discos most nights.

A good choice is the clean, quiet, three-story ★ **Sea Breeze Hotel** (5 Bekana Ln., tel. 666-0717, seabreezefiji@connect.com.fj, www.seabreezefiji.com, F$95 d), on the waterfront near the bus station. The 24 standard rooms have air-conditioning, refrigerators, and electric teapots. The pleasant lounge has a color TV, and a swimming pool overlooks the lagoon. It's Lautoka's best value and is often full, especially on weekends.

US$50-100

The upscale ★ **Northern Club** (11 Tavewa Ave., tel. 666-2469/666-0184, northernaccom@yahoo.com.au, F$125 s/d) rents six self-catering studios in a two-story block. The club has a large bar, swimming pool, and tennis courts just up the hill. It's clean and a good deal if you'd like to have a kitchen and amenities.

The 40-room **Cathay Hotel** (Tavewa Ave., tel. 666-0566 or 776-2203, cathay@fiji4less.com, www.fiji4less.com) has a swimming pool, TV room, and bar. The charge is F$79 double with fan and private bath, F$94 with air-conditioning. The renovated rooms are F$102. Ask the receptionist if there will be a towel in the room. Some of the rooms in less desirable locations have been divided into backpacker dormitories, with 3-6 beds or bunks for F$27/31 per person with fan/air-conditioning. Each dorm has its own toilet and shower.

Saweni Beach Apartment Hotel (Saweni Beach Rd., tel. 666-1777 or 776-2204, saweni@fiji4less.com, www.fiji4less.com), a kilometer off the main highway south of

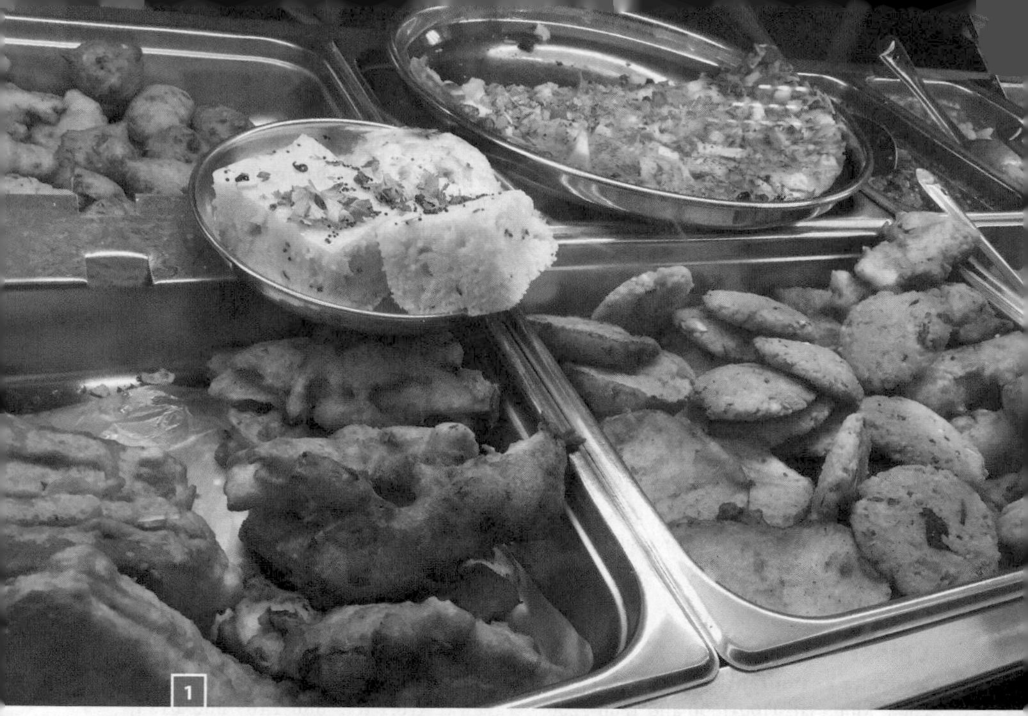

1

2

Lautoka, caters to seniors, families, and couples looking for quiet, inexpensive beach accommodations. A bed in a four-bed dorm is F$26 per person. The six self-catering apartments are F$120 if you just use the fan, F$151 if you use the air-conditioning. Additional adults/children are F$26/13. Guests unwind by the pool or head to the beach behind the hotel. During the season, it's typical to have more than a dozen yachts anchored offshore, and the crews often come ashore here for curry dinners in the restaurant in the main building.

US$100-150

Lautoka's most modern hotel is the **Tanoa Waterfront Hotel** (Marine Dr., tel. 666-4777, waterfront@tanoahotels.com, www.tanoawaterfront.com), a two-story building erected in 1987 and kept spick-and-span. The 47 air-conditioned rooms are F$210 single or double (children under 12 are free if no extra bed is required). The 26 "executive" rooms are F$280 single or double, and the family room is F$300 single or double (can sleep up to four adults). There's free Wi-Fi and an attractive swimming pool. The Fins Restaurant serves dinner mains around F$25.

Over US$150

Fiji Orchid (Saweni Beach Rd., tel. 628-3099 or 628-0097, info@fijiorchid.com, www.fijiorchid.com, F$660) is a boutique resort near Saweni Beach in an orchid garden formerly owned by actor Raymond Burr. (Burr, who starred in the 1957-1966 television show *Perry Mason,* owned Naitaba Island in the Lau Group and had a passion for breeding orchids, including at his Lautoka nursery.) The luxurious bungalows include breakfast. A restaurant, bar, and swimming pool are on the premises. Airport transfers from Nadi are included.

1: Indian food in Lautoka 2: the bustling streetscape of Lautoka.

INFORMATION AND SERVICES

Money

ATMs are found at the Westpac Bank branch on Vitogo Parade, a little west of the post office beyond the station, and at the ANZ Bank on Vitogo Parade kitty-corner to the post office. Other ANZ Bank ATMs are found next to Rajendra Prasad Foodtown on Yasawa Street opposite the bus station and at Village 4 Cinemas. Westpac and Colonial National Bank ATMs, accessible 24 hours a day, are at the Sugar City Mall next to the bus station.

Western Union Currency Exchange (161 Vitogo Parade, tel. 665-1969 or 992-0969, Mon.-Fri. 0800-1800, Sat. 0800-1600), just up from the ANZ Bank, and **Lotus Foreign Exchange** (tel. 666-7855) in the Sugar City Mall offer similar exchange rates and services.

Health

The emergency room at the **Lautoka Hospital** (tel. 666-0399), off Thomson Crescent south of the center, is open 24 hours a day.

If your problem is not life-threatening, you're better off attending the **Avenue Clinic** (Dr. Mukesh C. Bhagat, 47 Drasa Ave., tel. 665-2955 or 995-2369, Mon.-Fri. 0830-2100, Sat. 0900-1630). You'll receive good service at this convenient suburban office.

Dr. Suresh Chandra's **dental office** (tel. 666-0999, Mon.-Fri. 0800-1700, Sat. 0800-1300) is opposite Village 4 Cinemas on Namoli Avenue.

Public Toilets

Free public toilets are next to Bay No. 1A on the back side of the bus station, facing the market; in Shirley Park behind the police post opposite the Lautoka Hotel; and at the botanical gardens. The Tappoo City department store has clean, modern restrooms that can be used for a fee of F$0.50.

Internet

Jeri-Cho Internet Café (tel. 666-4477, daily 0800-2200) at Village 4 Cinemas on Namoli

Avenue charges F$4 an hour. It's often full of kids playing online games.

Immigration

The **Immigration Department** (tel. 666-1706) is on the ground floor of Rogorogoivuda House on Tavewa Avenue almost opposite the Sri Krishna Kaliya Temple. Customs is in an adjacent building.

GETTING THERE AND AROUND

The main Lautoka **bus station** (0600-1700) is a whirring place on Tukani Street next to the market. This is the terminus and transfer point for all buses on the Kings Road from both Nadi and Suva, so it's easy to find a bus heading here from main stations along the northern route. It's also easy to find a bus leaving here to main stations along the northern route; buses leave here every half hour, from about 0600 until at least 1700. To Suva, it's about six hours (F$18 express). To Nadi, it's about an hour (F$3 local).

Car rentals are available in Lautoka from **Central** (75 Vitogo Parade, tel. 666-4511) and **Budget** (4 Walu St., tel. 666-6166).

★ KOROYANITU NATIONAL HERITAGE PARK

This park, which takes its name from the range's highest peak, **Mount Koroyanitu** (1,195 m), preserves Fiji's only old-growth mountain forest by creating a small tourism business for the local villagers. With help from New Zealand, the reserve was created in 1992 in the Mount Evans Range, 15 kilometers east of Lautoka. Six villages cooperate to maintain the park, and everyone wins: The village carrier that transports visitors also carries local children to and from school, women earn money by staffing the office or arranging room and board, and men work as drivers, guides, and wardens. Entry is at the **Abaca Visitor Centre** (tel. 664-5431, 992-1517, or 719-3194, abacaecopark@yahoo.com, F$15 per person), located in the village of Abaca (am-BAA-tha) at the base of the mountain.

Recreation

From the visitor centre, there are beautiful short **walks** in the dakua (*Aganthis macrophylla*) forest; these trees, also known locally as *kauri* or *makadre*, can live to 1,000 years old. You can swim in the pools at **Vereni Falls,** a five-minute walk from the park

sunset in Koroyanitu National Heritage Park

lodge. Picnic shelters are provided. From the viewpoint above the falls, it's 15 minutes up the Navuratu Track to **Kokobula Scenic Outlook,** with its 360-degree view of the park and coast.

To trek farther, a guide is required. You can hike across the open grassland to **Savuione Falls** (about two hours, F$15 pp), passing the ruins of an ancient village site. The finest hike here is to **Mount Batilamu** (about five hours round-trip, F$25), where the reward is stunning views of the Mamanuca and Yasawa Islands; this part of the mountain range is also known as the Sleeping Giant for how its form appears from Nadi. You can also pay F$40 for an overnight guide, taking in the sunrise and sunset from the mountaintop. More ambitious hikes to higher peaks can be arranged, and the bird-watching throughout the park is spectacular.

Tours

George Prince's **Round the Island Tours** (tel. 992-1517, george_prasad@hotmail.com) charges F$30 per person, one-way, for transfers between Lautoka and Abaca, or F$40 from Nadi; inquire about rates from anywhere else. He also offers a full day tour including transportation from Nadi, meals, entry fees, guide, and a gift for the village.

Talanoa Treks (tel. 998-0560, info@talanoa-treks-fiji.com, https://talanoa-treks-fiji.com) occasionally leads small groups on a 72-hour, three-peak hiking challenge that starts with Mount Batilamu. Pickup can be in Nadi or Suva, and it's F$1,290 per person including all meals, three nights of accommodation, and village *sevusevus*. It's co-owned by a New Zealand couple and the villages en route.

Exotic Holidays Fiji (Thomson Crescent, Lautoka, tel. 701-2305, info@exoticholidaysfiji.com, http://exoticholidaysfiji.com) offers day trips to the Mount Batilamu summit, mostly for cruise passengers from Denarau. Inquire about rates depending on where you're staying.

Great Sights Fiji/Tourist Transport Fiji (Nadi Airport, tel. 672-3311, enquiries@greatsightsfiji.com, www.touristtransportfiji.com/greatsightsfiji) operates a morning tour (Mon.-Fri.) to the Koroyanitu National Park. Pickup from Denarau/Nadi hotels is at 0830/0845; an air-conditioned 4WD vehicle carries guests through Abaca, follows the Sabeto River inland, and stops at Navilava village inside the park for a *sevusevu* ceremony and snack. This trip is more about scenery than exercise, but a guide can take you on a short trek.

Accommodations

Bookings for all accommodations inside the park are arranged through the **Abaca Visitor Centre** (tel. 664-5431 or 992-1517, abacaecopark@yahoo.com) and include the park entry fee. Children age 2-14 are half price. There are three options:

Experience highland village culture by staying with a family in **Abaca village** for F$80 per night, including all meals. A *lovo* and *meke* can be arranged for groups of four or more. Observe village etiquette at all times, and don't arrive at the village during Sunday church service (1000-1200).

Nase Lodge, an old colonial lodge about 100 meters uphill from the village, has 12 bunk beds, a living area, cooking facilities, a cold-water shower, and a toilet. Campsites are F$35 per person, beds in the dorm are F$50. You can order meals at the village for F$13-25, but you should also take groceries, as there is no village store.

Mount Batilamu Hut, on the peak, is F$150 per person (minimum two people) including all meals and a guide to stay overnight with you. There's no electricity or phone reception up here, just a cabin to keep out the elements.

Getting There

This is an easy site to visit on your own and requires only transport, not necessarily the full guided tour treatment, since extensive hikes must be accompanied by guides from the mountain itself. Still, you'll need a 4WD vehicle or good strong legs to traverse the

10-kilometer unpaved road to Abaca. During the rainy season, floods can close the road to traffic.

The closest **public bus** stop is Abaca Junction on the Tavakuba bus route from Lautoka. From the stop, it's 10 kilometers to the visitors center.

Yavala (tel. 867-6523), a driver who works with the local village, offers rides from Lautoka, Nadi, and elsewhere.

Northwest Coast and Interior

East of Lautoka are several towns that serve as gateways to the rugged interior. None of the towns are frequented by tourists, but you might make a pit stop here to break up your drive or stay a night to experience small-town life in Fiji. There are some interesting sights along the way, and they have services such as ATMs, places to top off your prepaid cell phone, restaurants, and small lodgings.

Fiji's highest mountains and deepest valleys are accessible from the villages along this section of the Kings Road, and some spectacular hikes await those willing to veer off the beaten path. The frequent local buses between Lautoka and Suva stop at these towns, as do the Sunbeam Transport express buses.

Self-guided trips and even hikes are possible if you have your own **4WD transport** to the access points. Be familiar with village etiquette and be patient as you ask permission to pass through, as many seemingly wild areas are still the designated domain of villagers. Otherwise, you can opt to visit this region with a guided tour.

TOURS

The best way to truly experience interior Viti Levu is through a day hike, an overnight trip, or a four-night trek with **Talanoa Treks** (tel. 998-0560, info@talanoa-treks-fiji.com, https://talanoa-treks-fiji.com). Owners Marita and Matt Manley are passionate hikers who've trekked all over the island since coming to Suva in 2006. Upon invitation of the chiefs they met while hiking little-used trails in the highland villages, they have worked to set up cooperative ventures. While many tour operators do hire local guides, Talanoa Treks is one of the few in which the people of the villages make decisions, set rates, and reap an equal share of the profits. A four-day itinerary may include visiting the beautiful waterfall in Nabalesere, climbing Mount Tomaniivi, and visiting the small villages between Ba and Navala. Trips start in Suva, but other arrangements can be made. You get the chance to explore areas of Fiji that see fewer than a hundred tourists a year.

Fiji EcoTours (Nadi, tel. 672-4312, 975-7146, or 774-3586, sales@fijiecotours.com.fj, www.fijiecotours.com.fj) arranges day and overnight trips to Navala and other nearby sights (Abaca, Mount Batilamu). Cruise passengers often take the day trips, which are F$235-270 per person, depending on the destination. Children 6-12 are half price. For overnight stays, the price is a bit out of sync with the rustic conditions because a minimum of two people for two nights is required: F$258-360 per person per night, plus F$144-160 for transport each way.

Rosie Holidays (tel. 672-2755, www.rosiefiji.com), at Nadi Airport and numerous resorts, offers a full-day hiking tour of the Nausori Highlands (Mon.-Sat., F$74 including lunch). Entry is via the Nadi side rather than from Ba.

Nautilus Adventure Tours (tel. 628-1326, 801-1584, or 509-0967, info@nautilusfiji.com, www.nautilusfiji.com) offers half-day and full-day tours of the Nausori Highlands in a modern, air-conditioned 4WD vehicle, with minimal walking. Nadi resort guests often book these trips for early-morning birdwatching. The longer trips include lunch in a village and a dip in a small waterfall at 550 meters above sea level. The kava ceremony and school visits are all rather staged, but it's a decent introduction for those who won't see a village any other way. Bring your own drinking water. Tours are F$220-320 per adult and F$99-199 per child, including pickup and drop-off in Nadi; other locations can be accommodated.

BA AND THE NAUSORI HIGHLANDS

Ba, about 45 minutes from Lautoka via Kings Road, is the gateway to the **Nausori Highlands,** a vast mountainous area of western Viti Levu (not to be confused with Nausori town near Suva). This lush region is home to numerous villages connected by rough roads that see little tourism traffic. You'll find pleasant hiking, refreshing river swimming holes and small waterfalls, and some of the most beautiful scenery in Fiji.

Ba

The large Indo-Fijian town of **Ba** (population 18,500), on the Ba River, is seldom visited by tourists. Nearly half of Fiji's Muslims live in Ba Province, and there's an attractive mosque in the center of town. Small fishing boats depart from behind the service station opposite the mosque, and it's fairly easy to arrange to go along on all night trips. A wide belt of mangroves covers much of the river delta. Ba's original townsite was on the low hill where the post office is today, and the newer lower town is subject to flooding. Ba is well known in Fiji for the large Rarawai Sugar Mill, built by the Colonial Sugar Refining Co. in 1886. In 2002, the transnational company Nestlé established a large food-processing plant at Ba.

FOOD AND DRINK

Of the many places along Main Street in Ba serving Indian and Chinese meals, your best choice is probably **Chand's Restaurant** (tel. 667-0822, Mon.-Sat. 0800-2100, Sun. 1100-1500), just across the bridge from the mosque. Their upstairs dining room serves an Indian vegetarian *thali* for F$12.

For drinks, it's the **Central Club** (tel. 667-4348) on Tabua Park. The club's kitchen (Mon.-Tues. 1100-2100, Wed.-Sat. 1100-2100, Sun. 1100-1900, F$9), on the lower level, serves meals of reasonable quality for the price.

GETTING THERE AND AROUND

Ba is a stop on all the Kings Road local and express buses (F$5 from Nadi, F$20 from Suva). If you don't have your own car, you can take a private taxi or a public bus (F$2, departing roughly in the morning, noon, and midafternoon) along the partly paved road from Ba to Navala and beyond.

Navala

Navala, 25 kilometers southeast of Ba, is the last fully thatched village on Viti Levu, and the villagers have made a conscious decision to keep it that way. Its *bures* stand picturesquely above the sloping right bank of the Ba River against the surrounding hills. The installation of aboveground power lines means the village is not quite as photogenic as it once was.

Sightseers are welcome, though there is a F$25 per person admission fee to enter the village (this fee also applies if you only take photos from across the bridge). Tourists are sometimes asked to pay more, along with a gift of kava roots; if you get that treatment, ask to be taken to the *turaga-ni-koro* (village herald).

When water levels are right, white-water rafters shoot the rapids through the scenic Ba River gorge near here, and guided hiking or horseback riding can also be arranged in the village for an extra "tip"—up to F$100 per person depending on the activity and the size of the group that day.

Bukuya

The road climbs another 20 kilometers south to **Bukuya,** a village in the center of western Viti Levu's highland plateau. This village is far less traditional than Navala, and some of the only thatched *bures* in the village are those used by visitors on hiking and village-stay

1

2

3

4

tours organized by backpacker travel agencies in Nadi. The Tui Magodro, or high chief of the region, resides here. During the Colo War of 1876, Bukuya was a center of resistance to colonial rule.

Nubutautau

East of Bukuya, a rugged logging track runs along a very high ridge and then drops down to **Nubutautau** on the northernmost arc of the Sigatoka River. The Reverend Thomas Baker, the last missionary to be clubbed and devoured in Fiji (in 1867), met his fate at Nubutautau. Jack London wrote a story, "The Whale Tooth," about this incident, and the ax that brought about Reverend Baker's demise is kept in the village; other Baker artifacts are at the Fiji Museum in Suva. In 2003, Baker's descendants traveled to Nubutautau from Australia for a *matanigasau* ceremony during which the villagers apologized for this old crime, and a curse that had hung over the village for 136 years was lifted.

Vaturu Dam

If, from Bukuya, you turn west instead of east, the road toward Nadi passes **Vaturu Dam,** which supplies Nadi with fresh water. Gold strikes nearby may herald a mining future for this area, if the water catchment can be protected. The forests here were logged out in the 1970s, but the open scenery of the grassy highlands still makes a visit well worthwhile.

TAVUA AND INTERIOR

Tavua

Tavua, an important junction on the north coast, is a small agricultural town along Kings Road. It is the gateway to interior sights such as the gold mine at nearby Vatukoula and the impressive Mount Tomaniivi.

1: the market in Ba **2:** houses in Nubutautau **3:** a volleyball net on a beach along the Sunshine Coast **4:** Talanoa Treks leads multiday hiking tours into interior Viti Levu.

FOOD AND DRINK

New China Restaurant (tel. 668-1401), opposite the Total service station in Tavua, serves fast food from the warmer (F$7) or made-to-order meals from the menu on the wall (F$8-15).

Socialize at the **Tavua Club** (tel. 668-0265) on Nasivi Street.

ACCOMMODATIONS

The two-story **Tavua Hotel** (Nabuna St., tel. 668-0522, www.tavuahotel.com), a wooden colonial-style building on a hill, is a 10-minute walk from the bus stop. Dating from 1938 and last renovated in 2002, the seven-bed, fan-cooled dormitory is F$45 per person. The 11 air conditioned rooms with bath are a value at F$125 single or double, and air-conditioned family rooms are F$172-203 for three persons. This hotel looks like it's going to be noisy due to the large bar downstairs, but all is silent after the bar and restaurant close at 2100. Dinner is F$19-30 here.

GETTING THERE AND AROUND

Tavua is a stop for all Kings Road local and express buses (F$8 from Nadi, F$17 from Suva). To reach the interior, you'll need a 4WD vehicle. It's possible to hitch a ride along the way or on a truck from behind Tavua Market (offer about F$15 for a one-way ride).

Yaqara

From the Kings Road about 10 kilometers east of Tavua, tear your gaze away from the dramatic coastline to look inland up the **Yaqara River** valley and you'll see the large, flat white factory that bottles Fiji Water for the world. Canadian David Gilmour opened the plant here in 1996, and the premises are guarded after a couple of tourists tried to jump the fence. Also here is the 7,000-hectare Yaqara Cattle Ranch, where Fijian cowboys keep 5,500 head of cattle and 200 horses.

Vatukoula

From Tavua, you can drive about 12 minutes south to reach the gold-mining town of

Vatukoula. You can't enter the mine, but you can see it from the road eight kilometers south of Tavua. **Vatukoula** is a typical company town with education and social services under the jurisdiction of the mine, and the mostly iTaukei labor force living in considerably worse conditions than the senior staff and management. The Australian-owned Emperor Gold Mine opened in 1935 and by 2006 had produced 7 million ounces of gold, worth over US$4 billion at today's prices, though it's evident that little of this wealth flowed to the local community. Despite several major labor strikes and ownership changes, at one point involving both a South African company and the Fijian government, the mine continues to yield both silver and gold. An estimated 5 million ounces of gold remain underground and will take 20 years to extract.

Nadarivatu

An important forestry station is at **Nadarivatu,** a small settlement at 900-meter altitude, which means a cool climate and fantastic panorama of the northern coast from the ridge. In its heyday, Nadarivatu was a summer retreat for expatriates from the nearby Emperor Gold Mine at Vatukoula, but there are no accommodations now. Beside the road right in front of the Forestry Training Center is the **Stone Bowl,** the official source of the Sigatoka River. A five-minute walk from the center is the **Governor-General's Swimming Pool,** where a small creek has been dammed. The trail to the fire tower atop **Mount Lomalagi** (Mount Heaven) begins nearby; it's a one-hour hike each way. The tower itself has collapsed and is no longer climbable, but the forest is lovely, and you may see and hear many native birds. Pine forests cover the land.

★ Mount Tomaniivi

Mount Tomaniivi (formerly Mount Victoria), the highest mountain in the country (1,323 m), is a challenging yet rewarding trek. The two great rivers of Fiji, the Rewa and the Sigatoka, originate on the slopes of the mountain. Bright red epiphytic orchids *(Dendrobium mohlianum)* are sometimes in full bloom, and if you're very lucky, you might spot the rare red-throated lorikeet or pink-billed parrotfinch. Mount Tomaniivi is on the divide between the wet and dry sides of Viti Levu, and from the summit you should be able to distinguish the contrasting vegetation of these zones.

The trail up the mountain begins near the bridge at **Navai,** 10 kilometers southeast of Nadarivatu. Turn right up the hillside a few hundred meters down the jeep track, then climb through native bush on the main path all the way to the top, where there's a flat area suitable for camping. Beware of misleading signboards. There are three small streams to cross; no water is available after the third. On your way back down, stop for a swim in the largest stream.

Allow about six hours for the round-trip. This is one of the steepest hikes in Fiji, with a vertical elevation of 600 meters. It's rated 4 (on a scale of 5) for both difficulty and track roughness by the guides at Talanoa Treks, so you'll want to be in good shape to brave it. **Local guides** (F$20) are advisable, but permission to climb the mountain is not required.

Monasavu Hydroelectric Project

The largest development project ever undertaken in Fiji, this massive F$230 million scheme at Monasavu, near the center of Viti Levu, took 1,500 men six years to complete. An 82-meter-high earthen dam was built across the Nanuku River to supply water to the four 20-megawatt generating turbines at the Wailoa Power Station on the Wailoa River, 625 meters below. The dam forms a lake 17 kilometers long, and the water drops through a 5.4-kilometer tunnel at a 45-degree angle, one of the steepest engineered dips in the world. You can get a view of the lake and dam from the road or from the southern slope of Mount Tomaniivi. For more information on visiting, contact the Fiji Electricity Authority (tel. 331-3333, www.fea.com.fj) in Suva.

The Sunshine Coast

The **Sunshine Coast** is the area encompassing Rakiraki, Nananu-i-Ra Island, and the surrounding bays. The northernmost tip of Viti Levu offers beautiful scenery, a range of activities and accommodations, and dry (but windy) weather. It makes a good weekend reprieve from rainy Suva.

RAKIRAKI AND VICINITY

Rakiraki is used to refer to the region as a whole, but it's also commonly used interchangeably with the name of the region's main town, officially named **Vaileka,** where the Penang Sugar Mill was erected in 1881. There are three banks, a Western Union Currency Exchange, and a large produce market in Vaileka, but most visitors simply pass through on their way to one of the resorts or Nananu-i-Ra Island, a few kilometers east.

Sights

It's worth a pause just 100 meters west of the turnoff to Vaileka to pay your respects at the **grave of Ratu Udre Udre,** the onetime ruler of this region. He is alleged to have consumed 872 corpses of his enemies, and he holds the Guinness World Record as the planet's "most prolific cannibal."

A rocky hill named **Uluinavatu** (stone head), a few kilometers west of Vaileka, is reputed to be the jumping-off point for the disembodied spirits of the ancient Fijians. A fortified village and temple once stood on its summit. Uluinavatu's triangular shape is said to represent a man, while a similar-looking small island offshore resembles a woman with flowing hair.

Recreation

NAKAUVADRA RANGE

The **Nakauvadra Range,** which you can see towering south of here, is the traditional home of the Fijian serpent-god Degei, who is said to dwell in a cave on the summit of Mount Uluda (866 m). This "cave" is little more than a cleft in the rock. To climb the Nakauvadra Range, which the local Fijians look upon as their primeval homeland, permission must be obtained from the chief of Vatukacevaceva village, who will provide guides. A *sevusevu* must be presented.

VOLIVOLI POINT

A few kilometers east of Rakiraki is the scenic **Volivoli Point,** with a pleasant beach bay stretching toward a wharf. This region is the gateway to some of the best scuba diving in Fiji thanks to the reefs that are so treacherous that they almost sank Captain William Bligh, of HMS *Bounty* fame. In 1789, after being cast adrift by his own crew, Bligh and 18 others in a seven-meter longboat were chased by two Fijian war canoes through what is now called the Bligh Waters. His men pulled the oars desperately, headed for open sea, and managed to escape, while somehow charting the Fijian waters along the way. In 2017, director Baltasar Kormákur shot the Hollywood film *Adrift,* about a couple stranded after a massive hurricane, in these wild, scenic waters.

TOURS

Dhiren Naidu of **Getaway Tours** (tel. 938-0175, getawaytours2016@gmail.com) offers day tours as well as taxi services originating in Rakiraki and has a good vehicle.

Accommodations

Tanoa Rakiraki Hotel (Kings Rd., tel. 669-4101, www.tanoarakiraki.com), a couple of kilometers north of Vaileka, has 36 air-conditioned rooms with fridge and private bath at F$165/185/195 standard/superior/executive. The reception area, restaurant, and old wooden wing occupy the core of the original hotel, which dates to 1945; the two-story accommodations blocks were added much later. Extensive gardens surround the hotel and the

Cannibalism

the gravesite of Ratu Udre Udre near Rakiraki

In precontact times, the warring tribes of Fiji created an entire set of cultural practices around battle, including songs to praise the deities and dances choreographed to ensure victory. One of these practices was eating the enemy: The leaves of a certain vegetable *(Solanum uporo)* were wrapped around the human meat, which was then cooked in an earthen oven. Because the fingers and lips of chiefs and priests were taboo, and the attendants who normally fed them were banned from the spirit house during cannibal feasts, the chiefs used wooden forks to feed themselves. These objects themselves became taboo as a result and were kept as relics.

Most of the early European accounts of Fiji emphasized this tradition to the exclusion of almost everything else; for a time, Fiji appeared on European maps as the "Cannibal Isles." The ferocity of the inhabitants is credited with staving off European colonizers and missionaries for far longer than many other nations during the Age of Exploration. Ratu Udre Udre is said to have consumed 872 people and made a pile of stones, one for each victim, to record his achievement. He died around 1840, and a missionary who interviewed his son in 1849 reported that the son "assured me that his father ate all this number of human beings.... He ate them all himself, he gave to none."

Today, many cannibalistic artifacts have been repurposed as tourist attractions, perhaps to win the war against poverty. Replicas of specialized weapons such as neck-breakers and stomach scoopers are widely available, from keychains all the way up to monumental wall pieces. Still, they do carry deep meaning for Fijians and should be treated with respect. Don't be that jerk who makes the Fijian staff grimace politely with your crass jokes about whether they'll eat you if you don't tip.

outdoor bowling green draws lawn-bowling enthusiasts from Australia and New Zealand. Those folks like the old-fashioned "colonial" touches, such as the typed daily menu featuring British-Indian curry dishes, and gin and tonic in the afternoon. The Tui Ra (or king of Ra) lives in the village across the highway from the hotel. Only the local buses will drop you off right in front of the hotel; express buses take you into Vaileka. A taxi from Vaileka is F$5.

★ **Volivoli Beach Resort** (tel. 992-0942 or 992-5557, U.S. tel. 844/210-9802, info@volivoli.com, www.volivoli.com, F$365-585) is on sandy Volivoli Point at the northernmost tip of Viti Levu. Built on a steep hillside, all rooms have air-conditioning and ocean views from along a winding concrete pathway. The restaurant, lobby, pool (with a swim-up bar), and dive shop are down at the beach level. Volivoli is an ideal place to stay if scuba diving is a priority, as Ra Divers operates from here; packages including meals and/or diving are available, and fishing charters can be arranged as well. The snorkeling, kayaking, and hiking are all good. Day visitors can enjoy a scenic, if pricey, lunch (F$21-28 for sandwiches, fish-and-chips, or pizza) and a dip in the pool or sea by registering a credit card at the lobby. A taxi from Rakiraki is F$15.

The upscale **Wananavu Beach Resort** (tel. 669-4433, www.wananavu.com, US$179-714) is stylish but inconvenient. Built on a steep point facing Nananu-i-Ra Island, four kilometers off Kings Road, it has 34 air-conditioned bungalows varying in price based on size and location. The beachfront *bures* are right on a sweet strand with hammock chairs that's nice for snorkeling at high tide, but then you must climb the mountain for every meal, or even water (nothing is delivered to the rooms, although a staff member might promise to bring you something). The honeymoon *bures,* with private plunge pools, are luxurious and at the same level as the parking lot and restaurant, but there's little to do so far from the beach. There's a small swimming pool and tennis court, but the indifferent service doesn't match the prices.

One hill over from Wananavu is the self-catering accommodation **Starfish Blue** (tel. 999-6746, www.starfishblue.com). A villa for 1-3 people is F$350 and a villa for up to 6 is F$400. You can cook your own meals or, for a fee, ask the staff to do so. They'll also do laundry or babysit for a fee. A small ocean-front pool is in front of the building, and guests may use the facilities of the Wananavu Resort. **Suncoast Taxis and Tours** (tel. 669-4366) bring guests here from Nadi Airport for F$150-180 depending on number of people and suitcases.

Getting There

Vaileka is a stop for all Kings Road local and express buses (F$10 from Nadi, F$10 from Suva).

★ NANANU-I-RA ISLAND

The small (355-hectare) **Nananu-i-Ra Island,** three kilometers off the northernmost tip of Viti Levu, is a good place to spend some quality time amid tranquility and beauty. The climate is dry and sunny, and there are great beaches, reefs, snorkeling, walks, sunsets, and moonrises over the water—and no roads. Seven or eight white sandy beaches lie scattered around the island, and it's big enough that you won't feel confined. In the early 19th century, disease and tribal warfare wiped out Nananu-i-Ra's original Fijian inhabitants, and an heir sold the island to Europeans whose descendants now operate a few small resorts.

Most of the northern two-thirds of Nananu-i-Ra Island was once owned by Procter & Gamble heiress Louise Harper of Southern California, who bought it for a mere US$200,000 in 1968. Until Harper's death in 2005, her cattle grazed beneath coconuts on the 219-hectare Harper Plantation, and the land has remained largely untouched.

The island lies within the **Vatu-i-Ra Conservation Park,** which encompasses more than 100 square kilometers of reefs north of Rakiraki. This is a protected corridor for humpback whales migrating August-October, and has spectacular walls, soft corals, and thousands of schooling fish.

Recreation

It's possible to **hike** most of the way around Nananu-i-Ra in four hours or less during low tide, as the entire coastline is public, but thick mangroves make the western side of the island difficult to cover. The easiest and most picturesque route is to hike up the eastern side of the island to deserted One Beach on the northern side, and then return the same way. Even at low tide, at some point you'll probably have to take off your shoes and wade through ankle-high water or scramble over slippery rocks. Avoid becoming stranded by high tide.

The **diving** here is spectacular only if you observe the details—there's not the profuse marinelife or huge reefs you'll find elsewhere, though the underwater photographer will like it. This area is good for wreck diving: the 33-meter *Papuan Explorer* was scuttled in 1990 in 22 meters of water off the west side of Nananu-i-Ra, 150 meters off a 189-meter jetty that curves out into the sheltered lagoon. The interisland ferry *Ovalau* is 26 meters down in the open sea off northern Nananu-i-Ra.

Ra Divers (tel. 669-4511, www.volivoli.com), based at Volivoli Beach Resort, has been diving the waters around Nananu-i-Ra since the 1980s. They offer scuba diving at F$190/360 for one/two tanks (gear extra). Night diving is F$190. Snorkeling trips are

1

2

3

Joining the Great Fiji Shark Count

Sharks worldwide are in decline, and Fiji's pelagic population is no exception. Traditional fishing practices include spearing or sportfishing for sharks, but the Asian market for shark fins has provided aggressive incentives for locals to kill sharks faster than the fish can reproduce. In 2011, Fiji saw its first campaign to stop people from fishing for sharks. The export of shark fins brings in F$4 million a year, but Suva-based marine biologist and ecologist Helen Sykes argues that living sharks are far more valuable: shark- and diving-related tourism brings in F$42 million per year.

a shark in the Koro Sea

In 2012, Sykes and Stuart Gow started the **Great Fiji Shark Count** (www.fijisharkcount.com/participants), working with volunteer groups and dive operators across the country. It uses the same methodology as the Global Shark Count (www.eoceans.co) and aims to build awareness as well as establish a baseline for scientific research. In 2017, fifteen dive operators recorded 4,000 observations, and with five-plus years of data in the bank, a comparative analysis of changes over time can now begin.

It's easy to participate: Just go diving or snorkeling in Fiji during **April** or **November** with one of the participating operators listed on the website After each outing, your guide will note down how many sharks you've sighted, by species, along with manta rays and turtles. And voilá—you've done your part for science.

possible. They pick up clients regularly from all area resorts and their equipment is first-rate. Ra Divers uses the aluminum *Bligh Explorer* to take as many as 16 divers to Bligh Water and Vatu-i-Ra Passage, while the smaller *Phantom* frequents Sailstone Reef.

Safari Lodge Fiji (tel. 669-3333, 628-3332, or 948-8888, www.safarilodge.com.fj) on Ellington Wharf offers a variety of water sports activities, often with a minimum of two persons. The on-site Coconut Café serves coffee and meals. Boat transfers and day trips to Nananu-i-Ra can be arranged for F$50 per person. Travelers enjoy the atmosphere and rate the windsurfing and kitesurfing instruction highly, but the attached lodge is not recommended. The PADI dive shop gets mixed reviews; make sure the divemaster on the day you're diving has local knowledge. If not, Ra Divers will be a better bet.

1: the beach at Volivoli Beach Resort 2: the honeymoon suite at Wananavu Beach Resort 3: looking out to Nananu-i-Ra and Yanuca islands.

Accommodations

Accommodation prices on Nananu-i-Ra have crept up in recent years, especially June-August, the peak windsurfing season. Beds in the dorms are usually available, but advance bookings are necessary if you want your own room. All the budget places have cooking facilities, and a few also serve snacks and meals. MacDonald's and Betham's have mini-marts with a reasonable selection of groceries (including beer). Also take the opportunity to buy groceries in Vaileka on the way to Nananu-i-Ra. Bring cash, as most places don't accept credit cards.

★ **MacDonald's Nananu Beach Cottages** (tel. 628-3118, www.macsnananu.com) offers two attractive beach houses and one garden house, all with bath and fridge, at F$135 single or double, plus F$12 per additional person to four maximum. A duplex is F$90 for each of the two units, while a larger two-story house accommodating up to six is F$145 for the first two people. The four-bunk dorm is F$25 per person. All units have access to cooking facilities, and a three-meal package is available at F$40 per person. Mabel MacDonald's Beachside Café serves excellent grilled cheese sandwiches and pizzas, and also sells groceries. Dinner must be ordered by 1500. A Fijian *lovo* feast is arranged once a week. The property is peaceful and attractive, with excellent snorkeling (lots of parrot fish) from the long private wharf off the beach. Ryan MacDonald takes guests on a snorkeling trip to the outer reef, and kayaks are available for rent.

Right next to MacDonald's and facing the same white beach is **Betham's Beach Cottages** (tel. 628-0400, www.bethams.com.fj). The mixed dormitory with four ancient beds is F$40 per person. Each of the four units, in two cement-block duplex houses, sleeps up to six. It's F$116 single/double for the private room. There's also a wooden beachfront bungalow for FJ$170 single/double. Additional people are F$16 each. There's no hot water, but cooking facilities and a fridge are provided. Noisy parties are actively discouraged here. A paperback lending library is at your service. Betham's impressive grocery store also sells alcohol, and its well-stocked beachfront bar serves dinner.

Bulavou Beach Bungalows (tel. 628-3103, www.bulavoubeachbungalowsfiji.com) is on a mile-long picture-postcard beach. There are six apartments in three buildings, each accommodating up to six people at F$199 for the first four persons, then F$55 for each additional person. Each unit has a large fridge but no cooking facilities; it's F$55/70 per person for the meal plan (two/three meals).

Far more upscale is **Dolphin Island Resort** (tel. 378-5791, www.dolphinislandfiji.com), which is technically on the connected Yanuca Island (not to be confused with two other Yanuca Islands off the Coral Coast). It's F$5,850 per couple, all inclusive, with a two-night minimum.

Getting There

Coming from Nadi, you will have to change buses in Lautoka. From Lautoka, take an express bus along Kings Road to Vaileka (Rakiraki), then a taxi to the landing at Ellington Wharf for F$20. If you don't have much luggage, you can get off the express bus later, at the turnoff from the Kings Road to Ellington Wharf, and walk two kilometers to the wharf.

From the wharf, boat transfers to the island are F$25-40 per person round-trip (20 minutes), though the resorts may levy a surcharge for one person alone. Check prices when you call to book your accommodation.

Northeastern Viti Levu

From Rakiraki, you can continue east along the Kings Road east into the interior to Korovou. It's a pretty, paved drive, with some notable stops along the way.

Viti Levu's northeastern coast, also known as **the Tailevu Coast** (see page 194), is best accessed from Suva. Even if you're coming from Rakiraki, it's better to drive south into the interior on Kings Road to Korovou, and then travel up the coast.

NAISERELAGI

About 25 kilometers southeast of Rakiraki along the Kings Road is **Naiserelagi,** notable for the old Catholic church of St. Francis Xavier on a hilltop above Navunibitu Catholic School. It's beautifully decorated with frescoes painted by Jean Charlot in 1962-1963. Typical Fijian motifs, such as the *tabua, tanoa,* and *yaqona,* blend together in the powerful composition behind the altar. Charlot had previously collaborated with the famous Mexican muralist Diego Rivera, and his work (restored in 1998) is definitely worth stopping to see. Flying Prince Transport (tel. 669-4346) runs buses from Vaileka to Naiserelagi two times a day (FJ$3.15); otherwise, all the local Suva buses stop there. A taxi from Vaileka might cost F$50 round-trip with waiting time.

★ NABALASERE ECOTOURISM FOREST PARK

It takes a little work to find this idyllic spot, but you'll be rewarded with a waterfall and a wonderful swim in cool, refreshing waters when you do. About 50 kilometers south of Rakiraki, after Ra High School, turn right and go 13 kilometers along the road to Nalawa. There, a dirt road leads to Nabalasere. After a *sevusevu*, guides can take you 1 kilometer to the waterfall and swimming hole.

Twenty-five of the 30 homes in this village were destroyed in 2016 by Cyclone Winston, but the resilient village rebuilt. The entire region is in the process of being transformed into the **Nabalasere Ecotourism Forest Park** thanks to a partnership between the village, the government, and trail designers from the New Zealand Department of Conservation. **Talanoa Treks** (tel. 998-0560, info@talanoa-treks-fiji.com, https://talanoa-treks-fiji.com), of which the village is a key partner, includes this as a hiking trip with lunch in a full-day excursion from Suva.

WAILOTUA

Continuing southeast on the Kings Road, two neighboring villages share a name at Wailotua, 112 kilometers south of Rakiraki and 18 kilometers west of Korovou town. To stretch your legs, pause at Wailotua No. 1 to stroll through a large **"snake cave"** (admission F$10), easily accessible from the road. One stalactite in the cave is shaped like a six-headed snake.

KOROVOU

There are numerous places throughout Fiji named **Korovou,** which means "new village." The small crossroads town here, 47 kilometers north of Suva, is home to a hospital, a well-stocked **Nayan's Supermarket,** an ATM, a gas station, and a college. It's a landmark for directions and is the last major stop before Nausori and Suva.

It's also the turnoff point from the Kings Road for the coast north of Suva, known as the Tailevu Coast.

Vanua Levu

Fiji's second-largest island has an altogether different feel from Viti Levu, though it's only 40 miles to the north. Once called Sandalwood Island, 5,587-square-kilometer Vanua Levu has rain-heavy mountain ranges in the south and dry sugar-friendly flatlands in the north, with excellent roads and a variety of gorgeous scenery from coast to peak. It is wealthy in rivers too, including Fiji's deepest river, the Dreketi, and its most shark-infested, the Wainikoro. Daily flights and several ferries make it easy to reach, and it's a convenient stopover en route to Taveuni.

The southern town of Savusavu is a pleasant place to hang out for a few days, with a local Fijian feel and diverse recreational opportunities, including great snorkeling and diving, bird-watching, and natural

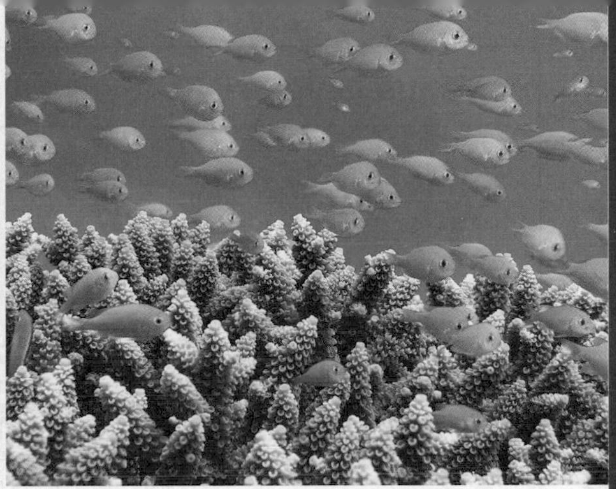

Highlights

Look for ★ to find recommended sights, activities, dining, and lodging.

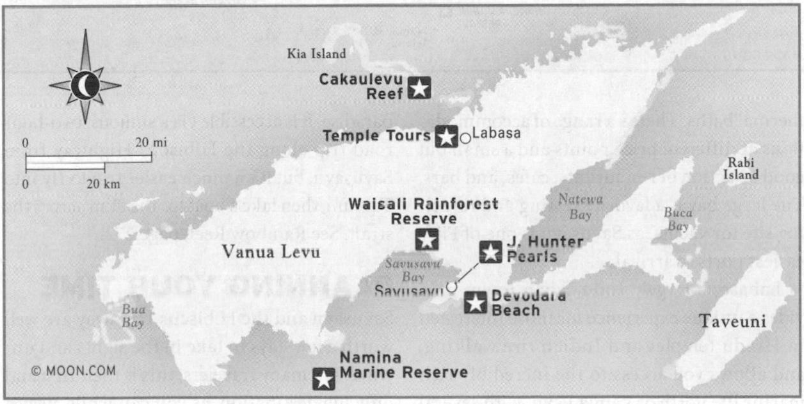

★ **J. Hunter Pearls:** Take a pleasant morning boat trip into Savusavu Bay to see how baby oysters grow into pearl-makers—then cool off by snorkeling amid giant clams (page 236).

★ **Waisali Rainforest Reserve:** Just off the highway between Savusavu and Labasa, this mountain forest is home to unexploited stands of native trees and dozens of rare and endemic Vanua Levu bird species (page 236).

★ **Devodara Beach:** This beach and lagoon is Vanua Levu's best, with uncrowded stretches of sand, shallow turquoise water, and a fine snorkeling reef (page 247).

★ **Temple Tours:** Several colorful Hindu temples in and around Labasa give you a chance to experience Indo-Fijian community life (page 251).

★ **Cakaulevu Reef:** The third-longest coral reef in the world is a magical turquoise underworld that's 95 percent unexplored (page 252).

★ **Namena Marine Reserve:** This is the largest no-take marine reserve in Fiji, with stunning, healthy coral reefs and Fiji's best all-around diving (page 256).

Vanua Levu

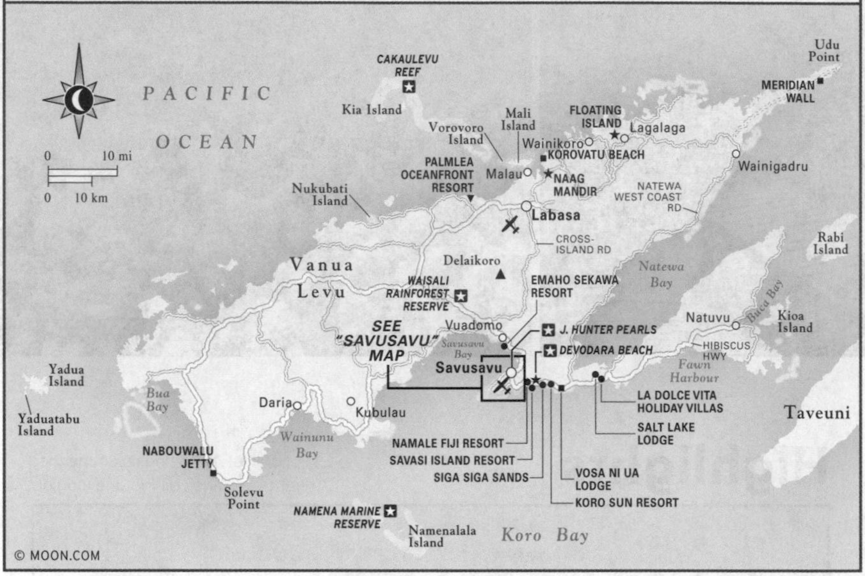

thermal baths. There's a range of accommodations at different price points and a small but good selection of restaurants, cafés, and bars. The large bay is a favorite resting and refueling site for yachts, as Savusavu is one of Fiji's easiest ports of arrival.

Labasa, a largely Indo-Fijian town, provides a unique experience for those interested in Hindu temples and Indian fire walking, and allows you access to the incredibly rich marine life north of Vanua Levu, with several lovely islands and one of the world's longest coral reefs.

In between, along the Hibiscus Highway, several bayside resorts provide a relaxing contrast and scenic views of the sea between the big island (Viti Levu) and Vanua Levu. To the west are several small towns.

The remote southeastern tip of Vanua Levu is the closest spot to the premier dive sites of the **Somosomo Strait,** which makes it a divers' paradise. It is accessible via a sinuous, two-hour road trip along the Hibiscus Highway from Savusavu, but it's a much easier trip to fly into Taveuni, then take a boat for the 8km across the strait. See Rainbow Reef, page 272.

PLANNING YOUR TIME

Savusavu and the Hibiscus Highway are well worth a few days to take in the sights and unwind. For many travelers, this is their first and only Fiji destination, as you can while away a week or more enjoying tranquil resorts, small-town Fiji, and adventures in the bay, ocean, or waterfall-rich jungle.

It's also a popular stopover en route to Taveuni. An excellent itinerary is to fly from Nadi to Savusavu, spending two nights there, and then continue eastward via a scenic bus trip and short ferry ride across the Somosomo Strait to spend three nights on Taveuni Island. From Taveuni, you can fly to Suva, touring

Previous: Lesiaceva Point, with Koro Island in the distance; looking out on Savusavu Bay; blue-green chromis school in the Namena Marine Reserve.

Find Your Beach

- **Devodara Beach** (page 247): The best swimming beach on Vanua Levu is off the Hibiscus Highway. It's also known locally as the Blue Lagoon (not to be confused with the movie-famous Blue Lagoon in the Yasawas).
- **Lesiaceva Point** (page 235): The nicest public beach near Savusavu is along Lesiaceva Point, near the Jean-Michel Cousteau Fiji Islands Resort. It makes for a nice stroll and picnic.
- **Korovatu Beach** (page 252): This is the best choice near Labasa. Snorkeling is also possible here.
- **Nawi Island** (page 235): Off Savusavu, this little island has several fine, secluded little beach coves accessible by boat.

more of Viti Levu before making your way back to Nadi.

Direct flights from Nadi or Suva are offered more cheaply and frequently to Labasa than to Savusavu, so you may find yourself passing through the northern town. Labasa is worth a half day or maybe a night, and only if you're interested in the workaday town side of Fijian culture. Unless your destination is a resort on the northern side of Vanua Levu, you can hustle through that part of the island.

GETTING THERE

If price and scheduling allow, it's most convenient to fly into Savusavu from Nadi or Suva. Alternatively, you can fly into Labasa (which is usually cheaper), about 90 minutes north of Savusavu along a fine paved road.

If you're on a budget, a ferry-plus-bus route will get you to Savusavu or Labasa somewhat weary and dusty. The trip is about 10 hours from Suva and 6 from Taveuni, most of which is via an open-air bus. The roads are paved, but seats on the buses and ferries are less than luxurious.

Air

Fiji Airways has direct flights to Labasa and Savusavu, daily from Nadi and several days a week from Suva.

Sea

Captain Cook Cruises (www.captaincookcruisesfiji.com) runs seven-night Colonial Fiji Discovery Cruises on the *MV Reef Endeavour.* The ship stops at Savusavu, as well as Ovalau and Taveuni. This cruise is offered about twice a year; see the website for upcoming dates. It's possible to join or leave the cruise in Savusavu.

Several ferries travel to and from Vanua Levu on a confusing variety of routes. Ferry tickets also include bus fare for the hours-long journeys to reach the towns from the two main arrival points. Some of these journeys are overnight. If you're coming from Viti Levu, you'll most likely depart from Natovi Jetty north of Suva and arrive at **Nabouwalu Jetty,** at the southwestern tip of Vanua Levu. If you're coming from Taveuni, you'll come into **Natuvu Jetty** on Buca Bay, at the eastern terminus of the Hibiscus Highway on Vanua Levu.

Patterson Brothers Shipping (tel. 331-5644, fijisearoad1@gmail.com, www.fijisearoad.com) operates the "Sea-Road" bus/ferry/bus service between Vanua Levu and Viti Levu. There are two offices in Labasa: in the Telecom Building behind the post office (tel. 881-2450), and on Nasekula Road opposite St. Mary's Primary School (tel. 881-2444). There's also an agent in Savusavu (tel. 885-0469). Boarding begins at 0430 at the Suva Flea Market (opposite the main bus stand); the ferry reaches Natovi Jetty at 0700 and Nabouwalu Jetty on Vanua Levu at 1130. From there, it's another four hours by bus to Labasa, or you can get off halfway and transfer to the Savusavu bus, which takes about the same amount of time. The return trip leaves Labasa at 0730 and leaves Nabouwalu Jetty at 1130. It takes about 10 hours right through, and costs F$56 one-way. There are discounts for children of various ages, and infants travel free but must still have a ticket. It's old-school: there's no prebooking by phone, email, or web, and you must to go to one of the shipping offices or to the bus/ferry itself for a ticket. Offices are open Monday-Friday 0830-1600 and Saturday 0900-1200.

The 350-passenger *Princess Moana,* operated by Savusavu-based **Miller Shipping** (tel. 755-6672, 755-6673, or 968-1127), links Suva, Vanua Levu (at both Nabouwalu jetty on the southwestern tip, and Natuvu on the eastern end), Rabi Island, and Taveuni. A Taveuni-to-Savusavu fare is F$15; to Labasa, it's F$20. Weekly departures from Taveuni's Lovonivonu wharf, near Waiyevo, are at 1730 Wednesdays and 0730 and 1330 Thursdays. There are many other scheduled trips; the company's Facebook page is the best source for current timetables as well as a long list of phone numbers, depending on where you want to start your journey. To book in person in Savusavu, visit the Miller Shipping office opposite the post office on Main Street. On Viti Levu, Patterson Shipping offices can also book these trips.

Grace Shipping (tel. 885-0448 or 995-0775) operates the latest iteration of the *Taveuni Princess;* the current boat was constructed in 2017, but ferries with this name have been plying the route for 52 years. A bus starts in Labasa at 0430, picks up most of its passengers at the main bus station in Savusavu, and then travels east to Natuvu for the ferry transfer, reaching Taveuni at 1100. On alternate days, the return trip leaves Taveuni at 0730 and reaches Labasa at 1330. The ferry has a variable schedule; call for timing and rates.

In 2018, **Goundar Shipping** (tel. 777-5463, goundarshipping@kidanet.com.fj) began running the 130-meter *Lomaiviti Princess V* for trips from Suva to Savusavu (12 hours) and Taveuni (an additional 3 hours). The 53-year-old Canadian vessel is now the largest ship plying the waters of Fiji, with a capacity of 164 vehicles and 1,000-plus passengers, as well as a play area for children and an onboard restaurant. Trips are said to be daily but are often canceled, and passengers have complained to the government's maritime department about overcrowding and being charged arbitrarily for "extras" such as using the restrooms and plugging devices into onboard electrical outlets. The entire journey is F$70 including bus fare.

Savusavu and Vicinity

The charms of this picturesque little town start with the superlative view: across a sparkling bay to cloud-forest mountains, and along a seemingly infinite coast out to sea. In the 1860s, Europeans arrived to establish coconut plantations here. The copra business went bust in the 1930s, but their descendants and the Fijian villagers still supply copra to a coconut-oil mill eight kilometers west of **Savusavu,** giving this side of Vanua Levu a pleasant agricultural air. In 2000, the first black pearl farm was established on the far side of Nawi Island in the bay, and J. Hunter pearls are now available at Prouds outlets throughout Fiji.

In addition to iTaukei and Indo-Fijians, Savusavu has a large white expat community drawn by the fact that a huge former copra plantation was parceled out and sold as freehold land, meaning it can be purchased outright (rather than leased from iTaukei landowners). It won't take you long to feel like everyone knows your name in this town of 7,000.

Cruise ships often anchor in the sheltered bay. The surrounding mountains and reefs also make Savusavu a well-protected hurricane refuge. The diving possibilities of this area were recognized by Jean-Michel Cousteau in 1990, when he selected Savusavu

Savusavu Vicinity

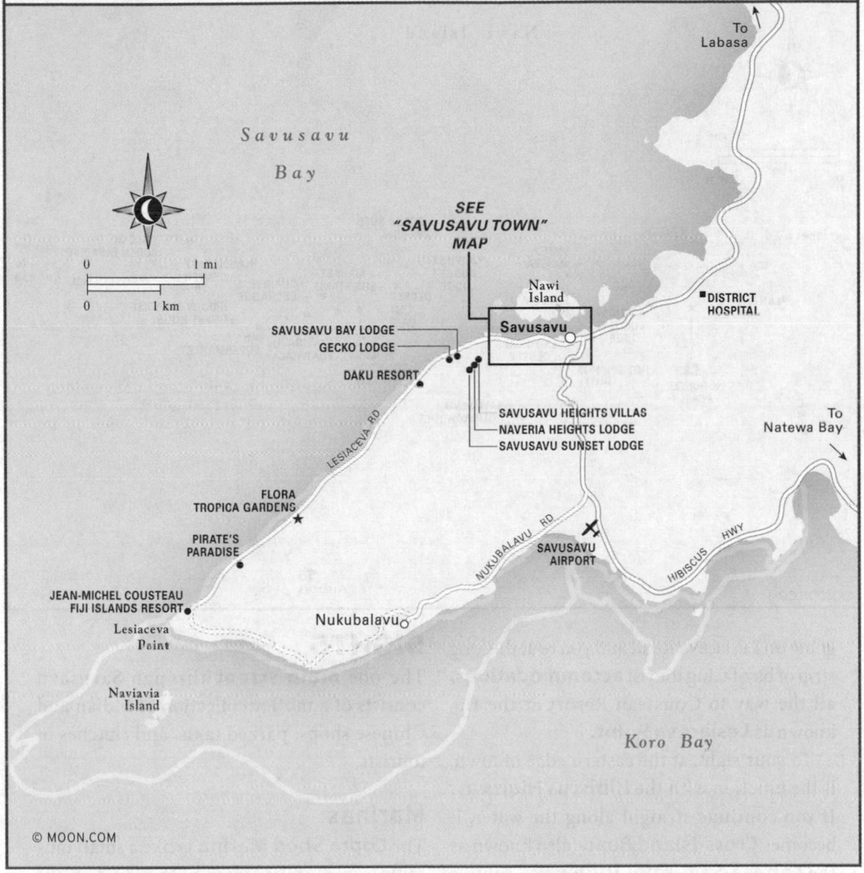

as the base for his Project Ocean Search. The nicest public beach near town is on Lesiaceva Point, just outside the Jean-Michel Cousteau Fiji Islands Resort. Although much smaller than Labasa, Savusavu is the administrative center of Cakaudrove Province and has three banks, a large pharmacy, and a supermarket.

ORIENTATION

Savusavu is tiny—you can walk from one end of downtown to the other in five minutes—but I always get confused about which way is which. That's because, although it's on the southern side of Vanua Levu, the town's main street actually faces *north* across **Savusavu Bay.** Green little **Nawi Island** is in the foreground, and the rainy coast of the northern side of the bay forms a stunning, mountainous background.

It's easy to get oriented if you stand at the **central market and bus stand,** facing the water. The road running behind you is called **Lesiaceva Road.** To your left the **Copra Shed Marina** anchors the western end of town. A hundred paces past that, small **Nakama Lane** rises uphill, but without going too far you can see the small natural hot spring bubbling up next to a school. Keep

Savusavu

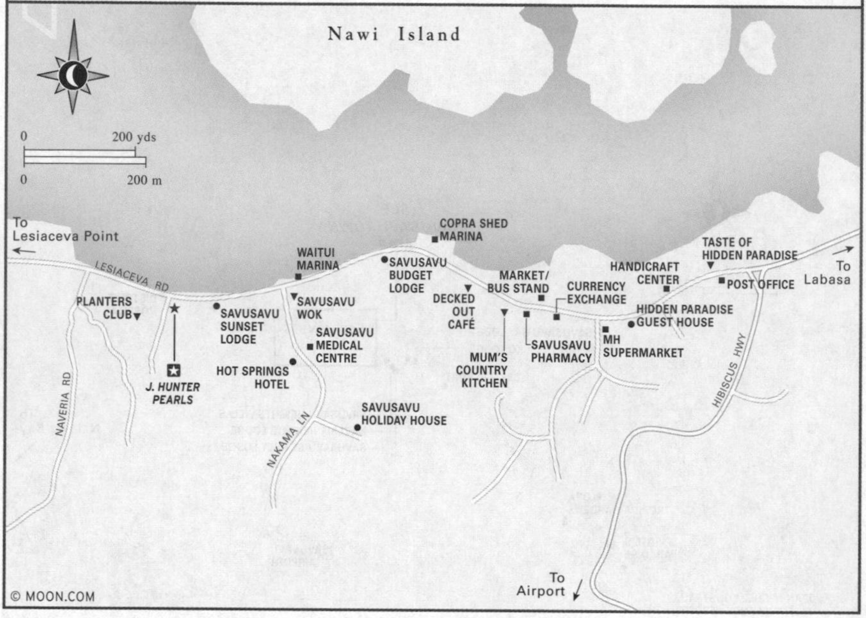

going on Lesiaceva Road and you're at the long strip of bay-facing tourist **accommodations,** all the way to Cousteau Resort at the tip, known as **Lesiaceva Point.**

To your right, at the eastern edge of town, is the junction with the **Hibiscus Highway.** If you continue straight along the water, it becomes **Cross-Island Road** (also known as the **Labasa-Savusavu Highway**), rounds the bay, and heads north and west. At a T-junction, you can turn right (northeast) for **Labasa.** Otherwise, go left (west and then south) to loop past **Bua Bay**—where the first European sandalwood traders put in, stripping an entire forest between 1800 and 1814—to **Nabouwalu Jetty**, the western ferry junction point.

If, instead, you take a right turn out of town, you'll go south to **Savusavu Airport,** which has lovely views of the big island, Viti Levu. Beyond the airport, you can head east along the coastline of **Natewa Bay** (next section).

SIGHTS

The one **main street** through Savusavu consists of a motley collection of Indian and Chinese shops, parked taxis, and clutches of tourists.

Marinas

The **Copra Shed Marina** is like a small museum/community center, with map displays and historical photos, information boards, fancy boutiques, and many of Savusavu's tourist services. In front of the marina is a stone dated 1880, which is said to be from Fiji's first copra mill.

A little west along the waterfront is Savusavu's second yachting center, the **Waitui Marina.** A wonderful scenic viewpoint (and romantic spot to watch a sunset) is on the hill just above and west of the Hot Springs Hotel, above the Waitui Marina.

Hot Springs

There are small **hot springs** boiling out

A Coastal Stroll

Savusavu Bay

This scenic walk from Nukubalavu to Savusavu should be timed for low tide.

Start by taking a bus or taxi from Savusavu past the airport to **Nukubalavu village** (bus F$1.15, departs daily 0930, 1300, and 1700; taxi F$8), located six kilometers down the road along the south side of the peninsula.

From here you can walk west along the beach to the Cousteau Resort on **Lesiaceva Point** in about an hour at low tide. On your way, you'll have picturesque views of the yachts, Nawi Island, and the mountainous side of Vanua Levu. You can often see the mist of rain falling through cathedral-like rays of sun on the distant peninsula.

Try to avoid cutting through the resort at the end of the hike, as the Cousteau management disapproves (though all beaches in Fiji are public up to two meters above the high-tide mark). From Lesiaceva, it's six flat kilometers by road back to Savusavu, which you can either walk—keep the sea to your left—or travel by taxi.

among fractured coral below and behind the Hot Springs Hotel. These and other springs throughout the area are reminders that the whole area was once a caldera. It's far too hot to bathe here; locals use the springs to cook meat and vegetables, almost like a *lovo*. If you happen by while cooking is in progress, you'll be invited; offer to return with beverages or some other contribution to the feast.

A few meters away, at the **Savusavu Medical Centre** (tel. 998-1786, ishaqfiji@yahoo.co.uk, Mon.-Fri. 0800-1600 or later by request, F$15/session) you can arrange a therapeutic bath in three cement pools where the sulfur water is piped in and allowed to cool enough to relax (104°F) rather than boil you. There's no fancy spa atmosphere here—just hot, soothing mineral water. Call ahead so the baths can be filled with fresh water for you. You must wear a swimsuit and bring a towel as well as drinking water.

Nawi Island

In Savusavu Bay, you'll see privately owned **Nawi Island** just a swim's length away, but you can't visit. It's under development, with a few rest *bures*, a bar, and a yacht repair dock. The island has been under development for more than a decade, with a proposal involving a resort and residential villas. In 2014, as part of the construction work, six graves of Solomon Islander laborers were dug up and relocated to Vanua Levu. The grave of a Samoan princess, Lalomauga, who married into Fiji's Miller family in the first half of the 19th century, will remain on the island as a historic site. The J. Hunter Pearls farm is right off Nawi Island.

★ J. Hunter Pearls

For a fascinating look into how pearls are made (and a chance to ogle the pearls themselves), take a tour at the farm of **J. Hunter Pearls** (tel. 885-0821, info@fijipearls.com, www.fijipearls.com, weekdays at 0930, other times and Saturdays by appt., F$25), beside Nawi Island. Call to make a reservation (required) and then meet at the showroom, next to the Planters Club.

After a 15-minute explanation and video, you're taken out to the water to see the operation. Bring along a mask and snorkel if you want to swim afterward between the clam racks in a lovely cove behind Nawi Island.

At the end, you'll have a chance to shop, of course. When looking for a valuable pearl, keep in mind luster, shape, and color. The most valuable pearls have more luster (a thicker coat of pearl), are rounder, and are lighter. Grades can be Gem, A, B, C, or D (D having visible marks or scratches).

Flora Tropica Gardens

Flora Tropica Gardens (Lesiaceva Point Rd., tel. 921-4600, floratropicafiji@gmail.com, www.floratropica.com) is a private botanical garden five kilometers from Savusavu town, on the bay side, with wooden walkways and stone paths winding through five lovely acres of hillsides and creek flats. There are beautiful views of Savusavu Bay, and it's a peaceful place to spend an hour or so wandering, perhaps bird-watching. Orchids, heliconia, water lilies, and 250 varieties of palm trees make this a place popular with cruise ship passengers and wedding photographers. Call ahead to book. Guided tours are held Monday-Friday at 1000 (F$20 pp); self-guided admission, Monday-Friday, is the same price; a guided tour at another time is F$30 per person, minimum two. A taxi from town is F$8, or it's a pleasant (mostly flat) bicycle ride. Take insect repellant and water, as nothing is for sale on-site.

★ Waisali Rainforest Reserve

For some mountain hiking, book a taxi or ask a bus driver to drop you at the entrance to the **Waisali Rainforest Reserve** (tel. 828-0267, Mon.-Sat. 0900-1500, F$10, www.nationaltrust.org.fj), about 25 kilometers northwest of Savusavu. This 116-hectare reserve protects one of Vanua Levu's last unexploited tropical rainforests, with native species such as the *dakua, yaka,* and *yasi* well represented. Thirty orchid species and some of Fiji's few remaining giant kauri trees are here. The rare red-breasted musk parrot, black-faced shrikebill, and orange dove are among the dozens of rare and endemic species recorded here.

A short but strenuous nature trail leads to viewpoints offering sweeping vistas. In all, two hours of hiking is available. Bring water and mosquito repellent. The guard closes up and goes home if no guests arrive, so it's best to call ahead. Birders can ask to arrive early; 0630 is best. **Daku Resort** (tel. 885-0046, reservations@dakuresort.com, www.dakuresort.com/bird-watching-tours) offers a four-morning guided birding tour that includes the rainforest, as well as other spots in Savusavu and Buca Bay.

On the Cross-Island Road

Many of the resorts and tour agencies in Savusavu head northwest, along the road to Labasa, to treat you to wilderness sights. The **thermal mud pools** past Levuka village are a favorite. At the 17.2-kilometer mark from town, you can pause at the small settlement, shout "hello," and wait for Mika or his family members to come out and lead you to the very pleasant **Waisile waterfall.**

About half a kilometer farther north, just past Emaho Sekawa resort, is friendly

Vuadomo village. This is the site of a fine waterfall that's a favorite of wedding photographers in the area. Look for the brick bus shelter adjacent to a (tiny!) road sign for Vodomo Road (a different spelling). Follow the steep slope down to the village and pause at the chief's house to present a *sevusevu* (you can buy a kava bundle in Savusavu or Labasa town, at the market). You may also be offered the chance to buy handwoven mats. Village etiquette applies here, so cover your shoulders and knees. For permission to visit the waterfall, pay F$10 per person, go back uphill to the road, and continue to the first right. Park at the hut and follow the sound of water a few minutes up along a clear and easy trail. There are no amenities, so take what you need and pack your garbage out with you. At the falls, feel free to shed your sulu (or wedding gown) and swim in the large, pleasant pool.

SPORTS AND RECREATION

Diving

The **Namena Marine Reserve** offers the best diving in this area. It surrounds tiny Namenalala Island, about 40 kilometers south of Savusavu. For more information on the diving here and a list of outfitters that will take you, see page 256.

Yachting

The **Copra Shed Marina** (tel. 885-0457, coprashed@connect.com.fj) near the bus station allows visiting yachts to moor for F$15 a day. This includes use of the facilities by the whole crew, but a F$10 refundable key deposit is required for the shower. You can have your laundry done for F$9 (wash and dry). The bulletin board here is a good place for up-to-date information and to connect with others about services and opportunities, or lurk around in the early morning and ask for Geoff Taylor to get the scoop. Yacht Club membership is complimentary for 90 days after you arrive by yacht in Savusavu.

Waitui Marina (tel. 885-3057 or 925-7111, waituimarinafiji@gmail.com) offers similar services.

Yachts can clear Fiji customs in Savusavu. Arriving yachts should call Savusavu Port Control on VHF 16. Customs, biosecurity, and immigration officials will board the vessel with all of the necessary paperwork. If you need to contact these officials directly, the customs office (tel. 885-0727, Mon.-Fri. 0800-1300 and 1400-1600) is next to Savusavu Budget Lodge west of the Waitui Marina, and the Immigration Department (tel. 885-0800) is across the street from the Waitui Marina. If you check in after 1630 or on weekends or holidays, there's an additional charge on top of the usual quarantine fee.

The Yacht Shop (tel. 778-0301, yssavusavu@tradewinds.com.fj, www.yachtshop.com.fj, Mon.-Thurs. 0800-1700, Fri. 0800-1600, Sat. 0800-1200) at the Copra Shed Marina sells local nautical charts, British charts, and boating necessities. If you have an urgent need after hours, try Vishwa at 925-4339.

Fishing

Several resorts have their own fishing boats. In addition, **Savusavu Fishing**'s Trevina and Terry Gray offer charter fishing trips on board the *Searov* (tel. 885-0674, savusavufishing@gmail.com, www.savusavufishing.com). Transfers to other islands and harbor tours are also possible, and they keep their blog (http://savusavufishing.blogspot.com/) up to date with honest posts about current fishing conditions and catches.

Tours

Savusavu Tours (tel. 838-0406, savusavutours@gmail.com, http://rafasadventuretours.weebly.com) owner Elayne Bennett offers a thermal mud pool excursion, available with or without a waterfall and village visit (F$75/F$120). The volcanic mineral springs bubble up at 37°C and coat the bottom of a pool that's like a natural hot tub, easily big enough for 15 people. It's very soothing in a goopy way, and your skin feels

Making Fiji's Pearls

THE INDUSTRY

Cultured pearl farming began in Japan in the early 1900s, and in the 1980s an attempt was made to establish a Japanese pearl farm in Fiji. It failed, however, and it took a Fiji-raised American to launch the industry here.

Justin Hunter, a marine biologist from a pearl-farming family in Washington State, returned to his childhood home in Savusavu in 1999 to establish **J. Hunter Pearls.** Using the uniquely colored oyster shells that grow naturally in nutrient-rich Savusavu Bay, the company cultivates pearls in an array of iridescent pastel grays, blues, purples, and greens not found elsewhere in the world.

Working closely with the nine Fijian villages around the bay that hold the traditional water rights, J. Hunter trains and employs Fijian marine biologists as well as villagers who plant, maintain, and harvest the pearl lines in 120 hectares of deep water in Savusavu Bay. Oysters require pristine conditions, so the business creates an incentive to keep the waters pure. Dividends fund projects such as a new community hall/hurricane shelter.

Two Japanese technicians arrive regularly at the company's larval tanks, north of Savusavu, to perform the highly skilled operation of "seeding" and grafting the pearls by implanting 100,000 *Pinctada margaritifera* oysters per year, which produce upwards of 30,000 pearls annually.

THE PEARLS

The life cycle of a pearl-making oyster in Fiji begins with spawning in October and November. The free-swimming larvae are swept up by "spat collectors," intentionally ragged nylon-rope structures that are 220 meters long and arranged into loose grids, trailed by boats through the spawning grounds.

At 20 days old, the baby oysters attach to whatever they can find to make their permanent homes—including the spat collectors. These are kept in a special nursery area to protect them from predators such as triggerfish and turtles, and moved through a series of homes as they grow in size.

baby-soft when you wash it off. Snacks and transportation from the Copra Shed Marina are included. The gregarious Elayne also offers intertidal reef walking, snorkeling (F$35-65), paddleboarding, horseback riding, and custom trips. If you find that you can't bear to leave Savusavu, she even sells real estate.

New Zealander **Clark Murphy** (tel. 929-8437, fijilodge@hotmail.com, www.flyseastay.com) teaches kitesurfing, paragliding, and surfing on a fine beach along the Hibiscus Highway, and rents out bicycles. There's also a strenuous reef walk to a private island with an interesting limestone cave that you can raft across.

A pleasant half-day trip is the **Natewa Bay tour** offered by La Dolce Vita (tel. 828-0824 or 991-3669, ladolcevitafiji@connect.com.fj). You'll be picked up in Savusavu and taken for a scenic drive along the Hibiscus Highway. Snorkel in the sparkling waters of Natewa Bay, where spinner dolphins often appear. A lunch of authentic pizza, cooked in the hotel's Italian-made wood-fired oven, is included. It's F$95 per person, for 4-10 people, with 24 hours' notice.

Trip'N Tour Travel (tel. 885-3154, 992-8154, or 932-2280, tripntour@connect.com.fj, Mon.-Fri. 0900-1300 and 1400-1630) in the Copra Shed Marina offers a range of excursions as well as scooter rentals. If the owner/agent Emily isn't there, she might be in the Art Gallery shop down the corridor.

Everyone knows **Jack Deo** (tel. 932-9207), and he knows everyone and everywhere. You can hire him and his (non-air-conditioned) taxi for F$10 from town to the Savusavu airport, F$100 to the Labasa airport, or anywhere

J. Hunter workers sort pearl oysters.

At nine months, they're full-size, but only when they're three years old are they ready to make pearls. Pearl technicians from Japan insert a tiny organic bead made from Mississippi River mussel into the reproductive organ of the host, so that the oyster will secrete calcium layers to protect itself from this irritant. At the same time, the technicians implant the desired color from the mantle of a finely hued oyster. This technique is called grafting.

Eighteen months later, a pearl is born. A single oyster can go through this process only three or four times.

you want to go for F$30/hour or F$150 for a full-day tour.

Ayush Paradise Cabs (tel. 995-6026 or 885-0521) owner Parmesh Maharaj arranges rides in and around Savusavu, as well as driving tours, in air-conditioned minivans.

ENTERTAINMENT

The bar at the **Copra Shed Marina** (daily 1100-2200) is rather hidden in the northeast corner of the building—ask someone for directions. Happy hour is 1730-1830. Remove your hat as you enter. A five-man band of local dive shop owners plays 1700-2000 every Sunday night.

Drinkers can repair to the old-school **Planters Club** (tel. 885-0233, Mon.-Thurs. 1100-2100, Fri.-Sat. 1100-2200, Sun. 1000-2000), a vintage colonial club toward the wharf. This place never runs out of Fiji Bitter, and the weekend dances are local events. There's also a billiards table, squash court, and a restaurant where everything is F$10, whether it's goat curry or a burger or fish with cabbage. Despite the Members Only sign, visitors are welcome.

The **Waitui Marina** (tel. 885-3031 or 997-2558, daily 1000-2200) has a pleasant bar that occasionally organizes *lovo* or barbecue nights, and has good fish-and-chips.

Savusavu's only nightclub is the loud **Uroso's Nite Club** (tel. 885-0366 or 923-8422, 1900-0100), upstairs in the building opposite the post office. It's the place to be for locals on Thursday-Saturday nights, but the party doesn't get started until about 2100.

1

2

3

4

SHOPPING

Most shops are open 0830-1700 Monday-Friday, and half days on Saturday.

The **market** in the center of town always bustles but is biggest early Saturday morning. Notice the kava dens at the back. Nearby, the **Handicraft Center** (Mon.-Fri. 0730-1700, Sat. 0730-1500), behind the Savusavu Town Council opposite the ANZ Bank, displays a mixture of kitschy and well-crafted souvenirs. **MH Supermarket** has the best variety of groceries, and next to it is the **Savusavu Wine Market.**

In the Copra Shed Marina, **Tako Handicrafts** sells a variety of beach- and boat-friendly women's clothing. **The Art Gallery** (Mon.-Fri. 0900-1300 and 1400-1630) has a selection of small, easy-to-pack souvenirs and locally created postcards.

FOOD

★ **Surf and Turf** (tel. 885-3033 or 867-3965, Mon.-Sat. 1100-1630 and 1700-2100), on the back side of the Copra Shed Marina, has a fine deck overlooking the bay. Owner-chef Vijendra Kumar was a chef at Namale and other resorts in the area before opening his own place, and his daughter Natasha, a former chef at the Cousteau resort, is set to take over when he retires. This place specializes in seafood and steaks, obviously, but there are also burgers, curries, stir-fries, and even quesadillas. Dinner is in the F$15-25 range; lobster is F$65. The Thursday night seafood barbecue, including snapper, rock lobster, king prawns, and crab, plus dessert and salad, is F$70 and reservations are required.

The less formal **Captains Café** (tel. 855-0511) on the front side of the Copra Shed Marina serves up entertaining entries such "nightmare steaks" (F$29) and "palatable chicken" (F$16), along with cold beer.

The **Decked Out Café** (tel. 885-2929, F$6-14), just east of the Copra Shed Marina and across the street, is also known as Kunal's Wine & Dine. On a large deck you can consume Asian- and Fijian-inspired vegetarian, lamb, prawn, chicken, and fish dishes.

Pizza Buzz (tel. 938-5141, F$16.50 pizzas), at the eastern end of the town strip, sells chicken and vegetarian pizzas as well as chicken wings and salads.

A few places offer Indian food in Savusavu. The **Sea View Cafe** (tel. 885-0106) has good fish curry and omelets, serves beer, and has a fine view of the marina.

Taste of Hidden Paradise (in the LTA building at the far end of the wharf, tel. 920-9781, F$8-14) is family-owned and unassuming in appearance, but serves up the tastiest Indian and Thai curries in Savusavu.

Mum's Country Kitchen (across from the bus station, tel. 927-1372, F$4-10), is popular for takeout, served in little plastic baggies. You should be familiar enough with Indian food to know what you want here, as it's a fast-moving place.

If it's Chinese you want, then it's **Savusavu Wok** (on the main road downtown, tel. 885-3688, F$8-14). Vegans will appreciate the tofu dishes and the Mongolian eggplant, though there are plenty of meat options as well.

For a splurge, call ahead and see if there's room at the restaurant of the **Jean-Michel Cousteau Fiji Islands Resort** (tel. 885-0188, www.fijiresort.com). Chef Raymond Lee whips up Fijian, continental, and fusion entrees such as curried New Zealand lamb and local pelagic fish. Meals are included for hotel guests; nonguests are allowed only when the hotel is not full, and reservations are required.

ACCOMMODATIONS

Savusavu is built on a slope, so almost all of the accommodations here require climbing at least one flight of steps and/or a steep driveway. None are wheelchair-accessible. Because much of this area is freehold land, expatriates have a lot of homes here, and Airbnb and other vacation rental sites have numerous listings.

1: Savusavu Bay **2:** soaking in a thermal mud pool in the Waisali Rainforest Reserve **3:** a dock at the Copra Shed Marina **4:** paddling off the Savusavu shore.

Under US$50

Rachel Lal's **Savusavu Holiday House** (tel. 885-0149 or 942-1370, F$35/45 s/d), just below the Hot Springs Hotel, is run-down but very cheap; rooms share baths. You might be allowed to camp here for F$8. Breakfast is not provided but there's a common kitchen. A cacophony of dogs, roosters, and the neighbor's kids will bid you good morning.

Savusavu Budget Lodge (tel. 885-3127 or 999-3127, www.savusavubudgetlodge.com), a two-story concrete building on the main street, has standard rooms with bath at F$50/75 single/double and air-conditioned rooms at F$80/100. Breakfast is included. The air-conditioned rooms have TVs and coffee makers. Signs say no beef, pork, or alcohol can be brought in, but the bottle shop below is open 0800-midnight.

Savusavu Sunset Lodge (tel. 926-2476, sunsetlodge@connect.com.fj, F$65-180), a two-story guesthouse near the Government Wharf, offers good views from the upper deck. Some rooms share a bathroom and some have only cold water, so check your room before you accept it. Drinking is not allowed on-site. You can buy recharge plans for your phone's SIM card here. The well-kept rooms have hot-water kettles, TVs, air-conditioning, and mini-fridges.

Savusavu Bay Lodge (tel. 885-0602 or 946-7266, ssvbaylodge@gmail.com, F$90) has several bedrooms, some with views and some without, off a shared balcony. The kitchen is available to all guests and closes at 2100, and drinking (including kava) is not allowed after 2300. The energetic director, Suresh Narayan, also runs tours for other lodges to all of the local sights by minivan or speedboat.

Hidden Paradise Guest House (tel. 873-7845 or 994-6540, hiddenparadise@connect.com.fj), just beyond Morris Hedstrom, has rather hot wooden rooms at F$25 for a dorm bed, F$55 for a single, or F$65 for a family room for up to four, including a good breakfast. There's air-conditioning and a shared bath. Cooking and washing facilities are provided.

US$50-100

Savusavu Heights Villas (Hugh St., Narains Heights, tel. 938-4573, 850-0999, or 885-0806, raaj@connect.com.fj, from F$120) is a set of modern apartment-cottages on stilts, high up on a hill behind town. Owner Suresh and his wife live on-site and lead trips in their 15-seater van or speedboat. The rooms have air-conditioning, fridges, and cable TV; some have kitchens. Two connecting rooms are F$250. No meals are provided, but there's access to a clean common kitchen, and free Wi-Fi.

Gecko Lodge (tel. 921-3181 or 885-3453, geckolodgefiji@yahoo.com, www.geckolodgefiji.com, F$140-180) is a home converted into a lodging. The more expensive rooms have ocean views; all include free Wi-Fi and use of bicycles and kayaks. The spacious air-conditioned rooms with fridges and simple metal-frame beds are clean and tasteful, with pleasant touches such as mosaic tile décor on the patios and bathrooms. Owner Saras, who formerly worked at Koro Sun Resort, keeps the place spick-and-span, including the shared outdoor kitchen. Meals can be prepared for you upon request.

Hot Springs Hotel (tel. 885-0195 or 885-0060, www.hotspringsfiji.com), on the hillside overlooking Savusavu Bay, has 48 clean, simple rooms, all with balconies offering splendid views. It was built as a Travelodge and entirely gutted and renovated in 2017. An air-conditioned room with a queen bed is F$175, while a two-bedroom apartment with kitchenette is F$410. No beach is nearby, but the swimming pool terrace is pleasant, and sunset views from the bar are excellent.

Friendly, lively ★ **Daku Resort** (tel. 885-0046, reservations@dakuresort.com, www.dakuresort.com), one kilometer west of the ferry landing, was founded as an Anglican Church retreat and is now an "upscale budget" property with a pleasant pool and restaurant. Owners Delia and John Rothnie-Jones often host group courses here, many through **Paradise Courses** (www.paradisecourses.com), including landscape painting, writing, and yoga in a large hilltop yoga platform with fantastic sunrise and sunset views. A standard air-conditioned bungalow in the nicely landscaped grounds is F$110, an excellent value (two beds can fit). A larger *bure* on the hilltop with a view is F$380 (you'll climb one or two flights of steps). When the owners are away, you can rent their four-bedroom home for F$420. Breakfast and so-so Wi-Fi are included, and other meals are buffet style, with one iTaukei chef and one Indo-Fijian chef to provide variety. Some *bures* have mini kitchens. You can cross the road to snorkel off a not-much beach, and it's an easy stroll to town. Visitors can call ahead to drop in for lunch (1200-1600) or dinner (1700-2130), or for a signature banana-leaf-wrap massage (F$80 foot treatment with pedicure, F$170 full body).

US$100-250

Naveria Heights Lodge (tel. 885-0348 or 936-4808, justnaveria@connect.com.fj, www.naveriaheightsfiji.com, F$250-550) is a bright, cheery four-room place perched on a hilltop a kilometer above the Government Wharf. Owner Sharon Wild, a Canadian nutritionist and psychotherapist who lived in Singapore for many years, envisions the place as a fitness and healing sanctuary, offering detox courses, a weight-loss boot camp, herbal medicine, and yoga. You can also just enjoy it as an upmarket bed-and-breakfast. There's a wonderful view from the poolside exercise bike. Breakfast is included in the rate. Activities such as hiking, river tubing, and bareback horse riding can be arranged for F$65-175 and are also available to nonguests. Only 4WD vehicles can climb the gravel road; you can scale it on foot or call and ask to be picked up from the main road.

The American-owned **Pirate's Paradise** (tel. 833-3710 or 912-7751, piratesparadisefiji@gmail.com, www.piratesparadisefiji.com, US$231), close to the Cousteau resort, comprises two luxury bungalows overlooking the bay. The Pod House for two is up 70 steps while the two-bedroom House of Bamboo, for up to four people, is up 125 steps. Once you make it, each villa has its own saltwater plunge pool, a fully equipped kitchen, fast Wi-Fi, flat-screen TV and entertainment system, barbecue grill, and indoor/outdoor dining and seating areas. Snorkel gear is provided, and kayaks and paddleboards can be rented. This is the closest place you can stay to Lesiaceva Point that isn't Cousteau. Tip the staff well—they help you carry your stuff up and down.

Over US$250

The ★ **Jean-Michel Cousteau Fiji Islands Resort** (tel. 885-0188, www.fijiresort.com, F$2,000-6,000) stylishly re-creates a Fijian village—if that village was stocked with every luxury you could dream up. Oceanographer Jean-Michel Cousteau, son of the famous Jacques, purchased the site in 1994 to build the resort and is sometimes in residence. Major renovations took place after Cyclone Winston crashed coconut-palm-high waves over the resort in 2016, damaging many buildings.

Room rates include all meals, airport transfers, babysitting 0830-2100, glass-bottom boat excursions, and snorkeling trips, including night snorkeling to see bioluminescent life forms. If you stay five nights, the sixth is free. In eco-luxe style, there are no TVs, and only one of the *bures* has air-conditioning (the fans and ocean breezes are enough). There's attention to every detail here, from the bleach-free organic cotton bedspreads to the on-site gardens that supply 40 percent of the food served to guests. Nonguests can call ahead to reserve at the fine-dining restaurant, which is pricey but delicious. Tuesday is *lovo* and kava night. There's an adults-only pool and add-on romantic possibilities such as private island picnics and pier dining by candlelight. Children under six are assigned their own nanny, and older children get a "Bula Buddy."

Due to its sheer scale, the resort is an industry of its own and attempts to be a responsible one. One of Cousteau's passions is the School Under the Sea, where children can go out with a marine biologist to plant coral or mangroves and learn about the marine ecosystem. Through the Savusavu Community

1

2

3

Foundation, the resort raises funds from guests and secures in-kind donations, such as medications and transport, for neighboring villages, many of whose residents are on the 220-person resort staff or contribute in other ways; one village produces all the cold-press coconut oil used at the Cousteau spa, for example.

INFORMATION AND SERVICES

Tourism

The **Savusavu Tourism Association** has an informative website (www.fiji-savusavu.com) and a helpful Instagram account (www.instagram.com/savusavu_fiji).

Eddie's 1Stop Agency (tel. 885 0469 or 955-0116, edwinrama123@gmail.com) sells tickets for the Patterson ferry, Northern Air, and Fiji Link flights, and can make room reservations for your next destination.

Money

Three banks have **ATMs** on the main street; the BSP charges the lowest service fee for international withdrawals. **Currency Exchange** (tel. 885-1566) does what it says and is also a Western Union outlet.

Health and Wellness

The **District Hospital** (tel. 885 0444, 0830-1600) is two kilometers east of Savusavu on the road to Labasa.

Savusavu Medical Centre (Hot Spring Rd., tel. 885-0721 or 998-1786, ishaqfiji@yahoo.co.uk, Mon.-Fri. 0800-1230 and 1400-1600, Saturday 0900-1200), near the Hot Springs Hotel, is run by Dr. Mohammed Ishaque, who will see you for F$50. This nonprofit center is funded by the Naqaqa Giving Foundation and your donations. The doctor will also make resort visits from 1230 to 1400, while the clinic is closed for staff lunch. In an emergency he can see you after hours and on Sundays by appointment—he lives right next door.

Say hi to my cousin, the pharmacist, if you have need of the **Savusavu Pharmacy** (Main St., Mon-Fri 0800-1800, Sat. 0800-1700).

Violet Ravitu of **Pacific Island Massage** (tel. 802-5883) will come to your hotel room to give you a Swedish, deep-tissue, or hot stone massage at reasonable rates.

Internet

If it's your computer that's ill, **Paradise Computers** (Main St., upstairs, tel. 885-3184, paradisecomputers211@gmail.com) does repairs and is also an Internet café.

GETTING AROUND

The Savusavu airstrip is beside the main highway, three kilometers east of town. It's little more than an open-air shed, with basic bathrooms around the corner, but the local shop across the main road has cold drinks and snacks if you need a little something to tide you over. Local buses to Savusavu pass the airport about once an hour, or you can take a taxi for F$5. If you're renting a car, call ahead to one of the companies listed below and ask them to deliver it to the airport.

Bus

The Savusavu **bus** terminal is right in town; you can't miss it. **Vishnu Holdings** (tel. 885-0276) operates public buses on the island, and updates about closures and route changes are posted on its Facebook page. Call for information; there's nothing much posted at the bus station. Regular buses leave Savusavu for Labasa (94 km, three hours, F$7) at 0730, 0930, 1130, 1300, 1430, and 1530. This ride over the Waisali Saddle is one of the most scenic in Fiji, and the paved highway is excellent.

Taxi

Numerous taxis congregate next to the bus station at Savusavu market; they're quite affordable for short trips in the vicinity. A taxi between Labasa and Savusavu is F$100 and takes about 90 minutes.

1: the entrance to Gecko Lodge **2:** the grounds of the Daku Resort **3:** yoga on the dock at the Jean-Michel Cousteau Fiji Islands Resort.

Car

Cars can be rented from **James Rentals** (at Main St./Airport junction in Marimuttu's petrol station, tel. 885-0455 or 989-8556); **Northpole Rentals** (tel. 992-4664 or 881-8008, 4wd@northpole.com.fj, www.northpole.com.fj), which has some 4WD options; **Avis** (the Labasa office will deliver to Savusavu, tel. 672-2233, www.avis.com/car-rental/location/ASP/FJ/Labasa/LB6); **Budget** (tel. 881-1999, www.budget.com.fj); and **Vanua Rentals** (tel. 881-1060 or 990-8248, vanua.rental@cisgroup.com.fj, www.cjsgroup.com.fj/vanua.html). Day rates are typically F$120-227 and go down for three-day and seven-day rentals.

Scooter

Trip n Tour Travel Agency (in the Copra Shed Marina, tel. 885-3154) rents scooters for F$60/day, a pleasant way to zoom around the island without having to depend on taxis. All of the island's main arteries are paved and well marked, but there are plenty of curves and no streetlights, so it's best to scoot about in the daytime. Some gravel side roads will be inaccessible by scooter.

Around Natewa Bay

Massive **Natewa Bay** is the largest bay in the South Pacific, almost bisecting Vanua Levu diagonally. Its sheltered waters are excellent for sea kayaking, and you're likely to spot the resident school of dolphins, even from the shore.

Along the bay's southeastern coast, the lovely coastal **Hibiscus Highway** offers fine sights and a smattering of resorts for tourists traveling out of Savusavu. Its farthest point is the ferry port, **Natuvu Jetty** on Buca Bay.

Along the bay's northwestern coast, the scenery is gorgeous along the Natewa West Coast Road. Its easternmost point is a century-old lighthouse at **Udu Point.** From here you could travel back west and along the northern shore of Vanua Levu toward Labasa. If you're traveling from Savusavu to Labasa, this seven-hour journey is not the quickest route, but is certainly the most scenic.

GETTING AROUND

The main roads on either side of Natewa Bay are paved and have little traffic, so the driving is some of the most relaxing in Fiji. Renting a car or taking a taxi from Savusavu is a great way to explore the southeastern coast on your own. Tour companies in Savusavu offer trips around this area.

Along the Hibiscus Highway to Buca Bay, buses leave Savusavu weekdays at 1030, 1300, and 1430 and weekends at 1030 and 1400 (three hours to Natuvu Jetty, F$7). Along the Natewa West Coast Road, the bus departs Savusavu at 0900 daily (four hours to Udu Point, F$9; or a total of seven hours all the way to Labasa, F$14). You could travel this route with any of the Savusavu-based travel options. If you're flying into Labasa first, it would make sense to rent a car or hire a taxi in Labasa (see below) and go east to Udu Point, then veer southwest toward Savusavu for the seven-hour trip. A bus makes the same trip starting at 0900 from Labasa.

ALONG THE HIBISCUS HIGHWAY

Among the palms lining the southeastern shore of Natewa Bay, you'll spot old frame mansions from the heyday of the 19th-century planters, as well as 21st-century homes of newly arrived foreigners. The resorts here are within half an hour of Savusavu Airport, but most feel as if they're isolated from the world amid green lawns, dramatic seascapes, and wide-open skies. The easternmost point is Natuvu Jetty on Buca Bay.

★ Devodara Beach

Also known as Blue Lagoon (not to be confused with the movie-famous Blue Lagoon in the Yasawas), the public **Devodara Beach,** Vanua Levu's best, is wide and expansive enough that you'll never feel crowded—and it's just fifteen minutes from town. The bigger resorts bring their honeymooners here for romantic picnics under the tall, swaying palms. A round barrier of white sand forms a fine shallow lagoon that makes this beach good for swimming even in low tide, and safe for children and swimmers of all levels. Beyond the breakers is excellent snorkeling along a soft coral reef. There are no amenities here, so bring everything you need from Savusavu or from your accommodation, including snorkeling gear. However, the **Siga Siga Sands** resort (tel. 885-0000 or 807-4240, U.S. tel. 626/404-7600, fiji@theultimateparadise.com, www.theultimateparadise.com) is right on the beach and may be able to arrange beach-delivered meals by Chef Sunita, as well as hiking excursions to its forest reserve, if you call in advance.

Salt Lake

Farther east, about 30 minutes from Savusavu, the **Qaloqalo Salt River** leads from the Koro Sea to Fiji's inland **Salt Lake.** A strange natural phenomenon, the waterway surges at high tide, carrying even large ocean-dwellers such as barracuda and stingrays in, before receding at low tide and stranding them. It's a favorite spot for local fishing, and a small boat can take you out in calm weather.

Buca Bay

About 78 kilometers east of Savusavu town the highway ends at Buca Bay. This is a recognized "hurricane hole" where ships can find shelter during storms. Here you'll find **Natuvu Jetty,** the portal for boats headed for Taveuni, Kioa, and Rabi Islands. A handful of humble stalls here sell snacks and sodas. Offshore, you'll see tiny flowerpot islands where the sea has undercut the coral rock.

ALONG THE NATEWA WEST COAST ROAD

It takes about four hours by car from Savusavu to get all the way to the northeastern tip of Vanua Levu, **Udu Point**. The rugged scenery is capped by a **lighthouse** that dates from 1912. It's the northernmost lighthouse in Fiji.

Also at Udu Point, just west of Vunikodi village, the **Meridian Wall** was built in 1999 to mark where the 180-degree longitudinal meridian and international date line cut across the island. Both sunset and sunrise can be observed from the wall. To get there, you must "charge" (charter) a boat from Wainigadru, where the Natewa Bay buses call.

It's possible to cruise through this area on the scenic seven-hour bus ride that makes a long loop between Labasa and Savusavu; the bus leaves both towns at 0900 daily. Other buses also go toward Udu from both towns.

ACCOMMODATIONS

Under US$500

At ★ **Siga Siga Sands** (tel. 885-0000 or 807-4240, U.S. tel. 626/404-7600, fiji@theultimateparadise.com, www.theultimateparadise.com, F$75-275), the beachfront Seahorse Bungalow is a steal at F$175, with a polished style comparable to much posher resorts, facing a near-private bay and large white-sand beach. Three other well-spaced cottages are also available. Weekly and monthly discounts apply. American owner Gene Calvert lives on site and fusses and hustles to make everything up to snuff; his Wi-Fi may be the fastest on the island. Chef Sunita shops and cooks to order: Give her a couple of hours' notice, and Indo-Fijian meals will magically arrive at your cottage door, or be delivered to you on the beach, 1030-1730 daily. Tuesdays and Fridays are vegetarian days only. The resort draws fresh spring water and backs onto 99 acres of forest trails, with a swimming pool in the forest. This place is conveniently located, in between the airport (10 minutes) and the activity-packed Koro Sun Resort

1

2

3

4

(another 10 minutes), but it feels like it's in the middle of nowhere, in the best way possible.

New Zealander Clark Murphy operates **Vosa Ni Ua Lodge** (tel. 929-8437, fijilodge@hotmail.com, www.flyseastay.com, F$200), with a handful of well-outfitted buildings on a very nice beach. There's also a big house that sleeps eight. Clark is the person to teach you adventure sports such as kitesurfing, paragliding, and surfing; package deals are available. There's also a strenuous reef walk to a private island with an interesting cave and formations.

La Dolce Vita Holiday Villas (tel. 828-0824, 991-3669, or 728-0824, www.ladolcevitaholidayvillas.com) is the last resort on the stretch, 30 kilometers east of Savusavu. Much of it was destroyed by Cyclone Winston, and it reopened with new buildings in late 2017. Owners Margaret, who hails from Levuka, and her husband Luigi, an Australian-Italian fisherman, live on-site. The spacious, luxurious, air-conditioned hexagonal villas include studios (US$460) and two-bedroom units (US$720). The price includes airport transfers, laundry, and all meals including excellent pizzas from the wood-fired oven. There's a large swimming pool facing the sea, and kayaks and a paddleboat are free to use. Dolphins are frequently sighted on the bay tours (F$95), and a boat takes snorkelers out.

Salt Lake Lodge (tel. 717-8200, U.S. tel. 720/414-2873, www.saltlakelodgefiji.com) is on Salt Lake Road, a five-minute walk from the junction with the Hibiscus Highway. There are just two *bures*; Kingfisher (US$195) is larger and closer to the main area, while Riversong (US$175) is more private. Only one party of guests is accepted at a time. The decks face a private river beach and swimming pontoon on the tidal Qaloqalo River, with water access to the picturesque Salt Lake, which you will have almost to yourself for fishing, swimming, and chasing crabs on the beach. There's no Wi-Fi. You can use the communal kitchen, gas barbecue, and fire pit; if so, stock up in Savusavu, as there are no groceries out this way, but there are free fruits and vegetables from the owners' nearby organic farm. Otherwise, chef Jose will cook up what you like, including the fish you catch, for the US$68 per person meal plan.

Koro Sun Resort (tel. 885-0262 or 885-3247, U.S. tel. 877/567-6786, marissa@korosunresort.com, www.korosunresort.com) is a large, attractive resort 14 kilometers east of Savusavu. The most fun rooms are the Edgewater Floating Bures (F$1,092), where you can jump right from your deck into the lagoon, and your own private kayak is tied up next to you. Other cottages, with a surprising variety from garden to treetop to lighthouse, are F$620-920. Optional meal plans are F$105/$168 for two/three meals. Set in a coconut grove, the Koro Sun has many interesting caves, pools, trails, falls, ponds, and lakes nearby to explore, as well as plenty of activities and facilities: a spa, pools, a waterslide, and tennis courts. The snorkeling is fine, but the nearest good beach is a kilometer away. Scuba diving is with **Namena Divers** (www.namenadiversfiji.com), and the deep-water pinnacle Dream House is right at your lagoon's front door.

Over US$500

The fanciest place around used to be the **Namale Fiji Resort** (U.S. tel. 800/727-3454, www.namalefiji.com), set on a beach nine kilometers east of Savusavu. *Bures* and villas start at US$800, including meals, alcohol, transfers, many activities, luxurious surroundings, unlimited shuttling around the property on golf carts, and very attentive service. Motivational seminars with owner Tony Robbins in a 60-seat conference center are Namale's stock in trade. Children under 12 aren't allowed. Discount packages including airfare are sometimes available via Costco travel.

In 2009, a Namale imitator opened on an adjacent island connected to Vanua Levu by

1: a cottage at Siga Siga Sands **2:** looking down at Devodara Beach **3:** the dining room at La Dolce Vita Holiday Villas **4:** a village along the Natewa West Coast Road.

a causeway. The seven secluded oceanfront *bures* and villas at **Savasi Island** (tel. 850-1192/8850124, www.savasiisland.com, from US$660) include meals, Wi-Fi, airport transfers, bicycles, and kayaks. You can rent the whole place for up to 26 people for US$7,500 per night, minimum three nights. Children are allowed in the larger villas, but the management says, "We believe Savasi is best suited to children 10-plus, and recommend a nanny/buddy for younger ages."

The all-inclusive **Emaho Sekawa Resort** (tel. 972-5515 or 979-5131, info@emahofiji.com, www.emahofiji.com, US$955-3,400) is the newest contender on the scene, with three super-luxurious villas nestled in rainforest, far away from each other. Each has a private pool and ocean view. A buggy takes you down to an exclusive two-kilometer-long beach. Gourmet meals are supplied in the central pavilion, on the beach, or in your own villa from the resort's own organic garden. Diving with an in-house PADI divemaster, fishing, and hiking tours are extra.

Labasa and Vicinity

Labasa is a busy market town that services Vanua Levu's major cane-growing area. Indo-Fijian descendants of indentured workers built this town and make up most of its 28,000 inhabitants, and continue to farm the sugar, rice, and vegetable fields in the surrounding countryside. It's Fiji's fifth-largest town, with four banks, and it is the Northern Division and Macuata Province headquarters.

Labasa was built on a delta where the shallow Labasa and Qawa Rivers enter the sea; maritime transport is limited to small boats. The Qawa River has been heavily polluted by waste from the mill. Large ships anchor off Malau, 11 kilometers north, where Labasa's sugar output is loaded.

Other than providing a fine base from which to explore the surrounding countryside and northern islands, as well as a good choice of places to spend the night, Labasa has little to interest the average tourist. That's its main attraction: Because few visitors come, there's adventure in the air and inexpensive food in the restaurants. Labasa's not beautiful, but it is real.

SIGHTS

Labasa town has an attractive riverside setting, with one long main street lined with shops and restaurants. The park along the river's left bank near the **Labasa Club** is quite pleasant.

Labasa Sugar Mill

The **Labasa Sugar Mill,** beside the Qawa River two kilometers east of town, opened in 1894. At the height of the crushing season (May-Dec.) there's usually a long line of trucks, tractors, and trains waiting to unload cane at the mill. From the road here, you get a view of **Three Sisters Hill** to the right.

Hanging Bridge

Just east of the sugar mill, you can pick up one of the frequent yellow-and-blue buses to the **hanging bridge,** a suspension footbridge at Bulileka, six kilometers east of Labasa. Get off the Bulileka bus at Boca Urata where it turns around. The hanging bridge is 150 meters down the road from that point (ask). Cross the bridge, and continue through the fields a few hundred meters to the paved road, where you can catch another bus back to Labasa. The main reason for coming is to see this picturesque valley, so you may wish to stroll part of the way back.

Delaikoro

You can get a view of much of Vanua Levu from the telecommunications tower atop the

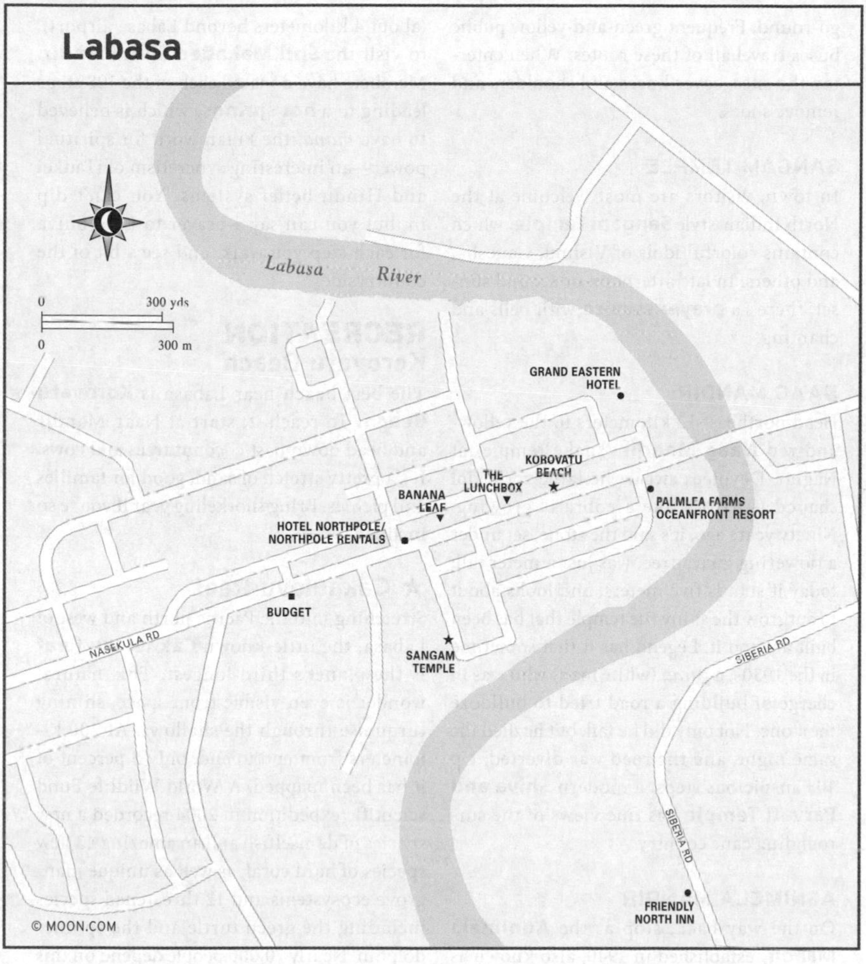

mountain of **Delaikoro** (941 m), 25 kilometers south of Labasa, farther down the same road past the airport. Only a 4WD vehicle can make it to the top.

Floating Island

Farther afield is the **Floating Island** at Kurukuru, between Wainikoro and Nubu, 44 kilometers northeast of Labasa (accessible on the Dogotuki, Kurukuru, and Lagalaga buses). It's an island floating in a circular section of a small river, and is said to have magical properties: A priest singing a sacred tune can cause the island to float from one bank to the other. It's a 45-minute walk from the turnoff at Lagalaga to Kurukuru. If you're in your own vehicle, the best way to find it is to ask a local child to hop in your car and steer you there for F$10. The 14th season of the American television series *Survivor* was filmed nearby, at Vunivutu Bay near Lagalaga.

★ Temple Tours

It's easy to do a daylong temple tour, or *yatra*, in Labasa, propitiating several different gods worshipped by Hindu Indo-Fijians in one go-round. Frequent green-and-yellow public buses travel all of these routes. When entering the sites, cover knees and shoulders and remove shoes.

SANGAM TEMPLE

In town, visitors are most welcome at the North Indian-style **Sangam Temple,** which contains colorful idols of Vishnu, Ganesha, and others. In late afternoon or around sunset, there's a **prayer service** with bells and chanting.

NAAG MANDIR

Head northeast 12 kilometers to the yellow-and-red **Naag Mandir** (snake temple) at Nagigi. Devotees swear the large rock idol shaped (sort of) like a cobra is growing. Ninety years ago, it's said the stone, set under a flowering guava tree, was just a meter tall; today it stands five meters, and looks about to outgrow the shiny tile temple that has been built around it. Legend has it that sometime in the 1930s, a *goraa* (white man) who was in charge of building a road tried to bulldoze the stone. Not only did he fail, but he died the same night, and the road was diverted. Up 108 auspicious steps, a modern **Shiva and Parvati Temple** has fine views of the surrounding cane country.

AGNIMELA MANDIR

On the way back, stop at the **Agnimela Mandir,** established in 1940, also known as the Sangam Mahamariamman Firewalking Temple, at Vunivau five kilometers northeast of Labasa. Large statues of Shiva, seated with a cobra around his head, and Hanuman, carrying a mace, flank the entry. Indian **fire walking** takes place once a year here during the full moon that falls in late July or early August. Worshippers fast and pray for a week, then walk across a bed of hot ash and coals as an act of devotion to the goddess Mariamma.

SHRI MAHADEO SHIU MANDIR

Pass back through Labasa and head to Waiqele, 14 kilometers southwest of town (about 4 kilometers beyond Labasa airport), to visit the **Shri Mahadeo Shiu Mandir.** Members have donated each of the 108 steps leading to a **hot springs,** which is believed to have *mana,* the Fijian word for spiritual power—an interesting syncretism of iTaukei and Hindu belief systems. You can't dip in, but you can say a prayer to Lord Shiva for each step you walk, and see a bit of the countryside.

RECREATION

Korovatu Beach

The best beach near Labasa is **Korovatu Beach.** To reach it, start at Naag Mandir and head down past coconut trees and cows. It's a pretty stretch of sand, good for families and picnics. Bring snorkeling gear if you're so inclined.

★ Cakaulevu Reef

Stretching into the Pacific north and west of Labasa, the little-known **Cakaulevu Reef** is the planet's third-longest. This natural wonder is even visible from space, shining turquoise through the shallows. At 200 kilometers from end to end, only 5 percent of it has been mapped. A World Wildlife Fund scientific expedition in 2004 recorded a new species of damselfish and an amazing 43 new species of hard coral, as well as unique mangrove ecosystems and 12 threatened species including the green turtle and the spinner dolphin. Nearly 70,000 people depend on this marine ecosystem, sometimes called the Great Sea Reef, for their livelihood and subsistence, and the local chiefs have put in place strict restrictions on fishing in vast stretches, which helps the fish population rebound and remain plentiful in the limited fishing zones.

Great Sea Reef Divers (tel. 903-3404, lbvokai@hotmail.co.uk, daily 0800-1600), based on neighboring Mali Island just north of Labasa, takes divers out to Cakaulevu Reef. PADI-certified dive instructor Leone Vokai grew up freediving the reef and is passionate about reef health and conservation. All levels of certification are possible, and you can

Choosing a Sunscreen

Every year, 14,000 tons of sunscreen end up in coral reefs around the world. Much of that contains the common UV-filtering chemical oxybenzone, which bleaches (kills) the adult coral and deforms the DNA of coral larvae, making it impossible for the reefs to regenerate. Hawaii outlawed the chemical in 2018, and other jurisdictions are likely to follow suit.

You can download the app from the **Environmental Working Group** (www.ewg.org/sunscreen), which rates sunscreens as well as lip balms and other products based on both effectiveness and environmental safety. The app is particularly helpful if you might be buying unfamiliar brands while traveling.

Chemical sunscreens can destroy delicate reef life.

Here are some guidelines to keep yourself and our fragile reefs safe:

- If possible, skip all hygienic products when snorkeling or diving.
- Rash guards and wet suits are as effective as sunscreen at blocking damaging rays. Cover your limbs with these water-friendly fabrics instead of slathering on product.
- Seek out biodegradable sunscreens and mineral-based sunblocks (such as titanium dioxide and zinc oxide).
- Don't use sunscreens with "nano" size particles, which are easily ingested by corals.
- Look for products with the reef safety certification seal (www.haereticus-lab.org/protect-land-sea-certification).

be picked up at Labasa or any of the northern islands.

Biking

Every August, New Zealand-based **Escape Adventures** (tel. 643/525-8783, info@escapeadventures.co.nz, www.escapeadventuresnz.com/cycle-tours/fiji-islands-2, NZ$2590) offers a 9-day bicycle tour in Fiji. It starts in Labasa, crosses the island of Vanua Levu, and continues on Taveuni Island, with snorkeling, village stays, and waterfall hikes in the mix. An optional 3-day trek up Viti Levu's Mount Batilamu can be added.

ENTERTAINMENT

Labasa has a lively nightclub scene from 1800 to 0100. **Fusion Nightclub** (Naseskula Rd., https://rhythmtravels.com/venue/fusion-nightclub-fiji, daily) bills itself as stylish and modern; head to the VIP lounge if you don't want to be jostled. **Pontoon Nightclub** (tel. 881-7005, www.cjsgroup.com.fj/night_club/index.html, pontoon@cjsgroup.com.fj, Wed.-Sun.) plays hip-hop as well as Bollywood hits. **StarBar Nightclub** (see Facebook) is the newest arrival, in 2018, and occasionally brings in Australian DJs.

FOOD

Labasa is, alas, not a foodie's paradise. Outside of hotels, you'll find the most choices along Nasekula Road, including fast food, Fijian, Chinese, and Indian meals for F$5-10; spots include **The Lunchbox** (tel. 992-4997), below the Hotel Northpole, which serves spicy fried chicken. Vegetarians will find sanctuary at **Govinda's,** which is also an Internet café. The **Banana Leaf** (tel. 881-6900), up a flight of stairs, serves up good *thalis*.

Next to the bus station, the **Oriental Restaurant & Bar** (2 Jaduram St., tel. 881-7321, F$10) is reasonable, with Chinese food and cold longnecks of Fiji Bitter.

MH Supermarket (Rosawa St., tel. 881-1211), next to the entrance to the Grand Eastern Hotel, has a clean, inexpensive food bar perfect for a fast lunch.

An excellent choice outside of town is ★ **Palmlea Farms Oceanfront Resort** (tel. 828-2220, palmleafarms@yahoo.com, www.palmleafarms.com, F$17-28), 14 kilometers west of Labasa. The attractive restaurant draws from the resort's organic farm to offer a range of dishes, including wood-fired pizzas, pastas, goat curry, and lobster cooked in a coconut shell. Wash it all down with sangria.

ACCOMMODATIONS

Under US$50

The basic but clean **Friendly North Inn** (Siberia Rd., tel. 881-1555, fni@cjsgroup.com.fj, http://cjsgroup.com.fj/friendly_north_inn.html) opposite the hospital is about a kilometer from the bus station (F$3 by taxi). The air-conditioned rooms are F$90-110, with TV and fridge, and rooms without air-conditioning are F$60. The inn's large open-air bar (Mon.-Fri. 1600-2000, Sat.-Sun. 1200-2200) is a pleasant place for a beer.

US$50-100

The **Grand Eastern Hotel** (Gibson St., tel. 881-1022 or 990-8053, grandeastern@cjsgroup.com.fj, http://cjsgroup.com.fj/grand_eastern.html, F$180) overlooks the river, just a few minutes' walk from the bus station. It's a classic colonial-style hotel with air-conditioned rooms with terraces. The Grand Eastern's atmospheric dining room and bar are brimming with vintage charm, and serve pizza and Western standards.

A stylish place to stay in downtown Labasa is the ★ **Hotel Northpole** (Nasekula Rd., tel. 992-4664, 881-8008, 881-8009, or 999-7224, resv@northpole.com.fj, www.northpole.com.fj). Air-conditioned rooms are F$150 and have Wi-Fi. Room-plus-car rental deals are also offered, and reduced rates can be found Friday-Sunday. The Northpole caters mostly to business travelers but it's a good mid-priced choice. The Good Times Bar and Grill downstairs has all-day breakfast, "lunch" from 1000 to 2000, and Fiji Bitter on tap.

Over US$100

★ **Palmlea Farms Oceanfront Resort** (tel. 828-2220, palmleafarms@yahoo.com, www.palmleafarms.com) is a working organic farm (guests love the baby goats!) and resort 14 kilometers west of Labasa. It's really away from it all, with no other tourists in sight.

The one-bedroom *bures* are F$295 and the two-bedroom villas are F$390; you can fit up to six people for an additional charge, depending on whether they're adults or children. Significant discounts are often available. Breakfast, transfers from Labasa Airport, and kayak use are included. The rooms have only fans and can be hot at peak season, December-January. There are no TVs and the Wi-Fi is limited.

There's an attractive **restaurant** (mains F$17-28) that draws from the farm, a 25-meter lap swimming pool, and a speedboat for surfing and fishing trips. There's also a secluded golden **beach** 10 minutes by rowboat from the resort jetty. The managers pack a picnic lunch and beverages for their guests to have the beach all to themselves. A half-day boat trip to a good snorkeling spot is $65 per person (minimum of two), and boat trips to the Cakaulevu Reef are also possible.

A taxi from the resort to Labasa will be about F$20 one-way, or you can catch a bus into town if you trek out to the highway (4 km down a gravel road).

1: an Indian *thali* (combo plate) **2:** devotees at the Raath Yatra festival in Labasa **3:** legumes and vegetables in the Labasa market.

1

2

3

INFORMATION AND SERVICES

The ANZ Bank is opposite the bus station, and the Westpac Bank is farther west on Nasekula Road. Both have **ATMs** outside their offices. **Western Union Money Exchange** (tel. 881-4147, Mon.-Fri. 0715-1715, Sat. 0715-1515) is on Nasekula Road near the Centerpoint Hotel.

Northern District Hospital (tel. 881-1444), northeast of the river, is open 24 hours a day for emergencies.

For pharmaceutical needs, try **Babasiga Pharmacy** (Nasekula Rd., tel. 881-8099, Mon.-Fri. 0800-1800) or **Labasa Pharmacy** (in the Just Jeans Building, tel. 881-8117 or 705-1701, labasapharmacy@gmail.com, Mon.-Fri. 0800-1800, Sat. 0800-1700, Sun. 1000-1200).

GETTING AROUND

From town to the airport, 10 kilometers southwest of Labasa, a taxi is about F$8 or the hourly green-and-yellow Waiqele bus is F$1.15.

Vishnu Holdings (tel. 885-0276) operates public buses on the island, and updates about closures and route changes are posted on its Facebook page. Call for information; there's nothing much posted at the bus station. Buses from Labasa leave for Savusavu (94 km, three hours, F$7) at 0815, 0930, 1215, and more frequently throughout the afternoon until 1615. It's a very beautiful ride on an excellent paved highway over the Waisali Saddle between the Korotini and Valili mountains and along the palm-studded coast. To Natewa Bay, the bus departs at 0900 daily, and takes seven hours to reach Savusavu the long way. There are regular buses to Nabouwalu (210 km, six hours), to Kubulau via Wailevu, and to Daria.

Cars can be rented from **James Rentals** (tel. 885-0455 or 989-8556); **Northpole Rentals** (tel. 992-4664 or 881-8008, 4wd@northpole.com.fj, www.northpole.com.fj), which has some 4WD options; **Avis** (at Asco Motors next to Jame Mosque just outside town, tel. 672-2233, www.avis.com/car-rental/location/ASP/FJ/Labasa/LB6); **Budget** (at the Mazda dealership on Zoing Place, tel. 881-1999, www.budget.com.fj); and **Vanua Rentals** (in the Mobil service station on the corner of Nanuku and Jadaram Sts., tel. 881-1060 or 990-8248, vanua.rental@cisgroup.com.fj, www.cjsgroup.com.fj/vanua.html). Day rates are typically F$120-227 and go down for three-day and seven-day rentals.

Labasa taxis have meters that start at F$1.50 flag fall (or F$2 from 2200 to 0600), after which it's F$0.50 a kilometer. A taxi between Labasa and Savusavu is F$100 and takes about 90 minutes.

Islands Around Vanua Levu

Vanua Levu's tiny neighbors are a smattering of curiosities: one with some of the best diving in Fiji, one that's a barely-more-than-camping social justice camp, one that's an adults-only upscale resort, two that are populated entirely by non-Fijians from other island nations, and finally, one that's reserved exclusively for a rare iguana. Browse the possibilities and prepare for a trip like no other.

NAMENALALA ISLAND

Cyclone Winston destroyed the only resort on this tiny island, as well as the lush forest and seabird nesting grounds. However, the diving here is still fantastic.

★ Namena Marine Reserve

Surrounding Namenalala Island, the **Namena Marine Reserve** (tel. 885-3035, 740-0704, or 906-0109, VHF channel 14, didi@coral.org, www.namena.org) offers

The Crested Iguana

the crested iguana on the F$5 bill

In 1979, a new species of lizard, the **crested iguana** *(Brachylophus vitiensis),* was discovered on uninhabited **Yaduatabu Island,** a tiny 70-hectare dot in Bligh Water off the west end of Vanua Levu. These iguanas are similar to those of the Galapagos Islands, and they may have arrived thousands of years ago on floating rafts of vegetation. The same species was later found on some islands in the Yasawa and Mamanuca Groups.

Crested Iguanas are shiny emerald green with white stripes and a yellow snout, and they turn black when alarmed. The females have longer tails, growing up to 90 centimeters in length. They're not to be confused with the more common banded iguana found elsewhere in Fiji, the male of which is also green with white stripes, while the female is totally green.

Yaduatabu is separated from neighboring Yadua Island by only 200 meters of shallow water, and at the time of their discovery the iguanas were being threatened by a large colony of feral goats that was consuming their habitat. Fortunately, the National Trust of Fiji took over management of the island, created an iguana sanctuary with an honorary warden from the Fijian village on Yadua, and eliminated the goats.

Today, about 6,000 lizards are present, basking in the sun in the canopy during the day and coming down to the lower branches at night.

Tourist boats cannot land here, but it's possible to visit by taking the ferry to Nabouwalu, then hiring a local boat to Yadua, where guides can be arranged. Prior permission must be obtained from the National Trust for Fiji Islands office in Suva.

some of the best diving in Fiji. Managed by the 10 village chiefs of **Kubulau District** in cooperation with international conservation experts, Namena is the largest no-take marine region in Fiji. The soft corals here are among the finest in the world, and the diversity of species is even greater than on Australia's Great Barrier Reef.

Cyclone Winston reshaped some Namena reefs, but left many others intact, including favorite dive sites such as **Grand Central Station, Two Thumbs Up,** and **Kansas**—whose pinnacles are flourishing—and snorkelers' favorites such as **Golden Nuggets.** Divers can see large manta rays, big-eyed trevally, whitetip and gray reef sharks, and schools of surgeonfish here, showing the incredible resilience of marinelife. Scalloped hammerhead sharks frequent the **Dream House** site.

The Namena reserve, created in

partnership with the Coral Reef Alliance and World Conservation Society Fiji, is a model conservation project that has been widely studied. A F$30 "goodwill fee" tacked on for every diver (good for a year) contributes to the preservation of this region, including patrolling it to prevent poaching and other destructive practices. The funds have allowed the community to keep out commercial fishing, to install and maintain mooring buoys at dive sites to reduce anchor damage, and to train local children in ecological practices and careers as fish wardens. You can buy T-shirts and other goods online to support the reserve (www.zazzle.com/namena_marine).

DIVING OUTFITTERS

Divers in this area are lucky to have three great operators, so choose based on where you're staying and what kind of diving you want. Check sites for rates and reviews by recent divers. Prebooking can mean cheaper rates for multiday dives, but locks you into one operator; refunds are not usually given.

Namena Divers (www.namenadiversfiji.com) formerly operated on Namenalala Island itself but, due to damage from Winston, now operates from Koro Sun Resort. Dives are at 0830 and 1330 daily. It's F$160/$255 for a one/two tank dive, plus gear rental. Trips to Namena and Somosomo are considered "premium excursions" and are almost twice as expensive.

Confusingly, **Koro Sun Divers** (tel. 934-1033, 885-2452, or 934-1033, www.korosundive.com) is now based at Savasi Island. Locals know Colin Skipper as an expert at finding the hammerheads at the Dream House site. It's F$150/$270 for a one/two tank dive, including all equipment. Snorkelers can climb aboard for F$50.

Jean-Michel Cousteau Diving (tel. 885-0694, VHF channel 69, www.jeanmichelcousteaudiving.com) is the most experienced and high-end dive operation in the area. A marine biologist is present on many dives, and Cousteau himself dives with guests when he's in town. Towels and refreshments are provided, and no corners are cut here. Rates are F$220/$390 for a one/two tank dive, plus F$75 for gear rental. If you're staying at one of the budget accommodations in town, you may be able to get the local rate, F$150/F$275 for one/two tanks, plus F$60 for gear rental. Fishing trips (F$250 per hour, minimum of two hours) are also possible, and snorkelers can join for day trips. You'll

kayaking with Jean-Michel Cousteau Fiji Islands Resort near Savusavu

need to arrange your own transport to the Cousteau resort.

KIOA ISLAND

The 25-square-kilometer **Kioa Island** is a touch of Polynesia in Fiji, inhabited by the descendants of people who bought it because their own island was overcrowded and had weak soil. In 1946, after earning some money from American armed forces during World War II, 37 people from Vaitupu Island in Tuvalu (the former Ellice Islands), a thousand kilometers north, landed here to make their new home. Today about 300 Tuvaluans live here. The women make baskets for sale to tourists in Savusavu, while the men go fishing alone in small outrigger canoes.

Getting There

The island is sometimes visited by yachts and liveaboards, but there are no facilities for tourists. To visit, negotiate with the fishing boats tied up near the Labasa Club. Village boats sometimes also dock at the Government Wharf on the other side of town.

Some tour operators from Taveuni and eastern Vanua Levu come to the **Black Magic** snorkel site, at the base of Kioa Island, which features hundreds of blue starfish, large clams, and rare black coral.

RABI ISLAND

Little **Rabi Island,** just 66 square kilometers, has been through a lot. In 1855, a Tongan army conquered the local Fijians who were at war with the chief at Taveuni. When the Tongans left, that chief sold Rabi to the Australian firm Lever Brothers, which ran a coconut plantation. It was the first place in Fiji to purchase Indian indenture labor, in 1879. Then the British government bought the island to resettle the Banaba people from their strip-mined, bombed-out home in the Gilbert Islands after World War II.

Today, Rabi Island's four villages are named for the four villages on Banaba where the current residents originated. **Tabwewa** is the administrative center, and neighboring **Nuku** has the post office, courthouse, and wharf. The local language is Gilbertese. Most people walk or ride horses around the island, or you can hail a pickup truck "taxi" along the island's single 23-kilometer road. Part of the island is still coconut plantations whose oil is processed in a **Nature Pacific** (www.naturepacific.com, banabanvco@gmail.com) factory for export and sale under the label Banaban Virgin Coconut Oil.

To visit, you'll need to know someone and ask them to arrange the necessary permit to land there, as well as to stay in the small government-run Rabi Council Guest House (tel. 330-3653).

Getting There

Every week, the 350-passenger *Princess Moana* operated by Savusavu-based **Miller Shipping** (tel. 755-6672, 885-3180, or 835-0211) makes a trip to Rabi Island. On Wednesday, the ferry leaves Taveuni at 1730 and arrives in Rabi at 1845. The next morning, Thursday, it departs Rabi at 0345 and arrives in Natuvu, on Vanua Levu, at 0500. This entire route takes about 24 hours from Suva, at F$70 for the entire trip; you pay only for the segment you travel. Natuvu to Rabi only is F$10. The company's Facebook page is the best source of updated information.

In 2018, **Goundar Shipping** (tel. 777-5463, goundarshipping@kidanet.com.fj) began offering trips along the Natuvu-Taveuni-Rabi route on the *Lomaiviti Princess IV.* The daily loop goes from Natuvu in eastern Vanua Levu to Taveuni (1 hour), then Rabi Island (2.5 hours), then back to Natuvu (45 minutes). Each leg is F$20, plus bus fare of F$5 from Natuvu to Savusavu or F$7 from Natuvu to Labasa.

At other times, catch the daily Napuka bus at 1030 from Savusavu to Karoko. A chartered speedboat from Karoko to the wharf at Nuku on the northwest side of Rabi costs F$70 each way, less if others are going over with you.

The Tragedy of Banaba

In 1899, the Sydney-based Pacific Islands Company discovered phosphates on Banaba, also known as Ocean Island, a tiny, six-square-kilometer raised atoll in the Micronesian Gilbert Islands. The company negotiated an agreement with the Banaba chiefs to gain exclusive access to the phosphate for 999 years—in exchange for just £50 a year. Little did the islanders know what this deal would truly cost them.

A few years later, the British government took over the island and reduced the term of the lease to a more realistic 99 years. But the company didn't need that long. By 1909, 15 percent of Banaba had been stripped of both phosphates and food trees. The mining continued despite islanders' protests, with the British turning a blind eye to the environmental devastation being wreaked.

In 1941, when World War II arrived on the island, the island was already mined out. The British blew up the mining infrastructure rather than have it fall into Japanese hands—evacuating white company officials, but leaving local laborers to the mercy of the 500 Japanese soldiers who landed on Banaba. Beheadings and electrocutions on the company's electric fence ensued, and eventually the Japanese deported almost all of the 2,413 local mine laborers and their family members to work on neighboring Tarawa, Nauru, and Kosrae. About 150 Banabans were kept back to serve the Japanese forces.

At the end of the war, when the British reclaimed the island, not a single local village was still standing. Later, an emaciated Gilbertese man, Kabunare Koura, would tell his story to a military court:

> We were assembled together and told that the war was over and the Japanese would soon be leaving. Our rifles were taken away. We were put in groups, our names taken, and then marched to the edge of the cliffs where our hands were tied and we were blindfolded and told to squat. Then we were shot.

Koura survived by falling off the cliff as the shots were fired. Unhurt, he fell into the sea and kicked his way to some rocks, then severed the string that tied his hands. He crawled into a cave and watched the Japanese pile up the bodies of his companions and toss them into the sea. After two nights, he made his way inland, where he survived on coconuts for three months until he was sure the Japanese had left. He was the sole survivor. Following the postwar trial on Guadalcanal, the Japanese commander of Banaba was hanged for his crimes.

Meanwhile, the British decided to take advantage of the devastation to get rid of the original inhabitants and their claims once and for all. Using £25,000 of the phosphate royalties that had by then been placed in a provident fund for the Banaban people, the British purchased **Rabi Island** off Vanua Levu in Fiji and turned it into a new homeland for the Banabans. Strip-mining of Banaba for phosphates resumed.

From 1945 onward, the Banabans worked to adapt to their mountainous new home while being assured that they retained some rights over their original island. Ever since, various efforts to gain reparations and compensation have been undertaken with the British government, the Australian profiteers, and the new independent government of Kiribati, whose constitution granted the natives free entry to Banaba.

In 1981, the Banabans accepted AU$10 million compensation, plus interest, from the British, though they refused to withdraw their claim to Banaba. By 1991, much of the money had "disappeared" during a period of corruption in the Rabi Council of Leaders. It was, anyway, a pittance compared with the AU$614 million trust fund from phosphate proceeds that fell into the hands of the Kiribati government, none of which has been released to the Rabi islanders. Even their status as Fijians was uncertain until, in 2005, Fiji granted them full citizenship.

VOROVORO ISLAND

Tiny **Vorovoro Island,** next to Mali Island near the port of Malau off Labasa, has been the site of a unique social experiment. From 2006 to 2011, the chief at Mali leased the mile-long islet to an Internet community, **Tribe Wanted** (www.tribewanted.com), whose 5,000 members rotated in and out for 1-4-week stays. They built a sustainable tourism village complete with *bures,* compost loos, gardens, and a kitchen. They were the subject of a five-part BBC documentary, *Paradise or Bust.* At the end of the five-year lease, they turned the project over to the Tui Mali.

As of 2018, U.S. company **Bridge the Gap Vorovoro** (U.S. 317/296-4883, info@btgvorovoro.com, www.btgvorovoro.com) has reopened the island to the public for a few months each year. Rates are US$44.50 per person, with children 12 and under staying free (one-week minimum stay). Be prepared for a camping-like environment with minimal amenities but tons of activities: cooking classes, kava sessions, fishing from the beach, a medicinal plant tour, and snorkeling. Some activities are free while others cost US$10-15 per person. The island also has hammocks, volleyball nets, and four rugged peaks for hikers. Classes in cultural skills such as mat-weaving are held at the **Vorovoro Cultural Center,** and study-abroad groups are regularly hosted from U.S. universities. Guests can also help with community projects such as building a new kindergarten classroom for the village school. Diving is possible with **Great Sea Reef Divers.** Generous meals are included, as well as a sulu and a bundle of kava to present during your own *sevusevu* arrival ceremony.

Taxi and boat transfers from Labasa airport are included with Bridge the Gap stays; it's about a 40-minute speedboat ride.

NUKUBATI ISLAND

Only guests at the upscale **Nukubati Private Island Resort** (tel. 603-0919, reservations@nukubati.com, www.nukubati.com, US$792-1,140) visit **Nukubati Island,** which sits one kilometer off the north shore of Vanua Levu, 40 kilometers west of Labasa. Rates include gourmet meals, drinks, laundry, and nonmotorized activities. This is a very couples-oriented place and markets honeymoons, weddings, and vow-renewals strongly; you can rent the whole island for US$5,500 a night for seven couples. Children

Rabi Island

are not allowed. Meals (emphasis on seafood, especially lobster) are included, but sportfishing and scuba diving are extra. Owners Jenny and Peter Bourke are usually on-site. This is the closest upscale resort to the Great Sea Reef, so the scuba diving and snorkeling possibilities are virtually unlimited. There's no pool, but the beach is white coral sand.

Transfers from Labasa airport, one hour by car and then half an hour by boat, are included with a stay.

Taveuni

Known as the Garden Island, Taveuni is a natural paradise. On Fiji's third-largest island, you can hike a volcanic peak to find a rare red flower, slide down a series of small waterfalls, or stroll along a pristine white-sand beach. Off the coast, the secluded coves of eastern Vanua Levu are accessible from here, as well as a few tiny island resorts.

Taveuni's 16-kilometer-long, 1,000-meter-high volcanic spine was the first land in Fiji sighted by a European, Abel Tasman, in 1643, who from his ship mistook its multiple peaks for several separate islands through the clouds. It contains Uluigalau (1,241 m), Fiji's second-highest peak, and Des Voeux Peak (1,195 m), which is the highest point in the country accessible by road. In southwestern Taveuni, Mount Vuna

Highlights

Look for ★ to find recommended sights, activities, dining, and lodging.

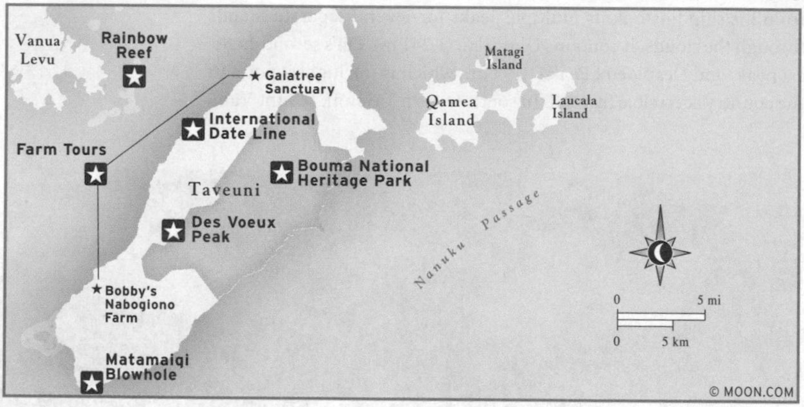

★ **International Date Line:** Visit the marker of the world's true 180-degree longitude and take a selfie with one foot in "today" and the other in "yesterday" (page 269).

★ **Des Voeux Peak:** The eight-kilometer climb to Taveuni's second-highest peak can be a bumpy ride or an all-day grind on foot—but it's worth it for the lake views, rich bird-watching, and chance to see the rare Tagimoucia flower (page 271).

★ **Matamaiqi Blowhole:** The sight of foamy whitecaps thrusting several meters into the air through pitch-black lava rock formations is a must for photographers (page 271).

★ **Rainbow Reef:** This famous spot offers possibly the best diving in Fiji. The soft corals of the Great White Wall here are awesome (page 272).

★ **Bouma National Heritage Park:** This accessible nature reserve has three waterfalls, good hiking and snorkleing, and sustainable tourism projects that directly assist the local communities (page 281).

★ **Farm Tours:** Taveuni's lush, rain-fed soils make it the perfect place to take in a farm tour. Choose between the fancy **Gaiatree Sanctuary** (page 269) and the down-home **Bobby's Nabogiono Farm** (page 271).

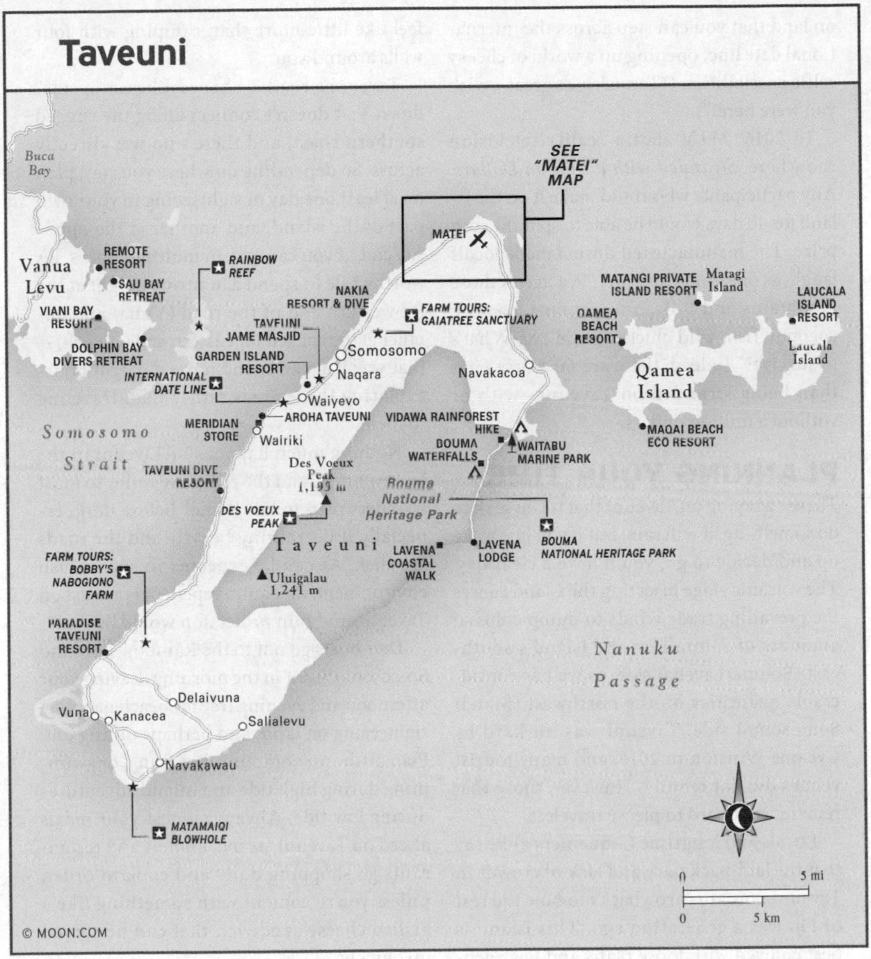

is considered Fiji's most active volcano, having erupted within the past 350 years, even though it's dormant now.

The entire island is actually the top of a gigantic volcano that goes all the way down to the bottom of the Pacific Ocean. The surrounding reefs are among the world's top dive sites, and the rugged southeastern shore is home to naturally occurring blowholes as the surf crashes up through openings in the black lava rock.

Above water, Taveuni is a lush 42 kilometers long, 15 kilometers wide, and 442 square kilometers in area. Most of the 12,000 inhabitants live on the gently sloping northwest side. About 60 percent of the land is tropical rainforest, and almost all of Fiji's coffee is grown here. The deep, rich volcanic soil nurtures indigenous floral species not found elsewhere, and there are many rare endemic birds to be spotted. The island also has a unique tourist attraction: It's the only place

Previous: an aerial view of the Rainbow Reef off Taveuni; view from the hike up Des Voeux Peak; live crabs bound and ready for sale.

on land that you can step across the international date line, opening up a world of cheesy selfie possibilities. ("Tomorrow's great—wish you were here!")

In 2016, MTV shot a reality television show here, *Stranded with a Million Dollars*. Any participants who could make it on the island for 40 days would be able to split the cash prize. The manufactured drama made locals laugh; as one guide told me, "We live in those mountains and hills. You get taro, papaya, coconut, fish, wild chicken, wild pig. What's to survive?" Indeed, there are far worse fates than being stranded on Taveuni—with or without a million dollars.

PLANNING YOUR TIME

There's a saying on Taveuni that if you plan to do something, it will rain, but if you just wake up and decide to go, you'll have a clear day. The volcanic ridge bisecting the island causes the prevailing trade winds to dump colossal amounts of rainfall on the island's southeast (Bouma/Lavena) side, as well as considerable quantities on the northwest (Matei/Somosomo) side. Taveuni was hit hard by Cyclone Winston in 2016, and many tourist venues did not rebuild. However, those that remain work hard to please travelers.

Locals and longtime frequenters alike say that the laid-back pace and lack of crowds in Taveuni now are throwbacks to how the rest of Fiji was a generation ago. This island is best enjoyed with loose plans and few agendas, so you can enjoy the slow pace and follow nature's cues. It's not worth going for less than two nights, and there's plenty for outdoor adventurers to keep busy for a week or more.

Most visitors stay on the western side of the island around Matei (airport), Somosomo, and Waiyevo, where the majority of the resorts, wharfs, and other facilities are concentrated. If you plan to use public transportation for sightseeing, stay in Somosomo/Naqara, where the central bus depot is located. The eastern side of the island (Lavena) is less equipped for tourists, and accommodations feel like little more than camping with four walls around you.

Taveuni's road is shaped like an upside-down V; it doesn't connect along the rugged southern coast, and there's no way directly across. So depending on where you stay, plan on at least one day of sightseeing in your own part of the island, and another at the opposite end. If you can stay in multiple places, it's worthwhile to spend a luxurious night at the far western end of the road (Vuna) and another at the rugged far eastern end (Lavena)—that way you can spend more daylight hours exploring those areas rather than traveling to them.

Nothing much happens in Taveuni in the late evenings, and the roads are unlit, so most islanders plan to be "home" before dark, especially if it's raining heavily and the roads are slick. As can be expected in such a lush environment, mosquito repellent is a must on Taveuni, and rain protection would be wise.

Dive boats go out to the Rainbow Reef and Somosomo Strait in the morning, leaving your afternoon and evening free for beach napping, sightseeing on land, and perhaps dining out. Plan offshore snorkeling, kayaking, or swimming during high tide and inland adventures during low tide. Always request your meals ahead on Taveuni, as most hotels and restaurants go shopping daily and cook to order, unless you're content with something like a grilled cheese sandwich that can be served up quickly.

GETTING THERE

Air

One of the most beautiful air landings in the world is at **Matei Airport,** where you descend low enough to see individual fish in the clear turquoise waters. There are no services at the airport, but there's a convenience store across the road.

Airfare to Taveuni on **Fiji Airways** (www.fijiairways.com) can vary widely depending on the time of year and how close you are to your departure date, running F$300-600 one-way, with several flights a week from Nadi (90

Find Your Beach

- **Matei** (page 269): About a kilometer southwest of the Matei Airport, the **public beach** adjacent to Maravu Lodge is the best centrally located swimming beach. The beach **east of Matei Pointe** is pleasant at high tide but turns into a broad mudflat at low tide.
- **Lavena Coastal Walk** (page 282): By far the **finest beach** on Taveuni is along on the eastern shore, accessible via the Lavena Coastal Walk at Bouma National Heritage Park.
- **Islands off Taveuni's Coast** (page 285): The outlying Qamea Island, Matagi Island, Laucala Island, and eastern Vanua Levu coast have great beaches, but **can only be accessed by resort guests.** The pricier resorts usually offer a boat ride out to an uninhabited islet with a beach cove where you can picnic privately for an afternoon.

minutes) and Suva (60 minutes). Book in advance if possible, as the small flights fill up during busier periods. If Taveuni is your first or primary destination, it's probably cheaper to buy your international ticket as a direct flight to Taveuni. But you'll still be held to the 15-kilogram check-in baggage limit, so you may need to stash a suitcase in the locked luggage room at Nadi Airport.

For a group, you may wish to charter a flight with Northern Air (from Suva only; www.northernair.com.fj) or Island Hoppers (www.islandhoppersfiji.com).

Sea

It's a tenth of the price but ten times more arduous to reach Taveuni from Suva by ferry than by air. It's preferable to start on Vanua Levu, either at Savusavu or at Buca Bay on the far eastern tip. Due to weather conditions and route changes, it can be difficult to figure out the exact ferry schedule; call the companies directly, or ask your hotel to do so. (Emails tend to go unanswered.)

Captain Cook Cruises (www.captaincookcruisesfiji.com) runs seven-night Colonial Fiji Discovery Cruises on the *MV Reef Endeavour*. The ship stops at the Bouma waterfalls in Taveuni, as well as Levuka and Savusavu. This cruise is offered about twice a year; see the website for upcoming dates. It's possible to join or leave the cruise in Taveuni.

Venu Shipping (tel. 339-5000 Suva office, 14 Baka Place, Laucala Beach, Suva; tel. 888-0382 Taveuni office, in Naqara town) sends the *MV Suilven* on one trip a week, originating at Walu Bay in Suva, stopping 12 hours later in Savusavu, and then going on to Taveuni a few hours later. The schedule is irregular and depends on tides, weather, and demand. But departure time from Suva is usually scheduled for 1800, to arrive at the Savusavu wharf around 0600. Assuming that all goes well, it should arrive around 1030 at Taveuni's Wairiki Wharf, where public buses and taxis are poised to pick you up. Most passengers start in Suva, and the price is F$75 per person steerage, F$100 for the first-class lounge, and F$120 for sleeper class—well worth it if you are taking the entire 16-hour journey. Prebook at the office in Suva if you want a premium ticket, or buy a ticket at the wharf; you must board two hours before departure. In Savusavu, you can just walk up to the ship. For the return journey from Taveuni, buy a ticket at the office in Naqara town.

Goundar Shipping (Tofua St., Walu Bay, Suva, tel. 330-1035, www.goundarshipping.com) operates the *MV Lomaviti Princess* once or twice a week. Departure time from Suva is either 1800 or midnight, arriving in Savusavu about 12 hours later before continuing to Taveuni's Wairiki Wharf. You can make inquiries and book tickets at the office on the main road in Somosomo village.

The **Grace Ferry** (tel. 927-1372 Savusavu or 888-0320 Taveuni, F$35 ferry plus F$5 bus) is a small, 50-person ferry that travels about four times a week. It's an adventure to board the bus around 0830 at Savusavu's bus terminal, then take the gorgeous but bumpy two-hour Hibiscus Highway east to Natuvu town on Buca Bay, and then board the ferry around 1130. From here it takes less than two hours to cross the Somosomo Strait. Bookings are essential, as this ferry fills up.

GETTING AROUND

Infrequent buses and expensive taxis make Taveuni a bit of a challenge to navigate. If you're not on organized day trips from your hotel, you might choose the public bus for longer excursions, and taxis for shorter runs. The good news: there's only one main road, so it's almost impossible to get lost.

Bus

The open-windowed public buses operated by **Pacific Transport** (tel. 888-0278, 931-1355, or 999-4368) are cheap but only run thrice a day on weekdays and Saturday, and once on Sundays. The buses stay overnight in villages, so that they can start in the morning either at the far western end of the route (Navakawau, at Vuna Point, 0530) or at the far eastern end (Lavena, 0545). They meet in the middle at Naqara, where the last buses depart at either 1640 (going west to Navakawau/Vuna) or 1630 (going east to Lavena). The eastern route to/from Lavena stops in Matei.

This is all very convenient for bringing people to their jobs in the center, and just fine if you want to move about early in the day, but it means you can't get a bus back toward the center after about 1400 most days. On Sundays, there's only one round-trip per day: leaving Navakawau/Vuna at 0700 and returning to the west from Naqara at 1530; and leaving Lavena at 0730, returning to the east from Naqara at 1530. An Australian travel agency keeps an updated schedule at www.taveuni.com.au/services/bus.htm, or just ask a local; most people know when the bus goes by. There are designated bus stands, but the driver will generally stop where you ask them to. Fares are F$5 one-way to either end of the island, less if you're only going part of the way.

The best way to understand your options is to ask a staff person at your accommodation, as they probably take the bus to and from work.

Taxi

Taxis on Taveuni do not have meters, so always negotiate the fare before you get in. Other than at the airport, empty taxis don't linger about, so it's best to have your accommodation or restaurant call one for you. If you're planning on going up the mountain or down to Vuna Point, or if it's raining, be sure to specify that you want a 4WD vehicle. From the airport, expect to pay about F$30 to reach most resorts, F$90 if you're going to the far western end (Vuna). You can book a taxi for a full day of sightseeing for about F$180. If your accommodation isn't calling a cab for you, try **Aloha Taveuni** (Samir Mohammed, tel. 902-8375, alohataveuni@gmail.com), **Taxi Matei** (tel. 844-0804 or 781-6407), **Veilomani Taxi** (tel. 991-1358), or **Kava Taxi** (tel. 945-5429).

Car

The sole car rental agency on the island is **Ruz Rentals** (tel. 888-0094 or 869-0843), F$210 for a four-wheel-drive vehicle. Locals sometimes rent out their cars for about F$130; note that you won't have insurance or any protection if the car breaks down.

Taveuni is exceedingly safe and it's fine to accept a ride from a local or allow your taxi driver to pick up other people. It may be one of the few places in the world where hitchhiking isn't risky. Drivers can generally identify who's driving every vehicle you encounter along the way, as well as what village they come from and a full rundown of gossip about each family member.

Matei and Western Taveuni

MATEI

Matei, on the northern tip of the island, is where the airport is located. There are several resorts and private rental properties. There's a fine **beach** about a kilometer south of the airport, next to Maravu Lodge, and another beach just past the northernmost **Matei Pointe** that is good only at high tide.

Civa Fiji Pearls Boutique (tel. 888-1260 or 935-6168, www.civafijipearls.com, Mon.-Fri. 0800-1600, Sat. 0800-1200) is the Matei retail outlet for an operation that farms pearls in and around Qamea Island. No tours are available, but staff will explain the pearl-making process to you at the store, which has a small selection of jewelry for sale. Most of the lustrous colored pearls are exported to Europe, with 2.5 percent of revenue going to the Fijian communities that own water rights to the region.

SOMOSOMO AND NAQARA

The next town, 16 kilometers west, is **Somosomo.** This is the chiefly quarter, with the personal residence of Taveuni's ruler, the Tui Cakau, on the hill directly above the bridge (no entry). Beside the main road below is the large hall built for the 1986 meeting of the Great Council of Chiefs. Missionary William Cross, one of the creators of today's system of written Fijian, died at Somosomo in 1843 and is buried in the attractive church next to the meeting hall.

Across a small stream and virtually indistinguishable from Somosomo is **Naqara,** the island's commercial center, with several stores, shipping offices, and the island's bank, with the only ATM on Taveuni. Pacific Transport has its bus terminus here, and the island's largest mosque, **Taveuni Jame Masjid,** is visible from the main road, on the left as you travel west.

★ Farm Tour

Gaiatree Sanctuary (tel. 992-8034, gaiatree@icloud.com, www.gaiatreesanctuary.com, Thurs.-Sat. 1000-1500, F$150), near the Nakia Resort north of Somosomo, is an organic farm with white domes designed to be cyclone-proof, established by a Canadian couple who came to Taveuni because it was on their "bucket list." The Spice of Life Tour includes a two-hour horticultural tour followed by a three-course vegetarian meal, and round-trip transfers from the Qila Road bus stand (near the Nakia Resort). It's a bit pretentious (organic botanical elixirs! superfood nectar shots! gluten-free jungle gnocchi!), but the earnestness of the hosts makes it a pleasant day. Reservations are required.

WAIYEVO

On a hilltop at **Waiyevo,** four kilometers west of Naqara, are Taveuni's police station, hospital, and government offices. On the coast below are the island's post office and its largest hotel, the Garden Island Resort. Across the road from the resort is a good barbecue stand—stop by in the afternoon to see what's cooking.

★ International Date Line

Five hundred meters up a small road near the Garden Island Resort is a display marking the 180th degree of longitude, the true **international date line.** It's cheesy fun to take a selfie with a foot in each day. Legend has it that one early Taveuni trader overcame the objections of missionaries to his doing business on Sunday by claiming the international date line ran through his property. According to him, when it was Sunday at the front door, it was already Monday around back. Similarly, European planters are said to have manipulated their laborers into working seven days a week by having Sunday at one end of the plantation and Monday at the other.

Matei

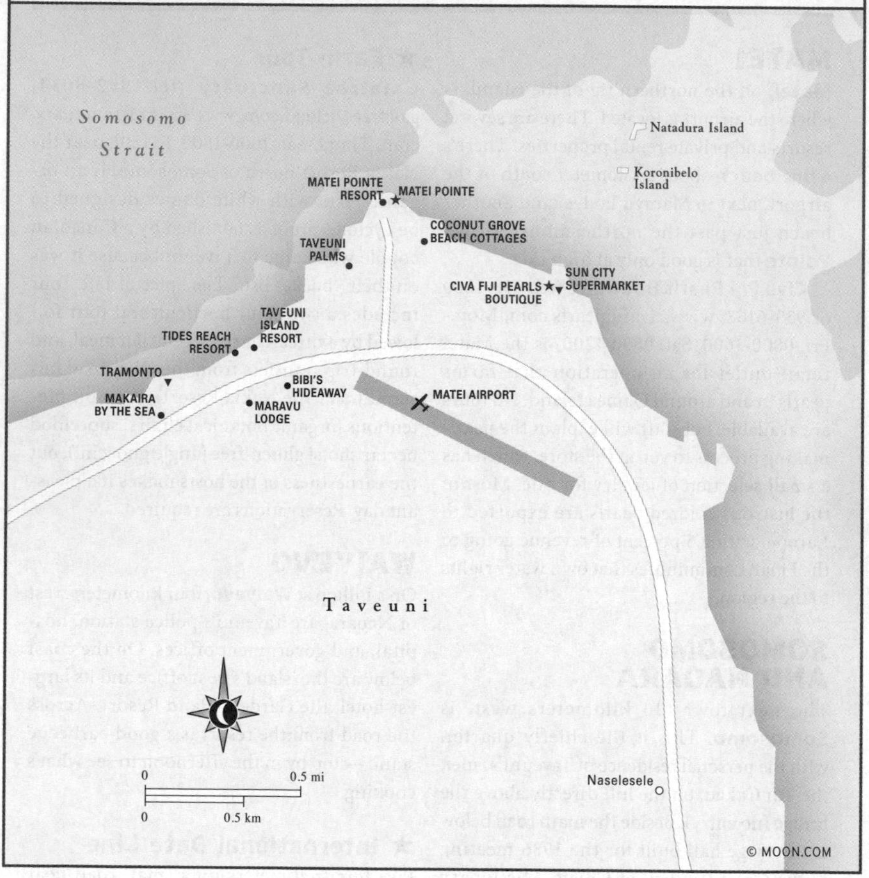

An 1879 ordinance ended the confusion by ordaining that all of Fiji is a single time zone, but it's still the most accessible place in the world that is crossed by the 180th meridian.

Waitavala Sliding Rocks

For an exhilarating natural waterslide, check out the free **Waitavala Sliding Rocks.** Walk north from the Garden Island Resort about five minutes on the main road, then turn right onto Waitavala Road. Take the first road to the right up the hill, and when you see a large metal building on top of the hill, turn left and go a short distance down a road through a plantation to a clearing on the right. The jungle trail up the river to the sliding rocks begins here. The waterslide is especially fast after heavy rains, yet the local kids go down standing up! It's busy on Sundays, when most people have the day off. Wear a bathing suit and start at one of the lower levels rather than the topmost. It looks scary, but the constant flow of water has worn the rocks silky smooth.

WAIRIKI

At **Wairiki,** two kilometers south of Waiyevo, are a few stores and the picturesque **Catholic mission,** with a large stone church containing interesting sculptures and stained glass. There are no pews: The congregation sits on the floor Fijian-style. From Wairiki Secondary School, you can hike up a tractor track to the large **concrete cross** on a hill behind the mission (30 minutes each way). You'll be rewarded with a sweeping view of much of western Taveuni and across Somosomo Strait. A famous 19th-century naval battle occurred here when Taveuni warriors turned back a large Tongan invasion force, with much of the fighting done from canoes. The captured Tongans ended up in Fijian ovens, and the French priest who gave valuable counsel to the Fijian chief was repaid with laborers to build his mission.

★ Des Voeux Peak

A rugged dirt road climbs from Wairiki to the two telecommunications towers atop **Des Voeux Peak.** At 1,195 meters, this is Taveuni's second-highest volcanic mountain. From the top you can gaze on the mountain's crater lake, **Lake Tagimoucia,** where the rare tagimoucia flower grows.

It's four arduous hours to hike the eight kilometers up and another two to walk back down. A guide is necessary, as there are many forks in the trail; request one in Wairiki or ask your hotel to arrange one. To reach the lake involves another half-hour of wading through knee-deep mud in the crater. The vegetation-covered lake is only about five meters deep; it's better appreciated from afar.

You can skip the hike altogether and hire a 4WD vehicle to the viewpoint. The first five kilometers pass open areas with varied views, while the upper three kilometers are through largely undisturbed forest.

October-January, keep an eye out for the tagimoucia *(Medinilla waterhousei),* a climbing plant with bright red-and-white flower clusters 30 centimeters long, and its cousin *Medinilla spectabilis,* whose blooms hang in clusters like red sleigh bells. Tagimoucia grows only around Taveuni's 900-meter-high crater lake and on Vanua Levu, and cannot be transplanted.

This peak is one of Taveuni's best bird-watching venues, and the rare monkey-faced fruit bat *(Pteralopex acrodonta)* survives only in the mist forest around the summit. Almost all of Taveuni's endemic species of birds have been seen here.

VUNA AND VICINITY

If you continue southwest from Wairiki, you'll find a gorgeous, less touristy part of the Garden Island. After passing the Taveuni Dive Resort, then Paradise Taveuni, you'll reach the large village of Vuna, followed by Kanacea, before reaching the South Cape and Navakawau.

★ Farm Tour

Bobby's Nabogiono Farm (Vuna, tel. 923-8612 or 844-1097, nabogiono@yahoo.com.au) is a sprawling farm inland from Vuna that showcases the best of wild, natural Taveuni. An Indo-Fijian who inherited the farm from his family, Bobby Shankaran has resolutely refused to sell the land to developers, and has instead bought the adjacent rainforest and land all the way to the rocky shore. The views over the jungle toward the sea are spectacular, and Bobby is the best guide you could imagine to Taveuni's special wildlife; from herbs to birds, butterflies to fish, he knows it all. Nonguests can call and ask to visit for bird-watching, nature hikes, fishing, waterfall trips, or tours to other natural spots on Taveuni, as well as a pleasant family-style lunch. Rates vary depending on the size of your group and your interests, but you'll find it all very reasonable. Taxi drivers on Taveuni know the turn-by-turn directions to get here, or you can call ahead to have Bobby meet you at the main junction at Vuna.

★ Matamaiqi Blowhole

Just east of South Cape is the **Matamaiqi Blowhole,** where waves, driven by trade winds, crash into the unprotected black volcanic rock. Geysers of sea spray soar skyward 15 meters or more, especially on a southern swell. The viewpoint for this dramatic sight is just

The Legends of Tagimoucia

the rare tagimoucia flower

Every Taveunian has their own story of the tragic, flamboyant tagimoucia flower. Here are a few:

- A young woman was fleeing from her father, who wanted to force her to marry a crotchety old man. As she lay crying beside the lake, her tears turned to flowers. Her father took pity on her and allowed her to marry her young lover.
- A princess had an arranged marriage but was in love with another man, so she fled up the mountain. Exhausted, she fell asleep crying, and her tears turned into the lake, from which sprung the flower. If you go there and see the flower, the person you are with will become your true love.
- A chief and a village woman fell in love, but could not marry because of custom. She took a knife and fled to the mountains, with the villagers in hot pursuit. When she was cornered, she stabbed herself, and her blood turned to flowers as it flowed out of her body, to remind the villagers forever of what they'd done.
- Two lovers escaped from their disapproving families, but the villagers chased and killed them. Blood from their wounds nourished the vines of the mountain, which sprouted red flowers.
- For a modern rendition of the legend that also makes a groovy hiking soundtrack, download local band Kula Kei Uluivuya's reggae hit named for the flower, "Tagimoucia." It was Fiji's Song of the Year in 2014, and you can still hear it blaring proudly from speakers all over the islands.

off the main road, and it's a great place to snap edge-of-the-world photos. You can clamber over the rocks, all the way down to the water if you dare. It's only worth going at high tide.

RECREATION

★ Rainbow Reef

Taveuni and its surrounding waters have earned a reputation as one of Fiji's top diving areas. The fabulous 32-kilometer Rainbow Reef is off the south coast of eastern Vanua Levu, just across the **Somosomo Strait** from Taveuni. It boasts 20-50-meter visibility and a range of wall, reef, and drift diving. The reef abounds in turtles, fish, overhangs, crevices, and soft corals, all in an easy 5-10 meters of water.

Favorite sites here include Annie's Boumie

(Annie still works as a divemaster at the Garden Island Resort), Blue Ribbon Eel Reef, Cabbage Patch, Coral Garden, Jack's Place, Jerry's Jelly, Orgasm, Pot Luck, the Ledge, the Zoo, and White Sandy Gully. At the Great White Wall, a tunnel in the reef leads past sea fans to a magnificent drop-off and a wall covered in awesome white soft coral.

Unfortunately, the hard corals of the Rainbow Reef have been heavily impacted by coral bleaching. The soft corals are still okay, and the White Wall is as spectacular as ever. Currents can be strong, so check with divemasters about tidal conditions.

Snorkelers can go along on dive boats, and it's well worth your time because there is plenty to see just a meter or two below the surface.

DIVING OUTFITTERS

Paradise Dive Centre (www.paradiseinfiji.com), located at Paradise Taveuni Resort, has the best boats on the island. They're mostly for in-house guests, but you can call to ask if there's space. It's F$300 for a two-tank dive plus F$40 for gear rental. Dive-stay packages are a good deal here because in addition to the multi-dive discount, you can also shore dive as much as you like. Overnight berths for two couples at a time are possible on the 45-foot *Taveuni Explorer*, built on Taveuni in 1997 and fully refurbished in 2018; you can book a sleepover dive expedition to the Namena Marine Reserve.

Dive Academy Fiji (tel. 725-8184 or 725-8167, info@diveacademyfiji.com, www.diveacademyfiji.com) is the newest operator, with brand-new equipment as of late 2017. It's the only operator in the region to offer manta ray dives and special events such as a yoga-dive retreat. A two-tank dive is F$290, plus F$48 gear rental, with discounts for prebooking and multiple-dive packages. The boat takes only four divers per trip and picks up at a number of sites in Taveuni; arrange for a transfer based on where you're staying. Based at Viani Bay Resort on Vanua Levu, they're close enough to most Rainbow Reef dive sites to use the resort's beach for surface intervals, which is more pleasant than lingering on the boat. Snorkel tours can also be booked at F$150. It's the only place in Fiji that offers PADI certification in freediving—the owner is a certified instructor from Germany.

Garden Island Diving (tel. 888-0286), at the Garden Island Resort, does daily dives at F$300 per two-tank trip, plus F$35 a day for gear. This is the closest dive shop to the famous Rainbow Reef, and one of the divemasters, Annie, was among the original Fijian divers who mapped the reef. The Annie's Boumie site is named for her.

Taveuni Dive (tel. 828-1063 or 997-1535, info@taveunidive.com, www.taveunidive.com) operates out of Taveuni Dive Resort, located on freehold land in Taveuni Estates (Soqulu Plantation), south of Wairiki. It's F$280 for a two-tank dive, plus F$40 for gear rental. Snorkelers can go along for F$125 if there's room on the boat. Check the Great White Wall diving schedule on the website for optimum dates.

Fishing

Sportfishing is offered by **Makaira Charters** (tel. 888-0680, www.fijibeachfrontatmakaira.com/fishing.htm), above the Tramonto Restaurant in Matei, at US$450 half day/$800 full day. Captain John Lllanes is a third-generation fisherman from Hawaii, and he steers a 32-foot fiberglass fishing boat built in 2014. It's custom-built for big-game fishing, including marlin, tuna, giant trevally, and barracuda.

Paradise Dive Centre (www.paradiseinfiji.com) offers fishing charters aboard the *Taveuni Explorer* from two hours to a two-day fishing trip through the basaltic cinder cones of the Koro Sea. A range of rates and options are available, all including gear, lures, lunch, local crews who know the waters, and dinner prepared by a sashimi chef upon your return. It's F$400 to charter the boat for one or two people after a scuba trip, or F$2,500 to charter the boat for 10 hours for a group. A sunset fishing cruise is F$50 per

TOP EXPERIENCE

Polish Your Binoculars

With 150 species of birds, including 28 endemics and 34 considered rare or endangered, Fiji is a haven for bird-watchers. Fijian bird-names often imitate their calls: kaka (parrot), ga (gray duck), and kikau (giant honeyeater).

Be sure to **ask locally** about bird-watching spots. The online shop of Suva-based nonprofit NatureFiji-MareqetiViti (https://naturefiji.org/product-category/books) sells several excellent **bird books** and pocket guides.

Here are the best places in the country to get your feathered fix.

TAVEUNI

Because Taveuni is free of mongooses, there are many wild chickens, *kula* lorikeets, red-breasted musk parrots, honeyeaters, silktails, fern-tails, goshawks, and orange-breasted doves, making this a special place for bird-watchers. Here you'll still find the jungle fowl, banded rail, and purple swamp hen, all extinct on Viti Levu and Vanua Levu. The Fiji flying fox and mastiff bat are also seen only here.

- For the best chance to see all four of Taveuni's endemic bird species, hike **Des Voeux Peak** (page 274).
- Visit **Bobby's Nabogiono Farm** (page 271) for a chance to see the elusive orange dove.

VITI LEVU

Fiji's largest island still has plenty of wild areas, so it's easy to spot birds found nowhere else in the world: the Fiji goshawk, swamp harrier, golden dove, barking imperial pigeon, colored lory, and more.

- Most of Viti Levu's endemic birds can be seen in one convenient location: the **Colo-i-Suva Forest Park** (page 191) just 15 minutes from Suva's airport. The onsite lodge's website (www.coloisuva.com.fj) has excellent information, including photos, for birding throughout Fiji.
- Each September, bar-tailed godwits arrive at **Suva Point** (page 169) after flying nine days nonstop overseas from Alaska. Each flock rests on the mudflats for about a day before carrying

person including cocktails (minimum four passengers), with the crew trawling for fish and you assisting if a big one bites.

Bird-Watching

Avian aficionados set their sights (and binoculars) on four main targets for Taveuni: the orange dove, red shining parrot, chatting giant honeyeater, and silktail. Keep an eye out everywhere, but if you're short on time, the best place to try spotting all four is **Des Voeux Peak.** From your hotel, hire a 4WD taxi to take you up just before daybreak and ask the driver to wait for three or four hours. Make sure he takes you up far enough, to the Digicel or Vodafone tower gate, about eight kilometers from the main road; lower than that and you may not see some specimens. Just downhill from the gate, take the left-hand trail to the south. As you walk into the forest and downhill, look for the silktail. The village at the bottom of the mountain levies a small fee to go up, so if you didn't pay it in the predawn darkness on the way in, be sure to stop on the way out; it's payable at the last house in the village (the first house as you are coming down).

The orange dove is elusive, even on the mountain peak, but one spot for sightings is **Bobby's Nabogiono Farm** (tel. 923-8612 on to New Zealand to complete their southward migration.

- The best place to spot the rare pink-billed parrotfinch is on the winding uphill **Namosi Road** (page 159), between Kilo Eco Adventure Park and Namosi village, north of Pacific Harbour.

- The bird-watching throughout **Koroyanitu National Heritage Park** (page 214), inland from Lautoka on the island's northern side, is spectacular. Hikes of two-five hours take you deep into the park, and overnight stays can be arranged to see species who are most visible at sunset and sunrise.

the Fiji woodswallow

OTHER ISLANDS

- **Kadavu Island** (page 199) has four endemic birds: the velvet dove, crimson shining-parrot, kadavu honeyeater, and kadavu fantail. All can be seen just a few kilometers from the airport, along the road between Namara village and the six-way roundabout in the center of the main town, Vunisea.

- On **Vanua Levu,** the old-growth **Waisali Rainforest Reserve** (page 236) is home to the rare black-faced shrikebill and the Vanua Levu subspecies of the long-legged warbler, as well as some of the species found on neighboring Taveuni.

- In the **Lomaiviti Group,** Gau, Koro, and Ovalau all have robust and biodiverse avian populations almost everywhere.

or 844-1097, nabogiono@yahoo.com.au). Call ahead to book a farm visit. Bobby won't charge you if you don't see the bird.

Golf

There's a bit of territorialism over the nine-hole golf course in the Taveuni Estates residential area. It's owned by the **Garden Island Resort** (Waiyevo, tel. 888-0286, relax@gardenislandresort.com, www.gardenislandresort.com), which charges F$40 for a tee time, but is closer to **Taveuni Dive Resort** (tel. 891-1063, inquiry@taveunidiveresort.com, www.taveunidiveresort.com), which often takes its own guests there off the books. You can book and rent clubs through either.

FOOD

Most hotels in Taveuni are happy to accommodate outside guests for meals; resort entrees are typically F$20-30. Other eateries are listed below, from west to east along the main road. In either case, always call ahead for mealtimes, as most places are fairly small, and food is purchased and cooked to order. Supermarkets and hotel restaurants are your only options on Sundays.

Tramonto (Matei, tel. 888-2224, F$20-30), on a hilltop at the southwest end of the

Hike Across South Cape

Before you reach Vuna, the road detours left, looping inland and uphill to Delaivuna before returning to the coast and heading down through Navakawau before reaching Kanacea and Vuna again. In this area, you'll pass through massive coconut plantations, their neatly lined rows inhabited by some of Fiji's only Australian magpies (large, chatty black-and-white birds).

It's possible to make this detour a **hike,** if you're willing to ignore the Private Property signs—just be sure to close any gates that you open to prevent cattle from escaping.

From Vuna, take the morning bus and get off west of Paradise Taveuni. Follow the road up and east to Delaivuna, and then hike an hour down through the coconut plantation to a junction with two gates, just before a small bridge over a (usually) dry stream.

Continue walking 30 minutes down the road straight ahead across the bridge to reach **Salialevu,** site of the Bilyard Sugar Mill (1874-1896), one of Fiji's first. A tall chimney, boilers, and other equipment remain below the school. After a look around, return to the two gates at the bridge and follow the other dirt road southwest for an hour through the coconut plantation to Navakawau, where you can catch the bus back to Vuna.

tourist strip, serves up pizza, fresh fish-and-chips, stir-fried chicken, and other classics, along with beer. The view of the beach and Somosomo Strait from the open-air dining room is superb.

The best-stocked grocery store on the island is **Sun City Supermarket** (Matei, tel. 888-0462, Mon.-Sat. 0730-1800, Sun. 0800-1100). It also carries toiletries, and there's a bottle shop and petrol pump next door.

If you're farther west, the **Meridian Store** (Wairiki, tel. 888-0266, daily 0630-1730) and the **MH Supermarket** (Somosomo, tel. 888-0053) are also good options. MH has a small bakery and fast-food station.

Ria Poni's Wine & Dine Restaurant (Somosomo, tel. 888-0000, ponipate_ratumudu@yahoo.com) serves up soda, beer, wine, and hearty Indian, Fijian, and Chinese dishes such as chili chicken (F$8) in an unpretentious café environment.

ACCOMMODATIONS

Places to stay are scattered around the northern and northwestern coast of Taveuni, with a cluster within walking distance of the Matei airport. Listings under each price category below start at the Matei airport and go southwest.

Six proprietors have banded together to create a local booking service, **Taveuni Rental Accommodations** (www.fiji-rental-accommodations.com), where you can rent anything from a single room with a view to an entire four-bedroom villa with private pool. Most are around Matei. Owners may be on-site, as well as local staff; one even includes a car and driver/guide. Many of these properties are also listed on Airbnb, so compare rates, which range US$190-320 per night. Discounts kick in with stays longer than seven nights. One of these is Yanuyanu, a bungalow owned by Dolphin Bay Divers, which may put you up here if you're ending your dive vacation there with an early-morning flight out of Taveuni.

Under US$100

Bibi's Hideaway (Matei, tel. 888-0443 or 831-7253), about 600 meters south of the airport, has some of the gracious atmosphere of neighboring properties, but without the sky-high prices. The film crew making *Return to the Blue Lagoon* camped out here for three months, and with the extra income, the owners built a couple of *bures* on their lush, spacious grounds. It's F$50 to stay in their guestroom, F$130 for a small *bure* that sleeps two, and F$150 for the family cottage that can

1: the Waitavala Sliding Rocks **2:** posing at the international date line **3:** funnel-shaped corals in the Rainbow Reef.

1

SNL
2

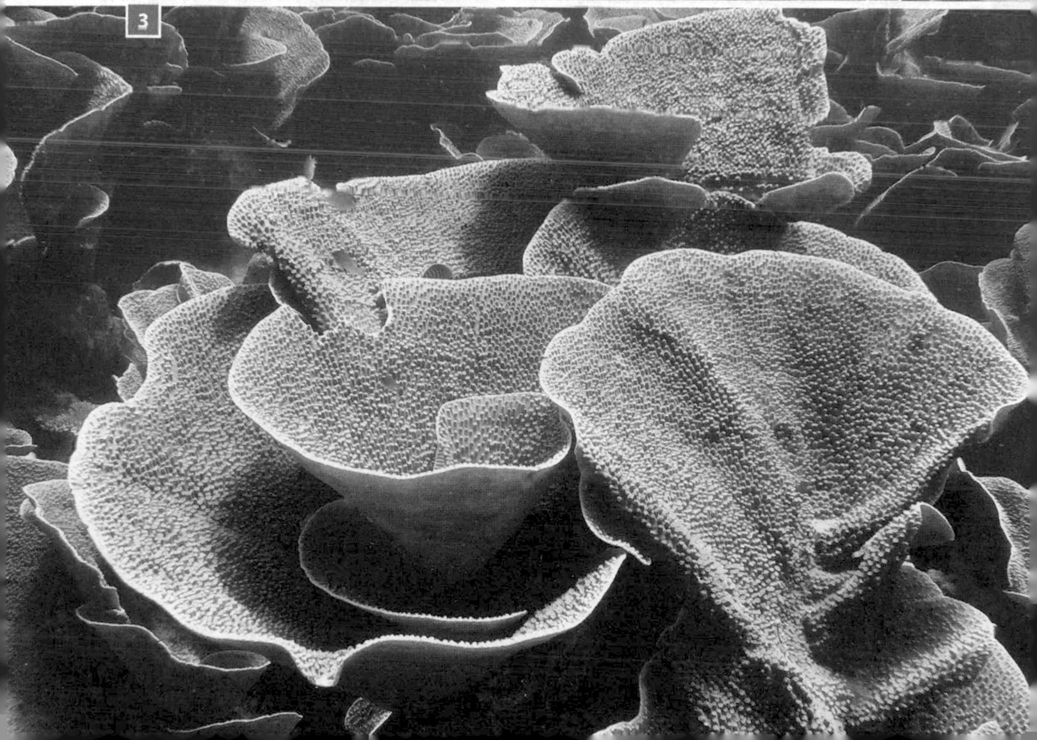
3

accommodate six people (tightly). Everyone has access to shared cooking facilities and a fridge. There is no pool or beach.

Maravu Lodge (Matei, tel. 888-0555, bula@travellersfiji.com, http://maravulodge.com) is a low-budget option with a five-star view. Everything's a bit shabby, but if you go with hostel-level expectations, you'll probably be satisfied. A bed in the dorm is F$38, and private rooms are F$120-260. It's set in the jungle, so there are sea views but no beach; it's about a 10-minute walk down to the beach. Wi-Fi, air-conditioning, and fans are available throughout, including in the dorm. There's a pool, bar, and occasional evening entertainment. Meals are monotonous here, but it's a fine base if you plan to be out and about. Bring insect repellent.

Guests at ★ **Bobby's Nabogiono Farm** (Vuna, tel. 923-8612 or 844-1097, nabogiono@yahoo.com.au) can enjoy good meals and excellent hiking all over the diverse property: through orchards and fields, up forested hills, and down toward the rocky coast. F$40 gets you a bed in a basic room in the old colonial-style house. Mealtimes are family-style, and you'll be woken in the mornings by abundant birdsong and jungle life. There is no pool or beach. This is the best place to experience the real Taveuni while still having some privacy, and you couldn't ask for a more knowledgeable guide than Bobby.

US$100-250

Coconut Grove Beach Cottages (Matei, tel. 888-0328 or 761-6999, ronna@coconutgrovefiji.com, www.coconutgrovefiji.com, US$195-265 d) has three fan-cooled *bures*, all just a few steps away from a white sandy beach. The rate includes transfers to the airport (just a few minutes away), kayaks, snorkel gear, and Wi-Fi in the gift shop. If you stay five nights, you get a free half-hour massage and a cooking class with the staff. A tasty all-inclusive meal plan is US$55 and includes packed lunches. They accommodate early check-in, but checkout is also early, and you'll be charged a half-day rate if you check out after 0900. If you book the smaller *bure* but the larger ones are vacant, they'll probably upgrade you. The **Coconut Grove Restaurant** gets rave reviews and is influenced by California cuisine; offerings change daily and can include anything from red Thai curry to homemade fettuccini to a lobster club sandwich.

Matei Pointe Resort (Matei, www.mateipointe.com) was under new ownership and closed for a much-needed overhaul at press time. Check the website for updates. The lovely site consists of freestanding bungalows opposite the airport.

Makaira by the Sea (Matei, tel. 888-0680, www.fijibeachfrontatmakaira.com, US$162-250) is actually located across the road from the sea, on a high bluff. It's a short hike down to a sandy bay where snorkeling and kayaking are available (and included in the rate). The house kayaks are outfitted for fishing, and you can have a speedboat tow you out to the best spots. Guests can help with the resort's coral reef gardening project. There are three *bures,* each with a private plunge pool, and a 10 percent discount is given for a seven-night stay. The larger *bure* has two bedrooms and can comfortably sleep four. Meals are of high quality, often sourced from the day's fishing charter, and a tuna catch results in sushi night; two of the cabins have kitchenettes if you prefer to cook. Plan to laze around for at least one morning to enjoy the sunrise from your bed—it's the best view on the island.

★ **Nakia Resort & Dive** (Nakia, tel. 888-1111, http://nakiafiji.com) sits on a bluff overlooking Somosomo Strait between Somosomo and Matei Airport. It's a true eco-resort run by a family from Northern California, harnessing wind and solar power (with generator backup) and home to an organic garden. It has three regular cottages (US$245-270 d), plus a spacious two-bedroom cottage that sleeps up to eight adults (US$450). Weekly rates are

---

1: the Catholic mission at Wairiki **2:** the view from the pool at the Garden Island Resort in Waiyevo **3:** a *lovo* (cooking) site) on Taveuni.

1

2

3

discounted about 40 percent, and seven-night dive/eat/sleep packages are available with the family-owned **Taveuni Ocean Sports** (tel. 867-7513), which is on-site. A two-tank dive is US$120 plus $20 if you're renting gear. There's a 40-foot pool but no beach. Baking is a specialty at the **Cliffhouse Restaurant,** which is organic.

★ **Garden Island Resort** (Waiyevo, tel. 888-0286, relax@gardenislandresort.com, www.gardenislandresort.com, F$440-520) was built as Taveuni's premier hotel by the Travelodge chain in the 1960s. It's been through a number of owners since, and the most recent, Hong Kong-based CHI, renovated it in 2009. A new manager hired in 2016 has brought some needed discipline back to the staff. The 30 air-conditioned rooms in an attractive two-story building all have unobstructed sea views. The patios of the ground-floor units open directly onto to a sandy beach with hammocks. Children under 12 are free when sharing with adults. There's an on-site dive shop. Airport transfers are F$40. Continental breakfast is included at the elegant, breezy **Garden Island Restaurant,** where sometimes there's a *meke* and *lovo* if enough paying guests are present. The restaurant is open to visitors 1200-1400 for lunch and 1900-2100 for dinner, but reservations are required, preferably a day ahead. It's the only non-cottage-style hotel on Taveuni.

Aroha Taveuni (Waiyevo, tel. 888-1882, www.arohataveuni.com, F$315 d), run by New Zealanders, is set on a reasonable beach just south of Wairiki Wharf. The two buildings have five air-conditioned rooms, each with its own bathroom as well as large outdoor showers; rooms can be configured with a king bed or two singles, or connected for larger groups. There's a 10-meter infinity pool, and the snorkeling offshore is good on an incoming tide. The seaside **Kai Time Restaurant** is a destination for its wood-fired pizzas and its Friday fish-and-chips night.

Taveuni Dive Resort (tel. 891-1063, inquiry@taveunidiveresort.com, www.taveunidiveresort.com, F$500) is at the center of the western coast, five kilometers south of Wairiki town. The eight fan-cooled bungalows, built in 2015, are more luxurious than at a typical dive resort. They're designed for couples but spacious enough to add a third if you like. The resort has no beach but a fine pool, and is set in a tropical garden environment on freehold land in Taveuni Estates (Soqulu Plantation), with sustainable practices including solar power (with backup generator), rainwater harvesting, and close monitoring of fuel consumption. It's American-run, so expect strong opinions from the management about what to do and how to do it during your stay. Stay-and-dive packages are the specialty, and the marina is just out back. It's a 10-minute walk through a swatch of jungle to the beach or to a nine-hole golf course. Airport transfers are F$30 per person, waived if you stay three nights or more. Guests can use free Wi-Fi at the restaurant, **The Salty Fox,** which serves up a range of Western and Fijian dishes either a la carte or as part of an all-inclusive meal plan (F$125).

Over US$250

Taveuni Palms (Matei, tel. 888-0032 or 891-5869, info@taveunipalms.com, www.taveunipalms.com, US$1,500 d) has two luxury villas on a high plateau above a white-sand beach and regularly wins awards in luxury travel categories. Each two-bedroom air-conditioned villa has its own plunge pool and spa, and is surrounded by a whole acre for privacy. Rates include meals, a one-hour massage, Wi-Fi, Bose speakers, airport transfers, some activities, and constant attention from your own personal staff of seven people per villa, including a nanny for children if you bring them. Alcohol, spa services, and activities requiring a boat with crew are extra. Stay-five-pay-four deals are often available, and it's pleasant to be dropped off for an afternoon at the private Honeymoon Island.

Taveuni Island Resort (Matei, tel. 888-0441 or 912-5574, resort@taveuniislandresort.com, www.taveuniislandresort.com) has received numerous awards as one of the top properties in the world. The original New Zealand proprietors, Dorothy and Ric Cammick, are widely credited with mapping and naming the Rainbow Reef, but there's no longer a dive shop on-site, and at press time the property was for sale. A pleasant cliffside lodge, pool, and lawns lead down to a beach. The luxurious *bures* include kitchenettes and boast ocean views from every bed. Rates start at US$1,143 and go up depending on the size of and view from your *bure*, and include meals and transfers. Discounts of 40 percent are often available. You can order room service 0630-2100.

The upper-crust **Tides Reach Resort** (Matei, tel. 888-2080, U.S. tel. 888/466-0740, info@tidesreachresort.com, www.tidesreachresort.com, US$875-1275 d), on the sea opposite Maravu Plantation, has two luxury villas with all the trimmings—Wi-Fi, flat-screen satellite TV, Belgian linens, robes, and more. There's an in-house dive shop as well as deep-sea fishing and spearfishing. It's owned by Malibu realtor Eytan Levin, originally from South Africa, and it must be said that the overall feel is more Malibu than Fiji. But the beach is sandy, the spa towels are fluffy, and it's the place to be on Taveuni for all-inclusive pampering.

★ **Paradise Taveuni Resort** (Vuna, tel. 778-0123, info@paradiseinfiji.com, www.paradiseinfiji.com) is a high-end dive resort and the southwesternmost accommodation on Taveuni, on beautifully landscaped grounds just before Vuna Point. It was almost entirely rebuilt after Cyclone Winston, and the new lodgings are luxurious without being ostentatious or overly sanitized. All of the 16 cottages have ocean views, a king bed, an outdoor shower over pretty lava rocks, a deck, and air-conditioning. The largest can accommodate up to three adults and two children. Rates start at F$825 for two people, but half-off specials are frequently available. Yachties will find a warm welcome here, as there are moorings offshore (call marine channel 16). There's a pool and a rocky beach with good snorkeling. Everything is artistically appointed by Australian expats Terri and Allan Gorton, who live across the road with their three Fijian children. Allan serves as the head chef and also runs the top-notch on-site dive shop, **Paradise Dive Centre.** The restaurant-bar is open to nonguests throughout the day and evening, and you can rent snorkel gear.

INFORMATION AND SERVICES

Bank South Pacific (Naqara, tel. 888-0433, weekdays 0900-1600) has the island's only ATM.

ZINTEC Computers (Naqara, tel. 912-3986, zinteccomputers@yahoo.com) sells components and camera memory cards, and can repair your devices in a pinch.

Taveuni's main **post office** and the **hospital** (tel. 888-0444) are in Waiyevo.

Eastern Taveuni

East of the swanky resorts of Matei is the wilder coast of Taveuni. There are villages here, but no hotels. The nature reserves of eastern Taveuni make it an ideal ecotourism destination, and four of its natural attractions have been set up as sustainable ecotourism projects that support the local communities. Local accommodations are possible at Lavena, and camping is available at Bouma and Waitabu.

TOP EXPERIENCE

★ BOUMA NATIONAL HERITAGE PARK

This important nature reserve between Bouma and Lavena villages was developed with New Zealand aid money, which put the land in trust for 99 years beginning in 1990. It covers 40 square kilometers and several distinct ecologies, from rainforest to beach. It's considered a model ecotourism development, as your tourist dollars allow the local communities to turn away offers from big logging companies who are always eyeing the rainforest. There are four distinct experiences, managed by four separate villages, and each one will entertain you for at least a half day if you go all in. They're closed on Sundays. They're described below from north to south.

Waitabu Marine Park

In the village of Waitabu is **Waitabu Marine Park** (tel. 820-1999 or 957-9876, www.waitabu.org), a lagoon area that has been declared a "no fishing" sanctuary. The F$30-75 per-person tour price includes snorkeling gear, transportation, lunch, and a knowledgeable local snorkeling guide. Discounts for children are available. The departure time varies according to tide and weather conditions, and sometimes the park is closed to allow the reefs to "rest." Snorkeling is not allowed at low tide, when fins can damage the reef. Call ahead, or book through a dive shop, as they sometimes run organized trips here. Because it's been a sanctuary for nearly two decades, the biodiversity is abundant, with a remarkable 298 species of hard coral and 1,198 species of reef fish in just 27 hectares of water and coastline. Snorkelers are guaranteed to see giant clams, which breed here, and likely to see silvertip reef sharks who come to dine on the abundant octopi and pelagic fish.

Vidawa Rainforest Hike

The challenging **Vidawa Rainforest Hike** (tel. 822-0361, 7 km/6 hrs. round-trip) starts at Vidawa village. Local guides introduce the birdlife, flora, and archaeological sites as you scramble over volcanic ridges offering spectacular views. Here you'll find ancient village sites with their temple platforms and ring ditches still clearly visible. Your guide brings it all to life with tales of the old ways of his people. Bring your own water and lunch (extra for the guide will be appreciated), and you'll have a pleasant picnic near a spring-fed stream deep in the interior. The trek ends at **Bouma Waterfalls,** where hikers are rewarded with a refreshing swim. The F$40 per-person cost includes park entry fees and a guide, and reservations by phone are necessary.

Bouma Waterfalls

The **Bouma Waterfalls,** also known as the Tavoro Falls, are just south of Bouma village (admission F$30 adults, F$10 children under 12). These three lovely, pristine falls are fit for swimming and clambering. From the information kiosk on the main road, it's an easy 10-minute walk on a broad path along the river's right bank to the lowest falls, which plunge 20 meters into a deep pool that you can swim in. Changing rooms, toilets, picnic tables, and a barbecue are provided.

A well-constructed trail leads up to a second falls in about 40 minutes, passing a spectacular viewpoint overlooking Qamea Island and Taveuni's northeast coast. You must cross the river once, but a rope is provided for balance. Anyone in good physical shape can reach this second falls with ease, and there's also a pool for swimming.

To reach the third falls, a muddy trail slip-slides for 40 minutes up across two rivers with just rocks—there's nothing to hold onto, and it would be unpleasant in the rain. But this trail cuts through the most beautiful portion of the rainforest with the richest birdlife, and these upper falls are perhaps the most impressive of the three: The river plunges over a black basalt cliff, which you can climb and use as a diving platform into the deep pool. The water here is very sweet.

Lavena Coastal Walk

At the end of the road—literally—lies the **Lavena Coastal Walk,** along the best beach on Taveuni. It's a great stroll even in the (frequent) rain. Start at the Lavena Lodge Visitor Center, located at the very end of the main road. Pay an admission fee

1: one of the Bouma Waterfalls **2:** the shoreline at Waitabu Marine Park.

beaches and only one Fijian village in the southwest corner. At high tide, when the sea is calm, some of Fiji's best snorkeling is here. There's even a two-hole golf course.

Accommodations

Naigani Island Resort (tel. 331-2433, www.naiganiresort.com), also known as "Mystery Island" (why? that's a mystery!), is on a shallow beach on the southeast side. There are 12 two-bedroom villas, running F$375 for a four-person garden villa or F$425 for a five-person beachfront villa, continental breakfast included. There are no TVs in the villas. The meal plans are F$60/75 per person for two/three meals, or you can order a la carte (no cooking facilities). Children under 13 are charged half price for meals and transfers. There's a swimming pool with a waterslide and special activities for children. Some nonmotorized water sports are free, but fishing trips cost extra. The day trip to Picnic Beach on Canabuli Bay at the north end of the island is F$35 per person (there's good snorkeling if you swim straight out). At the south end of the golf course is a sign indicating the start of a trail to the top of the southern hill on the island. There's a good view of the resort's bay 300 meters beyond the summit. Scuba diving, to sites like Nursery and Swim Through, costs F$210 for up to four tanks.

Getting There

From Suva, take a taxi to Natovi landing (F$120 one-way), then the boat to Naigani Island (F$70 pp round-trip). The 1300 Patterson Brothers bus can also take you to Natovi (F$5) if there's room.

From Levuka, call the resort and arrange to be collected by the speedboat at Taviya or Rukuruku villages on the northwest side of Ovalau (F$75 pp).

CAQALAI ISLAND

Caqalai Island (THANG-ga-lai) is a palm-fringed isle owned by the Methodist Church of Fiji, a short hop by boat from Ovalau. Visitors can dress up for Sunday choir service in the village church and enjoy the *lovo* that afternoon.

There's excellent snorkeling in turquoise waters all around the island, where the diverse coral reef sprawls about 30 meters from shore before the drop-off. Along the edge of tiny Snake Island, banded sea snakes congregate, along with octopuses and reef fish. If you have reef shoes, you can walk out on a sandbank to Snake Island at low tide: Enter the water to the

islets west of Ovalau in the distance

1

2

Tabua: The Treasured Tooth

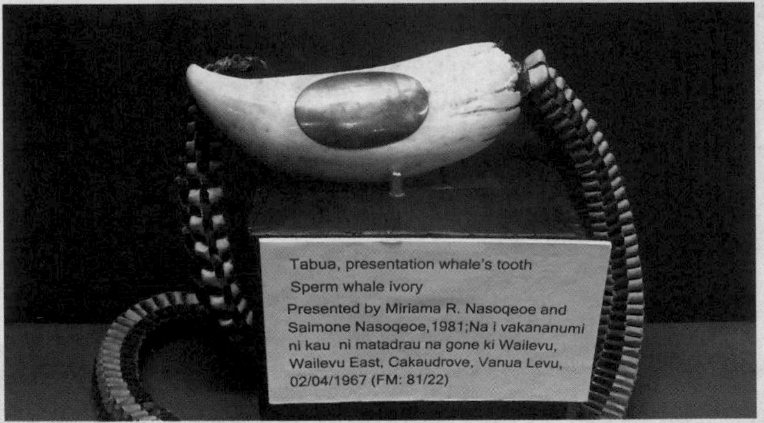
Tabua, presentation whale's tooth
Sperm whale ivory
Presented by Miriama R. Nasoqeoe and Saimone Nasoqeoe, 1981;Na i vakananumi ni kau ni matadrau na gone ki Wailevu, Wailevu East, Cakaudrove, Vanua Levu, 02/04/1967 (FM: 81/22)

tabua, a ceremonial whale's tooth

Teeth obtained from the lower jaw of the sperm whale, ***tabua,*** have always played an important part in Fijian ceremonies. In the 19th century, they were hung around the necks of warriors and chiefs during festivals, and were often buried with the men to continue their positions of high esteem in the afterlife. Today they are rarely worn, but are presented to distinguished guests and are exchanged at weddings, births, deaths, and reconciliations, as well as to seal an important pact. The color can range from a natural creamy shade to a rich brown, as they are sometimes smoked or rubbed with coconut oil and turmeric.

One of the earliest Western accounts of *tabua* comes from Taveuni, where a missionary describes several rituals in which a chief presented *tabua* to a priest at the Somosomo temple to seek the god's blessing for a series of upcoming battles—which he won. Later missionaries attempted to use *tabua* as currency, ignoring their religious significance, but had little success in persuading the chiefs to trade land, women, or goods in exchange for *tabua*.

Today, because whale teeth acquired ethically are so rare, it's illegal to trade in *tabua* or to take them out of the country without express permission from a number of government agencies. In the early 19th century, the European and American craze for "scrimshaw," the art of carving whalebone, resulted in thousands of fake *tabua* made from elephant and walrus tusks entering Fiji. Those ivories are also illegal to trade, so beware of transporting even replica *tabua*.

You can see several authentic *tabua* in the Fiji Museum in Suva, and they are often proudly displayed in glass cases at historical sites and chiefs' quarters throughout Fiji. The Royal Collection Trust in London holds a *tabua* that the Fijian Council of Chiefs presented to Queen Elizabeth II during her visit in 1953. The Duke and Duchess of Sussex (Prince Harry and Meghan Markle) were presented with a *tabua* during their 2018 tour of Fiji.

(F$25) to gain access to the walk. From the visitors center, you can hike the five kilometers down the Ravilevo Coast to **Wainibau Falls** (about 10 km/3 hrs. without stopping, round-trip).

You'll pass Naba village, where the descendants of blackbirded Solomon Islanders live to this day, and a suspension bridge over the Wainisairi River, which drains Lake Tagimoucia in Taveuni's interior. The last

15 minutes entail a scramble up a creek bed that can be very slippery. You'll then reach the Wainibau Falls, comprising two falls that plunge into the same deep basalt pool. During the rainy season you must actually swim a short distance to see the second pool. Diving into either pool is excellent fun. Be on guard while in the creek bed, as mild flash flooding often occurs; to be safe, keep to the left near the base of the falls. Several lovely beaches and places to stop are along the trail.

You can kayak here (F$65 pp), passing countless cliffs and waterfalls, or take a guided boat trip, which will run F$120-300 (depending on how many waterfalls you want to take in) for one or two people. Up to three more people can be added for a fee. The boat goes to the gorgeous **Savulevu Yavonu Falls,** which plummet off a cliff directly into the sea. These activities can be arranged at the visitors center.

ACCOMMODATIONS

There's a campground just 200 meters off the main road at the **Waitabu Marine Park** (tel. 820-1999), charging F$15 per person in your own tent. You can order meals at F$10 each or cook for yourself.

At the **Bouma Waterfalls,** visitors can camp by the river behind the park information kiosk (tel. 820-4709) at F$15 per head. Toilets and showers are provided. Meals can be ordered, or you can cook your own in a communal kitchen.

Lavena Lodge (tel. 820-3639 or 715-7682), next to Lavena village at the end of the bus route, is a basic building with running water (most of the time) and lantern lighting. A bed in one of the four rooms (two doubles and two three-bed dorms) is F$30 per person the first night, then F$20 per person additional nights—and the rate includes admission to the Lavena Coastal Walk, normally F$25. Sinks are provided in the rooms, but the bath is shared. Dinner can be ordered for F$10. The village was decimated by Cyclone Winston, and rebuilding has been slow. Two tiny trade stores are nearby, but it's better to bring groceries with you—as well as mosquito coils, which are essential.

Off Taveuni's Coast

Much of Taveuni's beauty is found underwater in the reefs and shoals that cover a vast, pristine marine area that stretches out past the surrounding islands. The rugged eastern coast of Vanua Levu, much of which is accessible only from Taveuni, and the outlying islands of Qamea, Matagi, and Laucala are favorites for travelers who want to be away from any hint of hustle and bustle, and who plan to spend most of their time on or beyond the beach. There is little commercial fishing or other activity here to despoil the waters.

There are several small upscale resorts, as well as a budget *bure* option on Qamea and a dive resort on Vanaira Bay. The islands of Matagi and Qamea are accessible only to guests of their own resorts.

EASTERN VANUA LEVU

The remote southeastern tip of **eastern Vanua Levu** is the closest spot to the premier dive sites of the Somosomo Strait, which makes it a divers' paradise. Some of it is accessible via a sinuous two-hour road trip along the Hibiscus Highway from Savusavu, but it's a much easier trip to fly into Taveuni and then take a boat the eight kilometers across the strait. Each of these resorts, whether budget or luxury, has a tiny-island feel because the coves are separate from each other, and many do not connect to Vanua Levu roads.

Dolphin Bay Divers Retreat (tel. 828-3001 or 992-4001, info@dolphinbaydiversfiji.com, www.dolphinbaydivers.com) is secluded and a true dive resort—there's little here to interest non-divers, but it's beautifully situated for the Rainbow Reef. It's one of the few places in Fiji where shore diving is possible, so you can go and visit the friendly "house turtles" without a guide (but always take a dive buddy!) for just F$40. Bamboo-and-hardwood *bures* are F$190 single or double, including mosquito nets. Jungle tents with mosquito screens and shared bathrooms are F$40 single, F$90 double, but some visitors have complained that their tents were not maintained, with holes in the screens or broken poles. Dive packages, including two tanks a day and shore diving, start at F$790 for three days. Accommodations are basic, but there is often Wi-Fi. Solar lighting results in dim indoor light, and the water system is unreliable, but staff try to make up for it by heating water over a fire and bringing it to you when you need it. Divers who don't mind the non-luxurious digs are euphoric about this place, with many returning year after year to see the stunning undersea sights. From Matei Airport, take a prearranged F$65 one-way transfer by boat across the eight kilometers of sea, to Vanaira Bay. (It's F$40-45 if you make your own way to one of the wharfs on Taveuni.)

Sau Bay Retreat (tel. 992-0051 or 992-0046, info@saubay.com, www.saubay.com) is a deluxe resort with just four cottages and a tent located on 100 acres overlooking a cove. It's owned by Nigel and Carol Douglas but ruled by their four friendly dogs. There are three cottages for couples (US$225), a two-bedroom, two-bathroom villa that sleeps up to six people (US$400), and a secluded, luxurious safari-style tent (US$450) for two adults only. Discounts are often available on third-party sites. All of the cottages have ocean views and mosquito nets, and it's F$35 extra if you turn on the air-conditioning. Meals are nicely presented, with fresh Fijian-influenced dishes and baked goods; you'll likely need a meal plan (F$110 adult/F$60 child per day), as there's nowhere else to dine on this cove. Honeymooners or recluses can opt for private meals on your patio or out on the beach. Excellent diving and fishing trips are extra. Airport transfers from Matei are F$90.

Viani Bay Resort (tel. 725-8184 or 725-8167, info@diveacademyfiji.com, www.diveacademyfiji.com) opened in late 2018 as a single 20-square-meter, solar-powered

Children attend school by boat in eastern Vanua Levu, accessible only from Taveuni.

bungalow with private veranda, owned by a German couple, Marina and Jone Walser. It's F$400 double or F$290 single, including a full meal plan. Transfers are arranged from Taveuni (a 20-minute taxi ride plus 15 minutes by boat) or Savusavu (a 1-hour taxi ride plus 40 minutes by boat). **Dive Academy Fiji** is based here.

The adults-only **Remote Resort** (Fiji tel. 802-2151, Aus. tel. 07/3040-2331, U.S. tel. 323/825-5005, request@theremoteresort.com, www.theremoteresort.com) occupies a 64-acre peninsula jutting into Buca Bay. A fan-cooled "villa" is US$563, while an air-conditioned "retreat" is US$744; both have king beds, private plunge pools, and a spacious 750-foot layout. Rates include a welcome foot rub, water/coffee/tea, guided snorkeling, nonmotorized watersports, and other activities. Meals are extra, either a la carte or US$120 for a meal plan—worthwhile if you're inclined toward the more expensive steak and lobster entrees. Transfers must be prebooked; it's US$95 from Savusavu or Labasa airport, or US$195 from Taveuni's Matei airport (one-way, per villa).

QAMEA ISLAND

Qamea Island (ngga-ME-a), just 3 kilometers east of Taveuni, is 10 kilometers long, with lots of lovely bays, lush green hills, and secluded white-sand beaches. At the beginning of the breeding season in late November or early December, land crabs *(lairo)* are harvested in abundance here during their migration to the sea. The birdlife is rich thanks to the absence of mongooses.

Accommodations

★ **Maqai Beach Eco Resort** (tel. 990-7761 or 834-0550, info@maqai.com, www.maqai.com), at the island's southern tip, is set up for surfers. It's a step up from "glamping," with nine simple *bures* that have en suite bathrooms. The Beachfront Bures (F$250) sleep one or two people, while the Family Beach Bures (F$350) can accommodate three adults, or two adults plus two children under age 12. The meal plan is F$110 per adult and FJ$75 per child, and much of the food comes from the organic garden on-site. It's all solar powered with generator backup. There are two surf breaks within 800 meters of Maqai's sandy beach, making it a great place to enjoy or even learn, perhaps through a five-night "awesome learner adventure package" (F$2,195-2,795), which includes three surf lessons, two boat trips to more remote surf breaks, five days of board rental, and a one-hour coconut back massage. Other activities include snorkeling, fishing, kayaking, hiking, and scuba diving if arranged with operators on Taveuni.

Young honeymooners are the target audience of the upscale **Qamea Beach Resort** (U.S. tel. 866/867-2632, Fiji tel. 888-0220, www.qamea.com, reservations online or via international phone only) on the island's west side. Guests must be 13 or older, and Honeymoon Bure guests must be 16 or older. This is a welcoming resort for gay and lesbian travelers. The 17 air-conditioned *bures* start at F$1,210 double for the Ocean View Bure, up to F$2,200 for the Royal Beach House. The minimum stay is usually seven nights, but there are sometimes five-night specials on the website. All units have a ceiling fan, mini-fridge, giant outdoor shower, lawn furniture, and hammock-equipped front deck. Rates include breakfast, or you can opt for an all-inclusive meal plan for F$274 per person. Meal plans must be booked at the time of reservation. Meals are served in a tall central dining room and lounge designed like a *burekalou* temple, and a trio sings around dinnertime. Drink prices are astronomical, so bring along a duty-free bottle. You can swim in the lava pools that emerge off Qamea's beach at low tide, and there's a small freshwater swimming pool. Some activities are included in the basic price, but tours to Taveuni, fishing, scuba diving, and spa treatments are extra.

Getting There

Hotels arrange round-trip transfers from Matei Airport to Qamea Island at F$160 per person; reserve at time of booking.

If you'd like to pop over on your own, outboards from villages on Qamea Island land near Navakacoa village on the northeast side of Taveuni. For a day visit, the best times to try for a ride over are Thursday and Friday afternoons. You won't be allowed to enter the resorts or villages, but you can stroll around the beaches.

MATAGI ISLAND

The tiny, horseshoe-shaped volcanic **Matagi Island** just north of Qamea features a sunken crater framed by a lovely palm-fringed bay. The 240-acre island is privately owned by the Douglas family, which has been producing copra on Matagi for five generations. In 1988, the family diversified into the hotel business.

Adults-only **Matangi Private Island Resort** (U.S. tel. 888/628-2644, tel. 888-0260 or 778-0061, info@matangiisland.com, www.matangiisland.com), 10 kilometers northeast of Taveuni, has three special tree house *bures* (US$770), usually reserved by honeymooners, and eight circular *bures* (US$500-860) scattered among the coconut palms below Matagi's high jungle interior. The layout makes each *bure* feel private. This resort went through some growing pains but has since turned around, and now gets high marks for those seeking quiet luxury, snorkeling, bird-watching, great meals, and attentive service. Divers can enjoy the local reefs, but it's a long boat ride (with a fuel surcharge fee) to reach the more famous dive sites in the Somosomo Strait. All-inclusive meal packages are an additional US$200 per *bure*, and transfers from Taveuni are F$188 round-trip. Children under 16 are not accepted. The website frequently offers deals including stay-seven-pay-five nights, dive packages, and wedding specials.

LAUCALA ISLAND

Laucala Island, which shares a barrier reef with Qamea, has a turbulent history. In the mid-19th century, the locals sided with Tongan chief Enele Ma'afu in his war against the chief of Taveuni. In retaliation, when the Taveuni chief won, he sold the 12-square-kilometer island to Europeans, who forced the entire local population to leave. They settled in other parts of Fiji, and their island eventually became the property of the Australian company Morris Hedstrom, which sold it to New York billionaire Malcolm Forbes for US$1 million in 1972. Forbes built the airstrip, wharf, and roads; knocked down the old village; and opened a small resort. He was buried on the island in 1990, and his former private residence stands atop a hill overlooking a copra-making village. During Fiji's 2000 coup, the resort managers were beaten and held captive for 24 hours. In 2003, the island was sold to Dietrich Mateschitz, the Austrian founder of the energy-drink producer Red Bull, for US$10 million. He reopened the exclusive resort in 2008.

Laucala Island Resort (tel. 888-0077, info@laucala.com, www.laucala.com) offers 25 luxurious *bures* with 1-3 bedrooms, all with private pools, starting at F$6,000 a day, with a minimum stay of three nights. Meals, drinks, a spa treatment, scuba diving, tennis, horseback riding, laundry, and just about everything else is included. There's even an 18-hole golf course designed by Scottish champion David McLay Kidd. The direct charter flight from Nadi will be extra.

The Lomaiviti Group

The Lomaiviti Group lies in the Koro Sea, right

between the two large islands of Viti Levu and Vanua Levu—yet these islets feel worlds away. Whether you're laid-back, nature-oriented, or a history buff, you'll find something to love here.

Lomaiviti ("central Fiji") has played a key role in Fijian history. The country's first capital, Levuka, was founded on the island of Ovalau in 1830 as a commercial whaling hub, and it became the center of British authority in 1874. Its well-preserved colonial architecture makes it distinctive among the South Pacific islands, and the entire town center was named a UNESCO World Heritage Site in 2013.

The climate here is moderate, neither as wet and humid as Suva, nor as dry and hot as Nadi. Of the group's nine main volcanic islands,

Highlights

Look for ★ to find recommended sights, activities, dining, and lodging.

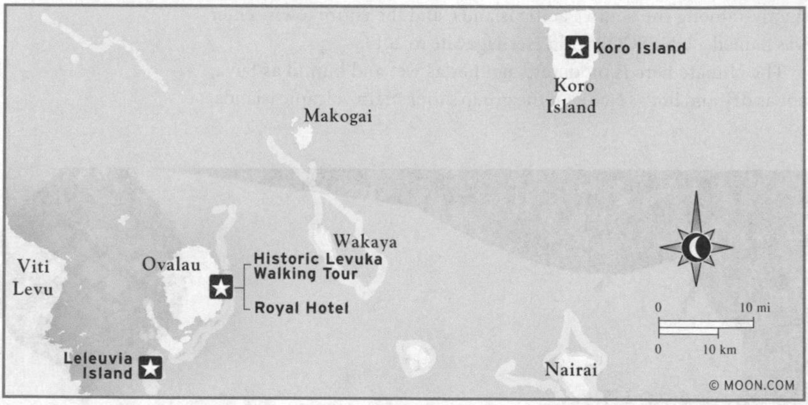

★ **Historic Levuka Walking Tour:** You'll feel like you're on a Wild West movie set while strolling through the historic sites of old Levuka town (page 294).

★ **Royal Hotel:** The South Pacific's oldest operating hotel hasn't changed much in the past century—and that's a good thing (page 296).

★ **Leleuvia Island:** One of Fiji's most authentic ecotourism destinations is also an art gallery, marine sanctuary, and outrigger sailing canoe base (page 305).

★ **Koro Island:** You can't get any closer to the "real Fiji" than this lush beautiful island (page 309).

Lomaviti Group

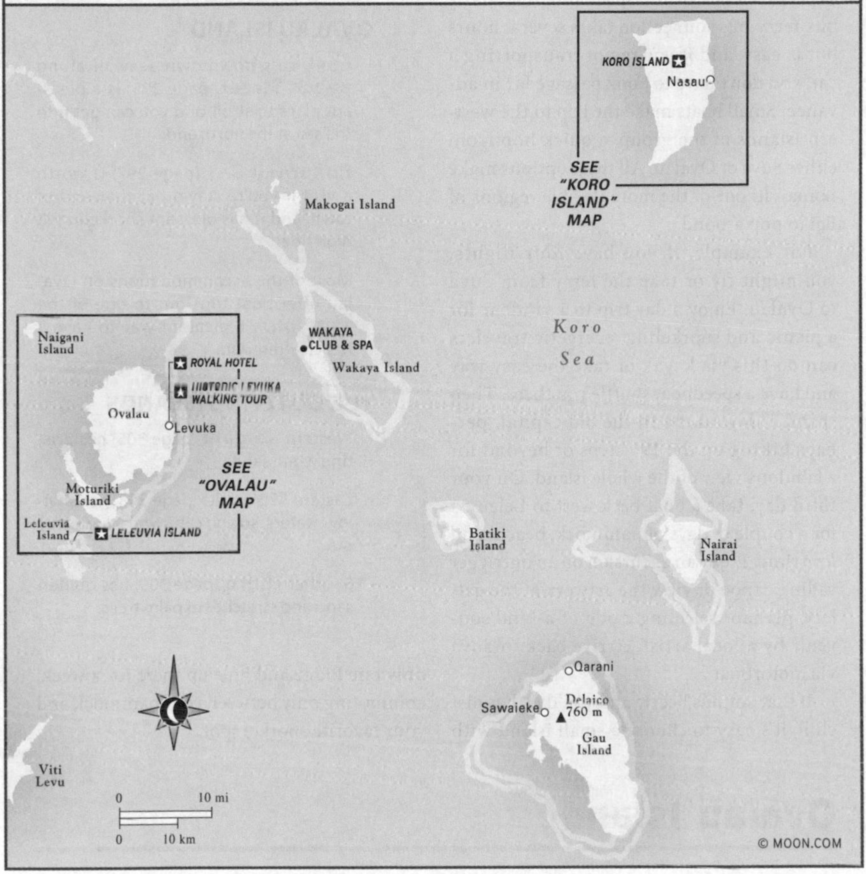

Ovalau, Gau, and Koro are among the largest in Fiji. The inner islands include both those with fully developed resorts and less developed islands that see only a few outsiders a year. The waters among them, particularly near the barrier reefs at Gau, Batiki, and Nairai, are filled with giant trevallies that can weigh up to 50 kilograms each, earning the Lomaiviti Group the reputation of being the "big fish" capital of Fiji.

To dive off any of the islands, you'll need to book a cruise on a liveaboard dive boat. There's excellent hiking on all these islands, and the small islands west of Ovalau (Caqalai, Leleuvia, and Yanuca Lailai) have good snorkeling. It's nice to just hang out on any of the quiet, peaceful islands of the Lomaiviti Group and enjoy the laid-back atmosphere.

PLANNING YOUR TIME

Levuka can be visited in a day trip from Suva if you fly over in the morning and back in

Previous: wild cassava fields at Kauwai Guesthouse on Ovalau; a storefront in downtown Levuka; the clock at the Church of the Sacred Heart in Levuka.

the afternoon. For a longer trip, there are accommodations at both the cheap and very expensive ends of the spectrum. The daily bus-ferry-bus connection takes several hours but is easy, and if you're not transporting a car, you don't have to book passage far in advance. Small boats make the trip to the western islands of the group, a quick hop from either Suva or Ovalau. All these options make Lomaiviti one of the more flexible regions of Fiji to pop around.

For example, if you have four nights, you might fly or take the ferry from Suva to Ovalau. Enjoy a day trip to a sandbar for a picnic and snorkeling; energetic travelers can do this via kayak or take the easy way and have a speedboat shuttle you there. Then spend a day taking in the old capital, perhaps hiking up the 199 steps or beyond for a fabulous view of the whole island. On your third day, take a boat back west to Leleuvia for a couple of days of hammock, beach, and *lovo* time. Enjoy an excursion on an outrigger sailing canoe or view the artwork at the gallery, perhaps selecting a one-of-a-kind souvenir by a local artist. Arrive back in Suva via motorboat.

If that sounds hectic and you'd rather just chill, it's easy to choose a small island with only one lodge and hole up there for a week, commuting only between your hammock and your favorite snorkel spot.

Find Your Beach

OVALAU ISLAND

- **Levuka**'s downtown seawall along **Beach Street** (page 295) is a pleasant place to stroll, and you can get into the sea at the north end.
- **Rukuruku Bay** (page 297) is worth a visit if you're staying at that end of town, and it has pleasant snorkeling at high tide.
- Most of the accommodations on Ovalau offer boat trips out to one of the **sandbars,** a pleasant way to have a beach afternoon.

THE OUTLYING ISLANDS

- Western **Naigani** (page 305) has pristine white sand.
- Eastern **Moturiki** (page 308) has shallow waters, so you can swim a long way out.
- Southern **Koro** (page 309) has golden sand and stretches of palm trees.

Ovalau Island

Ovalau Island, a large volcanic island just east of Viti Levu, is the main island of the Lomaiviti Group. Almost encircled by high peaks, the Lovoni Crater forms a deep valley in the center and is essentially the only flat land on the island. Its rim is pierced by the Bureta River, which escapes through a gap to the southeast. The highest peak is 626-meter Nadelaiovalau ("the top of Ovalau"), behind Levuka. Alas, the hiking trail across the center was washed out by Cyclone Winston.

Ovalau lacks the magnificent beaches found elsewhere in Fiji, which has kept the package-tour crowd away, and upscale scuba divers have better places to go—so it's still one of the most peaceful, pleasant, picturesque, and historic areas to visit and relax in the South Pacific.

LEVUKA

The town of **Levuka** is Fiji's first UNESCO World Heritage Site, designated in 2013 as "an outstanding example of late 19th century Pacific port settlements." Founded as a whaling settlement on Ovalau's east side in 1830, Levuka became the main center for European traders in Fiji, and a British consul was appointed in 1857. The cotton boom of the 1860s

Ovalau Island

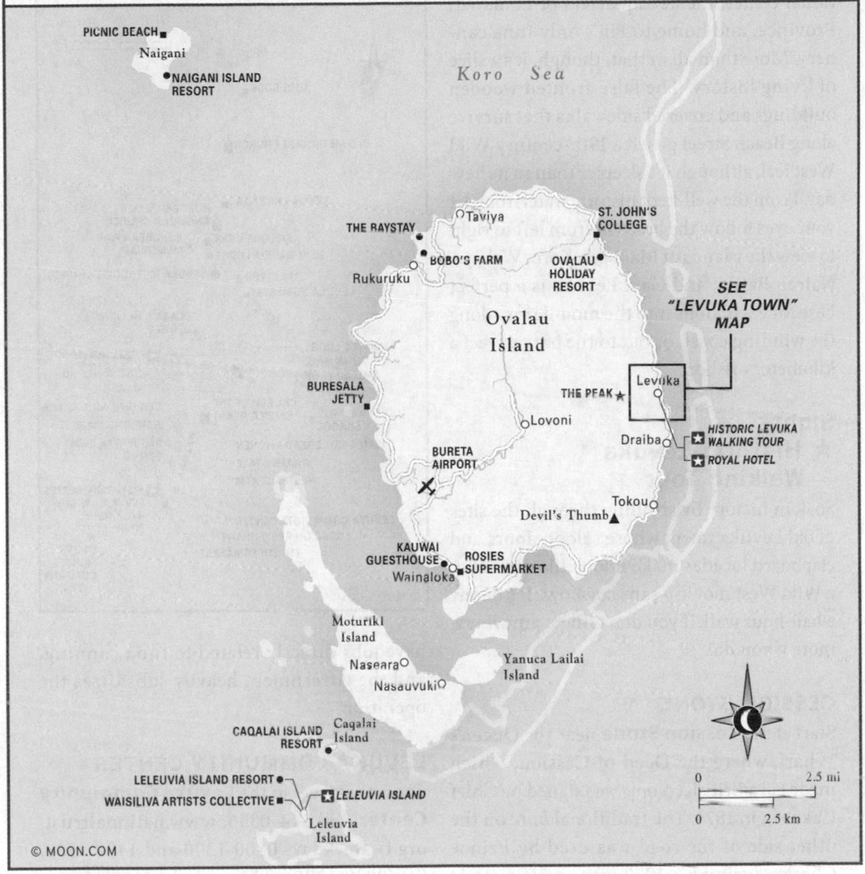

brought new settlers, and Levuka quickly grew into a boisterous town, with 60-plus saloons opening their swinging doors to entertain sailors and ship passengers along Beach Street. Escaped convicts and debtors fleeing creditors in Australia swelled the throng, until it was said that a ship could find the reef passage into Levuka by following the empty gin bottles floating out on the tide. The honest Aussie traders felt the need for a stable government, so in 1871 Levuka became the capital of Cakobau's Kingdom of Fiji. The rogue white traders countered by forming Fiji's one and only chapter of the Ku Klux Klan, and resolved to mount armed resistance against any form of indigenous Fijian authority.

The conflicts in Levuka subsided with the British annexation of Fiji on October 10, 1874. While Ovalau's central location seemed ideal for trade, the lush green hills that rise behind the town did not allow for expansion of the city. In August 1882, Governor Sir Arthur Gordon moved his government to Suva. Levuka remained the collection center for the Fiji copra trade right up until 1957, after which it converted to fishing in 1964.

Today Levuka is a quiet, quirky place, where smoking is not allowed at all, but drinking outdoors is permitted (unlike elsewhere on Ovalau). It's a minor educational center, the headquarters of Lomaiviti Province, and home to Fiji's only tuna cannery. More than all of that, though, it's a slice of living history. The false-fronted wooden buildings and covered sidewalks that survive along Beach Street give it a 19th-century Wild West feel, although it's sleepier than in its heyday. From the well-kept historic waterfront, let your eyes follow the horizon from left to right to view the islands of Makogai, Koro, Wakaya, Nairai, Batiki, and Gau. Levuka is a perfect base for excursions into the mountains, along the winding coast, or out to the barrier reef a kilometer offshore.

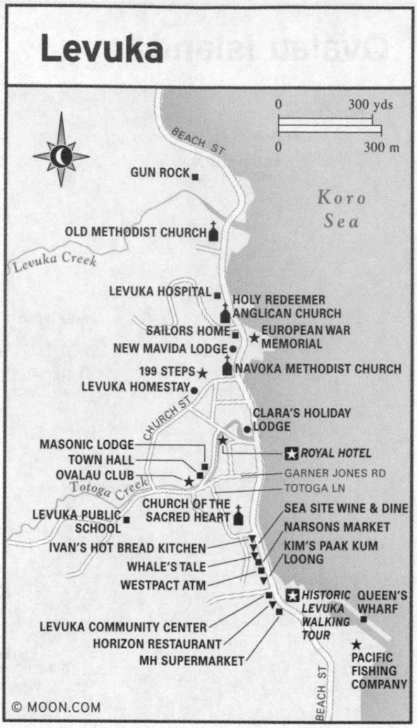

Sights

★ Historic Levuka Walking Tour

Soak in history by strolling through the sites of old Levuka town, whose saloon doors and clapboard façades make it look like the set of a Wild West movie—sans cowboys. It's barely a half-hour walk if you don't linger anywhere, more if you do.

CESSION STONE

Start at the **Cession Stone** near the Queen's Wharf, where the Deed of Cession, which made Fiji a British colony, was signed by Chief Cakobau in 1874. The traditional *bure* on the other side of the road was used by Prince Charles during his 1970 visit to officiate at Fiji's independence. The huge building with a blue roof next door is the venue of provincial council meetings. The nearby European-style bungalow is **Nasova House** (1869), the former Government House, or residence of the governor.

To the south, away from town, you can see the busy plant of the **Pacific Fishing Company,** founded by a Japanese firm and now owned by the Fiji government; it supplies the U.S. seafood company Bumble Bee in San Diego, California. Nearly 1,000 residents of Ovalau (85 percent of them women) have jobs directly related to tuna canning, and the government heavily subsidizes the operation.

LEVUKA COMMUNITY CENTER

Cross the street to the **Levuka Community Center** (tel. 344-0356, www.nationaltrust.org.fj, weekdays 0800-1300 and 1400-1630, Sat. 0830-1300). This was the first Morris Hedstrom general store, erected by Percy Morris and Maynard Hedstrom in the 1880s, great-granddaddy of today's Pacific-wide MH chain. The store closed when the lease expired in 1979, and the building was turned over to the National Trust, which reopened it as a museum and library in 1981. Cannibal forks, clay pots, and old photos vie for your attention. Some relics of the *Joyita,* a mysterious "ghost ship" whose crew and goods disappeared without a trace in Samoan waters in 1955 and was towed to Fiji for investigation, are on display here. Admission is by

Hikes Around Levuka

THE PEAK

If you want a real workout with some rewarding views, hike to the Peak, the picturesque green hill that's visible from much of Levuka.

From the Levuka Public School, continue straight up Garner Jones Road for about 20 minutes, past the lovely colonial-era houses, and you'll eventually reach a gate at the entrance to the town's water catchment. You may see a No Trespassing sign here, but everyone ignores it. A trail on the right immediately before the gate leads to a **pool** in the river below the catchment where you can swim. Look overhead for the swallows that live in a cave just upstream. The path to the Peak branches off to the left between a large steel water tank and the gate at the end of the main trail.

It takes about an hour to scale the Peak through the dense brush, and an experienced guide is the best way to go (arranged through your hotel or the Levuka Community Center). At the end of the challenging hike, you'll have a view over much of the island's east side.

LOVONI TRAIL

One of Fiji's most rewarding hikes begins at Draiba village, a kilometer south of the Cession Monument. A road to the right, around the first bend and just after a small bridge, marks the start of the 4.5-hour hike through enchanting forests and across clear streams to **Lovoni,** a region of six villages in the crater of the extinct volcano. Go straight back on the side road. At the end of the road, the unmarked Lovoni trail begins at the foot of the hill. This trail is no longer used by the locals and requires attentiveness to follow, so consider hiring a guide if you're not a very experienced hiker. Be sure to reach Lovoni before 1500 to be able to catch the last carrier back to Levuka.

If you go with a guide, they may recommend that you enter the Lovoni valley by another route, either up a five-kilometer dirt road starting from the Bureta airstrip, or from the north at Bobo's Farm; follow local advice about which trail is best for the season.

donation; the Community Center receives no funding, so history lovers keep this place going. Here you can also request a guide for other Levuka sights and hiking trails.

BEACH STREET

Stroll north on **Beach Street,** stopping if you like for a drink or a meal. This street includes Fiji's first newspaper (1869), bank (1876), and municipal council (1877). The seawall protecting the street and storefronts was originally constructed by the Royal Engineers in 1874.

CHURCH OF THE SACRED HEART

The wall ends at the **Church of the Sacred Heart,** erected by French Marist priests who arrived in 1858. The church's square stone tower was added in 1898 to commemorate the first priest. Its green neon light lines up with another green light farther up the hill to guide mariners into port. The tower's clock strikes the hour twice, with a minute interval in between. Through the gate behind the church is the formidable **Marist Convent School** (1882), originally a girls' school operated by the sisters and still a primary school.

TOWN HALL

Totoga Lane leads north from the convent to a small bridge over Totoga Creek and the **Ovalau Club** (1904), adjoining the old **Town Hall** (1898), also known as Queen Victoria Memorial Hall. Next to the town hall is the gutted shell of the **Masonic Lodge building,** erected in 1913 but burned down in 2000 by parishioners from Lovoni whose preacher told them it was a center of devil worship.

LEVUKA PUBLIC SCHOOL

Follow Garner Jones Road west up the creek to **Levuka Public School** (1881), the birthplace of Fiji's present public education system. Before World War I, the only Fijians allowed to attend this school were the sons of chiefs. The school was rebuilt after a 2005 fire.

CHURCH STREET

Turn left onto Church Street, and follow it around past the Nasau Park sports field—the site of the original Fijian village here. You can catch Sunday service at 1015 at the active **Navoka Methodist Church** (1862). Beside this church, 199 steps ascend Mission Hill to Delana Methodist High School. The original mission school formed here by the Reverend John Binner in 1852 was the first of its kind in Fiji. A stairway leads down through the high school to the hospital.

EUROPEAN WAR MEMORIAL

On a low hill farther north along the waterfront is the **European War Memorial,** which recalls British residents of Levuka who died in World War I. The 1870s cottage on the hilltop across the street from the monument is called **Sailors Home,** after the steamship that worked the England-to-China route in the 1850s. The **Holy Redeemer Anglican Church** (1904) farther north has period stained glass windows.

OLD METHODIST CHURCH

Follow the coastal road north from Levuka to a second bridge, where you'll see the **old Methodist church** (1869) on the left. Ratu Cakobau worshipped and converted to Christianity here. In the small cemetery behind the church is the grave of the first U.S. consul to Fiji, John Brown Williams (1810-1860).

TOMB OF AN OLD KING

Levuka Creek here marks the town's northern boundary. In the compound across the bridge and beneath a large *dilo* tree is the **tomb of an old king** of Levuka. The spacious house in front of the tree is the residence of the present Tui Levuka, chief of this area; don't enter the compound without permission.

GUN ROCK

Directly above this house is **Gun Rock,** atop which early Fijians had a fort. In 1849 the captain of the HMS *Havanah* used it as target practice for his ship's cannon, in a show of force intended to intimidate the local chiefs. Ask permission of the Tui Levuka (the "Roko") or a member of his household to climb Gun Rock for a splendid view of Levuka. If a small boy leads you up and down, it wouldn't be out of place to give him something for his trouble.

★ Royal Hotel

Circle back into town to end your tour with refreshments at the **Royal Hotel** (Robbies Lane, Levuka, tel. 344-0024, royal@connect.com.fj, www.royallevuka.com), a long wooden building alongside Totoga Creek. Originally built in 1852, the Royal is the oldest operating hotel in the South Pacific.

It was destroyed by fire and rebuilt on its original foundations in 1913 by Captain David Robbie, with extra-thick walls to resist the elements. It's the last of the 60 saloons that once lined Levuka's raucous waterfront, and the long wooden bar on the main floor looks like something straight out of a Hollywood Western. In the lounge, ceiling fans revolve above the rattan sofas and potted plants, and Fijian artifacts and historical photos hang from the walls. Generations of Levuka locals have played on the century-old billiard table. The platform on the roof is a widow's watch, where wives would watch for the overdue return of their husbands' ships.

Non-guests can visit for meals (a toasted sandwich is just F$3.50) or just wander through the atmospheric dining room on the main floor (open to the public).

NORTH OF LEVUKA

Shipwreck

As you drive up the road from Levuka, you'll see a wreck on the beach as you round the bend at Toki village: the *Sinu-i-Wasa Tolu,* run aground by Cyclone Winston. No one is taking responsibility for cleaning up the wreck, although the owner of Ovalau Holiday Resort aspires to turn it into a casino—which seems unlikely. This shoreline is a public swimming spot.

Waitovu Village

About two kilometers north, at **Waitovu village,** there's a beautiful deep pool and waterfall. You may swim here, but don't skinny-dip, and avoid arriving on a Sunday.

Mausoleum and Stone Church

At Cawaci, farther north, is a small white **mausoleum** (1922) high up on a point, with the tombs of Fiji's first and second Catholic bishops. The large coral **stone church** (1893) of St. John's College is nearby. This is the original seat of the Catholic Church in Fiji, and the sons of the Fijian chiefs were educated here from 1894 onward. The French-style church's walls are three meters thick around the buttresses.

Rukuruku Bay

You'll need to catch a ride to the bay near Rukuruku village, which has a pleasant **beach** where **snorkeling** is possible at high tide. Toilets and day showers are available for a fee at **The Baystay** (tel. 803-8789 or 360-9569, www.thebaystayfiji.com).

SOUTH OF LEVUKA

Town Cemetery

If you continue south on the main road, you'll come to the old **Town Cemetery.** Many of the graves here date back to the early colonial period.

Devil's Thumb

A few kilometers farther is the **Devil's Thumb,** a dramatic volcanic plug towering above **Tokou village,** one of the scenic highlights of Fiji. Catholic missionaries set up a printing press at Tokou, five kilometers from Levuka, in 1889 to produce gospel lessons in Fijian. In the center of the village is a sculpture of a lion made by one of the early priests.

RECREATION

Beaches

You'll need to catch a ride to the bay near Rukuruku village, which has a pleasant **beach** where **snorkeling** is possible at high tide. Toilets and day showers are available for a fee at **The Baystay** (tel. 803-8789 or 360-9569, www.thebaystayfiji.com).

Swimming Holes

From the Levuka Public School, continue straight up Garner Jones Road for about 20 minutes, past the lovely colonial-era houses, and you'll eventually reach a gate at the entrance to the town's water catchment. You may see a No Trespassing sign here, but everyone ignores it. A trail on the right immediately before the gate leads to a **pool** in the river below the catchment where you can swim. Look overhead for the swallows that live in a cave just upstream.

At high tide, the **river mouth** near the Royal Hotel is a popular swimming hole for the local kids (and some tourists). The rest of the day, some locals cool off by just sitting in the water fully dressed.

About two kilometers north, at **Waitovu village,** there's a beautiful deep pool and waterfall. You may swim here, but don't skinny-dip, and avoid arriving on a Sunday.

Tours

The two-hour **Historical Town Tour** from the Levuka Community Center (Beach St., tel. 344-0356) operates Monday-Friday at 1000 and 1400, Saturday at 1000, and costs F$10 per person. Groups of four or more can book a tour on Sunday by prearrangement.

For a **guided walking tour**, contact Noa "Nox" Vueti (tel. 344-0777), a staff member of Levuka Homestay. Possibilities include a more extensive historical town tour, a hike up the Peak, a seven-kilometer beach hike from Cawaci in the north back down to Levuka, or a plantation walk with botanical information.

Day visitors are welcome to book a tour at **Bobo's Farm** (tel. 993-3635 or 947-2277, bobosfarm@connect.com.fj, www.bobosfarm.

WHALE'S TA
RESTAURAN
KISHORE INVESTMENT LTD
WHOLESALERS & RETAILERS
SUPERMARKET
HARDWARE
1

2

3

4

Human Trafficking of the 1800s

The people of Ovalau, as elsewhere in the South Pacific, suffered from "blackbirding"—the practice of kidnapping and selling people to labor on plantations throughout the region, usually for designated periods of indenture.

Wainaloka village on the southwest side of Ovalau is inhabited by descendants of Solomon Islanders from the Lau Lagoon region whom European planters blackbirded more than a century ago. After their enslavement ended, and with no way to return home, they settled on Ovalau.

The people of the **Lovoni valley** were renowned for their resistance to colonial influence. They were the only tribe that the legendary Ratu Cakobau could not subdue by military might. In 1855, they burned down the European trading outpost of Levuka, and continued to make incursions until 1871. Cakobau finally defeated them through trickery: During a purported "truce," his soldiers captured them, then sold them off. Most entered the well-established blackbirding system and were trafficked to European-owned plantations on Ovalau and elsewhere as enslaved laborers.

At the same time, the American railroad circus of Barnum, Coup, and Costello purchased three people from Lovoni, on a three-year lease: a priest with dwarfism and two warriors. A slain Lovoni chief's "battle arm" was also sold. These joined the circus's "Feejee mermaid" hoax, actually the top half of a monkey skeleton stitched to the bottom half of a fish skeleton, which drew crowds into the freak show where the Lovoni people were forced to perform. The priest died within a year, and the two warriors never returned home. A photo of them is at the Fiji Museum in Suva.

The sale of the Lovoni people brought nearly 6,000 British pounds into Cakobau's coffers—conveniently, about the same amount he needed to pay off his debts to the trader colonists, at least for a while. With the last holdout tribe out of the way, four years later Cakobau and the now-united chiefs ceded the country to the British. The new government ended the enslavement policy, and the surviving Lovoni villagers returned to their valley, where their descendants live today.

com) near Rukuruku, in the northeast. Bobo knows the island inside and out. Possibilities, depending on tides and weather, include a trek to the natural waterslides, a hike up to the ruins of a fort surrounded by ancient vesi trees, a beach picnic at the Naigani Island lagoon, or a spearfishing trip (F$35-150 pp).

Tutu, aka David Kirton of **Tutu's Tours and Taxi** (tel. 994-8766), can show you the island or just drive you to where you need to go.

EVENTS

In October, Vodafone sponsors the weeklong **Back to Levuka Carnival,** with a Ferris wheel, beauty pageant, music, and food stalls. A highlight is the reenactment, with period costumes and pomp, of the somber ceremony on October 10, 1874, in which the high chiefs of Fiji signed the deed of cession to Queen Victoria. A translation was read aloud in Fijian, and two copies of the English deed were signed, one kept in the National Archive in Suva, the other in London. Ratu Cakobau presented Her Majesty's representatives with his ancient war club, symbolizing the end of traditional Fijian law and submission to the principles of Western rule.

1: the storefronts of downtown Levuka **2:** The 1874 Cession Stone **3:** 199 steps off of Church Street, leading up to Fiji's first mission school **4:** the bay at Rukuruku.

SHOPPING

There's no leisure shopping on Ovalau, but a few places supply the necessities.

MH supermarket (Beach St., Levuka, tel. 344-0467) is on the southern end of the downtown strip.

Narsons Market (Beach St., Levuka, tel. 344-0664, Mon.-Sat. 0900-1800, Sun. 0900-1000), next door to the Whale's Tale, has general goods and some electronics. You can buy camera memory cards here.

On the western side of Ovalau, **Rosies**

Supermarket (near Wainaloka village on the main road) opened in 2018 and is operated by the owners of the Kauwai Guesthouse, importing fresh produce and other goods via the Patterson ferry from Viti Levu.

FOOD

Outside the accommodations, all the island's eateries—four restaurants and a few takeaway stalls—are in Levuka town along Beach Street.

★ **Horizon Restaurant** (tel. 344-0429, Mon.-Sat. 0800-1400 and 1700-2100, Sun. 1700-2100), at the southern end of town next to the MH supermarket, is owned by Sarojani Devi. She was the longtime chef at its predecessor, Koromakawa, and many locals still know the restaurant by that name. Prawn curry with capsicum (green bell peppers), tuna steaks, delicious pizzas, and more are served for lunch and dinner. The club area of the restaurant is relaxed and modern, with air-conditioning, and is popular with locals, expats, and tourists alike.

Whale's Tale (tel. 344-0235, Tue.-Sat. 0930-1400 and 1800-2100, Sun.-Mon. 1800-2100, F$9-13.50) serves burgers, wraps, and pastas. There's a three-course special (F$27.50) offered at dinner. You can get a beer with your meal, and the percolated coffee is the best in town. They also sell bags of pounded kava (F$2).

Sea Site Wine & Dine (tel. 344-0553, Mon.-Sat. 1100-1400 and 1800-2000, closed Sun., F$10-15) has a very diverse menu, with spicy fried chicken, curries, pizza, chop suey, ceviche, sushi, and fish-and-chips. The front of the building is for fast food, takeaway, and ice cream, and the back is a full restaurant and bar (with air-conditioning). The Sea Site delivers if you're staying in town.

Ivan's Hot Bread Kitchen & Café (no phone) looks like a shop with biscuits and packaged foods, until you notice the fresh baked goods at the counter. Savory and sweet pastries are the specialty, sometimes with a festive dose of food coloring. There's no seating. It's one of the only storefronts open on Sundays.

Kim's Paak Kum Loong (tel. 344-0059, Mon.-Sat. 0700-1500 and 1700-2100, Sun. 1800-2100, F$15) is just fine for Chinese food and some Western dishes, but the real draw is the people-watching from the open-air veranda. Sometimes there's a noisy diesel generator running. There's no alcohol license, but you can bring your own or ask a waiter to bring you a beer from the supermarket next door. Everyone feels free to request dishes not on the blackboard menu. Portions are large but service is sometimes slow.

ACCOMMODATIONS

Under US$50

For the full colonial throwback experience, stay at the **Royal Hotel** (Robbies Lane, Levuka, tel. 344-0024, royal@connect.com.fj, www.royallevuka.com). The 15 fan-cooled rooms with private bath upstairs in the original colonial building are shabby-chic, with much-needed mosquito nets provided, but there's cold water only. Each room in the main building is in a different style, some with balconies facing the green mountainsides of Ovalau, others overlooking the Koro Sea, so check out your room first; there are singles (F$35.20) and doubles (F$58.30). The newer section has air-conditioned cottages arranged around a pool at F$99-F$157.50. Rooms there are big enough for 3-6 people; some have kitchenettes. The bar, beer garden, snooker tables, dartboards, pool, gym, and movie nights are strictly for guests, but outsiders can come for meals or just wander through the atmospheric dining room on the main floor (open to the public). Service can be inconsistent.

★ **Kauwai Guesthouse** (near Wainaloka village, tel. 710-5437 or 999-2321, kauwaifiji@gmail.com, www.kauwai.com), 10 kilometers southwest of the ferry landing, is operated by the charming Cloud Voigt and David Patterson. It was David's grandmother's home, converted by the energetic young couple into a low-key spiritual eco-retreat. There are no gurus or hard-sell courses here, and it's not fancy, but the beautiful yoga pavilion looks out on flawless sunsets and starry nights. Cloud (Claudia), who is from Germany, met David at a yoga retreat in Rishikesh, India, and both are certified teachers. They share a passion for educating visitors about Fiji's natural ways. Hammock chairs hang from trees on the wide lawn, and you can take kayaks out yourself, or pay extra for a boat trip for fishing or to lounge at a sandbar. A couple of bedrooms in the main house are available, and an outlying dorm has two separate rooms; mosquito nets are provided. It's F$50 per person for a double-occupancy room with its own bathroom, or F$40 per person for a double- or triple-occupancy room, with a bathroom/shower shared home-style. There's also a refreshing outdoor shower with rainwater catchment. The food is local and tasty, with each ingredient selected with care. Breakfast is included, and lunch (F$15 vegetarian) and dinner (F$20 pescatarian) are also delicious. Non-yogis are always welcome, and yoga fans can join the mailing list to learn about upcoming yoga weeks. Groups can rent a whole building and, depending on how cozy you want to be, the price would work out to barely F$10 per person per night for up to 12 people.

Clara's Holiday Lodge (Beach St., tel. 344-0013, 907-4975, or 762-1295) is a low-slung building at the far northern end of Beach Street, and you can cross the road to dip in the sea here. It's basic and a little run-down, but very clean, and more spacious inside than it looks. European budget travelers seem to find their way here, and locals may know it by the old name, Mary's Lodge. Breakfast is included for all, whether you're in a dorm (F$25) or in a single/double/triple room (F$40/55/75). Meals are offered, but it's just as easy to walk a few steps to town. You can cook here for F$10 per stay. Alcohol isn't allowed on the premises. They'll do your laundry for F$15 per load.

★ **Bobo's Farm** (tel. 993-3635 or 947-2277, bobosfarm@connect.com.fj, www.bobosfarm.com) near Rukuruku provides accommodations for four people in a two-room garden bungalow at F$60/80 single/double, plus F$13/15/22 for breakfast/lunch/dinner. There's also a small kitchen you can use, and two hot-water bathrooms. Owners Karin and Bobo Ahtack live on-site and are fantastic guides to the farm, natural landscape, and the island as a whole. You can relax in the lush, rambling premises, hike to the Na Vu Wai waterslides and waterfall for a swim, or snorkel on the coast. For a fee, Bobo can take you to a sandbank where the snorkeling is even better, or out to an islet for line fishing and spearfishing. Bobo's is an excellent choice for families—children love this place and can splash in a shallow swimming pool. Drinking water from the wells is pure and fresh. This could be the best place in the country to get a feel for rural Fiji without staying in a village.

US$50-100

New Mavida Lodge (Beach St., tel. 344-0477, newmavidalodge@connect.com.fj) is clean and modern, and a good base for exploring town. It is constructed from solid concrete, done so after a fire leveled the old Mavida Lodge. The nine air-conditioned rooms with TVs and modern bathrooms are F$86 double. The two ocean-view rooms upstairs are F$162, and there's also a 10-bed dorm with separate male/female washrooms at F$27 per bed. All rates include an ample breakfast and you can order dinner. There's a communal kitchen and fridge.

The new ★ **Ovalau Holiday Resort** (tel. 344-0329/930-0874/996-7766, ohrfiji@gmail.com, https://resort.owlfiji.com) opened in 2018 after Cyclone Winston leveled an older resort on the same pleasant site. It's about three kilometers north of Levuka, near the village of Toki, on a sandy bay whose most prominent feature is the enormous wrecked ferry *Sinu-i-Wasa Tolu*. Ten modern air-conditioned cottages are accompanied by a dive shop, a late-night restaurant-bar serving Fijian and Italian food, and the only swimming pool on Ovalau. A one-bedroom cottage sleeps two people (F$115) and a two-bedroom sleeps four (F$190); all rates include breakfast, Wi-Fi, and satellite TV. Laundry and room service are available for a fee, and the energetic proprietor

1

2

3

4

Chris works hard to make guests happy. Long-term stay rates are negotiable.

★ **The Baystay** (Rukuruku, tel. 803-8789 or 360-9569, info@thebaystayfiji.com, lizaditrich@hotmail.com, www.thebaystayfiji.com) is a small, rustic lodge set in a coastal garden on the northwest coast, near Bobo's Farm. Snorkeling is possible in the bay at high tide, as well as boat trips to a sandbank and a waterfall walk, and there's a tiny rock pool. You can also trek to a village inside the Lovoni crater from here. A dorm bed is F$35, a thatched *bure* for one/two people is F$116/133, and a family-size double *bure* for F$266 sleeps 4-8 people. Slow Wi-Fi is included, along with continental breakfast. For other meals, you can use the kitchen for F$10 per person for the whole stay, or have a hot breakfast (F$17.40), lunch (F$17.40), and dinner (F$25). There are hot showers, fans, and mosquito nets. Kayaks, snorkels, swim floats, table tennis, volleyball, and mountain bikes are available. A taxi from the wharf is F$30; from the airport, F$35; to town and back, it's F$50 plus F$5 per hour. Day guests can come and hang out here to use the barbecue facilities for F$15 per person if you bring your own food, or F$40 per person if you want Baystay to organize your transportation and food. Excursions are expensive from here and require a minimum of four people.

The beloved **Levuka Homestay** (Church St., Levuka, tel. 344-0777 or 970-1341, levukahomestay@connect.com.fj, www.levukahomestay.com), behind the Royal Hotel, is a good bed-and-breakfast choice for the fussy traveler who doesn't mind going up and down stairs for everything—it's custom-built on five levels. The four well-appointed rooms with bath and fridge are F$167/188 single/double, including a hearty breakfast and smoothie. Every room has a bathroom, veranda, and its own entrance from a verdant outdoor staircase that leads to the breakfast/lounge area. The three lower air-conditioned rooms with queen beds are preferable to the fourth fan-cooled room, with double plus single beds, tucked away directly below the owners' apartment. Australians John and Marilyn Milesi will make you feel right at home, and the gardener Nox has worked wonders, making the entire place feel like a tropical leisure garden.

1: inside a cottage at The Baystay Resort **2:** goats at pasture on Ovalau **3:** lush greenery at Bobo's Farm **4:** wind chimes at the friendly Kauwai Guesthouse.

INFORMATION AND SERVICES

The website of the **Levuka Tourism Association** (www.levukafiji.com) is useful.

Elaine at the **Whale's Tale** restaurant (tel. 344-0235) will be happy to give you a tip or two about local sights and characters—invaluable when planning a trip.

The **Levuka Community Center** (Beach St., Levuka, tel. 344-0356) may have information on offshore island resorts, transportation, and various land tours around Ovalau. You can borrow one or two books from the Community Center library by becoming a member for an annual fee of F$5.

Cyclone Winston destroyed **Ovalau Watersports**, leaving Ovalau without a dive operator, though the website (www.owlfiji.com) still has good general information about the island.

Narsons Market (Beach St., Levuka, tel. 344-0664, Mon.-Sat. 0900-1800, Sun. 0900-1000), next door to the Whale's Tale, has an air-conditioned "Internet & Gaming Zone" in the back with high-speed connections. After school and on holidays, it's packed with excited young boys playing video games—one of the few forms of entertainment in town.

The Westpac Bank on Beach Street has an **ATM.**

Levuka's **hospital** (tel. 344-0088) is on the north side of town, past New Mavida Lodge. The emergency room is open 24 hours, and other departments are open 0800-1600 Monday through Friday.

GETTING THERE

The island's two main entry points are Bureta Airport and Buresala Jetty, both on the western side.

Air

By plane, **Northern Air** (tel. 347-5005, www.northernair.com.fj) offers a 12-minute flight between Suva and Ovalau (LEV) at 0800 Monday through Saturday, and at 1530 Monday, Wednesday, and Friday. Return flights are about 40 minutes later. Trying to book online can be frustrating because so many flights fill up in advance, but the staff are lovely on the phone and will help you find an available seat. A one-way ticket is about F$85.

Sea

Captain Cook (www.captaincookcruisesfiji.com) runs seven-night Colonial Fiji Discovery Cruises on the *MV Reef Endeavour*. The ship stops at Levuka and Makogai in the Lomaiviti Group, as well as Savusavu and Taveuni. This cruise is offered about twice a year; see the website for upcoming dates. The ship takes two nights to cruise from Nadi to Levuka, and five nights to cruise back. It's possible to join or leave the cruise in Levuka.

Patterson Brothers Shipping (tel. 331-5644, fijisearoad1@gmail.com, www.fijisearoad.com) operates the "Sea-Road" bus/ferry/bus service between Suva and Ovalau. It should take just less than five hours right through, and costs F$30 one-way. There are discounts for children of various ages, and infants travel free but must still have a ticket. It's old-school: There's no prebooking by phone, email, or web, and you must to go to one of the shipping offices for a ticket. Offices are open Monday-Friday 0830-1600 and Saturday 2100-1200; the offices are closed Sundays, although the ferry and bus run seven days a week.

Buses depart the main Suva bus stand at 1300. Buy tickets before midday at the Suva office (Epworth House, tel. 331-5644). Note that sometimes there's more than one bus, and you may not board the same bus that your suitcase does; let the driver or loader know so you'll be reunited at the ferry and can transfer it. It takes about 3.5 hours by bus to Natovi Landing (don't get off at the market stop just a few minutes beforehand; wait till you see the wharf), followed by a few minutes of waiting around and then one hour on the ferry. Follow the crowd and retain your payment receipt, as you'll need to show it here and again on the next bus. Disembarking at Buresala Jetty, you board the bus again. It drops everyone off at the Levuka bus station, but if your accommodation is en route, you can see if the driver will stop for you.

If you happen to be at the Suva airport already, you can also catch this bus in Nausori so that you don't have to go all the way back to downtown Suva. Buy tickets at the Patterson Brothers office (north end of Main St., tel. 347-8335) and join the queue for the bus just across the street.

From Levuka, the bus departs at a brutal 0400 to reach the ferry landing by 0500. If you haven't booked a round-trip already, buy your ticket the day before at the Levuka office (Beach St., tel. 344-0125).

GETTING AROUND

Both the airport and the ferry landing are on the western side of the island, opposite Levuka town. It's about an hour by road all the way around. The bus is a bit slower because it stops everywhere people need to get on or off, but it's comfortable enough.

In Levuka, both taxis and carriers park across the street from the Church of the Sacred Heart. Due to steep hills on the northwest side of Ovalau, there isn't a bus all the way around the island, but cars can go; 4WD is required on rainy days. Carriers leave Levuka for Taviya (F$3) near Rukuruku village Monday-Saturday at 0730, 1145, and 1600 along a beautiful, hilly road. During school holidays, only the 1145 trip may operate. Occasional carriers to Bureta, Lovoni, and Viru park across the street from Kim's Paak Kum Loong Restaurant. To Lovoni, they leave Levuka at 0630, 1100, and 1700 (Saturday at 1100 only). There's no service on Sunday.

West of Ovalau

Between Ovalau and the big island of Viti Levu are several jewels whose location makes them accessible from both east and west. They make delightful stopovers on an all-over-Fiji tour or perfect little day trips, and they are set in some of the most untouched waters of Fiji thanks to local marine conservation efforts that began at the turn of this century. Leleuvia is a destination in its own right.

★ LELEUVIA ISLAND

The lovely 17-hectare **Leleuvia Island,** a reef island off the coast of Motoriki, is conveniently situated between Ovalau and Viti Levu. It's home to a resort operated by one of Fiji's true ecotourism leaders, Colin Philp. Due largely to his efforts and the local community's commitment, the protected marine area around the island is more than 60 times the size of the land, and it is monitored by 24-hour patrols to prevent illegal fishing. That means a stunning natural abundance of sealife for snorkelers and divers to enjoy responsibly.

Worth seeing is the **Waisiliva Artists Collective** (tel. 999-2340 or 838-4365, info@waisiliva.com, www.waisiliva.com) gallery, a showplace for the 30-plus local artists who contribute work. The proceeds go directly to the artists, 75 percent of whom use it as their family's sole source of income. Visual art, spoken word, and storytelling are part of the exhibitions, and some have been picked up for international travel—without fossil fuels, using wind- and solar-powered boats. Waisiliva means "silver waters" and is the local name for the sea surrounding the island, as it sparkles silver under moonlight.

Accommodations

★ **Leleuvia Island Resort** (tel. 838-4365 or 890-1049, www.leleuvia.com) was originally built in the 1980s as a backpacker place and underwent a complete overhaul in 2012. Skilled craftspeople from eight villages on neighboring Motoriki and Caqalai built the 20 *bures,* two 20-bed dormitories, and an 80-seat restaurant using traditional construction practices. A priority was to enable village elders to transfer the skills, now going out of style, to unemployed youth. As a result, the construction craft was restored, and several of the villages began to replace their modern tin-shed homes with traditional homes. The sustainability ethic carries on at the resort, where guests are invited to become "ocean ambassadors" by participating in conservation programs alongside the local communities, such as turtle tagging and coral farming. Outrigger canoeing and canoe sailing are unique activities available here. The snorkeling is lovely, and *lovo* feasts are held when there are enough guests.

It's F$69 for a bed in a single-gender dorm. A private *bure,* with a queen bed and a twin bed, is F$225 and can sleep three people, with shared bath and toilet facilities. A deluxe *bure* has its own bathroom, at F$313. Extra beds can be added, up to six people total in a *bure* (it would be a tight squeeze), and there are weekday discounts. Children younger than 12 can't stay in the dorms. All guests must buy a meal plan (F$107 adults, F$54 children under 12), which—oddly—doesn't include dessert.

Getting There

Transfers are scheduled via a 45-minute powerboat ride every morning between Leleuvia and Bau Landing (north of Suva), and every afternoon except Sunday (F$88 pp one-way). It's also possible to arrange a transfer from Levuka (F$112.50). Children are half price.

NAIGANI ISLAND

Naigani Island, 11 kilometers off Viti Levu, is a lush tropical island near Ovalau at the west end of the Lomaiviti Group. It's just the right size for exploring on foot, with pristine

Sustainable Marine Conservation

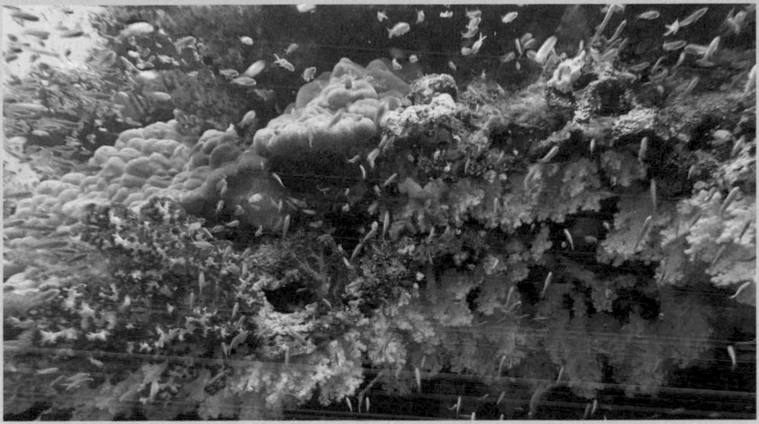

The Fiji Locally Managed Marine Area Network protects fragile coral ecosystems like these near Taveuni.

Globally, ocean fish populations have dropped by 50 percent in the last 40 years due to commercial overfishing and habitat destruction. Alifereti Tawake, a marine researcher from Kadavu, aimed to stem the tide when he founded the **Fiji Locally Managed Marine Area Network** (http://lmmanetwork.org) in 2000. The program has been so successful that the model has been exported throughout the Pacific and Asia. In the Lomaiviti Group alone, the initiative has protected seven vulnerable reefs.

Tawake's program is built on the traditional Fijian practice of *tabu*, in which villages set aside a portion of their own fishing grounds as a no-take zone for 100 days after the death of a chief. This is a sign of respect for the chief, and also ensures a far richer harvest for the feast that marks the end of the mourning period: The bigger the catch, the greater the power of the chief in the afterlife.

The LMMA network revived this traditional practice by setting up longer *tabu* periods—sometimes years, or even permanent decrees—through joint agreements with the people and the chief (no death necessary). A *tabu* applies only to about 10-20 percent of the fishing ground, preserving wild areas while also increasing the productivity of the open fishing zones. Traditional *tabu* rites and ceremonies are performed, neighbors are notified, and villagers patrol their areas against fishing incursions. The strength of the *tabu*, and the resulting benefits for tourism, help communities to resist tempting monetary offers to allow destructive commercial overfishing in areas facing resource decline and with few alternative livelihoods. Colin Philp of Leleuvia described the work, with slides, at a 2017 TED-style event sponsored by the Suva-based Genda Project (watch at https://youtu.be/V2SSYUFArew).

In 2015, the World Wildlife Fund honored Tawake with its Duke of Edinburgh Conservation Medal. "A crisis is coming," Tawake said in his acceptance speech. "It was not too long ago that the scientific community and governments refused to believe that communities could lead the way. But this award is recognition of what communities can do if given the chance, and what they can contribute to the global efforts to conserve our planet."

left just before reaching the island and swim around the island to the coral. Rowdy voluntourism youth groups from the United States and Australia sometimes come here en masse and can be a nuisance.

Accommodations

The church operates a small backpacker resort, **Caqalai Island Accommodation** (tel. 362-0388, caqalairesort@yahoo.com). The *bure*-style buildings have bunk beds and mosquito nets, but no window screens; expect critters and pretend you're cabin-camping. A bed in the dorm is F$65 and a private *bure* for two is F$100. Flush toilets, a shower shed (no hot water), snorkel gear, and palm-shaded hammocks are provided. No alcohol is sold on the island, but you can always get a coconut fresh from a tree. Caqalai is rustic but adequate, and the island and people are great.

Getting There

From Levuka, you can book a boat at the Royal Hotel in Levuka for F$30 per person each way, for either overnight or day trips. The Royal Hotel also arranges day trips to Caqalai.

From Suva, take the bus 90 minutes north to Waidalice Landing, where you can catch a boat across to Caqalai. The resort arranges this transfer, but travelers have complained about frequent miscommunication; luckily, if their boat misses you, another boat is probably going the same way.

Those already staying on Caqalai can make shopping trips to Levuka at F$10 per person each way.

OTHER ISLANDS

The Lomaiviti Group was hard hit by Cyclone Winston, and the two islands below have not yet rebuilt their resorts. Day visits are easy, though, as they're tucked in close to the southwest shore of Ovalau. Take all the water and food you'll need, as there are no tourist facilities. The snorkeling and fishing (where allowed) around these islands are some of the best.

In 2002, a 2,600-year-old female skeleton was discovered on the southeast coast of **Moturiki Island,** 10.1 kilometers from Ovalau. The burial style and fragments of Lapita pottery found nearby suggest a connection with Santa Cruz in the Solomon Islands dating back as far as 3,170 years. The finest beaches are on the east side of Moturiki. Camping is officially discouraged, but possible.

It was on tiny **Yanuca Lailai Island,** just off the south end of Ovalau, that the first 463 indentured Indian laborers to arrive in Fiji landed from the ship *Leonidas* on May 14, 1879. To avoid the introduction of cholera or smallpox into Fiji, the immigrants spent two months in quarantine here; some ruined buildings, and their ghosts, remain.

Getting There

In 2007, 21-year-old Jona Moli Bukasoqo made headlines when he swam from his village on Moturiki to interview for a carpentry apprentice program in Levuka. If you're not feeling up to that challenge, small outboards to Moturiki Island depart from Ovalau most afternoons, and both Yanuca Lailai and Moturiki are within kayaking distance. Almost all the resorts on Ovalau have boats, so you may inquire about taking a trip with your hosts.

East of Ovalau

The Koro Sea washes through the triangle between Ovalau to the west, Vanua Levu to the north, and Taveuni to the east, bringing deep, nutrient-rich currents through the wide channel, feeding small creatures who in turn feed the larger creatures. Thus, the islands below are excellent bases for sightings of whales, sharks, barracuda, eagle rays, and dolphins. Almost everywhere you turn, there are colorful soft corals, healthy hard corals, an array of huge schools feeding from them, and crystal-clear visibility.

★ KORO ISLAND

Koro Island is 8 by 16 kilometers and shaped like a shark's tooth. It was the hardest hit by Cyclone Winston, with nary a tree left untouched. The coastal coconuts and mangos, as well as the great tree ferns and rainforest of the interior, are slowly recovering, as are the 14 large villages on the island—but you'll see traces of the devastating winds and rains everywhere. The *kava* here is said to be Fiji's finest.

The best beach is along the south coast, between Mudu and the lighthouse at **Muanivanua Point.** Among Koro's 14 large Fijian villages is **Nasau,** the government center, with a post office, hospital, and schools. On the north coast, the road to **Vatulele** village climbs from Nasau to the high plateau at the center of the island. A ridge traverses the island from northeast to southwest, reaching 561 meters near the center. The track south runs along a golden palm-fringed beach between Nacamaki and Tua Tua. A 30-minute hike up a steep trail from **Naqaidamu** brings you to a waterfall and an idyllic swimming hole.

Accommodations

Dere Bay Resort (tel. 331-1075 Suva office, 778-3300 Koro Island, derebayresort@gmail.com, fijimiller@connect.com.fj, www.derebayresort.com, F$250 pp) is the only Koro resort that's been able to rebuild. The bungalows are simple but sweet, and breakfast is included. Other meals are F$25 per person.

Getting There

Koro has an unusual inclined **airstrip** on the east side of the island near Namacu village: You land uphill and take off downhill. **Fiji Link** flies from Suva's Nausori Airport to Koro at 1005 Mondays, returning at 1125 the same day.

Goundar Shipping departs Suva's Walu Bay at 1800 Monday and arrives on Koro at 0600 Tuesday; the ferry turns around and departs Koros at 1800 Tuesday and arrives in Suva at 0600 Wednesday.

Given the schedules, you'd typically spend a week on Koro. However, you could also opt to fly in on Monday morning and depart by ship on Tuesday evening (one night) or arrive by ship on Wednesday morning and fly out on Monday (five nights). (That's assuming neither flight nor boat is canceled, as sometimes happens due to weather.) Private passage by boat from Savusavu is sometimes available,

Koro Island

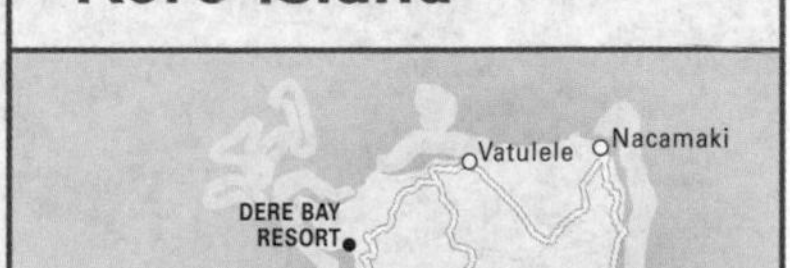

as it's less than an hour by speedboat; inquire with Dere Bay or at the Copra Shed Marina in Savusavu.

WAKAYA ISLAND

The eight-square-mile **Wakaya Island** has a colorful history. A high cliff on the west coast is known as **Chieftain's Leap**, for a young chief who threw himself over the edge of the hill fort to avoid capture by his foes. Chief Cakobau sold Wakaya to Europeans in 1840, and it has since had many owners. In 1862, David Whippy, the forefather of today's Patterson family on Ovalau, set up Fiji's first sugar mill on Wakaya. During World War I, the German raider Count Felix von Luckner was captured by a British officer and four Indian soldiers on Wakaya. The count was interned in Auckland as a prisoner of war and wrote a book, *The Sea Devil*, about his experiences in the Pacific.

Only resort guests may set foot on these ritzy shores, but everyone can snorkel from a boat on Wakaya's glorious reefs, and liveaboard dive boats often pass this way. Blue Ridge on the northern side of the island's outer reef is named for its blue ribbon eels; lionfish are common at the Lion's Den; and Wakaya Passage off the island's south point is the place for manta ray and hammerhead shark encounters.

In 1973, Canadian industrialist David Harrison Gilmour bought the island for US$3 million, and in 1990 he and his wife, Jill, opened a resort there; they are sometimes in residence. In 1996, Gilmour cofounded Fiji Water on Viti Levu.

Accommodations

The all-inclusive **Wakaya Club & Spa** (tel. 344-8128, U.S. tel. 949/650-1911, www.wakaya.com, from US$3,000) has nine spacious cottages, the most luxurious of which is a three-bedroom hilltop villa (US$9,000). There is a five-night minimum and children under 16 are not accommodated. The snorkeling is superb, and there's scuba diving, a nine-hole golf course, a swimming pool, and Wi-Fi. Only sportfishing and massage cost extra. As you might expect at these prices (Fiji's highest!), it's all very tasteful and elegant—just ask notables like Pierce Brosnan, Carol Burnett, Russell Crowe, Tom Cruise, Céline Dion, Bill Gates, Nicole Kidman, or Michelle Pfeiffer. It's a sort of country club for the rich and famous, rather than a trendy social scene. A third of Wakaya has been subdivided into 100 parcels, which are available for building

Dere Bay Resort on Koro Island

Coral Reef Adventure on the *Nai'a*

the *Nai'a* liveaboard

Since 1993, the liveaboard *Nai'a* (www.naia.com.fj) has been the flagship of Fiji's diving industry, discovering and naming many remote sites now regularly visited by other boats. In 2000-2001, the MacGillivray Freeman Films IMAX production ***Coral Reef Adventure*** was filmed in Fiji by Howard Hall, who selected *Nai'a*'s Cat Holloway and Rob Barrel as his guides, both topside and under water.

One of the highlights of every *Nai'a* voyage is an afternoon spent in a village on the island of Gau, which impressed Howard and Michelle Hall when they first visited as *Nai'a* passengers. *Nai'a* divemaster Rusi Vulakoro also has a starring role in the film, and *Nai'a* passengers will recognize their favorite Lomaiviti dive sites on the giant screen, as well as the sharks, turtles, manta rays, sea snakes, gobies, and shrimp that they have come to love.

In addition to *Nai'a*'s regular cruises around Fiji, its humpback whale tours to Tonga and scientific expeditions to the shark-rich waters of Kiribati are annual events.

private homes; red deer imported from New Caledonia run wild across the rest.

Getting There

Wakaya has an airstrip for charter flights, an additional F$2,000 round-trip per couple from Nadi.

OTHER ISLANDS

The following islands don't have accommodations.

Gau Island is the fifth-largest island in Fiji, with 16 villages and 13 settlements. There's a barrier reef on the west coast and a fringing reef on the east. The Takalaigau (high chief of Gau) resides in **Sawaieke village,** and the remnants of one of the only surviving pre-Christianity temples *(bure kalou)* in Fiji are beside the road at the village junction. The high stone mound is still impressive. From there, it's possible to climb **Delaico** (760 m), the highest peak on the island, in four hours, of which the first hour is the hardest. The summit offers a sweeping view. The Fiji petrel, a rare seabird of the albatross family, lays its eggs underground on these jungle-clad peaks. Only two specimens have ever been taken: one by the survey ship *Herald* in 1855, and a second by writer Dick Watling in 1984. Ships from Suva arrive irregularly at the government station of **Qarani** at the north end of Gau. The east coast is redolent with waterfalls, of which the most impressive are behind **Lekanai** village and up Waiboteigau Creek, both an hour's walk off the main road. Look for the "weather stone" on the beach, a five-minute walk south of **Yadua village.** Bad weather is certain if you step on it or hit it with another stone.

Seven Fijian villages are found on 336-meter-high **Nairai Island** between Koro and Gau. The inhabitants are known for their woven handicrafts. Hazardous reefs stretch out in three directions, and in 1808 the brigantine *Eliza* was wrecked here. Among the survivors was European mercenary Charles Savage, who gained chiefly favor by introducing firearms to Fiji.

Batiki Island has a large interior lagoon of brackish water flanked by mudflats and is surrounded by a broad barrier reef. Four Fijian villages with a total population of about 300 are on Batiki, and you can walk around the island in four hours. Fine baskets are made on Batiki. Due to hazardous reefs, there's no safe anchorage for ships. **Bula Batiki** (www.bulabatiki.co.uk) cold-pressed coconut oil is made here and, through a sustainable development partnership with a U.K. company, sold worldwide, with each small-batch bottle labeled with the name of the family on Batiki that made it.

Makogai Island shares a figure-eight-shaped barrier reef with neighboring Wakaya. The anchorage is in Dalice Bay on the northwest side of the island. From 1911 to 1969, this was a leper colony staffed by Catholic nuns, and many of the old hospital buildings still stand. Among the 1,241 souls interred in the patients' cemetery on the hill are Mother Marie Agnes, who ran the facility for 34 years, and Maria Filomena, a Fijian sister who worked at the colony from its inception. After contracting leprosy in 1925, Maria Filomena joined her patients and continued serving them for another 30 years. The colony was phased out after treatment for leprosy was introduced in 1948. Today, Makogai is owned by the Department of Agriculture, which runs an experimental sheep farm here, with some 2,000 animals.

Getting There

For Gau Island, it's a three-hour motorboat ride from Suva, or a trip on the irregular monthly Goundar Shipping ferry; inquire at Walu Bay. Otherwise, almost all the resorts on Ovalau have boats, so you may inquire about taking a trip with your hosts. Even if they can't land, the snorkeling and fishing (where allowed) on the reefs around these islands are some of the best in Fiji. Yachts and liveaboards visit these islands or their waters.

The people at the Levuka Community Center (tel. 344-0356) may know about other local boats from Levuka to Gau, Koro, and other eastern islands. If you just show up at the Levuka Wharf around 1000, you may be able to arrange a spot on a boat leaving for one of the islands.

The Outer Islands

You've traveled so far to get to Fiji—why not go

a little farther to experience truly unspoiled beaches and seas? Words like *pristine* and *idyllic* seem to have been invented for Fiji's outer islands, and the friendliness of the local people is renowned.

Some of the Lau islands, at the eastern edge of Fiji, see only a couple dozen visitors a year, while northern Rotuma is so remote that it doesn't even make it onto most maps of Fiji. These islands are especially rewarding for tourists who are ready to go with the flow, as flights and boats are infrequent, and there are no flashy activities. Here, you'll do as the locals do—take in picturesque views, feast on fresh seafood and fruit (abundant on these lush tropical isles), and enjoy some of the most fantastic beaches in the world.

Look for ★ to find recommended sights, activities, dining, and lodging.

Highlights

★ **Nakama Hot Springs:** These natural mineral waters on Vanua Balavu Island are private, relaxing, and said to be therapeutic (page 319).

★ **Limestone Caves:** Lakeba Island's numerous limestone caves are fun to explore (page 323).

★ **Ono-i-Lau Island:** Snorkel a coral-filled lagoon in an ancient volcanic crater. It'll just be you and the fish (page 324).

★ **Sisilo Hill:** This hill is the burial place of the last kings of Rotuma, and a few historical relics can still be seen (page 327).

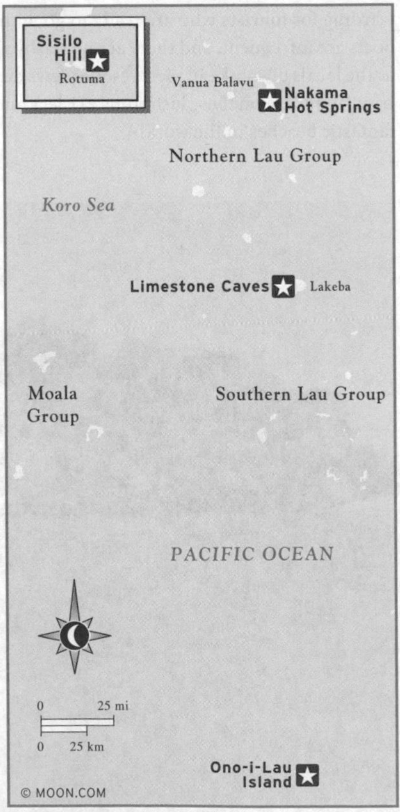

Each island has its own unique culture and dialect, distinct from the "big island" Fijians and more akin to those of neighboring Tonga and Samoa. You can travel by cargo ferry or plane, or if you're lucky, as part of a private yacht crew. There are no regular hotels, restaurants, bars, or dive shops anywhere in these islands, but your hosts should be able to arrange small boats for snorkeling or island visits. There are no banks, so bring all the Fijian currency you think you'll need. Whichever island you choose, you won't regret adding this once-in-a-lifetime journey to your Fiji adventure.

The Lau Group

The **Lau Group** is Fiji's most remote region, its 57 islands scattered over a vast area of ocean between Viti Levu and Tonga. All are relatively small and vary from volcanic islands to uplifted atolls. It's easy to feel that the landscape hasn't changed much since a century ago, when Methodist missionary William Reed wrote, "Here in the cool depths of the glassy sea are reflected sunny peaks draped in gossamer clouds. If fairies dwell anywhere, it must surely be in such enchanted realms as these."

Fairies or not, a thrilling array of species do inhabit this biodiverse region. During a 2017 Lau expedition, Conservation International scientists discovered six new marine species here, including new varieties of tiny coral dwarf goby fish not found anywhere else in the world.

Roughly half of the islands are inhabited. Many of the islands of northern Lau are freehold and owned by outsiders, while the isles of southern Lau are communally owned by the Fijian inhabitants. Historically, the chiefs of Lau have always had a strong political influence in Fiji. Today, more than 45,000 Lauans live on Viti Levu, leaving less than 11,000 on their home islands.

Vanua Balavu (52 square km) and **Lakeba** (54 square km) are the largest islands and the only ones with organized visitor accommodations. Vanua Balavu has more to see and do. Few of these islands are prepared for tourism, so it helps to know someone before you go.

GETTING THERE

Air

It's barely an hour's flight from Suva to the islands, but each flight goes only once a week. From Suva, **Fiji Link** connects with Cicia on Tuesdays (1015 from Suva, 1140 return), with Vanua Balavu on Wednesdays (0645 from Suva, 0825 return), and with Lakeba on Thursdays (1015 from Suva, 1155 return). **Northern Air** connects with Moala on Thursdays (1130 from Suva, 1245 return).

Sea

Twice a year, **Captain Cook** (tel. 670-1823, U.S. tel. 424/206-5275, enquiries@captaincookfj.com, www.captaincookcruisesfiji.com) offers an 11-day cruise that stops at the Lau Group. After a day on Taveuni, the cruise goes to the northernmost Lau island, Wailagilala, and then takes you through half-day stops on several other islands. The exact itinerary depends on tides and local conditions, but you're guaranteed isolated beaches far from other tourists at several of these: Vanua Balavu; Oneata (where you may also take in a village church service); an extinct volcanic crater at either Fulaga or Komo; Vuaqava; and Totoya. On

Previous: an islet in the southern Lau group; sunset in the Lau Islands; plant fiber crafts, a Lau specialty.

The Outer Islands

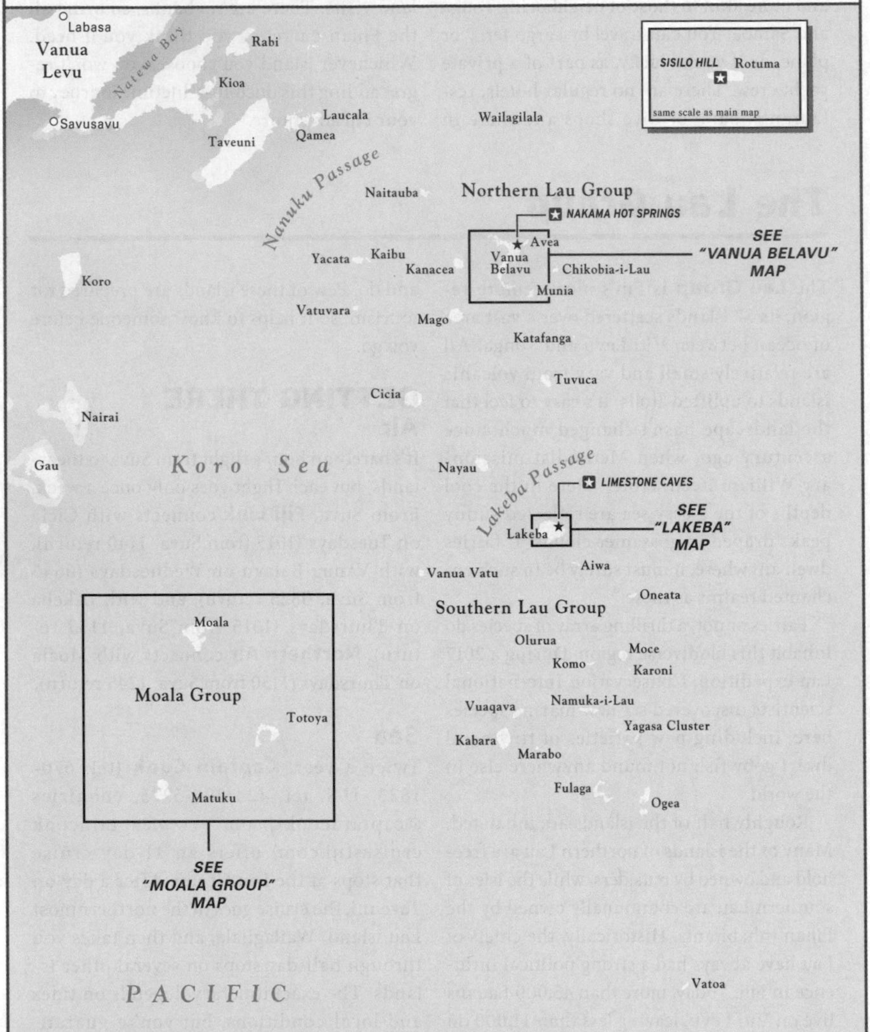
Labasa
Vanua Levu
Natewa Bay
Rabi
Kioa
Savusavu
Laucala
Taveuni
Qamea
Wailagilala
SISILO HILL
Rotuma
same scale as main map
Nanuku Passage
Naitauba
Northern Lau Group
NAKAMA HOT SPRINGS
Avea
SEE "VANUA BELAVU" MAP
Yacata
Kaibu
Vanua Belavu
Kanacea
Chikobia-i-Lau
Koro
Munia
Vatuvara
Mago
Katafanga
Tuvuca
Cicia
Nairai
Gau
Koro Sea
Nayau
Lakeba Passage
LIMESTONE CAVES
SEE "LAKEBA" MAP
Lakeba
Aiwa
Vanua Vatu
Oneata
Southern Lau Group
Moala
Olurua
Moce
Komo
Karoni
Moala Group
Namuka-i-Lau
Totoya
Vuaqava
Yagasa Cluster
Kabara
Marabo
Matuku
Fulaga
Ogea
SEE "MOALA GROUP" MAP
Vatoa
PACIFIC OCEAN
ONO-I-LAU ISLAND
0
25 mi
0
25 km
Ono-i-Lau
© MOON.COM

Find Your Beach

SOUTHERN LAU

- The best beach on Lakeba Island is **Nukuselal** (page 322), just a few minutes' walk from the historically important and attractive village of Tubou.
- **Fulaga Island** (page 324) has a stunning beach, accessible by permission of the neighboring village.

ROTUMA

- Some of Fiji's most gorgeous white-sand beaches are on Rotuma, like **Oinafa** near the wharf and **Vaioa** near the Solroroa Bluff (page 327). Locals can tell you where to surf for excellent breaks, as well as where to find *fuliu,* freshwater rock pools perfect for a refreshing swim.

the island of Kabara or Komo, you can share a Tongan-influenced *meke* and *lovo* that are quite different from what you'll see elsewhere in Fiji.

Cruising **yachties** can inquire at their point of entry into Fiji (either Vuda Point Marina in Nadi or the Copra Shed Marina in Savusavu) about accessing the private **Bavatu Plantation** (https://fijimarinas.com/vanua-balavu-lau/) on the scenic **Bay of Islands,** at the northwest end of Vanua Balavu. A recognized hurricane shelter, it has a lovely harbor with moorings for 30 yachts. The plantation is owned by Fiji's number one yachting family, the Philp family, who will be happy to host you and arrange guides to show you around if they are in residence.

Copra-collecting ships circulate through Lau every couple of weeks, usually calling at five or six islands on a single trip. Several commercial carriers take passengers as well. Food is usually included in the price, and on the outward journey it will probably be okay, but on the return don't expect much more than rice and tea. If you're planning a long voyage by interisland ship, gifting a big bundle of kava roots to captain and crew as a token of appreciation for their hospitality works wonders. It can take up to four days to reach your destination. In Suva, some carriers:

Maritime Shipping Line (tel. 357-2972), in a green container on Muaiwalu Wharf, operates the barge *Sea-Link* from Suva to northern or southern Lau every fortnight.

Western Shipping (tel. 331-4467, westernshipping@connect.com.fj), in a yellow container on Muaiwalu Wharf, operates the *Cagi Mai Bu* to the Lau and Lomaiviti Groups.

Bligh Water Shipping Ltd. (tel. 331-8247, www.blighwatershipping.com.fj) operates the *Suilven* from Taveuni to Vanua Balavu and Cicia on the first Saturday of every month (F$75/125 economy/sleeper).

Also check **Seaview Shipping Services** (tel. 330-9515, www.seaviewshippingfiji.com), at the side of the yellow building between the Consort Shipping and Bligh Water Shipping offices on Matua Street. They sometimes have a ship to Lau.

The small wooden copra boat *Adi Lomai* runs to Lomaiviti, Lau, and Rotuma. Other small boats operate from Suva to Lau every week or two. Ask the crews of vessels tied up at Muaiwalu Jetty on Walu Bay for passage; you may need to ask several people before you are pointed in the right direction.

NORTHERN LAU

Vanua Balavu Island

The name **Vanua Balavu** means "long land." Here the villages are impeccably clean, the grass cut and manicured. Large mats are made on the island, and strips of pandanus can be seen drying in front of many houses. The southern portion of this unusual, sea-horse-shaped island is mostly volcanic, while the north is uplifted coral. This unspoiled environment of palm-fringed beaches backed by long grassy hillsides and sheer limestone cliffs is a wonderful area to explore. Varied vistas and scenic views appear on all sides. To the east is a 130-kilometer barrier reef enclosing a 37-by-16-kilometer lagoon.

Vanau Balavu Island

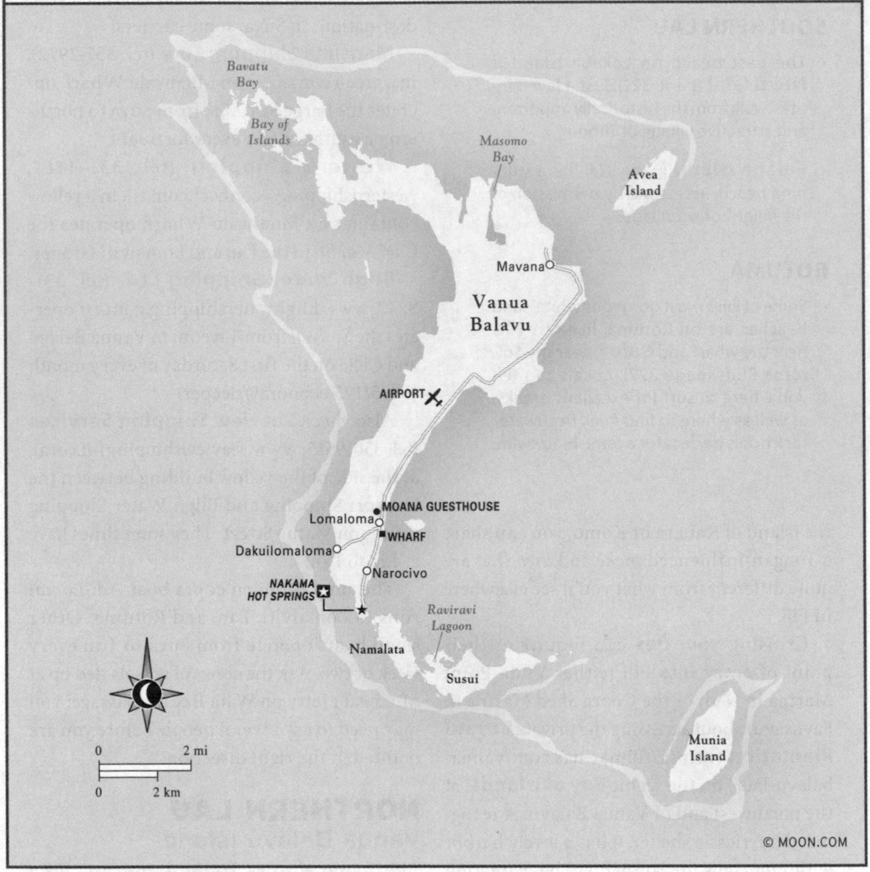

LOMALOMA VILLAGE

In 1840, Commodore Charles Wilkes of the U.S. Exploring Expedition named Vanua Balavu and its adjacent islands within the barrier reef the "Exploring Isles." In the days of sail, **Lomaloma,** the largest settlement, was an important Pacific port. Today it's a big, sleepy village with a coconut-oil mill, a hospital, and a couple of general stores. A modest monument flanked by two cannons on the waterfront near the wharf recalls the battle of 1855, when the great Tongan prince Enele Ma'afu conquered northern Lau from the chiefs of Vanua Levu and made Lomaloma the base for his bid to dominate Fiji.

A road runs inland from Lomaloma up and across the island to **Dakuilomaloma.** The small communications station on a grassy hilltop midway affords an excellent view.

NAROCIVO VILLAGE

Follow the road south from Lomaloma three kilometers to **Narocivo village,** then continue two kilometers beyond to the narrow passage that separates Vanua Balavu and Malata islands. At low tide, you can

The Coconut Palm

a fruit-laden coconut tree

Copra is the Lau Group's major export, and human life would not be possible on most of the Pacific's far-flung atolls without this all-purpose tree. It reaches maturity in eight years, then produces about 50 nuts a year for 60 years. Aside from the tree's aesthetic value and usefulness in providing shade, the water of the green coconut provides a refreshing drink, and the white meat of the young nut is a delicious food. The harder meat of more mature nuts is grated and squeezed, which creates a coconut cream that is eaten alone or used in cooking. The oldest nuts are cracked open and the hard meat removed, then dried, to be sold as copra. It takes about 6,000 coconuts to make a ton of copra. Copra is pressed to extract the oil, which in turn is made into candles, cosmetics, and soap. Scented with flowers, the oil nurtures the skin.

The juice or sap from the cut flower spathes of the palm provides toddy, a popular drink; the toddy is distilled into a spirit called arrack, the whiskey of the Pacific. The sap can also be boiled to make candy. "Millionaire's salad" is made by shredding the growth cut from the heart of the tree. For each salad, a fully mature tree must be sacrificed.

The nut's hard inner shell can be used as a cup and makes excellent firewood. Rope, cordage, brushes, and heavy matting are produced from the coir fiber of the husk. The smoke from burning husks is an effective mosquito repellent. The leaves of the coconut tree are used to thatch the roofs of the islanders' cottages or are woven into baskets, mats, and fans. The trunk provides timber for building and furniture.

easily wade across to **Namalata village.** Alternatively, work your way around to the west side of Vanua Balavu, where there are isolated tropical beaches. There's good snorkeling in this passage.

★ NAKAMA HOT SPRINGS

You'll need a guide to show you to the **Nakama Hot Springs,** nestled among burial caves and high limestone outcrops between Narocivo and Namalata. This can be easily arranged at Nakama, the tiny collection of houses closest to the cliffs, upon payment of F$30 per group. Small bats inhabit some of the caves. You can get right in the hot springs and soak, which is reputed to be very therapeutic. It's relaxing to sit back in the soothing water and gaze at the dramatic limestone views.

RAVIRAVI LAGOON

Rent a boat to take you over to the **Raviravi Lagoon** on Susui Island, the favorite picnic spot near Lomaloma for the locals. The beach and snorkeling are good, and there's a lake where sea turtles are kept.

CHRISTMAS RITUAL AT MASOMO BAY

If you happen to be here around Christmas, you might catch an annual rite at **Masomo Bay,** west of Mavana village. Villagers enter the waters wearing skirts of *drauniqai* leaves to stir up the muddy bottom, which, coupled with a bit of ancient magic, stuns the mullet fish (*yawa*), rendering them easy prey for waiting spears. A Fijian legend tells how the *yawa* were originally brought to Masomo by a Tongan princess. Peni, the *bete* (priest) of Mavana, controls the ritual. No photos are allowed. This provides enough food for the village's Christmas feast.

ACCOMMODATIONS

Most of the barely two dozen visitors a year to Northern Lau stay at the cozy ★ **Moana Guesthouse** (37 Vanua Balavu Island, Northern Lau, tel. 718-2886, 784-5511, or 719-0929, moanaguesthouse2010@gmail.com, www.facebook.com/Moana-Guesthouse-885600288159299, F$77 including meals). You sleep in a cabana (which holds up to four people, technically, but you'd be more comfortable with two) right next to north-facing Sawana beach, share a bathroom, and eat hearty meals cooked in the kitchen by the Fotofili family, which traces its ancestry to Tongan warriors who accompanied Prince Ma'afu to Fiji in the early 1800s. This is where government and business travelers to the Lau Group generally stay. You'll also share your beach with giant coconut crabs, which grow up to nine pounds and crack open coconuts to binge on the contents.

GETTING AROUND

From the airstrip, you can hitch a ride to Lomaloma with the Fiji Link agent for a small fee or hire a carrier to Moana's Guesthouse for F$20. On departure, after checking in for your flight, you might have time to scramble up the nearby hill for a good view of the island.

Several carriers a day run from Lomaloma north to Mualevu, and some continue to Mavana.

Other Islands of Northern Lau

After setting himself up at Lomaloma in 1855, Chief Ma'afu encouraged the establishment of European copra and cotton plantations in Lau, and several islands are freehold land to this day. You're most likely to see these picturesque spots as sunset-lit mounds on the horizon from Vanua Balavu or as you pass by them on the ferry.

Mago (20 square km) belongs to U.S. actor Mel Gibson. **Kanacea** (13 square km) has seven volcanic peaks, was used during the American Civil War as a cotton plantation, and is up for sale by its current owner, a biotech executive. **Katafanga** once belonged to Australian aviator Harold Gatty, who founded Fiji Airways, but now investors are being sought for a half-finished luxury resort project. **Wailagilala,** northernmost of the Lau Group, has a cast-iron lighthouse built in 1909, now automated to signal to ships entering Nanuku Passage, the northwest gateway to Fiji. It's uninhabited aside from protected seabird and turtle nesting grounds.

Cicia (34 square km) is Fiji's first entirely organic island, covered by coconut plantations that export virgin coconut oil, tended by people from five villages. Fiji Link has a flight to and from Cicia every Tuesday, but there are no tourist accommodations.

There's a single Fijian village and a gorgeous white-sand beach on **Yacata Island.** Next to Yacata and sharing the same lagoon is 260-hectare **Kaibu Island.** Kaibu and another island to the south, **Vatuvara Island,** are owned by Jim Jannard, the billionaire founder of Oakley and RED Digital Camera. On Kaibu, he operates the exclusive **Vatuvara Private Islands resort** (http://vatuvara.com/), consisting of three ultra-luxury villas for US$4,300-5,800 per night. If you have children, you're required to do the whole "island buyout" for up to six people at US$15,000 per night. There's a four-night minimum, and rates include your private flight from Suva or Nadi as well as everything you can imagine needing during your stay. Vatuvara was listed as the world's most expensive island in 2006, at an asking price of US$75 million, perhaps because there is reputed to be buried treasure there. Its circular, 314-meter-high central limestone terrace, which makes the island look like a hat when viewed from the sea, gives it its other name, Hat Island.

1: the Bay of Islands **2:** Lau Islander Salote displaying crafts woven by the community **3:** on a stand-up paddleboard in the Lau waters **4:** boats heading for the long beach of Fulaga Island.

1

2

3

4

Naitauba is a circular island about 186 meters high and 2.4 kilometers across, with high cliffs on the north coast. Once owned by Hennings Brothers Drilling Company, in 1983 it was purchased from TV star Raymond Burr for US$2.1 million by the California spiritual group Johannine Daist Communion, currently known as Adidam (www.adidam.org). Longtime Adidam members travel to the island for intensive meditation retreats and, more recently, to help locals rebuild after Cyclone Winston. Adidam's founder and teacher, said to have attained enlightenment in Hollywood in 1970, was buried here after his 2008 death.

SOUTHERN LAU

Lakeba Island

Lakeba Island is the largest of the Southern Lau archipelago, tucked in the most remote corner of Fiji's eastern waters. Its rolling interior hills reach 215 meters and their red soil has been planted with pine. The low coastal plain, with eight villages and all the people, is covered with coconuts. To the east, a barrier reef encloses a wide lagoon.

A 29-kilometer road runs all the way around Lakeba. Forestry roads have been built throughout the interior, so you can walk across the island in a couple of hours, enjoying excellent views along the way. A bus connects the airstrip to the largest village, Tubou, and buses run around the island several times a day. A radio station, powered by solar energy, operates near the center of the island.

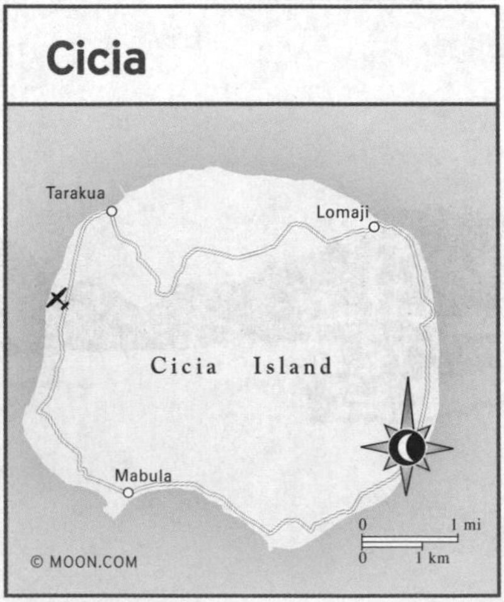

TUBOU VILLAGE

The main village, **Tubou,** is one of the largest and most prosperous in Fiji. It's the seat of the paramount chief of the Nayau clan, the Tui Nayau, who rules all of southern Lau. From the 1970s to the 1990s, the Tui Nayau, the late Ratu Sir Kamisese Mara, served as prime minister and later as president of Fiji.

From the **Catholic church,** you get a good view of the whole village, including the hospital, wharf, several stores, and the Lau provincial headquarters. Just inland, you can see the foundations of former houses of the original village site. Farther inland on the same road is the forestry station and a nursery.

Near the wharf behind the Provincial Office is the stepped **platform grave** of the Tongan prince Enele Ma'afu, who died in 1881. It was Ma'afu who united the scattered eastern islands into the Lau Confederation and took the title Tui Lau after invading in 1847 to advance the spread of Christianity. Two years later, he accepted the supremacy of Cakobau's Kingdom of Fiji, and in 1874 he signed the cession to Britain. Alongside Ma'afu are the graves of Ratu Sir Lala Sukuna (1888-1958), an important figure in the development of indigenous-Fijian self-government, and of Fiji's first prime minister, Ratu Sir Kamisese Mara (1920-2004).

The **beach** just opposite is where David Cargill and William Cross, the first Methodist missionaries to arrive in Fiji, landed on October 12, 1835. Blame them for the Fijian consonants you have to memorize, as they created the system of written Fijian still in use.

The number one beach near Tubou is **Nukuselal Beach,** which you can reach by walking east along the coastal road as far as the Public Works Department workshops. Turn right onto the track, which runs along the west side of the compound to Nukuselal Beach.

Lakeba Island

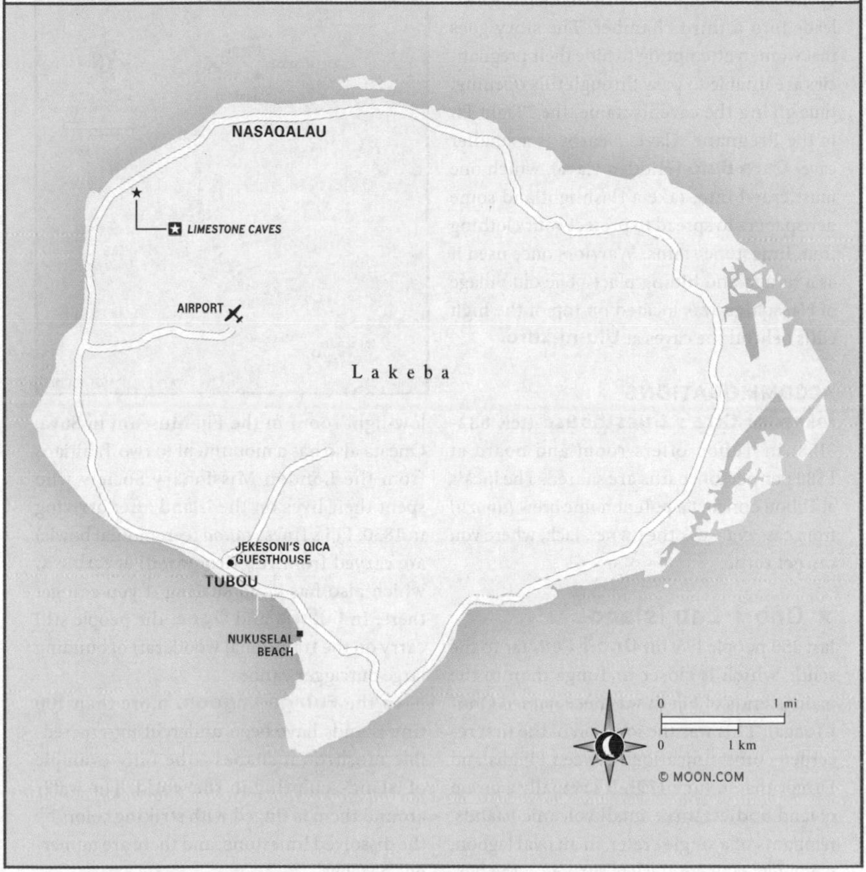

Aiwa Island, which can be seen to the southeast, is owned by the Tui Nayau and is inhabited only by flocks of wild goats.

NASAQALAU VILLAGE

On the northwest side of Lakeba is **Nasaqalau** village, home to the Nautoqumu clan and notable for its annual **shark-calling ritual** in October or November. A month before the ritual, a priest *(bete)* plants a post with a piece of tapa tied to it in the reef offshore from the village. He then keeps watch to ensure that no one comes near the area, while performing a daily kava ceremony. When the appointed day arrives, the caller wades out up to his neck and repeats a chant. Not long after, a large school of sharks led by a white shark arrives and circles the caller. He leads them to shallow water, where all but the white shark are killed and eaten.

★ LIMESTONE CAVES

The finest **limestone caves** on the island are 2.5 kilometers southwest of Nasaqalau village. The whole area is owned by the village, where you can arrange for a guide to show you around for a fee. **Oso Nabukete** is the largest of the caves; the entrance is behind a raised limestone terrace. You walk through two chambers before reaching a small, circular opening about one meter in diameter, which leads into a third chamber. The story goes that women attempting to hide their pregnancies are unable to pass through this opening, thus giving the cave its name, the "Tight Fit to the Pregnant" Cave. Nearby is a smaller cave, **Qara Bulo** (Hidden Cave), which one must crawl into; take a flashlight and some newspapers to spread to protect your clothing from limestone stains. Warriors once used it as a refuge and hiding place. The old village of Nasaqalau was located on top of the high cliffs behind the caves at **Ulu-ni-koro.**

ACCOMMODATIONS

Jekesoni Qica's Guesthouse (tel. 882-3188) in Tubou offers room and board at F$80 per person; baths are shared. The locals at Tubou concoct a potent home brew *(uburu)* from cassava—ask the owner, Jack, where you can get some.

★ Ono-i-Lau Island

Just 350 people live on **Ono-i-Lau,** far to the south, which is closer to Tonga than to the main islands of Fiji (it was once named Ono-i-Tonga). This was the location of the first recorded communication between Fijians and Europeans, in June 1791. It's actually a group of land bodies: three small volcanic islands, remnants of a single crater, in an oval lagoon, plus a few tiny coral islets sitting on the barrier reef. The snorkeling here is exquisite. The highest point on Ono-i-Lau is 113 meters and the total land area is 7.9 square kilometers. The people of Ono-i-Lau make the best *magi* (sennit rope) and *tabu kaisi* mats in the country, upon which only high chiefs may sit.

Other Islands of Southern Lau

Komo is famous for its dances *(meke),* which are performed whenever a ship arrives. In a pool on **Vanua Vatu,** locals summon red prawns with a certain chant. **Moce** and **Oneata** are renowned for their tapa cloth, of which grand samples are housed in a special low-light room in the Fiji Museum in Suva. Oneata also has a monument to two Tahitians from the London Missionary Society who spent their lives on the island after arriving in 1830. Fiji's finest *tanoa* (ceremonial bowls) are carved from *vesi* (ironwood) at **Kabara,** which also has good surfing if you can get there. In **Fulaga** and **Ogea,** the people still carry on the traditional woodcraft of building large outrigger canoes.

In the **Fulaga Lagoon,** more than 100 tiny islands have been undercut into incredible mushroom shapes—the only example of island-sculpting in the world. The water around them is tinged with striking colors by the dissolved limestone, and there are numerous beaches.

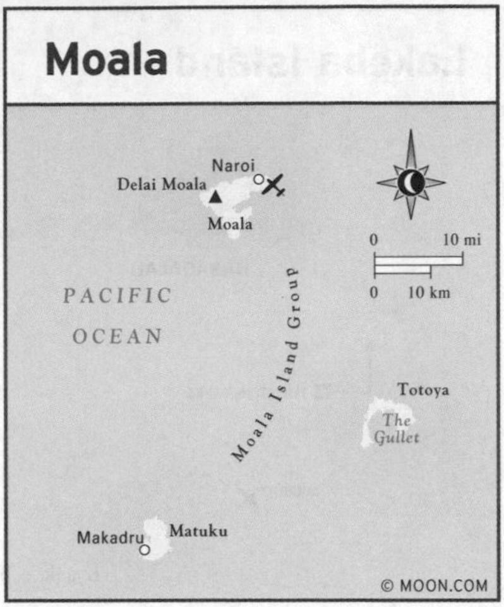

Getting There

From Lakeba, you may be able to arrange day trips to these islands, where ferries and copra boats also travel. Ono-i-Lau once had air service from Suva; today the airstrip is maintained for emergency use, but there are no regular flights and the only access to the

1: Gerry Allen, a Conservation International scientist, scouting for undiscovered species in the Lau waters **2:** a new species of coral dwarf goby recently discovered in the Lau Islands **3:** students at Moala Island's college **4:** an islet in the southern Lau group.

1

2

3
YASAYASA MOALA COLLEGE
SEEK LEARN PERSEVERE
EST 1971

4

island is occasional visits by vessels such as the barge *Sea-Link* or the copra boat *Adi Lomai.* For information on departures, inquire at Muaiwalu Wharf in Suva.

Yachts can enter the surreal Fulaga Lagoon through a narrow pass.

THE MOALA GROUP

Unlike the rest of the Lau islands, the western **Moala Islands** are closer to Viti Levu culturally as well as geographically. They were conquered only briefly by Tongan prince Enele Ma'afu. All three high volcanic islands have gorgeous scenery, with dark green rainforests above grassy slopes, good anchorage, many villages, and abundant food. There are no tourist facilities.

Triangular **Moala Island** is an intriguing 68-square-kilometer island, the ninth largest in Fiji. Two small crater lakes on the summit of Delai Moala (467 m) are covered with matted sedges that will support a person's weight. Though the main island is volcanic, an extensive system of reefs flanks the shores. Ships call at the small government station of Naroi, also the site of a disused airstrip.

Totoya is a horseshoe-shaped high island enclosing a deep bay on the south. The bay, actually the island's sunken crater, can only be entered through a narrow channel known as the Gullet, and the southeast trade winds send high waves across the reefs at the mouth of the bay, making this a dangerous place. Better anchorage is found off the southwest arm of the island. Five Fijian villages are found on Totoya, while neighboring **Matuku** has seven.

Getting There

The Moala islands are relatively close to Suva by boat, but there are no regularly scheduled tourist trips. Ask the crews of vessels tied up at Muaiwalu Jetty in Walu Bay on Suva for passage and schedules. You may need to persist and ask more than one person.

The anchorage for yachts, in a submerged crater near Makadru village on the west side of Matuku, is one of the finest in Fiji.

Rotuma

There's a saying in Fiji that if you can find Rotuma on a map, then it must be a *really* good map. Lush and verdant, **Rotuma** is a little piece of Polynesia in Melanesian Fiji. Two bodies of land, almost like twin islands, are joined by the Motusa Isthmus; the whole island is just 5 by 14 kilometers, surrounded by more than 322 kilometers of open sea. Because it's closer to the equator, it is more tropical—think heat and humidity—than elsewhere in Fiji. Rotumans grow Fiji's juiciest oranges and its strongest kava, and the women weave beautiful mats.

Most visitors to Rotuma are relatives or friends of local residents, and the number of foreign tourists arriving here is negligible. This is on purpose: In 1985, wary of tourism taking over their land and their way of life, 85 percent of Rotumans voted against opening up the island. A 2004 film, *The Land Has Eyes,* directed by Vilsoni Hereniko, explores the downside of this cultural conservatism, a conformism that some find stifling. For greater mobility and jobs, the great majority of Fiji's 10,335 Rotumans (according to the 2017 census) now live elsewhere in Fiji, especially Suva and its suburbs, with just 2,800 remaining on Rotuma.

The busiest season in Rotuma is **Fara,** a six-week festival starting **December 1,** when family members return home if possible and everyone celebrates with dancing and parties. You might find people to connect with in Suva, or via online groups (www.rotuma.net or www.facebook.com/groups/rotumans).

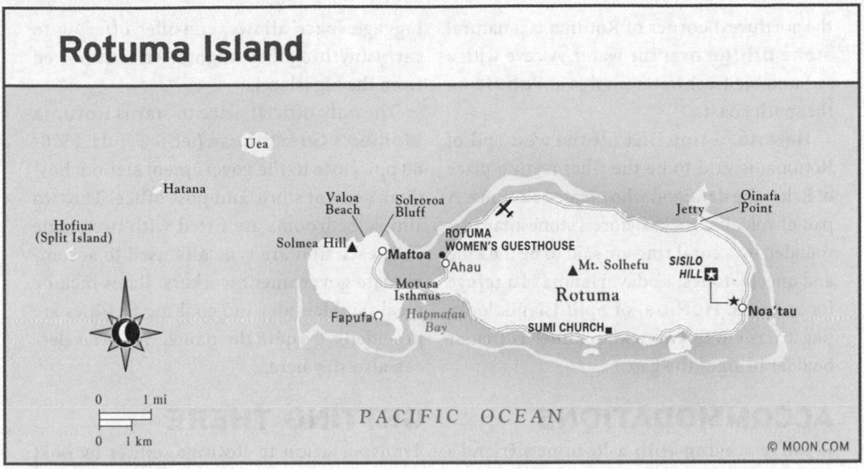

SIGHTS

Ships arrive at a wharf on the edge of the reef, connected to Oinafa Point by a 200-meter coral causeway that acts as a breakwater. The airstrip is to the west, between Oinafa and Ahau, the capital and government station. **Ahau** has a post office (tel. 889-1003), which also serves as a Western Union and convenience store. It's near a health clinic, police station, and district administrator's office. There's no bank on Rotuma.

Visitors are expected to **request permission** before visiting sites like Sisilo or the cave at Fapufa. Inquire at Ahau about whom to ask. Permission is always given unless something peculiar has come up, but this courtesy is expected and will avoid unpleasant misunderstandings.

★ Sisilo Hill

This archaeological site near Noa'tau features the massive Kine'he'he Platform and the burial place of the *sau* (kings) of yore. In 1824, 20 well-maintained stone tombs were recorded here. Each consisted of four coral slabs: a large one at the head, a smaller one at the foot, and two long slabs along the sides. Traditional feasts would be held here, with kava poured on the kings' graves. The last *sau* to be interred here was a man named Maraf who was killed during a battle between the island clans in 1845. He was buried with a defective cannon as his headstone. The old burial ground on Sisilo Hill is now overgrown with brush, and a local guide will be necessary if you want to see anything. In any case, it's important to ask permission of the elders in Noa'tau before visiting a sacred spot such as this.

Other Sights

There's a lovely white **beach at Oinafa.** Look for the fine stained glass windows in the Catholic church at **Sumi** on the south coast. Inland near the center of the island is **Mount Solhefu** (256 m), the highest peak; climb it for the view.

Maftoa, across the Motusa Isthmus, has a graveyard with huge stones brought here long ago. It's said that four men could go into a trance and carry the stones with their fingers. The yacht anchorage in Hapmafau Bay is well protected from northern winds.

Solroroa Bluff (218 m), above Maftoa, can be climbed, though the view is obstructed by vegetation. Deserted **Vaioa Beach,** on the west side of Sororoa Bluff, is one of the finest in the Pacific. A kilometer southwest of Vaioa Beach is **Solmea Hill** (165 m), with an inactive crater on its north slope. On the coast at the northwest corner of Rotuma is a natural **stone bridge** over the water. A cave with a swimmable freshwater pool is at **Fapufa** on the south coast.

Hatana, a tiny islet off the west end of Rotuma, is said to be the final resting place of Raho, the demigod who created Rotuma. A pair of volcanic rocks before a stone altar surrounded by a coral ring are said to be the king and queen stones. Today, Hatana is a refuge for seabirds. **Hofliua,** or Split Island, looks like it was cut in two with a knife; a circular boulder bridges the gap.

ACCOMMODATIONS

If you're staying with a Rotuman friend's family, as most travelers do, ask your friend what you should take along as a gift. It's also appropriate to make a financial contribution to your host family soon after you arrive, in order to compensate them for your stay (F$100 a day per couple is the minimum you should offer). When deciding on the amount, bear in mind that groceries purchased in the small stores around Rotuma cost about double what they would on Viti Levu. If your luggage space allows, consider offering to carry anything they might need transported from the big island.

The only official place to stay is **Rotuma Women's Guesthouse** (tel. 889-1011, F$70-80 pp), close to the government station, hospital, general store, and post office. The two simple bedrooms are fitted with two single beds each and are typically used to accommodate government workers. Rates include meals and laundry (no cooking facilities are provided). Despite the name, male travelers can also stay here.

GETTING THERE

Transportation to Rotuma, either by boat or plane, can be erratic, and you should be as flexible as possible. It's not uncommon for the boat from Suva to be delayed two weeks with engine trouble, and flights can be canceled.

Fiji Link flies on Friday from Nadi or Suva to Rotuma in the morning, and back in the afternoon (F$660 each way).

Ships operate from Suva to Rotuma once a month, a two-day trip for hardy

a golden beach on Rotuma

A History of Encounters

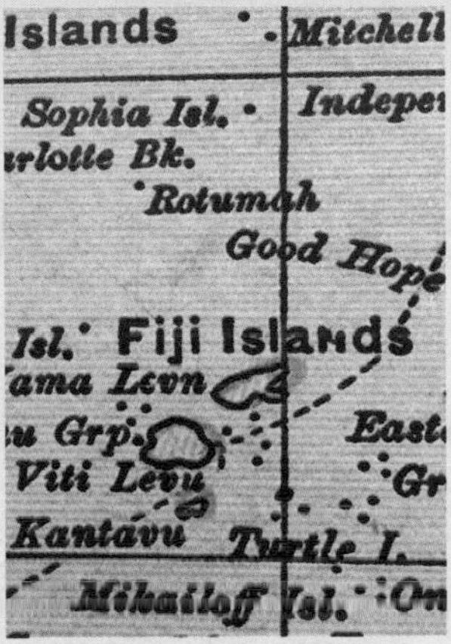

A colonial-era map shows a FIJI that does not include "Rotumah," to the north.

According to legend, Rotuma was formed by Raho, a Samoan folk hero who dumped two basketfuls of earth here to create the land. Tongans conquered Rotuma in the 17th century and ruled from Noa'tau. The first recorded European visit was by Captain Edwards of the HMS *Pandora* in 1791, while he was searching for the *Bounty* mutineers. Tongan Wesleyan missionaries introduced Christianity in 1842, followed in 1847 by Marist Roman Catholics. Their followers fought pitched battles in the religious wars of 1871 and 1878, with the Wesleyans emerging victorious.

Tiring of strife, the chiefs of Rotuma asked Britain to annex the island in 1879. Cession officially took place in 1881, and Rotuma has been part of Fiji ever since. European traders ran the copra trade from their settlement at Motusa, until local cooperatives took over.

Today Rotuma's administration is in the hands of a district officer, who in turn is responsible to the district commissioner at Levuka. Most decisions of the 15-member Rotuma island council pertain to local concerns. Occasionally Tonga makes noises about reclaiming the island, which remains remote from the rest of Fiji, while some Rotumans feel a desire for independence from both nations.

travelers only. There is also a government-operated ship and the small wooden copra boat *Adi Lomai* that goes once a month to Rotuma. Ask the crews of vessels tied up at Muaiwalu Jetty in Walu Bay on Suva for passage and schedules. You may need to persist and ask more than one person. **Bligh Water Shipping Ltd.** (tel. 331-8247, www.blighwatershipping.com.fj) occasionally has a ship to Rotuma from Lautoka.

Background

The Landscape

OCEAN

Less than 1.5 percent of the 1,290,000 square kilometers of Fiji's territory is dry land. The rest is the Pacific Ocean. The Pacific Ocean has a greater impact on the world's climate than any other geographical feature on earth. By moving the sun's heat away from the equator and toward the poles, it expands the area of our planet that is habitable. Without this redistribution of heat, we'd be squeezed into a tiny temperate zone between a waistband of scorched desert and huge polar caps.

Broad, circular currents (gyres) flow across the tropical Pacific. North of the equator, they swirl clockwise around Hawaii, bringing warm water from Southern California across to Japan and then Alaska. South of the equator, they flow counterclockwise, moving warm water from Peru to Australia, then swinging down toward Antarctica. At the northwestern rim of the **Southern Pacific Gyre** lies Fiji.

LAND

Millions of years ago, underwater volcanoes erupted again and again. Their lava flows cooled as they touched the sea, resulting in the islands known today as Fiji, 5,100 kilometers southwest of Hawaii and 3,150 kilometers northeast of Sydney. If every speck of dry land above sea level were counted, the isles of Fiji would number in the thousands, adding up to a surface area about the size of Connecticut. However, a mere 322 islands are judged large enough for human habitation, and of those, only 106 are inhabited. The rest lack fresh water or are too far away from any other land to have been settled.

All of Fiji's volcanoes are dormant or extinct, but this geological history means that there are as many as 50 active **hot springs** and thermal mud sites throughout the islands, some in use by local communities as well as tourists. Some islands are **coral atolls,** formed as coral skeletons pile up on the rim of a volcanic crater lagoon. When the last volcanic material finally disappears below sea level, the coral rim, known as a **barrier reef,** remains as an indicator of how big the crater once was.

Orientation

The seemingly scattershot shape of Fiji makes sense if you remember you're just seeing the tips of a dramatic underwater topography. Coconut-shaped **Viti Levu** ("great Fiji") lives up to its name, being twice as large as any of the other islands, about 100 by 150 kilometers. It has the biggest cities and 75 percent of the people. It's taller, too: Mount Tomaniivi, the country's highest peak, rises to 1,323 meters, and there are 28 other distinct peaks in the interior.

About half its size is **Vanua Levu** (5,587 square km) to the north, wide and shaped a bit like a shark's jaw, with the region's largest bay, Natewa Bay, almost dividing it in two. Below its lower "lip" is the much smaller "garden island," green and wet **Taveuni** (434 square km).

All around these anchors are scattered hundreds of smaller islands: the **Lomaiviti Group** tucked into the central Koro Sea, the **Mamanucas** and **Yasawas** cupping the northwestern sea border, **Beqa** and **Kadavu** to the south, and tiny **Rotuma** all on its own 587 kilometers north of Viti Levu. Stretching east is the **Lau Group,** made not of lava, but layers of limestone (dead coral) built up over millennia.

Climate

Along the coasts the weather is warm and pleasant, without great variations in temperature. The southeast trade winds prevail June-October, the best months to visit. In February and March, the wind often comes directly out of the east, dumping rain. Fiji's winter, May-November, is cooler and less humid, making these the preferred months for mountain trekking. During the drier season, the reef waters are clearest for scuba diving. Yet even during the rainy summer months (Dec.-Apr.), bright sun often follows the rains, and the rain is only a slight inconvenience. Summer is hurricane season, with up to five tropical storms annually.

Previous: a new species of damselfish recently discovered in the Lau Islands

In the Wake of Cyclone Winston

a home destroyed by Cyclone Winston

When Fiji presided over the United Nations Climate Change talks in 2017 in Bonn, Germany, it did so with moral authority. Fiji experienced only 12 tropical cyclones 1941-1980, but now at least a few come close every year. Fiji has also permanently taken in refugees of ecological disasters on the neighboring islands of Banaba, Kiribati, and Tuvalu.

On February 19-20, 2016, climate change quite literally hit home when Severe Tropical Cyclone Winston reached Category 5 intensity, with winds of 280 kilometers per hour, and struck several of the islands of Fiji. It killed 44 people, damaged or destroyed 40,000 homes, and cut communications with 80 percent of the population as well as six entire islands. Nearly 40 percent of the population—approximately 350,000 people—suffered losses or were displaced due to the storm. Several villages and most of the town of Rakiraki were leveled, and 229 schools collapsed. Koro Island had not a building untouched, while Mel Gibson's private communication tower on Mago Island toppled. In the Lomaiviti Group, 42,000 tons of debris had to be cleared.

A nationwide state of emergency lasted for 60 days, during which New Zealand, Australia, and international aid organizations sent relief while Fijians desperately tried to stay alive and rebuild. Damages totaled F$3 billion. It was the worst storm in Fiji's recorded history.

Today, Fiji and other island nations, threatened by rising sea levels as well as climate disaster, are in the position of trying to persuade those of us in larger industrialized nations to change our behavior. As Fiji's prime minister, Frank Bainimarama, told the world body, "As Pacific Islanders, we are fighting for our very survival....We are all in the same canoe, not just the island nations but the whole world. No one is immune to the effects of climate change."

Plants and Animals

PLANTS

More than 2,000 species of plants grow in Fiji, of which 476 are indigenous to the country; 10 percent of those are found only here. The absence of leaf-eating animals in Fiji has allowed the vegetation to develop largely without the protective spines, thorns, and itchy toxins found in vegetation elsewhere.

Trees

The wetter sides of the high islands are heavily forested, with occasional thickets of **bamboo** and scrub. Natural forests cover 40 percent of Fiji's total land area, and about a quarter of these forests are classified as suitable for logging. The last stands of the towering **dakua** or **kauri** tree are now being logged on Vanua Levu. Since the 1960s, many native forests have been replaced by **mahogany** plantations. The native **yaka** is a conifer whose wood has an attractive grain, and **vesi** trees are commonly harvested for furniture.

Coconut groves fill the coastal plains, creating palm-fringed shorelines, while **Caribbean pine** has been planted in many dry hilly areas. Well-drained shorelines often feature **ironwood,** or ***nokonoko,*** a casuarina appreciated by woodcarvers. **Mangroves** are commonly found along high island coastal lagoons, and their roots play an important role in preventing erosion and protecting coastlines, as well as providing nesting spots for tiny mudflat dwellers. Around Christmas, ***poinciana,*** or **flame trees**, bloom bright red.

Vegetation

Many of Fiji's forest plants have **medicinal** applications, which have recently attracted the attention of patent-hungry pharmaceutical giants. The sap of the **tree fern** *(balabala)* was formerly used as a cure for headaches by Fijians, and its heart was eaten in times of famine; its trunks are often carved into fanciful faces. Rainforest guided hikes are a treasure of apothecary information, and farm tours allow appreciation of all the cultivated species.

On the drier sides of the islands, open **sawgrass** savanna *(talasiga)* predominates where the original vegetation has been destroyed by slash-and-burn agriculture.

Sugarcane

Though only introduced to Fiji in the late 1860s, sugarcane probably originated in the South Pacific. On New Guinea the islanders have cultivated the plant for thousands of years, selecting vigorous varieties with the most colorful stems. In Fiji, you'll see cane farms, trains, and trucks all over.

ANIMALS

Some Fijian clans have totemic relationships with eels, prawns, turtles, and sharks, and are able to summon these creatures with special chants. Tribe members never eat their own patron animal.

Mammals

The first Fijians brought with them **pigs, dogs, chickens,** and **gray rats** from elsewhere in Melanasia. The only native mammals are the monkey-faced fruit **bat**, or flying fox, called ***beka*** by the Fijians, and the smaller, insect-eating bat. **Dolphins** and **whales** ply the waters offshore.

Planters introduced the Indian **mongoose** in the 1880s to combat rats, which were damaging the plantations. Unfortunately, no one realized at the time that mongooses hunt by day, whereas rats are nocturnal, so the two seldom meet.

Birds

The mongoose is the scourge of chickens and **native ground birds,** though Kadavu, Koro, Gau, Ovalau, and Taveuni are

Coral in Crisis

Oceanographer Jacques Cousteau marveled at Fiji's undersea variety, calling it "the soft coral capital of the world." More than 800 species of coral make their home in the Pacific (compared to only 48 in the Caribbean), and Fiji stands out for having no less than 33 large barrier reefs around the islands. Coral reefs are the world's oldest ecological system, and among the most fragile, taking 7,000-10,000 years for a single reef to form. They provide food and shelter for countless species of fish, crustaceans (shrimps, crabs, and lobsters), mollusks (shells), and other animals.

Scientists classify corals as part of a broad class of stinging invertebrate animals that also includes jellyfish. Only those with calcium carbonate exoskeletons and a single hollow cavity within the body are considered **true corals.** A single organism, called a **polyp,** may be no bigger than a pinhead, and a small piece of coral is actually a **colony** composed of large numbers of polyps. Corals reproduce both asexually, by budding into genetically similar clones, and sexually, by releasing streams of gametes into the water, where they find and fertilize each other. Dead corals are white, while living corals—even if they're hard and don't seem to move—are every color of the rainbow. Young corals grow on the consolidated skeletons of their ancestors. All the organic **limestone** in the world is ancient coral, cemented and mushed together with water and sediment.

You'll encounter three main types of coral in Fiji:

- Stony or **hard corals** such as brain, table, staghorn, honeycomb, and mushroom corals have rigid external skeletons and an open "mouth" ringed by six hard tentacles. Shallow waters are ideal for the colorful symbiotic algae that live in their nooks and crannies, which photosynthesize sunlight and nourish the coral. This makes hard coral particularly vulnerable to climate events and human presence close to the ocean's surface. Their skeletons form the bulk of the world's coral reefs.
- **Soft corals,** including sea anemones, don't rely on algae to feed them; they nibble on plankton by trapping it with eight fuzzy tentacles. Instead of a hard exterior, they have tiny "sclerites," bony spikes and flakes that keep them supple but tough. They're plush and colorful, but don't be fooled by how cuddly they look; many secrete toxins to fend off predators.
- **Fire corals** aren't true corals, as they belong to a different class, but they're found in the same reefs. They don't look particularly incendiary, but their stinging toxins can burn painfully for up to an hour. Watch out for yellow-green to brown brush-like growths that look like branching seaweed on a reef. Better yet, don't touch anything at all.

Alas, the global coral crisis hasn't spared Fiji. While many reefs are still strong and healthy, others are showing the bleaching effects of warming ocean temperatures and climate-change-exacerbated hurricanes, which can cover reefs with sand.

Travelers can help by following **best practices:**

- Don't touch coral (a bit of oil from your skin can kill a whole colony).

mongoose-free (and thus the finest islands for bird-watching). Feral cats do the same sort of damage.

Of the 57 breeding species of land birds, 26 are endemic. Some **150 bird species** have been recorded in Fiji, including broadbills, cuckoos, doves, fantails, finches, flycatchers, fruit doves, hawks, herons, honeyeaters, kingfishers, lorikeets, owls, parrots, pigeons, rails, robins, silktails, swallows, thrushes, warblers, whistlers, and white-eyes. The Fijian names of some of these birds, such as the *kaka* (parrot), *ga* (gray duck), and *kikau* (giant honeyeater), imitate their calls. Red and green *kula* lorikeets are often seen in populated areas collecting nectar and pollen from flowering trees or feeding on fruit.

Introduced species are the Indian

a thriving coral reef off Vanua Levu

- Don't stand or walk on living coral.
- Respect local restrictions on access to sanctuary and reef regeneration areas.
- Speak up to educate other tourists and tour operators when you see someone hurting the reefs.
- Yachties in Fiji should use moorings whenever possible. If you must anchor, avoid poking holes in the reef by using a recording depth sounder to help locate sandy areas if you can't see the bottom. Always use environmentally friendly pronged anchors with plastic tubing over the end of the chain to soften the impact.
- If you have snorkeling or diving skills (including enough buoyancy control to avoid brushing reefs with your hands and fins), you might enjoy joining a resort's coral-planting project for an afternoon.

Your individual impact may seem small, but considering that most of the 840,000 annual visitors to Fiji do check out the reefs by boat, snorkel, or scuba, the tourist impacts add up fast. The **Coral Reef Alliance** (www.coral.org) offers more guidelines and ways to help. **Wildlife Conservation Society Fiji** (https://fiji.wcs.org/) is working with local communities to protect and manage pristine marine ecospheres.

mynah, with its yellow legs and beak, the Indian bulbul, and the Malay turtledove. The hopping common mynah bird *(Acridotheres tristis)* was introduced to many islands from Indonesia at the turn of the 20th century to control insects, which were damaging the citrus and coconut plantations. The mynahs multiplied profusely and have become major pests, crowding out native species and inflicting harm on the very trees they were brought in to protect.

Of the **seabirds,** boobies, frigate birds, petrels, and tropic birds are present.

Reptiles and Amphibians

Three of the world's seven species of **sea turtles** nest in Fiji: green, hawksbill, and leatherback. Nesting occurs

November-February, on nights when there is a full moon and a high tide. Sea turtles lay their eggs on the same beach from which they themselves hatched. In the 1980s, more than 10,000 hawksbill turtle shells were exported to Japan, but the turtles and their eggs are now protected by law.

Geckos and **skinks** are small lizards often seen on the islands. The skink hunts insects by day; its tail breaks off if you catch it, but a new one quickly grows. The gecko is nocturnal, has no eyelids, and often lives indoors, eating insects attracted by electric lights.

One of the more unusual creatures found in Fiji and Tonga is the **banded iguana,** a lizard that lives in trees and can grow up to 70 centimeters in length (two-thirds of which is tail). The iguanas are emerald green, and the male is easily distinguished from the female by his bluish-gray cross stripes. Banded iguanas change color to control their internal temperature, becoming darker when in direct sun. In 1979, a new species, the **crested iguana,** was discovered on Yaduataba Island.

Two species of **snakes** inhabit Fiji: the very rare, poisonous *bolo loa* and the harmless Pacific boa, which can reach lengths of two meters. Venomous **sea snakes** are common on some coasts, but they're docile and easily handled. Fijians call the common banded black-and-white sea snake the *dadakulaci.*

Land- and tree-dwelling native **frogs** are noteworthy for the long suction discs on their fingers and toes. Because they live deep in the rainforests and feed at night, they're seldom seen.

In 1936, the **giant toad** was introduced from Hawaii to control beetles, slugs, and millipedes. When this food source is exhausted, they tend to eat each other. At night, gardens and lawns may be full of them.

Sealife

Fiji's richest store of life is found in the silent underwater world. It's estimated that half the fish remaining on our globe are swimming in the Pacific. In 2017, a Conservation International team recorded 527 species over just 11 days in the waters around the Lau Islands in southeastern Fiji, including nine potential new species whose identity will be confirmed by DNA analysis.

In the **open sea,** the food chain begins with phytoplankton, which flourish wherever ocean upwelling brings nutrients such as nitrates and phosphates to the surface. Large schools of fast-moving tuna ply these waters feeding on smaller fish, including reef fish, mollusks, and crustaceans. Other big swimmers include bonito, mahi-mahi, swordfish, wrasses, giant trevally, and the larger sharks.

In **lagoons** surrounded by barrier reefs, coral pinnacles on the lagoon floor provide a haven for smaller fish like angelfish, butterfly fish, damselfish, groupers, soldierfish, surgeonfish, triggerfish, trumpet fish, and countless more. Larger fish such as barracuda, jackfish, parrotfish, pike, stingrays, and small sharks range across lagoon waters as well as the ocean side of the reef.

Dangerous, spiky sea urchins are found on **rocky shores and reefs,** while spiny stonefish and crown-of-thorns starfish can rest on the seafloor. The tiny blue-ring octopus is only five centimeters long but packs a poison that can kill a human. Eels hide in reef crevices by day; most are harmful only if you inadvertently poke your hand or foot at them. Luckily, Fiji is free of poisonous jellyfish.

People and Culture

The story of Fiji's peoples is intrinsically tied to the land. While the country may seem tiny by continental standards, Fiji is a regional power, with more land and humans than all of the other South Pacific islands combined. Because rugged volcanic peaks collect water that flows down toward the coasts, most of Fiji's 900,000 people live along the river valleys—blessed with rich volcanic soil—or the shorelines, where they have access to sea-fishing and trade. Three quarters live on the largest island, Viti Levu.

DIVERSITY

Fiji's 2013 constitution recognizes the equality of four groups of Fijians: the **iTaukei (indigenous)** people of Fiji, the people of **Rotuma,** the **Indo-Fijians** descended from indentured laborers in British India, and the descendants of all other settlers and immigrants. This final category includes the 3,000 Fiji-born descendants of **white** planters and traders; descendants of **Solomon Islanders** who were forcibly brought to Fiji and settled here; a small number of longtime resident **Chinese** families; climate refugees from neighboring **Banaba, Kiribati,** and **Tuvalu;** and a smattering of **Samoans, Tongans,** and other neighbors, many of whom came to Fiji for an education at the regional universities in Suva. Some 98 percent of the country's population was born in Fiji.

Despite this rich mix of peoples, a generation ago Fiji was a fairly segregated society. It was normal to see only white settlers, "part-European" people of multiracial descent, and Indo-Fijians in the towns, while iTaukei (indigenous) people lived mainly in villages with traditional clan structures, under the rule and protection of their chiefs. Today, though, people of various ethnicities mingle in all of the towns. Workplaces and social circles are more integrated, and even intermarriages—once unthinkable—are now commonplace. There are still distinct "Indian" and "Fijian" villages, though, and all of the peoples of Fiji are quite proud of their own heritage.

As a tourist, you may also notice at many resorts that white owners/managers are making the decisions, while iTaukei or Indo-Fijian staff are doing the labor. How well this works out depends entirely on the managers' skill in working with their local staff, and there's a real range.

It might help to know that at most sites, the iTaukei are actually the landowners. Most resorts—even the big ones—operate on 99-year leases, by making deals not only to pay for use of the land, but also to employ the local people at a designated wage. This creates an incentive to treat workers well, as they are the real landowners and have robust workers' rights.

It's always appropriate to be polite and respectful of the local staff, and you may find that these relationships get you better treatment than if you ask the managers to make demands on your behalf.

Religion

Religious lines are largely ethnic in Fiji. Among iTaukei, the main churches are Methodist (290,000, or 78 percent), Catholic (76,500), Assembly of God (47,500), and Seventh-day Adventist (32,500). After the 1987 military coups, an avalanche of well-financed American fundamentalist missionary groups descended on Fiji, and membership in the Assembly of God and newer Christian sects has grown at the expense of the Methodists. These sects use Fiji as their base to proselytize in neighboring island nations. Indo-Fijians are mainly Hindu (233,500) and Muslim (52,500), and there are also small Sikh and Christian populations. Europeans in Fiji are mostly Christian, with about 60 Jewish people in Fiji.

Island Ecotourism

a mangrove planting project to prevent shore erosion

Sustainability and ecotourism are buzzwords these days, but how can you gauge what's truly responsible and what's just marketing? Here are three main questions that the experts ask when deciding whether a resort is truly "green," or just greenwashed.

- **Does it have environmentally sustainable practices?** Solar and wind power, rainwater harvesting, recycling, responsible waste and sewage disposal, composting or low-flush toilets, water-limiting showers, and landscaping that fits the natural conditions are good. Lawns that devour water, trash on the beach, sewage that runs into the sea, and reliance on disposable plastic (water bottles, bags, straws) are bad.
- **Is it socially responsible in creating local economic sustainability?** This is harder to judge as a tourist, but schools, medical projects, scholarship programs, and mentoring are good indicators, as is a happy workforce. Profit-sharing or co-ownership with local communities is ideal. Dive operations that focus on training local people rather than only hiring an ever-rotating crew of foreign divemasters are a good example.
- **Does it educate?** Look for signage and information about the local ecology, scientific and conservation-oriented interpretation, activities that allow you to learn as you have fun, and briefings that include not only personal safety but also how to minimize your impact on the marine or land environment.

The ecumenical **Pacific Conference of Churches** (https://pacificconferenceofchurches.org), headquartered in Suva, began in 1961 as an association of the mainstream Protestant churches throughout the South Pacific, but since 1976 many Catholic dioceses have been included as well. Both the Pacific Theological College (founded in 1966) and the Pacific Regional Seminary (opened in 1972) are in southern Suva, and serve as regional hubs for aspiring ministers.

LAND RIGHTS

Fiji is one of the few former colonies in the world in which indigenous people retain their land and traditional ways of living. A full 83 percent of the land is inalienable iTaukei communal land, which can be leased (about 30 percent is, typically on 99-year leases) but never sold. It's administered on behalf of some 6,600 clan groups (*mataqali*) by the iTaukei Land Trust Board, and each hereditary chief decides, in consultation with his people, how to best use the land. Many large resorts lease land from the villages, in exchange for not only annual rent but also agreements to employ village inhabitants.

Another 7 percent is government land, while just 10 percent is known as "freehold" land, which can be bought and sold on the free market. Most expatriates prefer to settle on freehold land, resulting in little colonies of foreigners in Savusavu, around the airport on Taveuni, and in a few other patches.

PROSPERITY

Although Fiji's economy is in a growth phase, 28 percent of the population lives below the poverty level, including 80 percent of the mostly Indo-Fijian cane farmers. Among city dwellers, single-parent urban families cut off from the extended-family social safety net are most affected, especially Fijian women trying to raise families on their own.

However, literacy is high at 87 percent, and 98 percent of children attend school even though education is not compulsory. Government and foreign investment and aid projects have made significant improvements to infrastructure over the past 15 years, including roads, ports, airports, water systems, and sewage management.

Tourism and **sugar** account for most of the country's F$8 billion gross domestic product. As the top tourist destination in the South Pacific, Fiji draws 840,000 visitors a year, largely from Australia, New Zealand, and the United States, followed by Europe and China. Despite ups and downs due to political events, tourist numbers are increasing and new developments are constantly underway. But much of the profit from the F$1.8 billion industry goes back overseas to international chains or foreign investors. Most resort and restaurant staff work for the minimum wage, F$2.68 an hour, but unionizing hospitality workers has met with stiff opposition from hoteliers.

Because of this, **sugar** is actually more beneficial to the country's economy. A quarter of Fiji's population relies on sugar for its livelihood. Almost all of Fiji's sugarcane is grown by some 22,000 independent farmers who belong to a national union. They provide cane on contract to the government-owned **Fiji Sugar Corporation.** These mostly Indo-Fijian farmers cultivate holdings that average four hectares, leased from around 2,000 indigenous Fijian landowners. Seasonal laborers cut the cane, and truck drivers and mill workers round out the workforce. The F$250 million industry seems to have been on the verge of collapse for a long time but somehow chugs along, helped by subsidies and foreign aid deals. Fiji's four aging, inefficient sugar mills are in urgent need of modernization, yet major new investments are unlikely, as the FSC has been operating at a loss since 1997. Various countries provide technical assistance and buy sugar at above-market rates as a means of foreign aid.

The **government** is the next largest employer, with schools, hospitals, administrative offices, the military, and other divisions accounting for a large portion of the workforce.

Other **significant industries** include timber, mineral water, garment manufacturing, gold mining, vegetables, rice, kava, and coconut products. **Subsistence agriculture** is important to rural areas, where manioc, taro, yams, sweet potatoes, and corn are the principal crops. **Fish** is now Fiji's second-largest export, with chilled sashimi-grade tuna heading to Hawaii and Japan and the rest to canneries in the United States. Coastal subsistence **fishing** is twice as important as commercial fishing in terms of actual catch. Two **pearl-farming** operations nurture thousands of oysters.

History

PREHISTORY

According to iTaukei oral tradition, the great serpent Degei and the hawk Turukawa were the first divine beings. When Turukawa disappeared and Degei went to look for her, he found only two eggs in her nest. He took them home for safekeeping, and they hatched into humans. He traveled with them in search of a place they could thrive and arrived at what is now the village of **Viseisei,** near Lautoka, which all Fijians recognize as the first human settlement.

EARLY HISTORY

The first archaeological evidence of human presence in Fiji is from around 1600 BC, when the **Lapita** people left shards of pottery all over the islands, as well as elsewhere in Melanesia and Polynesia. Their distinctive creations, decorated in horizontal geometric bands and dated from 1290 BC, were excavated from the sand dunes near Sigatoka and can be seen at the Fiji Museum in Suva. Later waves of people from elsewhere in the South Pacific arrived by large canoe, starting in 500 BC.

Their descendants developed a patrilineal warrior culture in which ancestral spiritual power was embodied in the *turaga* (chief), who could subdue or negotiate with other chiefs to form a larger, more powerful *vanua* (confederation). Cannibalism was thought to imbue the devourer with the power of his defeated enemies. Villages were built along ridges or terraced hillsides or fortified with ring ditches; one of the most prominent examples is the **Laucala Ring Ditch,** near Suva. The villagers built great oceangoing double canoes (*drua*) up to 30 meters long; constructed large, solid thatched houses (*bure*); performed marvelous song-dances (*meke*) for battle and other occasions; and made tapa, pottery, and skillfully plaited mats.

COLONIAL ENCOUNTERS

Fiji's fierce warriors and treacherous reefs kept it safe from colonization much longer than many other nations. In 1643, Dutchman **Abel Tasman** became the first European to sight Fiji—spying a string of mountain peaks in Taveuni—although he could not land. In 1774, British captain **James Cook** anchored off Vatoa in southern Lau but failed to proceed farther or land. British captain **William Bligh** was chased out of Fijian waters by canoe-loads of Fijian warriors just north of the Yasawas, but he managed to create the first European map of the islands. It was only in 1800, when a survivor from the shipwrecked American schooner *Argo* brought back word that **sandalwood** grew in abundance along the Bua coast of Vanua Levu, that profiteers determined to land in Fiji—to devastating ecological effect. A load of sandalwood, bought from the islanders for $50 worth of trinkets, could be sold in Canton, China, for $20,000, to be made into joss sticks and incense. By 1814, the traders had stripped the forests.

The first Europeans to mingle with Fijians were escaped convicts from Australia, who gained favor with chiefs as arms dealers, selling them European muskets to use against their enemies. From 1820 to 1850, traders collected **bêche-de-mer,** a sea cucumber that, when smoked and dried, also brought a good price in China. More followed in their footsteps, including the Frenchman **Dumont d'Urville** (1827), who offended his hosts by turning up his nose at kava and drinking his own wine instead; the American **Charles Wilkes** (1840), who produced the first modern map of Fiji but slaughtered 87 Fijians on Malolo Island over a misunderstanding; and the Englishman **H. M. Denham,** whose accurate navigational charts of 1855-1856 paved the way for future foreign visits. White "beachcombers" arrived to act as middlemen between traders and Fijians, living luxuriously and sometimes agitating local conflicts for profit. Some men of this period settled in Fiji for long periods of time, fathering local children whose descendants are still known in Fiji as "part-Europeans." A motley assortment of Europeans and Americans formed a settlement at Levuka, which whalers and traders used as a supply base. At its peak, 60-plus saloons and brothels lined the waterfront.

As the traders opened up the routes, the missionaries sought entree to Fijians' spiritual lives and afterlives. Methodists at Lakeba rendered the Fijian language into writing and print 1835-1840, but their catechism made little headway until the conversion of the powerful chiefs. As late as 1867, an Australian reverend was clubbed and eaten in central Viti Levu for touching the chief's head.

DIVIDING, CONQUERING

Europeans capitalized on and sometimes created divisions among islanders. In a heinous practice known as "blackbirding," planters kidnapped people from the Solomon Islands and New Hebrides to work on the sugar and copra plantations of Fiji, a human trade that ended only with the Polynesian Islanders Protection Act of 1872.

Meanwhile, **Ratu Seru Epenisa Cakobau** was building coalitions and attempting to unite Fiji under his rule even as he battled other local warlords. He faced another challenge when, in 1847, **Enele Ma'afu** of the Tongan royal family arrived in Lau and began building a personal empire in the name of Christianity. Europeans at Levuka also accused Ratu Cakobau of twice ordering their town set afire. Conflicts ensued, with rogue pirates and official navies duking it out at sea and warriors raiding each other's areas on land.

On July 4, 1849, a cannon exploded during the American consul's fervent celebration of his Independence Day, burning down his two-story wooden home on Nukulau Island. Local Fijians "rescued" various items from the flames, and the American—who had purchased the entire island for only $30—blamed Ratu Cakobau for his losses. The bill eventually mounted to US$45,000, and American gunboats arrived to order Ratu Cakobau to pay up.

Under pressure, in 1854 Ratu Cakobau accepted Christianity in exchange for an alliance with England's King George. The following year, the king himself arrived and, alongside 2,000 Tongans, helped Ratu Cakobau put down a local revolt at the Battle of Kaba. In the process, however, the Tongan leader Ma'afu became the dominant force in Lau, Taveuni, and Vanua Levu.

Meanwhile, both British and American presence increased, including a brief cotton rush in Fiji in the 1860s as the U.S. Civil War led to a temporary worldwide shortage of cotton. To bring order, Ratu Cakobau and planter John Thurston established the first national government at Levuka in 1871. But infighting and intrigue continued, as well as American threats over the "debt."

Unwilling to cede more land or tax his people into starvation, Ratu Cakobau begged Britain to take over his lands in exchange for paying off the Americans. This "tragic episode," as Leo Tolstoy called it in an essay against imperialism, ended in 1874 with Britain taking possession of the more than three hundred islands of Fiji. All Fijians became subjects of Queen Victoria, even those who tried to resist: the hill tribes of Viti Levu succumbed after a battle in 1876, Rotuma was annexed in 1881, and the government moved to Suva in 1882, displacing a local village to the other side of Suva Bay.

SUGAR, INDENTURE, PROFIT

The first Englishman in charge of Fiji was Governor-General **Arthur Gordon**, and his first challenge was the imperial policy that every British colony had to turn a profit. Gordon decided it was best to rule through the chiefs, so to protect their power, he ordered that native land could never be sold—only leased. He also decided not to conscript the native Fijians, who after all had voluntarily

The Flag of Fiji

Fiji's current national flag was adopted in 1970, when the country achieved independence from Great Britain. The Union Jack in the upper left corner recalls Fiji's 96 years as a British colony. On the right side of the flag is a shield with a golden imperial lion on a red background holding a cocoa pod between its paws. The red cross below the lion divides the lower part of the shield in four: stalks of sugarcane, a palm tree, a banana bunch, and a dove of peace. The flag's light blue background represents the Pacific Ocean. Though Fiji has been a republic since 1987, the symbolism of British royalty remains on its flag and currency.

A flag flies at the Fiji Museum in Suva.

given their country to the Crown. Besides, the Fijians were considered poor workers: they were under the illusion that the land would provide, as it had since creation.

Fresh from postings in Trinidad and Mauritius, where indentured Indian labor had converted tropical jungle to lucrative plantations, the governor decided to apply once again the magic formula of sugarcane plus free labor. In 1879, the first Indians arrived in Fiji.

The **indenture** system had started in 1834, just a few weeks after actual slavery was outlawed throughout the British Empire. Without the labor of enslaved Africans, the plantation economies of the colonies verged on collapse. Panicked memos traveled back and forth to London; a scheme to keep former slaves as unpaid "apprentices" failed when the slaves learned of their liberation. The Crown compensated owners for the loss of "property," but money alone could not harvest the crops.

Casting about for a practical solution, the imperial eye landed on India. There, legions of peasants were languishing in idle poverty, eager for work, if only they could afford the sea passage. So it was decided: they would mortgage the trip with their years.

Abolitionists cried foul, but over the next several decades an old system of travel and bondage was reincarnated and implemented on a grand scale: indenture. Weeks after Emancipation Day, the process of replacing slave labor began at the docks of Calcutta. It was the beginning of the modern Indian diaspora.

White colonists found the scheme nearly as cost-effective as slavery. The Indians signed up for 5-10 years of bonded labor, six days a week, nine hours a day. In return, they received round-trip passage on a converted slave ship plus a small wage, with deductions for food and illness. Those who enlisted called it the **girmit** system, a mispronunciation of the word *agreement*.

Perhaps the phonetic abridgment was appropriate, for as an agreement the system left much to be desired. Poor Indians were lured, tricked, or kidnapped outright by profit-hungry agents, who received a commission for each worker they managed to deliver. Largely illiterate, the new recruits relied on these agents to translate the English contracts. As one recruiter promised in 1893, "What is Fiji? It is heaven! . . . You will eat a lot of bananas and a stomach-full of sugar cane, and play flutes in relaxation." New recruits signed the papers with thumbprints and X's, committing them to field labor oceans away. Those who tried to leave their jobs were beaten, whipped, or imprisoned.

By the time the first "girmityas" arrived in Fiji, the system was well oiled, and it would reshape Fiji's population and landscape. Most of the Indians brought to Fiji worked for the Australian-owned Colonial Sugar Refining Company, which controlled the sugar industry from 1881 right up until 1973, when the Fiji government paid $14 million to nationalize it.

TOWARD INDEPENDENCE

At the beginning of European colonization, about 200,000 people lived in Fiji; by 1921, just 84,000 indigenous Fijians remained. Meanwhile, indenture was outlawed in 1916, leaving 63,000 Indians in Fiji. Together with the "Europeans" (a word that in Fiji also included white Australians, New Zealanders, and Americans), they would form a nation.

The first inkling of representative government came in 1904, when a legislative council was formed with six Europeans elected by the European population, plus two Fijians nominated by the Great Council of Chiefs, itself an instrument of colonial rule. In 1916, the governor appointed an Indian member to the council. Membership expanded over time but was still divided racially, and it was only an advisory body. Still, Indians inspired by Mahatma Gandhi began agitating for equal rights as citizens of the British Empire. In 1963, European women and indigenous Fijians of both genders got the vote for the first time.

After a series of agitations and the example of numerous other colonies being granted independence, a constitutional convention for Fiji was held in London. Fiji became a fully independent nation in 1970, exactly 96 years to the day (October 10) of cession. The first prime minister was **Ratu Sir Kamisese Mara**, considered the nation's founding father, and the first Fijian governor-general was **Ratu Sir George Cakobau**—great-grandson of the chief who had worked so hard to unite Fiji. For the first time, Fijians of all ethnic backgrounds had an equal vote. Fiji remained part of the Commonwealth, and Queen Elizabeth II was decreed Queen of Fiji.

A SERIES OF COUPS

As Fiji formed various new political parties, racial divisions at times dominated local politics. Four coups have attempted to pit indigenous and Indo-Fijian rights against each other, and this thread continues in Fiji's politics today.

In 1987, a multiethnic coalition defeated Ratu Mara at the polls. Its cabinet had a majority of Indo-Fijian members, and none of the indigenous Fijian members were chiefs. In response, in May a lieutenant colonel in the military, **Sitiveni Rabuka,** took command of the government. Although the Supreme Court ruled the coup unconstitutional and the political parties negotiated a truce, Rabuka staged a second coup in October, solidifying his rule. Both coups were largely bloodless, but highways were barricaded, Fijians rallied and marched, and Indian-owned businesses were firebombed. Rabuka declared Fiji a republic and deposed Queen Elizabeth II in absentia. Fiji was expelled from the British Commonwealth. In December, Rabuka reappointed Ratu Mara as prime minister of the new republic, made himself Minister of Home Affairs, and added several of his army officers to his cabinet.

Australia, New Zealand, the United States, and the United Kingdom suspended all foreign aid, and Australia—Fiji's largest trading partner—instituted an embargo on all shipments to Fiji. The Fiji dollar was devalued, inflation and food prices skyrocketed, and civil servants (half the workforce) had to accept a 25 percent wage cut as government spending was slashed. Food prices skyrocketed, causing serious problems for many families.

Indo-Fijians, feeling the backlash, began seeking ways to emigrate. By 1996, more than 58,300 left for Australia, Canada, New Zealand, and the United States, including a significant portion of the country's administrators, professionals, and technical workers—a serious loss for a country with a total population of less than 750,000. Fiji embarked on an International Monetary Fund/World Bank-style structural adjustment program.

A new constitution in 1990 gave increased power to the Great Council of Chiefs and greater voting control to indigenous Fijians, while also making Christianity the official religion. Elections held under these terms in May 1992 resulted in Rabuka becoming prime minister. A more egalitarian constitution followed, and Fiji was welcomed back into the British Commonwealth. In 1999, Fiji's 419,000 eligible voters participated in the first free election in a decade. Rabuka himself was elected, but his party was wiped out almost entirely. The new "People's Coalition" winners included seven women elected to Parliament, and the first Indo-Fijian prime minister was chosen: **Mahendra Chaudhry**, who began to wage a war against corruption and poverty. Rabuka quit parliament and became chair of the Great Council of Chiefs.

In 2000, a businessman named **George Speight,** who had been bankrupted when Chaudhry's government canceled his contracts due to corruption charges, stormed Fiji's Parliament along with three dozen armed soldiers and ex-soldiers. Parliament was in session, and Speight took its members—including Chaudhry—hostage for 56 days. In central Suva, mobs looted or burned 160 Indian shops. The commander of the Fiji Military Forces, **Voreqe (Frank) Bainimarama,** did not support the coup and ordered his men to surround the parliamentary compound, but declined to use force to free the captives for fear of triggering a bloodbath. Eighty-year-old President Mara dismissed the elected government and stepped down after Speight threatened to kill his daughter, yielding power to Bainimarama. Meanwhile, Speight's supporters invaded Fiji's main television station to dispute critical coverage, occupied tourist resorts, blocked highways, and burned down the Masonic lodge in Levuka. Bainimarama, realizing the military wasn't capable of dealing with all the unrest, appointed a prime minister, **Laisenia Qarase,** and granted amnesty to the rebels if they disarmed and released the hostages.

After the hostages were freed, Speight's agitating continued, with Bainimarama now the target. Speight was arrested and his followers rounded up for carrying weapons, in contravention of the amnesty deal. He was sent to Nukulau Island to await trial for treason. Pro-Speight soldiers raided army headquarters in an attempt to murder Bainimarama. Loyal officers helped Bainimarama escape down a gully, and in the ensuing gun battle, five rebels and three government soldiers died, and two dozen people were wounded.

The American-educated, part-Fijian Speight was an unlikely flagbearer for indigenous Fijian rights—and as it turned out, he was more interested in who would gain the rights over Fiji's US$60 million mahogany trade. He had worked for a Seattle lumber company favored by the Rabuka government, but the incoming Chaudhry government announced it intended to give the contract to the British-based Commonwealth Development Corporation. The Seattle lumberman, Marshall Pettit, told Fiji TV and the *New York Times* that his payments to Speight were for services rendered, not bribes. Whatever the case, as the *Times* concluded in its 2000 investigative report, "It does seem likely that Mr. Speight intended to emerge from the coup as the mahogany king."

Eventually, Speight pled guilty to treason, thus avoiding a trial that might have revealed his motivations and backers. His death sentence was commuted to life in prison, and most of his coconspirators served only brief terms.

Australia and New Zealand imposed sanctions, since no elections seemed forthcoming. By the end of 2000, more than 7,400 Fijians

Key Dates

A statue in front of the Government Buildings in Suva depicts the first Ratu Cakobau.

1600-1300 BC	Lapita people inhabit Fiji
500 BC	Melanesians reach Fiji by canoe
1600s-1700s	European explorers try and fail to enter Fiji
Early 1800s	Sandalwood and bêche-de-mer trade booms
1830s	Christian missionaries arrive
1847	Enele Ma'afu (Tonga) invades Lau
1854	Ratu Cakobau converts to Christianity
1865	Fijian chiefs form confederacy
1871	Levuka becomes capital
1874	Ratu Cakobau cedes Fiji to Great Britain
1879-1916	Indentured Indian laborers arrive
1881	First large sugar mill built
1881	Rotuma annexed to Fiji
1882	Capital moved from Levuka to Suva
1928	First flight from Hawaii lands at Suva
1939	Nadi Airport built
1953	Queen Elizabeth II visits Fiji
1968	University of the South Pacific established
1970	Fiji becomes independent
1973	Sugar industry nationalized
1987	Two military coups led by Rabuka; Fiji becomes a republic
1999	Labor Party under Chaudhry elected
2000	Coup led by Speight
2006	Coup led by Bainimarama
2013	New egalitarian constitution
2016	Cyclone Winston
2017	Fiji presides over UN Climate Change talks

had lost their jobs, and tourism had dropped to a quarter of its previous level; the industry was losing US$1 million a day.

A lawsuit resulted in a ruling that the 1997 constitution remained in force, and elections were called in 2001. Qarase's rule was legitimized, and in 2004, his government organized a "National Week of Reconciliation" at which many Fijian participants in the coup violence offered verbal apologies and asked forgiveness for their actions in the traditional Fijian way, but no reparations to coup victims were offered. By early 2006, some 2,000 people had been investigated for crimes relating to the coup and 728 had been charged.

In 2006, Bainimarama himself staged a coup, objecting this time to Qarase's introduction of number of measures favored by the Speight camp: amnesty for coup crimes, exclusive clan rights to coastlines and waters, and a separate tribunal process allowing the chiefs to lay claim to more of Fiji's wealth. He exiled Qarase to his home on remote Vanua Balavu, and fired the entire government.

Fiji's fourth coup was different from the previous three in that the army claimed to be acting against a clique of corrupt politicians in the name of multiculturalism. A state of emergency was in place for six months, but by mid-2007 all soldiers had been withdrawn from the streets and the roadblocks removed. In April 2007, the Great Council of Chiefs, which had backed the Qarase government, was shut down. Many of the high chiefs had become wealthy as members of powerful statutory bodies and had come to be viewed as corrupt by ordinary Fijians.

The Bainimarama regime cracked down on freedom of speech and the press. The New Zealand High Commissioner to Fiji was expelled, as was the Australian publisher of the *Fiji Sun* newspaper. Australia and New Zealand resumed sanctions against Fiji, and tourism and the value of the Fiji dollar again dropped.

RETURN TO DEMOCRACY

A new constitution in 2013 restored Fiji to a one-person-one-vote system, without racial reservations. Sanctions were lifted, the economy has recovered, and tourism is booming, although human rights advocates note a marked chill over speech and press freedoms. Executive power is in the hands of the cabinet, presided over by the prime minister, who in turn is elected by the majority party or coalition in Parliament. Bainimarama has continued to hold this position. The president, **George Konrote,** of Rotuma, is also the commander in chief of the military. Their FijiFirst party was formed in 2014 and has held power since.

At present, the most significant opposition parties also have military leaders: Rabuka as the leader of the Social Democratic Liberal Party, and retired Lieutenant-Colonel **Pio Tikoduadua** for the National Federation Party. This has raised concerns among some Fijians that the country is in the grip of a "coup culture," with election results ever-vulnerable to overthrow if someone doesn't like them, since all the party leaders have soldiers at their disposal. But for now, the country is enjoying an interval of peace and democracy.

Essentials

Getting There

AIR

In 1931, an Australian aviator set a record by flying around the world in eight days. He later settled down on his own island in western Fiji, and it took him 20 more years to create his real legacy: **Fiji Airways** (Fiji tel. 672-0888 or 330-4388, U.S. tel. 800/227-4446, Aus. tel. 800/230-150, NZ tel. 800/800-178, reservations@fijiairways.com, www.fijiairways.com). After a series of ownership changes over the decades, the government of Fiji now holds the majority share and Qantas Airways is the most significant minority stakeholder.

Fiji's geographic position makes it a convenient hub to points all around the Pacific Rim, and 30 international flights a day land at **Nadi International Airport** (NAN, 5.5 km north of Nadi town). Besides Fiji Airways and Qantas, you can catch a ride on Aircalin, Air Kiribati, Air New Zealand, Air Niugini, American Airlines, Cathay Pacific, Hong Kong Airlines, Korean Air, Jetstar, Nauru Airlines, Solomon Airlines, and Virgin Australia.

For U.S. travelers, it's an 11-hour direct flight to Nadi from Los Angeles or San Francisco. During sales, round-trip fares can drop as low as US$898, but $1,100 is a more typical price. Sydney to Nadi is about 4 hours costing AU$600 round-trip, while Auckland to Nadi is about 3 hours, NZ$600.

Baggage allowances vary by airline and class of seating. You can usually check your folding kayak, golf clubs, and surfboard as oversize baggage (for a fee), but sailboards may have to be shipped as airfreight.

SEA

By sea, major towns such as Suva and Lautoka are destinations for Pacific cruises, while international yachts are welcome at five ports of entry across Fiji (Lautoka, Levuka, Savusavu, Suva, and Rotuma).

Getting Around

AIR

Within Fiji, Nadi International and Nausori Airport north of Suva are the two main domestic hubs. Allow at least a day between flights, in case weather or machinery malfunction cancels a flight.

See **Fiji Airways** (www.fijiairways.com/bookings/domestic-flight-fares) for a current list of where the national airline flies within Fiji, along with the fares. Passengers on domestic flights, which are usually in small planes, are limited to one checked bag of 15 kilograms. Fiji Airways accepts excess baggage on a space-available basis only; this happens only after they weigh every passenger to make sure the small plane is not overloaded, meaning you can't prebook space for your luggage. You don't pay until they accept your excess baggage at the airport, and even then, it may come on the next flight rather than with you. Additional "peak period" excess baggage fees apply May 15-July 15 and November 15-December 31.

See www.ars.northernair.com.fj/Booking/FlightSchedules for a list of where private provider **Northern Air** flies within Fiji. The website can be a little frustrating to navigate, but it works. If you get fed up, call, as representatives are very friendly on the phone. Try the three numbers till you get through on one: 347-5005, 995-8162, or 773-2449. The flights are small and do book up, but you can make a tentative reservation by phone without a credit card, and then pay within 24 hours online, by phone (there is a 4 percent credit card surcharge), or in person at the office in Nadi or Suva. The same baggage restrictions apply.

SEA

Reservations are recommended when possible. Specific times and fares can be found in transportation sections throughout the book.

From Nadi to the Mamanuca and Yasawa Islands:

Most travelers take the fast catamarans that leave daily from the Marina at Port Denarau in Nadi. If you're booking travel to the Mamanucas through a hotel tour desk in Nadi, chances are you'll end up on a vessel belonging to **South Sea Cruises** (tel. 675-0500,

Previous: Flying into or around Fiji comes with a perk: spectacular aerial views of coral reefs.

Fiji Airport Codes

- ICI — Cicia
- KDV — Kadavu
- KXF — Koro
- LBS — Labasa
- LEV — Levuka
- LKB — Lakeba
- MFJ — Moala
- MNF — Mana
- NAN — Nadi
- NGI — Gau
- PTF — Malololailai
- RTA — Rotuma
- SUV — Suva
- SVU — Savusavu
- TVU — Taveuni
- VBV — Vanua Balavu

info@ssc.com.fj, www.ssc.com.fj, staffed by phone daily 0700-2000). For higher budgets, there's **Golden Charters** (tel. 992-1999 or 999-5999, bookings@goldenchartersfiji.com, www.goldenchartersfiji.com); for lower budgets, there's the **Ratu Kini Cruiser** (tel. 999-1246 or 672-1959, diveratukini@gmail.com) or the **Mana Flyer** (tel. 930-5933). To reach the Yasawa Islands, most travelers take the "yellow boat," the *Yasawa Flyer II,* operated by **Awesome Adventures** (tel. 675-0499, www.awesomefiji.com), which is owned by South Sea Cruises. An alternative to the *Yasawa Flyer* is the 46-seat **Fiji Seabus** (tel. 666-2648, 924-9770, or 904-3723, www.seabusfiji.com, tavewaseabus@coral.com.fj), also known as the Tavewa Seabus or simply the "red seabus."

From Viti Levu to Vanua Levu/Taveuni: Several ferries travel to and from Vanua Levu on a confusing variety of routes. Ferry tickets also include bus fare for the hours-long journeys to reach the towns from the two main arrival points. Some of these journeys are overnight. If you're coming from Viti Levu, you'll most likely depart from Natovi Jetty north of Suva and arrive at **Nabouwalu Jetty,** at the southwestern tip of Vanua Levu. If you're coming from Taveuni, you'll come into **Natuvu Jetty** on Buca Bay, at the eastern terminus of the Hibiscus Highway on Vanua Levu. The most popular service is via **Patterson Brothers Shipping** (tel. 331-5644, fijisearoad1@gmail.com, www.fijisearoad.com), which operates the "Sea-Road" bus/ferry/bus service between Vanua Levu and Viti Levu. Other companies include Savusavu-based **Miller Shipping** (tel. 755-6672, 755-6673, or 968-1127), which links Suva, Vanua Levu (at both Nabouwalu jetty on the southwestern tip, and Natuvu on the eastern end), Rabi Island, and Taveuni; **Grace Shipping** (tel. 885-0448 or 995-0775), which links Taveuni and Vanua Levu; and **Goundar Shipping** (tel. 777-5463, goundarshipping@kidanet.com.fj), with trips from Suva to Savusavu and Taveuni.

BUS

Scheduled public bus service is available on Viti Levu, Vanua Levu, Taveuni, and Ovalau, and the fares are low. It's the cheapest way to travel and the one most likely to bring you in proximity to locals. Some buses are open-air, without glass windows, while certain express buses even have air-conditioning. In towns, bus stations are usually at the local market. A bus that says "Via Highway" is a slow local, while an "Express" skips many stops; be sure to inquire when you board. The times of buses can be hard to look up, but keep asking passengers and drivers until you get a good answer. Local buses might run late, but long-distance express buses depart right on time.

On Viti Levu, the most important routes are between Lautoka and Suva, the biggest cities. If you follow the southern route via Sigatoka, you'll be on Queens Road, the smoother and faster of the two. Kings Road via Tavua is longer, but you get to see a bit of the interior. Fares from Suva are F$5.40 to Pacific Harbor, F$11.25 to Sigatoka, F$15.70 to Nadi, F$16 to Nadi Airport, F$18 to Lautoka, and F$20 to Ba. Fares average just more than F$3 for each hour of travel.

TAXI

Taxis are plentiful and also relatively cheap, except in certain tourist areas such as Denarau. On Viti Levu, taxis are metered, and meters are required for trips under 16 kilometers. For longer trips, or on other islands, you'll need to negotiate. You don't need to accept the first "flat rate" you hear; haggling aggressively in Fiji is not customary, but you can often get the driver to budge by at least 10% if you're friendly. It's affordable to hire a taxi for a half-day or whole-day tour, especially for two or more people. Show the driver a list of everything you might want to see before setting out and be sure the price is clearly understood. If your driver is well chosen, you'll have a relaxing day with a local guide. Estimated rates for common trips are included in the location chapters.

CAR

Rental cars are available on the two biggest islands: Viti Levu (in Nadi, Suva, Lautoka, and Sigatoka towns) and Vanua Levu. (On other islands, only informal arrangements for borrowing cars exist; beware, as these are uninsured deals.) Rates can vary widely, especially between the local companies and international franchises. The local companies tend to have lower rates but older cars. Make reservations in advance.

The roads in Fiji are generally good, and if you can adjust to driving on the left side of the road, you should have no trouble. Consider whether you'll be going off the highways, in which case you may want a 4WD vehicle, especially if it's rainy during your trip. Some companies' contracts don't allow you to go into the mountainous interior or to take your rental car on an interisland ferry.

Note that many gas stations are closed on Sunday. Hitchhiking is common and expected on the smaller islands where bus and taxi service is infrequent.

There's a lot of fine print when it comes to renting a car in Fiji:

- Drivers must be over 21 and have a valid driver's license from their home country, but some companies charge more for drivers under 26. A few don't rent to drivers under age 25.
- You'll pay extra if you want to return a car to a different place from where you picked it up.
- Some companies forbid taking a rental car on the inter-island car ferries; be sure to ask if you plan to do this.
- A stamp duty of F$10 per rental is levied on top of all taxes and fees.

If you're not already at the airport, most companies will deliver the car to your hotel or give you a free transfer to the airport to pick up your car. Here's a complete list of rental car companies operating from the Nadi airport. The prices quoted below are for a single day; rates go down by as much as 50 percent for multiday rentals.

- **Avis** (tel. 672-2233 or 999-1451, info@avis.com.fj, www.avis.com.fj) has vehicles from a compact (F$123) to an eight-seater luxury SUV (F$331).
- **Budget** (tel. 672-2735, reservations@budget.com.fj, www.budget.com.fj) has options from subcompacts (F$82) to a five-seater SUV (F$165). Note that Budget has a higher age threshold; you must be 25 or over and have held your license for two years.
- **Bula Car Rentals** (tel. 670-1209, 990-8990, or 999-9718, reservations@bulacarrentals.com.fj, www.bulacarrentals.com.fj) can be booked directly or through Tappoo shops. A scooter is F$89 and a subcompact is F$99, with rates increasing up to a nine-seater van for F$219. You can also book a chauffeur for F$70 a day, from 0800 to 1700, with 48 hours advance notice.

- **Europcar** (tel. 672-5957 or 999-3407, reservations@europcarfiji.com.fj, europcarfiji@connect.com.fj, www.europcar.com.fj) has subcompacts (F$67) up to small SUVs (F$106).
- **Satellite Rent-A-Car** (tel. 670-2109 or 999-2109, satelliterentals@connect.com.fj, www.satelliterentacar.com.fj) has compacts (F$159) up to 11-seater vans (F$350).
- **Thrifty Car Rental** (tel. 672-2755, www.thriftyfiji.com) has three categories: compact sedan (US$92), midsize hatchback (US$154), and five-seater SUV (US$201). Rosie Holidays operates joint desks with Thrifty in many hotels.
- **True Blue Rent-A-Car** (tel. 670 7470, 999-7368, or 929-7368, renttrueblue@connect.com.fj, www.truebluerentacar.com) has vehicles ranging from a hybrid Toyota Prius (F$90) to a 4WD SUV (F$180). The minimum rental is two days.

Tours

ORGANIZED TOURS

While packaged travel isn't for everyone, reduced group airfares and discounted rates at top hotels make some tours an excellent value. For two people with limited time and a desire to have all meals and activities included, a package tour may be the cheapest way to go. Solo travelers will pay a healthy supplement. You'll probably get prepaid vouchers to turn in as you go along. Alcohol is usually not included in the package price. Do check all the restrictions.

Fiji Holidays (www.fijiairways.com/fiji-holidays), a service of Fiji Airways, offers flight-plus-hotel deals at four- and five-star resorts.

Travel Agencies

Travel agencies at home can help you organize a trip with various levels of customization. Spend some time surfing through their websites, and crosscheck the resorts they offer using the listings in this guide.

From the **United States and Canada:**

- www.fijitravel.com
- www.fijivacations.com
- www.islandsinthesun.com/fiji
- www.otadventures.com/countries/fiji/
- www.pacific-destinations.com/product-category/fiji/
- www.tropicalfiji.com
- www.zicasso.com/fiji

From **Australia:**

- www.essencetours.com.au
- www.hideawayholidays.com.au/fiji/

From **New Zealand:**

- www.ginz.com
- www.goholidays.co.nz
- www.hootholidays.com.au/fiji

If you're booking with a foreign tour company, chances are they've outsourced your trip. You might be able to cut out the middleman and save a percentage by dealing with the inbound Fiji agency directly, if you don't mind some long-distance emails. The following Nadi-based agencies are reputable:

Argo Travel & Foreign Exchange (269 Main St., tel. 670-2308) has an office in town. It exchanges money and books local, regional, and international flights.

ATS Pacific (at Nadi Airport and many resorts, tel. 672-2811, www.atspacific.com), **Coral Sun Fiji** (at Nadi Airport, tel. 934-4411, www.coralsunfiji.com), and **Fiji's Finest Tours** (Port Denarau, tel. 675-0646, www.fijisfinesttours.com) all offer similar tours and services; compare rates or go with the one that's most convenient to you.

Rosie Holidays (at Nadi Airport and

many resorts, tel. 672-2755, www.rosiefiji.com) works with most of the upscale resorts and many foreign travel agencies, catering to international visitors with special touches such as garlands and welcome drinks. If you booked your trip through a foreign travel agency, chances are you'll be greeted by Rosie's staff at the Nadi airport office, which is open 24 hours.

TTF, or **Tourist Transport Fiji** (at Nadi Airport, tel. 672-3311, www.touristtransportfiji.com), handles the "Feejee Experience" backpacker bus tours around Viti Levu.

Be sure that you leave their offices understanding which vouchers you need for which trips, and make sure any important details are in writing on your vouchers (two queen beds, not one king bed, for example; breakfast, Wi-Fi, etc.). It can be difficult to get a refund from an agent if something goes wrong. The best arbiter of disputes is probably your international credit card.

Sea-Based Tours

If you can't be bothered with wasting time on land, book an all-inclusive trip that focuses on being in, on, or under the sea. All meals are included, and usually as much of your chosen activity as your stamina allows.

Two local **cruise** companies can take you around Fiji in style, with frequent excursions for beach and adventure time. **Blue Lagoon** is more upscale but has a limited range, going only to the Mamanucas and Yasawas. **Captain Cook** follows a similar pathway, but also cruises through the Lau Islands and Lomaiviti Group several times a year. These all-inclusive trips draw plenty of elders and families with young children, the occasional honeymooners, and a smattering of others.

For scuba, pretty much anywhere in Fiji you can strap on your gear, walk into the sea, and see something amazing. But for the most devoted water bunnies, there's nothing better than a **scuba liveaboard** experience: Wake up, roll into the water, rinse and repeat. Snacks and meals are provided for your surface intervals, and you can snorkel and dive as much as your stamina—and PADI chart—allow. The ***Aggressor*** (www.aggressor.com/fiji.php) is a 30-meter cruiser with five cabins based at the Novotel in Suva; it travels south through the Great Astrolabe Reef. The 34-meter, eight-cabin ***Nai'a*** (www.naia.com.fj) starts in Lautoka and travels west through the Bligh Waters and Rainbow Reef. Both include land excursions. The Nai'a is more expensive, and dive reviews say it's worth it.

Calm coastlines sheltered by barrier-reef halos make Fiji an excellent place for kayaking, and almost every resort has a couple of kayaks that guests can take out. If you long for more paddling time, weeklong **ocean kayaking** tours are offered in the Yasawas and around Kadavu. Beginners are welcome if you have the stamina, as kayaking isn't hard to learn.

Surfing package deals are popular around the famous Cloudbreak.

Land Tours

Talanoa Treks (tel. 998-0560, info@talanoa-treks-fiji.com, https://talanoa-treks-fiji.com) offers a four-night hiking and village stay tour that benefits people of the highlands communities in lush, mountainous Viti Levu. There's about six hours of hiking a day. These high-quality adventures with excellent guides give you the chance to explore areas of Fiji that see fewer than a hundred tourists a year.

Feejee Experience (672-5950, www.feejeeexperience.com), represented by Tourist Transport Fiji at Nadi Airport, offers organized low-budget bus tours around Fiji. These tours get very mixed reviews and are nonrefundable. For budget travelers, it's worth checking out the suggested itineraries online—and then booking them yourself for about half the price.

Tours for Students

Rustic Pathways (tel. 800/321-4353, www.rusticpathways.com) operates a variety of programs in Fiji for high school students ages 14-18. The base house, at Momi Bay, is for students only, and isn't open to other tourists. Most tours involve some study and hours that count toward community service credits, combined with travel and adventure sports. Prices start at US$1,995 plus airfare.

Tours for Seniors

Hawaii-based **Pacific Islands Institute** (tel. 808/732-1999, www.explorethepacific.com) operates educational tours in cooperation with **Road Scholar** (www.roadscholar.org; formerly **Elderhostel**) for those 55 and over. Younger spouses are welcome. The Fiji trip includes walking and snorkeling in Savusavu (at Daku Resort) and Taveuni (at Paradise Taveuni) for 11 days at US$5,699, including round-trip airfare from Los Angeles. A marine biologist and other experts guide the group.

YACHTS

Fiji has five ports of entry for **yachts:** Lautoka, Levuka, Savusavu, Suva, and Rotuma.

To crew on a yacht, you must be willing to wash and iron clothes, cook, steer, keep watch at night, and help with engine work. Other jobs might include changing and resetting sails, cleaning the boat, scraping the bottom, pulling up the anchor, and climbing the mainmast to watch for reefs. Expense-sharing crew members pay US$70 or more a week per person. If you have crewing skills or are ready to learn, the best places to look for a boat are the Royal Suva Yacht Club and Novotel Marina in Suva; the Vuda Point Marina, Port Denarau Marina, and Musket Cove Resort, all near Nadi; and the Copra Shed Marina at Savusavu. Cruising yachts are recognizable by their foreign flags, wind vane steering gear, sturdy appearance, and laundry hung out to dry. Good captains evaluate crew on personality, attitude, and willingness to learn more than experience, so don't lie. Be honest and open when interviewing with a skipper—a deception will soon become apparent. Prime season is May-October.

If you're on your own yacht, Fiji's Ports Authority can be contacted over VHF channel 16. Calling at an outer island before clearing customs is prohibited. Levuka is the easiest place to check in or out, as all of the officials have offices right on the main wharf; Savusavu is also convenient. Lautoka is the most inconvenient, as the popular yacht anchorages off western Viti Levu are far from the town. To visit the outer islands, yachts require a letter of authorization from the Ministry of Foreign Affairs in Suva, or the commissioner (at Labasa, Lautoka, or Nausori) of the division they wish to visit. Yacht clubs in Fiji can advise on how to obtain permission. **Yacht Help Fiji** (www.yachthelp.com) and **Fiji Shores & Marinas** (www fijimarinas.com) have tons of useful information for yachties.

Food and Accommodations

TAXES

A 9 percent Value-Added Tax (VAT) is applicable to all goods and services in Fiji. Visitors staying in hotels and resorts are also subject to a 6 percent Service Turnover Tax (STT) and an Environment & Climate Adaptation Levy of 10 percent on all meals and accommodations. When booking rooms, check whether this hefty 25 percent tax is included in your rate or not; often the whole thing is called VAT tax, though it's three separate taxes. Menus typically list pretax prices. Many places levy a credit card surcharge of 3-5 percent.

FOOD

Fiji's diverse cuisine reflects the many populations who share the islands.

Fijian restaurants once served up unimaginative copies (either passable or poor) of continental cuisine. But these days, nouveau chefs are offering innovative twists on local specialties. **Yams** (*tivoli*), ocean and river

fish, coconut in all its forms, **duruka** (a cane shoot, with a texture and mild taste similar to water chestnuts), ***nama*** ("sea grapes," a type of seaweed), and **taro** and **cassava** (potato-like root vegetables) play starring roles. Look for **kokoda,** Fiji's version of ceviche, in which the "cooking" agent is vinegar instead of lime and is mellowed out with fresh coconut milk. ***Vakalolo*** is fish and prawns baked in coconut cream, while ***kuita*** is smoked octopus. Taro leaves are used to make a dish called ***palusami,*** often stuffed with corned beef; the same leaf is known as ***rourou*** when soaked in coconut cream. Taro stems are cut into a marinated salad called ***baba.*** Cassava is peeled, diced, and soaked in water for three days, then mashed together with sugar and grated coconut to make thin vasili leaf-wrapped tubes of a snack called ***bila***. Seasoned chicken (*toa*) is wrapped and steamed in banana leaves to produce ***kovu. Miti*** is a delicious sauce made of coconut cream, oranges, and chilies, served over fish.

Tropical fruits are abundant year-round. Don't miss the pineapple, papaya, passionfruit, mangoes and other beauties that populate every market and buffet spread. Wash it all down with **coconut water** fresh from a tree; most places, there will be someone offering to scramble up 10 meters to retrieve one for a few bucks.

Most resorts and some restaurants offer a ***lovo*** **feast** every few nights, prepared in an impromptu oven-stove. A shallow fire pit is covered with large lava rocks and set alight. After the rocks reach peak barbecuing temperature, a lattice of banana fronds forms a sort of grille on which food, wrapped in banana leaves, is cooked: root vegetables, fish, coconut, and spices.

Indian dishes are spicy, often **curries** with rice and **daal** (spiced lentil stew). Breads include the flat, tortilla-like **roti** or **chapati,** the smaller deep-fried **puri,** or the stone-oven-baked **naan,** similar to pita bread. **Papadam** is a crispy lentil-flour cracker, while **pulao** is a mixture of rice, peas, and other vegetables. **Lamb kebabs** and **goat curry** are a specialty of the Gujarati community of Fiji. Deep-fried **samosas** are usually stuffed with a spicy potato mixture, while deep-fried **pakoras** are made of gram flour, chili, and onion or other chopped vegetables. Spicy chutney, pickle, and yogurt are common accompaniments. A **thali** is a round metal plate with several compartments for rice, daal, curries, breads, and chutney, and can be either vegetarian or nonvegetarian. Yogurt mixed with water and salt makes a refreshing drink called **lassi.** South Indian vegetarian dishes like **idli** (steamed white rice cakes) and **masala dosa** (a crispy rice pancake folded over a potato-onion mixture), both served with a spicy lentil soup called **sambar,** are breakfast favorites. Some Indian places serve a dizzying and colorful array of sweets and trail-mix-like spicy snack mixes to go; take a few flavors to sample on a long road or boat trip.

It's not uncommon for a single restaurant to serve up standards from these two cuisines alongside **Chinese** noodles and stir-fries, as well as **Western** dishes such as pizza and burgers. Recent additions to the culinary landscape in Fiji include **Japanese, Thai,** and **Korean** restaurants in the larger cities and resorts.

For **groceries**, the big supermarket chains (with bakeries and fast-food counters) are open seven days, but most smaller shops close on Sundays and open only for a half day on Saturdays. **Bakeries** usually have the freshest goods before 1400.

It's always cheaper to eat outside a fancy hotel, and inside a basic one. Many **hotels** in Fiji are the only operation on the whole island, so you may not have much choice other than to go with the resort's **meal plan**. If you do have a choice, try it for just a day; see whether the food is to your liking. Sometimes it's also possible to choose a two-meal plan (breakfast and dinner) instead of three, which gives you flexibility to be away from the resort at lunchtime or to enjoy fruits or snacks midday.

Fiji is getting better at catering to **vegetarians,** but you'll want to carry your own protein bars if you're staying in a budget place and are on the meal plan; sometimes the "vegetarian" option is just vegetables, fruit, and starch. Outside hotels, an Indo-Fijian restaurant is a vegetarian's best bet.

DRINK

Amazing herbal teas, sodas, and juices are widely available in Fiji, and worth trying. Lemon leaf tea (*drau ni moli*) is a village specialty, while *moli* (a citrus) makes a refreshing juice. Juice stalls near the markets and an increasing number of cafes offer a wide variety.

Fiji's most potent offering is **yaqona,** also known as **kava** or (if you're English) grog: a fermented potion distilled from the powdered root of a plant that belongs to the pepper family. It's an acquired taste, and the effect can range from a mellow stoned feeling to a face-numbing euphoria. The pleasure of kava is more communal than gastronomic; it is usually enjoyed in a group that passes around a shared coconut husk, a carved wooden bowl, or—thanks, globalization!—a plastic tub. Fijians spend an estimated F$750,000 a day on kava, adding up to a F$276 million industry.

If you prefer not to numb your tongue, Fiji has several fine **rum** distilleries, thanks to the sugarcane industry. Look for Ratu Rum, Samaroli Fiji Rum, and several varieties of Seven Tiki rum. The famous Fiji Bitter **beer** is brewed in Suva by a Coca-Cola subsidiary. Locals also make a kind of moonshine from cassava or taro, known as **boro**, and a palm wine, **tadi** (toddy). If you're planning on buying whole bottles to consume during your stay, the duty-free shop in Nadi Airport's arrivals hall has good prices, and stores in towns are always cheaper than stores at or near resorts.

HOTELS

The word "resort" is rather loosely applied in Fiji. A backpacker resort may consist of little more than a cluster of thatched huts with communal bathing and eating facilities. At the other end of the market are the designer resorts that offer en suite bathrooms with marble floors, personal butlers and maids, and chefs capable of pleasing the most demanding gourmet. Most Fijian resorts lie somewhere in between, providing cleanliness and adequate comfort, either in low-rise blocks of rooms or in freestanding cottages, which are often called "*bures*" or "villas" regardless of building materials and size.

When picking a hotel, price is not always an indicator of quality and service. Owner-operated properties in Fiji are generally more likely to be responsive to travelers' needs than places owned by distant overseers. Bear in mind that although a thatched bungalow is cooler and more aesthetic than a concrete box, it's also more likely to have insect problems, especially at a budget property. Carry repellent and ask for mosquito coils. With luck there will be a resident lizard or two to feed on the bugs.

You don't have to accept the first room offered; feel free to look at several before choosing. If a place isn't full, they'll often upgrade you for free. If you don't mind sleeping in a dorm or are packing a tent, you might show up without reservations, but this is risky during high season.

Read the fine print on the hotel's cancellation policy, which you should expect to be rigorously applied. There's often a 100 percent charge unless you cancel 30 days in advance.

If your group includes infants and children—or conversely, if you hope to avoid children—don't hesitate to make a special request with the resort. Many have free and paid kids' clubs, all-day babysitters, and/or adults-only areas.

Getting the Best Deal

The rack rates quoted throughout this book are about double what you can pay in practice. Nadi travel agents tack on a 30 percent commission, which they pass on to international partner travel agents, so you'll certainly do better if you bypass a travel agent.

In the low-to-medium price range, you'll often get the best deals by walking in or booking just a day or two ahead. Budget places don't have a lot of wiggle room or incentive to give discounts ahead of time, but as a walk-in, your 50 percent is better than leaving the room empty. Dorm beds are the cheapest stays, and dorms are usually mixed-gender; if the dorm already has several people of the other gender, you might see if the place will upgrade you to a single room at the same price, to keep everyone comfortable.

At the higher end, you can often get a substantial discount by booking well ahead of time, with or without a package tour. The best rates are often through a third-party travel site (TripAdvisor, Travelocity, Expedia, Agoda, hotels.com, and booking.com are all active in Fiji). At the large international chains, loyalty programs often give you benefits such as free Wi-Fi or breakfast, so it's worth joining even if you don't plan to rack up any more stays.

When tourism is slow—most likely in February, March, and November—many resorts offer specials, and prices become negotiable. Christmas is a busy time, as are the Australia and New Zealand school holiday weeks (in April, July, and October). Always check the "deals" area of a resort's website to find out about seasonal packages and discounts, and if none are listed, email or call to inquire. A free night is often given on stays of more than four days.

CAMPING

Only resorts owned by Fiji nationals are allowed to offer camping facilities.

Away from these spots, remember that all land is owned by someone in Fiji; get permission before pitching your tent, and present a *sevusevu* if it's iTaukei land. Asking to camp *inside* a village implies that people's homes are not good enough for you. Instead, seek permission to camp at a scenic spot nearby.

Travel Tips

WHAT TO PACK

If you're flying domestically, keep your luggage light: The limit on small-plane flights is one bag of 15 kilograms per passenger. Be sure to pack **mosquito repellant, sunscreen** that's free of oxybenzone, a **sun hat, water bottle, reef shoes** or sandals that will survive sand and water, and as many **swimsuits** as you want. A **mask** and **snorkel** are essential—you'll be missing half of Fiji's beauty without them.

Attire is casual everywhere. Loose-fitting cotton washables, light in color and weight, suit the tropical climate. In midwinter (July-August), it can be cool at night, so a light sweater, shawl, or windbreaker may come in handy.

In addition to personal **medications,** you might want a motion-sickness remedy, a diarrhea remedy, aspirin, antibacterial ointment, anti-itch calamine lotion, hand sanitizer, and baby powder to prevent prickly heat rash.

Your devices will need a 240 volt-compatible battery charger, plus an adapter with two flat plugs at angles (the same as used in Australia and New Zealand). A spare battery or power pack will come in handy; many of the smaller resorts have limited electricity.

VISAS AND OFFICIALDOM

Citizens of most countries do not need a visa to enter Fiji for four months or less; see the list of exempt nations at www.fijihighcom.com. All travelers should be prepared to show:

- a passport valid at least six months after arrival;
- a ticket for departure from Fiji and the appropriate visa or document for entering your next destination; and
- up-to-date vaccinations for tetanus, hepatitis A and hepatitis B.

If you're staying more than four months, you must apply for a two-month extension at the immigration offices (tel. 331-2622, www.immigration.gov.fj, Mon.-Fri. 0830-1230) *before* your current permit expires. There are offices in Lautoka, Savusavu, Levuka, Labasa, Rotuma, Suva (in the Civic Tower behind the library on Victoria Parade), or Nadi Airport (departures hall). Bring the F$96 fee, your passport, onward or return ticket, accommodation booking or letter for the remainder of your stay, and proof that you have sufficient funds to continue traveling in Fiji. After six months, you must leave and stay away at least four days, after which you can return and start on another four months. Yachties can obtain extensions for up to one year.

CONSULATES

The following diplomatic missions are in Suva:

- Australia: 37 Princes Road, Samabula, tel. 338-2211, www.fiji.embassy.gov.au
- Chile: Suite 1 Q.B.E. Centre, 18 Victoria Parade, tel. 330-0433
- China: 183 Queen Elizabeth Drive, Nasese, tel. 330-0215, http://fj.china-embassy.org/eng/lxwm/
- European Union: Fiji Development Bank, 360 Victoria Parade, tel. 331-4866
- Federated States of Micronesia: 37 Loftus Street, tel. 330-4566
- France: Pacific House, 2nd Floor, Butt Street, tel. 331-0526, https://fj.ambafrance.org/-The-Embassy
- Germany: 80-82 Harris Road, tel. 331-2633, www.wgfiji.com.fj
- India: LICI Building, Level 7, Butt Street, tel. 330-1125, www.indianhighcommissionfiji.org
- Indonesia: Ra Marama House, 6th floor, 91 Gordon Street at Thurston, tel. 331-6697
- Japan: BSP Life Centre, Level 2, Thomson Street, tel. 330-4633
- Kiribati: 36 McGregor Road, tel. 330-2512
- Korea: Vanua House, 8th Floor, Victoria Parade, tel. 330-0977, 330-0683, or 330-0709
- Malaysia: Pacific House, 5th Floor, Butt and MacArthur Streets, tel. 331-2166, www.kln.gov.my/web/fji_suva/
- Marshall Islands: 41 Borron Road, Samabula, tel. 338-7899
- Nauru: Ratu Sukuna House, 7th Floor, Victoria Parade and MacArthur Street, tel. 331-3566
- New Zealand: Reserve Bank Building, 10th Floor, Pratt Street, tel. 331-1422
- Papua New Guinea: 1 Central Street, 1st Floor, tel. 330-4244
- Solomon Islands: 33 Ellery Street, Downtown Boulevard, Plaza 1, Level 3, Government Buildings, tel. 310-0355
- South Africa: 16 Kimberly Street, tel. 331-1087
- Taiwan: Pacific House, 6th Floor, Butt and MacArthur Streets, tel. 331-5922
- Tuvalu: 16 Gorrie Street, tel. 330-1355
- United Kingdom: 47 Gladstone Road, tel. 322-9100, www.gov.uk/guidance/living-in-fiji
- United States: 158 Princes Road, Tamavua Heights, tel. 331-4466, http://suva.usembassy.gov

CONDUCT

Respect—for humans, the land, and all life—is one of the most important aspects of Pacific life, and humility is also greatly appreciated. Fijians may not show open disapproval if their social codes are broken, but don't underestimate them. **Land rights** are especially important; never trample on a village's right to the land and sea surrounding it, and err on the side of asking permission if you're uncertain.

Be friendly; it's customary to smile and say hello or *bula* to people as you pass. Try to take an interest in local people, not as servant-bots or as a collection of exotic stories, but as people with families and the same range of human joys and sorrows as you.

The *Sevusevu* and Village Etiquette

Fijian villages are communally held private property, and you should only enter after you've been formally welcomed and your *sevusevu* accepted on behalf of the community.

The *sevusevu* is a reciprocal gift, expressed in advance to thank your hosts for the hospitality you're receiving. This can be money, but it's usually a 500-gram "pyramid" of whole kava roots (not powder), which can be easily purchased at any Fijian market for about F$20. The same applies if you wish to surf off the coast of a village, picnic on a village beach, or fish in the lagoon near a village, or if you'd like permission to stay overnight in the village.

If you're not with a tour group, wait until someone greets you, and then say you wish to be taken to the *turaga-ni-koro* (village herald). Place the bundle on the ground in front of him; don't hand it to him. If he accepts by touching the package, he'll grant you permission to look around and assign a villager to act as your guide and host. Permission is usually given unless something important is happening, such as a funeral, feast, or church service (avoid arriving on a Sunday).

Shake hands with your hosts and introduce yourself by name; be sure to learn their names. Children are beloved in Fiji, so your children can expect a warm welcome, and it's always appropriate to compliment someone on the beauty of their children.

Take off your hat while walking through a village, where only the chief is permitted to wear headgear. Carry backpacks, handbags, and cameras in your hands rather than slung over your shoulders. Don't point at people or raise your voice. Always ask before taking pictures of individuals or inside buildings. Before eating, wait until grace has been said. If you're offered kava, clap once with cupped hands, take the bowl with both hands, say "*bula,*" and drink it all in one gulp. Then hand the bowl back to the same person and clap three times, saying "*vinaka*" (thanks).

Many villages have only minimal electricity, running water, toilets, and furniture. Don't use up their precious resources by demanding to charge your cell phone. Bring your own bottled water, and if you need to use the facilities, don't expect toilet paper.

Before entering a *bure,* take off your footwear, and stoop as you walk around inside. It's offensive to walk in front of a person seated on the floor, so go around behind the person, and always say "*tulou*" ("excuse me") as you pass. When you join people already seated on mats on the floor, clap three times.

Inside a *bure,* men should sit cross-legged, women with their legs to the side. Standing, lying down, sitting with your legs stretched out in front, or sitting with your knees up during presenta-

If things work differently (more slowly, less explicably) than they do back home, try to feel gratitude that you're among the few lucky globetrotters who have the privilege to travel and have these new experiences. Don't stress out if things, people, and events run late. Relax, smile, take a breath, and marvel at how out of sync you are with **"bula time."**

In Fijian villages, wrap a **sulu** around you to cover up bare legs and/or shoulders. In town, skirts and shorts should cover the upper legs while seated, and men should always wear a shirt. It's fine to lounge on your hotel's beach in just a bathing suit, though.

Get consent before **photographing** individuals. If they ask for money, which happens rarely, you can either make a contribution or say no; both parties have the right to walk away, of course. At markets, smile and say something friendly to the vendors before and after taking photos of their wares. Show your subjects their pictures on your screen, and offer to email copies to them.

ACCESS FOR TRAVELERS WITH DISABILITIES

Facilities for travelers with disabilities are not well developed in Fiji, although Fiji ratified the United Nations Convention on the Right of Persons with Disabilities in 2007 and created a strategic plan covering the years 2008-2018. The **Fiji National Council for Disabled Persons** maintains a

Men prepare kava for a *sevusevu* ceremony in the Nausori Highlands in northwestern Viti Levu.

tions is disrespectful. After a meal or during informal kava drinking, you can stretch your legs out, but never point them at the chief or the kava bowl. Don't sit in doorways. Never put your hand on a person's head or touch their hair or headgear.

If you're staying overnight, donate at least F$50 per guest per night to the family that's hosting you, presenting it with both hands as a *sevusevu* in advance to the man of the house. When you depart, give some money to the lady of the house as your goodbye *sevusevu*; she may demur at first but will not be offended. If you're headed for a remote outer island without hotels or resorts, you could take some gifts along for your host family or the local school, but don't give alcohol, cigarettes, or coffee. It's not much considering they'll be feeding, housing, and guiding you, and setting aside their other activities for the duration of your visit.

discouragingly small list of hotels that are partially wheelchair-accessible (www.fncdp.org/docs/accessible_hotels.pdf). The nongovernmental **Fiji Disabled Peoples Federation** (3 Brown St., FNCDP Complex, Suva, tel. 331-1203 or 867-9687, fdpfoffice@fdpf.org, www.fdpf.org) is a coalition whose members advocate for policy and practical changes and offer training.

In practice, travelers with disabilities will need to ask plenty of questions in advance and firmly advocate for accommodations when they arrive. Very little is available in Braille or with sign-language interpretation. International chains are more likely to have at least one room set aside for wheelchair access, but resorts in Fiji are often designed with scenic multilevel architecture that disrupts wheelchair access; be sure to verify that you will be able to get to the breakfast restaurant and other necessities/amenities. Although facilities may not be up to Western countries' standards of accessibility, most tourism-oriented staff are cheerful about adapting as needs arise—lifting you and your wheelchair onto a boat will be considered a good solution if there is no ramp, for example.

TRAVELING WITH CHILDREN

Fiji is a safe, family-friendly country. Taking your children along can be a rewarding experience for both them and you, and there are many discounts and facilities for children.

Destination Weddings and Honeymoons

Chiaroscuro sunsets and moonlit walks with gentle waves lapping on idyllic, secluded shores—what could be more romantic? Fiji has been a popular honeymoon destination for decades, and has recently become a trendy spot for destination weddings as well as for couples renewing their vows. Whether you want to say "I do" underwater in scuba sign-language, or host your family and friends by renting out an entire island, every resort in Fiji would love to make your dream come true.

It's a buyer's market, so here are some tips to make your special occasion go smoothly:

The average wedding package in high season runs about F$8,000, but can vary wildly; you might score a $1,500 deal in low season or spend six figures for your own private seven-star island holiday. A typical package includes the ceremony, flowers, cake, photography, a wedding coordinator, a minister, the honeymoon suite, and perhaps singing by the village choir and an escort of Fijian warriors for the bride. Check carefully to make sure you understand what's included in your "all-inclusive" wedding package and what will cost you extra: additional guest rooms, alcohol, food, extra prints of photographs, kava for the band, or a sunset cruise, among other items.

Compare estimates from several sites (www.fijiweddings.com, www.fijibride.com.au, www.destinationweddings.com/Destinations/Fiji.aspx, www.fijiairways.com/inspiration/getting-married-in-fiji/) to get a sense of what packages can include. Do your own research to find the resort that's right for your party's size and interests, read reviews, and then contact the resort directly for a quote. Eliminating the 30 percent or more commission is likely to save you money, but you might prefer to have an agent in your own country to negotiate in case things start to go wrong.

Bring the required documents to make your marriage binding: passports, birth certificates, a statutory declaration proving the parties are not already married, a letter of consent from the father of any bride or groom under the age of 21, and decrees of divorce or the death certificate of a previous spouse if applicable. Additional requirements may apply if either party is a current or former resident of Fiji.

Purchase a wedding license in person on a weekday at the registry or district office in the

Many resorts offer a deal on children's meal plans, have kids' clubs with staff-supervised activities, and allow children to stay in their parents' room for free. Backpacker dorms don't usually allow children, but instead provide a family-size room with more space and beds. Fiji also has upscale "adults-only" resorts, so be sure to check the fine print when you book, especially for teenagers who may fall in between categories.

WOMEN TRAVELING ALONE

Tourists of all sorts, including solo women, have been coming to Fiji for decades now and can expect friendly, respectful treatment. Off the tourist track, Fiji is a family-oriented culture, so women traveling alone might face questions about their mysteriously absent husband/boyfriend/parents. Women's rights are enshrined in the constitution, though, and common crimes against women tend to be domestic violence rather than stranger attacks. Street heckling is less common than in most of the world's cities, but may still happen. Take the normal precautions, don't tell a strange man where you're staying, and don't accept nighttime rides or go to isolated areas with strangers.

LGBTQ TRAVELERS

Fiji's 2013 constitution is one of the world's most progressive, banning discrimination based on sexual orientation and gender identity or expression. However, same-sex couples do not have legal rights in Fiji; Prime Minister Frank Bainimarama called the idea "rubbish" in 2016 and said gay couples should move to

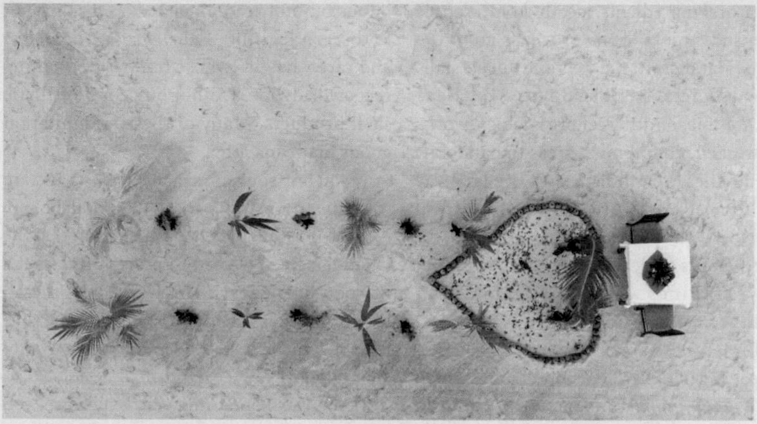

Palm fronds, flowers, and shells are arranged next to a picnic table for a romantic meal.

province in which you intend to marry. The ceremony can be carried out by the district registrar or a minister who has registered as a marriage officer. The marriage certificate will list the bride's maiden name.

If you don't need the legal marriage paperwork, renewal of vows ceremonies are readily available for tourists who are already married, and private honeymoon *bures* can be booked ahead with amenities such as champagne and couples massages. If you've paid for a standard room only, it doesn't hurt to mention when you check in that it's your honeymoon/anniversary; an upgrade might be available, or at least some heartfelt congratulations.

Iceland, as gay marriage would not be legalized in Fiji in his lifetime. Societal discrimination and bullying are not uncommon. Most people follow a conservative Christian, Hindu, or Islamic faith, so public displays of affection aren't common for people of any sexual orientation.

There is an active LGBTQ movement here, however, especially in urban centers such as Suva, Lautoka, and Labasa. You can connect on Facebook with the **Rainbow Pride Foundation** (LGBTQ human rights), **Diva For Equality** (women), and **Haus of Khameleon** (transgender advocacy).

Fiji's hospitality industry is one of the few routes that can provide working-class gay, lesbian, bisexual, and transgender Fijians with the opportunity to break out of religion-dominated families and communities and embark on local travel. Feel free to make connections, but don't make assumptions; norms vary widely across cultures. Whenever I think someone might be at my end of the Kinsey scale, I've found the best approach is to quietly come out myself, without asking any invasive personal questions.

TRAVELERS OF COLOR

Fiji is one of the world's most multicultural societies, but its tourism base is largely white Australians, New Zealanders, and Americans, along with a recent boom in travelers from mainland China. If you're a tourist of color, you'll be something of a novelty and may garner a few extra glances, but Fijians will be welcoming and delighted to connect.

WHAT TO BUY

To share a taste of the islands with folks back home, look for goods made with Fiji's signature natural ingredients, ideally from a source that ensures most of the proceeds go to the makers. Handicrafts markets and village stalls are good sources, as is **Rise Beyond the Reef** (http://risebeyondthereef.org), which works with women from remote areas to handcraft home textiles even though they live far away from tourist hotspots. Merchandise from **Nature Fiji** (https://naturefiji.org/shop/) directly benefits critical conservation work.

Several lines of **beauty and skin products** with luscious coconut oil and floral fragrances are available, and coconut soap packaged in bark is a popular gift. Fijian **chocolates** made of local cacao come in inventive flavors such as "island chai white chocolate" and "chili dark." In addition, look for:

- **Tapa** cloth: a stiff, pounded bark on which traditional designs and sayings are painted.
- Souvenir **kava bowls and cups,** carved from the hard, dark wood of the yesi tree.
- **Woven mats,** baskets, and other handicrafts in the traditional village manner, from placemat- to room-sized.
- **Sulus,** cotton wrap skirts worn by Fijian men, or stitched clothing with bold, bright sulu prints.
- Contemporary **art**, including sketches and paintings, made by emerging artists who show at galleries in Suva, Nadi, and elsewhere.

Seashell jewelry and decorations are ubiquitous but not recommended, as it's difficult to discern legitimate shells from the illegal and rare varieties whose trade is decimating reefs worldwide. Do not buy coral or turtle shell products. Many of these are imitation goods made in China.

If you buy souvenirs made of wood and are traveling to Australia or New Zealand, be sure to ask the retailer for documentation that the wood has been treated to prevent the spread of wood-borne pests. This will come either in the form of a sticker or a statement on your receipt, which you'll need to show as you enter Australia or New Zealand.

If you buy something very expensive, you might be able to negotiate a small discount even at a chain store. Be sure to ask them to process the paperwork for your 9 percent VAT refund if you buy goods worth more than F$500 (over your entire visit). You must keep your VAT goods in your carry-on, in original condition (unworn), and be prepared to show them after you go through passport control; it's a separate line to apply for the refund. Retailers participating in the Tourist VAT Refund Scheme (TVRS) post a sign in their shops and are also registered with the **Fiji Revenue and Customs Service** (tel. 324-3325 or 673-4337, www.frcs.org.fj). You'll need to show your passport as you shop to get the correct paperwork.

Health and Safety

Fiji's sea and air are healthy and rarely polluted. Health care is decent, with an abundance of hospitals, health centers, and nursing stations scattered around the country. The crowded government-run medical facilities provide free medical treatment to local residents but have special rates for foreigners. It's usually no more expensive to visit a private doctor or clinic, where you'll receive much faster service since everyone is paying.

To call an ambulance, dial 911. To call police, dial 917. There's a dive recompression chamber (tel. 321-5525) at the Colonial War Memorial Hospital in Suva.

ACCLIMATING

As you recover from **jet lag,** rest as much as you need, and drink plenty of water. It's wise to forgo dehydrating coffee and alcohol for the first couple of days.

If you're **diving,** make sure you wait 24 hours before flying.

If you start feeling **seasick** on board a ship, stare at the horizon, which is always steady. Anti-motion-sickness pills are effective only *before* you start feeling queasy. Chewing on ginger or ginger candy helps quell the uneasiness. If you must throw up, do so off the side of the boat; no one minds, and you'll feel better instantly.

Your **stomach** will be adapting to new bacteria, too, but Fiji is easier than some other places. The tap water is usually drinkable, except immediately after a cyclone or during droughts, when care should be taken. If in doubt, boil it or drink bottled water. If the water's unfit to drink, avoid brushing your teeth or drinking ice made of it, too. Wash or peel fruit and vegetables if you can. Cooked food is safer than raw.

NATURE

Although Fiji's **weather** is generally pleasant, avoid dehydration on humid and hot days by drinking plenty of water and electrolytes (sugars and salts). In the event of (rare) cyclone and flood danger, abide by local warnings and never hesitate to evacuate if advised.

In the sea, do not enter the ocean while bleeding (sharks!), touch corals, or provoke the cute, zebra-striped, highly venomous sea snakes. Fiji has no stinging jellyfish.

Fiji does not have any dangerous wildlife on land.

AILMENTS

Cuts become infected easily in the tropics, and bites by sand flies itch for days and can become infected. Prevent infection by immediately washing wounds with soap and fresh water, then rubbing in vinegar, alcohol (rum will do), an antiseptic such as hydrogen peroxide, or an antibacterial ointment such as Neosporin. Islanders usually dab coral cuts with lime juice.

Pure aloe vera is good for **sunburn,** as well as scratches and even coral cuts.

Prickly heat, an intensely irritating rash, is caused by wearing heavy clothing that is inappropriate for the climate. When sweat glands are blocked and the sweat is unable to evaporate, the skin becomes soggy, and small red blisters appear. Synthetic fabrics like nylon are especially bad in this regard. Take a cold shower, apply calamine lotion, dust with talcum powder, switch to cotton, and avoid physical activity that makes you sweat until you improve.

Fiji has its share of **mosquitoes** but they do not carry malaria. **Dengue fever** outbreaks occur from time to time, and the **zika** virus arrived in 2016. Avoid bites by using repellent, coils, and mosquito nets (stretch them tight around the bed so that the net does not touch you as you sleep). Symptoms of both diseases are similar, may appear 2 to 14 days after a bite by an infected mosquito, and include headaches, sore throat, pain in the joints or behind the eyes, fever, nausea, and rash. Dengue symptoms are typically more sudden and severe, requiring treatment, while Zika often resolves itself without hospitalization but can spread from a pregnant woman to her fetus. No vaccines exist, so just try to avoid getting bitten by the *Aedes aegypti,* a black-and-white-striped mosquito that bites only during the day.

Sexually transmitted diseases (STDs) are present, especially in Nadi and Suva, and the number of AIDS cases in Fiji is modest but growing; a pack of condoms costs under a dollar at any pharmacy in Fiji.

If you're traveling to the peaks of mountains, stay alert for signs of **altitude sickness**: headache, fatigue, breathlessness, and nausea. The best recourse is to descend immediately.

CRIME

Fiji is generally safe. Violent crime occurs much less frequently than in most countries from which tourists come. Property crimes exist, particularly in the cities, but usually target residential or business areas rather than tourist venues.

Still, tourists should take normal precautions such as locking doors and belongings, staying in known areas after dark, and not allowing taxis to pick up unknown passengers along the way. Stay aware of your surroundings, lock up valuables, and don't flash wads of money or expensive devices in front of people who have less than you. On the beach, keep an eye on your stuff. If you have a rental car, keep everything in the trunk; don't leave belongings visible when you're out sightseeing.

On the streets of Nadi and Suva, beware of high-pressure touts who may try to lure you into their shops, and self-appointed guides who offer to help you find the "best price." If you frequent local bars, know your limit as well as when to stop buying drinks for your new companions.

Political violence can flare up from time to time. Tourists need not worry generally, but may wish to stay away from large demonstrations to avoid being caught up in the action.

Drugs are illegal in Fiji, and the penalties are severe; stick with kava.

Information and Services

MONEY

Fiji isn't cheap the way some other countries are, but its money may be some of the most beautiful in the world—adorned with colorful designs of native species. It starts with the five-cent coin starring the delicious *nuqa,* a rabbitfish whose scientific name, *Siganus uspi,* honors the University of South Pacific (USP), and goes all the way up to $500 bill featuring the *nanai,* a rare beetle that emerges only every eight years and is a local food source. (Next sighting: 2025.) The Fiji petrel can now be seen only on the $20 bill, as the bird is, alas, thought to be extinct; the last sighting was in 2009.

The Fiji dollar is stable at a bit under two to one to the U.S. dollar. To obtain the current rate, visit www.xe.com/ucc. Only F$500 in Fiji banknotes may be imported or exported; unless you're a collector, avoid taking any Fiji banknotes out of the country, as they're difficult to change outside Fiji. Exchange rates at the airport are as good as anywhere.

Banks are open Monday-Thursday 0930-1500 and Friday 0930-1600, and there are several 24-hour banks and exchange offices at Nadi Airport. Western Union and private exchanges, found in the larger towns, are open later and on Saturdays. Large hotels will change bills for guests any day, but the rate is often unfavorable. It's a good idea to plan ahead and change enough money to see you through the weekends. It's usually not possible to change foreign banknotes in rural areas or on the outer islands, and many drivers and small shops don't have change. Always carry an ample supply of small Fijian banknotes in your wallet.

Most banks on Viti Levu have automated teller machines (ATMs) outside their branches accessible 24 hours a day, and these provide local currency at good rates against most debit cards. Be aware, however, that both your bank and the one providing the ATM may charge a stiff service fee for each transaction, as well as a foreign exchange fee. Ask your own bank how much they'll charge if you use an ATM in Fiji. If you have a choice among banks in Fiji, look for the many outlets of the **Bank South Pacific (BSP),** which does not charge a foreign exchange commission and has the lowest ATM fees.

Credit cards are accepted in cities and resorts, but often there's a fee of up to

5 percent. The most useful cards to bring are MasterCard and Visa. Check with your card before leaving home to see if there's an additional foreign transaction fee, and shop around for a card that doesn't add one (Capital One and many credit unions, for example).

Bargaining is the order of the day in smaller shops and handicraft markets, but rarely in shops with glass fronts. You can also try to bargain for longer excursions with taxi drivers, but be aware that some rates are more set than they seem, and it may not be fair to ask one driver in a particular area to undercut his brethren. Almost any service, from scuba diving to mani-pedis, will be more expensive at a high-end or European-owned outfit than if it's provided by a Fijian national.

Tipping is new to Fiji, and is viewed with pleasure but not expectation. Some resorts have staff Christmas funds to which contributions are always welcome.

TIME

Fiji time is Greenwich Mean Time (GMT) plus 12 hours. When it's noon on Monday in Fiji, it will be midnight in London, 1000 in Sydney, 1600 Sunday in Los Angeles, and 1900 Sunday in Toronto. To look at it another way, Fiji is 20 hours ahead of California and two hours ahead of Sydney. If you need to call Fiji from North America, do it in the afternoon or evening Sunday through Thursday, so that you'll reach Fiji during business hours a day later.

Fiji's daylight savings time turns the clocks forward on the first Sunday of November, and backward on the second Sunday of January. There isn't much twilight in the tropics, so sunrises and sunsets are dramatic and quick. When the sun begins to go down, you have less than half an hour before nightfall.

TOURIST INFORMATION

Alas, there are no visitors centers with objective information for tourists in Fiji. **Tourism Fiji** (tel. 672-2433, www.fiji.travel.com) is a marketing organization, unhelpful to visitors; you can pick up brochures in the lobby in Colonial Plaza, Namaka, Nadi, but don't expect assistance. The website has extensive but often outdated accommodations listings.

Instead, a host of private travel agencies provide information, generally skewed toward their own commissions. Even the Information Desk at the international airport is staffed by tour agents who will steer you toward their

Each bill features an endemic species.

own cubicles for even the simplest informational requests. Do your research ahead of time and ask more than one person for advice, and then just go with the flow.

COMMUNICATIONS

Post

Post offices are open weekdays 0800-1600. Postcard postage is inexpensive. For a surcharge, Post Fiji's *fast* POST service guarantees that your letter or parcel will get on the first international flight to your destination.

Phone

To call Fiji from abroad, dial your own international access code (from the United States, it's 011), then Fiji's country code, **679,** and then the phone number.

If you're in Fiji and want to make an international call, dial 00, then your country code (to Canada and the United States, it's 1), then the area code and phone number. To call collect (billed to your party at the higher person-to-person rate), dial 031 instead of 00.

The best place to get a temporary SIM card for your mobile phone is right inside the arrivals terminal at Nadi International Terminal. Fiji's two main providers, **Airtel** and **Vodafone,** both have counters there and are efficient in getting you set up within 15 minutes or so. Plans sold at the airport include international calling and texting, unlike what's available in town. Both carriers are similar on Viti Levu, but if you're traveling to other islands, Vodafone is better on Taveuni and Airtel is better on Ovalau. If you're staying longer than 30 days, you can buy the SIM card here and top it off later online or at a retail outlet in one of the towns.

Viti Levu and the larger tourist centers have 4G coverage. On other islands, many places have more than one phone number because the lines are not very good, so try all the numbers to get through.

Otherwise, you can find public phone facilities at the Fintel office in Suva. Calling internationally from hotels is expensive and not recommended. It's better to use your own device to access a Wi-Fi network, then use an Internet app such as WhatsApp, Skype, Viber, or Messenger (all widely used in Fiji) to make phone calls.

You can search for any telephone number in Fiji at www.whitepages.com.fj and www.yellowpages.com.fj.

Internet

Fiji is the most advanced country in the South Pacific as far as the Internet goes. Many hotels offer Wi-Fi, either for free (at least in the lobby or public areas) or for an hourly or daily fee. Some also have terminals you can use, often in the business center. If you're at a big resort, check in advance whether signing up for the chain's loyalty program will give you free Wi-Fi. It's almost never fast enough for streaming, and at cheaper places, it may not be fast enough for much of anything. Most towns have Internet cafés, which we've listed.

Most tourism-related businesses in Fiji now have email addresses and websites, making communication from abroad a lot cheaper and easier. In this guide, we've embedded the website and email addresses in the listings whenever possible. If no website is listed, search Facebook, as even small resorts and restaurants in Fiji have figured out how to set up a "Page"; these are often more up-to-date than the websites, and respond more speedily than email.

Useful Numbers

- Emergency: 911
- Domestic directory assistance: 011
- International directory assistance: 022
- Domestic operator: 010
- International operator: 012
- Updates in case of natural disaster: 915
- Hyperbaric chamber (Suva): 999-3506 or 999-3500

Resources

Glossary

adi: title for women of chiefly rank, prefixed to their name
balabala: tree fern
balawa: pandanus, screw pine
balolo: a reef worm *(Eunice viridis)*
beka: flying fox
bete: a traditional priest
bilibili: a bamboo raft
bilo: a kava-drinking cup made from a coconut shell
buli: Fijian administrative officer in charge of a *tikina;* subordinate of the *roko tui*
bure: strictly speaking, a thatched house built in the traditional manner; now used informally for an array of cottages and bungalows
cassava: manioc; the starchy edible root of the tapioca plant
ciguatera: a form of fish poisoning caused by microscopic algae
dalo: taro root; a starchy elephant-eared tuber *(Colocasia esculenta)* that is a staple food
drua: an ancient Fijian double canoe
dugong: a large plant-eating marine mammal; called a manatee in the Caribbean
ika: fish
iTaukei: the official term since 2010 for indigenous Fijian people and culture; this is preferable to "native," "tribal," or "real Fijian" as a descriptor. It is used interchangeably with "indigenous" throughout this book.
ivi: the Polynesian chestnut tree *(Inocarpus edulis)*
kai: freshwater mussel
kaihidi: an Indo-Fijian
kaivalagi: a white person
kaiviti: an indigenous Fijian; non-Fijians should avoid using this term, however, as it sometImes carries offensive overtones
kava: a Polynesian word for the drink known in the Fijian language as *yaqona*
kerekere: asking for or borrowing something from a member of one's own group
kokoda: chopped raw fish and sea urchins marinated with onions and lemon
koro: village; non-Fijians should avoid this term, as it has come to carry a connotation of "backwards" and can be offensive
kumala: sweet potato *(Ipomoea batatas)*
kumi: stenciled masi cloth
lali: a hollow-log drum hit with a stick
lapita: a style of pottery made by the ancient Polynesians 1600 BC-500 BC
lolo: coconut cream
lovo: an underground, earthen oven
magimagi: coconut rope fiber
magiti: the root crops that form the basis of a feast
mana: authority, prestige, virtue, "face," psychic power, a positive force
marama: woman/women
masa kesa: freehand-painted masi cloth
masi: a cloth made from the bark of the paper mulberry tree *(Broussonetia papyrifera)*, soaked and beaten with a mallet to flatten and intertwine the fibers, then painted with geometric designs; called *tapa* throughout the Pacific, *masi* only in Fiji
matanigasau: forgiveness/reparations ceremony
mata ni vanua: an orator who speaks for a high chief

mataqali: a landowning extended family, a clan lineage

meke: traditional song and dance

pandanus: screw pine with slender stem and prop roots, whose sword-shaped leaves are used for plaiting mats and hats

qara: cave

qoliqoli: traditional fishing rights claimed by Fijian clans

rara: a grassy village square

ratu: title for men of chiefly rank, prefixed to their names

roko tui: senior Fijian administrative officer

salusalu: garland, lei

sennit: braided coconut-fiber rope

sevusevu: a formal ceremony in which a guest requests permission to be accepted into a village, including its lands and its waters

sulu: a wraparound skirt or loincloth similar to a sarong

tabu: a no-fishing area created and protected by the village that owns the fishing rights

tabua: a whale's tooth; a ceremonial object

takia: a small sailing canoe

talanoa: to chat or tell stories

talatala: reverend

tanoa: a special wide wooden bowl in which *yaqona* (kava) is mixed; used in ceremonies in Fiji, Tonga, and Samoa

tapa: a Polynesian word for the bark cloth known in Fiji as *masi*

tavioka: tapioca, cassava, manioc, arrowroot

teitei: a garden

tiki: a humanlike sculpture used in the old days for religious rites

tikina: a group of Fijian villages administered by a *buli*

tui: king

turaga: man/men

turaga-ni-koro: village herald or mayor

vakaviti: in the Fijian way

vale: house/home

vale lailai/vale vo: toilet

vale ni lotu: church

vanua: land, region, custom, people

vu: an ancestral spirit

wai: water

wai tui: ocean/sea

waka: a bundle of whole kava roots, dried or fresh

yaqona: a drink made by squeezing a mixture of the grated root of the pepper shrub *(Piper methysticum)* and cold water through a strainer of hibiscus-bark fiber; called *kava* throughout the Pacific, *yaqona* only in Fiji

yasana: an administrative province

Phrasebook

Most Fijians speak at least two languages: English and their mother tongue. The three official languages are English; Fijian, of which there are many dialects, the standard being the eastern Fijian dialect of Bauan; and a dialect of Hindi known locally as "Fiji Hindi" or Hindustani. Other languages include Rotuman, Tongan, Samoan, Banaban, Tuvaluan, Gilbertese, Cantonese, Urdu, Gujarati, and Punjabi. It's worth practicing a few simple greetings just to be friendly, and learning a few simple phrases can help you feel oriented and connected.

FIJIAN

Greetings

bula simple greeting, hello

dua oo said by males when they meet a chief or enter a Fijian dua

Kocei na yacamu? What's your name? (formal)

Cei na yacamu? What's your name? (informal)

Iko mai vei? Where are you from?

Iko sa lako kei vei? or Iko lako e vei? Where are you going?

Au lako mai Kenada. I come from Canada.

Spelling and Pronunciation

Thanks to the early British missionaries who created the system of written Fijian according to some sort of mysterious 19th century logic, the following five letters in Fijian are not what they seem:

- If you see *b*, say "mb" as in *lamb*.
- If you see *c*, say "th" as in *the* (not *thing*).
- If you see *d*, say "nd" as in *land*.
- If you see *g*, say "ng" gently, as in *long*.
- If you see *q*, say "ngg" harshly, like you mean it, as in *longer*.

Practice by mentally changing the pronunciation as you read this book: Nadi is pronounced *Nandi*, Mamanuca is *Mamanutha*, Beqa is *Mbengga*, Sigatoka is *Singatoka*, and so on.

Once you master these simple transformations, you'll find the rest of Fijian pronunciation to be extremely straightforward.

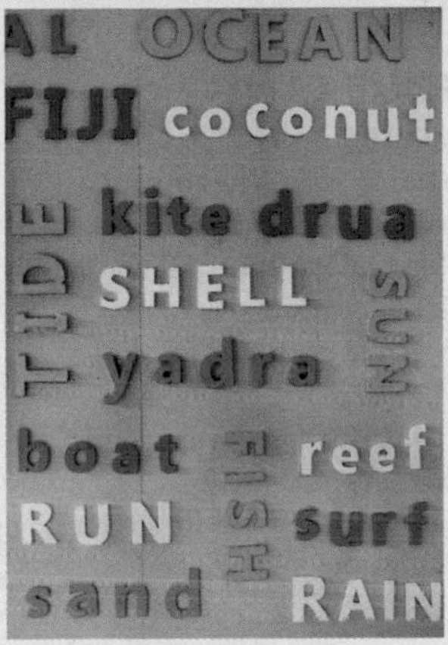

a vocabulary-building display

ni sa bula or sa bula or bula vinaka Hello, how are you?
an sa bula vinaka I am well.
yadra or ni sa yadra good morning
marama ma'am, madam
turaga sir, Mr.
tulou excuse me
uro a provocative greeting for the opposite sex (you may hear this, but don't use it!)

Mealtime

kana eat
mai Kana come and eat
Na cava oqo? What is this?
maleka delicious

Farewells

Loloma yani Please pass along my regards.
moce goodbye
ni sa moce good night
sota tale see you again

Hanging Out

ken datou lako Let's go
sa veca na kaloko What's the time?
sa vinaka it's okay
io yes
kauta mai bring
kauta tani take away
lako mai come
lako tani go

Gratitude

yalo vinaka please
vinaka thank you
vinaka vakalevu thank you very much
sega na leqa you're welcome, no worries

Quantity

ya vica how much
lailai small
levu big, much
sega no, none
tale more
dua tale one more or once more
vaka lailai a little, small
vaka levu a lot, great
vaka malua slowly
vaka totolo fast
dua one

rua two
tolu three
va four
lima five

HINDUSTANI

Greetings

Kaise hai? Hello, how are you?
namaste greeting (Hindu)
as-salaam alaykum greeting (Muslim)
Theek hai I'm fine
accha Okay, good

Directions

chaalo let's go
Kahaan jata hai? Where are you going?
seedhe jauo go straight
kahaan where
yahin here
wahin there
kab when
khana food
paani water

Shopping

Yeh kyaa hai? What's this?
Kitna? How much?
haan yes
nahi no
bahut julum very beautiful (slang)
ek aur one more
chhota small
maaf kijiye excuse me, I'm sorry
dhaniavaad thank you

Suggested Reading

Fiji's notable writers in English include the fiction masters **Raymond Pillai** and **Subramani**; poets **Pio Manoa** and **Sudesh Mishra**; memoirists **Satendra Nandan** and **Joseph Veramo**; and playwrights **Vilsoni Hereniko** and **Larry Thomas**. The best place to find their works is the University of the South Pacific's campus bookstore near Suva. The books below will help you get to know the rich cultures, ecosystems, and peoples of Fiji.

ART AND PHOTOGRAPHY

Geraghty, Craig, Glen Geraghty, and Paul Geraghty. *Children of the Sun.* Gympie, Australia: Glen Craig Publishing, 1996. This photo book is like one big Fiji family picture album in glorious color.

Stephenson, Dr. Elsie. *Fiji's Past on Picture Postcards.* Suva: Fiji Museum, 1997. Some 275 old postcards of Fiji from the Caines Jannif collection.

Thomas, Nicholas. *Oceanic Art.* A cogent overview organized thematically with 182 illustrations, 26 in color.

Traditional Handicrafts of Fiji. Suva: Institute of Pacific Studies, 1997. The significance and history of Fijian handicrafts.

UNDERWATER LIFE

Allen, Gerald, and Roger Steene. *Indo-Pacific Coral Reef Field Guide.* El Cajon, CA: Odyssey Publishing, 1998. Essential for identifying the creatures of the reefs.

Allen, Steene, Ned DeLoach, and Paul Humann. *Reef Fish Identification, Tropical Pacific.* Jacksonville, FL: New World Publications, 2005. A comprehensive guide with 2,500 color photographs.

Nimmerfroh, Achim. *Fiji's Wild Beauty.* Germany: Nimmerfroh Dive Productions, 2006. A photographic guide to the coral reefs of the South Pacific with more than 750 images of marine creatures.

Randall, John E., Gerald Robert Allen, and Roger C. Steene. *Fishes of the Great Barrier Reef and Coral Sea.* Honolulu: University of Hawaii Press, 1997. An identification guide for amateur divers and specialists alike.

Ryan, Paddy. *The Snorkeler's Guide to the Coral Reef, from the Red Sea to the Pacific Ocean.* Honolulu: University of Hawaii Press, 1994. A take-along guide with 200 color photographs. The author spent 10 years in Fiji.

NATURE AND ECOLOGY

Nunn, Patrick D. *Pacific Island Landscapes.* Suva: Institute of Pacific Studies, 1998. A leading geographer demystifies the geology and geomorphology of Fiji, Samoa, and Tonga, with emphasis on the origin of the islands.

Ryan, Paddy. *Fiji's Natural Heritage.* Auckland: Exisle Publishing, 2000. With 500 photos and 288 pages of text, this is probably the most comprehensive popular book on any Pacific island ecosystem.

Watling, Dick. *A Guide to the Birds of Fiji & Western Polynesia.* Suva: Environmental Consultants, 2001. The guide has detailed accounts for the 173 species with confirmed records in the region, and notes a further 22 species with unconfirmed records. Copies can be ordered through www.pacificbirds.com.

Watling, Dick. *Mai Veikau: Tales of Fijian Wildlife.* Suva: Fiji Times, 1986. A wealth of easily digested information on Fiji's flora and fauna. Copies are available in Fiji bookstores.

Wheatley, Nigel. *Where to Watch Birds in Australasia and Oceania.* Princeton University Press, 1998. The descriptions of nature reserves and forested areas will interest any ecotourist.

Whistler, W. Arthur. *Flowers of the Pacific Island Seashore.* Honolulu: University of Hawaii Press, 1993. A guide to the littoral plants of Hawaii, Tahiti, Samoa, Tonga, Cook Islands, Fiji, and Micronesia.

HISTORY AND POLITICS

Derrick, R. A. *A History of Fiji.* Suva: Government Press, 1946. A classic, still in print, by the former director of the Fiji Museum, covering Fiji before British cession in 1874.

Donnelly, Quanchi, and Kerr. *Fiji in the Pacific: A History and Geography of Fiji.* Australia: Jacaranda Wiley, 1994. A high school text on the country.

Field, Michael, Tupeni Baba, and Unaisi Nabobo-Baba. *Speight of Violence: Inside Fiji's 2000 Coup.* Honolulu: University of Hawaii Press, 2005. A powerful account of events that continue to haunt Fiji, as told by a former hostage, the hostage's wife on the outside, and a veteran Pacific reporter.

Fraenkel, Jon, and Stewart Firth, eds. *From Election to Coup in Fiji.* Suva: IPS Publications, 2007. A panel of political observers discusses the 2006 election campaign and its aftermath.

Kikau, Eci. *The Wisdom of Fiji.* Suva: Institute of Pacific Studies, 1981. This extensive collection of Fijian proverbs opens a window to understanding Fijian society, culture, and philosophy.

Lal, Brij V. *Broken Waves: A History of the Fiji Islands in the 20th Century.* Honolulu: University of Hawaii Press, 1992. Accessible language.

Lewis, David. *We, the Navigators: The Ancient Art of Landfinding in the Pacific.* This engaging classic examines how Stone Age Polynesians may have navigated the Pacific.

LITERATURE

Griffen, Arlene, ed. *With Heart and Nerve and Sinew: Post-Coup Writing from Fiji.* Suva: Marama Club, 1997. An eclectic collection of responses to the first coups and life in Fiji thereafter.

Hereniko, Vilsoni, and Teresia Teaiwa. *Last Virgin in Paradise.* Suva: Institute of Pacific Studies, 1993. The Rotuman Hereniko has written a number of plays, including *Don't Cry Mama* (1977), *A Child for Iva* (1987), and *The Monster* (1989).

Joseph, Paul. *Precious Cargo: Mark Twain and I Take Our Families Across the South Pacific.* Madison: University of Wisconsin, 2019. The author, an American peace studies professor with a wry sense of humor, follows the trail and provides a critical lens on Twain's journey to Fiji and elsewhere, as documented in his 1897 memoir *Following the Equator.*

Kamali, Daren. *Squid Out of Water: The Evolution.* CreateSpace, 2014. Honoring the Pacific Ocean and its many cultures and stories, this is the second collection by the poet, who is of Fijian and Wallis and Futuna descent.

Khelawan, Rajni Mala. *Kalyana.* Toronto: Second Story Press, 2016. This compelling and at times brutal novel, told in the voice of a young girl growing up in Suva in 1965, elegantly intertwines the effects of patriarchy, colonialism, slavery, and second-wave feminism in a story about a young woman losing and then finding her voice.

Mishra, Sudesh. *The Lives of Coat Hangers: Poems.* Dunedin: Otago University Press, 2016. Mishra, a poet of humble philosophy, heads the School of Language, Arts and Media at the University of the South Pacific, and is the author of several volumes of poetry and criticism.

Sharma, Kamlesh. *Rahul's Road: Memories of a Fijindian Childhood.* Amazon, 2016. This self-published semiautobiographical novel tells a story of growing up in a poor Indo-Fijian village. The writing is amateurish but the details are compelling.

Tarte, Daryl. *Fiji: A Place Called Home.* Canberra, ANU Press, 2014. A gossipy, anecdotal autobiography of growing up in Taveuni and elsewhere in Fiji, by a sixth-generation European Fijian. Access it free online through the publisher (https://press.anu.edu.au/publications/fiji-place-called-home/download).

Veramu, Joseph C. *Moving Through the Streets.* Suva: Institute of Pacific Studies, 1994. A fast-moving novel providing insights into the lifestyles, pressures, and temptations of teenagers in Suva. Veramu has also written a collection of short stories called *The Black Messiah* (1989).

Wendt, Albert, ed. *Nuanua: Pacific Writing in English Since 1980.* Honolulu, University of Hawaii Press, 1995. This worthwhile anthology of contemporary Pacific literature includes works by 10 Fijian writers.

REFERENCE

Capell, A. *A New Fijian Dictionary.* Suva: Government Printer, 1991. Scholars generally have a low opinion of this work, which contains hundreds of errors, but it's still a handy reference. Also see C. Maxwell Churchward's *A New Fijian Grammar.*

Douglas, Ngaire, and Norman Douglas, eds. *Pacific Islands Yearbook.* Suva: Fiji Times, 1994. First published in 1932, this is the 17th and final edition, but it remains an indispensable reference work.

Lal, Brij V., and Kate Fortune, eds. *The Pacific Islands: An Encyclopedia.* Honolulu: University of Hawaii Press, 2000. This important book combines the writings of 200 acknowledged experts on the physical environment, peoples, history, politics, economics, society, and cultures.

MAPS

Bier, James A. *Reference Map of Oceania.* Honolulu: University of Hawaii Press, 2007. A fully indexed map of the Pacific Islands with 51 detailed inset maps of individual islands. Useful details such as time zones are included.

International Maps. Hema Maps Pty. Ltd., P.O. Box 4365, Eight Mile Plains, QLD 4113, Australia (tel. 07/3340-0000, www.hemamaps.com.au). Maps of the Pacific, Fiji, Solomon Islands, Vanuatu, and Samoa.

Lands and Survey Department Map Shop (CK Patel Building, 94 Raojibhai Patel St., Suva, tel. 331-8631, Mon.-Fri. 0800-1600). This government department sells detailed island-by-island maps of Fiji. It's tucked behind the back entrance to the building, up a flight of stairs. A complete list of maps for sale and current prices is at www.lands.gov.fj/ (scroll down the left for Map Shop fees). Simpler maps are available for purchase at post offices throughout Fiji.

Internet Resources

Until you can hit the waves, spend some time surfing these enjoyable sites.

CULTURE

ARTtalk Fiji
https://artalkfiji.com
A beautifully designed online magazine edited by Suva poet Peter Sipeli, who has his finger on the pulse of the best local photographers, artists, fashionistas, and makers.

The Contemporary Pacific
www.uhpress.hawaii.edu/t-the-contemporary-pacific.aspx
This journal, published twice a year, highlights the work of one or more Pacific Islander artists in every issue and publishes an interesting mix of scholarly and popular articles. Back issues are free online.

Fiji Museum Online
www.fijimuseum.org.fj
A virtual tour of the museum, with special online exhibitions.

Genda Project
www.thegendaproject.com/genda-disrupt/
If you like TED talks, you'll love these short, well-paced videos by Fiji's best thinkers, lovingly curated by Sharon Narayan. Join the mailing list (thegendaproject@gmail.com) to see if you can attend a live event while you're in Fiji.

National Trust of Fiji Islands
www.nationaltrust.org.fj
Learn about Fiji's natural and cultural heritage, including detailed descriptions of the eight National Trust protected areas and three community parks.

Talanoa
http://talanoa.com.au
A digital storytelling site with well-produced mini-videos and profiles of ordinary people in the Pacific, encompassing topics from climate change to fashion to music.

Taste of Paradise
http://tasteofparadise.tv
Drool at the food *and* the scenery, as the affable Lance Seeto, Fiji's top chef, takes you on a foodie tour of a different island or locale in each episode.

FOR CHILDREN

Little Learners Fiji
Available via the ios App Store
Designed for kids, this US$0.99 app for iPhones and iPads is a fun way for learners of any age to build a basic Fijian vocabulary, with virtual flashcards for colors, months, days of the week, weather conditions, body parts, numbers, objects, clothes, and people.

Tui's Gang
www.tuisgang.com
This joyful set of books illustrated with bright images by expat artist Penelope Casey follows the adventures of young Tui and his friends, all while building readers' Fijian vocabulary. In Fiji, look for the books at Tappoo stores. There's even a *Tui's Gang Coloring Book*.

REFERENCE

Bureau of Statistics
www.statsfiji.gov.fj
A wealth of data in accessible tables and graphics.

Fiji A to Z
www.fijiatoz.com
A great overview of the islands in a user-friendly alphabetical format.

Fiji Government Online
www.fiji.gov.fj
All you need to know about official stuff.

TRAVEL

Exquisite Fiji
www.exquisitefiji.com
This site is notable for its useful chart with price comparisons of various resorts and hotels all around Fiji.

Fiji Hotels
www.fiji-hotels.com.fj
Located in Nadi, this booking agency's website provides accurate hotel information and competitive rates, with a level of detail not available elsewhere.

Live Feeds
www.amazing-fiji-vacations.com/fiji-webcams.html#needs
A collection of live webcams on various islands.

RECREATION

Fiji Rucksack Club
https://sites.google.com/site/fijirucksackclub/home
The website is nothing fancy, but connecting with the Rucksack Club, established in 1963, is a great way to meet local travelers interested in out-of-the-way spots and outdoor activities in Fiji. Upcoming trips are listed in monthly newsletters.

Surfbirds
www.surfbirds.com/Trip%20Reports/fiji.php
Detailed birding trip reports from Fiji.

***Surfer* magazine**
www.surfermag.com
Search the site for the latest news and videos from Fiji's surfing scene, and check current conditions via the Swellwatch feature. Creating a free account allows you to customize your settings, track particular buoys, and log your surf sessions.

***Undercurrent* newsletter**
www.undercurrent.org
An online consumer-protection-oriented resource for serious scuba divers. Unlike virtually every other diving publication, *Undercurrent* accepts no advertising or free trips. Some information is free online; full reviews are behind a paywall.

NEWS

Fiji Broadcasting Corporation

www.fbc.com.fj

Livestreams of six AM/FM radio stations in Fiji, television schedules, and frequently updated news stories.

Fiji Live

www.fijilive.com

Fiji's largest news and information portal with a wide range of topical content. This is a good place to look for upcoming sports events (and results).

Fiji Meteorological Service

www.met.gov.fj

Daily weather bulletins and regional forecasts.

Fiji Sun

http://fijisun.com.fj

A daily tabloid that also publishes online.

Fiji Times

www.fijitimes.com

The online portal for "the first newspaper published in the world every day," founded in 1869.

Islands Business

www.islandsbusiness.com

The online portal of a monthly newsmagazine, this site posts daily news stories as well as in-depth coverage of political and economic trends around the Pacific. An overseas subscription to the print edition is US$52/NZ$65/AU$45.

Index

A

B

C

H

IJ

K

L

T

UV

List of Maps

Front Maps

Discover Fiji

Nadi and Vicinity

The Mamanuca and Yasawa Islands

The Coral Coast

Suva and the Kadavu Group

Northern Coast and Interior Viti Levu

Vanua Levu

Taveuni

The Lomaiviti Group

The Outer Islands

Photo Credits

Title page photo: vomo island, fiji;

All interior pohots © Minal Hajratwala, except: page 2 © jean-michel cousteau fiji islands resort; page 3 © south sea cruises; page 8 © (top left) caroline steinmetz; (top right) caroline steinmetz; page 9 © (bottom right) conservation international/mark erdmann; page 10 © (top) chris mclennan/tourism fiji; page 11 © (top) natalie stirling; (bottom right) mark snyder/tourism fiji; page 14 © jean-michel cousteau fiji islands resort; page 15 © (top) talanoa treks/matt manley; (bottom) tourism fiji; page 17 © (top) aaron march/tourism fiji; page 18 © vou dance fiji; page 20 © (bottom) grand pacific hotel; page 23 © (bottom) skyward industries/tourism fiji; page 29 © jean-michel cousteau fiji islands resort; vomo island, fiji; page 31 © (bottom) jean-michel cousteau fiji islands resort; page 47 © vou dance fiji; page 55 © jean-michel cousteau fiji islands resort; page 68 © (top right) nayan hajratwala; page 75 © (bottom) nayan hajratwala; page 80 © chris mclennan/tourism fiji; page 85 © caroline steinmetz; page 90 © vomo island, fiji; page 96 © (top) tourism fiji; (left middle)vomo island, fiji; (right middle)natalie stirling; (bottom) south sea cruises; page 98 © natalie stirling; page 106 © (top) south sea cruises; (bottom) captain cook cruises fiji; page 108 © south sea cruises; page 114 © (right middle) caroline steinmetz; (bottom) caroline steinmetz; page 116 © south sea cruises; page 133 © (left middle) adi lawake; (right middle) nayan hajratwala; (bottom) nayan hajratwala; page 139 © chris williams/vomo island, fiji; page 142 © (right middle) rob rickman/hot glass fiji; page 149 © natalie stirling; page 158 © (bottom) namosi eco retreat; page 160 © fijian government; page 173 © rainbowpridefiji; page 175 © (top right) nayan hajratwala; (bottom) grand pacific hotel; page 193 © (top left) nayan hajratwala; page 198 © south sea cruises; page 200 © captain cook cruises fiji; page 204 © talanoa treks; page 212 © (top) adi lawake; page 214 © rob rickman/talanoa treks; page 218 © (left middle)rob rickman/talanoa treks; (bottom) rob rickman/talanoa treks; ppage 225 © jean-michel cousteau fiji islands resort; page 228 © chris mclennan/jean-michel cousteau fiji islands resort; page 239 © j. hunter pearls fiji; page 240 © (left middle) savusavu tours; (bottom) jean-michel cousteau fiji islands resort; page 244 © (bottom) jean-michel cousteau fiji islands resort; page 248 © (top) sigasiga sands resort; (left middle)sigasiga sands resort; (right middle)margaret giuliani; (bottom) fijian government; (top right) shratika naidu; (bottom) captain cook cruises fiji; page 258 © chris mclennan/jean-michel cousteau fiji islands resort; page 261 © rob edwards/it's time foundation; page 275 © tourism fiji; page 277 © (top left) caroline steinmetz; (top right) nayan hajratwala; (bottom) natalie stirling; page 279 © (top left) mark snyder/tourism fiji; page 283 © (top) caroline steinmetz; page 286 © rob edwards/i]ts time foundation; page 307 © natalie stirling; page 310 © chris mclennan/tourism fiji; page 311 © tourism fiji; page 313 © dcim\100gopro\gopr0071.jpg; page 321 © (top) natalie stirling; (right middle)natalie stirling; (bottom) captain cook cruises fiji/david kirkland; page 326 © (top) conservation international/photo by mark erdmann; (left middle)conservation international/photo by mark erdmann and gerry allen; (bottom) natalie stirling; page 330 © conservation international/photo by mark erdmann; page 332 © fijian government; page 335 © jean-michel cousteau fiji islands resort; page 359 © talanoa treks/rob rickman; page 361 © south sea cruises;

Acknowledgments

FROM THE AUTHOR

It's impossible to write a book like this without the help of hundreds of hands. I'm grateful to all of my cousins, aunts, and uncles in Fiji, who hosted and fed me and made all manner of helpful suggestions during the research for this book. Many fellow travelers generously shared their own favorite sites, contacts, photographs, and more, especially Caroline Steinmetz, Natalie Stirling, Rob Edwards, my awesome brother Nayan Hajratwala, and Lakshmi Shubha. These heroes went out of their way to make introductions, show me around, and share detailed information: Marita Manley, Sudesh Mishra, David Patterson, Kris Prasad, Delia Rothnie-Jones, Jolene Sami, Sachiko Soro, Helen Sykes, and Christine Tawake. For meticulous research assistance over many months, I'm deeply indebted to Ed P. Lee.

For making this book gorgeous and saving me from countless errors, an enormous *vinaka* to the talented and patient team at Moon: Rachel Feldman, Lucie Ericksen, Albert Angulo, Karin Dahl, Nikki Ioakimedes, Holly Birchfield, Kimi Owens, and to the first author of *Moon Fiji,* David Stanley. All errors are, of course, mine. For corrections or updates for future editions, please email me at MoonFiji2019@gmail.com.

This book is dedicated to my mother, Bhanu Hajratwala, born in Tavua, for being a delightful travel companion as well as instilling my first love of Fiji.

FROM THE PUBLISHER

This 10th edition of *Moon Fiji* is the first one not researched and written by the incomparable David Stanley, one of Moon's founding authors and a guiding light for our philosophy of travel publishing. In the introduction to the first edition of his *South Pacific Handbook* in 1979, David wrote:

> We are entering an era when exotic destinations are becoming more available. Much of the South Pacific is still virgin territory from the travel industry standpoint. It is actually the world's most recent travel area, only opened up in 1768-9 when Capt. James Cook voyaged through as an explorer and observer ... But the experience of tourism in the Pacific Islands is a touchy one. For this reason, this book has been written for the traveler rather than for the conventional free-spending tourist.

David has embodied this spirit in his own travels. Over the course of four decades, he crossed six continents overland and visited almost every country in the world. His travel guidebooks to the South Pacific, Micronesia, Alaska, Eastern Europe, and Cuba opened those areas to independent travelers for the first time. Like any true traveler, David was supremely adaptable, always willing to make changes in response to evolving travel regulations, tourism infrastructure, series guidelines, and of course, the Internet. He was a pleasure to work with; and for many of us at Moon, a true friend. You can learn more about David and the South Pacific at his website, www.southpacific.org.

Trips to Remember

Epic Adventure

Beachy Getaways
MOON.COM
@MOONGUIDES
MOON
ARUBA
BAHAMAS
BAJA
Including Cabo San Lucas
JENNIFER KRAMER
BELIZE
CAPE COD
MARTHA'S VINEYARD & NANTUCKET
RAY BARTLETT
COASTAL CALIFORNIA
DOMINICAN REPUBLIC
LEBAWIT LILY GIRMA
FIJI
FLORIDA
HAWAII
JAMAICA
LOS ANGELES
SAN DIEGO
IAN ANDERSON
TULUM
YUCATÁN PENINSULA

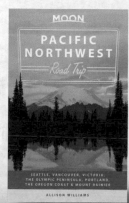

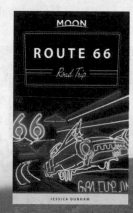

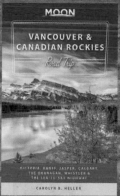

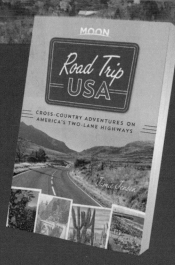

MAP SYMBOLS

- Expressway
- Primary Road
- Secondary Road
- Unpaved Road
- Feature Trail
- Other Trail
- Ferry
- Pedestrian Walkway
- Stairs
- City/Town
- State Capital
- National Capital
- Point of Interest
- Accommodation
- Restaurant/Bar
- Other Location
- Campground
- Airport
- Airfield
- Mountain
- Unique Natural Feature
- Waterfall
- Park
- Trailhead
- Skiing Area
- Golf Course
- Parking Area
- Archaeological Site
- Church
- Gas Station
- Glacier
- Mangrove
- Reef
- Swamp

CONVERSION TABLES

°C = (°F - 32) / 1.8
°F = (°C x 1.8) + 32
1 inch = 2.54 centimeters (cm)
1 foot = 0.304 meters (m)
1 yard = 0.914 meters
1 mile = 1.6093 kilometers (km)
1 km = 0.6214 miles
1 fathom = 1.8288 m
1 chain = 20.1168 m
1 furlong = 201.168 m
1 acre = 0.4047 hectares
1 sq km = 100 hectares
1 sq mile = 2.59 square km
1 ounce = 28.35 grams
1 pound = 0.4536 kilograms
1 short ton = 0.90718 metric ton
1 short ton = 2,000 pounds
1 long ton = 1.016 metric tons
1 long ton = 2,240 pounds
1 metric ton = 1,000 kilograms
1 quart = 0.94635 liters
1 US gallon = 3.7854 liters
1 Imperial gallon = 4.5459 liters
1 nautical mile = 1.852 km

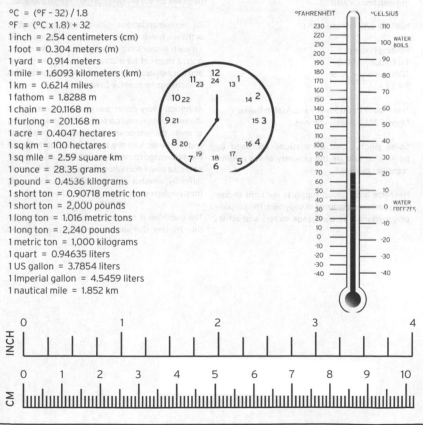

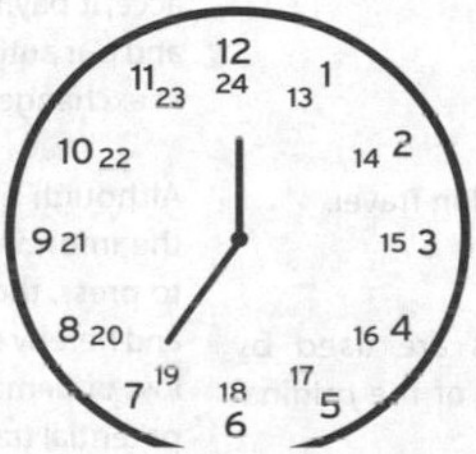

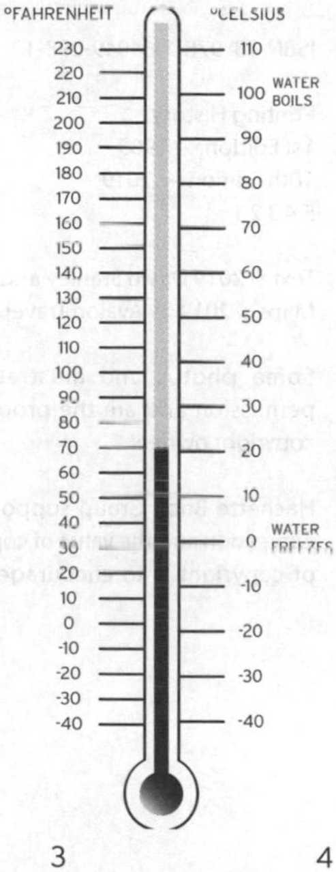

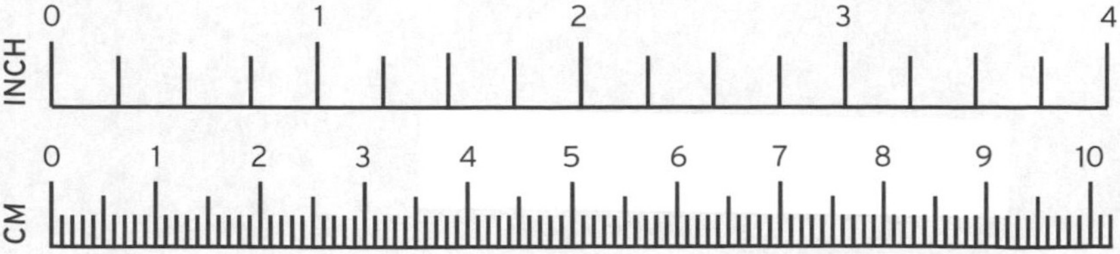

MOON FIJI

Avalon Travel
Hachette Book Group
1700 Fourth Street
Berkeley, CA 94710, USA
www.moon.com

Editor: Rachel Feldman
Series Manager: Kathryn Ettinger
Copy Editor: Brett Keener
Graphics Coordinator: Lucie Ericksen
Production Coordinator: Lucie Ericksen
Cover Design: Faceout Studios, Charles Brock
Interior Design: Domini Dragoone
Moon Logo: Tim McGrath
Map Editor: Albert Angulo
Cartographers: Karin Dahl, Andy Dolan, and Albert Angulo
Proofreader: Rosemarie Boucher Leenerts
Indexer: Greg Jewett

ISBN-13: 978-1-64049-298-1

Printing History
1st Edition — 1985
10th Edition — 2019
5 4 3 2 1

Front cover photo: Martin Valigursky / Alamy Stock Photo
Back cover photo: waterfall in Suva © Sorin Colac | Dreamstime.com

Printed in China by RR Donnelley.